NATION SHAPES

NATION SHAPES

THE STORY BEHIND THE WORLD'S BORDERS

Fred M. Shelley

ABC-CLIO

Santa Barbara, California • Denver, Colorado • Oxford, England

Copyright 2013 by ABC-CLIO, LLC

All rights reserved. No part of this publication may be reproduced, stored in a retrieval system, or transmitted, in any form or by any means, electronic, mechanical, photocopying, recording, or otherwise, except for the inclusion of brief quotations in a review, without prior permission in writing from the publisher.

Library of Congress Cataloging-in-Publication Data

Shelley, Fred M., 1952–
   Nation shapes : the story behind the world's borders / Fred M. Shelley.
      p. cm.
   Includes bibliographical references and index.
   ISBN 978-1-61069-105-5 (hardcopy : alk. paper) — ISBN 978-1-61069-106-2
(ebook) 1. Boundaries. 2. Political geography. I. Title.
   JC323.S55 2013
   320.1'2—dc23   2012035416

ISBN: 978-1-61069-105-5
EISBN: 978-1-61069-106-2

17 16 15 14 13   1 2 3 4 5

This book is also available on the World Wide Web as an eBook.
Visit www.abc-clio.com for details.

ABC-CLIO, LLC
130 Cremona Drive, P.O. Box 1911
Santa Barbara, California 93116-1911

This book is printed on acid-free paper ∞

Manufactured in the United States of America

CONTENTS

INTRODUCTION: NATIONS, STATES, TERITORIES, AND BOUNDARIES

The world is divided into nearly 200 separate countries, each of which is separated from others by boundaries. How might the land boundaries of each country be described? Why have these boundaries evolved as they have over the course of history? And what conflicts over territory are being faced by each country? The purpose of this book is to address these questions.

NATIONS AND STATES

In describing the countries of the world and their boundaries, it is important to recognize the difference between a nation and a state. A nation is a group of people living in a particular area who share common cultural, ethnic, linguistic, or religious characteristics. A state is a political unit recognized by the international community of states. According to this definition, Americans, Swedes, Chinese, French, and Japanese are nations. The United States, Sweden, China, France, and Japan are states. Confusion arises in some cases because some countries, including the United States, Mexico, India, and Germany, consist of multiple units that are termed "states." From the perspective of international political geography, however, these countries are considered states.

Throughout history, conflicts have arisen because states and nations do not match up with each other. Some nations and states are closely linked to each other. For example, most Japanese people live in Japan, and most residents of the state of Japan are Japanese nationals. However, many nations extend across several states while many individual states include multiple nations.

For example, Arabs represent the majority of people who live in several states in Southwest Asia and North Africa. There are several definitions of what constitutes the Arab nation. Three commonly used definitions include being descended from people who lived in ancient or medieval Arabia, speaking Arabic as one's first language, and being a citizen of a country that is a member of the League of Arab States. Any or all of these definitions can be used to identify a person as a member of the Arab nation. However, there is no single Arab state. There are many states, including Saudi Arabia, Egypt, Libya, and Qatar, in which a very large percentage of the population consists of Arabs.

On the other hand, many states contain multiple nations. For example, India consists of many different nations, distinguished from one another on the basis of language and culture. Conflict between members of different nations within states has occurred frequently. Many of these conflicts are associated with differences in language, religion, and other cultural characteristics. These conflicts are especially intense in cases in which a majority group attempts to impose its culture, language, or religion on minority groups. In some cases, cultures of indigenous populations are also suppressed by governments, again leading to political turmoil and conflict.

The designation of a language as an official language is often a source of controversy, particularly among persons who do not speak the official language of the state. States that have identified official languages generally require that government business and education be conducted in the official language. Knowledge of the official language is sometimes a requirement for citizenship. For example, someone who wishes to become a citizen of Estonia is required to pass a test about Estonian culture, history, and political structures in the Estonian language. About 25 percent of Estonian residents are of Russian ancestry and many of these persons cannot speak or read Estonian, therefore precluding them from obtaining Estonian citizenship.

Not only do many states contain multiple nations, but there are many nations that do not have their own states. Frequently, nationalist movements have arisen within such states. Nationalists support political independence, or at least higher levels of political autonomy, for members of minority nations within their states. Among the many nations that currently lack states and in which nationalist movements are active are Kurds in Southwest Asia, Basques in Spain and France, and Uighurs and Tibetans in China.

CITIZENSHIP AND SOVEREIGNTY

What constitutes a state? Geographers and political scientists have identified several criteria associated with recognizing a place or region as a state. In order for a state to be considered a state, it needs to meet several requirements. These include a territory, a population, an economy, a government, and a system of infrastructure including transportation, education, and communications.

The world's states vary dramatically in terms of land area, population, history, and other characteristics. For example, San Marino in Europe has a land area of 24 square miles, or a third of the size of the District of Columbia. Its population is about 30,000. On the other hand, China has a land area of 3.7 million square miles, making it the third-largest state in the world by land area behind Russia and Canada. Its population of about 1.3 billion makes China the most populous country in the world. Some states, such as the United Kingdom, Spain, China, and Japan, have been in existence for hundreds of years. Others such as South Sudan, which became independent of Sudan in 2011, have been added to the world political map only recently. Yet all of these countries meet the criteria for states.

The fact that states must include territory and population leads to the concepts of citizenship and sovereignty. Citizenship represents the rights and responsibilities linking a person to the state. However, the definition of citizenship varies from one state to another. In the United States and many other countries, citizenship is related to the state and is unrelated to nationality. To become a naturalized American citizen, one must pass a test demonstrating knowledge of U.S. history and government. A person who does so is eligible for citizenship regardless of national origin. In other countries, national origin is an important criterion for citizenship. For example, it is difficult for someone who cannot prove that he or she has German ancestry to become a German citizen. This has been a question of considerable controversy in Germany because many residents of Germany are descended from people who moved to Germany from Turkey, the Middle East, and elsewhere 50 or more years ago. Estonia is a country that also bases citizenship on nationality. Persons who can prove that they are descended from ancestors who were Estonian citizens between 1918 and 1940, when Estonia was an independent state, are exempt from the requirement to pass a test on Estonian history and government in the Estonian language.

Sovereignty is recognition by the international community of a state's right to rule its territory. The legitimacy of a new state is related to the degree to which the new state is recognized by existing states. In some cases, sovereignty results from agreement between existing states. For example, many new states were established and recognized in Europe after World War I. In other cases, sovereignty is contested. Rival factions or governments may claim sovereignty over particular territories. National groups have often claimed sovereignty over the territories in which these nations live. Rejection of these claims by the international community means generally that the proposed new state will not be recognized as a new state.

BOUNDARIES

Sovereignty is associated with control of territory. In order to determine the geographic limits of sovereignty, boundaries have been established. There are many different types of sovereignty. They can be classified on the basis of their physical form or by the degree to which those drawing the boundaries are aware of circumstances on either side of the boundary.

Boundaries can be divided on the basis of their physical form between natural boundaries, geometric boundaries, and cultural boundaries. Natural boundaries are boundaries that follow natural features on the landscape such as rivers or mountains. Examples of natural boundaries that follow rivers are the Rio Grande, which separates the United States and Mexico, and the Paraná River separating Paraguay and Brazil. However, the locations of boundaries within rivers vary. Some river boundaries follow the center of the stream, equidistant from the two banks. Other river boundaries follow the thalweg of the river, or the line connecting the deepest point within the river. In other cases, the boundary is located along one of the banks, with all of the river itself belonging to the other country. The location of a boundary within a river can be important—for example, when a country controlling the entire river across to the opposite bank can restrict navigation potential on the part of the other country.

Other physical boundaries follow mountain ranges. For example, the boundary between Spain and France follows the crest of the Pyrenees Mountains. Still other boundaries follow drainage divides that separate streams flowing into different rivers. For example, part of the boundary between Colombia and Brazil follows the drainage divide between the two major rivers of northern South America. Streams on the Brazilian side of the boundary flow into the Amazon River, while those on the Colombian side flow into the Orinoco River.

Geometric boundaries are straight lines that separate states from each other. Usually, geometric boundaries are agreed upon by the two countries via treaty. Some geometric boundaries are parallels of latitude or meridians of longitude. Examples are the 49th parallel of north latitude between the United States and Canada and the western and southern boundaries of Egypt in the Sahara Desert. Some straight-line segments are lengthy. For example, the boundary between the United States and Canada follows the 49th parallel for more than 1,500 miles. Many other straight-line boundary segments are very short. Some are as short as 300 feet in length, or no longer than the length of a football field.

Cultural boundaries are drawn in order to separate people on the basis of national origin or some other cultural characteristic. The boundary between India and Pakistan is a well-known example. The present-day countries of India, Pakistan, and Bangladesh were a single British colony prior to World War II. After the war ended, the British prepared to grant the colony its independence. Before independence was granted, it was decided to divide the colony into two countries: one with a Hindu majority (India) and one with a Muslim majority (Pakistan). After the boundaries were announced, many people decide to move. An estimated 15–20 million people moved across the boundary immediately prior to or after independence. Most were Muslims moving into Pakistan or Hindus and Sikhs moving into India. Much of this movement took place in western India. An estimated 200,000–500,000 people lost their lives during this population exchange. Millions of other persons lost their homes, land, and other property.

At the time of independence, Pakistan included West Pakistan (present-day Pakistan) and East Pakistan (present-day Bangladesh). The two parts of Pakistan shared Muslim majorities but were separated by 1,000 miles and had very different cultures, economies, and physical environments. In 1971, Bangladesh seceded from Pakistan and became a separate independent state, which it remains to this day. The boundaries of other countries such as Georgia and Croatia were drawn in such a way as to include as many members of their national groups as possible, as well as to exclude people belonging to other national groups. Cultural boundaries can follow straight-line segments, natural features, or both.

ANTECEDENT AND SUBSEQUENT BOUNDARIES

Boundaries can also be categorized as to the extent to which those drawing the boundaries knew about what was on either side of the border before the boundary lines were drawn. Antecedent boundaries are boundaries drawn without prior knowledge of the territory being separated. The 49th parallel between Canada and the United States is an example. Subsequent boundaries are boundaries drawn with knowledge of the territory being separated. Because knowledge of the human and physical geography of the earth's surface is now comprehensive, any present-day boundary change would involve subsequent boundaries.

Most of Africa's boundaries are also antecedent boundaries. They were drawn by European diplomats in the late 19th century. At that time, Europeans had very little knowledge of the African interior, and they did not know what people, natural resources, or physical features were located on either side of the boundaries that were drawn. As a result, many of Africa's boundaries separated nations and cultures between colonies governed by different European powers.

That many of Africa's boundaries are antecedent boundaries is evident from the fact that many boundaries separating states in Africa today are drawn perpendicular to the coast. These boundaries were drawn perpendicular to the coast because each European colonial power focused its attention on port cities, through which trade between Africa and Europe took place. Many of the boundaries were drawn around port cities that had already been established by various European powers. After most African countries became independent during the 1950s and 1960s, the boundaries drawn by the European colonial powers continued to be used. Some African countries continue to find it difficult to promote state identity as opposed to identity as a member of a nation or cultural group. However, in addressing boundary-related disputes, the African Union has generally taken the view that existing boundaries should be preserved when possible, even though most of these boundaries were antecedent boundaries that had been drawn by Europeans who had little knowledge of the African interior.

EXCLAVES AND ENCLAVES

The boundaries of most states enclose contiguous territory, all of which is under the sovereignty of the country circumscribed by these boundaries. However, some countries are sovereign over territory that is separated from the rest of that state's territory by land belonging to another country.

An exclave is a territory that is part of a particular state but that cannot be reached by land from the rest of that state without crossing territory belonging to another state. For example, Spain is sovereign over the exclaves of Ceuta and Melilla, which are located on the southern coast of the Mediterranean Sea and are both surrounded by Moroccan territory. Russia is sovereign over Kaliningrad Oblast, which has a land area the size of Connecticut and is home to nearly a million people. Kaliningrad Oblast is bounded by Lithuania, Poland, and the Baltic Sea, and it is separated from the rest of Russia by more than 200 miles by road.

An enclave is a territory that is surrounded entirely by territory under the sovereignty of another country. For example, there are nearly 200 enclaves along the boundary between India and Bangladesh, with 92 Bangladeshi enclaves surrounded by India and 106 Indian enclaves surrounded by Bangladesh. Many enclaves are also exclaves and vice versa. However, Kaliningrad Oblast is an exclave of Russia that is not an enclave given that the Oblast has borders with both Lithuania and Poland.

THE DEVELOPMENT OF THE MODERN STATE SYSTEM

States are currently defined on the basis of territory over which they are recognized as sovereign, and which is delineated by boundaries. Individual regimes have claimed control of particular regions for thousands of years. However, the idea of using boundaries to delineate the geographic limits of sovereignty is the product of European history beginning in the 17th century.

The word *territory* derives from the Latin word *territorium*—a conjunction of "earth" or "land" with "belonging to" or "surrounding." Originally, the idea of a territory pertained to land surrounding a city and under the authority of this city. From a geographic perspective, this territory was not defined precisely until after the Middle Ages. Not until the 17th century was the concept of territory connected to the concept of the state.

The modern state system as we know it today began to develop in Western and Central Europe during and after the Renaissance. Throughout history, ruling regimes have levied taxes in order to raise revenues. After the collapse of the Roman Empire, most of Europe was organized under feudalism. Under feudal societies, taxes were levied on the basis on occupation and social status, and these relationships were not tied closely to location. Because people were not taxed based on the locations of their lands or where they lived, there was not much need to delineate boundaries precisely.

The feudal system began to break down as urban centers oriented to trade and commerce began to develop. The growing independence of these urban centers led to the development of the modern system of sovereign states. The Hanseatic League was an important development in the transition between feudalism and the modern state. The Hanseatic League was a confederation of cities and towns that developed among communities located along the Baltic Sea during the 12th century. Residents and leaders of cities in the Hanseatic League demanded freedom of commerce and resented the person-centered authority of rural-based feudal societies. At that time, cities were associated with commercial, political, and artistic freedom relative to the conservatism and traditionalism of the countryside as controlled by the feudal nobility. The word *bourgeoisie*, which we now use to describe a middle-class person, comes from the word *burgher*, meaning a city dweller.

The linkage between the concept of territory and the idea of the state began with the Peace of Westphalia. The Peace of Westphalia was actually two treaties (the Treaty of Münster and the Treaty of Osnabrück), which were signed in 1648 to end the Thirty Years' War in Central Europe. The Peace of Westphalia established the principle that individual rulers could determine the official religion within areas under their control. Under terms of the Peace of Westphalia, a ruler could choose among Catholicism, Lutheranism, and Calvinism as the religion of the territory controlled by that ruler. Citizens who were not of the same religion as the ruler could practice their religion privately without persecution by the ruler, but taxes could be levied by the ruler to support the church of the ruler's choice.

In establishing this principle, the Peace of Westphalia established the principle of state sovereignty over territory on the earth's surface. It also established the concept of equality among sovereign states. States could not interfere in one another's internal affairs. The linkage between the state and geographically bounded territory meant also that states began to draw maps showing their territories specifically. Treaties between states specified the locations of boundaries between them. When sovereignty was transferred between states, the agreement identified the location of the territory to be transferred, identifying the boundaries as appropriate.

The first instance in which the Peace of Westphalia's principles were used in resolving an international territorial dispute was the Treaty of the Pyrenees in 1659. This treaty established the boundary between Spain and France that remains in place today.

Currently, of course, many disputes between countries are associated with disagreements over control of territory. In many cases, two and sometimes more countries have claimed sovereignty over the same territory. Control of additional territory has often been an important objective of a country's foreign policy. This is particularly true when the territory in dispute contains valuable resources or is considered important from the point of view of military strategy.

Disputes over territorial sovereignty have led to many wars throughout the past three centuries. Some wars have resulted in the direct conquest of territory. In other cases, agreements made following the end of the war involve redrawing boundaries. Generally speaking, territory is ceded from the losing country or countries to the victorious country or countries. For example, the Franco-Prussian War of 1870 resulted in the military defeat of France. The resulting Treaty of Frankfurt specified that the territory of Alsace-Lorraine in northeastern France would be transferred from French to Prussian sovereignty. On a larger scale, agreements made among belligerents after wars have ended have resulted in major boundary changes. For example, the map of Europe was redrawn via the Congress of Vienna following the Napoleonic Wars. It was redrawn again after World War I via the Treaty of Versailles.

STATE SYMBOLS AND FLAGS

Throughout the world, states symbolize themselves in many ways. Flags, national anthems, memorialization of historical figures and events, currency, coins, postage stamps, plants, and animals all symbolize states. Since ancient times, people have used symbols to identify members of their cultural groups.

Flags and banners, which are lightweight, easy to carry, and easy to see from a distance, were invented in China several thousand years ago. The use of flags made from silk or other fabrics to identify tribes and cultures had spread throughout Europe and Asia by the Middle Ages. Once the modern system of sovereign states developed, states began to design and use flags in order to symbolize themselves. Flags are also used by nationalist movements and indigenous peoples seeking autonomy and recognition.

Every state in the world now has an official flag. The oldest state flag still in use is the Dannebrog, whose name means "Danish Cloth" and is the flag of Denmark today. The Dannebrog is known to have been used by 1400 and may have been used even earlier. The Dannebrog's design includes the Nordic, or Scandinavian, cross. This design includes a cross in which the horizontal and vertical portions of the cross intersect on the hoist side of the flag, or to the left of center from the observer's point of view. The Nordic-cross design of the Dannebrog appears on the flags of other Scandinavian countries, including Norway, Finland, and Iceland. Autonomous regions in and near Scandinavia, such as the Faeroe Islands of Denmark and the Aland Islands of Finland, also have flags whose designs are based on the Nordic cross. Other substate units such as Scotland's Orkney Islands and Shetland Islands, whose histories are associated with Scandinavia or the Vikings, also have flags including the Nordic cross.

Flags used in other parts of the world also contain common elements. The stars and stripes of the flag of the United States symbolize the unification of the Thirteen Colonies into a single federal state. A similar design with stripes appears on the flags of Liberia, Uruguay, and several other countries.

Particular colors or color combinations are associated with various parts of the world, and these color combinations are often found on state flags. For example, red, white, and blue are the "Pan-Slavic" colors. These colors appear on the flags of Slovakia, Slovenia, Croatia, and Serbia, along with Bulgaria (where green replaces blue) and Russia (where orange replaces red). The "Pan-African" colors are red, green, and either gold or black. These colors appear on the flags of more than half of the states in sub-Saharan Africa.

Similarly, most state flags in the Arab world, including those of Morocco, Algeria, and Tunisia, use the "Pan-Arab" colors of red, white, and green. The flag of Oman includes these three colors, along with the emblem (crossed swords over the traditional curved dagger, or *khanjar*) of the Albusaidi Dynasty, which rules Oman as an absolute monarchy. The crescent and star are symbols of Islam. These symbols appear on the flags of many Islamic-majority countries inside and outside of the Arab world, including Algeria, Tunisia, Turkey, Azerbaijan, and Uzbekistan. During the period of communist rule, the Soviet Union's flag contained a gold hammer and sickle, symbols of communism, on a red field. The hammer-and-sickle motif and the red and gold colors continue to influence several flags today, including those of China and Mozambique. The flags of Guatemala, El Salvador, Honduras, and Costa Rica all include two blue stripes and one white stripe, in recognition of their history as part of the United Provinces of Central America between 1823 and 1841.

Some national flags contain plants, animals, or natural features symbolic of the states that they represent. For example, the maple leaf is a symbol of Canada, and it appears on the Canadian flag. The flag of Guatemala includes an image of the quetzal (*Pharomachrus mocinno*), that country's national bird. The flag of Papua New Guinea includes an image of a bird of paradise, many species of which live in that country. The Papua New Guinea flag also includes a representation of the Southern Cross, a constellation visible in the Southern Hemisphere that also appears on the flags of Australia and New Zealand.

Throughout the world, nationalist movements have been active in promoting independence, or at least greater autonomy. Nationalist movements often design and use flags. The use of these flags is often seen as an act of defiance against an established government, and in some cases their use is illegal. The flags of nationalist movements often become part of state flags after the country achieves independence. For example, many Uighurs in northwestern China seek independence. About 11.5 million Uighurs live in Central Asia. Most Uighurs live in Xinjiang Province in northwest China, although some Uighurs live in neighboring Russia, Kazakhstan, and Kyrgyzstan. Most Uighurs are Muslims, and they speak a Turkic language that is closely related to the languages of Central Asia rather than to Chinese. Religious and linguistic differences have put the Uighurs at odds with the Chinese government, which is officially atheistic. Uighur activists have also accused the Chinese of attempting to dilute their culture by encouraging the migration of Han Chinese into Uighur-majority areas of Xinjiang. Some Uighurs would prefer that Uighur-dominated territories of northwest China and Central Asia become an independent country named "East Turkestan" or "Uighurstan." The flag used by supporters of Uighur secession contains the crescent-and-star emblem used on the flags of other Islamic-majority countries of Central Asia.

Many other nationalist movements are also associated with their own flags. These nations include Tibet, the Kurds, and the Basques of northern Spain and southwestern France. In many cases, the display of these flags is discouraged or banned. For example, flying the Kurdish nationalist flag is against the law in Syria; flying the Basque flag was illegal in Spain between 1938 and 1977. Indigenous populations within countries have also designed flags. These flags often symbolize movements to promote political independence or increased local autonomy. In some cases, the flags are recognized and given official status by state governments. In Australia, for example, Aborigine activists designed a flag in 1971. The flag was recognized by the Australian government and given official status in 1995. The Maoris of New Zealand, the Sami of northern Scandinavia, and the Ainu of Japan are among the other indigenous populations that have designed and used flags representing their identities.

OTHER NATIONAL SYMBOLS

In addition to their flags, states throughout the world have many other symbols. These include national anthems and mottoes, national heroes, and national holidays. The use of these symbols is undertaken to encourage identification with a state on the part of its residents. National symbols are often depicted on artwork and on currency, coins, and stamps. Throughout the world, state leaders memorialize famous persons associated with the histories of their states. Many states recognize famous historical figures in various ways. Cities, airports, highways, streets, public buildings, and natural features are named in honor of national heroes, and statues of these persons have been built and displayed prominently in public places.

Legends about the heroic deeds of such persons are perpetuated in order to associate these national heroes with the virtues attributed to the states in which they live, even though these legends may have little or no basis in fact. For example, there is no historical evidence to support the often-repeated story that the young George Washington chopped down a cherry tree and later admitted the misdeed to his father with the words "I cannot tell a lie." Nevertheless, the story of George Washington and the cherry tree has been told to generations of American children in order to promote the virtues of honesty and truthfulness.

Frequently, a government's decision to promote, or to prevent, public memorials of historic figures or events results in public controversy. Historic figures who may be considered heroes by some people are considered villains or outcasts by others. Especially in autocracies or dictatorships, regime changes trigger changes in memorialization. For example, the city of St. Petersburg was renamed Leningrad after the death of the first leader of the Soviet Union, Vladimir Lenin, after Lenin died in 1924. After the collapse of the Soviet Union in 1991, the post-communist Russian government renamed the city St. Petersburg. The Dominican Republic's capital city of Santo Domingo was renamed Ciudad Trujillo by its dictator, Rafael Trujillo, in 1930. After Trujillo was assassinated in 1961, the original name of the city was restored. In other cases, one national group within a state may have a favorable image of historical figures or events that are viewed negatively by other groups. In Estonia, for example, the government built a statue of a Red Army soldier to commemorate the Soviet Army's efforts in liberating Estonia from Nazi control during World War II. As time went on, many ethnic Estonians came to identify the Soviets as well as the Nazis as oppressors. In 2007, the post-communist Estonian government dismantled and moved the statue over the objections of Russian Estonians who saw the memorialization of the Red Army's activities in a more positive light.

UNITARY AND FEDERAL STATES

The world's sovereign states can be divided between unitary states and federal states. In unitary states, all government power is held by the central government. Local government exists to administer decisions made at the central level. In federal states, power is shared formally between the central government and local governments. As a general principle, unitary states tend to be smaller and have more homogeneous populations than federal states, which are larger and more heterogeneous. Many of the large and diverse countries of the world, including the United States, Canada, Mexico, Germany, the United Kingdom, India, Nigeria, Australia, and Brazil, are federal states. China, Japan, and France are among the large and prominent unitary states in the world today.

The 10th Amendment to the United States Constitution, which reads, "The powers not delegated to the United States by the Constitution, nor prohibited by it to the States, are reserved for the States respectively, or to the people," establishes that the United States is a federal state. In practice, however, the federal government assumes responsibility for various functions that are state responsibilities under the Constitution.

SYSTEMS OF GOVERNANCE

Each of the world's states has a government, but systems of governance vary considerably from state to state. A convenient means of classifying the various types of government structures currently used in the world is to distinguish between democracies and autocracies. An autocracy is a state in which opposition to the current ruling regime is suppressed. Autocracies can be absolute monarchies or dictatorships. They can also be states ruled by military juntas or ruling parties such as the Communist Party in the former Union of Soviet Socialist Republics. In a democracy, all or most adults have a formal voice in the government, and opposition to the government is allowed.

A few countries can be regarded as anocracies, or states lacking any central authority to maintain order. Social relationships are based on personal allegiances to leaders, and these allegiances are often based on kinship, tribal, or ethnic communalities. Anocracy was common in many parts of the world prior to the modern era but is seldom found today. However, states that are regarded generally as "failed states" can be identified as anocracies. Perhaps the best example of an anocratic state is Somalia, which has lacked a functioning central government for nearly two decades.

ORGANIZATION OF THE BOOK

This book includes an overview of the states in each of seven major regions of the world: Europe, the Americas, sub-Saharan Africa, Southwest Asia and North Africa, Central and East Asia, South and Southeast Asia, and Australia and Oceania. These overviews form the core of chapters 1 through 7 respectively.

In each of these chapters, the overview is followed by a vignette with specific information about each country in the region. The initial section of each vignette provides an overview of the country, including its land area, its population, and a description of its boundaries with its neighbors. This overview is followed by discussion of the historical context underlying the development of that country and the evolution of its boundaries. The final section of each vignette describes contemporary conflicts over boundaries and other contemporary tensions between the country and nearby countries.

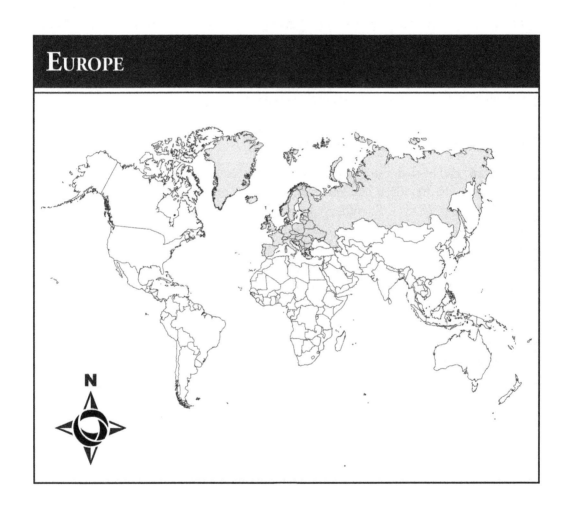

CHAPTER 1

EUROPE

Europe has been the center of global geopolitics for several hundred years. The concepts of nation, state, sovereignty, and boundaries as we know them today originated in Europe during and after the Renaissance. Through the process of colonialism, European civilization spread from Europe to the rest of the world. Today Europe is one of the most developed and prosperous parts of the world.

Europe today contains more than 40 independent states. The European state system as we know it today has developed over the past 2,000 years. To examine the development of the European state system as we know it today, it is useful to begin with the Roman Empire. Much of Western, Central, and Southern Europe was united under the Roman Empire 2,000 years ago. At its maximum extent, the Roman Empire included present-day Portugal, Spain, France, Italy, Belgium, and the Netherlands as well as southern Great Britain, southern Germany, and the countries of the Balkan Peninsula. It also included the lands along the Mediterranean coast of Africa along with much of present-day Egypt, Israel, Jordan, Syria, Lebanon, and Turkey.

The area controlled politically by empires such as the Roman Empire was the same as the area controlled economically. From the empire's center in Rome, the empire enforced control of outlying areas by forcing people living in these areas to pay tribute and taxes to support the empire. Tribute and taxes were paid in the form of money, produce and other goods, or labor. In order to expedite control over the empire, the Romans built an extensive system of roads. The labor was provided by local residents under the supervision of Roman legions and engineers. The purpose of the roads was to speed movement of military personnel and also to integrate commerce within the empire. Some of the roads can still be seen today.

Over time, Rome became wealthy at the expense of peripheral areas, whose residents resented having to pay tribute or contribute taxes and rebelled when strong enough. In order to maintain control of its outlying areas, the Romans needed an ever larger army. Eventually, the empire became stretched too thin to maintain control of outlying territories. After about AD 300, the authority of Rome over its outlying territories declined. People living in outlying areas refused to accept Roman authority or pay taxes and tribute to Rome, and the Roman state was no longer strong enough to enforce Roman authority or payment of taxes and tribute. In AD 395, the empire split formally between the Western Roman Empire, which was based in Rome, and the Eastern Roman Empire, which was based in Constantinople (present-day Istanbul, Turkey). By this time, the area under effective control of the Western Roman Empire was limited to Italy, parts of present-day Switzerland and Austria, and the lands along the eastern coast of the Adriatic Sea in present-day Slovenia and Croatia. In AD 476, the last Roman emperor, Romulus Augustus, was deposed by a Germanic army.

Once the Roman Empire collapsed, much of Europe was ruled by local landlords and kings under the system of feudalism. Feudalism was a rural-based system; a large majority of people were serfs who were bound to the lands on which they lived and which they cultivated. The feudal system began to break down as urban centers oriented to trade and commerce began to develop. The growing independence of these urban centers, including those belonging to the Hanseatic League, led to the development of the modern system of sovereign states in Europe and elsewhere in the world.

The Reformation was another key element in the development of the modern concept of sovereignty. In the 16th century, theologians including Martin Luther and John Calvi, protested the excesses of the Roman Catholic Church, eventually breaking with the church. Europe became divided between Catholicism and various branches of Protestantism. Conflict over the relationships between religion and the state led to the Thirty Years' War in Central Europe. The Peace of Westphalia, which ended the war, also established the concept of state sovereignty and created the need to delineate and maintain boundaries between sovereign states.

European states contested with one another for influence and territorial control within Europe and throughout the world over the next 300 years. During this period, European influence spread throughout the world. Most of the non-European world was at one time under the direct or indirect control of one or more European powers between the 17th and the mid-20th century. However, European dominance of the global economy ended with World Wars I and II. The end of World War II left the United States and the Soviet Union as the leading political powers in the world. For the first time in several hundred years, Europe was no longer the most powerful region of the world. Instead, many Europeans saw their homeland as a potential battleground between the West and the East as the Cold War developed.

These considerations underlie the development of the European Union. The "Iron Curtain" symbolized the Cold War in Europe. The term "Iron Curtain" came from a famous speech made by Sir Winston Churchill (1874–1965) in Westminster, Missouri, on March 5, 1946, less than a year after World War II ended. Churchill stated, "From Stettin in the Baltic to Trieste in the Adriatic, an 'iron curtain' has descended across the Continent. Behind that line lie all the capitals of the ancient states of Central and Eastern Europe. Warsaw, Berlin, Prague, Vienna, Budapest, Belgrade, Bucharest, and Sofia; all these famous cities and the populations around them lie in what I must call the Soviet sphere, and all are subject, in one form or another, not only to Soviet influence but to a very high and in some cases increasing measure of control from Moscow."

Recognizing increased Soviet influence in Eastern Europe, the United States and her Western European allies took several steps to curb further Soviet expansion during the late 1940s. The North Atlantic Treaty Organization (NATO) was established in 1949. A year earlier, the governments of Belgium, France, the Netherlands, Luxembourg, and the United Kingdom agreed to the Treaty of Brussels, which established the Western European Union's Defense Organization (not to be confused with the European Union itself). The Defense Organization can be thought of as a precursor to NATO in that it promoted collective security and mutual defense among its members. However, the Defense Organization differed from NATO in two important ways. First, it was concerned about the threat from a potentially resurgent Germany as well as the Soviet Union; second, it regarded the concept of collective security against German and Soviet expansion as a purely European response.

The Soviet blockade of West Berlin in 1949 persuaded members of the Defense Organization that Soviet communism was a much greater threat to Western Europe than was the possible resurgence of the Nazis in Germany. They also recognized the importance of including the United States in the collective security process. NATO was formally established in 1949. In 1955, West Germany was invited to join NATO.

The United States also responded to the threat of Soviet expansion in Europe by establishing the Truman Doctrine and the Marshall Plan. The Truman Doctrine stated that the United States would provide military and economic assistance to any country that was threatened by communist takeover. It was first applied in 1947 in Greece and Turkey. President Truman also applied it to justify the Berlin Airlift, in which the United States responded to the Soviet blockade of West Berlin by having the U.S. Air Force fly food, medical supplies, and other goods into the city. The Marshall Plan was a corollary to the Truman Doctrine. The Marshall Plan was an effort to provide U.S. economic aid to rebuild the war-torn economies of Europe. In implementing the Marshall Plan, the United States saw foreign aid as a means of promoting European prosperity and therefore helping resist communist influence.

These considerations, along with concerns that nationalism within European countries would cause further wars in Europe, led Western European leaders to consider ways to unify Europe. Between the 1950s and the end of the Cold War, the European Union was established and expanded its membership and influence to encompass most of the continent. The first step toward the establishment of the European Union was the establishment of the European Coal and Steel Community (ECSC) in 1951. The ECSC's members were France, West Germany, Italy, the Netherlands, Belgium, and Luxembourg. The ECSC eliminated all tariffs and trade barriers in the production and distribution of coal, steel, and steel products. In 1957, the ECSC decided to eliminate tariffs and barriers in the trade of all manufactured goods and services. The name of the organization was changed to the European Economic Community and was then changed to the European Community in 1967.

Between 1967 and 1994, the European Community expanded its membership. It also expanded its jurisdiction from economic to political, cultural, and other activities. It also adopted its present name, becoming the European Union (EU). Six countries joined the European Community during the 1970s and 1980s. These included the United Kingdom, Ireland, Denmark, Spain, Portugal, and Greece. Spain and Portugal were not original members of the Community because both were ruled by dictators in the 1950s and 1960s. Once their dictatorships were replaced by functioning democracies, both were invited to join the Community.

The Community also established the European Parliament in 1979. Since that time, voters in member countries have voted directly for members of the European Parliament, which is headquartered in Strasbourg, France. The Community also designed and began using the current EU flag in 1986. The European Community became the European Union after the Treaty of Maastricht, named for the Dutch city in which it was negotiated, went into effect in 1993. The treaty created the governmental structures of the contemporary European Union.

The transition from the European Community to the European Union coincided with the collapse of communism in the Soviet Union and Eastern Europe between 1989 and 1991. As Soviet communism collapsed, members of the European Community recognized that the original rationale for forming the Community— the development of a political and economic counterweight to Soviet influence during the Cold War—was no longer critical. Various issues involving European unification, such as a common currency, language, the judicial and legal system, and immigration, had been on the back burner prior to the end of the Cold War but now became much more significant to Europe's leadership. The currency issue has become particularly critical today and threatens the continued stability of the European Union.

The collapse of communism in the Soviet Union also led to its growth. The EU has continued to grow since its formal inception in 1993. Sweden, Finland, and Austria joined the EU in 1994. At that time, Norway was also invited to join but declined the invitation. Twelve additional countries have joined since that time. These include several former Soviet satellites including Poland, the Czech Republic, Slovakia, Hungary, Romania, Bulgaria, and Slovenia. Three former Soviet republics— Estonia, Latvia, and Lithuania—have also become members of the EU. The other two new members are Cyprus and Malta.

Several other countries have applied to join the EU, but their applications are pending. As a general principle, any new member of the EU must agree to the conditions of the Copenhagen Criteria concerning EU membership. The Copenhagen Criteria were approved by EU members at a meeting of the European Council in June 1993. According to the Copenhagen Criteria, "Membership requires that candidate country has achieved stability of institutions guaranteeing democracy, the rule of law, human rights and respect for and protection of minorities, the existence of a functioning market economy as well as the capacity to cope with competitive pressure and market forces within the Union. Membership presupposes the candidate's ability to take on the obligations of membership including adherence to the aims of political, economic and monetary union."

Currently Turkey, Croatia, and Macedonia are under consideration for EU membership.

Immigration has become a significant concern throughout the European Union. Given its aging population and low birth rates, Europe relies heavily on immigrants from less developed countries as a source of labor. However, members of the EU have experienced difficulty in coordinating their policies concerning immigration and political asylum. The EU is a very attractive destination for migrants from Africa, Southwest Asia, and other less developed countries of origin. In 2006, more than 1 million people moved legally to the European Union, and nearly 300,000 people sought political asylum. However, immigrants are not evenly distributed across the European Union. The countries of Southern Europe, including Spain, France, and Italy, which border the Mediterranean Sea and are geographically closest to Africa, receive the most migrants. More than half of the 2006 migrants to the EU came to Spain. All three of these countries have made efforts to crack down on immigration. For example, government officials in Italy have proposed to make illegal immigration into Italy a felony offense, punishable by prison. On the other hand, countries such as Estonia, Finland, and Latvia attract relatively few migrants and have expressed opposition to EU efforts to standardize immigration policy.

Members of the EU also disagree about appropriate ways to deal with the global economic recession of 2008–2009. Rising levels of unemployment have resulted in tensions between countries whose jobs are threatened by the downturn. For example, both France and Germany have engineered efforts to protect jobs in automobile manufacturing in their respective countries. These disagreements intensified into the Eurozone crisis of 2011–2012, and it remains uncertain whether the Euro can survive as the EU's common currency.

ALBANIA

OVERVIEW

The Republic of Albania is located on the Balkan Peninsula in southeastern Europe. It has a land area of 11,100 square miles, about the size of the state of Maryland. Its population is about 2.8 million.

Albania's neighbors are Montenegro to the north and west, Kosovo to the northeast, Macedonia to the east, and Greece to the south. To the west is Albania's coastline on the Adriatic Sea. Most of Albania's boundaries follow mountain ranges and other natural features. Much of the boundary between Albania and Montenegro follows the Buna River, which is known in Montenegro as the Bojana River. The Buna represents the boundary from its mouth along the Adriatic upstream to Lake Scutari, which is also known as Lake Skadar and is the largest natural lake on the Balkan Peninsula. From Lake Scutari, the boundary follows the crest of the Prokletije, or Albanian Alps, in a northeasterly direction.

Near the Albanian town of Vermosh, the crest of the mountain range extends in a generally eastward direction to the tripoint between Albania, Montenegro, and Kosovo. From this tripoint, the boundaries between Albania and Kosovo and between Albania and Macedonia continue in a southeasterly direction along the crests

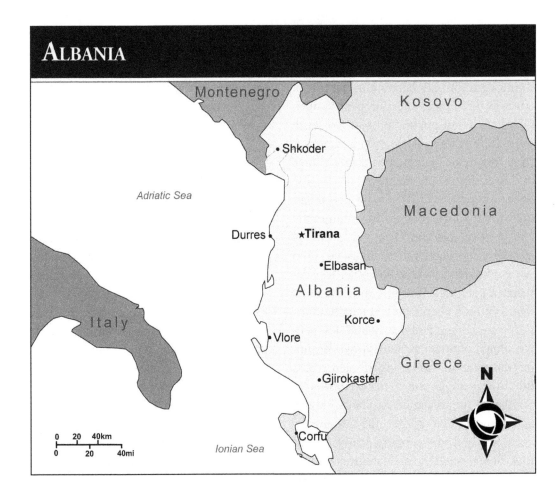

ALBANIA

of local mountain ranges. Lake Ohrid and Lake Prespa, which are the second- and third-largest natural lakes on the Balkan Peninsula respectively, are located near the southern end of the border between Albania and Macedonia. The tripoint between Albania, Macedonia, and Greece is located in Lake Prespa.

From Lake Prespa, the boundary between Albania and Greece trends in a southwesterly direction to the Ionian Sea, which separates the Adriatic Sea from the Mediterranean Sea. Much of this boundary also follows the crest of the mountain range, known locally as the Southern Mountain Range, that separates the two countries. Near the Adriatic coast, the boundary trends westward until it enters the Adriatic opposite the Greek island of Corfu.

HISTORICAL CONTEXT

The Albanians have been recognized as a distinctive national group for more than 2,000 years. The Albanian language, although it is part of the Indo-European language family, forms a distinct subfamily and is related only distantly to other Indo-European languages. Although present-day

Albania has been occupied by a succession of foreign powers since Roman times, Albania has managed to maintain its cultural identity in part because it is isolated from its neighbors by the rugged mountains that form its boundaries today.

Present-day Albania was known as Illyria. Illyria was part of the Roman Empire until AD 395, when the empire was divided between its eastern and western portions. Illyria became part of the Eastern Roman Empire, which became the Byzantine Empire. It remained under Byzantine rule until it was taken over by the Bulgarian Empire in the ninth century AD. For the next several centuries, portions of what is now Albania were ruled at various times by locally based principalities and kingdoms and at other times by foreign-based kingdoms and empires. In the late 14th and early 15th centuries, Albania was conquered by the Ottoman Empire. The Ottoman conquest of Albania was completed by 1485, and all of Albania remained under Ottoman control until 1912. During the period of Ottoman rule, many Albanians converted from Christianity to Islam. According to recent estimates, the population of Albania today is about 70 percent Muslim, 20 percent Orthodox Christian, and 10 percent Roman Catholic.

In the early 20th century, Albanian nationalists protested the increasing Turkish influence on the Ottoman Empire. Albania declared its independence in 1912, and Albanian independence was confirmed by the Treaty of London in 1913. The boundaries of newly independent Albania were approximately those in place today. They were delineated primarily with the intention of separating ethnic Albanians within Albania from people of other national origins in neighboring countries. These boundaries were formalized during the 1920s. Albania remained independent until 1939, when its government was overthrown by Italian forces under Benito Mussolini's regime.

Shortly after World War II, communist leaders dominated Albania and proclaimed the People's Republic of Albania in 1946. The People's Republic, under the leadership of Enver Hoxha, was dedicated to Stalinist principles, and it broke with the Soviet Union after its de-Stalinization policies were put into effect in the late 1950s. During the 1960s, Albania became a close ally of China, but this alliance deteriorated in the 1970s and 1980s as China opened itself to increased interaction with the West. After Hoxha died in 1985, anti-communist activity increased. The People's Republic, which had been renamed the People's Socialist Republic in 1976, dissolved in 1990, and the first free elections were held in March 1991. An anti-communist, pro-democracy party took power a year later. Since then, Albania has maintained itself as a parliamentary democracy. Albania became a member of NATO in 2009.

CONTEMPORARY ISSUES

Although the boundaries of Albania have remained intact since shortly after World War I, tension continues between Albania and some of its neighbors. Many of these conflicts are associated with the rights of Albanian nationals living outside Albania, an issue that has been an important objective of Albanian foreign policy since the collapse of the communist regime.

The most significant conflict has involved Kosovo. After World War II, what are now Montenegro, Kosovo, and Macedonia were all part of Yugoslavia. After Yugoslavia's breakup in the early 1990s, Kosovo and Montenegro became part of the State Union of Serbia and Montenegro, which dissolved in 2006 when Montenegro became an independent country.

Kosovo had been established as an autonomous region in Yugoslavia in 1945. Nearly 90 percent of Kosovo's people are of Albanian ancestry and speak Albanian as their first language. During the ongoing conflict over Kosovo's status, Albania became a strong supporter of Kosovo's independence. Several hundred thousand Kosovars moved across the boundary to Albania during and after the Kosovo civil war, although many of these refugees have returned to Kosovo. Albania became one of the first countries to recognize Kosovo as an independent country after Kosovo declared its independence from Serbia in 2008. Serbia has not recognized Kosovo's independence, contributing to tension between Albania and Serbia although the two no longer share a boundary.

See also   Greece, Kosovo, Macedonia, Montenegro

Further Reading

Paulin Kola. *The search for greater Albania.* London: Hurst and Company, 2003.

Nick Thorpe. "Uncovering Albania's role in the Kosovo War." *BBC News,* May 17, 2010, http://news.bbc.co.uk/2/hi/8687186.stm.

Gus Xhudo. "Tension among neighbours: Greek-Albanian relations and their impact on regional security and stability." *Studies in Conflict and Terrorism,* 18 (1995), pp. 111–143.

ANDORRA

OVERVIEW

The Principality of Andorra is located in the Pyrenees Mountains between France to the north and Spain to the south. It has a land area of 181 square miles (about 2.5 times the land area of Washington, DC) and a population of about 84,000. Andorra's boundaries with France to the north and Spain to the south include short straight-line segments along with lines that follow the crests of the mountains located in the border region.

HISTORICAL CONTEXT

Andorra owes its origin to conflict within Europe between the Moors of present-day Spain and the French. In 795, Charlemagne established the Marca Hispanica as a buffer region between his Christian Frankish kingdom and the Muslim Moors, who controlled most of present-day Spain. The Marca Hispanica extended across present-day northern Spain from Barcelona on the Mediterranean coast to Pamplona to the northwest. Charlemagne's grandson, Charles the Bald, gave Andorra to the Diocese of Urgell in Catalonia. Today, Andorra is the only independent state that was once part of the Marca Hispanica.

In 1278, the Diocese of Urgell agreed to share control over Andorra with the Count of Foix, which controlled what is now Southern France north of the Andorran boundary. The Count of Foix and the Bishop of Urgell became joint heads of the Andorran state. The last Count of Foix ascended the French throne in 1589 as King Henry IV. With Henry's accession, cosovereignty over Foix was transferred to the

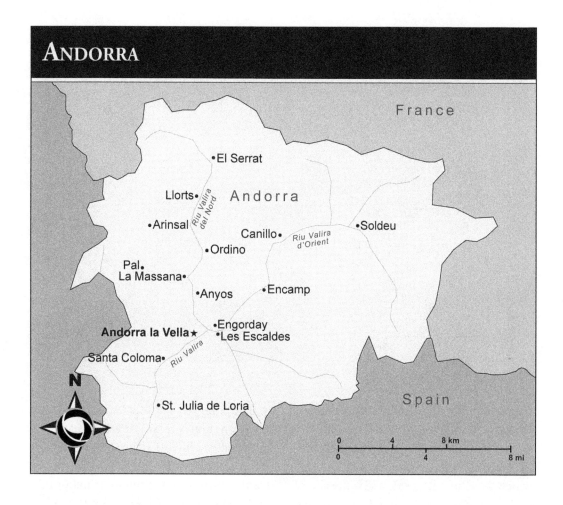

ANDORRA

France

•El Serrat

Llorts•   A n d o r r a

Riu Valira del Nord

•Arinsal   Canillo•   •Soldeu

Riu Valira d'Orient

•Ordino

Pal•
La Massana•

•Anyos   •Encamp

•Engorday
Andorra la Vella★ •Les Escaldes

Santa Coloma• *Riu Valira*

N

•St. Julia de Loria

Spain

0   4   8 km

0   4   8 mi

French state. Today, the bishop of Urgell remains the joint head of state of Andorra along with the president of France. In 2000, Andorra and France agreed to an exchange of territory so that Andorra could build a new access road from France without the road cutting back and forth between Andorran and French territory.

See also France, Spain

Further Reading

Hugh O'Reilly. "Andorra: The forgotten principality." Translated and based upon Philippe Delorme, *Andorre, La Principaté Oublié Point de Vue*, September 29, 1989, pp. 40–41.

AUSTRIA

OVERVIEW

The Republic of Austria is located in Central Europe. It has a land area of 32,377 square miles, or about the size of South Carolina. Austria's population is about 8.5 million. Much of western and southern Austria contains part of the Alps and is rugged and mountainous. However, the valley of the Danube River in northern Austria crosses relatively flat, fertile land. Austria's capital city of Vienna is located on the Danube.

Austria is landlocked, and it borders eight other countries: Germany and the

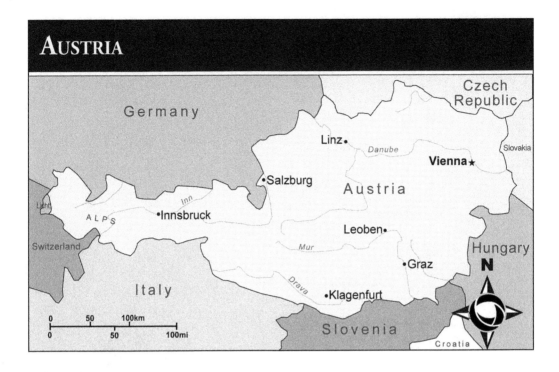

Czech Republic to the north, Slovakia and Hungary to the east, Slovenia and Italy to the south, and Switzerland and Liechtenstein to the west. Lake Constance, into which the Rhine River flows, is the site of the tripoint between Austria, Germany, and Switzerland. From this tripoint, the boundary between Austria and Germany extends through mountainous and sparsely populated territory. From Lake Constance, it extends generally eastward and then turns southward. Near the town of Wolfegg, it turns northeastward. The boundary follows the crest of the Bavarian Alps and the drainage divide that separates rivers that flow southward into Austria from those that flow northward into Germany. Near the village of Renbach, the boundary turns more directly eastward. At this point, a small section of Austrian territory, about three square miles in land area, is nearly surrounded by German territory.

The boundary between Austria and Germany continues in an irregular but generally easterly direction. It follows the Inn River northward before resuming its eastward course from the Inn to its major tributary, the Salzach River. From this point, the boundary follows the Salzach northward, passing the city of Salzburg, to its confluence with the Inn near the town of Braunau am Inn. It then follows the Inn downstream to its confluence with the Danube. The boundary follows the Danube downstream and eastward for a short distance before it turns northward to the tripoint between Austria, Germany, and the Czech Republic. From this tripoint, the boundary between Austria and the Czech Republic follows a series of short geometric segments until it reaches the Thaya River, which is known as the Dyje River in the Czech Republic. The western portion of this boundary generally follows the drainage divide between the Danube on the Austrian side of the border and the Vltava River, which flows northward and drains much of the western Czech Republic, on the Czech side. The boundary follows the line of the Thaya southeastward to its confluence with the Morava River. The tripoint between Austria, the Czech Republic, and Slovakia is located at this confluence.

The Morava forms the boundary between Austria and Slovakia before it empties into the Danube. The Danube itself forms a brief portion of the boundary between Austria and Slovakia until the boundary turns southward near the outskirts of Slovakia's capital city of Bratislava. From this point it follows a series of straight-line segments in a generally southward direction to the tripoint between Austria, Slovakia, and Hungary. The boundary between Austria and Hungary is also geometric. It follows a series of straight-line segments southward until it turns eastward abruptly at a point south of the Austrian village of Hansaghof. It continues in a westerly direction, following more straight-line segments, to Lake Neusiedl. A few miles west of the lake, it turns southward again and follows additional straight-line segments to the tripoint between Austria, Hungary, and Slovenia.

In contrast to the boundary between Austria and Hungary, much of the boundary between Austria and Slovenia follows natural features. Part of this boundary follows the Mur and Drava rivers, both of which are tributaries of the Danube. West of the Drava, the boundary enters mountainous terrain. The tripoint between Austria, Slovenia, and Italy is located near Mount Petzen, which is the highest mountain in the Alpine range that separates Austria and Slovenia.

The crest of the eastern Alps forms the boundary between Austria and Italy. The boundary region is mountainous, sparsely populated, and relatively inaccessible by European standards, with few roads crossing the border.

Austria has two borders with Switzerland, separated by its boundary with Liechtenstein. The southern portion of the boundary crosses mountainous Alpine terrain. The northern portion of the boundary, north of the northern tripoint between Austria, Switzerland, and Liechtenstein on the Rhine, follows the Rhine northward into Lake Constance, which contains the tripoint between Austria, Switzerland, and Germany. Between the two boundaries with Switzerland, the boundary between Austria and Liechtenstein follows straight-line segments that extend generally from south to north.

HISTORICAL CONTEXT

What is now Austria was inhabited by Celtic tribes about 5,000–6,000 years ago. Much of present-day Austria south of the Danube was part of the kingdom of Noricum, which became a province of the Roman Empire in approximately 50 BC. For several centuries, the Danube represented the frontier between the Roman Empire to the south and lands controlled by Germanic tribes to the north. After the breakup of the Roman Empire, the area was settled also by Germanic tribes from the north and west and by Slavic tribes from the east. A variety of principalities ruled parts of Austria throughout the Middle Ages.

Beginning in the 11th century, the Hapsburg family became prominent in Austria. By the 15th century, the Hapsburgs controlled most of present-day Austria and Slovenia. This region was located on the southeastern periphery of the Holy Roman Empire but played a prominent role in the empire's political system and administration. All of the Holy Roman Emperors who reigned between 1438 and 1740 were members of the Hapsburg dynasty. In 1458, the region ruled by the Hapsburgs directly became known as the Archduchy of Austria.

The Hapsburgs continued to rule the Archduchy into the early 19th century. In 1804, the last Holy Roman emperor, Francis II, formally dissolved the Holy Roman Empire and proclaimed himself the emperor of Austria. The new Austrian Empire included not only Austria but all of the present-day Czech Republic, Slovakia, Hungary, and Slovenia along with territory in what is now Italy, Croatia, and Romania. In 1867, the Austrian Empire became the Austro-Hungarian Empire following a power-sharing agreement between the Hapsburgs and the government of Hungary. This agreement led to what would become known as the dual monarchy, in which the Hapsburg ruler was sovereign over both Austria and Hungary but each maintained a separate parliament and responsibility for its internal affairs.

The Austro-Hungarian Empire fought on the side of Germany during World War I, and the empire was dissolved in 1918 after the war ended. Most of the German-speaking areas of the empire became the Republic of Austria. In 1938, Hitler invaded Austria, initiating the Anschluss. The republic was dissolved, and Austria was incorporated into Nazi Germany.

After World War II, Austria was separated once again from Germany. Like Germany, it was divided into British, French, American, and Soviet occupation zones. The city of Vienna was also divided into occupation sectors. The Soviet occupation zone included Vienna and much of the Danube valley, and a division between a communist East Austria and a Western-oriented West Austria—a situation analogous to the Cold War division of Germany—became a distinct possibility. In 1955, however, the four occupation zones were united under a promise that Austria would remain neutral in the Cold War. The country became independent, and the Second Republic of Austria was constituted. Austria remained officially neutral until the end of the Cold War, after which it joined the European Union in 1994.

Most of Austria's present boundaries were delineated before World War I, with the others specified immediately after the war. Austria's oldest extant boundaries are those with Liechtenstein, which have been in place since 1719, and with Switzerland, which were established in conjunction with the Congress of Vienna in 1815. The boundary between Austria and Germany was agreed upon in 1866, after the German Confederation under the leadership of Prussia defeated Austria-Hungary in the Austro-Prussian War, also known as the Seven Weeks' War. No territory changed hands as a result of the war, although the war resulted in a shift of power in Central Europe from Austria-Hungary to what would become the German Empire under the leadership of Prussia. After World War II, Austria and Germany were separated again, and the 1866 boundaries were reaffirmed.

The boundary between Austria and Hungary also was delineated after the Austro-Prussian War. Recognizing its decline in power relative to the German Empire, Austria pushed to formalize the agreement with Hungary that created the dual monarchy. The boundaries agreed upon remained the boundaries of Austria and Hungary after the dissolution of the Austro-Hungarian Empire. The boundary between Austria and Italy were agreed upon in a treaty between Austria-Hungary and Italy signed in 1866 during the period of Italian unification in the 19th century. In this treaty, Austria ceded control of the area around the city of Venice to the new Italian state. Austria ceded a portion of the Tyrol region near the Brenner Pass in the Alps to Italy in 1919. A subsequent agreement between Austria and Italy, signed in 1955, confirmed these boundaries.

Austria's boundaries with the Czech Republic, Slovakia, and Slovenia were determined as part of the Treaty of Paris after World War I. At that time, the Czech Republic and Slovakia were the single country of Czechoslovakia. After Czechoslovakia was split between the Czech Republic and Slovakia in 1993, the existing boundaries remained in place.

CONTEMPORARY ISSUES

Austria's boundaries have remained stable since its independence from Nazi Germany was recognized at the end of World War II. During the Cold War, East Germany and Czechoslovakia fortified areas along their boundaries to prevent people from escaping from these communist countries to the west. Barbed wire and land mines were used to restrict movements further. These fortifications were dismantled after the Cold War came to an end in the late 1980s and early 1990s.

See also   Czech Republic, Germany, Hungary, Italy, Liechtenstein, Slovakia, Slovenia, Switzerland

Further Reading

Nicole Alecu de Flers. *EU foreign policy and the Europeanization of neutral states: Comparing Irish and Austrian foreign policy.* London: Routledge, 2011.

Steven Beller. *A short history of Austria.* New York: Cambridge University Press, 2007.

Gunter Bischof, Fritz Plasser, Anton Pelinka, and Alexander Smith (eds.). *Global Austria: Austria's place in Europe and the world.* New Orleans, LA: University of New Orleans Press, 2011.

BELARUS

OVERVIEW

The Republic of Belarus is located in northeastern Europe. It has a land area of 80,155 square miles, slightly smaller than Kansas. Its population is about 9.6 million.

Belarus borders Russia to the north and east, Ukraine to the south, Poland to the west, Lithuania to the northwest, and Latvia to the north. Most of Belarus's boundaries are irregular. Some follow physical features on the landscape, while most of the others are short geometric lines that connect boundary posts and pillars. In general, the boundaries of Belarus were delineated in order to place people of Belorussian ancestry in the Belorussian state.

The central portion of the boundary between Belarus and Latvia follows the

BELARUS

Western Dvina River, which is known in Latvia as the Daugava River. Northeast of the Western Dvina, the boundary follows a complex series of short geometric lines that trend generally from southwest to northeast until it reaches the tripoint between Belarus, Latvia, and Russia. The boundary between Belarus and Russia also consists of numerous short straight-line segments, trending generally from northwest to southeast. It was created with the intention of separating people of Belorussian ancestry from those of Russian ancestry to the east.

The boundary between Belarus and Ukraine was also delineated to separate Belarusians to the north and Ukrainians to the south. This boundary is also irregular and consists primarily of very short straight-line segments. Chernobyl, the site of the world's worst nuclear accident in 1986, is located in Ukraine less than 10 miles from its boundary with Belarus. Given the prevailing wind patterns at the time, it is believed that as much as two-thirds of the fallout from the accident fell on Belarusian territory.

Belarus's western boundaries with Poland and Lithuania are also complex and irregular, with numerous straight-line segments. The southern section of the boundary between Belarus and Poland follows the Bug River downstream and to the north to a point northwest of the Belarusian city of Brest-Litovsk. The Bug flows westward into Poland where it empties into the Vistula River, but the boundary between Belarus and Poland turns northeastward to a point near Belarus's Bielaviezskaja Forest. It then turns northward to the tripoint between Belarus, Poland, and Lithuania. The boundary between Belarus and Lithuania extends in a generally northeastward direction, following many short straight-line segments. A small section of Lithuanian territory about 80 square miles in land area extends into Belarus's territory south of the Lithuanian capital city of Vilnius. From this near enclave, the boundary between Belarus and Lithuania extends in a more northerly direction to the tripoint between Belarus, Lithuania, and Russia.

HISTORICAL CONTEXT

The name of Belarus is derived from the name of the Belorussian people, whose name translates to "White Russians" in English. The Belorussian people are related closely to other Northern Slavic peoples living in present-day Poland, Ukraine, and Russia. Their identity as a separate nation derives from Belarus's history of contestation between larger Eastern European powers dating back hundreds of years.

During the Middle Ages, White Russia was also known as Ruthenia. Ruthenia was part of the Grand Duchy of Lithuania. In 1569, Ruthenia was absorbed into the Polish-Lithuanian Commonwealth, which also included most of present-day Poland, Ukraine, and Lithuania. The

commonwealth was dissolved in 1795, with its territory absorbed into those of larger and more powerful neighbors. What is now Belarus was absorbed by the Russian Empire, where it remained until 1918 when the Russian Empire dissolved.

Belarus declared its independence in 1918 as the Belarusian People's Republic. It claimed sovereignty over those areas that had Belorussian population majorities. On January 1, 1919, the Soviet Union absorbed the People's Republic, which became the Byelorussian Soviet Socialist Republic (BSSR). During the period of Soviet rule, the Soviets imposed various territorial changes to the BSSR. For example, sovereignty over part of eastern Poland was transferred to the BSSR in 1939 after Poland fell to the Germans and the Soviets at the outset of World War II. In 1945, the United Nations Charter gave the BSSR a seat in the United Nations General Assembly, although BSSR remained a part of the Soviet states.

With the dissolution of the Soviet Union in 1991, Belarus became an independent state. Today about 81 percent of Belarus's population is of Belorussian ancestry. Eleven percent are of Russian ancestry, with smaller percentages of Poles, Ukrainians, and other minorities.

CONTEMPORARY ISSUES

Despite Belarus's volatile history, and despite the fact areas of present-day Belarus were contested among the larger European powers for hundreds of years, Belarus's contemporary boundaries are stable and uncontested. In recent years, Belarus has negotiated agreements with its neighbors to address minor boundary issues. In 2010, Belarus signed treaties with both Lithuania and Ukraine. These treaties formalized Belarus's boundaries with these respective countries and dealt with other boundary-related questions such as border-crossing issues.

Whether Belarus will remain an independent state or will be absorbed eventually into Russia is an open question. Given its long history of absorption into neighboring countries, Belarusian national identity is weak relative to that of Estonia, Latvia, Lithuania, Ukraine, and other former Soviet satellites. The lack of distinctive national identity along with the close historical ties between Belarus and Russia has encouraged many Belarusians to support closer ties with Russia, including full political unification. In December 2008, a public opinion survey showed that 46.3 percent of Belarusians would vote in favor of unification, with 35.3 percent opposed. In 2011, Russian prime minister Vladimir Putin announced his support for unifying Belarus and Russia.

See also Latvia, Lithuania, Poland, Russia, Ukraine

Further Reading

Deutsche Welle. "Belarus rejects Putin's call for unification with Russia." August 4, 2011, http://www.dw.de/dw/article/0,15295158,00.html.

Elena Korosteleva. "Belarusian foreign policy in a time of crisis." *Journal of Communist Studies and Transition Politics*, 27 (2011), pp. 566–586.

Sarah Rainsford. "Belarus cursed by Chernobyl." *BBC News*, April 26, 2005, http://news.bbc.co.uk/2/hi/europe/4485003.stm.

BELGIUM

OVERVIEW

Belgium, located in northwestern Europe, has a land area of 11,787 square miles (slightly larger than Maryland), with a population of about 11 million. Belgium consists of two major regions, Flanders and Wallonia. Flanders, in northern Belgium, is inhabited by Dutch-speaking Flemish people; Wallonia in the south is inhabited by French-speaking Walloons. About 58 percent of Belgium's people are Flemish and about 40 percent are Walloons. A small population of German speakers lives in eastern Belgium near the German border. Dutch, French, and German are the official languages of their respective regions.

Although Belgium borders Dutch-speaking Netherlands, French-speaking France, and German-speaking Germany and Netherlands, language has not been an important consideration in determining Belgium's boundaries with these countries. Nor do most of Belgium's boundaries follow rivers or natural features. Rather, Belgium's contemporary boundaries are the result of centuries of conflict among its larger and more powerful neighbors, including France, Germany, and the Netherlands. Since the Middle Ages, all of these powers, along with Spain, Austria, and Britain, have competed for influence and territorial control within present-day Belgium. Belgium has been the scene of many pivotal battles in European history, including the Battle of Waterloo in 1815 and major battles during World Wars I and II. Belgium's contemporary boundaries result from the historical struggle for control over its present-day territory.

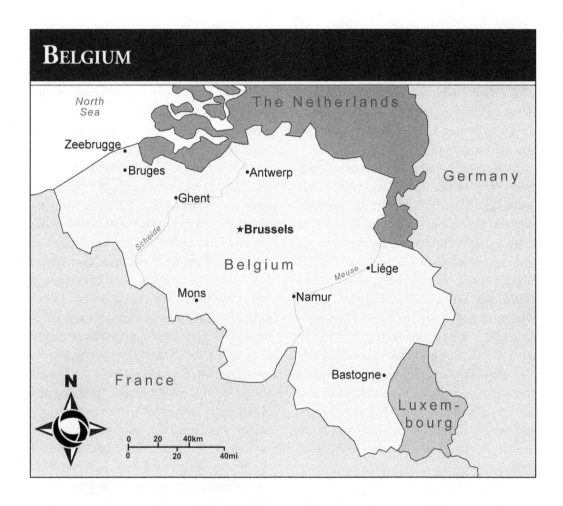

BELGIUM

The boundary between Belgium and France is highly irregular but trends generally from northwest to southeast. It extends southeastward from the North Sea near the town of Adinkerke to its boundary with Luxembourg. The boundary region near the North Sea separates Flanders from France. To the southeast, the boundary separates France from Wallonia. The boundary between Belgium and Luxembourg is also irregular but trends generally in a north-south direction. It was created during the 19th century in order to separate French speakers in Belgium from German speakers in Luxembourg. Belgium's boundary with Germany is also irregular, but it also trends in a north-south direction. Belgium, the Netherlands, and Germany meet near the German city of Aachen. Belgium's boundary with the Netherlands trends from this point northwestward to the North Sea near the city of Brugge, which is known in English as Bruges. It too is highly irregular, with numerous enclaves and exclaves on both sides of the boundary.

HISTORICAL CONTEXT

Ancient Romans referred to the Celtic and Germanic tribes who lived in present-day Belgium as the "Belgae," and much of the area was part of the Roman province of Gallia Belgica, or "French Belgium." During the Middle Ages, various parts of what is now Belgium was ruled at different times by France, the Netherlands, Spain, the Holy Roman Empire based in present-day Germany, and Austria.

Modern Belgium owes its origins and boundaries to the end of the Napoleonic Wars. The United Kingdom of the Netherlands, which includes present-day Belgium along with present-day Netherlands and Luxembourg, was established in 1815. Much of what is now Belgium had been part of the "Austrian Netherlands," which was ruled nominally by Austria-Hungary, although it was still claimed by France. At the 1815 Congress of Vienna, which created the Kingdom, the boundary between the Austrian Netherlands and France was confirmed as the boundary between France and the Kingdom. This boundary remains the boundary between Belgium and France today.

The United Kingdom was ruled by King William I, the head of a Dutch-speaking, Protestant royal family. However, the newly independent kingdom faced deep differences of opinion regarding language, religion, and economic policy. The government was Dutch speaking, Protestant, and supportive of free trade. However, Walloons in southern Belgium were French speakers, Catholics, and supporters of protective tariffs. Many believed that King William was determined to impose Dutch culture and economic institutions throughout the country.

Riots in Brussels in 1830 initiated the Belgian Revolution. Belgian leaders issued a declaration of independence on October 4, 1830. In 1831, a constitution was written, and Prince Leopold of Saxe-Coburg-Gotha, who had close connections to the royal families of Britain, France, and Germany, was installed as the first king of the Belgians. Britain and France recognized Belgian independence in 1831.

Tensions and skirmishes between newly independent Belgium and the Netherlands continued until the Netherlands formally recognized Belgium's independence in 1839. In that year, the Treaty of London was signed by the two countries along with the great European powers. The Treaty of London guaranteed Belgian independence. It also resolved the status of Luxembourg and delineated the boundary between Belgium and Luxembourg. Newly independent Belgium had claimed sovereignty over all of the Grand Duchy of Luxembourg, which had been a part of the United Kingdom of the Netherlands. Under terms of the treaty, the French-speaking western half of the Grand Duchy was recognized as part of Belgium. The predominantly German-speaking eastern half became recognized as the independent state that it remains today.

The boundary between Belgium and the Netherlands was agreed upon by both countries via the Treaty of Maastricht, which was signed in 1843. While negotiating the treaty, the two countries failed to reach agreement on the central section of the boundary, including the municipality of Baarle, northeast of Antwerp. Eventually, the two sides agreed to divide Baarle between the Belgian community of Baarle-Hertog, which was part of the Belgian province of Antwerp, and the Dutch community of Baarle-Nassau, which was part of the Dutch province of Noord-Brabant. As a result of the agreement, more than 20 Belgian enclaves, some less than 30 acres in land area, were surrounded by

Dutch territory. Some of these Belgian enclaves, such as one containing the town of Tommel, have Dutch enclaves within them. In 1892, the two governments negotiated to eliminate the enclaves by exchanging territories, but the proposed agreement was rejected by the parliaments of both countries.

The leadership of independent Belgium was primarily French speaking. Dutch-speaking residents of Flanders began to agitate for linguistic equality. In 1873, the government passed a law allowing government business in Dutch. In 1898, the government enacted the Law on Equality, which gave equal status to Dutch and French as the official languages of Belgium.

The division of Belgium into formal language areas began in 1962. This was followed by the establishment of Dutch, French, and German cultural communities. The existence and rights of these cultural communities were added to the Belgian Constitution in 1970. In 1980, they were renamed communities, and the Flemish and Walloon regions were also established. Each of these communities and regions was granted more and more autonomy. In 1993, the first article of the Belgian constitution was rewritten to read "Belgium is a Federal State which consists of Communities and Regions." Each community and each region was granted the authority to elect its own parliament.

CONTEMPORARY ISSUES

Despite this devolution of power associated with the creation of Belgium's communities and regions, linguistic conflict in Belgium continues. Some predict that this conflict will eventually result in splitting Belgium into two states, separating Dutch-speaking Flanders and French-speaking Wallonia. One cause of ongoing conflict stems from the fact that Flanders is more prosperous than Wallonia. Per capita income in Flanders is about 20 percent higher than in Wallonia, and unemployment in Wallonia is nearly twice as high as in Flanders.

The status of Belgium's capital city of Brussels is also a matter of controversy within contemporary Belgium. Brussels is located within Flanders, but more than 80 percent of its residents speak French. When Belgium's linguistic communities were established, Brussels was designated officially as a bilingual city. The establishment of the Flemish and Walloon regions was accompanied by the designation of the Brussels metropolitan area as the Brussels-Capital Region. The Brussels-Capital Region elects its own parliament, but as is the case elsewhere in Belgium, political parties are split largely along linguistic lines. The language issue has meant that Belgium no longer has a functioning central government, although day-to-day administrative functions continue. Some predict that Belgium will eventually split along linguistic lines into two separate countries.

An important issue has been the expansion of the growing Brussels metropolitan area outside the boundaries of the Brussels-Capital Region into the Flemish Region. Suburbs of Brussels have expanded into the Dutch-speaking countryside. Residents of these Dutch-speaking Flemish communities have expressed concern that continued suburbanization of French speakers from Brussels will dilute or eliminate their local Flemish culture.

See also   France, Germany, Netherlands

Further Reading

Henri Astier. "Rich Flanders seeks more autonomy." *BBC News*, September 30, 2008, http://news.bbc.co.uk/2/hi/europe/7640176.stm.

Steve Erlanger. "Belgium teeters on a linguistic edge." *New York Times*, May 13, 2008, http://www.nytimes.com/2008/05/13/world/europe/13iht-belgium.4.12857851.html.

Alexander B. Murphy. *The regional dynamics of language differentiation in Belgium: A study in cultural-political geography.* Chicago: University of Chicago Press, 1988.

Roland Willemyns. "The Dutch-French language border in Belgium." *Journal of Multilingual and Multicultural Development*, 23 (2002), pp. 36–49.

BOSNIA AND HERZEGOVINA

OVERVIEW

Bosnia and Herzegovina is located in southeastern Europe and is part of the former Yugoslavia. The country is shaped roughly like a triangle. Its land area is 19,741 square miles, or slightly larger than Vermont and New Hampshire combined. Its population is about 4 million.

Bosnia and Herzegovina's neighbors are Croatia to the west and north, Serbia to the east, and Montenegro to the south. All of Bosnia and Herzegovina's neighbors, like Bosnia and Herzegovina itself, were part of Yugoslavia before Yugoslavia was dissolved in 1991, and the boundaries were drawn in such a way as to separate different nations within Yugoslavia. However, the population of Bosnia and Herzegovina today is divided between Bosniaks, Serbs, and Croats. Most Bosniaks, who comprise about 48 percent of the population of Bosnia and Herzegovina, are Muslims, whereas most Serbs and Croats are Christians. Ethnic and religious tensions have affected Bosnia and Herzegovina's history profoundly, especially after 1991.

The boundary between Bosnia and Herzegovina and Croatia is considerably longer than Bosnia and Herzegovina's other two boundaries put together. It extends northwestward from the tripoint between Bosnia and Herzegovina, Croatia, and Serbia, and then it turns southeastward abruptly. From the tripoint between Bosnia and Herzegovina, Croatia, and Serbia on the eastern edge of Bosnia and Herzegovina, this boundary extends in a northwesterly direction along the Sava River to a point near the town of Male Kladusa on the Bosnia side of the boundary. Male Kladusa is located in the northwest corner of Bosnia and Herzegovina. Here it leaves the Sava and turns southeastward, paralleling the coast of the Adriatic Sea through the Dinaric Alps. Most of the eastern Adriatic coast is part of Croatia. However, Bosnia and Herzegovina has a short coastline of less than eight miles on the Adriatic. This coastline includes the town of Neum, which is Bosnia and Herzegovina's only port. The short coastal strip separates a Croatian exclave, which is about 35 miles long but less than 10 miles wide, from the rest of Croatia.

The tripoint between Bosnia and Herzegovina, Croatia, and Montenegro is located about 10 miles inland from the Adriatic coast and 2 miles north of the Croatian town of Dubravka. This boundary follows numerous very short straight-line segments extending northward. It includes the

BOSNIA AND HERZEGOVINA

eastern shore of Bilecko Lake, all of which is located in Bosnia and Herzegovina and which is the largest artificial lake in the Balkan Peninsula. From Bilecko Lake, it continues in a more northeasterly direction to the tripoint between Bosnia and Herzegovina, Montenegro, and Serbia. Most of the boundary between Bosnia and Herzegovina and Serbia follows the Drina River, which empties into the Sava at the tripoint between Bosnia and Herzegovina, Serbia, and Croatia.

HISTORICAL CONTEXT

A group of tribes known as the Illyrians occupied present-day Bosnia and Herzegovina and other parts of the western

Balkans during the first millennium BC. The Roman Empire began efforts to conquer the Illyrians beginning in 229 BC, but Roman conquest of the area was not completed until between AD 6 and 9. Present-day Bosnia and Herzegovina remained part of the Western Roman Empire until the fifth century AD. Subsequently, the area was conquered successfully by the Ostrogoths, Slavic tribes, and the Byzantine Empire.

Over the next several centuries, present-day Bosnia and Herzegovina was contested among kingdoms centered in Croatia, Hungary, and Serbia. The independent Kingdom of Bosnia arose in the early 14th century. By 1390, the kingdom had conquered most of the territory currently occupied by Bosnia and Herzegovina as well as neighboring territory along the nearby Adriatic coast. The Ottoman Empire deposed the Bosnian monarchy and took over the area in 1463. The Ottomans controlled Bosnia and Herzegovina until 1878, when it was transferred to the Austro-Hungarian Empire.

After the Austro-Hungarian Empire was dismembered following World War I in 1918, Bosnia and Herzegovina became part of the newly independent Kingdom of the Serbs, Croats, and Slovenes. The kingdom's name was changed to the Kingdom of Yugoslavia in 1929. Nazi Germany took control of Yugoslavia during World War II, and administration of Bosnia was transferred to the pro-Nazi state of Croatia. After the war, the kingdom was reconstituted as the Socialist Federal Republic of Yugoslavia. Bosnia and Herzegovina became one of the six constituent republics comprising the Federal Republic along with Slovenia, Croatia, Serbia, Montenegro, and Macedonia, all of which are now independent states also.

The Federal Republic broke apart in 1991. The parliament of Bosnia and Herzegovina voted to hold a referendum on Bosnia and Herzegovina's independence. However, Serb members of the parliament walked out before the vote was taken and urged Bosnian Serbs, many of whom preferred continued union with Serbia, to boycott the referendum itself. Many Serbs and Croats in Bosnia and Herzegovina did boycott the referendum, which passed with about 93 percent voting for independence. Bosnia and Herzegovina declared its formal independence over the objections of Serbia and Croatia on March 3, 1992. Three years of warfare broke out. An estimated 100,000 people in Bosnia and Herzegovina were killed between 1992 and 1995, when hostilities were ended following the signing of the Dayton Peace Accords by all three countries.

CONTEMPORARY ISSUES

Although armed violence among national groups in Bosnia and Herzegovina has subsided, ethnic tensions between the majority Bosniak population and the minority Serb and Croat populations continue. During and after the Bosnian War, many Serbs and Croats left Bosnia and Herzegovina and returned to Serbia and Croatia respectively.

Bosnia and Herzegovina and Croatia have disputed control of the small islands of Mali and Veliki Skolj in the Adriatic Sea. These islands are located near the Bosnia and Herzegovina's short coastline on the Adriatic. Although most of the islands' residents are of Croat ethnicity, Bosnia and Herzegovina has pushed its claim to the islands in order to secure maritime access to international waters and possibly to construct a new and modern port facility.

See also   Croatia, Montenegro, Serbia

Further Reading

Klaudina Rachel, Ruxandra Esanu, Alexandra McBain, and Brigitte Rohwerder. *Bosnia and Herzegovina: Post-conflict reconstruction.* St. Andrews, Scotland, UK: Centre for Peace and Conflict Studies, 2010.

Sabrina P. Ramet. *The three Yugoslavias: State-building and legitimation, 1918–2004.* Bloomington: Indiana University Press.

Guy M. Robinson, Sten Engelstoft, and Alma Pobric. "Remaking Sarajevo: Bosnian nationalism after the Dayton Accord." *Political Geography*, 20, pp. 957–980.

BULGARIA

OVERVIEW

The Republic of Bulgaria is located in southeastern Europe. It has a land area of 42,823 square miles, about the size of Virginia. Its population is about 7.6 million. About 84 percent of the population consists of ethnic Bulgarians, whose Slavic language is related closely to Russian. Turks make up nearly 10 percent of the population.

BULGARIA

Bulgaria's neighbors are Romania to the north, Turkey and Greece to the south, and Macedonia and Serbia to the west. Eastern Bulgaria borders the Black Sea. The Danube River forms most of the boundary between Bulgaria and Romania. To the south, the eastern section of the boundary between Bulgaria and Turkey follows the Rezovska River from its mouth at the Black Sea inland to its junction with its tributary, the Deliva River. The boundary follows the Deliva upstream for a few miles, then follows short straight-line segments in a westerly and southwesterly direction to the tripoint between Bulgaria, Turkey, and Greece. West of this tripoint, most of the boundary between Bulgaria and Greece follows ridges and drainage divides separating streams that flow northward into Bulgaria from those that flow southward into Greece. The boundary between Bulgaria and Macedonia and the boundary between Bulgaria and Serbia, which were delimited when both Macedonia and Serbia were part of Yugoslavia, also follow drainage divides. The tripoint between Bulgaria, Serbia, and Romania is located at the confluence of the Danube and its tributary, the Timok River.

HISTORICAL CONTEXT

Bulgaria's boundaries have undergone numerous changes over the course of its history. Bulgaria was absorbed into the Ottoman Empire in 1393. In 1877, the Russo-Turkish War broke out between the Ottoman Empire and Russia. Russia's victory resulted in the creation of the separation of present-day northern and western Bulgaria, along with parts of what are now Macedonia and Montenegro, from the empire. The Bulgarian state proclaimed its independence in 1908. After a series of wars with Serbia, Greece, and Romania, some of Bulgaria's territory was stripped and awarded to victorious neighboring powers.

Bulgaria allied itself with Germany and Austria during World War I. Many Bulgarians opposed Bulgarian entry into the war, in part because Bulgaria was also aligned with its traditional enemy, the Ottoman Empire, and was fighting against fellow Christian countries in the Balkans region. After World War I ended, Bulgaria was forced to cede additional territory to its neighbors. Many of these lost territories included Bulgarian population majorities. In 1921, Bulgaria and Turkey agreed upon its boundary.

In World War II, Bulgaria was allied once again with Germany until the Soviet army took over the country in 1944. The country was absorbed into the Soviet sphere of influence as the People's Republic of Bulgaria. The Treaty of Paris, signed in 1947, confirmed Bulgaria's present boundaries. Bulgaria remained a Soviet satellite until communist rule was terminated in 1990 and the country became the Republic of Bulgaria. Bulgaria joined NATO in 2004 and the European Union in 2007.

CONTEMPORARY ISSUES

Bulgaria's boundaries have been stable since they were confirmed through the Treaty of Paris in 1947. The most significant issue has involved the status of minority populations in Bulgaria.

About 10 percent of Bulgaria's population is of Turkish ancestry. During the period of communist rule, the Bulgarian government pursued a campaign of discrimination against its Turkish minority population. Bulgarian Turks were expected to give up their Islamic faith and to adopt Bulgarian names. Bulgaria justified these discriminatory policies by claiming that these Turks were descendants of Bulgarians who had been incorporated into Turkey and converted to Islam by the Ottoman Empire. As a result of persecution, many Bulgarian Turks fled the country and moved across the border into Turkey. Post-communist Bulgaria signed a treaty of friendship with Turkey in 1991, and in contrast to the communist government, the post-communist government allowed public schooling of Bulgarian Turkish children in the Turkish language. Turkish-oriented political parties are represented in the Bulgarian government at the national and local levels. However, some Bulgarian Turks continue to support the transfer of Turkish-majority territories within Bulgaria to Turkey.

See also   Greece, Macedonia, Romania, Serbia, Turkey

Further Reading

Birgul Demirtas-Coskun. "Turkish-Bulgarian relations in the post–Cold War era: The exemplary relationship in the Balkans." *Turkish Yearbook*, 32 (2001), pp. 26–60.

Venelin I. Ganov. *Preying on the state: The transformation of Bulgaria after 1989.* Ithaca, NY: Cornell University Press, 2007.

Stoimen Pavlov. "Bulgarian-Turkish relations are stronger than ever." Radio Bulgaria, March 21, 2012, http://bnr.bg/sites/en/Lifestyle/BulgariaAndWorld/Pages/2103BulgarianTurkishrelations.aspx.

CROATIA

OVERVIEW

The Republic of Croatia, located in southeastern Europe, is one of the seven contemporary states that were once part of Yugoslavia. Croatia's land area is 21,851 square miles, slightly smaller than West Virginia. Its population is approximately 4.3 million.

Croatia's territory includes two major sections of approximately equal land area. From the area surrounding Croatia's capital city of Zagreb, the western section extends southward along the coast of the Adriatic Sea, an arm of the Mediterranean. The eastern section extends eastward from the Zagreb area. Croatia's neighbors are its former fellow Yugoslav republics of Slovenia to the northwest, Serbia to the east, and Bosnia and Herzegovina and Montenegro to the south along with Hungary to the northeast. Western Croatia has a long coastline along the Adriatic. Along the northeastern Adriatic coast, Croatia's boundary with Slovenia is located only about 10 miles south of the Italian city of Trieste. More than 1,000 islands in the Adriatic are also part of Croatia.

In general, Croatia's boundaries have been drawn in order to separate people of Croatian heritage from those belonging to other ethnic groups. About 90 percent of Croatia's people are ethnic Croatians. Thus most of Croatia's boundaries follow numerous short straight-line segments, some of which are less than 100 feet in length— shorter than the distance across a football field. The boundary between Croatia and Slovenia extends in a generally east to northeastward direction from the Adriatic

CROATIA

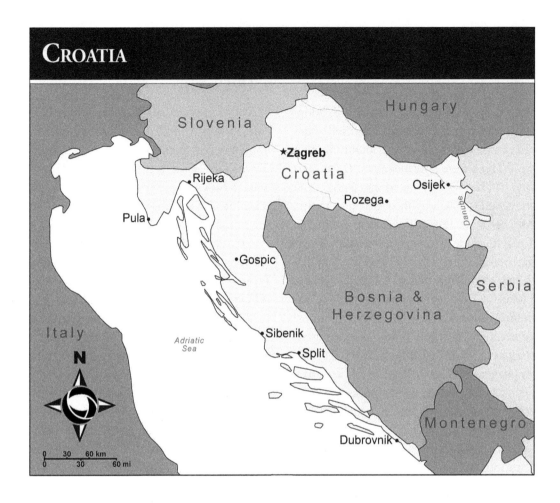

coast to the tripoint between Croatia, Slovenia, and Hungary on the Drava River, a major tributary of the Danube River.

Hungary is Croatia's only neighbor that was not once part of Yugoslavia. Most of the boundary between Croatia and Hungary follows the Drava southeastward from the tripoint between Croatia, Hungary, and Slovenia. However, one small section of about 20 square miles on the left (Hungarian) bank of the Drava belongs to Croatia. A somewhat larger territory on the left bank of the Drava and west of the Danube also belongs to Croatia. The northern boundary of this triangular territory, which extends eastward to the tripoint between Croatia, Hungary, and Serbia, is geometric.

The Danube itself forms the northern two-thirds of the boundary between Croatia and Serbia. In a few places, the boundary crosses the river. These crossings reflect changes in the course of the Danube that have occurred since the boundary was delineated. Near the Croatian town of Ilok, the Danube flows eastward into Serbia on its way to the Black Sea. The boundary between Croatia and Serbia follow short line segments southward to the tripoint between Croatia, Serbia, and Bosnia and Herzegovina on the Sava River, which is a major tributary of the Danube and empties into the Danube in Serbia.

Croatia's longest boundary is with Bosnia and Herzegovina. This boundary follows the Sava northwestward and upstream along the Sava to a point near the town of Rakovica. From that point, the boundary turns southeastward and parallels the Adriatic coast in the Dinaric Alps. Here Croatia's territory, known as Dalmatia, is narrow. Most of the coastline of the eastern Adriatic is located in Croatia. However, Bosnia and Herzegovina has a short coastline, less than eight miles in length, on the Adriatic, including the town of Neum. This coastline separates the southernmost portion of Croatia along the Adriatic, an exclave about 35 miles long and 5 to 10 miles wide, from the rest of the country. From this separated territory, the short boundary between Croatia and Montenegro extends northward and eastward to the tripoint between Croatia, Montenegro, and Serbia.

HISTORICAL CONTEXT

The ancestors of today's Croats are believed to have moved to present-day Croatia during the seventh and eighth centuries AD. The first Croatian kingdom was established in AD 925. This kingdom controlled much of present-day northern and eastern Croatia for nearly 200 years. In 1118, the kingdoms of Croatia and Hungary entered into joint rule. In 1526, Croatia became part of the Austro-Hungarian Empire. In 1867, Austria-Hungary became a dual monarchy, with the emperor ruling over both Austria and Hungary although these territories were administered separately. At this time, Croatia became part of the Hungarian portion of the empire.

Croatia remained under Austro-Hungarian rule until 1918, when the Austro-Hungarian Empire was dissolved following World War I. After the empire's dissolution, Croatia became part of the Kingdom of the Serbs, Croats, and Slovenes. The kingdom included most of present-day Croatia, Serbia, Slovenia, and Bosnia and Herzegovina. It was renamed Yugoslavia in 1929. Yugoslavia was invaded by German and Italian forces at the outset of World War II, and the pro-Nazi independent state of Croatia was established with a puppet government.

Following the war, Yugoslavia became a communist state under the leadership of Marshal Josip Broz Tito, who had been a leader of the anti-Nazi Yugoslav resistance movement known as the Partisans. Tito was of Croatian heritage and had been born in present-day Croatia. Although Tito was aligned with the Soviet Union at the outset of the Cold War, he refused to recognize Soviet hegemony of Yugoslavia. He broke with the Soviets in the late 1940s. Yugoslavia remained a communist state, but it began to steer a course independent of the Soviet Union. Croatia and the other republics constituting Yugoslavia had considerable autonomy over internal affairs. However, nationalist sentiment in Croatia, as well as elsewhere in Yugoslavia, increased especially after Tito died in 1980.

During the early 1990s, Croatia along with other non-Serbian republics in Yugoslavia broke away from Serbia. The breakup of Yugoslavia and the creation of independent states in what had been Yugoslav territory were motivated in part by ethnic tensions, and the breakup process fueled ethnic tensions that resulted in several full-scale wars. In 1991, a referendum on secession and independence was held in Croatia. More than 90 percent of the voters supported the referendum, and Croatia declared its independence from Yugoslavia in June 1991. However, many Serbs were living in Croatia, and many of these Croatian Serbs boycotted the referendum.

After Croatia's declaration of independence, war broke out between Croatian forces and forces loyal to the Serb-dominated government of what remained of Yugoslavia. The primarily Serbian Yugoslav army seized control of parts of Croatia. Many areas seized by Serbian forces, including the province of Eastern Slavonia, Baranja, and Western Syrmia located at the eastern end of the easternmost portion of Croatia near the tripoint between Croatia, Serbia, and Hungary, contained majority-Serb populations. The Croatian War for Independence continued until 1995, when Croatian troops with the support of troops from Bosnia and Herzegovina initiated successful military operations to expel Serbian troops from control of Croatian territory. In November 1995, Croatia and Serbia signed the Erdut Agreement, which called for the eventual reintegration of Eastern Slavonia, Baranja, and Western Syrmia into Croatia. Croatia has applied to join the European Union (EU).

CONTEMPORARY ISSUES

Tensions between Croatia and some of its ex-Yugoslav neighbors continue, particularly with Slovenia. Tensions have intensified since both countries became independent from Yugoslavia in 1991.

The ongoing boundary dispute between Croatia and Slovenia has involved both the land boundary between them and the maritime boundary between them in the Adriatic Sea. Slovenia has only a short and concave coastline on the Adriatic and has been anxious to secure the right of navigation in the Adriatic. On the other hand, Croatia has yet to ratify a proposed agreement that would secure maritime access to Slovenia and would give Slovenia control of maritime rights in the Pirin Bay off the Slovenian coast. Slovenia, which is a member of the European Union, has announced its intention to veto Croatia's membership in the EU until the boundary dispute has been resolved. In 2010, a majority of voters in Slovenia supported a referendum calling for referring this ongoing boundary dispute to international arbitration.

See also   Bosnia and Herzegovina, Hungary, Montenegro, Serbia, Slovenia

Further Reading

Ian Bancroft. "Bringing Croatia and Serbia together." *Guardian*, January 18, 2010, http://www.guardian.co.uk/com mentisfree/2010/jan/18/croatia-serbia-new-president.

BBC News. "Slovenia unblocks Croatian EU bid." September 11, 2009, http://news.bbc.co.uk/2/hi/europe/8250441.stm.

Sharon Fisher. *Political change in post-communist Slovakia and Croatia: From nationalist to Europeanist.* New York: Palgrave Macmillan, 2006.

CYPRUS

OVERVIEW

The Republic of Cyprus contains the island of Cyprus in the eastern Mediterranean Sea. Its land area is 3,572 square miles, or about two-thirds the size of

Connecticut. Cyprus's population is 1.1 million. Cyprus occupies the entire island and has no land neighbors. The closest countries to Cyprus across the Mediterranean are Turkey, 70 miles to the north, and Syria, 80 miles to the east.

HISTORICAL CONTEXT

Cyprus has been inhabited for at least 12,000 years. Archaeologists have excavated ruins of a village on the island, and these ruins have been dated to between 9500 and 10,500 BC. Greek traders began to visit the island between 1300 and 1500 BC. A large-scale migration to Cyprus from Greece is believed to have occurred between 1000 and 1100 BC.

Cyprus was controlled by various European, Asiatic, and African empires for more than 2,000 years following its conquest by Alexander the Great in the fourth century BC. After Alexander's death, the island was ruled by the Ptolemaic dynasty of Egypt until it was taken over by the Roman Empire in 58 BC. After the Roman Empire was split into its eastern and western portions, Cyprus became part of the eastern portion, which became the Byzantine Empire that was governed from

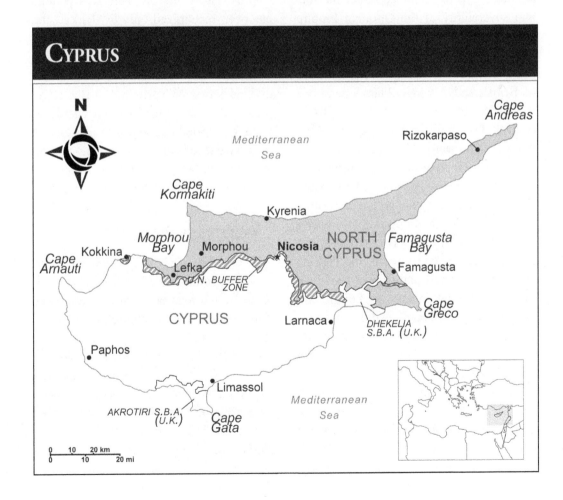

Constantinople (present-day Istanbul). Cyprus was contested between Christian and Muslim rule during the Crusades and became part of the Ottoman Empire in 1570. Although the Ottomans controlled Cyprus for more than 300 years, it retained its Greek culture and language, and the majority of its people remained Christians. An 1881 census showed that about three-quarters of the Cypriot population were Christians of Greek ancestry, while Turks who had moved to Cyprus during the Ottoman regime remained a minority.

The British Empire took over the administration of Cyprus in 1878 and established a British protectorate on the island, although Cyprus remained under the formal sovereignty of the Ottoman Empire until the empire's collapse before World War I. Britain annexed Cyprus formally in 1914. Cyprus became an important base of British and Allied military operations during World War I. Britain remains in control of two military bases that were established on the island at that time. After World War II, Cypriot leaders pushed for union with Greece. The majority of Cypriots of Greek ancestry supported this policy of *enosis*, which was opposed vigorously by most Turkish Cypriots. After negotiations between Britain, Greece, and Turkey, *enosis* was rejected, and Cyprus became a fully independent country in 1960. Public offices and government positions were allocated on a percentage basis by ethnicity, giving the minority Turkish population a voice in the government of Cyprus.

The postindependence period has been characterized by ongoing tension between Greek and Turkish Cypriots and between Greece and Turkey. In 1974, the Greek government attempted to annex Cyprus to Greece. In response, Turkish forces invaded Cyprus. Turkish troops seized control of the Turkish-majority northern third of the island. Thousands of Greek Cypriots moved to the area still controlled by the Greek-dominated government of Cyprus, while thousands of Turkish Cypriots moved into the Turkish-controlled region. This mass migration reinforced geographically the ethnic division of Cyprus into Greek and Turkish sectors. A cease-fire was proclaimed in December of 1974, but Turkish troops remained in northern Cyprus.

In 1983, leaders in the Turkish-controlled region of the country proclaimed the area to be the Turkish Republic of Northern Cyprus. However, the Turkish Republic has been recognized only by Turkey and was not recognized as a sovereign state by the United Nations. Today, most Turkish Cypriots continue to regard the island as divided between Cyprus and Northern Cyprus while most Greek Cypriots regard it as a single, unified country with jurisdiction over the entire island. The de facto boundary between the two sectors divides Nicosia, the capital and largest city on Cyprus.

CONTEMPORARY ISSUES

The status of Cyprus within the international community continues to be dominated by tensions between the Greek and Turkish Cypriot communities, with Greece supporting the former and Turkey supporting the latter. Supported by Turkey, Northern Cyprus continues to operate as a sovereign state with an elected government. About 30,000 Turkish troops are stationed in Cyprus. The government of Cyprus regards these troops as an illegal occupation force, and the United Nations Security Council has asked Turkey to withdraw its forces although Turkey has declined to do so. An estimated 200,000 Cypriots remain displaced nearly four decades after the conflict began. The issue was compounded after Cyprus joined the European Union in 2004 because Turkish Cypriots are European citizens but are unable to access Greek territory within Cyprus because of the military standoff. Negotiations between the two sides are ongoing. Some international observers have argued in favor of partition on the grounds that ethnic self-determination is a principle of the European Union, which Cyprus joined in 1997.

See also   Greece, Turkey

Further Reading

International Crisis Group. "Cyprus: Six steps toward a settlement." *Europe Briefing*, 61 (2011), http://www.crisisgroup. org/en/regions/europe/turkey-cyprus/cy prus/B61-cyprus-six-steps-toward-a-set tlement.aspx.

International Crisis Group. "Cyprus: Reunification or partition?" *Europe Report*, 201 (2009), http://www.crisisgroup. org/en/regions/europe/turkey-cyprus/ cyprus/201-cyprus-reunification-or-parti tion.aspx.

James Ker-Lindsay. *The Cyprus problem: What everybody needs to know.* New York: Oxford University Press, 2011.

CZECH REPUBLIC

OVERVIEW

The Czech Republic is located in Central Europe. It has a land area of 30,450 square miles, about the size of South Carolina. Its population is about 10.5 million. The Czech Republic contains three major regions: Bohemia in the west,

Moravia in the east, and Czech Silesia in the northeast.

The Czech Republic is landlocked. Its neighbors include Germany to the west, Poland to the north, Slovakia to the east, and Austria to the south. The tripoint between the Czech Republic, Germany, and Austria is located in the Bohemian Forest, part of which is preserved as the Sumava Biosphere Reserve in the Czech Republic. From this tripoint, the boundary between the Czech Republic and Germany extends northwestward along the drainage divide between the drainage basin of the Vltava River in the Czech Republic and the drainage basin of the Danube River in Germany. The western two-thirds of the Czech Republic, including its capital city of Prague, are located in the drainage basin of the Vltava and the Elbe River, into which the Vltava empties north of Prague. The location of this drainage basin roughly coincides with the historic frontiers of Bohemia.

The Czech Republic's northern boundaries parallel mountain ranges that separate streams flowing southward into the Vltava from those flowing northward into rivers that empty into the Oder-Neisse drainage basin and other rivers in Germany and Poland. Near the small city of Cheb, the boundary between the Czech Republic and Germany turns northeastward, north of and paralleling the crest of the Ore Mountains in the northwestern Czech Republic. This portion of the boundary is complex and follows a large number of short straight-line segments. East of the tripoint between the Czech Republic, Germany, and Poland, the general trend of the boundary shifts southeastward, following straight lines along and near the crest of the Sudeten Mountains to the tripoint between the Czech Republic, Poland, and Slovakia. At this

CZECH REPUBLIC

Germany

Poland

•Teplice   Liberec•

Elbe

Prague★   •Kolin

Plzen•

Czech Republic

Ostrava•

Vltava

Strakonice•   Prostejov•   •Prerov

Brno •   •Zlin

Znojmo•

Austria   Slovakia

0   30   60 km
0   30   60 mi

N

tripoint, the boundary between the Czech Republic and Slovakia turns abruptly westward. Here it generally follows the crest of the Carpathian Mountains in a west-southwesterly direction.

Near the village of Rohatec, the boundary between the Czech Republic and Slovakia reaches the Morava River, which is an important tributary of the Danube from which the Czech region of Moravia gets its name. The boundary follows the Morava for a short distance south-southwestward to its confluence with the Dyje River, which is called the Thaya River in Austria. The tripoint between the Czech Republic, Slovakia, and Austria is located at this confluence. From there, the boundary follows the Dyje upstream and westward, then follows a series of straight-line segments in a generally westward direction. In general, the western portion of this boundary separates the drainage basins of the Vltava and the Danube as is the case with the boundary between the Czech Republic and Germany.

HISTORICAL CONTEXT

The present-day Czech Republic was settled by Germanic tribes moving westward and southward from Germany and by Slavic peoples moving eastward and northward from the Black Sea region. As long ago as 1000 BC, control of the region was disputed among various kingdoms that controlled portions of the area. Most of Bohemia, which occupies the western two-thirds of the present-day Czech Republic, was united for the first time as the Kingdom of Bohemia in the ninth century AD. The Kingdom of Bohemia became part of the German-based Holy Roman Empire in AD 1002. Except for a period of about eight decades in the 15th and early 16th centuries, Bohemia remained a component of the Holy Roman Empire until the empire was dissolved in 1806. Control of what is now the Czech Republic was passed to the Austro-Hungarian Empire, of which the Czech Republic remained a part until the empire was dissolved after World War I.

The redrawing of Europe's political map after World War I led to the creation of Czechoslovakia. This new country included Bohemia and Moravia, both of which were populated largely by speakers of the Czech language. To the east, Czechoslovakia also included what is now Slovakia. Although Czech and Slovak languages are related closely, the regions of Czechoslovakia had very different political histories. Bohemia and Moravia had been part of the Austrian portion of the Austro-Hungarian Empire, whereas Slovakia had been administered by Hungary. Ethnic Germans and ethnic Hungarians living within the borders of newly independent Czechoslovakia agitated for reunification of their respective homelands.

Despite these ethnic tensions, Czechoslovakia became a stable, peaceful democracy that continued until 1938, when it was invaded by Nazi Germany. The Nazis justified their actions on the grounds that ethnic Germans in Czechoslovakia were destined as German nationals to be part of the expanding German state. An estimated 3 to 4 million people of German ancestry, known as Sudeten Germans, lived in Czechoslovakia in the 1930s, where they comprised about a quarter of Czechoslovakia's population. Although the Nazis' stated intention was to reunite the Sudeten Germans with Nazi Germany, the Germans took over the entire country and split Slovakia from the rest of Czechoslovakia. Most of what is now the Czech Republic became the Protectorate of Bohemia and Moravia, which was ruled by the Nazis directly. Leaders of the former Czechoslovakia formed a government in exile and cooperated with the Allies to expel the Germans. In 1944, Soviet forces secured control of the protectorate, forcing Germany to relinquish control of Bohemia and Moravia.

After World War II ended, the regions of Bohemia, Moravia, Czech Silesia, and Slovakia were reunited. Democracy was reestablished briefly, but the democratic government was toppled in a Soviet-backed coup d'état in 1948. Czechoslovakia was then ruled by the Communist Party, and it remained a Soviet satellite and a member of the Warsaw Pact until 1989. In 1968, Czechoslovakian leaders attempted to liberalize the country in what became known as Prague Spring. A new constitution guaranteed freedom of speech, freedom of the press, and freedom of religion. However, in August 1968 the Soviet Union, along with other Warsaw Pact countries, invaded Czechoslovakia and forced it to abandon these reform efforts.

After Prague Spring, the Czechoslovakian government reestablished communist principles, including central planning and the suppression of dissent. However, anticommunist activities continued and intensified in the late 1980s. In November 1989, a series of peaceful protests against the government began. Hundreds of thousands of people participated in the protests, which became known as the Velvet Revolution. The communist government relinquished power, and the first noncommunist government of Czechoslovakia in more than 41 years assumed office in December 1989.

In 1992, Czech and Slovak leaders agreed to separate the two components of Czechoslovakia and established the current boundary between the two countries. The separation between the Czech Republic and Slovakia took effect on January 1, 1993, and the Czech Republic joined NATO in 1999 and the European Union in 2004. The Czech Republic's boundaries with its neighbors are stable, and there are no significant border conflicts involving the Czech Republic.

See also   Austria, Germany, Poland, Slovakia

Further Reading

Oskar Krejci. *Geopolitics of the Central European region: The view from Prague and Bratislava.* Translated by Martin C. Styan. Bratislava, Slovak Republic: Institute of Political Sciences, SAS, 2005.

Robin H. E. Shepherd. *Czechoslovakia: The Velvet Revolution and beyond.* New York: St. Martin's Press, 2000.

Stefan Wolff. *Germany, Poland, and the Czech Republic since reunification.* New York: Taylor and Francis, 2007.

DENMARK

OVERVIEW

The Kingdom of Denmark is considered a Scandinavian country on the basis of its shared history and linguistic and culture communalities with Norway and Sweden. However, Denmark is separated from the rest of Scandinavia by the Baltic Sea. Denmark consists of the Jutland Peninsula on the European mainland along with over 400 islands in the Baltic. The capital and largest city, Copenhagen, is located on the islands of Zealand and Amager. Denmark's strategic location has allowed it to control or influence trade through the Baltic Sea throughout history.

Denmark has a land area of about 16,641 square miles, making it slightly larger than Maryland and Delaware combined. About two-thirds of Denmark's territory is on the Jutland Peninsula on the mainland, with the rest on Zeeland, Amager, and other islands. Its current population is about 5.5 million, with slightly less than half living on the Jutland Peninsula. Denmark is an active member of NATO and has been a member of the European Union since 1973.

Denmark is sovereign also over the Faeroe Islands, which are located in the North Atlantic Ocean midway between Scotland and Iceland. There are 18 islands in the archipelago, with a total population of about 50,000. The Faeroe Islands were settled by Vikings, who brought with them the Old Norse language that eventually evolved into the modern-day Faeroese language. Denmark retains partial sovereignty over Greenland. Greenland achieved partial independence in 2009, but Denmark remains responsible for Greenland's defense and foreign affairs.

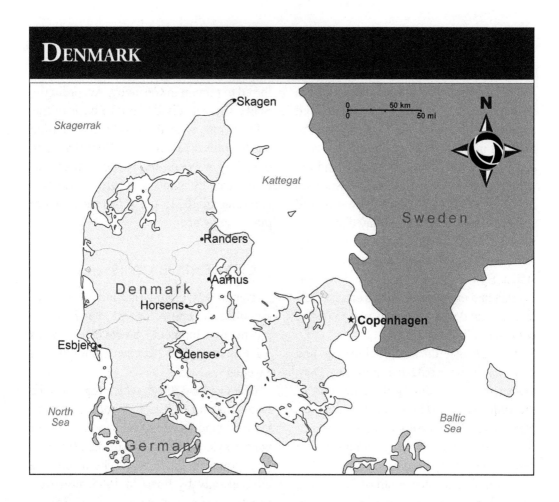

DENMARK

Skagen

Skagerrak

Kattegat

0   50 km
0   50 mi

N

Sweden

•Randers

•Aarhus

Denmark

Horsens•

★ •Copenhagen

Esbjerg•

Odense•

North
Sea

Baltic
Sea

Germany

Denmark's only land boundary is with Germany to the south. This boundary trends in an east-to-west direction across the southern end of the Jutland Peninsula. The North Sea adjoins Denmark to the west with the Baltic Sea to the north and east. From the Baltic, the Flensburg Fjord extends inland in an east-west direction, separating Denmark to the north from Germany to the south. The head of the fjord is located near the German city of Flensburg. From there, the boundary follows short straight-line boundaries to the North Sea coast. The Oresund Strait, which separates Denmark from Sweden, connects the Baltic with the North Sea. At its narrowest point, the Oresund Strait is than three miles in width. Since 1999, the two countries have been connected via the Oresund Bridge.

HISTORICAL CONTEXT

Most of present-day Denmark was unified under Danish kings by the 12th century. In the 13th century, Denmark also ruled over southwestern Sweden, across the Oresund Strait. In 1396, the Kalmar Union was formed, uniting present-day Denmark with Sweden and Norway. In 1523, Sweden broke away from the Kalmar Union, but Denmark and Norway remained united under Danish control and under the rule of the Danish royal family. At that time, the

Kingdom of Denmark referred to the rule of Denmark over its own territory as well as that of Norway.

Following the Napoleonic Wars of the 19th century, the Treaty of Kiel transferred sovereignty over Norway from Denmark to Sweden in 1814. Denmark remained sovereign over the Jutland Peninsula and the islands in the Baltic. The major issue facing Denmark in the 19th century involved its boundary with present-day Germany. At the time of the Treaty of Kiel, Germany remained divided between numerous small states. By the late 19th century, however, Prussia had emerged as the strongest German state and was well on its way to taking control of all of Germany.

Two Danish duchies, Schleswig and Holstein, were contested between Denmark and Prussia during the latter part of the 19th century. Denmark claimed sovereignty over these territories on the basis of the Treaty of Kiel, although a majority of people in southern Schleswig and in Holstein, which is located south of Schleswig, spoke German. In 1864, war broke out between Denmark and Prussia, with Austria involved in the war on the side of Prussia. After Denmark was defeated in the war, both Schleswig and Holstein became part of Prussia. Prussia promised to hold a plebiscite in northern Schleswig, a majority of whose people spoke Danish. However, this promise was never kept, and all of Schleswig remained in Prussian and later German hands.

The Schleswig question was resolved finally after World War I in keeping with the Treaty of Versailles. Residents of Schleswig voted on their preferences concerning becoming part of Denmark or part of Germany. About 75 percent of those

in northern Schleswig voted to become part of Denmark while in the central and southern part of Schleswig, 80 percent preferred to remain in Germany. Accordingly, Schleswig was divided on the basis of this referendum, with the pro-Danish portion of the province given to Denmark. The boundary between the two countries was formalized by agreement between the two countries in 1921, and it has remained in place ever since.

CONTEMPORARY ISSUES

Denmark's boundaries have been stable since the end of World War I. A key recent development, however, involves a land connection between Denmark and Sweden.

The Oresund Strait, which separates the Danish island of Zealand from the Swedish mainland, is one of the world's busiest waterways. Until the end of the 20th century, however, the Oresund Strait could be crossed only by boat. In 1995, however, construction began on the Oresund Bridge, which connects Denmark's capital city of Copenhagen with the Swedish city of Malmo. The bridge was opened in 1999. It connects the two countries by both road and railroad, and about 35 million passengers cross the bridge each year.

Denmark has laid claims to territory in the Arctic Ocean on the basis of its control over Greenland and its foreign policy. Denmark has claimed jurisdiction of the area from Greenland's Arctic coast northward to the North Pole. In response, both Canada and Russia have made similar claims to territory north of their own coastlines. Control of these territories is regarded as increasingly valuable because of the discovery of oil reserves and other minerals and because warming temperatures may result in the melting of sufficient ice in the Arctic to permit navigation in summer. The International Court of Justice is currently reviewing Danish claims and those of other countries that have coastlines on the Arctic Ocean.

See also Germany

Further Reading

Harriet Alexander. "Denmark's defiance over frontier controls has left European Union bordering on crisis." *Telegraph*, May 15, 2011, http://www.tele graph.co.uk/news/worldnews/europe/ denmark/8514180/Denmarks-defiance-over-frontier-controls-has-left-European-Union-bordering-on-crisis.html.

Per-Olof Berg, Anders Linde-Laursen, and Orvar Lofgren (eds.). *Invoking a transnational region: The making of the Oresund Region.* Copenhagen: Copenhagen Business School, 2000.

Zachary Fillingham. "Arctic ownership claims." *Geopolitical Monitor*, April 21, 2012, http://www.geopoliticalmonitor. com/arctic-ownership-claims.

ESTONIA

OVERVIEW

The Republic of Estonia is the northernmost of the three Baltic countries. It has a land area of 17,413 square miles, or about the size of Vermont and New Hampshire combined. Its population is approximately 1.4 million. About 69 percent of Estonia's people are ethnic Estonians, 25 percent are of Russian ancestry, and the rest belong to other ethnic groups. Estonia is culturally distinct from Russia, and the Estonian language is related closely to Finnish.

Estonia shares land boundaries with Russia to the east and Latvia to the south. The Baltic Sea is located to the west of Estonia, and Estonia includes several islands in the Baltic off the coast of the Estonian mainland. The Gulf of Finland, which is an arm of the Baltic, is located to the north of Estonia. The Estonian capital city of Tallinn is located on the south shore of the Gulf of Finland across from Finland's capital of Helsinki. The boundary between Estonia and Russia follows the Narva River southward from its mouth on the Gulf of Finland inland to Lake Peipus, which is the largest transboundary lake and the fifth-largest lake in Europe. South of Lake Peipus, part of the boundary follows the Piusa River, which empties into the southern end of the lake. The remainder of the boundary between Estonia and Russia is made up of numerous short straight-line segments that trend generally in a north-south direction to the tripoint between Estonia, Russia, and Latvia. The boundary between Estonia and Latvia consists of short segments and trends in an east-west direction from this tripoint west to the Baltic Sea.

HISTORICAL CONTEXT

For most of its history since the Middle Ages, Estonia has been controlled by foreign powers. Estonia was occupied by Denmark in 1219. It became part of the Swedish Empire in the 17th century. After the Swedish Empire was defeated by Russia in 1710, control of Estonia was transferred to Russia. The Russian Empire collapsed during World War I, and Estonia became an independent country in 1918.

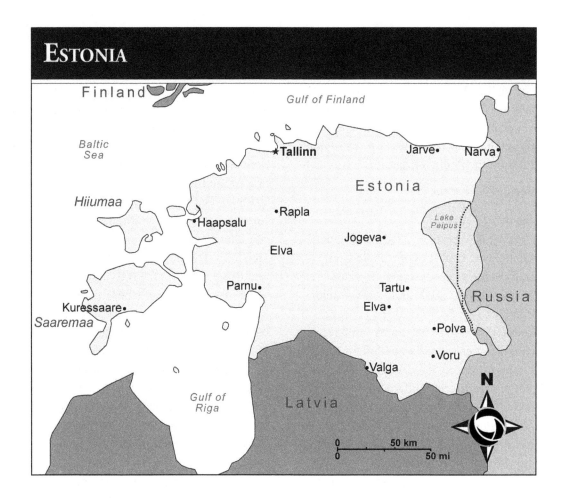

ESTONIA

Finland

Gulf of Finland

Baltic
Sea

★Tallinn   Jarve•   Narva•

Estonia

Hiiumaa

•Rapla

•Haapsalu

Lake
Peipus

Jogeva•

Elva

Parnu•

Tartu•

Russia

Elva•

Kuressaare•

Saaremaa

•Polva

•Voru

Gulf of
Riga

•Valga

Latvia

N

0   50 km
0   50 mi

At this time, the boundary between Estonia and the Soviet Union and the boundary between Estonia and Latvia were delineated.

In 1939, the Soviet Union demanded that it be allowed to establish military installations and station Red Army troops in Estonia. The Soviets formally invaded Estonia in 1940. The following year, Germany declared war on the Soviet Union and occupied Estonia until 1944, when the Soviets retook Estonia. Estonia was incorporated into the Soviet Union as the Estonia Soviet Socialistic Republic, although the United States and some other countries never recognized Soviet sovereignty over Estonia. In 1945, the Soviets adjusted Estonia's boundary by moving some small territories inhabited primarily by Russian speakers and located along the boundary from Estonia into Russia.

Estonia regained its independence as the Soviet Union disintegrated in 1991. In March 1991, a referendum was held in which 80 percent of those voting supported Estonian independence. Estonia formally declared its independence on August 20, 1991. Estonia joined NATO and the European Union in 2004.

Since independence, issues of citizenship and language have been controversial in Estonia. In conjunction with the Soviet Union's Russification policy, many ethnic Russians moved to Estonia during its period of Soviet rule. By 1991, about a quarter of Estonia's people were ethnic Russians. The newly independent Estonian government declared Estonian to be the country's official language and mandated the use of Estonian in schools and in transacting government business. Estonian law granted Estonian citizenship automatically to persons who were citizens of pre-Soviet Estonia and their descendants. Persons not descended from pre-1940 citizens had to be naturalized. A requirement for naturalization was knowledge of the Estonian language and Estonian history. Estonian citizenship is required for voting for the Riigikogu (Parliament) and the European Parliament, although noncitizen residents may vote in local elections.

In 1944, during World War II, the Soviet Union's Red Army recaptured Estonia's capital city of Tallinn from the Nazis. Three years later, the Soviets built and unveiled a statue memorializing the capture of Tallinn. The statue, which is known as the Bronze Soldier of Tallinn, depicts a soldier wearing the World War II uniform of the Red Army. The Bronze Soldier of Tallinn has been resented by many ethnic Estonians who regarded the Soviets as well as the Nazis as oppressors.

On February 20, 2007, the Estonian government passed a Law on Forbidden Structures. This law banned public display of monuments associated with the Soviet Union. On April 26, Estonian government officials dismantled the Bronze Soldier of Tallinn and moved it to a military cemetery. The statue's removal sparked riots in which one Russian Estonian was killed and hundreds of persons were arrested.

CONTEMPORARY ISSUES

Estonia's contemporary boundaries are stable. Controversy over language rights and cultural differences continues within Estonia, although the boundary with Russia remains uncontested. In addition to language-rights issues, one of Estonia's concerns is establishing its place in the 21st-century world as a small but increasingly prosperous country located between larger and more powerful neighbors.

Estonia has the highest per capita income of any of the former Soviet republics. Its prosperity is derived in part from its free-market economy and its establishment of trade links with the West, particularly Germany and the Scandinavian countries. Many Estonians believe that the key to future prosperity is to reinforce these linkages with Scandinavia and the West. Some Estonian politicians have proposed changing the Estonian flag to make it look more like the flags of the Scandinavian countries. The proposed change would retain Estonia's traditional colors of blue, black, and white but would adopt a design containing the Nordic cross that is used on flags throughout Scandinavia.

See also   Latvia, Russia

Further Reading

Toomas Hendrik Ilves. "Estonia as a Nordic country." Estonian Ministry of Foreign Affairs, 1999, http://www.vm.ee/?q=node/3489.

Anatol Levin. *The Baltic revolution: Estonia, Latvia, and Lithuania and the path to independence.* New Haven, CT: Yale University Press, 1994.

Toivo U. Raun. *Estonia and the Estonians.* Palo Alto, CA: Hoover Press, 2001.

FINLAND

OVERVIEW

The Republic of Finland is located in Northern Europe between the Scandinavian Peninsula and Russia. However, the Finnish language is unrelated to the languages of Norway, Sweden, and Denmark; it is a Ural-Altaic language more closely related to Hungarian and to various Asian languages. Finland's land area is 130,596 square miles, slightly smaller than Montana. Its population is about 5.2 million. As with Norway and Sweden, most of Finland's people live in the southern part of the country while northern Finland is sparsely populated.

Finland has coastlines on the Gulf of Finland to the south and the Gulf of Bothnia to the west. Both of these bodies of water empty into the Baltic Sea. Sweden is located on the opposite shore of the Gulf of Bothnia, and Estonia is located on the south shore of the Gulf of Finland. Finland has land boundaries with Sweden and Norway to the north and northwest and with Russia to the east.

The boundary between Finland and Sweden follows the Muonio River southward until it empties into the Torne River, then follows the Torne River until it empties into the Gulf of Bothnia. The Tana River, which is the longest in Scandinavia, forms the central portion of the boundary between Finland and Norway. Short straight-line boundary segments are located to the west and east of the Tana River. The entire boundary region is very sparsely inhabited, and there are very few permanent settlements or paved roads. The boundary with Russia, which has been contested frequently over several hundred

years, consists of numerous short straight-line segments that extend generally in a north-south direction before trending southwestward in a single longer segment to the Baltic Sea.

HISTORICAL CONTEXT

For much of its history, Finland has been controlled by Sweden or by Russia. Swedish forces invaded Finland on several occasions during the 12th and 13th centuries. Finland was incorporated formally into the Swedish Empire in 1249. For the next 500 years, Finland's political history was linked to that of Sweden. In 1721, Russia's defeat of the Swedish Empire during the Great Northern War resulted in the cession of territory in what was then the eastern part of Finland to Russia. However, most of what is now Finland remained under Swedish sovereignty.

In 1809, Sweden and Russia contested what became known as the Finnish War. After Sweden was defeated, Russia expelled the Swedes from present-day Finland and established the Grand Duchy of Finland. The grand duchy was a constitutional monarchy, and Russia allowed Finland to maintain its Lutheran state religion and its language. Beginning in 1899, Russia initiated efforts to impose Finnish integration into the Russian empire, including the forced conscription of Finnish soldiers into the Russian Army and mandating the use of Russian in administration of the grand duchy.

Finland declared its independence during the Russian Revolution in 1917, and it has remained independent ever since. In 1920, Finland and the Soviet Union signed the Treaty of Tartu. This treaty confirmed that the boundary between the

FINLAND

Grand Duchy of Finland and Russia would remain the boundary between independent Finland and the Soviet Union. Finland was also given sovereignty over the small northern territory of Petsamo, which included access to an ice-free port on the Arctic Ocean.

In 1939, the treaty signed by Germany and the Soviet Union at the outset of World War II identified Finland as part of the

Soviet sphere of influence. The Soviets invaded Finland in the winter of 1939–1940 and regained Petsamo while also taking over other areas of eastern Finland. Finland remained neutral during World War II but allowed German troops to transit the country. After World War II ended, Finland remained a neutral country during the Cold War, although it retained its status as a democracy and its boundaries with the Soviet Union were stabilized. Finland joined the European Union in 1994, after the Cold War had ended.

CONTEMPORARY ISSUES

Finland's long history as a nation with a distinctive culture located between powerful neighbors has affected its relationships with nearby countries since the Middle Ages. During the Cold War, Finland was ostensibly neutral although its economy was much more oriented to Scandinavia and Germany than it was to the Soviets and their allies. Today, Finland is allied closely with Scandinavia and Western Europe.

Trade relationships in the Baltic Sea have also affected Finland. One concern has been control over the Aland Islands, which are located at the entrance to the Gulf of Bothnia between the mainland of Finland and the mainland of Sweden. The Aland Islands have a population of 28,000, the majority of whom speak Swedish. However, sovereignty over the islands was given to the Grand Duchy of Finland when the grand duchy was founded in 1809. During the 19th and early 20th centuries, many islanders supported ceding sovereignty over the islands from Finland to Sweden. Today, the question of sover-

eignty over the Aland Islands has largely disappeared.

See also   Norway, Russia, Sweden

Further Reading

Juha Jokela. *Europeanization and foreign policy: State identity in Finland and Britain.* New York: Routledge, 2011.

Anssi Paasi. "Boundaries as social practice and discourse: The Finnish-Russian border." *Regional Studies*, 33 (1999), pp. 669–680.

Alan Palmer. *The Baltic: A new history of the region and its people.* New York: Overlook, 2006.

FRANCE

OVERVIEW

France is the largest country in the European Union by land area. Its European land area of 213,010 square miles makes it slightly smaller than the state of Texas. France considers several overseas colonies, including Guadeloupe and Martinique in the Caribbean and French Guiana in South America, to be an integral part of the French Republic. Including these territories, the overall land area of France is 260,558 square miles. The term "Metropolitan France" is used to refer to those portions of France located in Europe. France has a population of about 66 million, making it second in population only to Germany among the European Union's members.

France's neighbors are Belgium and Luxembourg to the north, Germany to the north and east, Switzerland and Italy to the east, Monaco to the southeast, and Spain and Andorra to the southwest.

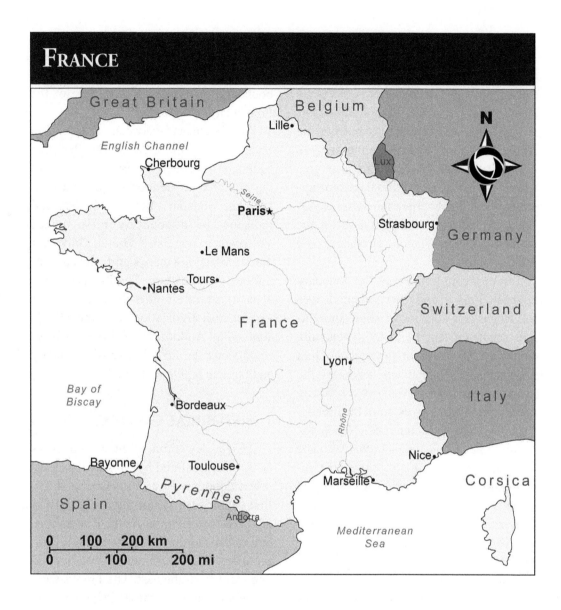

FRANCE

Great Britain

Belgium

English Channel

Lille•

Cherbourg•

Lux

N

Seine

Paris★

Strasbourg•

Germany

•Le Mans

Tours•

•Nantes

France

Switzerland

Lyon•

Bay of
Biscay

•Bordeaux

Italy

Rhône

Bayonne•

Toulouse•

Nice•

Pyrennes

Marseille•

Corsica

Spain

Andorra

Mediterranean
Sea

| 0 | 100 | 200 km |
| 0 | 100 | 200 mi |

Southeastern France has a coastline on the Mediterranean Sea. Western and northwestern France adjoin the Atlantic Ocean, with a coastline on the Bay of Biscay to the west. Northwestern France has a coastline on La Manche, which is known in the United Kingdom as the English Channel, and the North Sea. La Manche separates France and the United Kingdom and is about 20 miles wide at its narrowest point. France's European territory also includes the island of Corsica in the Mediterranean Sea.

Some of France's boundaries are physical boundaries, and others are cultural boundaries. The boundary between France and Belgium and the boundary between France and Luxembourg are highly irregular geometric boundaries. They trend generally from northwest to southeast from a point three miles northwest of Dunkerque on the North Sea to the tripoint between France, Luxembourg, and Germany. From this tripoint, the boundary between France and Germany also includes numerous short straight-line segments until it reaches the Rhine River about 30 miles northeast of the city of Strasbourg. The boundary then turns to the southwest and follows the Rhine upstream past Strasbourg to the Swiss city of Basel, which is located just south of the tripoint between France, Germany, and Switzerland.

Just upstream from Basel, the boundary between France and Switzerland leaves the Rhine and consists of short straight-line segments that trend in a generally southwesterly direction through the Jura Mountains. The boundary separates the historically French provinces of Savoy and Burgundy to the west from the French-speaking Swiss cantons of Neuchatel, Vaud, Geneva, and Valais to the east. The boundary continues in a southwesterly direction to a point west of the Swiss city of Geneva. It circles Geneva to Lake Geneva east of the city, then turns southward into the Alps to the tripoint between France, Switzerland, and Italy.

From this tripoint, the boundary between France and Italy follows high peaks in the western portion of the Alps toward the Mediterranean. This boundary includes the peak of Mont Blanc, which is the highest mountain in Europe. The boundary region represents the historic frontier between French and Italian civilizations and spheres of influence. Except near the coast, the boundary crosses very rugged and sparsely populated territory and was very difficult to cross prior to the development of mechanized transportation in the 19th century. The tiny country of Monaco is located on the coast of the Mediterranean about 15 miles west of the French-Italian boundary and about 15 miles east of the French city of Nice.

The boundary between France and Spain follows the crest of the Pyrenees Mountains between the Bay of Biscay to the west and the Mediterranean to the east. Like the boundary between France and Italy, most of this boundary crosses rugged and sparsely populated terrain. Only near the two coasts are there significant concentrations of population. The Pyrenees have been a natural frontier between French and Spanish civilization since the Middle Ages. Tiny Andorra in the Pyrenees is located along the French-Spanish boundary and borders both countries.

HISTORICAL CONTEXT

Present-day France, then known as Gaul, was inhabited by Celtic tribes until it was conquered by Julius Caesar in the first century BC. Gaul then became part of the Roman Empire. As the Roman Empire collapsed during the fourth and fifth centuries AD, Germanic tribes moved into Gaul from the east. The Franks were prominent among these invaders, and they gave France its present name. However, the area controlled by present-day France remained divided among various kingdoms throughout the sixth, seventh, and eighth centuries. Frankish tribes expanded their influence throughout this time until the late eighth century, when Charles the Great or Charlemagne united much of present-day France with what is now western and southern Germany and northern Italy.

After Charlemagne's death, his empire was divided among his heirs. What is now western France was ruled by his grandson Charles the Bald. This region became the core of the modern French state. France was ruled by kings throughout the Middle Ages, but these monarchs had little authority over individual regions, which retained substantial autonomy.

Beginning in the 15th century, the French monarchy consolidated its power and expanded its area of territorial control. Burgundy, Provence, Brittany, and other areas now part of France came under French control during this period. By the 1660s, all of present-day Metropolitan France except for the eastern part of the country and the island of Corsica had become part of the French state.

France was also an active participant in Europe's expansion to other parts of the world beginning in the early 16th century. France established colonies in many areas, notably Quebec and the Mississippi Valley in North America. After the Seven Years' War, France was forced to give up its North American territory, which was taken over by Britain and Spain. The western portion of the drainage basin of the Mississippi River, known as Louisiana, was retroceded by Spain to France in 1798 but was sold to the United States in 1803. During the 19th century, France expanded its colonial empire once again. Much of northwestern Africa became French territory, as did much of mainland Southeast Asia. Most of these former French colonies achieved independence after World War II.

The island of Corsica in the Mediterranean Sea became part of France in 1768. Corsica is closer to Italy than to mainland France and most Corsicans speak Italian as their first language. It is the fourth-largest island in the Mediterranean (following Sicily, Sardinia, and Cyprus), with about 300,000 residents.

The Valois and Bourbon dynasties ruled France as an absolute monarchy until the French Revolution began in 1789. The last Bourbon king, Louis XVI, was executed in 1793. After several years of turmoil, Napoleon Bonaparte emerged as the emperor of France in 1800. During the next 15 years, Napoleon attempted to expand the French empire throughout continental Europe. Following the pivotal defeat of Napoleon's armies at the Battle of Waterloo in 1815, the Napoleonic Wars came to an end. The map of Europe was redrawn at the Congress of Vienna in 1815.

Most of France's modern boundaries were delineated during this period. The boundary between France and Switzerland was agreed upon by the two countries in 1814. It has remained in place ever since, with minor adjustments made in 1953.

The boundaries between France and Belgium and between France and Luxembourg were established as part of the Congress of Vienna, which established the United Kingdom of the Netherlands, in 1815. The United Kingdom of the Netherlands was created as a buffer state between centers of power in France and Germany. It was divided into the present-day countries of the Netherlands, Belgium, and Luxembourg in 1839 with the boundaries between France and Belgium and France and Luxembourg remaining intact. The boundary between France and Spain has followed the crest of the Pyrenees Mountains since the Treaty of the Pyrenees was signed in 1659. The Treaty of the Pyrenees was the first international treaty after the Peace of

Westphalia that included specific reference to a delineated boundary between two sovereign countries.

The boundary between France and Germany, however, was contested between the two countries from the Middle Ages until after World War II. Much of this contestation involved Alsace-Lorraine, which is located on the French side of the Rhine River and extends northwestward to the contemporary boundary between France and Luxembourg. Its population is divided among French and German speakers, with a majority of people near the contemporary French-German border speaking German.

Control of Alsace-Lorraine has shifted back and forth between the two countries for several centuries. Alsace-Lorraine became part of Germany after France's military defeat by Prussia in the Franco-Prussian War of 1870. The territory was returned to France after World War I but annexed by Nazi Germany in 1940. After World War II ended, Alsace-Lorraine was returned to France. French policy suppressed the use of German dialects and mandated the use of French in schools and for government business, although this policy has been loosened in recent years. Alsace-Lorraine's principal city of Strasbourg became the headquarters of the European Parliament in 1979.

CONTEMPORARY ISSUES

France's boundaries are stable and uncontested. However, over the years separatist movements have arisen in various outlying areas of France. Many Basques in southwestern France are supportive of efforts among Basques in both Spain and France to create an independent Basque state. Separatists in the historic province of Brittany in northwestern France have also promoted independence.

Separatists have also been active on the island of Corsica. Some Corsicans have promoted full independence for the island, although these efforts are opposed by the French government. In 2010, a Corsican separatist party known as Corsica Libera, or Free Corsica, won 18 percent of the votes in Corsica's regional elections.

See also   Andorra, Belgium, Germany, Italy, Luxembourg, Monaco, Spain

Further Reading

Economist. "France, Germany, and the European Union: Future dreaming." October 22, 2009, http://www.economist.com/node/14704609.

Colette Mazzucelli. *France and Germany at Maastricht: Politics and negotiations to create the European Union.* New York: Taylor and Francis, 1997.

Peter Sahlins. *The making of France and Spain in the Pyrenees.* Berkeley: University of California Press, 1989.

GERMANY

OVERVIEW

The Federal Republic of Germany is located in north-central Europe. Germany has a land area of 137,847 square miles, slightly smaller than Montana. It has a population of 82 million, making Germany the largest state by population in the European Union.

Germany is bordered by Denmark to the north, Poland and the Czech Republic to the east, Austria and Switzerland to the

south, and France, Luxembourg, Belgium, and the Netherlands to the west. Northern Germany has a coast on the North Sea to the west of its border with Denmark and a coast on the Baltic Sea to the east of this border. The boundary between Germany and Denmark crosses the Jutland Peninsula and connects the North Sea and the Baltic Sea. To the west, German territory includes Sylt Island, which is the largest and northernmost of the Frisian Islands in the North Sea. A bridge connecting Sylt Island with the mainland was built and opened to traffic in 1929. From a point just north of the bridge, the boundary between Germany and Denmark follows short straight-line segments running in a generally westward direction to a point less than five miles north of the German city of Flensburg. Flensburg is located at the head of the Flensburg Fjord, which is an arm of the Baltic Sea. German territory is located south of the Flensburg Fjord, while the territory north of the fjord belongs to Denmark.

The boundary between Germany and Poland extends southward from the Baltic Sea near the Polish city of Szczecin. It follows the Oder River upstream and inland to its tributary, the Neisse River, and continues upstream and southward along the Neisse to the tripoint between Germany, Poland, and the Czech Republic east of the German city of Dresden. The Oder-Neisse Line was established as the boundary between Germany and Poland after World War II, and it was confirmed as the boundary between the two countries after Germany was reunified in 1990.

From the tripoint between Germany, Poland, and the Czech Republic, the boundary between Germany and the Czech Republic extends in a southwesterly direction, paralleling the crest of the Ore Mountains, which cross the northwestern portion of the Czech Republic. East of the town of Hof, the boundary turns southeastward. Here it is located along the drainage divide between tributaries of the Danube River in Germany and those of the Vltava River in the Czech Republic. The boundary continues in a southeasterly direction to the tripoint between Germany, the Czech Republic, and Austria.

The northwestern Czech Republic, Austria, and central and eastern Switzerland are inhabited primarily by German speakers. Thus these boundaries generally follow natural features. From the tripoint between Germany, Austria, and the Czech Republic, the boundary extends southward to the main channel of the Danube. It follows the Danube upstream briefly to the city of Passau. From Passau, the boundary turns southward along the Inn River, which is a tributary of the Danube. It continues along the Inn upstream to its confluence with the Salzach River, then follows the Salzach upstream and southward. South of the city of Salzburg, the boundary leaves the Salzach and turns westward, following generally the crest of the Bavarian Alps to the tripoint between Germany, Austria, and Switzerland in Lake Constance.

From Lake Constance, most of the boundary between Germany and Switzerland follows the Rhine River downstream and westward to the tripoint between Germany, Switzerland, and France near the Swiss city of Basel. Here the Rhine turns northward, and the boundary between Germany and France follows the Rhine to a point north of the French city of Strasbourg. At that point the Rhine continues northward into Germany, while the boundary between Germany and France turns to the west. It follows short and sometimes irregular straight-line segments westward past the city of Saarbrucken to the tripoint between Germany, France, and Luxembourg on the Mosel River, spelled "Moselle" in France, which is a tributary of the Rhine in Germany.

The boundary between Germany and Luxembourg follows the Mosel downstream and northward to its confluence with its tributary, the Sauer River. The Sauer enters the Mosel at right angles. The boundary then follows the Sauer northwestward, then continues along its tributary, the Our River, to the tripoint between Germany and Belgium. In contrast to many of Germany's other boundaries, the boundary between Germany and Belgium follows short straight-line segments rather than natural features. It extends in a generally northward direction to the tripoint between Germany, Belgium, and the Netherlands near the historically significant city of Aachen. From the vicinity of Aachen, the boundary between Germany and the Netherlands extends northward to the North Sea. This boundary was drawn historically in order to separate German speakers to the east from Dutch speakers to the west. The boundary was drawn through marshy and frequently flooded terrain, which was relatively sparsely populated and poorly suitable for agriculture before the marshes were drained and became farmed.

HISTORICAL CONTEXT

The concept of boundaries as we know it today originated in Germany. Since the Middle Ages, Germany has evolved from a patchwork consisting of hundreds of small, semi-independent principalities to the largest state in Europe. The boundaries of Germany have been changed many times over several centuries, often as a result of victory and defeat in wars.

What is now southwestern Germany was conquered by the Roman Empire in the first century BC. The Romans established an administrative center at Trier, on the banks of the Mosel, in 30 BC. However, most of modern Germany, including the valleys of the Rhine and Danube rivers, was occupied by Germanic tribes. Beginning in the third century AD, some of these Germanic tribes invaded outlying portions of the Roman Empire, and they continued to move to the southwest as the Roman Empire weakened in the fourth and fifth centuries AD.

The most powerful of these Germanic tribes were the Franks, who occupied much of modern western Germany along with neighboring portions of France and Belgium. Charlemagne, who was king of the Franks, was crowned by Pope Leo III as Holy Roman Emperor in AD 800. Charlemagne established his court at Aachen near the tripoint between present-day Germany, Belgium, and the Netherlands, where he died in AD 814. Charlemagne's empire was divided in 843, and the eastern portion of the realm, including much of present-day Germany, maintained the title of the Holy Roman Empire.

The Holy Roman Empire remained in existence until 1806. At its zenith, the empire included all of present-day Germany along with the Netherlands, Belgium, Switzerland, much of Austria, the western Czech Republic, and northern Italy. However, the empire included hundreds of small principalities, duchies, and other administrative units that were often in conflict with one another. Germany remained divided through the 15th, 16th, and 17th centuries whereas Britain, France, Spain, and other European countries had become unified and had established control over the territories that for the most part they continue to occupy today.

Germany was the birthplace of the Reformation, which was initiated when Martin Luther challenged the authority of the Roman Catholic Church in 1517. Many Germans, especially in northern Germany, converted to Lutheranism. By 1600, many German principalities had adopted Lutheranism as their official religions while others remained Roman Catholic and some adhered to Calvinism. Religious tensions between Protestants and Catholics contributed to the Thirty Years' War, which began in 1618 and continued until the Peace of Westphalia was signed ending the war in 1648. The Peace of Westphalia established the modern concept of sovereignty and hence created the need to define and delineate boundaries between states.

German unification began in the 19th century. After the Congress of Vienna ended in 1815, the German Confederation was established. The confederation included 39 German-speaking political units. It included almost all of present-day Germany along with Austria and parts of modern Poland. The two dominant members of the confederation were Austria and Prussia. Located in northeastern Germany and centered on the modern German capital city of Berlin, Prussia emerged as the most powerful member of the confederation by the 1860s. Prussia and Austria went to war in 1866. After the war the confederation collapsed, and Prussia emerged as the most powerful state in the region and the leader of the newly established North German Confederation. The confederation expanded after taking control of Schleswig and Holstein along the Danish frontier in 1866 and after a military victory over France in the Franco-Prussian War of 1870. In 1871, Prussia's King William I proclaimed himself as the kaiser, or emperor, of Germany.

The German Empire maintained its authority over the region until World War I. After the end of the war, Germany was forced via the Treaty of Versailles to cede a substantial amount of territory to the victorious Allies. The territories of Alsace and Lorraine in the southwestern corner of the empire were ceded to France and remain part of France today. A larger area of eastern Germany was ceded to the newly independent state of Poland. Western Prussia, which was ceded to Poland, included a coastline along the Baltic Sea known as the Polish Corridor. The Polish Corridor gave Poland access to the Baltic but divided East Prussia in far northeastern Germany from the rest of the country. Germany was also stripped of its overseas colonies and was forced to pay heavy indemnities to the Allies.

After Germany was forced to accept the terms of the Treaty of Versailles, the democratic Weimar Republic was established. In 1932 and 1933, the majority of seats in the Weimar parliament were held by communists or by members of the National Socialist or Nazi Party led by Adolf Hitler. Hitler was appointed as chancellor of Germany in 1933, and shortly thereafter he crushed all political opposition and established a totalitarian state. Germany rearmed and in the late 1930s annexed Austria and the Sudetenland area of the present-day Czech Republic. The German invasion of Poland in September 1939 triggered World War II, which raged throughout Europe for nearly six years and resulted in as many as 40 million military and civilian casualties. The Nazi regime was responsible for the slaughter of about 6 million Jews during the Holocaust.

After Germany surrendered at the end of World War II, its boundaries were redrawn once again. The boundary between Germany and Poland was moved westward to its current location along the Oder and Neisse rivers. The territory east of the Oder and Neisse rivers was given to Poland and to the Soviet Union. Germany was divided into four occupation zones. Each was occupied by Allied troops with the British occupation zone in the northwest, the French zone in the southwest, the American zone in the south, and the Soviet zone in the east. Germany's capital city of Berlin was also divided into British, French, American, and Soviet occupation zones.

In 1949, the four sectors became two separate countries. The British, French, and American occupation zones were united as the Federal Republic of Germany. The Soviet occupation zone became the German Democratic Republic under a communist dictatorship. The two Germanies were known as West Germany and East Germany, respectively. The Soviet occupation zone in Berlin, known as East Berlin, became the capital of East Germany. However, the rest of Berlin became an exclave of West Germany. During the 1950s, thousands of East Germans crossed from East Berlin to West Berlin in order to escape communist tyranny. With Soviet support, the Berlin Wall was constructed in 1961 in order to stem the flow of migration out of East Germany to the West.

In 1951, West Germany became a founding member of the European Coal and Steel Community, which evolved eventually into the European Economic Community and later into the European Union. West Germany's economy boomed while that of East Germany stagnated. The communist regime in East Germany collapsed in 1989, and West and East Germany were reunified in 1990. The seat of government of East Germany had been the city of Bonn, but the capital of reunified Germany was moved to Berlin in 1994.

CONTEMPORARY ISSUES

After reunification, Germany had to adjust to its sudden increases in territory and population. By the 1980s, the standard of living in East Germany had fallen far below that of West Germany. Once they were free to do so, many East Germans moved to the former West Germany in search of employment and other opportunities.

The reunification of Germany also affected populations of German ethnicity who had been living outside Germany during the Cold War. Substantial numbers of ethnic Germans lived in Hungary, Romania, the Czech Republic, the Soviet Union, and other former communist countries at the end of the Cold War. At the time, German law granted citizenship to anyone who could prove descent from German citizens. On this basis, many Eastern Europeans of German ancestry moved to Germany. These new arrivals were known as *auslanders*, or "outlanders."

The arrival of the *auslanders*, as well as people from the former East Germany, created tension in particular among Germany's immigrant populations. Since World War II, many people from Turkey, the Middle East, and southeastern Europe had moved to Germany. These migrants were not considered permanent residents of Germany and were known as *gastarbeiters*, or "guest workers." Most worked in factories or took various menial jobs.

Although the *gastarbeiters* were regarded as temporary, rather than permanent, inhabitants of Germany, by the early 1990s many *gastarbeiters* and their families had been living in Germany for as long as four decades. Many spoke fluent German and were assimilated into German culture and society. However, the same German laws that fast-tracked *auslanders* toward German citizenship made it difficult for people of non-German ancestry to become German citizens. Some *gastarbeiters* resented the newcomers, whom they saw as having been privileged by the government.

Germany has been involved in minor disputes with some of its neighbors since its reunification. For example, Germany and the Netherlands have disputed their maritime boundaries in the North Sea, including a disagreement over the location of the boundary within the Ems-Dollart estuary that separates the two countries.

Since the 1950s, Germany has been a strong proponent of the European Union and European integration more generally. German support for the European Union and the creation of a unified European political entity continued after unification. Today Germany has the largest population in the European Union and its strongest economy. Tensions between Germany and some fellow European Union members with weaker economies have intensified, and some Germans resent the responsibility of supporting these countries. Germany is an integral part of the Eurozone, or the region with a common currency within the European Union, but German economic strength contrasts with the struggles of Greece, Spain, and other members of the Eurozone that are in danger of having to default on their economic obligations.

See also   Austria, Belgium, Czech Republic, Denmark, France, Luxembourg, Netherlands, Poland, Switzerland

Further Reading

James Angelos. "What integration means for Germany's guest workers." *Foreign Affairs*, 2011, http://www.mmg.mpg.de/fileadmin/user_upload/Publikationen/Pdf/What_Integration_Means.pdf.

Ralph Beste. "A new era in international relations: Germany's government faces tough work abroad." *Der Spiegel Online*, September 29, 2009, http://www.spiegel.de/international/world/a-new-era-in-international-relations-germany-s-new-government-faces-tough-work-abroad-a-651808.html.

Bill Niven and J.K.A. Thomaneck. *Dividing and uniting Germany.* London: Routledge, 2001.

Stefan Wolff. *Germany, Poland, and the Czech Republic since reunification.* New York: Taylor and Francis, 2007.

GREECE

OVERVIEW

The Hellenic Republic, known as Greece, is located in southeastern Europe. Most of Greece occupies the southern portion of the Balkan Peninsula. Greece also includes more than 1,400 islands in the Mediterranean, Ionian, and Aegean seas, of which 227 are inhabited. The largest of these islands, Crete, is larger than the state of Delaware. The overall land area of Greece, including the islands, is 50,944 square miles, or the approximate size of Louisiana. The population is about 11.5 million.

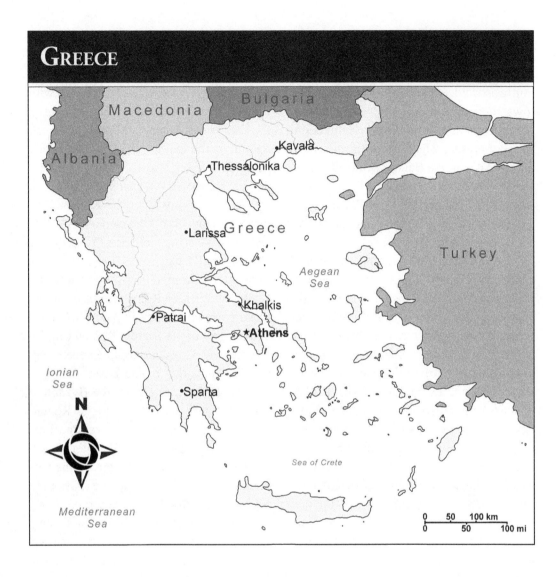

Greece's neighbors on the Balkan Peninsula are Albania, Macedonia, and Bulgaria to the north and Turkey to the northeast. The peninsula juts southeastward into the Mediterranean Sea, with the Ionian Sea to the west and the Aegean Sea to the east. In general, Greece's land boundaries follow mountain ranges that separate Greece from its neighbors. However, the boundaries also separate people of Greek nationality from people of other nationalities in neighboring countries. About 94 percent of Greece's population consists of people of Greek ancestry and ethnicity.

The boundary between Greece and Albania trends northwestward from the Ionian Sea. Northwest of the Greek town of Saglada, however, Greek territory includes a strip of land about 12 miles long and 1 to 2 miles wide along the Ionian Sea coast. Greek territory also includes the island of Corfu in the Ionian Sea northwest of the mainland, although the east coast of Corfu is closer to the coast of Albania

than to the Greek mainland. North of Saglada, the boundary follows generally the
Pindus Mountains northward, then turns
northeastward. Most of this boundary follows short straight-line segments. It continues in a generally northeasterly direction
to Lake Prespa, which is the third-largest
natural lake on the Balkan Peninsula. The
tripoint between Greece, Albania, and
Macedonia is located in Lake Prespa.

From Lake Prespa, the boundaries be-
tween Greece and Macedonia and between
Greece and Bulgaria extend eastward.
These boundaries follow the Rhodope
Mountains. Near the Greek town of Mikro
Dereio at the eastern end of the Rhodope
range, the boundary turns northward, separating the lowlands in Greece from the
higher elevations of southeastern Bulgaria.
It continues northward to the Maritsa River,
which is known also in Greece as the Evrus
River or the Hebros River. It follows the
Maritsa northward to the tripoint between
Greece, Bulgaria, and Turkey. Near this
tripoint, the Maritsa turns eastward and
southward to the Aegean Sea, forming the
entire boundary between Greece and Turkey. However, a small section of Turkish
territory is located on the west, or right,
bank of the Maritsa.

HISTORICAL CONTEXT

Various civilizations arose on the Greek
islands and on the mainland Greek peninsula as long ago as 3000 BC. These advanced civilizations were the first to arise
in all of Europe. The Minoan civilization, based on the island of Greece, became prominent beginning in about 2700
BC. The Mycenaean civilization emerged
about 2000 BC and dominated the Greek

mainland for the next thousand years. The
classical Greek civilization emerged in
Athens around 500 BC, but internal conflicts among Greek city-states along with
threats of conquest by the Persians caused
the decline of Athens and its main rival,
Sparta, as the major powers of the Greek
peninsula. Greek was ruled by the Macedonian empire of Alexander the Great in
the fourth century BC. The Roman Empire took control of Macedonia in 146 BC
and had taken over the rest of present-day
Greece by 27 BC.

When the Roman Empire was split between the Western Roman Empire and the
Eastern Roman Empire in AD 476, Greece
became part of the Eastern Roman Empire
centered on Constantinople (present-day
Istanbul in Turkey). The Eastern Roman
Empire was known also as the Byzantine
Empire, after Constantinople's Roman
name of Byzantium. The Byzantine Empire was dissolved in 1453, after which
most of Greece became part of the Ottoman Empire. Protests against Ottoman
rule, which many Greeks regarded as repressive, intensified in the 18th and early
19th centuries. In 1821, Greek nationalists
declared war on the Ottomans. After several years of fighting, Britain, France, and
Russia intervened on the side of Greek independence. Greece was recognized as an
independent kingdom by these and other
sovereign states in 1830. The kingdom of
Greece controlled much of present-day
Greece except for the northern portions
near its current boundaries with Albania, Macedonia, Bulgaria, and Turkey.
Throughout the rest of the 19th century,
the kingdom strove to expand its control to include Greek-majority territories
along its northern frontier. Some Greek

nationalists proposed that the expanded Greek kingdom include Constantinople, which at that time contained a large Greek population.

After World War I, the Ottoman Empire was dissolved. Many persons of Greek nationality moved from Istanbul and other parts of Turkey, as the successor state to the Ottoman Empire, into Greece. During World War II, Greek forces resisted Italian efforts to take over the country, but German forces later occupied Greece. After the war, communist and anti-communist forces grappled for control of the Greek government. U.S. president Harry Truman promulgated the Truman Doctrine, which provided American assistance to efforts to resist communist expansion in Greece at a time when the other states of the Balkan Peninsula had been taken over by communist regimes. Greece joined the European Union in 1981, but in the early 20th century, the Greek government has been engulfed in a crisis concerning its national debt.

CONTEMPORARY ISSUES

Greece's relationship with neighboring Turkey has been contentious since the early 19th century, when Greece broke away from the Turkish-dominated Ottoman Empire and became an independent kingdom. Since that time, Greece and Turkey have fought several wars, including conflicts in 1897 and before and after World War I. Many of these wars have involved territorial disputes, often associated with Greek efforts to incorporate ethnic Greeks into the Greek state.

Greece and Turkey have also contested the status of Cyprus, an independent state in the Mediterranean Sea. A majority of Cypriots are of Greek ancestry, but the island also contains a substantial Turkish minority. Throughout the 20th century, some Greek Cypriots demanded political unification with Greece. In 1974, after Greece announced support for this unification, Turkish troops invaded Cyprus and took control of Turkish-majority areas in northern Cyprus. The Turkish-majority areas declared the region to be the Turkish Republic of Northern Cyprus. The Turkish Republic is recognized as sovereign over this area only by Turkey, and not by the international community. However, Turkish forces continue to occupy Northern Cyprus.

Greece and Turkey have contested issues associated with sovereignty over islands in the Aegean Sea. Many of these islands are under Greek sovereignty but are located very close to the Turkish mainland. Because these islands are part of Greece, Turkey has little opportunity to claim maritime sovereignty in the Aegean. In addition to maritime territorial claims, Greece and Turkey have disputed the question of airspace over the Aegean and the question of whether Greece has the right to station troops on the islands located closest to the Turkish mainland.

Greece and Macedonia have also experienced conflict over Macedonia's name. From the Greek perspective, most of Macedonia's inhabitants are ethnic Greeks and therefore that Macedonia should be considered part of Greece. In light of these views, Greece does not recognize Macedonia by that name, recognizing it instead as the Former Yugoslav Republic of Macedonia.

See also   Albania, Bulgaria, Macedonia, Turkey

Further Reading

Faruk Birtek and Thalia Dragonas. *Citizenship and the nation-state in Greece and Turkey.* New York: Routledge, 2005.

Economist. "An economy crumbles: Uncertainty about whether Greece will stay in the euro is crippling its prospects." January 28, 2012, http://www.economist.com/node/21543522.

International Crisis Group. "Turkey and Greece: Time to settle the Aegean dispute." *European Briefing,* 64 (2011), http://www.crisisgroup.org/en/regions/europe/turkey-cyprus/turkey/B64-turkey-and-greece-time-to-settle-the-aegean-dispute.aspx.

GREENLAND

OVERVIEW

Greenland is located in the North Atlantic Ocean. At its closest point, Greenland is about 200 miles west of Iceland. The Arctic Ocean lies to the north of Greenland, with the North Atlantic Ocean to the west, south, and east. From the point of view of physiography, Greenland is considered part of America. However, its history is closely intertwined with that of Scandinavia, and from a political and economic standpoint, it is considered a part of Europe.

Greenland is the largest island in the world. Its land area of 837,000 square miles makes it slightly smaller than Alaska and Texas combined. However, Greenland contains the largest ice cap in the world outside Antarctica, and about 84 percent of Greenland is covered by ice. Settlement is limited to ice-free areas, primarily along the coast.

About 57,000 people live in Greenland. About 88 percent of Greenland's residents are of Inuit or mixed Inuit and Scandinavian ancestry, with most of the rest of European descent. Most Greenlanders speak both Danish and Greenlandic, an Inuit language. Both Danish and Greenlandic are official languages of Greenland.

HISTORICAL CONTEXT

Indigenous peoples from North America have visited and occasionally settled Greenland for several thousand years. The first Europeans to settle in Greenland were Viking explorers who first visited the island in the tenth century AD. The Vikings established two settlements along fjords in southwestern Greenland. The settlements disappeared during the 14th or 15th centuries, most likely because of worsening environmental conditions, famine, and attacks by Inuits and other indigenous peoples.

Even after the Viking settlements disappeared, Denmark continued to claim Greenland as a colony. However, Greenland has been granted increasing home rule in the last half century. In a referendum held on November 26, 2008, over 76 percent of Greenland's voters supported a plan to grant Greenland partial independence from Denmark. Partial independence from Denmark was granted in June 2009; however, Denmark retains authority over Greenland's defense and foreign policy. Greenland's economy is dependent on fishing, especially for shrimp. Minerals, including hydrocarbons and rubies, are increasingly important to Greenland's economy.

GREENLAND

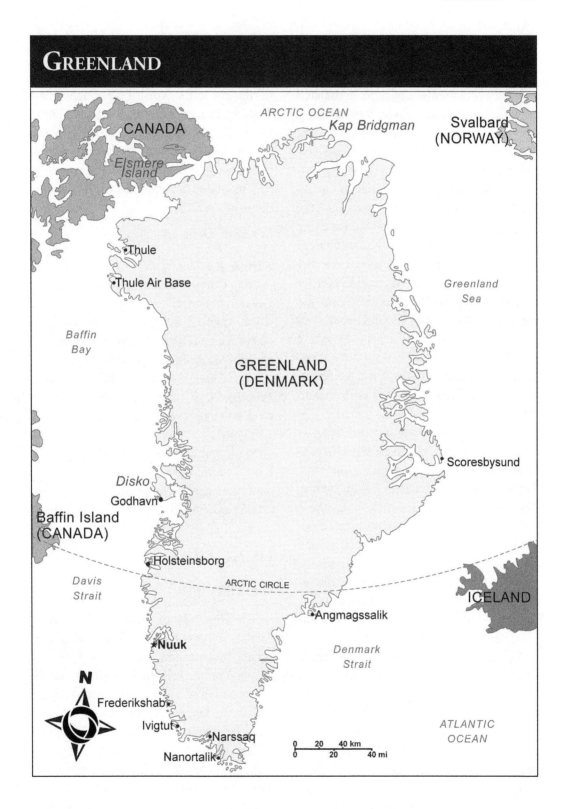

ARCTIC OCEAN

CANADA

Kap Bridgman

Svalbard
(NORWAY)

Elsmere
Island

•Thule

•Thule Air Base

Greenland
Sea

Baffin
Bay

GREENLAND
(DENMARK)

Scoresbysund

Disko

Godhavn•

Baffin Island
(CANADA)

Holsteinsborg

Davis
Strait

ARCTIC CIRCLE

ICELAND

Angmagssalik

★Nuuk

Denmark
Strait

N

Frederikshab

Ivigtut•

Narssaq

ATLANTIC
OCEAN

Nanortalik•

0   20   40 km
0   20   40 mi

CONTEMPORARY ISSUES

Greenland's foreign policy issues involve environmental concerns associated with global climate change, the discovery and exploitation of mineral resources, and Denmark's claim via Greenland to the Arctic Ocean.

Scientists monitoring the size of Greenland's ice cap have discovered that the ice cap may be shrinking. Should melting continue at current rates, the melting ice could cause an increase in global sea levels. Scientists from the National Center for Atmospheric Research have predicted that the continued melting of Greenland's ice cap would affect ocean currents in such a way that sea level rise would have especially pronounced effects along the Atlantic coast of Canada and the northeastern United States.

In recent years, large mineral deposits have been discovered in Greenland. Greenland is the site of what is likely the most lucrative supply of rubies in the world. Currently, ownership rights over these valuable ruby deposits are in dispute between the indigenous Inuit population and a Canadian company that owns the land— some of which has been exposed following melting of the ice at the edge of the ice cap—underneath which these deposits have been discovered.

Controversy over control of the Arctic Ocean also affects Greenland. Control over the Arctic is of increasing interest to countries adjoining the ocean because valuable oil deposits have been discovered, and also because warmer global temperatures and melting ice have increased the possibility that the ocean may become navigable in the summer months. On the basis of its control over Greenland's foreign policy, Denmark has claimed jurisdiction of the area from Greenland's Arctic coast northward to the North Pole. Canada and Russia have made similar claims. These territorial claims are under review by the International Seabed Authority, which evaluates territorial claims in the world's oceans under the auspices of the Law of the Seat Treaty.

See also   Denmark

Further Reading

John Carey. "Global warming: The Greenland factor." *Bloomberg Businessweek*, April 17, 2008, http://www.businessweek.com/bwdaily/dnflash/content/apr2008/db20080417_425304.htm.

Economist. "Nearly independent day." June 20, 2009, http://www.economist.com/node/13854765?story_id=13854765.

Mark Nuttall. "Self-rule in Greenland: Toward the world's first independent Inuit state?" *Indigenous Affairs*, 3–4 (2008), pp. 64–70.

HUNGARY

OVERVIEW

The Republic of Hungary, located in Central Europe, has a land area of 35,919 square miles (about the size of Indiana). Its population is about 10 million, nearly 95 percent of whom are ethnic Hungarians. Unlike the languages of Hungary's neighbors, Hungarian is not an Indo-European language; rather, it is a Finno-Ugric language more closely related to Finnish and Estonian. Historically, Hungary has been oriented to agriculture, and the country

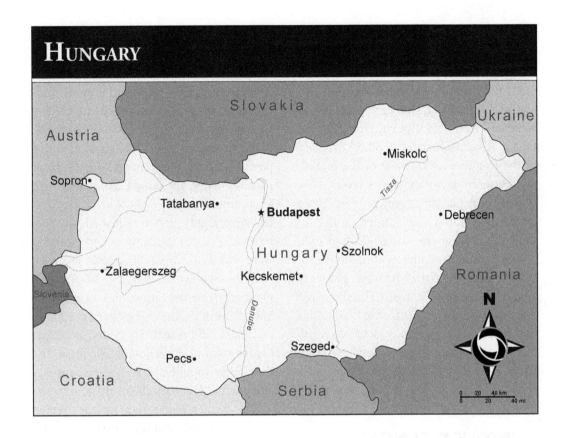

HUNGARY

remains largely self-sufficient in food production. During communist rule, heavy industry was developed, and it remains important to the Hungarian economy.

Hungary's neighbors are Slovakia to the north, Ukraine and Romania to the east, Serbia and Croatia to the south, and Slovenia and Austria to the west. Some of its boundaries follow rivers, whereas others were delineated on the basis of cultural factors. The tripoint among Hungary, Austria, and Slovakia is located along the Danube River, which becomes the boundary between Hungary and Slovakia before the Danube makes a sharp bend southward northwest of Budapest. From that point, the boundary extends in an east-northeast direction following numerous short straight-line segments.

The tripoint among Hungary, Slovakia, and Ukraine is located on the Tisza River, an important tributary of the Danube that flows through eastern Hungary before emptying into the Danube in northern Serbia. The Tisza is the boundary between Hungary and Ukraine for a short distance eastward from this tripoint. To the east, the boundary consists of short straight-line segments to the north of the river before it joins the Tisza once again upstream to the tripoint between Hungary, Ukraine, and Romania. Short segments extending in a generally northeast-to-southwest direction form the boundary between Hungary and Romania to their tripoint between Hungary, Romania, and Serbia.

Hungary's southern borders are also short straight-line segments separating Hungary from Serbia westward to the tripoint between Hungary, Serbia, and Croatia and separating Hungary and Croatia westward from this tripoint. However, the Drava River, which is another tributary of the Danube, forms most of the boundary between Hungary and Croatia. The downstream (southeastern) portion of the boundary follows the former course of the river, whose course has shifted over the years in accordance with natural processes. The boundaries between Hungary and Slovenia and between Hungary and Austria are complex geometric boundaries that extend in a generally south-to-north direction from the tripoint between Hungary, Croatia, and Slovenia to the tripoint between Hungary, Austria, and Slovakia.

HISTORICAL CONTEXT

The ancestors of today's Hungarians, known as the Magyars, moved westward into present-day Hungary as the Roman Empire collapsed during the fourth and fifth centuries AD. During the tenth century, several Magyar tribes united under the rule of St. Stephen, who was crowned as king of the Hungarians in AD 1000 with the support of Pope Sylvester II. St. Stephen's successors ruled the Hungarian Kingdom for the next 300 years. Much of Hungary became absorbed into the Ottoman Empire in the early 16th century.

In the early 18th century, Hungary became part of the Hapsburg Empire, which was centered in Vienna in present-day Austria. During the 18th and 19th centuries, some Hungary leaders pushed for separation from the empire, but their efforts were unsuccessful. After revolutionary activities failed to bring down the Hapsburg government in 1848, Emperor Franz Josef of Austria attempted to impose absolute rule on the empire. It became evident that this absolutist rule would not work, however, and in 1867 Austria agreed to a power-sharing arrangement with the Hungarians. This agreement, known as the Compromise of 1867, recognized Hungarian sovereignty and established the dual monarchy in which Austria and Hungary were ruled as separate kingdoms, each with its own set of laws, by the Austrian monarch. The dual monarchy came to be known as the Austro-Hungarian Empire and included present-day Slovenia, Croatia, Bosnia and Herzegovina, Slovakia, and the Czech Republic as well as present-day Austria and Hungary themselves.

The Austro-Hungarian Empire, which had been allied with the defeated Central Powers during World War I, was dismantled after the war ended. Hungary was recognized as one of the successor states to the Austro-Hungarian Empire. In 1920, the Allies and Hungary signed the Treaty of Trianon, which established the provisions by which Hungary's boundaries were to be delineated. Under the terms of the Treaty of Trianon, the new Hungarian state lost about 72 percent of its land area and 64 percent of its prewar population. Sovereignty over the rest of the former Hungarian kingdom was granted to neighboring states.

Nearly 90 percent of the residents of the postwar Hungarian state were of Hungarian ancestry. However, substantial numbers of Hungarians lived in areas that were transferred from the old kingdom of Hungary to neighboring countries. It has been estimated that about a third of ethnic Hungarians in Central Europe were living outside Hungary after the Treaty of Trianon was implemented. Even today, substantial numbers of people of Hungarian ancestry live in Slovakia, Romania, and other neighbors of present-day Hungary. Once the Treaty of Trianon was signed, Hungary's boundaries with its neighbors were delineated.

Before and during World War II, Hungary was allied with Germany and Italy. With German support, Hungary annexed portions of present-day Slovakia and Ruthenia, which is now part of Ukraine. Hungarian armies fought on the Axis side during the war. The Soviets gained control of Hungary in 1944. After the war ended, Hungary's prewar boundaries were reaffirmed and Hungary lost its sovereignty over the areas it had taken over in the late 1930s. A Soviet-supported government took office, and the country became known as the People's Republic of Hungary in 1949. The communists were expelled in 1989, and a democratic government took over. Hungary joined NATO in 1999 and the European Union in 2004. Although Hungary's economy has boomed over the past two decades, in recent years concerns have been raised that Hungary's government may be moving away from democracy toward a more authoritarian regime.

CONTEMPORARY ISSUES

With only minor adjustments, Hungary's boundaries have remained stable since the 1920s. However, the adjustment from communist rule to democracy has generated some controversies between Hungary and its neighbors.

The status of ethnic Hungarians outside of Hungary itself remains controversial. Recent estimates suggest that about 2.5 million people of Hungarian descent live in neighboring countries. About 60 percent of them live in Romania, primarily in those portions of Romania that were part of Hungary prior to the Treaty of Trianon. Hungary and Romania signed an agreement in 1995 through which Hungary agreed to give up all ongoing territorial claims to present-day Romanian territory. In exchange, Romania agreed to respect the rights of its Hungarian minority, whose rights as a minority within a sovereign state were reinforced by Romania's joining the European Union in 2007.

Another recent issue has been the development of hydroelectric power along the Danube River along the boundary between Hungary and Slovakia. In the 1960s, government officials in Hungary and Czechoslovakia began discussions to build a series of dams along the Danube River in order to generate hydroelectric power, prevent floods, and improve navigation. In 1977, the two countries signed a formal agreement to construct the dam. Construction of the Gabcikovo-Nagymaros Dams began in the 1980s, but the construction efforts were slowed down by a lack of financial resources in the two countries and by the prospect that the completed dam would cause the Danube to change course. In 1989, the post-communist government of Hungary announced that it would suspend work on the project and that it wished to end the 1977 treaty. Hungary's Parliament voted in 1992 to terminate the 1977 treaty unilaterally. Meanwhile, Czechoslovakia proceeded with its portion of the project. The Gabcikovo Dam was opened in 1992.

In 1993, the two countries agree to submit their dispute to the International Court of Justice. In 1997, the court ruled that the treaty remained binding on both countries, including Slovakia as the successor state to Czechoslovakia. The countries were required to reopen negotiations to complete the project, with Hungary required to pay damages if negotiations could not be completed. These negotiations have been impeded by evidence that the project has caused considerable environmental degradation.

See also   Austria, Croatia, Romania, Serbia, Slovakia, Slovenia, Ukraine

Further Reading

CBS News. "EU sues Hungary, fearing authoritarianism." January 17, 2012, http://www.cbsnews.com/8301-202_162-57360731/eu-sues-hungary-fearing-au thoritarianism/.

Bukhosi Fuyane and Ferenc Madai. "The Hungary-Slovakia Danube River dispute: Implications for sustainable development and equitable utilization of natural resources in international law." *International Journal of Global Environmental Issues*, 1 (2001), pp. 329–344.

Kim Lane Scheppele. "Hungary's constitutional revolution." *New York Times*, December 19, 2011, http://krugman.blogs.nytimes.com/2011/12/19/hungarys-constitutional-revolution/.

ICELAND

OVERVIEW

Iceland occupies the island of Iceland in the North Atlantic Ocean just south of the Arctic Circle. Iceland is located about 600 miles west of Norway on the European mainland. The closest inhabited places to Iceland are the Danish territory of the Faeroe Islands, 260 miles to the southeast, and Greenland, 200 miles to the west.

The island owes its origin to volcanic activity along the Mid-Atlantic Ridge, and several active volcanoes are located on Iceland. Iceland has a land area of approximately 39,780 square miles (about the size of Kentucky) and a population of about 320,000. Much of Iceland's land surface is covered with tundra, lava fields, or glaciers and is uninhabited. About two-thirds of Icelanders live near the southwestern coast in or near the capital city of Reykjavik.

HISTORICAL CONTEXT

Irish monks and hermits are believed to have visited Iceland temporarily in the seventh and eighth centuries AD. Viking explorers from Scandinavia established permanent settlements in Iceland beginning in AD 874. Between 874 and 930, Viking settlers claimed all of the island's arable land.

During the 13th century, feuds between families resulted in the murders of several prominent Icelandic chieftains. In order to eliminate these blood feuds, Iceland's leaders worked to establish formal union with Norway, from which their ancestors had moved to Iceland several centuries previously. The agreement known as the Gamli Sattmali, or "Old Covenant," was negotiated and agreed upon in 1262, when Iceland was formally made part of Norway. Control of Iceland passed to Denmark after the Norwegian and Danish kingdoms were united via the Kalmar Union in the 15th century. Iceland remained under Danish control after the Treaty of Kiel separated Norway from Denmark in 1814.

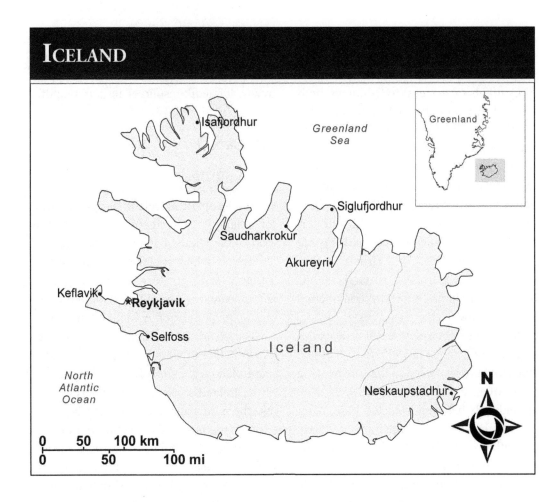

ICELAND

During and after the Middle Ages, Denmark forbade Icelanders from trading with any country other than Denmark. This policy, coupled with Iceland's geographic isolation, contributed to the fact that Iceland was among Europe's poorest countries prior to the 19th century. Iceland's problems were exacerbated by an ongoing series of epidemics, volcanic eruptions, and earthquakes. An eruption in 1784 killed 25 percent of Iceland's people and more than 90 percent of the livestock upon which many depended.

Denmark granted Iceland home rule in 1874, but Denmark remained in charge of Iceland's defense and foreign policy. Partial sovereignty was granted in 1921, and

Iceland became fully independent from Denmark in 1944. Iceland became a charter member of NATO in 1949. In 2009, Iceland's government announced its goal to apply eventually for membership in the European Union.

CONTEMPORARY ISSUES

As an island country, Iceland has no land boundaries. However, the North Atlantic in which Iceland is located is one of the richest fishing grounds in the world. Iceland's economy has been heavily dependent on the fishing industry throughout its history. Before 1900, fish accounted for virtually all of Iceland's export income. Although efforts to diversify Iceland's economy continue, even today fish account for nearly half of Iceland's export income.

Conflicts over access to fishing grounds have taken place between Iceland and other North Atlantic colonies over many years. These conflicts intensified in the 19th century, when steam-powered ships and other new technologies increased fish catches and resulted in overfishing. In 1899, Denmark claimed control over a 12-mile territorial limit around Iceland to keep out foreign fishing fleets, but Britain in particular ignored it. In 1958, Iceland claimed a similar 12-mile limit. In conjunction with the Law of the Sea Treaty, Iceland announced its control of a 200-mile exclusive economic zone in 1975. British objections to these limits led to the Cod Wars, a series of armed skirmishes that took place sporadically between 1958 and 1976. After Iceland threatened to close its NATO base at Keflavik, the British relented, and the Cod Wars ended.

Today, Iceland maintains control of a 100-mile exclusive economic zone. Icelandic control of this area has allowed it to restrict fishing rights, and some experts are optimistic that fish stocks are increasing. In 2010, Iceland accused the European Union and Norway of overfishing for mackerel (*Scomber scombrus*) and violating informal annual mackerel catch quotas.

Further Reading

Martin Beckford. "Iceland bank collapse: The history of the Cod War—Financial crisis." *Telegraph*, October 9, 2008, http://www.telegraph.co.uk/news/worldnews/europe/iceland/3167216/Iceland-bank-collapse-The-history-of-the-Cod-War-financial-crisis.html.

International Boundaries Research Unit. "Maritime jurisdiction and boundaries in the Arctic region." 2011, http://www.dur.ac.uk/resources/ibru/arctic.pdf.

IRELAND

OVERVIEW

The Republic of Ireland shares the island of Ireland with Northern Ireland, which is part of the United Kingdom. The Republic of Ireland, which contains about 82 percent of the island's territory, has a land area of 27,133 square miles (the size of West Virginia). Its population is about 4.6 million.

The island of Ireland is surrounded by the Atlantic Ocean, with the Irish Sea separating Ireland from Great Britain. The Republic of Ireland's only land boundary is with Northern Ireland, which occupies the northeastern portion of the island. Of Ireland's 32 traditional counties, 26 belong to the Republic of Ireland, while the remaining 6 are part of Northern Ireland. Thus the boundary between Ireland and Northern Ireland is associated with long-standing boundaries between Ireland's counties, many of which date back to the Middle Ages. Many parts of the boundary follow rivers or lakes. To the west, the two are divided by the River Foyle. The boundary trends southwestward, and at its narrowest point the Republic of Ireland is only six miles wide near the border between County Donegal to the north and County Leitrim to the south.

HISTORICAL CONTEXT

Ireland's contemporary status is closely associated with the island's relationship with Great Britain. During the Protestant

IRELAND

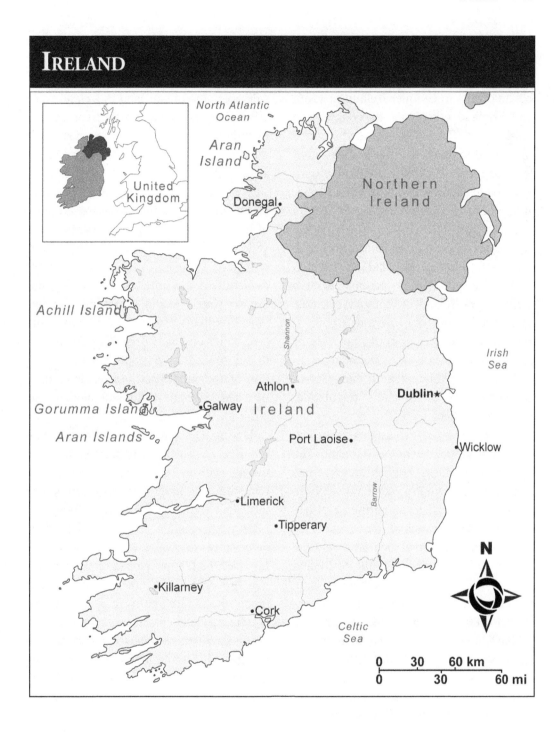

Reformation, England became Protestant whereas Ireland remained predominantly Catholic. King Henry VIII of England began efforts to conquer Ireland in 1536, and England completed its conquest in 1603. Irish Catholics regained control of Ireland in 1641, but the British under the leadership of Oliver Cromwell reconquered the island between 1649 and 1653. Ireland thus became a colony of Britain and part of the British Empire. After the British reconquest of Ireland, the British Parliament adopted the Penal Laws, which were directed largely against Roman Catholics in Ireland. Although they made up about 90 percent of Ireland's population, Roman Catholics could not vote or serve in the Parliament of Ireland.

In order to dilute the Roman Catholic dominance of Ireland's population, after Ireland became a British colony the British encouraged Protestants from England and Scotland to move to Ireland. The movement of these English and Scottish Protestants created Protestant majorities in the province of Ulster in northeastern Ireland. This demographic shift eventually resulted in the division of the island between the Catholic-majority Republic of Ireland and Protestant-majority Northern Ireland, which remains part of the United Kingdom. In 1801, the Act of Union was passed by the British Parliament and the Irish Parliament (which had no Catholic members). The Act of Union merged the Kingdom of Great Britain and the Kingdom of Ireland, creating the United Kingdom of Great Britain and Ireland.

During the 18th and 19th centuries, many in Ireland became active in promoting independence for Ireland. The independence movement accelerated after the Irish Potato Famine of 1845–1850. Under British rule, Irish commercial farmers produced grain and livestock for export. Considerable amounts of land in Ireland were given over to raising cattle to meet England's demands for beef. However, Irish farmers relied on "Irish" potatoes (which are actually native to South America) as a staple crop for day-to-day subsistence. A blight caused by a fungus destroyed most of Ireland's potato crop each year between 1845 and 1849. Despite the blight, Ireland continued to export potatoes and other foodstuffs, even after 1845. During the famine years, Ireland exported cattle and other livestock. Because of the crop failure, however, many Irish had no money to buy food. Between 500,000 and 1 million of Ireland's 8 million residents died between 1846 and 1849, and another 2 to 3 million emigrated.

During and after the Irish Potato Famine, many Irish activists blamed some of the misery on the policies of the United Kingdom, including land laws, tariff structures that encouraged export of food, and a tardy response by the United Kingdom government to alleviate hunger and suffering once the famine had begun. During the late 19th century, several bills to establish home rule for Ireland were considered by Britain's parliament. However, many Protestant landowners opposed home rule. A majority of Ireland's residents were supporters of a separate Irish state; however, many in the Protestant-majority northeastern part of Ireland were Unionists who supported keeping Ireland in the United Kingdom.

Tension between Catholics and Protestants affected the eventual creation of an independent Irish state. In 1914, the

British government passed the Third Home Rule Act, which provided for an independent Ireland. This law was opposed bitterly, however, by many Ulster Protestants who were opposed to having minority status within an independent Ireland. Implementation of the act was delayed until after the end of World War I but in 1919, Ireland declared its independence. In 1921, representatives of Ireland negotiated the Anglo-Irish Treaty with representatives of the United Kingdom's government. Under terms of this treaty, all of Ireland became a self-governing territory within the British Empire known as the Irish Free State. However, the counties of Ulster were given the right to remain part of the United Kingdom, and six of them exercised this right. The Irish Free State, including the remaining 26 counties, declared itself a republic in 1949 and in doing so withdrew from the British Commonwealth as the successor to the British Empire.

CONTEMPORARY ISSUES

The major boundary-related issue facing Ireland continues to be the status of Northern Ireland. For centuries, Irish independence activists have advocated the creation of an independent Republic of Ireland containing the entire island. However, many Protestants in Northern Ireland have remained firmly in favor of remaining part of the United Kingdom.

After Irish independence, the Republic of Ireland claimed sovereignty over all of the island of Ireland. Ireland continued to claim sovereignty over Northern Ireland until 1998, when it dropped this territorial claim following the Belfast Agreement. The Belfast Agreement involved revising the Republic of Ireland's definition of Ireland as a nation rather than a specific territory (including Northern Ireland). Article II of the Agreement reads, "It is the entitlement and birthright of every person born in the island of Ireland, which includes its islands and seas, to be part of the Irish Nation. That is also the entitlement of all persons otherwise qualified in accordance with law to be citizens of Ireland. Furthermore, the Irish nation cherishes its special affinity with people of Irish ancestry living abroad who share its cultural identity and heritage." Thus, this text identifies anyone of Irish heritage as part of the Irish nation. However, the agreement makes clear that Northern Ireland would become part of the Republic of Ireland at some future time if, and only if, this union was to be agreed upon by a majority of voters in Northern Ireland.

See also   United Kingdom

Further Reading

Dermot Keogh. *Twentieth-century Ireland: Nation and state.* Dublin: Gill and Macmillan, 1994.

Brigid Laffan and Jane O'Mahony. *Ireland and the European Union.* London: Palgrave Macmillan, 2008.

David McKittrick and David McVea. *Making sense of the Troubles: The story of the Troubles in Northern Ireland.* London: Penguin, 2000.

ITALY

OVERVIEW

The Italian Republic occupies the Italian Peninsula, which extends into the central Mediterranean Sea, along with territory between the peninsula and the southern ranges of the Alps. It has a land area of 116,346 square miles, or slightly smaller than Montana. Italy's population is about 60.5 million. Italy includes the islands of Sicily and Sardinia, which are the largest islands in the Mediterranean Sea, along with many smaller islands.

ITALY

Italy's neighbors are France to the northwest, Switzerland and Austria to the north, and Slovenia to the northeast. The boundaries between Italy and these neighbors extend through the Alps. The very small, independent countries of San Marino and Vatican City are surrounded completely by Italy. Western, southern, and eastern Italy adjoin the Mediterranean Sea, including the Tyrrhenian Sea to the west and the Adriatic Sea to the east.

Although the Alps trend from east to west in general, at the western end of the range the Alps turn southward almost to the coast of the Mediterranean. This range has represented the frontier between Italy and France since ancient times. Until the development of modern motorized transportation, the range was very difficult to cross. Today, most of the boundary between Italy and France follows the crest of the Alps. The highest peak in Europe, Mont Blanc, is located along the boundary between Italy and France.

The boundary between Italy and Switzerland also follows the trend of the Alps, extending from west to east. This boundary includes straight-line segments and drainage divides. Much of this boundary is located in mountainous and sparsely populated areas high in the Alps. However, some of it extends through more populated areas around Lake Lugano, which forms part of the boundary. The crest of the eastern Alps forms the boundary between Italy and Austria. This boundary crosses very sparsely populated territory and is crossed by few roads. At the tripoint between Italy, Austria, and Slovenia, Italy's boundary turns southward. It follows the crest of the Julian Alps southward nearly to the coast of the Adriatic Sea. Near the Adriatic coast, the boundary bends southeastward

to include the city of Trieste and neighboring territory on the northeastern coast of the Adriatic.

HISTORICAL CONTEXT

Present-day Italy was the center of the Roman Empire during ancient times. After the Roman Empire dissolved, what is now Italy was comprised of numerous small, independent city-states. Some of these city-states evolved into modern cities, including Milan, Florence, Genoa, and Venice. These Italian city-states became important centers of trade, commerce, and scholarship before and during the Renaissance. The Roman Catholic Church has been centered in Rome since long before the collapse of the Roman Empire, and the church has maintained substantial secular as well as religious authority throughout most of Italy's history.

Beginning in the 16th century, present-day northern Italy was ruled by foreign powers. It was controlled by Spain from 1559 to 1713 and by Austria from 1713 to 1796. In 1796, France under Napoleon invaded Italy. After the defeat of Napoleon, the Congress of Vienna in 1814 divided northern Italy into several independent kingdoms along with areas under foreign control. Meanwhile, central Italy, including Rome, had become the Papal States under the formal sovereignty of the pope. The Kingdom of Sicily controlled the southern portion of the mainland of the Italian Peninsula as well as the island of Sicily. The Kingdom of Sardinia controlled part of northwestern mainland Italy.

Italy became a unified state during the 19th century. Unification efforts began in northeastern Italy in opposition to Austrian rule over that area, and eventually the unification movement spread across Italy. By 1860, present-day Italy included three independent states—the Papal States in the center, Sicily in the south, and Sardinia in the northwest—while northeastern Italy remained under Austrian rule. After Italian unification, the question of temporal sovereignty over Rome and the Papal States continued until Italy and the Vatican signed the Lateran Accords in 1929. Under terms of the Lateran Accords, Italy recognized the temporal sovereignty of the church over Vatican City. The church relinquished temporal control over the rest of Rome and the Papal States. In exchange, Italy agreed to recognize the primacy of the Roman Catholic Church throughout the country.

The boundaries of unified Italy in the late 19th century approximated Italy's present-day boundaries, with minor adjustments. Many of these adjustments were made in order to accommodate construction of roads and railroads in order to reduce the number of border crossings or to facilitate administration of border territory. The major change in Italy's boundaries after unification involved the city of Trieste and neighboring territory near the boundary between Italy and present-day Slovenia. About 75 percent of Trieste's people were Italians, and about a quarter were Slovenes. Trieste, which had remained under Austrian control after Italy was reunified, was occupied by Italy during World War I and was formally annexed by Italy in 1920. After the fascist government of Benito Mussolini assumed control of Italy in the 1920s, Italy embarked on a policy of "Italianization," including banning the use of the Slovenian language.

At the end of World War II, Trieste was occupied by Yugoslavian troops. In 1947, the United Nations declared Trieste, including nearby territory along the Adriatic coast, to be a "free city" under United Nations administration. The territory comprising the "free city" was divided between Italy and Yugoslavia in 1954. Most of the territory, including the city of Trieste itself, was awarded to Italy. Italy and Yugoslavia confirmed the United Nations's division of territory by signing the Treaty of Osimo in 1975. This boundary was reaffirmed by Italy and Slovenia after Slovenia became independent following the breakup of Yugoslavia.

CONTEMPORARY ISSUES

Italy's boundaries have remained stable since the 19th century. Only minor adjustments have been made to Italy's borders over the past century. The only exception was the question of sovereignty over the Trieste and its environs, and this question was resolved amicably in 1975. However, Italy and its neighbors have questioned the European Union's border policies in light of ongoing immigration-related problems.

The major issue facing Italy is ongoing controversy regarding the political status of northern Italy. Since the Industrial Revolution, the Po Valley of northern Italy, including the cities of Milan and Turin, has been the most industrialized and most prosperous portion of Italy. Southern Italy, which is known as the Mezzogiorno, has been oriented historically to agriculture and is less developed and poorer.

Since the early 1990s, activists from northern Italy have advocated more autonomy for northern Italy. The Lega Nord (Northern League) is a coalition of political parties in northern Italy that advocates more autonomy for northern Italy in light of these regional disparities. Many members of the Lega Nord believe that the prosperous and highly industrialized north is being forced to subsidize the less developed Mezzogiorno. Many also believe that northern Italy's medieval history of self-governing city-states separates northern Italy from other parts of the country, which lack this tradition of urban independence and reliance on commerce and trade.

Some members of the Lega Nord have advocated that the north secede from Italy entirely and form a separate country. Such a country might be called Padania, after the Po River's Latin name of Padus. Were it to become an independent country, Padania would include about 55 percent of Italy's land area and about 55 percent of its current population.

In 1996, some members of the Lega Nord prepared and issued a Padanian Declaration of Independence. To date, Padanian independence has not been recognized by Italy or other sovereign countries. However, supporters of Padanian independence have designed a Padanian flag, identified a national anthem, prepared websites, and sponsored the election of an informal Padanian parliament. Secession is supported by a substantial number of people in northern Italy. A public opinion poll conducted in northern Italy in 2010 indicated that about 45 percent of respondents favored Padanian independence.

See also Austria, France, Slovenia, Switzerland

Further Reading
Benito Giordano. "Italian regionalism or 'Padanian' nationalism: The political project of the Lega Nord in Italian politics." In *Regions and regionalism in Europe*, edited by Michael Keating, pp. 378–404. London: Edward Elgar, 2004.

Stacy Meichtry. "France resurrects border with Italy." *Wall Street Journal*, April 6, 2011, http://online.wsj.com/article/SB100014240527487046300045 76249120727824628.html.

Michael Shin and John A. Agnew. *Berlusconi's Italy: Mapping contemporary Italian politics.* Philadelphia, PA: Temple University Press, 2008.

KOSOVO

OVERVIEW

The Republic of Kosovo, located in southeastern Europe, was part of the former communist country of Yugoslavia. Kosovo has a land area of 4,212 square miles, or about the size of Connecticut, with a population of approximately 1.8 million. Serbia does not recognize Kosovo as an independent state, considering Kosovo to be a part of Serbian territory that has attempted to break away from Serbia illegally.

Ethnic and religious differences underlie the conflict between Kosovo and Serbia. In 1981, a census revealed that about 77 percent of Kosovo's people are ethnic Albanians, most of whom are Muslims. By 2006, international observers estimated that the Albanian percentage had increased to 88 percent because of outmigration of ethnic Serbs and high birth rates among ethnic Albanians. Today

about 10 percent of Kosovo's population consists of Serbs.

Kosovo's neighbors are Serbia to the north and east, Macedonia to the south, Albania to the southwest, and Montenegro to the west. The delineation of the boundaries was based in general on the idea of separating ethnic Kosovars from other nearby cultural groups.

The boundary between Kosovo and the rest of Serbia generally separates Kosovars from ethnic Serbians, although Serbians are a majority in the northern part of Kosovo. The boundaries between Kosovo and Serbia, Macedonia, and Montenegro—all of whom, like Kosovo, were part of the former Federal Republic of Yugoslavia—consist of numerous short straight-line segments. The boundary between Kosovo and Albania also consists of straight-line segments, many of which follow the crest of a mountain range separating the two countries.

HISTORICAL CONTEXT

What is now Kosovo was part of the Ottoman Empire for hundreds of years prior to World War I. After the war ended, the territory became part of the new country of Yugoslavia. The boundaries between Kosovo and other parts of Yugoslavia, including present-day Serbia, Macedonia, and Montenegro, were delineated by the Yugoslavian government. The boundary between Yugoslavia and Albania was determined by an international boundary commission including France, Britain, and Italy. The commission's findings were used to determine this boundary in 1925.

After World War II, Kosovo's leadership pushed for union with neighboring Albania. The government of Yugoslavia refused this request. Instead, in 1946 Yugoslavia created the Autonomous Province of Kosovo and Metohija, with Kosovo's current boundaries. Yugoslavia's intention was to create a Kosovar-majority province within Serbia but excluding those portions of Ottoman Kosovo that had previously been assigned to Montenegro and Macedonia. The name of the Autonomous Province was changed to the Socialist Autonomous Province of Kosovo in 1974. The Socialist Autonomous Province requested recognition as a full-scale province of Yugoslavia,

with status equal to Serbia, Croatia, and the other Yugoslavian provinces. However, this request was also denied.

Yugoslavia was dissolved in 1990. After the breakup, a referendum was held within Kosovo, and 87 percent of the voters supported the creation of an independent, sovereign state of Kosovo. Despite local support for independence, Kosovo became a part of the Yugoslavian successor state of Serbia. Ethnic Albanians in Kosovo accused Serbia's government of discrimination and repression against them. Ongoing hostility between the Serbian government and Kosovar activists erupted into armed conflict in the late 1990s. Over a two-year period, the Kosovo War resulted in about 10,000 fatalities and displaced hundreds of thousands of ethnic Albanian Kosovars. In 1999, NATO authorized bombings in Kosovo with the idea of forcing Serbia to withdraw its forces from Kosovo.

In order to end the conflict, the United Nations Security Council passed Resolution 1244 in 1999. Resolution 1244 provided for temporary UN administration of Kosovo with the assistance of a peacekeeping force led by NATO. The resolution called for the autonomy of Kosovo within Serbia, but it also specified that Kosovo would remain part of Serbia as the legal successor to the defunct Federal Republic of Yugoslavia. In 2006, international negotiations concerning the long-unresolved status of Kosovo began. As an ally of Serbia, Russia made clear that it would oppose Kosovar independence unless Serbia agreed to the existence of an independent Kosovo. Because Russia is a permanent member of the UN Security Council, the threat of a Russian veto caused talks to break down.

Kosovo declared independence on February 17, 2008. The United States recognized Kosovo's independence, but Serbia, Russia, and many other countries did not. Some European Union countries, including Romania and Spain, have not recognized Kosovo's independence in part because of concerns that their own ethnic minorities might be motivated to declare independence also. In 2010, the International Court of Justice ruled that Kosovo's declaration of independence was legal, but it did not take a position on the legal status of Kosovo as an independent sovereign state. As of mid-2011, Kosovo's independence had been recognized by 75 countries, including all of its neighbors except for Serbia. Serbia continues to regard Kosovo as a United Nations–administered territory within Serbia.

CONTEMPORARY ISSUES

Kosovo's status in the international community remains uncertain, in part because the international community remains divided as to whether it should be recognized as an independent state. Major issues facing Kosovo are its recognition in the international community, ongoing conflict with Serbia, and its status relative to Albania.

Upon independence, Kosovo became a member of the International Monetary Fund. In 2011, Kosovo's new president, Atifete Jahjaga, announced that her government's goals included applying for membership in the United Nations and the European Union. United Nations membership may be problematic because Russia, which has permanent veto power in the UN Security Council, does not recognize Kosovo's independence. An application by Kosovo to join the European Union may also be controversial, again because of division among its members as to whether Kosovo should be recognized. A parallel issue is whether nations that are currently minorities within established states should be recognized as independent by the European Union. This issue is controversial in several European Union countries, including Scotland in the United Kingdom, Catalonia and Euzkadi in Spain, and Padania in Italy. (These conflicts are discussed in this volume as part of the entries for these countries.)

The status of North Kosovo is also a major point of contention between Kosovo and Serbia. North Kosovo includes Kosovo's three northernmost provinces, which are located along the boundary between Kosovo and Serbia. Together, these provinces have about 66,000 people who live in an area of about 500 square miles, half the size of Rhode Island. In contrast to the rest of Kosovo, North Kosovo has a Serbian majority. Kosovo has refused to grant autonomy to North Kosovo relative to the rest of the country.

For several decades, some Kosovars have advocated uniting Kosovar with Albania. The populations of both countries speak the same Albanian language, and a large majority in both states practices Islam. Kosovar leaders as well as international experts predict that union between Kosovo and Albania will become more and more likely as long as conflict between Kosovo and Serbia remains unresolved.

See also Albania, Macedonia, Montenegro, Serbia

Further Reading

International Crisis Group. "Kosovo and Serbia: A little goodwill could go a long way." *Europe Report*, 215 (2012), http://www.crisisgroup.org/en/regions/europe/balkans/kosovo/215-kosovo-and-serbia-a-little-goodwill-could-go-a-long-way.aspx.

Paul Latawski and Martin A. Smith. *The Kosovo crisis and the evolution of post–Cold War European security.* Manchester: Manchester University Press.

Dennis McShane. *Why Kosovo still matters.* London: Haus, 2012.

LATVIA

OVERVIEW

Latvia is one of the Baltic republics of Eastern Europe, located along the Baltic Sea between Estonia and Lithuania. Latvia's land area is 24,938 square miles, the size of West Virginia. Its population is about 2.2 million. Latvia's population has been declining because of low birth rates and because many ethnic Russians have emigrated.

Latvia's neighbors are Estonia to the north, Russia and Belarus to the east, and Lithuania to the south. Western Latvia adjoins the Baltic Sea. Culturally, Latvia is more closely related to Lithuania than to Estonia. Most Lithuanians and about half of Latvians are Roman Catholics, while the population of Estonia is predominantly Lutheran. The languages of Latvia and Lithuania are both Indo-European languages that are closely related to one another, while Estonian is a non-Indo-European language that is closely related to Finnish but not at all to Latvian.

Most of Latvia's boundaries are complex and consist of numerous short straight-line segments. The boundaries are primarily cultural in that they separate regions with predominantly Latvian populations from those whose populations are dominated by other nationalities. The boundary with Estonia extends from the Baltic coastline eastward to the tripoint between Latvia, Estonia, and Russia. From this tripoint, the boundary between Latvia and Russia extends southward. Like the Latvia-Estonia boundary, the boundary with Russia consists of many short segments, some less than 100 feet long.

The boundary between Latvia and Belarus extends southwestward from the Russian tripoint along a series of short straight lines that trend in a northeast-to-southwest direction to the Daugava River, which forms the central portion of this boundary. The Daugava, which is known in Belarus as the Western Dvina River, flows from east to west. From the Daugava, the boundary continues as a series of generally short straight lines in a southwestward direction to the tripoint between Latvia, Belarus, and Lithuania. This boundary region is marshy and wooded, with few settlements. The boundary between Latvia and Lithuania extends in a generally westward direction from the Belarus tripoint to the Baltic Sea. The Venta River forms most of the western portion of this boundary, although the mouth of the Venta is wholly within Lithuania.

HISTORICAL CONTEXT

The small and strategic territory occupied by the Latvian nation has been contested by various larger European powers

LATVIA

Baltic Sea

Estonia

Russia

Gulf of Riga

Ainazi

Valmiera

Aluksne

Ventspils

Talsi

Latvia

Gulbene

Jurmala

★Riga

Madona

Ogre

Ludza

Jelgava

Rezekne

Liepaja

Jekabpils

Daugava

Daugavpils

Lithuania

Belarus

N

0   30   60 km
0   30   60 mi

since the Middle Ages. Latvia's capital and largest city, Riga, was established on the Baltic coast by Germans in 1201. As the largest city on the eastern coast of the Baltic, Riga dominated trade in the eastern Baltic and retained substantial German influence.

German kingdoms continued to dominate present-day Latvia until the 1560s. After a series of conflicts, what is now southern Latvia was known as the Duchy of Courland and Semigallia. This territory became part of the Poland-Lithuania Confederation. The northern part of present-day Latvia, known is Livonia, came under

Swedish control. Swedish domination of Latvia continued until the 18th century. Tsar Peter the Great annexed Livonia, including Riga, in 1721. In 1795, the Duchy of Courland and Semigallia was also taken over by Russia.

Russian control of Latvia continued until World War I. In 1915, Germany took over Latvia. The Germans retained control of Latvia until 1918, when Latvia declared independence. After a series of civil wars, the independence of Latvia was recognized by the international community in 1921. Latvia remained independent until 1940, when it was annexed by the Soviet

Union along with Estonia and Lithuania. The Nazis occupied Latvia for three years beginning in 1941. Latvia remained under Soviet control until the collapse of the Soviet Union in 1991. On March 3, 1991, 73 percent of Latvians voted for complete independence. Latvia became fully independent on August 21. It became a member of NATO and the European Union in 2004.

The boundaries of Latvia changed frequently over its long history of foreign control. Latvia's boundaries with its Soviet neighbors of Estonia, Russia, Belarus, and Lithuania were delineated by the Soviets during and after World War II. After taking control of Latvia in 1940 and expelling the Nazis in 1944, the Soviets decreed boundary changes that removed territory from previously independent Latvia and added this territory to the Russian Soviet Federated Socialist Republic (RSFSR), which is now Russia. An area of about 400 square miles, which was part of a larger area known as the Abrene district, was transferred from Latvia to the RSFSR. The Soviet Union justified these territorial changes on the grounds that the territory removed from Latvia was inhabited primarily by Russians rather than Latvians.

CONTEMPORARY ISSUES

After Latvian independence, the boundary between Latvia and Russia remained in dispute. Latvia claimed the portion of the Abrene district that had been transferred to the RSFSR in the 1940s on the grounds that the Abrene district had been part of independent Latvia prior to 1940. The dispute was resolved when Latvia and Russia signed a boundary delineation treaty in 2007. The treaty specified that the previously transferred portion of the Abrene district would remain part of Russia.

Latvia's relations with Russia have been complicated by the fact that more than a quarter of Latvia's people are ethnic Russians. That so many people of Russian ancestry live in Latvia is the result of the Soviet Union's policy of Russification, through which the Soviets encouraged people of Russian ancestry to move to Latvia and other non-Russian Soviet republics. The status of Russian nationals in Latvia became controversial after Latvian independence because the government of newly independent Latvia did not grant automatic citizenship to residents of non-Latvian ancestry. Today, 27 percent of Latvia's residents are of Russian ancestry whereas only about 20 percent of the country's citizens are of Russian descent. Latvian is the country's only official language, and in February 2012 a majority of the voters of Latvia voted against a referendum that would have given equal status to Latvian and Russian as the country's official languages. Latvia's borders with its remaining neighbors are stable, although Latvia and Lithuania are negotiating over control of offshore regions in the Baltic that are believed to contain valuable oil deposits.

See also Belarus, Estonia, Lithuania, Russia

Further Reading

Associated Press. "Latvians reject Russian as official language." *Guardian*, February 18, 2012, http://www.guardian.co.uk/world/2012/feb/19/latvians-reject-russian-official-language.

Anatol Levin. *The Baltic revolution: Estonia, Latvia, and Lithuania and the path to independence.* New Haven. CT: Yale University Press, 1994.

Dietrich Loeber. "The Russian-Latvian territorial dispute over Abrene." *Parker School Journal of East European Law*, 2 (1995), pp. 537–559.

LIECHTENSTEIN

OVERVIEW

The Principality of Liechtenstein is a small, landlocked country located in the Alps of Central Europe. Liechtenstein's land area is 62 square miles, making it slightly smaller than the District of Columbia. Its population is approximately 35,000.

Liechtenstein and Uzbekistan are the only two doubly landlocked countries in the world, meaning they are landlocked countries themselves whose neighbors are all landlocked also. Liechtenstein's neighbors are Switzerland to the west and south and Austria to the east. All of Liechtenstein is north of the Rhine River, which forms most of the boundary between Liechtenstein and Switzerland. The southern boundary of Liechtenstein follows straight-line segments east of the Rhine. The boundary between Liechtenstein and

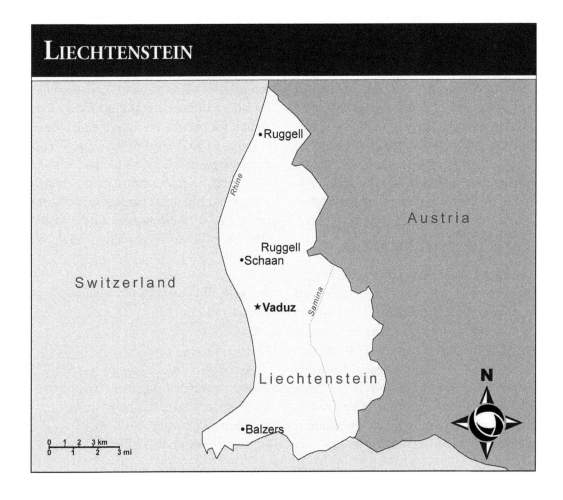

Austria consists of straight-line segments extending in a north-south direction. It extends through mountainous terrain, including the three peaks of Drei Schwestern (the Three Sisters) in the Alps. The northern tripoint between Liechtenstein, Switzerland, and Austria is located on the Rhine, while the southern tripoint between these countries is located about five miles east of the river.

HISTORICAL CONTEXT

Liechtenstein is named for the Liechtenstein family, whose members owned and occupied the Castle of Liechtenstein in nearby Austria beginning in 1140. The Principality of Liechtenstein was established in 1719. After the Napoleonic Wars, Liechtenstein remained tied closely politically and economically to Austria. It joined the German Confederation, which was led by Austria, in 1815 and remained a member until the confederation was dissolved in 1868. At that time, Liechtenstein declared its neutrality. It was neutral in World War I and World War II.

After the Austro-Hungarian Empire was dismantled after World War I, Liechtenstein became aligned more closely with Switzerland. Liechtenstein and Switzerland agreed that Switzerland would represent Liechtenstein's interests diplomatically, and Switzerland continues to do so today. In 2006, the boundaries between Liechtenstein and its neighbors were re-surveyed, and the more accurate measurement awarded Liechtenstein about 123 acres, or one-fifth of a square mile, of additional territory.

See also   Austria, Switzerland

Further Reading

BBC News. "Liechtenstein redraws Europe map." December 28, 2006, http://news.bbc.co.uk/2/hi/europe/6215825.stm.

LITHUANIA

OVERVIEW

The Republic of Lithuania is the southernmost of the three Baltic states along with Estonia and Latvia. All of the Baltic states were part of the Soviet Union from World War II until the early 1990s. Lithuania is the largest of the three Baltic states, with a land area of 25,174 square miles, or about the size of South Carolina. It has a population of approximately 3.2 million.

Lithuania's neighbors are Latvia to the north, Belarus to the east and southeast, Poland to the southwest, and the Russia exclave of the Kaliningrad Oblast to the west. North of Kaliningrad, Lithuania has a seacoast on the Baltic Sea. Most of Lithuania's boundaries consist of short straight-line segments, although a few follow rivers and physical features. In general, they were drawn to separate people of Lithuanian nationality and ancestry from non-Lithuanians elsewhere. The boundary between Lithuania and Latvia extends eastward and inland from the Baltic Sea. Much of the western portion of this boundary follows the Venta River, although the mouth of the river is located in Lithuania. North of the Lithuanian town of Birzai, the boundary turns southeastward and continues in that direction to the tripoint between Latvia, Lithuania, and Belarus north of Lake Druksiai in northeastern Lithuania. Lithuanian includes a small territory east of the eastern shoreline of the lake.

LITHUANIA

South of Lake Druksiai, the boundary between Lithuania and Belarus trends in a generally southwesterly direction along numerous short straight-line segments. At one point, an area of about 80 square miles of Lithuanian territory extends southeastward into Belarus's territory. This area is nearly an exclave in that it is connected to the west of Lithuania by a strip of territory less than a mile wide. The boundary was drawn in order to separate people of Lithuanian ancestry, who speak a Baltic language related to Latvian and are primarily Roman Catholics, from those of Belarusian ancestry who speak a language related very closely to Russian and who are primarily Russian Orthodox.

At the tripoint between Lithuania, Belarus, and Poland, the boundary between Lithuania and Poland trends in a northwesterly direction toward the tripoint between Lithuania, Poland, and the Russian exclave of the Kaliningrad Oblast. This tripoint is located just south of Lake Vistytis, which straddles the border but most of which is in Russia. North of Lake Vistytis, the boundary between Lithuania and the Kaliningrad Oblast extends northward. Part of this boundary follows the Liepona River. At the town of Smalininkai the boundary reaches the Nemunas River. The boundary follows the Nemunas westward and downstream until the river empties into the Curonian Lagoon on the Baltic Sea coast.

HISTORICAL CONTEXT

Present-day Lithuania has been populated since the end of the Ice Age about 10,000 years ago. For several thousand years, the area was inhabited by Baltic tribes. Most of Lithuania was united politically for the first time as the Kingdom of Lithuania in 1263. In 1440, Lithuania's ruling dynasty united Lithuanian and Poland. Lithuania and Poland formed the Polish-Lithuanian Commonwealth in 1569. Poland became the dominant partner in the alliance, but Lithuanian retained its separate currency, armed forces, laws, and other institutions. The commonwealth weakened during the 17th century, and Lithuanian territory came to be contested among Sweden, Poland, and Russia. Most of Lithuanian territory came under the control of the Russian Empire in the 19th century, but it was occupied by Germany during World War I.

Lithuania declared independence in February 1918, but Germany remained in control of Lithuanian territory and refused to recognize the new state. Lithuania became fully independent after the signing of the armistice ending the war on November 11, 1918. Shortly afterward, the Red Army invaded Lithuania and captured about two-thirds of Lithuania's territory. Germany supported the Lithuanian nationalists. The Lithuanian-Soviet War ended in 1920, and the Soviet Union recognized Lithuania as an independent state.

Lithuanian independence lasted only two decades. At the outset of World War II in 1939, Nazi Germany and the Soviet Union signed the secret Molotov-Ribbentrop Pact, which divided the territory between the German and Soviet spheres of influence. The Red Army invaded and took control of Lithuania in 1940. The Nazis invaded in 1941, but the Red Army retook Lithuania in 1944, incorporating Lithuania into the Soviet Union as the Lithuanian Soviet Socialist Republic. The Soviets pushed a policy of Russification, deporting thousands of Lithuanian nationals and encouraging Russian nationals to move into Lithuania. Lithuania remained under Soviet control until the breakup of the Soviet Union. However, resistance to Soviet domination of Lithuanian intensified in the 1980s. In 1991, Lithuania held a referendum on independence, and more than 90 percent of voters supported the referendum. After independence, Lithuanian began to transition from a Soviet planned economy to a free-market economy. It became a member of NATO and the European Union in 2004.

CONTEMPORARY ISSUES

Lithuania's borders with its neighbors are stable but have been fine-tuned since Lithuania became independent. In 1998, Lithuania and Belarus signed an agreement to demarcate their boundary and to regulate the movement of people and goods across their border. Lithuania and Russia have entered negotiations to clarify their maritime border in the Baltic Sea.

See also   Belarus, Latvia, Poland, Russia

Further Reading

Anatol Levin. *The Baltic revolution: Estonia, Latvia, and Lithuania and the path to independence.* New Haven, CT: Yale University Press, 1994.

Timothy Snyder. *The reconstruction of nations: Poland, Ukraine, Belarus, Lithuania, 1569–1999.* New Haven, CT: Yale University Press, 2003.

Galina Vascenkaite. "The discrepancy of Lithuanian foreign policy: 'Normative' deeds for 'Realpolitik' needs?" *Lithuanian Foreign Policy Review*, 25 (2011), http://www.lfpr.lt/uploads/File/2011–25/Vascenkaite.pdf.

LUXEMBOURG

OVERVIEW

The Grand Duchy of Luxembourg in Western Europe has a land area of 999 square miles, slightly smaller than Rhode Island. Its population is approximately 510, 000. Luxembourg's neighbors are Germany to the east, France to the south, and Belgium to the west and north.

The boundary between Luxembourg and Germany is riparian, following a waterway. From the tripoint between Luxembourg, Germany, and Belgium, it follows the Our River southward to its confluence with the Sauer River, then the Sauer southward until it empties into the Moselle River. The Moselle, which flows from south to north before emptying into the Rhine, forms that southern portion of the boundary southward to the tripoint between Luxembourg, Germany, and France. The boundary between Luxembourg and France, in contrast, is geometric and consists of numerous short straight-line segments. Luxembourg's boundary with Belgium is also irregular, consisting of short segments whose general orientation is from south to north. This boundary was created during the 19th century with the idea of separating French speakers in Belgium from German speakers in Luxembourg.

HISTORICAL CONTEXT

The territory now controlled by Luxembourg was recognized as part of the Holy Roman Empire in the 10th century. In 1354, Emperor Charles IV granted Luxembourg the status of a duchy. The duchy was ruled by the Hapsburg dynasty as part of the Austrian Netherlands until the early 19th century. It included the present-day independent state of Luxembourg as well as adjoining territory in what is now southeastern Belgium.

Present-day Luxembourg was established as part of the United Kingdom of the Netherlands, which was created via the Congress of Vienna at the end of the Napoleonic Wars in 1815. The United Kingdom included present-day Luxembourg, the Netherlands, and Belgium. What is now Luxembourg had been part of the Austrian Netherlands, which was under the nominal sovereignty of Austria-Hungary but was also claimed by France. The Congress of Vienna confirmed the boundary between France and the United Kingdom of the Netherlands. The contemporary boundary between Luxembourg and France has been intact ever since.

A Dutch-speaking, Protestant royal family was placed on the throne of the United Kingdom. However, most residents of southern present-day Belgium and present-day

LUXEMBOURG

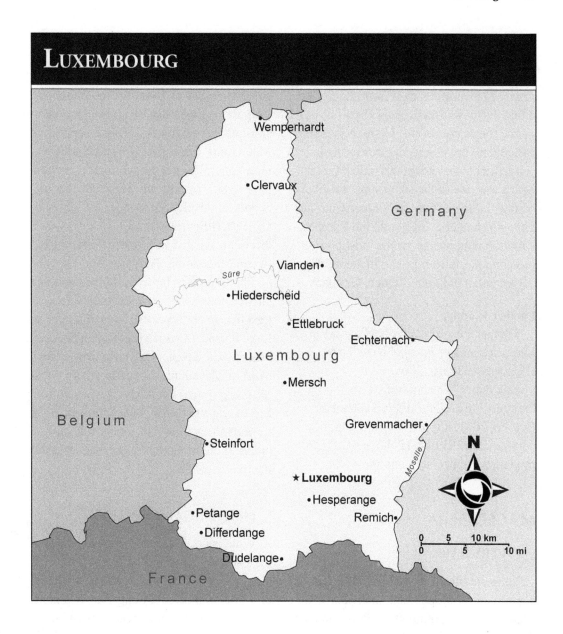

Luxembourg were Roman Catholics. Most spoke French, although the area that would become independent Luxembourg was primarily German-speaking. In 1830, Belgium, including Luxembourg, declared independence. Conflict between newly independent Belgium and the United Kingdom continued until 1839, when the Treaty of London was signed. Under terms of the Treaty of London, Belgium was recognized as an independent state.

The Treaty of London also resolved the status of Luxembourg and delineated the boundary between Belgium and Luxembourg. Newly independent Belgium had claimed sovereignty over all of the Grand

Duchy of Luxembourg, which had been a part of the United Kingdom of the Netherlands. Under terms of the treaty, the primarily French-speaking western half of the grand duchy was recognized as part of Belgium. The predominantly German-speaking eastern half became recognized as the independent state that it remains today. Luxembourg was one of the six original members of the European Coal and Steel Community, which later evolved into the European Union. It remains one of the most prosperous countries in Europe and in the world.

See also   Belgium, France, Germany

Further Reading

Thomas Eccardt. *Secrets of the seven smallest states of Europe.* New York: Hippocrene Books, 2005.

Eric Pape. "The lap of Luxembourgery." *Foreign Policy*, September/October 2011, http://www.foreignpolicy.com/articles/2011/08/15/the_lap_of_luxembourgery?hidecomments=yes.

MACEDONIA

OVERVIEW

The Republic of Macedonia is located in southeastern Europe. Its land area is 9,779 square miles, making it slightly smaller than Maryland. Macedonia has a population of about 2.1 million.

Macedonia's neighbors include Kosovo and Serbia to the north, Bulgaria to the east, Greece to the south, and Albania to the west. Most of its boundaries were delineated upon cultural grounds with the idea of concentrating people who spoke the Macedonian language in the same political unit. Macedonia, Kosovo, and Serbia were

part of Yugoslavia prior to the dissolution of Yugoslavia in 1991.

Given that Macedonia's boundaries are cultural, most of them are complex and irregular, consisting of many very short straight-line segments. Those separating Macedonia from Kosovo and Serbia extend generally in a west-to-east direction. From the tripoint between Macedonia, Serbia, and Bulgaria, Macedonia's boundary with Bulgaria extends in a north-south direction until it reaches the tripoint between Macedonia, Bulgaria, and Greece.

The boundary between Macedonia and Greece consists of short segments that extend in a generally east-to-west direction to Lake Prespa, in which the tripoint between Macedonia, Greece, and Albania is located. Most of Macedonia's boundary with Albania is a physical boundary. It extends from Lake Prespa to nearby Lake Ohrid and then extends along lines that connect the highest peaks in the mountain range that separates the two countries.

HISTORICAL CONTEXT

What is now Macedonia became part of the Ottoman Empire in the late 14th century. During the 19th century, the territory was contested among the Ottomans, Serbia, Bulgaria, and Greece. In 1878, the question of sovereignty over Macedonia was referred to the Congress of Berlin, which reaffirmed Macedonia and Greece as part of the Ottoman Empire. Macedonia remained part of the empire until its dissolution.

In 1913, the areas occupied by people of Macedonian heritage were divided into three regions—Pirin Macedonia, Aegean Macedonia, and Vardar Macedonia. Pirin

MACEDONIA

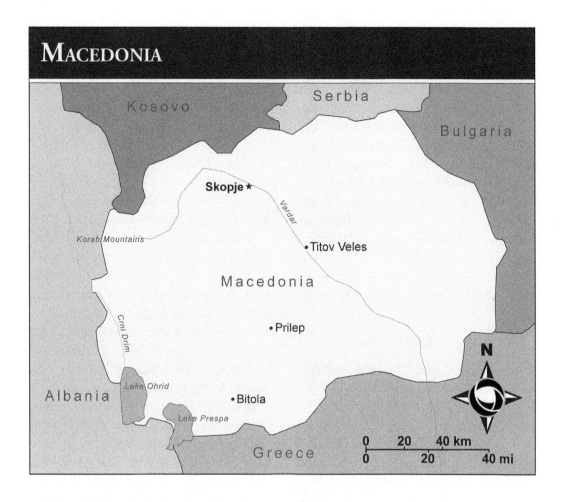

Macedonia was assigned to Bulgaria, and Aegean Macedonia was assigned to Greece. Vardar Macedonia, which included most of the present-day Republic of Macedonia, was assigned to Serbia. In 1918, Macedonia, along with the rest of Serbia, became part of the Kingdom of Serbs, Croats, and Slovenes, which became known as the Kingdom of Yugoslavia in 1929.

During World War II, Vardar Macedonia was occupied by Bulgaria and Italy, both of which were allied with the Germany and the Axis powers. After the war, Macedonia became a constituent republic within the Socialist Federal Republic of Yugoslavia. In giving Macedonia status as a constituent republic, the Yugoslav communists emphasized ethnic and linguistic differences between speakers of the Macedonian and Bulgarian languages, although these languages are very similar. Slavic Macedonia was also distinguished from the Greek province of Macedonia to the south. Many within Greece expressed concern that Yugoslavia would try to expand into Greek Macedonia, in part to obtain sovereignty over territory with a seacoast on the Aegean Sea.

The Socialist Federal Republic of Yugoslavia dissolved in 1991, and Macedonia became independent officially on November 20. After independence, Greece objected to the new Republic's use of the name "Macedonia." In 1993, the United Nations recommended that the new country be known internationally as the "Former Yugoslav Republic of Macedonia." With this caveat, the European Union and the United States recognized Macedonia. Today, the United States, most of Macedonia's neighbors, and many other countries recognize Macedonia under the name of the Republic of Macedonia although the United Nations continues to refer to the country as the Former Yugoslav Republic.

CONTEMPORARY ISSUES

Since independence, Macedonia has experienced disputes involving its boundaries with its neighbors. The most pervasive issue has been conflict with Greece, but issues involving some of Macedonia's other neighbors have also arisen. Many of these issues involve the fact that Macedonia's boundaries are not fully consistent with the distribution of Macedonia's ethnic and linguistic population. Many Macedonians live outside Macedonia in adjacent countries, whereas Macedonia's population includes substantial numbers of non-Macedonians. About 65 percent of the country's people are Macedonians. A quarter of them are Albanians, with the remaining 10 percent belonging to various other ethnic groups.

Relationships between Macedonia and Greece remained strained even after Greece, as part of the European Union, recognized the Former Yugoslav Republic of Macedonia in 1993. Greece remained concerned about possible Macedonian irredentism and expansion into Greek territory. In 1994, Greece imposed a trade embargo with Macedonia. The trade embargo was lifted in 1995, in exchange for Macedonia's revision of its constitution to eliminate any reference to possible Macedonian sovereignty over Greek territory. Conflict between Greece and Macedonia continues, however. Macedonian efforts to join NATO and the European Union have been hindered by Greek objections to its membership in these organizations.

Macedonia's relationships with Albania and Kosovo, with its largely Albanian population, have been affected by the status of the sizeable Albanian minority living in Macedonia. In the late 1990s, an Albanian secessionist movement known as the Albanian National Liberation Army was established. The Albanian National Liberation Army was associated closely with the Kosovo Liberation Army in neighboring Kosovo. A brief armed skirmish near the Macedonia-Kosovo boundary in early 2001 resulted in several dozen fatalities. With the looming possibility of civil war between the Macedonian government and the Albanian National Liberation Army, the two sides signed the Ohrid Agreement in 2001. The agreement provided more rights to ethnic Albanians in Macedonia, including recognition of Albanian as an official language of the country. In 2009, Macedonia and Kosovo signed a boundary agreement that left open the possibility of adjusting the boundary between the two countries on the basis of ethnicity.

See also　Albania, Bulgaria, Greece, Kosovo, Serbia

Further Reading

Josh Rogin. "What's in a name? For Macedonia, everything." *Foreign Policy*,

April 4, 2012, http://thecable.foreignpol
icy.com/posts/2012/04/04/what_s_in_a_
name_for_macedonia_everything.

John Shea. *Macedonia and Greece:
The struggle to define a new Baltic nation.* Jefferson, NC: McFarland, 1997.

Srdja Trifkovic. "Macedonia: The new
Kosovo?" *Jerusalem Post*, February 28,
2012, http://www.jpost.com/Opinion/Op-
EdContributors/Article.aspx?id=259806.

MALTA

OVERVIEW

The Republic of Malta is an archipelago
located in the central Mediterranean Sea.

The three largest islands, Malta, Gozo, and
Comino, are inhabited. The overall land
area of the republic is 121 square miles,
or slightly less than twice the size of the
District of Columbia. The population is
about 450,000. Malta is located about 50
miles south of the Italian island of Sicily
and about 180 miles east of Tunisia.

HISTORICAL CONTEXT

Malta's location between the European
and African coasts of the Mediterranean Sea
has given the islands considerable strategic
and economic importance for thousands of
years. Throughout its history, control of
Malta has been contested among various

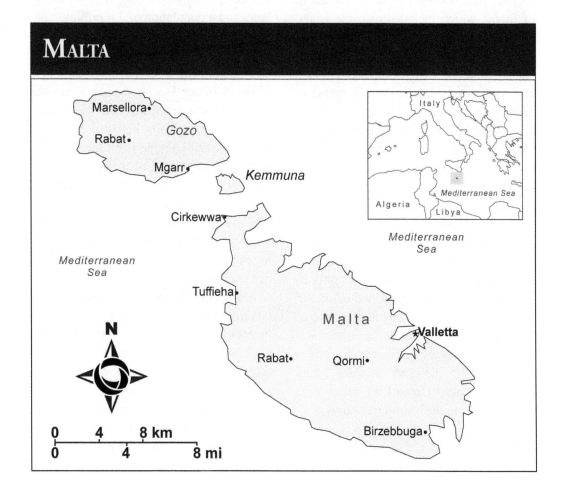

civilizations and empires centered in places along the European and African coasts of the Mediterranean. Archaeologists have discovered sites on Malta that were occupied at least 7,000 years ago.

In the first millennium BC, Malta became a Phoenician outpost. It became a colony of Carthage, which was situated in present-day Tunisia, around 400 BC. After the Punic Wars, Malta became part of the Roman Empire. It later became part of the Eastern Roman Empire, or the Byzantine Empire.

Muslim Arabs invaded and took over the islands around AD 870, and Malta remained under Arab control for the next two centuries. During the Crusades, the Normans from present-day France conquered Sicily. Malta became part of the Kingdom of Sicily, which included also the island of Sicily and the southern portion of the Italian peninsula. It was ruled by the Spanish kingdom of Aragon during the 15th century. Control passed to the Knights of Malta, a religious and military organization associated with the Roman Catholic Church, in the 16th century. Administration by the Knights of Malta ended when Napoleon Bonaparte seized control of the islands.

In 1814, Malta became part of the British Empire. Its strategic importance in the central Mediterranean Sea increased after the Suez Canal opened in 1869. Control of Malta was critical to the Allied efforts to recapture Italy from the Axis powers during World War II. Malta became independent in 1964 and joined the European Union in 2004. Disputes between Malta and the European Union have arisen over fishing rights in the Mediterranean Sea.

See also Italy

Further Reading

Ivan Camilleri. "EU row over fish controls." *Times of Malta*, June 14, 2012, http://www.timesofmalta.com/articles/view/20120614/local/EU-row-over-fish-controls.424194.

Daniel Flott. "How Europeanized has Maltese foreign policy become?" *Mediterranean Quarterly*, 21 (2010), pp. 104–110.

MOLDOVA

OVERVIEW

The Republic of Moldova is located in Eastern Europe. It has a land area of 13,067 square miles, slightly larger than Maryland, and a population of 3.6 million.

Moldova's neighbors are Romania to the west and Ukraine to the north, east, and south. The Prut River, which is a tributary of the Danube River, forms the boundary between Moldova and Romania. The southern tripoint between Moldova, Romania, and Ukraine is located near the town of Giurgiulesti near the confluence of the Prut and the Danube. From there, the boundary follows the Prut River upstream and north-northwestward. The northern tripoint between Moldova, Romania, and Ukraine is located on the Prut near the town of Criva.

The boundary between Moldova and Ukraine follows short straight-line segments in a generally northeasterly direction until it reaches the Dniester River near the town of Ocnita. It then follows the Dniester downstream and southeastward until reaching the town of Nimereuca. At that point the Dniester continues into Moldova, and the boundary is located east of its main

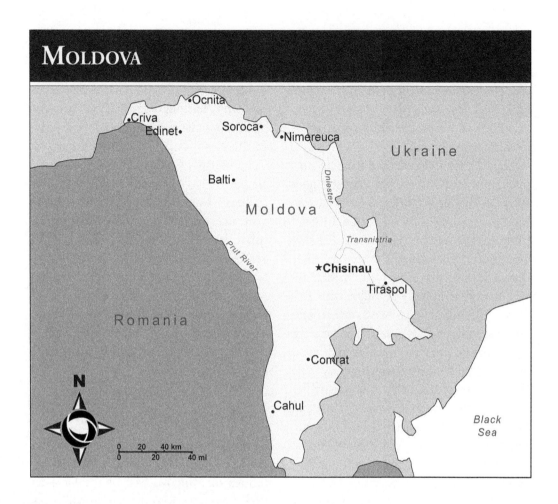

MOLDOVA

channel. The Dniester separates the main portion of Moldova from the territory of Transnistria, which includes those portions of Moldova east of the Dniester and which has claimed independence.

From Nimereuca, the boundary follows straight-line segments that extend in a generally southeasterly direction paralleling the course of the Dniester. South of the city of Tiraspol, the boundary extends back to the Dniester, which becomes the boundary again before entering Ukraine and emptying into Dnistrovsky Liman, or Dniester Lake, which is an arm of the Black Sea. Moldova is landlocked, but its southeasternmost point is located less than two miles from the Dnistrovsky Liman. From that point, the boundary leaves the Dniester and follows straight-line segments in a generally westward direction, then southward to the southern tripoint between Moldova, Ukraine, and Romania.

HISTORICAL CONTEXT

The history of Moldova is linked closely to that of neighboring Romania, and a Moldovan dialect of the Romanian language is the official language of Moldova today. In 1359, the Principality of Moldavia controlled all of present-day Moldova as well as areas of eastern Romania and western Ukraine adjacent to Moldova's current borders. In 1538, the Ottoman Empire took over the principality, but Moldavia was allowed to retain control of its internal affairs.

In 1812, the Ottoman and Russian Empires signed the Treaty of Bucharest. Under terms of this treaty, what is now eastern Moldova was transferred to the Russian Empire and became part of the Russian Oblast of Moldavia and Bessarabia. After World War I, the Moldavian parliament voted overwhelmingly to unite with Romania. The union of Moldavia and Romania was recognized by Western powers but not by the Soviet Union, which continued to claim Moldavia as Soviet territory. The Dniester became the de facto boundary between Romania and the Soviet Union, and Moldavian territory east of the Dniester became the Moldavian Autonomous Soviet Socialist Republic, which was administered via Ukraine.

At the outset of World War II, the Soviet Union reclaimed Moldavia in 1940 and created the Moldavian Soviet Socialist Republic. Over the next four years, present-day Moldova was the scene of conflict between the government of Romania, which was allied with Nazi Germany, and the Soviet Union. The Soviet Red Army recaptured Moldova from the Nazis in 1944, reconstituting the Moldavian Soviet Socialist Republic with its present boundaries. The Soviets worked to separate the republic from Romanian influence. Russians and Ukrainians were encouraged to move to the republic, and the Soviet government decreed that the Moldovan language would be written with the Cyrillic alphabet as opposed to the Latin alphabet. In 1991, Moldova declared its independence.

Moldovan politics have been characterized by ongoing tension between pro-communist and anti-communist political factions. In 2009, the ruling Party of Communists of the Republic of Moldova claimed to have won a majority of seats in Moldova's parliamentary elections. However, many observers claimed that the results were fraudulent. Protests followed, and because many protestors relied on social media to communicate with one another, the protest movement came to be known as the Twitter Revolution. Eventually, new elections were held, and a coalition of anti-communist parties achieved a parliamentary majority.

CONTEMPORARY ISSUES

The status of Transnistria remains unsettled. Transnistria consists of the territories of Moldova east of the Dniester River. In contrast to the rest of Moldova, Transnistria has substantial populations of ethnic Ukrainians and Russians. Only about a third of Transnistria's people are ethnic Moldovans, as compared to about 90 percent in the rest of the country. The overall land area of Transnistria is 1,607 square miles, or about 12 percent of the land area of the entire country. Its population is about 520,000.

In 1990, Transnistria declared its independence from Moldova. The declaration of independence was triggered in part by concerns that post-Soviet Moldova would reunite with Romania. War between Transnistrian secessionist, supported by Russia, and the Moldovan army broke out.

Armed skirmishes continued until 1992 when a cease-fire agreement was negotiated. The territory constituted itself as the Pridnestrovian Moldavian Republic (PMR). Moldova has not recognized the PMR's independence, and the sovereignty of the PMR over its territory is generally unrecognized by the international community. However, the PMR remains in de facto control of the area and has adopted its own constitution and its own flag. Moldova and Ukraine have worked together to control movement of people and goods in and out of the PMR.

See also   Romania, Ukraine

Further Reading

Economist. "Transdniestria: The black hole that ate Moldova." May 3, 2007, http://www.economist.com/node/9116439?story_id=9116439.

EU Business. "Romania, Moldova sign key border treaty." November 8, 2010. http://www.eubusiness.com/news-eu/romania-moldova.6uv.

Nathan Hodge. "Inside Moldova's Twitter Revolution." *Wired*, April 8, 2009, http://www.wired.com/dangerroom/2009/04/inside-moldovas/.

MONACO

OVERVIEW

The Principality of Monaco is located on the coast of the Mediterranean Sea. With a land area of about 490 acres (three-quarters of a square mile), Monaco is the second-smallest sovereign state in the world. Only Vatican City is smaller. Monaco has a population of about 36,000, making it the most densely populated independent country in the world. With an income generated largely by tourism, Monaco is one of the wealthiest independent jurisdictions in the world.

Located about halfway between the French city of Nice and the boundary between France and Italy, Monaco is completely surrounded by France. The land area is long and narrow, stretching from southwest to northeast along the shoreline. At its widest, Monaco is less than half a mile wide. Most of the boundaries between Monaco and France follow city streets in this heavily urbanized area.

HISTORICAL CONTEXT

Monaco was founded in 1215 as a colony of the Italian city-state of Genoa. The Grimaldi family, or House of Grimaldi, became Monaco's ruling family in 1297. Monaco was ruled by French and Spanish kings until the Grimaldis purchased the territory from the Spanish province of Aragon in 1419. During the French Revolution, the territory was annexed by France, but the Grimaldis were restored in 1814. A treaty between France and Monaco, signed in 1861, guaranteed Monaco's sovereignty upon the condition that a member of the Grimaldi family remain on Monaco's throne. The current prince of Monaco, Prince Albert II, is descended directly from Grimaldo, the 13th-century founder of the dynasty. France remains responsible for Monaco's foreign policy and defense. Currently, plans are under way to reclaim land from the Mediterranean, thereby expanding Monaco's land area.

See also   France

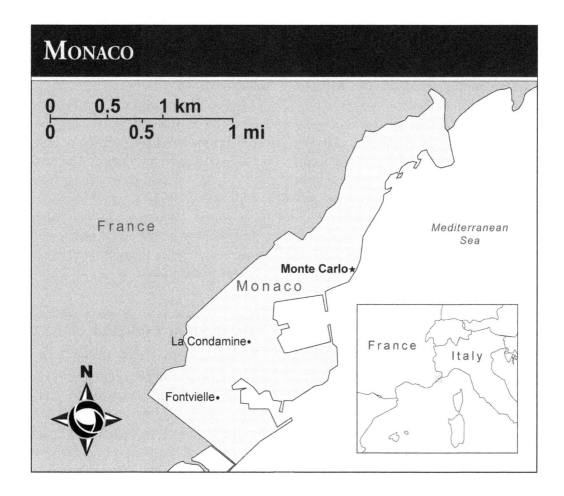

MONACO

0   0.5   1 km

0   0.5   1 mi

France

Mediterranean
Sea

Monte Carlo★

Monaco

La Condamine•

Fontvielle•

N

France

Italy

Further Reading

Thomas Eccardt. *Secrets of the seven smallest states of Europe.* New York: Hippocrene Books, 2005.

MONTENEGRO

OVERVIEW

Montenegro is located on the Adriatic Sea coast of the Balkan Peninsula in southeastern Europe. Montenegro has a land area of 5,019 square miles, slightly smaller than Connecticut. Its population is about 630,000. In contrast to other states in the Balkan peninsula, Montenegro's population is multiethnic. About 45 percent are ethnic Montenegrins, about 30 percent are Serbs, and the remainder belongs to other national groups, including Bosniaks and Albanians.

Montenegro is shaped roughly like a diamond. Its neighbors are Albania and Kosovo to the southeast, Serbia to the northeast, and Bosnia and Herzegovina to the northwest. It has a brief boundary with Croatia on the Adriatic coast to the northwest, and a coastline on the Adriatic to the southwest. The boundary between Montenegro and Albania follows the Buna River

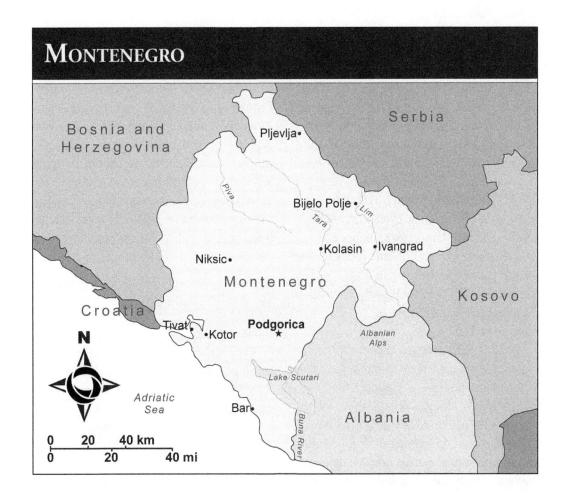

MONTENEGRO

Bosnia and Herzegovina

Serbia

Pljevlja•

Piva

Bijelo Polje •

Lim

Tara

•Kolasin   •Ivangrad

Niksic•

Montenegro

Kosovo

Croatia

•Tivat

Podgorica
★

•Kotor

Albanian Alps

Lake Scutari

N

Adriatic Sea

Bar•

Buna River

Albania

0	20	40 km
0	20	40 mi

upstream from its mouth on the Adriatic to Lake Scutari, which is the largest natural lake in the Balkans and is shared between the two countries. From Lake Scutari, the boundary extends northeastward into the Prokletije, or Albanian Alps. It then turns southeastward along the crest of this mountain range to the tripoint between Montenegro, Albania, and Kosovo.

From this tripoint, the boundary between Montenegro and Kosovo follows numerous short straight-line segments northeastward to the tripoint between Montenegro, Kosovo, and Serbia. The boundary between Serbia and Montenegro extends northwestward, also along straight-line segments. From the tripoint between Serbia, Montenegro, and Bosnia and Herzegovina, the boundary between Montenegro and Bosnia and Herzegovina follows straight-line segments south-southwestward toward the Adriatic. The tripoint between Montenegro, Bosnia and Herzegovina, and Croatia is located less than five miles from the Adriatic coast. The boundary between Montenegro and Croatia separates Montenegro from the southernmost portion of Croatia, which is an exclave of that country located southeast of the short Adriatic coast of Bosnia and Herzegovina. This boundary also follows straight-line segments, going southward and then southeastward to the Bay of Kotor on the Adriatic.

HISTORICAL CONTEXT

Most of the history of Montenegro is tied closely to the history of neighboring Serbia. The region was part of the Roman Empire beginning in the second century BC, then became part of the Byzantine Empire after the Roman Empire's split between the Western and Eastern Roman Empires in the late fourth century AD. Much of present-day Montenegro was included in the kingdom of Dujika, which arose in the 10th century AD and became independent of the Byzantine Empire in 1042. Serbia conquered Dujika in 1186, and present-day Montenegro became part of the Ottoman Empire in 1499.

In 1852, Montenegro became the independent Principality of Montenegro. The principality became a kingdom in 1910. Montenegro along with Serbia fought on the side of the Allies in World War I. After the war, Montenegro was incorporated into Serbia. Serbia and Montenegro became part of the Kingdom of the Serbs, Croats, and Slovenes after the war, and the kingdom was renamed the Kingdom of Yugoslavia in 1929. During World War II, Montenegro was occupied by Italy. Control of Montenegro passed to Germany after the Italians surrendered to the Allies in 1943. Montenegro became one of the six components of the Federal Republic of Yugoslavia after World War II ended.

Yugoslavia began to dissolve in 1990, and Slovenia, Croatia, and Bosnia and Herzegovina became independent. Serbia and Montenegro remained united as the reconstituted Federal Republic of Yugoslavia as the successor state to the older and larger pre-1990 Yugoslavia. Montenegro and Serbia remained unified until 2006, when a referendum on Montenegrin independence took place. In the referendum, 55.5 percent of the electorate voted for independence. In response to the referendum results, Montenegro declared its independence. The newly independent Montenegrin state was recognized by Serbia, and Montenegro has maintained its territorial integrity since that time. Montenegro has used the euro as its currency since before becoming independent in 2006, and it has entered negotiations with the European Union concerning possible EU membership.

See also Albania, Bosnia and Herzegovina, Croatia, Kosovo, Serbia

Further Reading

Economist. "Edging toward Europe: A small Balkan country knocks at Europe's door." June 16, 2012, http://www.econo mist.com/node/21556982.

Kenneth Morrison. *Montenegro: A modern history.* London: I. B. Tauris, 2007.

Ana Selic. *Influence of foreign policy to the EU accession process: Case study: Montenegro and Serbia.* Saarbrucken, Germany: VDM Verlag, 2010.

NETHERLANDS

OVERVIEW

The Netherlands is located in northwestern Europe. It has a total land area of 16,158 square miles, making it slightly smaller than Vermont and New Hampshire together. The Netherlands is one of the most densely populated countries in the world, with about 16.7 million residents. The Netherlands is sometimes referred to as "Holland," but the name Holland is

NETHERLANDS

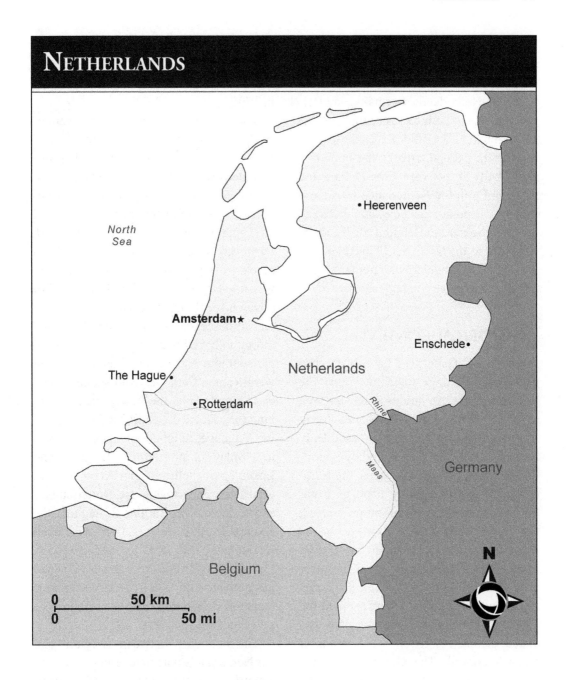

associated properly with only two of the country's 12 provinces. Some in the Netherlands prefer to identify their country as "Netherland," with the plural term "Netherlands" used to refer to the "Low Countries" of the Netherlands, Belgium, and Luxembourg. However, this linguistic distinction is not used outside the Netherlands itself.

The Netherlands borders Germany to the east and Belgium to the south, with the North Sea located to its north and west. The boundary between the Netherlands and Germany is complex and irregular, but it trends from north-northeast to south-southwest from the Ems-Dollart estuary in the North Sea to the north to the tripoint between the Netherlands, Germany, and Belgium at its southern end near the German city of Aachen. The Rhine River, the longest in Western Europe, crosses the boundary about halfway between Ems-Dollart and Aachen. From the Netherlands-Germany-Belgium tripoint, the boundary between the Netherlands and Belgium trends northwestward to the North Sea. This boundary is also highly irregular, with numerous enclaves and exclaves on both sides.

HISTORICAL CONTEXT

The "Low Countries" have been contested within Europe since the days of the Roman Empire. At various times, the area contained within the Netherlands today was controlled by the German-based Holy Roman Empire, by France, and by Spain.

During the late Middle Ages, the Netherlands began to identify itself as a nation. As the Age of Exploration ensued, the Netherlands took advantage of its maritime location to establish itself as an important economic and colonial power within Europe. In 1579, seven provinces in the present-day Netherlands signed the Union of Utrecht. In doing so, they declared themselves to be independent of Spanish control. The Union of Utrecht created the Dutch Republic, whose existence was recognized by Spain in 1609. The Dutch Republic became the world's leading merchant country, and the republic became one of the wealthiest countries in the world. The Peace of Westphalia recognized the Dutch Republic's independence

and sovereignty over the provinces associated with the Union of Utrecht. The Dutch Republic was absorbed into France in 1795.

The present-day state of the Netherlands is a successor state to the United Kingdom of the Netherlands, which also included present-day Belgium and Luxembourg. The United Kingdom of the Netherlands was established in 1815 as part of the Congress of Vienna, which dealt with territorial issues in Europe after the final defeat of Napoleon. The United Kingdom was ruled by King William I, the head of a Dutch-speaking, Protestant royal family whose descendants remain on the Dutch throne today. However, most residents of the southern part of the United Kingdom were Roman Catholics who spoke French or German. Thus the newly independent kingdom faced deep differences regarding language, religion, and economic policy. Many in present-day Belgium and Luxembourg believed that King William was determined to impose Dutch culture and economic institutions throughout the country. In 1830, Belgium (which included Luxembourg) declared its independence. France and Britain recognized Belgian independence in 1831. The Netherlands recognized Belgium and Luxembourg as independent countries in 1839.

The boundary between Belgium and the Netherlands was agreed upon by both countries via the Treaty of Maastricht, which was signed in 1843. While negotiating the treaty, the two countries failed to reach agreement on the central section of the boundary. In particular, they could not agree on the status of the municipality of Baarle, northeast of the Belgian city of

Antwerp. Eventually, the two sides agreed to divide Baarle between the Belgian community of Baarle-Hertog, which was part of the Belgian province of Antwerp, and the Dutch community of Baarle-Nassau, which was part of the Dutch province of Noord-Brabant. As a result of the agreement, more than 20 Belgian enclaves, some less than 30 acres in land area, were surrounded by Dutch territory. Some of these Belgian enclaves, such as one containing the town of Tommel, have Dutch enclaves within them. In 1892, the two governments negotiated to eliminate the enclaves by exchanging territories, but the proposed agreement was rejected by the parliaments of both countries, and the 1843 boundary remains in place today.

Historically, most of the border area between the Rhine River and the North Sea was swampy and poorly suited to agriculture and was very sparsely populated. This border region has been considered a frontier between Dutch culture to the west and German culture to the east since the Middle Ages. The northern section of the Dutch-German boundary extends across marshy lands that were unsettled until these marshes were drained by the Dutch government and later by the Germans. Today this area contains numerous canals and drainage ditches, some of which serve as boundary segments.

While the northern part of the boundary between the Netherlands and Germany crossed historically unsettled frontiers, the area south of the Rhine River supported dense populations and was contested between Dutch and German interests for hundreds of years. At various times in history, Dutch dominance of the border region has

shifted eastward into present-day Germany whereas German influence shifted westward into the Netherlands. The Congress of Vienna, which established and recognized the United Kingdom of the Netherlands as an independent country, also addressed the question of the United Kingdom's eastern boundary. The German territory along the boundary south of the Rhine was controlled by Prussia, which was a participant in the 1815 Congress of Vienna. The resulting treaty resolved Dutch and Prussian claims to the border region. In 1824, the Netherlands and the German state of Hanover, then an independent state, agreed upon what is now the northern section of the border between the Netherlands and Germany. With only minor adjustments, the boundaries as set forth by the Congress of Vienna remain in effect. In 1960, the Netherlands and Germany (then the Federal Republic of Germany, or West Germany) agreed to a treaty formalizing their boundary. This treaty went into effect in 1963 and remains in place today. The Netherlands was a founding member of the European Union, and its membership in the EU remains a cornerstone of Dutch policy.

CONTEMPORARY ISSUES

The boundaries between the Netherlands and its neighbors have been stable for more than 150 years. Nevertheless, a few tensions along these boundaries may become more significant in the years ahead. Continued increases in global temperatures could result in sea-level rise, which could threaten to inundate the northern boundary region between the Netherlands and Germany. Flooding on one side of the boundary, should it occur, could affect conditions on the other side. The border region south of the Rhine River is a heavily polluted industrial area, with the possibility that air and water pollution on either side of the boundary could affect people on the other side.

While the land boundary between the Netherlands and Germany is stable, the maritime boundary within the Ems-Dollart estuary remains in dispute. The Netherlands claims jurisdiction between its coastline and the middle of the estuary, while Germany's territorial claim includes much of the estuary close to the Dutch shoreline. In 2001, Google Earth produced and circulated a map that shows the maritime boundary running very close to the German shore although the Netherlands has never claimed the area between the center of the estuary and the German coast. This situation shed light on the extent to which Google Earth and other mapping sites will influence boundary disputes at present and in the future.

See also   Belgium, Germany

Further Reading

J.F.I. Klaever and A.W.M. Ode. *Civic integration and modern citizenship.* Groningen, Netherlands: Europa Law Publishing, 2009.

Giles Scott-Smith. "The future of Dutch foreign policy." *nrc.nl*, January 29, 2010, http://vorige.nrc.nl/international/opinion/article2471351.ece.

Richard S.J. Tol, Nicolien van der Grijp, Alexander A. Olsthoorn, and Peter E. van der Werff. "Adapting to climate: A case study on riverine flood risks in the Netherlands." *Risk Analysis*, 23 (2003), pp. 575–583.

NORWAY

OVERVIEW

Norway is located on the western part of the Scandinavian Peninsula. The long, narrow, and mountainous country has a total land area of about 149,000 square miles, slightly smaller than California. Norway's population is about 5 million, making it the second least densely populated country in continental Europe after Finland.

Norway shares a long boundary with Sweden to the east, a shorter boundary with Finland to the northeast, and a short boundary with Russia at its extreme northeast. Western and southern Norway has a coastline of more than 1,500 miles. The southern coast is located along the Skagerrak, a strait connecting the North Sea and the Baltic Sea. The western coast is located along the North Sea and the Norwegian Sea, both of which are part of the Atlantic Ocean. This coastline is indented by numerous fjords, or long, narrow, and often spectacular coastal inlets that were formed when glaciers carved out valleys through the underlying rock. For more than a thousand years, Norway's fjords and mountains have impeded land transportation, and Norway has been strongly oriented to the sea. Northern Norway adjoins the Barents Sea, which is part of the Arctic Ocean. Norway also is sovereign over the archipelago of Svalbard, which includes the island of Spitsbergen and is located in the Arctic Ocean north of the Norwegian mainland.

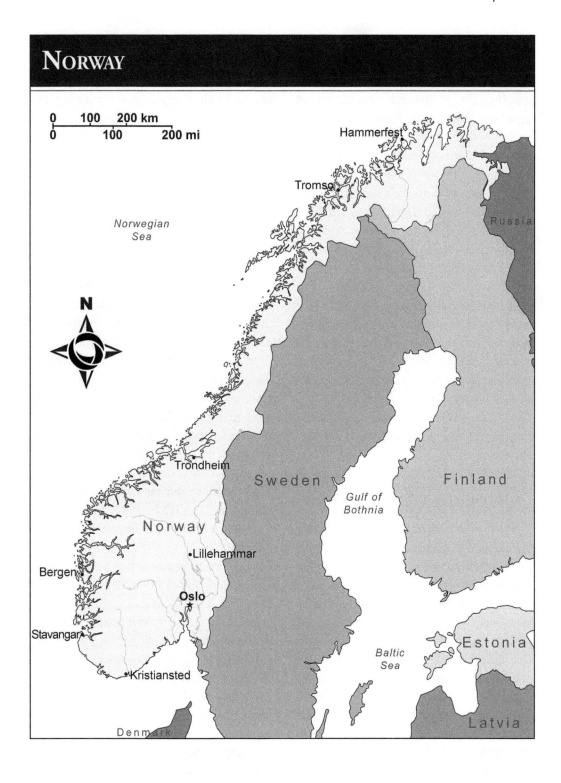

Norway's boundaries generally follow physical features. Its longest boundary with Sweden follows the crest of the Scandinavian Mountains, which extend across the length of the Scandinavian Peninsula. With Norway oriented to the sea and Sweden oriented to the east and south, the boundary region is very sparsely populated. Much of Norway's boundary with Finland follows the Tana River, which is the longest and largest river in northern Scandinavia. Straight-line segments separate Norway and Finland along the western and eastern portions of their boundary, with the Tana River in between. The boundary region on both sides is very sparsely inhabited, with few paved roads or permanent settlements. Most of the relatively short boundary between Norway and Russia follows the Pasvikelv and Jakobselva rivers. The Jakobselva discharges into the Varangerfjord, which is an arm of the Arctic Ocean.

HISTORICAL CONTEXT

Norway has been unified politically since approximately AD 800. Norway, along with Sweden and Denmark, was the home of the Vikings, who sent numerous expeditions of exploration, settlement, raiding, and conquest over the next several hundred years. Vikings raided and settled in the British Isles and other areas of continental Europe, including the French province of Normandy whose name refers to its history of settlement by the Vikings, or "Northmen," in the 9th and 10th centuries. They also discovered and settled Iceland and Greenland.

During the Middle Ages, Norway was at various times united with Denmark and/or Sweden. The three present-day countries were united as the Kalmar Union from 1396 until 1523, when Sweden broke away. Denmark and Norway remained united, with Copenhagen remaining the seat of government and the home of the royal family. Historians today use the term "Kingdom of Denmark" to refer to this union. In 1814, Norway was transferred from the Kingdom of Denmark to Sweden, following the kingdom's defeat during the Napoleonic Wars. Norway declared its independence, but Swedish forces invaded Norway in order to assert Swedish control over both territories. In 1826, Sweden and Russia agreed upon the boundary between the two countries, including the present-day boundary between Norway and Russia.

In the late 19th century, Norwegian nationalists promoted independence for Norway. The union between Sweden and Norway dissolved, and Norway became a fully independent country with its present boundaries in 1905. Norway experienced substantial devastation at the hands of Nazi Germany during World War II. Norway joined NATO in 1949. In 1994, following a nationwide referendum, Norway declined to join the European Union in part because its extensive oil and gas reserves have made Norway one of the wealthiest countries in the world. In 2010, Norway and Russia agreed upon a maritime boundary between Svalbard and the Russian archipelago of Novaya Zemlya to the east.

The boundary between Norway and Sweden, which then included Finland, was delimited in 1751. In 1809, Finland became part of the Russian Empire. The boundary between Norway as part of Sweden and Finland as part of Russia was agreed upon between Sweden and Russia in 1826. This boundary is reviewed by a joint commission between the two countries every 25 years, most recently in 2000.

CONTEMPORARY ISSUES

Norway's land boundaries have remained stable and uncontested since it became independent in 1905. The major location of boundary-related conflict occurs in the Arctic Ocean.

Norway is one of five countries (along with Russia, the United States via Alaska, Canada, and Denmark via Greenland) that have a seacoast along the Arctic Ocean. During the first decade of the 21st century, all of these countries articulated renewed interest in the Arctic, in part because of the discovery of extensive and valuable petroleum reserves and also because of the prospect that continued global warming would cause sufficient sea ice melting to make the ocean navigable. Russia, Canada, and Denmark have claimed sovereignty over those portions of the ocean north from their seacoasts to the North Pole. Norway has not made such a claim, but it has claimed control over areas of the continental shelf that extend more than 200 miles—the exclusive economic zone that can be claimed under the Law of the Sea Treaty. The claim includes territory in the northeastern Atlantic Ocean between Norway and Greenland as well as in the Arctic Ocean itself.

The cultural and political status of Norway's largest indigenous population, the Sami, has also been an issue of controversy. The Sami, who were known at one time as the Lapps, live in the northern part of Scandinavia. Their ancestors are believed to have lived in northern Scandinavia for as many as 10,000 years, since shortly after the end of the most recent Ice Age. The Sami language is distinct from the Indo-European languages spoken throughout most of Europe.

The Sami homeland, which was once known as Lapland, extends across northern Norway, northern Sweden, northern Finland, and the Kola Peninsula of northwestern Russia. The Sami are best known for semi-nomadic reindeer herding. However, other traditional Sami occupations have included fishing, fur trapping, and sheepherding. The total Sami population has been estimated at between 80,000 and 130,000, of whom about two-thirds live in Norway.

During the 19th and early 20th centuries, the Norwegian government made concerted efforts to integrate the Sami into Norwegian culture. The use of Norwegian was mandated in schools, and people were forbidden from speaking the Sami language in schools or in state-supported Lutheran churches. Knowledge of the Norwegian language was a requirement for purchasing property in the Sami-dominated areas of northern Norway.

Today, Sami rights are now recognized more fully by the governments of Norway and other Scandinavian countries. The Sami flag was recognized in 1986, and the Norwegian government established a Sami parliament in 1989. The Sami language was also given equal standing with Norwegian by the Norwegian government.

See also   Finland, Russia, Sweden

Further Reading

Olga Denisova. "Arctic fishing policy a source of disagreement between Russia and Norway." *Voice of*

Russia, June 6, 2012, http://english.ruvr.
ru/2012_06_06/77271953/.

Kirsty Hughes. "Non-EU Norway
'almost as integrated in union as UK.'"
BBC News Europe, January 17, 2012,
http://www.bbc.co.uk/news/world-
europe-16594370.

International Boundaries Research
Unit. "Norway and Russia announce historic maritime boundary agreement."
April 27, 2010, http://www.dur.ac.uk/
ibru/news/boundary_news/?itemno=9951
&rehref=%2Fibru%2Fnews%2F&resubj=
Boundary+news%20Headlines.

POLAND

OVERVIEW

The Republic of Poland is located in
north-central Europe along the Baltic Sea.
It has a land area of 120,696 square miles,
the size of New Mexico. Poland's population is about 38.5 million.

Poland's neighbors are the Russian
Oblast of Kaliningrad to the north, Lithuania to the northeast, Belarus and Ukraine
to the east, Slovakia and the Czech Republic to the south, and Germany to the west.
Northern Poland has a long coastline along
the Baltic Sea. The boundary between Poland and the Russian exclave of Kaliningrad extends in an easterly direction from
the Baltic to the tripoint between Poland,
Kaliningrad, and Lithuania near the Russian Lake Vistytis. This boundary follows
straight-line segments with very little devi-
ation from its general east-west orientation.
From the tripoint, it trends southeastward,
also following straight-line segments, to
the tripoint between Poland, Lithuania, and
Belarus. The boundary between Poland

and Belarus and the boundary between
Poland and Ukraine also consist of numerous short straight-line segments, generally
trending southward to the tripoint between
Poland, Ukraine, and Slovakia.

In contrast to Poland's northern and
eastern borders, Poland's southern borders
with Slovakia and the Czech Republic follow natural features. Both boundaries follow the trend of the Carpathian Mountains.
In general, the Carpathians form a drainage
divide between streams that flow into the
Baltic Sea to the north in Poland and those
that are part of the Danube River drainage basin to the south. From the tripoint
between Poland, the Czech Republic, and
Germany, the boundary between Poland
and Germany follows the Neisse River
northward to its confluence with the Oder
River and then follows the Oder northward
to its mouth in the Baltic Sea.

HISTORICAL CONTEXT

Poland has been inhabited since the end
of the most recent Ice Age about 10,000
years ago. Most of what is now the Republic of Poland was united by the Piast dynasty beginning in the 10th century AD.
The Piast dynasty's regime fractured during the 13th century, but much of Poland
was reunited by the Jagiellian dynasty,
which took power in 1386. The Jagiellons
united Poland and Lithuania, forming one
of the largest political entities in Europe in
the late Middle Ages. The union between
Poland and Lithuania was reinforced with
the establishment of the Polish-Lithuanian
Commonwealth in 1569.

In 1772, some of the territory belonging
to the commonwealth was divided between
Russia, Austria, and Prussia. The partition

POLAND

of Poland was completed in 1795, when the Polish-Lithuanian Commonwealth was dissolved. Throughout the 19th century, Polish nationalists promoted the recreation of a Polish state. However, Poland remained divided among foreign powers until after World War I. The collapse of the German Empire, the Austro-Hungarian Empire, and the Russian Empire at the end of World War I resulted in the recreation of a Polish state. The Second Polish Empire came into existence in 1918. Its eastern and western boundaries were located somewhat to the east of Poland's current territory. Much of what is now western Poland, near the Oder and Neisse rivers, was then part of Germany, while the Second Polish Republic included territory in what is now Belarus and Ukraine. The Second Republic included the Polish Corridor, an area that gave Poland access to the Baltic Sea but split Germany by dividing the territory around Kaliningrad, known as Konigsberg in Germany, from the rest of the country. The German area east of the Polish Corridor coincides roughly with Russia's Kaliningrad Oblast today.

The Second Republic retained its independence through the 1920s and most of the 1930s. In June of 1939, Nazi Germany and the Soviet Union agreed to the Molotov-Ribbentrop Pact, which called for the division of Eastern Europe into Nazi and Soviet spheres of influence. The Second Republic was divided between these two spheres of influence. Germany invaded Poland from the west on September 1, 1939, beginning World War II. On September 17, the Soviet Union invaded Poland from the east. The Second Republic surrendered to the invaders on September 28. After these invasions, the Second Republic was dismantled. Germany annexed western Poland while the Soviets annexed eastern Poland. However, a Polish government in exile was constituted and fierce underground resistance to Nazi and Soviet rule occurred throughout Poland during World War II. In 1944 and 1945, the Red Army drove the Nazis out of Poland and established a provisional government.

At the end of the war, Poland was reestablished as an independent state with its present boundaries. The eastern portion of the Second Polish Republic was transferred to the Soviet Union, while Poland took over those parts of Germany east of the Oder-Neisse Line, which forms the current boundary between Poland and Germany. Under increased Soviet influence, Poland became a Soviet satellite. However, many Poles rejected communism. Strikes, protests, and riots against the communist government occurred frequently over the next four decades.

Polish resistance to communist rule intensified after the election of the Polish archbishop of Krakow, Cardinal Karol Wojtyla, as Pope John Paul II of the Roman Catholic Church in 1978. John Paul II tacitly encouraged opposition to the communist regime and supported the efforts of the Solidarity trade union movement, which was based in the northern Polish city of Gdansk along the Baltic coast, to promote liberalization and democracy. Solidarity called for a general strike in 1980, after which it became part of a large and growing anti-communist movement across the country. In 1989, pro-Solidarity candidates won a majority of seats in Poland's National Assembly in the country's first democratic elections. The Communist Party was dissolved, and the country became the present-day Republic of Poland in 1990.

CONTEMPORARY ISSUES

Poland joined NATO in 1999 and the European Union in 2004. After joining the European Union, Poland and other new Eastern European members of the European Union subscribed to the Schengen Agreement. The Schengen Agreement eliminates the need for travelers within the European Union to show passports when crossing boundaries between member states. However, Poland and the other new European Union members were expected to increase the stringency of border security along their boundaries with non–European Union countries. Travelers from non–European Union countries, including Ukraine and Belarus, must have visas to enter the European Union. Ukrainians living near the Polish boundary, and those doing business in Poland, have protested this increased border security.

See also Belarus, Czech Republic, Germany, Lithuania, Russia, Slovakia, Ukraine

Further Reading

David Armitage, Marcin Zaborowski, Wess Mitchell, and Robert Kron. *Translating opportunity into impact: Central Europe in the European Union, 2010–2020.* Washington, DC: Center for European Policy Analysis, 2011.

Kerry Longhurst and Marcin Zaborowski. *Poland's foreign and security policy priorities.* London: Chatham House, 2007.

Timothy Snyder. *The reconstruction of nations: Poland, Ukraine, Belarus, Lithuania, 1569–1999.* New Haven, CT: Yale University Presss, 2003.

PORTUGAL

OVERVIEW

The Portuguese Republic occupies the southwestern portion of the Iberian Peninsula. It has a land area of 35,645 square miles, making it slightly smaller than Indiana. The population of Portugal is about 10.7 million. In addition to mainland Portugal, the country also includes the archipelagoes of the Azores and Madeira in the Atlantic Ocean.

Portugal's only land boundary is with Spain, which borders Portugal on the north and east. Southern and western Portugal has coastlines on the Atlantic. From the northwest corner of Portugal, the boundary follows the Minho River inland. The boundary trends eastward and then southward along the crests of several mountain ranges. The southern portion of the boundary follows the course of the Guadiana River southward until the river empties into the Gulf of Cadiz, which is part of the Atlantic. However, some territory east of the Guadiana is claimed by Portugal and remains in dispute between the two countries.

HISTORICAL CONTEXT

Portugal was part of the Roman Empire and along with the rest of the Iberian Peninsula was ruled by the Moors during the Middle Ages. After the Moors were expelled from present-day Portugal, it was recognized as part of the Kingdom of Galicia and Portugal in 1065. The two were separated during the 12th century, and Portugal has been recognized as an independent state ever since.

During the 14th, 15th, and 16th centuries, Portugal was instrumental in promoting exploration of other parts of the world outside Europe, including the first European circumnavigation of Africa and the colonization of Brazil. Portugal established the first major European colonial empire and became a major world power. The largest colony in the Portuguese Empire, Brazil, became independent in 1822. Portugal's last colonies became independent in 1975, and the Portuguese Empire ceased to exist.

The frontier between Portugal and Spain has been recognized informally since the Middle Ages, but it was formalized in a treaty signed by the two monarchies in

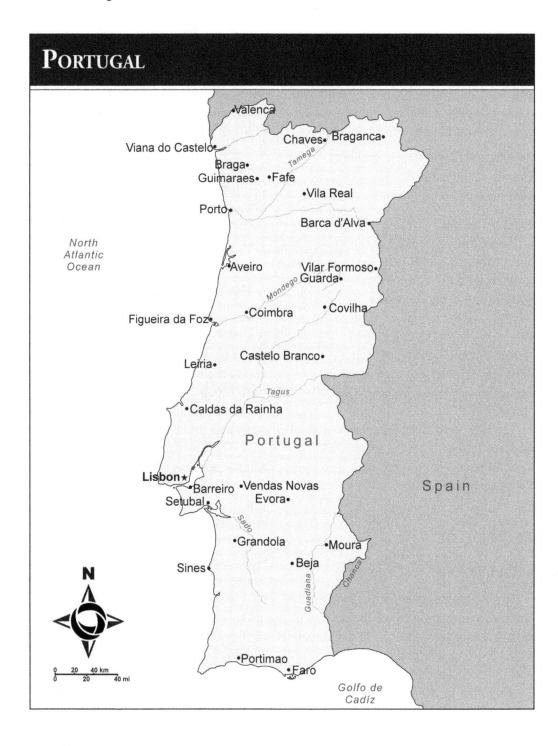

PORTUGAL

1864. Portugal was ruled by military dictators from 1926 until 1974, when its current democratic government was formed. In 1986, Portugal joined the European Union.

CONTEMPORARY ISSUES

The major issue facing Portugal is its ongoing territorial dispute with Spain. The area in dispute is located in southeastern Portugal and southwestern Spain, along the course of the Guadiana River near the Spanish city of Badajoz. This area has a land area of approximately 290 square miles and is located along the Caia River. The disputed territory including the town of Olivenza was occupied by Spain in 1801. Although the 1864 treaty awarded sovereignty over this area to Portugal, Spain continues to occupy and administer the area.

See also   Spain

Further Reading

Barry Hatton. *The Portuguese: A modern history.* Northampton, MA: Interlink, 2011.

Malyn Newitt. *Portugal in European and world history.* London: Reaktion Books, 2009.

ROMANIA

OVERVIEW

Romania is located in southeastern Europe and occupies the northeastern portion of the Balkan Peninsula. Most of Romania is located within the drainage basin of the lower Danube River. Romania has a land area of 92,043 square miles, slightly smaller than Michigan. Its population is about 19.2 million.

Romania has borders with Hungary to the northwest, Ukraine to the north and also to the east, Moldova to the northeast, Bulgaria to the south, and Serbia to the southwest. To the east, it has a coastline on the Black Sea. Many of Romania's borders follow rivers, but most of the boundary between Romania and Hungary is an exception. The tripoint between Romania, Hungary, and Serbia is located between the cities of Timisoara in Romania and Szeged in Hungary. From this tripoint, the boundary between Romania and Hungary extends in a generally northeasterly direction following short straight-line segments. Historically, the intent of this boundary has been to separate ethnic Romanians from ethnic Hungarians. However, about 6.5 percent of Romania's people are ethnic Hungarians, most of whom live in the northwestern portion of Romania near the Romania-Hungary border. The boundary reaches the tripoint between Romania, Hungary, and Ukraine north of the Romanian town of Satu Mare.

The boundary between Romania and Ukraine is also geometric, extending in a generally eastward and northeastward direction along straight-line segments to the Prut River, which is a major tributary of the Danube, just northwest of the Romanian town of Oroftiana. It then follows the Prut River eastward and downstream to the northern tripoint between Romania, Ukraine, and Moldova. The Prut forms the entire boundary between Romania and Moldova, and the southern tripoint between Romania, Moldova, and

ROMANIA

Ukraine is located near the confluence of the Prut and the Danube. From there a second boundary between Romania and Ukraine follows the Danube to its mouth on the Black Sea.

The Danube forms most of the boundary between Romania and Bulgaria. From the southern tripoint between Romania, Ukraine, and Moldova, the course of the Danube crosses Romania upstream from north to south. The Danube reaches the boundary between Romania and Bulgaria south of the Romanian town of Calarasi. East from this point, the boundary is located south of the Danube. It follows straight-line segments that extend in a south-southeasterly direction from the Danube to the Black Sea.

West of Calarasi, the Danube forms the boundary between Romania and Bulgaria upstream and westward to the tripoint between Romania, Bulgaria, and Serbia. The Danube continues upstream and northwestward as the boundary between Romania and Serbia to a point near the Deliblato Sands Nature Reserve. From here the boundary turns north-northwestward and follows straight-line segments to the tripoint between Romania, Serbia, and Hungary.

HISTORICAL CONTEXT

Dacian tribes occupied and governed what is now Romania for several centuries BC. Much of present-day Romania was ruled by the Dacian Kingdom until AD 106, when it was absorbed into the Roman Empire. The Romans encouraged people from all over the empire to move to Dacia. Roman influence today is seen in the name of the country as well as its language. Romanian is a Romance language that is related more closely to French, Spanish, and Italian rather than to the languages spoken in other Eastern European countries today.

Rome abandoned Dacia in AD 271. Over the next several centuries, present-day Romania was governed by many petty kingdoms and principalities. By the Middle Ages, what is now Romania included three distinct parts: Transylvania to the west, Wallachia in the center, and Moldovia in the east. The Ottoman Empire held sway over all three of these regions in the 15th and 16th centuries. In 1600, the three provinces were united for the first time since the fall of the Roman Empire by a Wallachian prince, Michael the Brave. However, Michael the Brave was assassinated during the following year, and the union between the three provinces dissolved. During the 19th century, Transylvania was a part of the Austro-Hungarian Empire while Wallachia and Moldavia remained part of the Ottoman Empire. In 1878, Wallachia and Moldavia were reunited as the independent Kingdom of Romania.

Romania entered World War I on the side of the Allies in 1916. At the end of the war, Romania gained territory inhabited by ethnic Romanians in present-day Hungary, and it included all of present-day Moldova. This expanded kingdom, known to history as Greater Romania, joined the Axis powers during World War II but later switched to the Allied side. After the war, Romania was occupied by the Soviet Union. The last king of Romania, Michael I, abdicated the throne and fled the country. Romania was reconstituted as a communist state known as the People's Republic of Romania, and it continued to be occupied by Soviet troops until the late 1950s.

In 1965, Nicolae Ceausescu became head of the Romanian state. Ceausescu tried to steer an independent course relative to other Soviet satellites in Eastern Europe. However, Ceausescu's regime became increasingly autocratic. As many as 2 million Romanians may have perished during the Ceausescu regime. In 1989, protests and riots against the regime led to the toppling of Ceausescu's regime. In contrast to the removal of communist regimes elsewhere in Eastern Europe, the Romanian Revolution was characterized by violence and resulted in more than 1,100 fatalities. Ceausescu was ousted from power and executed in December 1989. Romania became a member of NATO in 2004 and joined the European Union in 2007.

CONTEMPORARY ISSUES

Romania's boundaries are stable. However, Romania and Ukraine have disputed control of Snake Island in the Black Sea near the mouth of the Danube. Snake Island is only four acres in land area and has no permanent inhabitants. Its only residents are Romanian troops and some research scientists, and whether it should be classified as an island at all has been disputed. However, control of Snake Island has been important to both countries because its sovereignty affects the delineation of maritime boundaries in the Black Sea. In 2009, the International Court of Justice ruled that Snake Island is not an island. On this basis, the court issued guidelines for delineating the maritime boundary between the two countries.

Romania has also objected to Ukraine's plans to construct a canal from the Danube to the Black Sea through Ukrainian territory. Romania and Bulgaria also have initiated transnational efforts to promote navigability on the Danube. However, they have disputed control of a small area in the Black Sea.

See also Bulgaria, Hungary, Moldova, Serbia, Ukraine

Further Reading

Tom Gallagher. *Modern Romania: The end of communism, the failure of democratic reform, and the theft of a nation.* New York: NYU Press, 2008.

Agnes Nicolescu. "Changes in Romania's foreign policy from the perspective of NATO and EU membership." *Romanian Journal of European Affairs*, 10 (2010), pp. 1–13.

RUSSIA

OVERVIEW

The Russian Federation occupies northeastern Europe and northern Asia. Russia is by far the largest country in the world by land area. With a land area of 6,592,800 square miles, Russia is nearly twice as large as the United States. It is about 60 percent larger by land area than Canada, which is the second-largest country by land area in the world. However, Russia is sparsely populated by global standards. Its population of about 142 million ranks Russia eighth in the world. The large majority of Russians live in the European portion of Russia, whereas many areas of Asiatic Russia are virtually uninhabited.

Russia has boundaries with more neighbors than any other country in the world. Its neighbors are Norway, Finland, Estonia, Latvia, Belarus, and Ukraine to the west, Georgia, Azerbaijan, Kazakhstan, Mongolia, and China to the south, and North Korea to the southeast. Russian territory also includes the exclave of Kaliningrad, which is west of the main body of Russia and has boundaries with Poland and Lithuania. Eight of Russia's neighbors—Estonia, Latvia, Lithuania, Belarus, Ukraine, Georgia, Azerbaijan, and Kazakhstan—were part of the Soviet Union before 1991. Only Norway and Finland among Russia's neighbors were ruled by communist government between the late 1940s and 1990. In addition, Russian islands in the Pacific Ocean are located very near to Japan to the southeast and to the United States to the east.

Russia is one of three countries in the world that borders on three of the world's oceans. Kaliningrad and the area around St. Petersburg have coastlines on the Baltic Sea, which is an arm of the Atlantic Ocean. To the south, Russia also borders the Black Sea, which has water access to the Atlantic via the Mediterranean Sea. To the north, Russia has a very long coastline on the Arctic Ocean. Eastern Russia has long coasts on the Bering Sea and the Sea of Okhotsk, both of which are part of the Pacific Ocean. Russian territory also includes

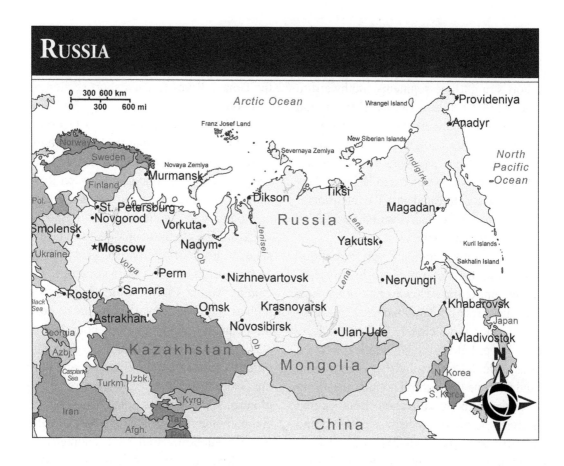

RUSSIA

0   300   600 km
0   300   600 mi

numerous islands in the Arctic and the Pacific, although with few exceptions these islands are uninhabited or very sparsely populated.

Russia's short boundary with Norway extends southward from the eastern and wider end of the Varangerfjord. The Varangerfjord is an arm of the Barents Sea, which in turn is a part of the Arctic Ocean. The boundary extends inland, upstream, and southward along the Jakobselva River to its confluence with the Pasvikelv River, then follows the Pasvikelv further inland to the tripoint between Russia, Norway, and Finland. From this tripoint, the much longer boundary between Russia and Finland follows short straight-line segments southward to the Gulf of Finland in the Baltic Sea. The region near the boundary between Russia and Finland is swampy, has numerous glacial lakes, is poorly suited to agriculture, and has few residents. The city of St. Petersburg, which is Russia's second-largest city and was its capital city prior to the Russian Revolution, is located at the mouth of the Neva River, which empties into the Gulf of Finland.

The boundary between Russia and Estonia follows the Narva River southward and upstream from the Gulf of Finland. The Narva forms the boundary southward to Lake Peipus, which is the largest lake in

Europe that is shared between two countries. South of Lake Peipus, the boundary follows the Piusa River, then follows short straight-line segments southward to the tripoint between Russia, Estonia, and Latvia. The boundary between Russia and Latvia continues southward along numerous straight-line segments to the tripoint between Russia, Latvia, and Belarus. This border was delineated with the intention of separating ethnic Russians to the east from ethnic Latvians to the west.

Estonia and Latvia are very much distinct from Russia in terms of history, language, and culture. However, the languages and histories of Belarus and Ukraine are related much more closely to those of Russia. Nevertheless, the boundaries between Russia and Belarus and between Russia and Ukraine are cultural boundaries. From the tripoint between Russia, Belarus, and Latvia, the boundary between Russia and Belarus extends in an east-southeast direction to a point west of the small town of Velizh. Here it turns southward, once again following straight-line segments to the tripoint between Russia, Belarus, and Ukraine. This boundary was drawn in order to separate ethnic Russians from ethnic Belarusians. Especially on the Russian side of the boundary, the border region is heavily forested and has few inhabitants.

From the tripoint between Russia, Ukraine, and Belarus, the boundary between Russia and Ukraine extends in a generally east-southeasterly direction. East of the Ukrainian city of Kharkov, it turns abruptly to the south-southwest and continues in that direction to the Sea of Azov. The Sea of Azov is an arm of the Black Sea, but it is nearly enclosed by the Crimean Peninsula in Ukraine to the west and by

Russian territory to the east. Most of the boundary between Russia and Ukraine follows short straight-line segments although the Donets River forms a short section of this boundary.

The Transcaucasian states of Georgia, Armenia, and Azerbaijan are located south of Russia between the Black Sea and the Caspian Sea. The boundary between Russia and Georgia that begins at the Black Sea extends across the crest of the Caucasus Mountains to the tripoint between Russia, Georgia, and Azerbaijan. Many of the highest peaks in the Caucasus range, including Mount Elbrus, which is Russia's highest mountain, are located on or near the boundary. In general, this boundary is also a cultural boundary that was drawn in order to separate ethnic Russians and ethnic Georgians. However, the Georgian regions of Abkhazia and South Ossetia have claimed independence from Georgia, with Russian support. Both have claimed independence that is recognized by Russia but not by Georgia. From the tripoint between Russia, Azerbaijan, and Georgia, the boundary between Russia and Azerbaijan continues southeastward along the Caucasus. It then turns northeastward, reaching the Caspian Sea south of the Russian town of Derbent. Much of this section of the boundary follows the Samur River downstream, although the Samur's lower reaches and its mouth are located north of the boundary.

The boundary between Russia and Kazakhstan is located east of the Caspian Sea. This boundary is the longest continuous land boundary in the world. From the Caspian Sea, it follows straight-line segments northwestward through the Ryn-Peski Desert, then turns to the northeast and then to the east. The boundary continues eastward to Lake Aike. The boundary between the Caspian Sea and Lake Aike consists primarily of numerous short straight-line segments. The complex pattern of straight-line segments continues northward and eastward from Lake Aike. The eastern section of the boundary between Russia and Kazakhstan is located in the Altai Mountains. The tripoint between Russia, Kazakhstan, and China is located near the peak of Mount Belukha, whose summit is at an altitude of 14,784 feet above sea level and is the highest peak in the Altai range.

Russia has two boundaries with China, which are separated by its border with Mongolia. The western boundary between Russia and China is much shorter than its eastern boundary. The tripoint between Russia, China, and Kazakhstan is only about 50 miles west of the western tripoint between Russia, China, and Mongolia. From the latter tripoint, the boundary between Russia and Mongolia extends eastward to Lake Uvs on the border. East of Lake Uvs, the boundary follows roughly the drainage divide between the Yenisey River, which flows into the Arctic Ocean, in Russia and southward-flowing streams flowing into Mongolia. However, the boundary to the east turns northward and crosses the southern end of the Yenisey drainage basin such that the extreme southern portion of this drainage basin is located in Mongolia. The boundary follows numerous short straight-line segments eastward to the eastern tripoint between Russia, Mongolia, and China.

Most of the boundary between Russia and China follows rivers. The boundary extends east-northeastward from the eastern tripoint between Russia, China, and Mongolia to the Argun River. It then follows the Argun northeastward and downstream to its confluence with the Shilka River. The confluence of the Argun and the Shilka forms the Amur River, which continues as the boundary for hundreds of miles southeastward to the confluence between the Amur and its major tributary, the Ussuri River. The boundary then turns southwestward and upstream along the Ussuri to its confluence with the Songacha River. It then follows the Songacha southward to Khanka Lake along the boundary. From Khanka Lake, it continues southwestward parallel to the Sea of Japan coast to the tripoint between Russia, China, and North Korea. Russia's major city of the Pacific coast, Vladivostok, is located on the coast but only a few miles east of the boundary. The boundary between Russia and North Korea, which is less than 10 miles in length, follows the Tumen River southward to its mouth in the Sea of Japan.

The Russian exclave of Kaliningrad is located on the Baltic Sea coast and is separated from Russia's main territory by about 200 miles. Kaliningrad has a land area of about 5,800 square miles, slightly larger than Connecticut, and a population of nearly 1 million. Kaliningrad borders Lithuania to the north and east, Poland to the south, and the Baltic Sea to the west. The boundary between Kaliningrad and Lithuania follows the Nemunas River eastward and inland from the Baltic Sea to its confluence with the Liepona River. It then turns southward, following the Liepona upstream, and then continues southward to the tripoint between Kaliningrad, Lithuania, and Poland near Lake Vistytis, most of which is in Russia. From this tripoint, the boundary follows long segments extending east to west to the Baltic.

Russian islands are also located close to both Japan and the United States. The southern tip of Russia's Sakhalin Island is less than 20 miles north of the northern tip of the island of Hokkaido in Japan. To the northeast, the southernmost and westernmost of Russia's Kurile Islands are located less than 15 miles east of Hokkaido. The four Kurile Islands that are closest to Hokkaido are claimed by both Russia and Japan. The mainland of far eastern Russia is only about 40 miles west of the mainland of the U.S. state of Alaska across the Bering Strait. Within the strait, Russia's Big Diomede Island and the United States's Little Diomede Island are separated by only about three miles.

HISTORICAL CONTEXT

Present-day Russia was inhabited by Slavic tribes who moved northward and eastward from Eastern Europe during the first millennium AD. In the ninth century, settlers from the Baltic Sea region moved into the region, probably from Scandinavia. The Rus people, from whom Russia gets its name, were prominent among these newcomers. The Rus established themselves around the city of Kiev in present-day Ukraine in the ninth century and ruled over much of modern western Russia. The Rus remained the major power in the region until the invasions of Mongols from Asia in the 13th century.

The region continued to be dominated by Mongols for the next hundred years. In the 14th century, however, the Grand Duchy of Moscow arose. The grand duchy expelled the remnants of the Mongols and united what is now northwestern and western Russia under Moscow's control. The grand duchy became the Russian Empire. Ivan IV, who is known to history as Ivan the Terrible, was crowned Russia's first tsar in 1547.

The history of the Russian Empire over the next 370 years is one of expansion and conquest of territory. In 1703, Tsar Peter the Great established the city of St. Petersburg on the Gulf of Finland and moved the empire's capital to St. Petersburg from Moscow. Thus Russia become more involved in the politics of Europe and began to contest with Britain, Germany, and other European powers for global economic and political power. Within Europe, Russia took over parts of the former Kingdom of Poland and Lithuania in the 18th century and later expanded into Finnish territory.

Russia also expanded to the east and south. It took control of Siberia in the 17th and 18th centuries. Russia expanded into northwestern North America, claiming Alaska and establishing forts and outposts along the Pacific coast of North America as far south as Fort Ross north of San Francisco. However, Russia sold Alaska to the United States in 1867 and gave up its territorial ambitions in North America. In the 19th century, Russian territory expanded to the Black Sea. Control of a coastline on the Black Sea was important to Russia in that it secured access to ice-free ports that could be used for shipping and trade year-round. Russia also expanded into what are now the Transcaucasian states of Georgia, Armenia, and Azerbaijan and into Central Asia, including modern-day Kazakhstan,

Uzbekistan, Turkmenistan, Tajikistan, and Kyrgyzstan.

The Russian Empire was deposed during the Russian Revolution in 1917. Civil war broke out after the revolution. By 1920, however, the Bolsheviks had secured control over Russia. The Soviet Union, which included Russia as well as Ukraine, Belorussia (present-day Belarus), and the Transcaucasian Republics, was formed in 1922. With the Soviet Union, present-day Russia was known as the Russian Soviet Federative Socialist Republic (RSFSR). The RSFSR was by far the largest of the Soviet republics in land area and population and was the dominant economic and political power within the Soviet Union throughout its history. The USSR incorporated the Central Asian republics in the 1920s and 1930s. During World War II, the Soviet state expanded to incorporate previously independent Estonia, Latvia, and Lithuania. However, the United States did not recognize the incorporation of these countries.

The Cold War, pitting the Soviet Union and its allies against the United States, began after World War II. By the 1970s and 1980s, however, the Soviet Union faced increasing economic difficulties and fell further and further behind the West in economic power. These economic problems in combination with repressive governance generated anti-Soviet independence movements throughout the Soviet Union. The Soviet Union dissolved in 1991, and the RSFSR became the independent Russian Federation. Since independence, Russia has made strides in improving its economy but is dealing with an increasingly autocratic government, serious environmental problems, and a steady decrease in its population due to emigration, low birth rates, and substandard public health.

CONTEMPORARY ISSUES

Russia is involved with several controversies involving its neighbors. These controversies include disputes over the status of the territories of Abkhazia and South Ossetia along the boundary between Russia and Georgia. Abkhazia is located along the northeast coast of the Black Sea, with a land area of 3,343 square miles, somewhat larger than Delaware. Its population is about 250,000. South Ossetia, about halfway between the Black Sea and the Caspian Sea, is about half as large as Abkhazia by land area with a population of about 75,000. During Soviet days, both were part of the Georgian Soviet Socialist Republic. However, as the Soviet Union began to disintegrate, both pushed for independence from both Russia and Georgia. Abkhazia declared independence in 1992, and war between Abkhazian separatists and the Georgian government broke out. Russia recognized the independence of Abkhazia and supported the Abkhazian secessionists. As many as 20,000 Georgians and Abkhazians may have lost their lives during the war.

A similar situation occurred in South Ossetia. Almost two-thirds of South Ossetia's people are ethnic Ossetians, a distinct nation from Georgia. South Ossetia declared independence from the Republic of South Ossetia in 1990. War between the Georgia government and South Ossetian separatists, supported by Russia, broke out in 1991 and again in 2004 and 2008.

Conflict over the status of Abkhazia and South Ossetia is ongoing. In 2008, the Georgian government enacted a law specifying that non-Georgians could enter Abkhazia and South Ossetia only through Georgian territory. Russia stationed soldiers near the border between Russia and South Ossetia but withdrew these troops in 2010. The status of Abkhazia and South Ossetia remains uncertain.

In East Asia, Russia and Japan have experienced a long-standing conflict over the status of the Kurile Islands. The Kurile Islands are an archipelago that extends southwestward from the southern tip of Russia's Kamchatka Peninsula to the northeastern portion of the Japanese island of Hokkaido. The 56 islands comprising the archipelago separate the Sea of Okhotsk to the west from the Pacific Ocean to the east. In 1875, Japan and Russia signed a treaty in which the two empires agreed to grant Japan sovereignty over the 18 southernmost islands in the Kurile chain. However, the entire archipelago was transferred to the Soviet Union after World War II. Today, Japan claims the four islands closest to Hokkaido. The four islands have a total population of about 17,000.

In several places, Russia and its neighbors have been involved in controversy over the status of ethnic Russians in the former Soviet republics. Prior to 1990, the Soviet Union pursued a policy of Russification. The goal of the policy was to promote a Russian cultural identity throughout the Soviet Union. Ethnic Russians were encouraged to move from Russia to the outlying Soviet republics, in part to dilute the influence of non-Russians in each of the republics. By 1990s, Russian nationals formed a majority of the people of Kazakhstan and substantial minorities in Estonia, Latvia, Lithuania, and other now-independent former Soviet republics. Russia has supported Russian minorities in their efforts to promote autonomy and to prevent the assimilation these Russian nationals into non-Russian states.

Russia's economy went through a boom period in the 1990s. However, more recently Russia's economy has stagnated in response to corruption, environmental damage, and population declines. How Russia deals with this malaise may be related to the long-standing question in Russian history about whether it should identify itself as predominantly European or increase its ties with Asia. A prominent Russian academic, Sergei Karaganov, has proposed that Russia consider moving its capital from Moscow to Vladivostok. Karaganov's argument is that this move would link Russia more closely to the growing economies of Asia relative to the less dynamic economies of Europe.

See also   Azerbaijan, Belarus, China, Estonia, Finland, Georgia, Kazakhstan, Latvia, Lithuania, Mongolia, North Korea, Norway, Poland, Ukraine

Further Reading

Kit Dawney. "Rising tensions over the Kurile Islands." *Current Intelligence*, March 2, 2011, http://www.currentintel ligence.net/chinadispatch/2011/3/2/rising-tensions-over-the-kurile-islands.html.

Irina Isakova. *Russian governance in the twenty-first century: Geo-strategy, geopolitics, and governance.* New York: Frank Cass, 2005.

Clifford J. Levy. "Russia backs independence of Georgian enclaves." *New*

York Times, August 26, 2008, http://www. nytimes.com/2008/08/27/world/europe/ 27russia.html?_r=1&ref=abkhazia.

Andrei P. Tsygankov. *Russia's foreign policy: Change and continuity in national identity.* Lanham, MD: Rowman and Littlefield, 2010.

Fareed Zakaria. "Would moving capital kick-start Russian economic reform?" *CNN Global Public Square Blog*, May 29, 2012, http://globalpublicsquare.blogs. cnn.com/2012/05/29/would-moving-capital-kick-start-russian-economic-reform/.

SAN MARINO

OVERVIEW

The Republic of San Marino is located on the eastern side of the Italian Peninsula, inland from the Aegean Sea. It is about 60 miles southeast of the Italian city of Bologna. San Marino is one of the world's smallest independent states, with a land area of 24 square miles (about a third the size of the District of Columbia) and a population of about 31,000. San Marino is surrounded entirely by Italy, with a total

boundary length of 24 miles. It is one of only three states in the world (along with Lesotho and Vatican City) that are completely surrounded by a larger state.

HISTORICAL CONTEXT

San Marino claims to be the world's oldest sovereign state. According to tradition, the country was founded in AD 301 by a Christian stonemason named Saint Marinus. Saint Marinus established a refuge for persecuted Christians on the slopes of Mount Titano, the highest peak in the country.

Until the 15th century, San Marino included only the town on the original site of Saint Marinus's community. In 1463, Pope Pius II added three nearby towns, and a fourth nearby town, Faetano, joined San Marino voluntarily. The boundaries of San Marino have remained intact ever since. During the Renaissance, various Italian kingdoms attempted to annex San Marino. In 1602, Pope Clement VIII signed a treaty with San Marino in which the Vatican recognized San Marino's independence within the Papal States.

After Italian unification, the new Italian government reaffirmed its support for San Marino's sovereignty and independence in a treaty signed in 1862. San Marino remained neutral in subsequent European conflicts, including World War I and World War II. It joined the United Nations in 1992.

See also   Italy

Further Reading

Thomas Eccardt. *Secrets of the seven smallest states of Europe.* New York: Hippocrene Books, 2005.

SERBIA

OVERVIEW

The Republic of Serbia is located in the Balkan Peninsula of southeastern Europe. Serbia has a land area of 34,116 square miles, the size of Maine. Its population is about 7.2 million.

Serbia is landlocked, and its neighbors include Hungary to the north, Romania and Bulgaria to the east, Macedonia and Kosovo to the south, and Montenegro, Bosnia and Herzegovina, and Croatia to the west. The boundary between Serbia and Hungary extends eastward from the tripoint between Serbia, Hungary, and Croatia. This boundary includes numerous short straight-line segments for most of its length. However, it follows the Tisza River upstream for a short distance south of the Hungarian city of Szeged. The tripoint between Serbia, Hungary, and Romania is located about 10 miles east of the Tisza near the village of Majdan.

From this tripoint, the boundary between Serbia and Romania extends in a southeasterly direction along straight-line segments to the Danube River, which reaches the boundary east of the Serbian capital city of Belgrade near the Deliblato Sands Nature Reserve in Serbia. It then follows the Danube southeastward and downstream to the tripoint between Serbia, Romania, and Bulgaria. Here the Danube leaves Serbia and flows eastward to the Black Sea, forming the boundary between Romania and Bulgaria. However, the boundary between Serbia and Bulgaria extends southward from the tripoint. It follows in general the drainage divide between tributaries of the Danube, with tributaries of the Great Morava

SERBIA

River (not to be confused with the Morava River of the Czech Republic) in Serbia from tributaries of the Osam River in Bulgaria.

The boundary between Serbia and Macedonia follows straight-line segments westward to the tripoint between Serbia, Montenegro, and Kosovo north of the Montenegran city of Kumanovo. From this tripoint, the boundary between Serbia and Kosovo extends northward, also along numerous short straight-line segments. The intent of this boundary was to separate ethnic Serbs from ethnic Kosovars, although some areas of northern Kosovo have

Serb-majority populations. The boundary between Serbia and Kosovo extends north-northwestward to a point near Kopaonik National Park in Serbia, then turns southwest to the tripoint between Serbia, Kosovo, and Montenegro. From here, the boundary between Serbia and Montenegro follows numerous short-line segments northwestward to the tripoint between Serbia, Montenegro, and Bosnia and Herzegovina.

North of this tripoint, the boundary between Serbia and Bosnia and Herzegovina reaches the Drina River. It follows the Drina River northward and downstream to the confluence between the Drina and the Sava River at the tripoint between Serbia, Bosnia and Herzegovina, and Croatia. From this point the Sava flows eastward into the Danube, but the boundary between Serbia and Croatia continues northward to the Danube itself, and it follows the Danube upstream and northwestward for most of its length before it reaches the boundary between Serbia, Croatia, and Hungary.

HISTORICAL CONTEXT

Present-day Serbia has been contested by various people from southern Europe, eastern Europe, and western Asia for more than 2,500 years. What is now Serbia was conquered by the Roman Empire in the second century BC, and the area became part of the Eastern Roman Empire, or Byzantine Empire, after the Roman Empire was divided in the late fourth century AD. After modern Serbia became part of the Byzantine Empire, Slavs moved into the Balkan Peninsula in the sixth century AD. The Slavs pushed the Byzantines southward

into Greece, although the Byzantines regained control of what is now the southern half of Serbia south of the Danube River in the 10th and 11th centuries.

The Serbian Empire arose in the 14th century, but the short-lived empire soon collapsed, and Serbia was taken over by the Ottoman Empire in the 15th century. The area remained under Ottoman control until the early 19th century. However, Serbia's location near the frontier between the Ottomans to the south and the Austrians and Hungarians to the north made Serbia the scene of frequent conflicts between these powers.

Beginning in 1804, Serbian nationalists began fighting for independence from the Ottomans. After 11 years of warfare, the Ottoman Empire recognized Serbia as an independent state in 1815. Serbia remained independent throughout the 19th century. After World War I, Serbia became part of the new Kingdom of the Serbs, Croats, and Slovenes along with present-day Croatia, Slovenia, Bosnia and Herzegovina, and Montenegro (which was then part of Serbia). The kingdom was renamed the Kingdom of Yugoslavia in 1929. Yugoslavia was overrun by German and Italian troops during World War II but regained its independence after the war. Postwar Yugoslavia included Macedonia in addition to the original members of the Kingdom of the Serbs, Croats, and Slovenes. A communist government seized power. At first Yugoslavia became a satellite of the Soviet Union, but by the 1950s, the Yugoslav government had moved away from Soviet control and began to steer an independent course.

Yugoslavia remained united until its ruler, Josef Broz Tito, died in 1980. Tensions between the constituent republics of Yugoslavia intensified after Tito's death. In 1989, Yugoslavia broke up. After the breakup, Serbia and Montenegro remained united as the Federal Republic of Yugoslavia. Montenegro remained part of the federal republic until 2006, when the two entities separated. In 1996, Kosovar independence advocates rebelled against the Serbian government. However, Serbia continued to regard Kosovo as a constituent component of the federal republic and refused to recognize Kosovo as an independent country. War broke out, and an estimated 10,000 people lost their lives in the Kosovo War. The United Nations negotiated a settlement of the conflict in 1999, calling for Kosovar independence within Serbia. A UN peacekeeping force was sent to Kosovo to enforce the settlement. The International Court of Justice ruled in 2010 that Kosovo's independence declaration was legal within the context of international law; however, Serbia still regards Kosovo as part of Serbia.

CONTEMPORARY ISSUES

Conflict over the status of Kosovo continues. A large majority of Kosovo's residents are ethnic Kosovars, most of whom are Muslims and whose nationality is related closely to Albania. Ethnic Serbs are a minority within Kosovo, but they represent a majority of the population in portions of northern Kosovo. Serbia has protested the treatment of the Serbian minority in Kosovo. Serbia has also protested the status of the minority Serb population in Bosnia and Herzegovina.

See also   Bosnia and Herzegovina, Bulgaria, Croatia, Hungary, Kosovo, Macedonia, Montenegro, Romania

Further Reading

Ian Bancroft. "Bringing Croatia and Serbia together." *Guardian*, January 18, 2010, http://www.guardian.co.uk/commentisfree/2010/jan/18/croatia-serbia-new-president.

David Bosco. "Why Kosovo independence is good for Serbia." *Foreign Policy*, July 23, 2010, http://www.foreignpolicy.com/articles/2010/07/22/why_kosovar_independence_is_good_for_serbia.

Melissa McConnell. "Serbia's foreign policy capacity." *Mediterranean Quarterly*, 20, no. 4 (2009), pp. 71–82.

Ana Selic. *Influence of foreign policy to the EU accession process: Case study: Montenegro and Serbia.* Saarbrücken, Germany: DM Verlag, 2010.

SLOVAKIA

OVERVIEW

The Slovak Republic is located in central Europe. The land area of the Slovak Republic is 18,932 square miles, or about as large as Vermont and New Hampshire combined. Its population is about 5 million.

Landlocked Slovakia has five neighbors, including Austria to the west, the Czech Republic to the northwest, Poland to the north, Ukraine to the east, and Hungary to the south. The boundaries between Slovakia and Poland and between Slovakia and Hungary are by far the longest boundaries of Slovakia. From the tripoint between Slovakia, Austria, and Hungary, the boundary between Slovakia and Austria follows a series of short straight-line segments that extend in a generally northward direction to a point just west

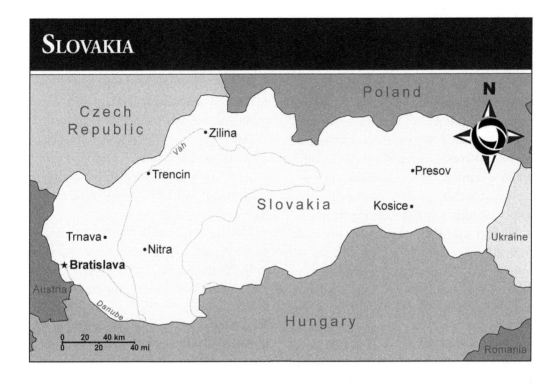

SLOVAKIA

of Slovakia's capital city of Bratislava, which is located less than 10 miles east of the international boundary. The boundary reaches the Danube River, which it follows briefly upstream and westward to the confluence between the Danube and Morava rivers. It then follows the Morava upstream and northward to the tripoint between Slovakia, Austria, and the Czech Republic. The boundary between Slovakia and the Czech Republic continues along the Morava in a north-northeast direction for a short distance until it turns east-northeast, following and paralleling the crest of the Carpathian Mountains to the tripoint between Slovakia, the Czech Republic, and Poland.

From this tripoint, the boundary between Slovakia and Poland continues along the Carpathians, including their highest peaks in the Tatra Mountains. In general, this boundary forms the drainage divide between streams flowing southward into the Danube in Slovakia from those that flow northward into the Baltic Sea on the Polish side of the boundary. The Dunajec River, most of which flows through Poland, forms a short section of this border. A short boundary between Slovakia and Ukraine extends southward from the tripoint between Slovakia, Poland, and Ukraine to the tripoint between Slovakia, Ukraine, and Hungary.

The tripoint between Slovakia, Ukraine, and Hungary is located on the Tisza River. The boundary between Slovakia and Hungary follows the Tisza southward and downstream for about four miles. It then turns westward and continues in this general direction until it reaches the Ipel' River, which is a tributary of the Danube. It follows the Ipel' westward and southwestward to its confluence with the Danube itself. The boundary then follows the Danube upstream until reaching a point near the town of Samorin. From there the boundary is located a few miles west of the Danube until it reaches the tripoint between Slovakia, Hungary, and Austria.

HISTORICAL CONTEXT

Modern-day Slovakia was occupied by Celtic peoples between 2,000 and 3,000 years ago. Between the second and sixth centuries AD, the area was invaded from the east by Huns and later by Slavic peoples, who brought with them what would become the Slovak language. Many of the Slovak tribes of present-day Slovakia were united for the first time as part of the Greater Moravian Empire starting in about AD 830. What is now Slovakia was integrated with Hungary beginning in the early 11th century AD. Slovakia was ruled by Hungarian kings, whose control of Slovakia continued for the next 900 years. During the 19th century, Slovakia was part of the Hungarian portion of the Austro-Hungarian Empire.

After World War I, the Austro-Hungarian Empire was dismembered, and the map of Europe was redrawn. Slovakia along with the Czech regions of Bohemia, Moravia, and Silesia became the independent state of Czechoslovakia. After a brief shooting war broke out between Czechoslovakia and Poland over control of certain territories along their boundary, Czechoslovakia's borders with its neighbors were confirmed by the Treaty of Trianon, signed in 1920. Although newly independent Czechoslovakia experienced ethnic tensions between Slovaks, Czechs, Germans, Hungarians, and other nationalities

within its borders, it became a successful democracy.

Democratic rule in Czechoslovakia came to an abrupt end in 1938, which it was invaded by Nazi Germany. The Nazis split Slovakia from the rest of Czechoslovakia. Slovakia was nominally independent during World War II, but it was governed by a German-sponsored regime until the Nazis were expelled by Soviet Red Army troops in 1944. After World War II ended, Czechoslovakia was reconstituted and democracy was restored briefly. However, a 1948 coup d'état, which was supported by the Soviet Union, toppled Czechoslovakia's government. The Communist Party took control of Czechoslovakia, which became a Soviet satellite and a member of the Warsaw Pact.

Anti-communist activities became more and more prevalent during the 1970s and 1980s. Protests in November and December of 1989 forced the communist regime of Czechoslovakia to relinquish power, and a democratic regime was inaugurated in December 1989 for the first time since 1948. In 1992, Czech and Slovak leaders agreed to separate the two components of Czechoslovakia and established the current boundary between the two countries. The separation between the Czech Republic and Slovakia took effect on January 1, 1993. Slovakia became a member of the European Union and NATO in 2004.

CONTEMPORARY ISSUES

The major issue of concern associated with Slovakia and its neighbors has involved conflict with Hungary over construction of a dam on the Danube River. In 1977, Czechoslovakia and Hungary signed the Budapest Treaty, which authorized the construction of a series of dams between the towns of Gabcikovo in Slovakia and Nagymaros in Hungary. These towns are located near the point at which the boundary between Slovakia and Hungary moves westward from the Danube toward the tripoint between Slovakia, Hungary, and Austria. The project was named for the two towns. The purpose of the project was to control floods, provide hydroelectric power, and improve navigability along the Danube. Both countries agreed to contribute to the costs of constructing and operating the dam.

In the 1980s, concerns arose in Hungary about the potential environmental impacts of the Gabcikovo-Nagymaros Dam. However, construction continued on the Czechoslovakian side of the border. After the communist government of Hungary was toppled, the new Hungarian government suspended work on the project. When Slovakia and the Czech Republic were separated in 1993, Hungary argued that the 1977 treaty was no longer binding. However, the International Court of Justice ruled in Slovakia's favor on this question in 1997. The court denied Hungary's request to end construction, required the two countries to attempt to negotiate a settlement, and required Hungary to pay damages to Slovakia in the event that a solution could not be negotiated. After negotiations, a treaty was drafted, but Hungary did not ratify this treaty, and the issue remains unresolved.

See also   Austria, Czech Republic, Hungary, Poland, Ukraine

Further Reading

Stanislav J. Kirschbaum. *A history of Slovakia: The struggle for survival.* New York: Palgrave Macmillan, 2005.

Oskar Krejci. *Geopolitics of the Central European region: The view from Prague and Bratislava.* Translated by Martin C. Styan. Bratislava, Slovak Republic: Institute of Political Sciences, SAS, 2005.

Gyorgy Moldova. "A tale of two dams: Slovakia, Hungary, and the Danube River." *UNESCO Courier*, October 2011, http://findarticles.com/p/articles/mi_m1310/is_2001_Oct/ai_79560853/.

SLOVENIA

OVERVIEW

The Republic of Slovenia is a former Yugoslav republic located in Central Europe. It has a land area of 7,827 square miles, slightly smaller than New Jersey. Its population is about 2.1 million.

Slovenia shares boundaries with Italy to the west, Austria to the north, Hungary to the northeast, and Croatia to the east and south. Slovenia has a short coastline on the Adriatic Sea to the west. In general, the boundaries of Slovenia separate people of Slovenian nationality and those of other nationalities. The boundary between Slovenia and Italy begins at the Adriatic Sea. It extends eastward to separate the Italian port of Trieste from Slovenian territory to the east, then parallels the Adriatic coast a few miles inland to a point east of the Italian city of Monfalcone. The boundary separates a strip of territory along the coast in Italy from Slovenian territory inland. At its narrowest point, the territory is less than three miles wide. From the vicinity of Monfalcone, the boundary follows the crest of the Julian Alps northward to the tripoint between Slovenia, Italy, and Austria. This tripoint is located near the peak

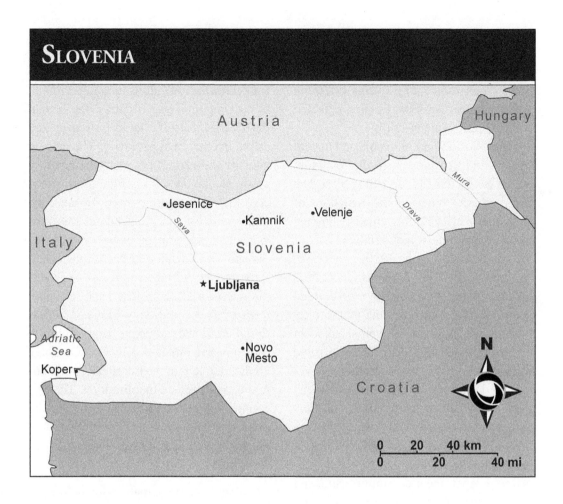

SLOVENIA

of Mount Petzen, the highest point in this portion of the Alps.

From Mount Petzen, the boundary between Slovenia and Austria extends eastward through mountainous terrain, then enters less rugged terrain. It reaches the Mur River, following this river eastward and downstream to the Drava River, which in turn empties into the Danube River in Croatia. Both the Mur and Drava form part of the boundary between Slovenia and Austria. The boundary between Slovenia and Hungary is a complex series of short geometric lines extending southward to the tripoint between Slovenia, Hungary, and Croatia on the Drava. From there, the boundary extends eastward and then southeastward to the Adriatic.

HISTORICAL CONTEXT

Present-day Slovenia was incorporated into the Roman Empire in the first century BC. During the third and fourth centuries AD, the region was invaded by various Germanic and Slavic tribes, and the Romans abandoned the area around AD 400. Slavic peoples who would become the ancestors of today's Slovenes moved into the area during the fifth and sixth centuries

AD. Slovene became part of the Hapsburg Empire, which was the forerunner of the Austrian Empire, in the 15th century. Napoleon took control of Slovenia briefly in 1809, but the Austrian Empire regained control of Slovenia in 1813.

After World War I, Slovenia united with Croatia and Serbia to form the Kingdom of the Serbs, Croats, and Slovenes. The kingdom was renamed the Kingdom of Yugoslavia in 1929. Slovenia became the wealthiest and most industrialized part of the kingdom during the 1920s and 1930s. During World War II, the kingdom was invaded by the Axis powers, who divided control of the country among themselves. Eastern and northern Slovenia, adjacent to German-speaking Austria, was ruled by Nazi Germany while western Slovenia, bordering Italy, was ruled by Fascist Italy. After the expulsion of Italy and Germany, Yugoslavia was reconstituted as the Federal People's Republic of Yugoslavia under communist rule. Slovenia continued to prosper under communist rule, and nationalist sentiment increased especially after the death of Yugoslavia's ruler, Marshal Josef Broz Tito, in 1980.

As Yugoslavia began to split apart, in 1990 a large majority of Slovenia's voters supported a referendum calling for an independent Slovenia. Slovenia declared its independence in 1991. It joined NATO and the European Union in 2004.

CONTEMPORARY ISSUES

Slovenia's main concerns with respect to its neighbors involve areas along and near its short coastline on the Adriatic Sea. Slovenia and Croatia dispute territory along the Dragonja River, a short river that empties into the Adriatic near the border between Slovenia and Croatia. Both countries claim territory along the southern bank of the Dragonja, with Croatia claiming that the Dragonja itself should be recognized as the international boundary. The dispute also involves control of maritime territory offshore. Given the configuration of the coastline of the northeastern Adriatic, the delineation of maritime boundaries seaward from the boundaries between Slovenia and Croatia and between Slovenia and Italy into the Adriatic could restrict Slovenia's territorial claim to a small offshore territory and could deny Slovenia access to international shipping lanes entirely. Slovenia has threatened to veto Croatia's application to join the European Union unless Croatia agreed to arbitration. The two countries agreed on a treaty to submit the question to international arbitration, and the arbitration proceedings began in January of 2012.

See also   Austria, Croatia, Hungary, Italy

Further Reading

David Armitage, Marcin Zaborowski, Wess Mitchell, and Robert Kron. *Translating opportunity into impact: Central Europe in the European Union, 2010–2020.* Washington, DC: Center for European Policy Analysis, 2011.

Bogomir Ferfila and Paul Phillips. *Slovenia's transition: From medieval roots to the European Union.* Lanham, MD: Lexington Books 2010.

Sharon Fisher. *Political change in postcommunist Slovakia and Croatia: From nationalist to Europeanist.* New York: Palgrave Macmillan, 2006.

SPAIN

OVERVIEW

The Kingdom of Spain occupies most of the Iberian Peninsula, which it shares with neighboring Portugal, in southwestern Europe. Spain has a land area of 194,610 square miles, or about the size of Colorado and Wyoming combined. Thus, Spain is the second-largest country in Western Europe by land area, behind only France. Its population is about 46 million.

Spain's large neighbors are Portugal to the west and France to the north. Northwestern Spain has coastlines on the Bay of Biscay and the Atlantic Ocean, and southern and eastern Spain has coastlines on the Atlantic and the Mediterranean Sea. Spain also borders the tiny country of Andorra, which is located in the Pyrenees Mountains between Spain and France. To the south, Spain borders the British Overseas Territory of Gibraltar. In addition to its mainland territory on the Iberian Peninsula, Spain includes two exclaves in northwestern Africa, the Balearic Islands in the

Mediterranean, and the Canary Islands in the Atlantic.

Spain's boundaries generally follow physical features. The boundary between Spain and France follows the crest of the Pyrenees Mountains, which separate the two countries. Except along the Atlantic and Mediterranean seacoasts, this boundary is located along rugged and sparsely populated terrain that formed a natural frontier between the two countries and was difficult to traverse prior to the development of modern transportation.

Spain's boundary with Portugal follows the Minho River from its mouth on the Atlantic Ocean inland to its tributary, the Barjas River. It follows the Barjas into mountainous territory and then trends eastward and then southward along the crests of several mountain ranges. The southern portion of the boundary follows the course of the Guadiana River southward until the river empties into the Gulf of Cadiz, which is part of the Atlantic. However, some territory east of the Guadiana is claimed by Portugal and remains in dispute between the two countries.

colonization of South America, Central America, and Mexico.

With only minor modifications, Spain's boundaries have been stable since the end of the Reconquista. The Pyrenees were recognized as the frontier between France and Spain during the late Middle Ages. The boundary was formalized in 1659 through the signing of the Treaty of the Pyrenees, which was the first significant treaty signed following the Peace of Westphalia involving the specific delimitation of marked boundaries. Similarly, the boundary between Spain and Portugal was recognized informally as early as the 13th century and was formalized in a treaty between the two countries signed in 1864.

Spain experienced several decades of autocratic rule beginning in the 1930s. After the death of dictator Francisco Franco in 1975, Spain became a constitutional monarchy and established a system of democratic government. Spain's economy, which had lagged behind the rest of Europe for much of the 20th century, soon prospered. Spain joined the European Union in 1986.

HISTORICAL CONTEXT

The Iberian Peninsula, including present-day Spain and Portugal, comprised the Roman province of Hispania. As the Roman Empire collapsed, it was invaded by Germanic tribes. In the eighth century AD, Spain was invaded by Muslim Moors from Africa. Over the next several centuries, Christian kingdoms gradually pushed the Moors southward. The Reconquista, or expulsion of the Moors, was completed in 1492. At the same time, Spain began to emerge as a world power through the

CONTEMPORARY ISSUES

Although Spain's boundaries have been stable for several hundred years, Spain and Portugal have an ongoing and unresolved boundary dispute. The major issues facing contemporary Spain, however, involve the Basques of northwestern Spain and the Catalonians of northeastern Spain.

Spain and Portugal have disputed control over an area along the Guadiana River, which forms much of their boundary. The area in dispute, which has a land area of approximately 300 square miles, is located in southeastern Portugal and southwestern Spain near the Spanish city of Badajoz. The disputed territory, including the town of Olivenza, was occupied by Spain in 1801. Although the 1864 treaty awarded sovereignty over this area to Portugal, Spain continues to occupy and administer the area.

The Basques are an ethnic group who live in northwestern Spain and southwestern France. The Basque homeland is located on the western end of the Pyrenees Mountains and along the Bay of Biscay. Anthropologists are uncertain about the prehistoric origins of the Basque people, who have inhabited their present homeland for at least 2,000 years. The Basque language, which is also known as Euskara, is unique and is unrelated to any other language in the world.

The Treaty of the Pyrenees, which delimited the boundary between Spain and France, separated the Basque population between the two countries. About 85 percent of Basques today live on the Spanish side of the boundary. The historically agricultural Basque country became heavily industrialized during the 19th century, attracting non-Basques from other parts of Spain who did not share Basque cultural identity.

During Franco's regime, the Spanish government tried to suppress Basque identity and culture. Resentment of these harsh laws spurred activism among Basque separatists, who founded the Euskada ta Askatasuna (Basque Country and Freedom Party, or ETA). These harsh laws were eased after the end of the Franco regime, and in 1978 the Basque region was recognized by Spain as the Basque Autonomous Community, which has a population of about 2.2 million and in which both Spanish and Basque are official languages. However, ETA and other Basque nationalists have pressed for complete independence of the Basque country from Spain and France for many years.

A secessionist movement is also active in Catalonia, which is located in the northeastern corner of Spain. Centered on the city of Barcelona, Catalonia is about the size of Maryland with a population of 7.5 million. Thus Catalonia contains about 6 percent of Spain's land area and 16 percent of its population.

The Treaty of the Pyrenees, which separated the Basque population between Spain and France, also separated Catalan culture. The northern part of Catalonia became and remains part of France, while the majority of Catalonia was part of Spain. During the 20th century, a nationalist movement arose in both the Spanish and French portions of Catalonia. The movement was based on the premise that Catalonia should be recognized as a distinct nation with its own cultural heritage and identity and the fact that the Catalan language is related to but distinct from Spanish.

As was the case with the Basques, the Franco regime attempted to suppress Catalan nationalism, but Catalonia gained increased autonomy in the 1970s. The Autonomous Community of Catalonia was established in 1978, with Spanish and Catalan both recognized as official languages. A referendum approved by the Catalonian electorate in 2006 expanded the powers of the Autonomous Community. However, several proindependence political parties remain active in Catalonia.

See also   Andorra, France, Portugal

Further Reading

Alfred W. McCoy, Josep M. Fradera, and Stephen Jacobson. *Endless empire: Spain's retreat, Europe's eclipse, America's decline.* Madison: University of Wisconsin Press, 2012.

Kenneth McRoberts. *Catalonia: Nation building without a state.* New York: Oxford, 2001.

Diego Muro. "Nationalism and nostalgia: The case of radical Basque nationalism." *Nations and Nationalism*, 11 (2005), pp. 571–589.

SWEDEN

OVERVIEW

The Kingdom of Sweden occupies the eastern part of the Scandinavian Peninsula. It is the largest Scandinavian country by land area and population. Its land area of about 173,000 square miles makes it slightly larger than California. Sweden's population is about 9.2 million.

Sweden's neighbors are Norway to the west and north and Finland to the east. The Baltic Sea separates Sweden from Denmark to the south. Eastern Sweden has a long coastline along the Gulf of Bothnia, which is part of the Baltic.

The boundary between Sweden and Norway extends across the Scandinavian Peninsula, generally in a north-south direction. This boundary follows the crest of the Scandinavian Mountains, which extend across the length of the peninsula. The boundary region is mountainous and very sparsely populated. The land boundary between Sweden and Finland trends in a north-south direction northward from the coast of the Gulf of Bothnia. The Torne River forms the southern portion of the boundary, with the northern portion following its tributary, the Muonio River.

HISTORICAL CONTEXT

Most of what is now southern and central Sweden became united culturally during the Middle Ages. Present-day Sweden was united with Norway and Denmark via the Kalmar Union in 1397. Sweden, including present-day Finland, broke away from the Kalmar Union in 1523 and became an independent country. Over the next century, the Swedish state expanded. By the late 17th century, what was then known as the Swedish Empire controlled present-day Estonia and Latvia as well as several ports on the southern coast of the Baltic in what is now Germany. Control of these territories allowed Sweden to control trade through the Baltic, which was one of Europe's major shipping routes.

During the first decade of the 18th century, Sweden and Russia fought for political supremacy in the Baltic region in what came to be known as the Great Northern War. After Sweden suffered decisive military defeats at the hand of Russia, Sweden ceded its territory east and south of the Baltic to Russia, Poland, and Prussia. Finland remained part of Sweden until 1809, when it came under Russian control following a Swedish defeat by Russian forces during what would become known as the Finnish War. In 1826, Sweden and Russia agreed upon their boundary. This boundary became the boundary between Sweden and Finland after Finland achieved independence in 1917, and it remains in place today.

SWEDEN

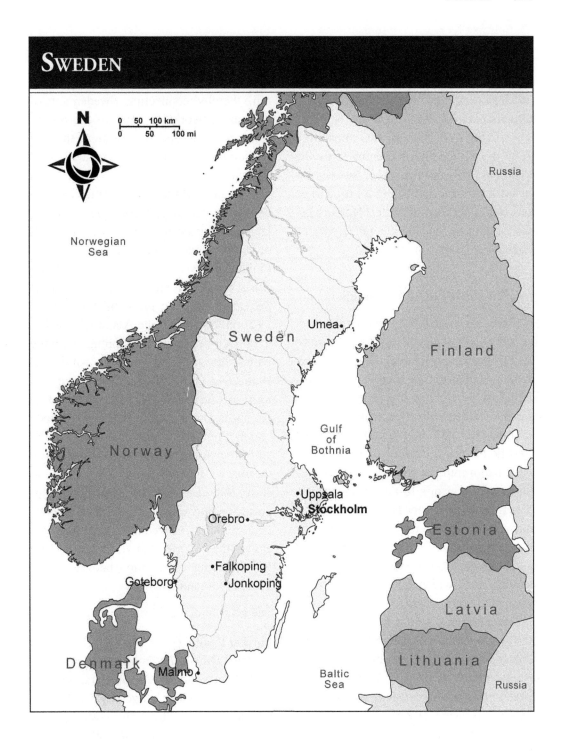

After Sweden left the Kalmar Union, Norway and Denmark remained united under the Danish crown. In 1751, Sweden and Denmark agreed upon the boundary between Sweden and present-day Norway. Sovereignty over Norway was transferred from the Kingdom of Denmark to the Kingdom of Sweden in 1814. Sweden invaded Norway in 1814 in order to enforce its sovereignty over the latter. Norway became a fully independent country with its present boundaries in 1905.

CONTEMPORARY ISSUES

Sweden's boundaries have been intact for more than two centuries. In part because they cross sparsely inhabited territory, they have remained uncontested. Today, Sweden's issues involving its geographic position involve the Baltic Sea, which has been an important maritime trading route since the Middle Ages. Control of Baltic trade was a major impetus underlying the Swedish Empire's efforts to take over what is now Estonia and other lands on the south and east shores of the Baltic. This was also a factor underlying Russia's military actions against Sweden in the early 18th century, after which Sweden gave up its trans-Baltic territories.

The Baltic Sea is connected to the North Sea and to the open Atlantic Ocean by the Oresund Strait, which is one of the busiest waterways in the world. The Oresund Strait separates southwestern Sweden from the Danish island of Zealand. At its narrowest point, the Oresund Strait is less than three miles wide. For centuries, the Oresund Strait could be crossed only by boat. In 1995, however, construction began on the Oresund Bridge, which connects the Swedish city of Malmo with the Danish capital of Copenhagen. The bridge connects the two countries by both road and rail, thereby connecting Sweden's road and rail networks to those of the rest of continental Europe. Today more than 35 million travelers cross the Oresund Bridge each year.

The status of the Aland Islands has also been a matter of concern. The Aland Islands are located at the entrance to the Gulf of Bothnia, which separates Sweden from Finland. They are located north of Sweden's capital of Stockholm but south of Sweden's coast on the Gulf. Given their location, control of the Aland Islands has long been important to shipping and trade within the gulf and therefore within the Baltic Sea Gulf. Although the large majority of the Aland Islands's 28,000 people speak Swedish, the islands have been under Finnish sovereignty since 1809, when they were ceded to Russia along with the rest of Finland. During the 19th and early 20th centuries, many islanders supported ceding sovereignty over the islands from Finland to Sweden. The conflict has eased since World War II, in conjunction with ongoing cooperation between Sweden and Finland.

See also   Finland, Norway

Further Reading

Bertil Oden. *The Swedish policy for global development: Implementation and changes.* Goteborg University, Center for Global Studies, 2009, http://www.global studies.gu.se/digitalAssets/1269/1269811_ perspectives12.pdf.

Martina Sprague. *Sweden: An illustrated history.* New York: Hippocrene Books, 2005.

SWITZERLAND

OVERVIEW

The Swiss Confederation is located in Central Europe. Switzerland has a land area of 15,940 square miles (roughly the size of New Hampshire and Vermont together) and a population of about 7.7 million.

The main range of the Alps extends across Switzerland, much of which is mountainous. Switzerland includes more than 100 peaks with elevations greater than 13,000 feet above sea level. Switzerland has a long history of political neutrality.

It has stayed out of most European conflicts since the Middle Ages and has not been at war since 1815. Its official name reflects the fact that Switzerland includes 26 provinces or cantons that have united to become a single country over several hundred years.

Switzerland's long history of peace and neutrality may be related to its mountainous environment, its location at the crossroads of several European cultures, and the fact that its population is multilingual. Switzerland has four official languages: German, French, Italian, and Romansch, which is a Romance language spoken in

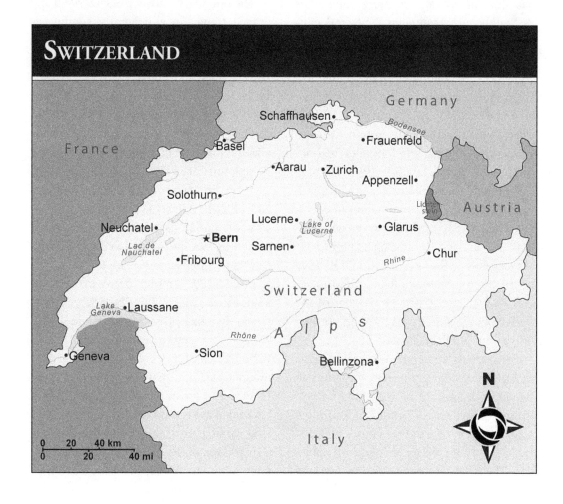

southeastern Switzerland and related to Italian and French. German, French, and Italian are the official languages of Switzerland's neighbors. All four languages were recognized as official national languages in the Swiss constitution of 1938.

In 2000, 63.7 percent of the people spoke German as their first language, or mother tongue. French was spoken as a mother tongue by 20.4 percent of the Swiss population. Italian was the mother tongue of 6.5 percent, with Romansch spoken as a mother tongue by 0.5 percent. Switzerland today consists of 26 cantons, each of which has considerable local autonomy. Each of the 26 cantons has designated one or more languages as "public use languages." Several cantons have two or three public use languages. Administrative functions and education are conducted in the public use language(s) within the cantons. German is the only public use language in 17 cantons. French is the only public use language in 4 cantons, and Italian is the only public use language in 1. Both German and French are public use languages in 3 cantons, and the canton of Graubunden in southeastern Switzerland has chosen German, Italian, and Romansch as public use languages. The Swiss population is divided nearly evenly between Roman Catholics and Protestants. About 48 percent of the Swiss people are Roman Catholics and 40 percent are Protestants.

Switzerland's neighbors are Austria and Liechtenstein to the east, Germany to the north, France to the west, and Italy to the south. Switzerland's boundaries follow a combination of natural features and historical divisions between medieval societies. The Rhine River rises in Switzerland and flows northwestward, forming most of the boundary between Switzerland and Liechenstein and much of the boundary between Switzerland and Austria. The Rhine empties into Lake Constance, within which the tripoint between Switzerland, Austria, and Germany is located. It leaves Lake Constance at the western end of the lake and flows westward, forming much of the boundary between Switzerland and Germany. However, in a few places Swiss territory extends north of the Rhine. The tripoint between Switzerland, Germany, and France is located near the Swiss city of Basel, where the Rhine turns northwestward.

The boundary between Switzerland and France trends in a generally southwestward direction from Basel to Geneva. This boundary represents the historic dividing line between the Swiss cantons of Basel, Jura, Neuchatel, and Vaud and the French regions of Burgundy and Savoy. The city of Geneva at the western end of Switzerland is surrounded nearly completely by French territory. The boundary then turns eastward to Lake Geneva. From the east end of Lake Geneva, the boundary consists of numerous straight-line segments extending southward between the Swiss canton of Valais and French territory until it reaches the tripoint between Switzerland, France, and Italy. The boundary between Switzerland and Italy includes both straight-line segments and drainage divides. Much of this boundary is located in mountainous and sparsely populated areas. However, some of it extends through more populated areas around Lake Lugano. This lake forms part of the boundary, although a small area of the Swiss canton of Ticino, known as Mendricio, is located south of the lake and is unconnected with the rest of Switzerland by land.

HISTORICAL CONTEXT

Present-day Switzerland originated as the Old Swiss Confederacy in 1291, when leaders of three rural areas in the central Alps—Uri, Schwyz, and Unterwalden—agreed to provide military assistance to one another in the event any of them were attacked. During the 14th century, the cantons of Zug and Glarus and the cities of Zurich, Berne, and Lucerne affiliated themselves with the Old Swiss Confederacy, which expanded to 13 members by 1513. Swiss independence was guaranteed as part of the Treaty of Westphalia in 1648. The remaining cantons were added to Switzerland between 1803 and 1815.

In 1798, France invaded and conquered Switzerland. After the Napoleonic Wars ended with the defeat of France and the end of French control of Central Europe, the Congress of Vienna established and recognized Switzerland as an independent state. In general, the boundaries between Switzerland and its neighbors as established during the Congress of Vienna remain in place today. However, at the time of the Congress of Vienna neither Italy nor Germany were united politically. Thus Switzerland's boundaries were delineated through agreements with individual political units that would later become part of Italy or Germany. Later treaties between Switzerland and Italy and between Switzerland and Germany reaffirmed the boundary agreements. The boundaries between Switzerland and its neighbors have been adjusted slightly through later agreements. The Swiss-Italian border has been modified in order to promote "administrative convenience"—for example, to facilitate the construction of railroads, highways, and reservoirs in such a way as to prevent these features from crossing the boundary.

In recognizing Swiss independence, the Congress of Vienna also guaranteed Swiss neutrality. The Swiss have not been involved in any war since 1815. Switzerland remained neutral during World War I and World War II. It did not join the United Nations until 2002 and has not joined either NATO or the European Union.

In large part because of its long history of neutrality, Switzerland has long been home to the headquarters of many international organizations. For example, Geneva was the headquarters of the League of Nations after World War I before its dissolution shortly before World War II. Although Switzerland is not a member of the United Nations, several UN agencies, including the World Health Organization, are headquartered in Geneva. Influential international nongovernmental agencies such as the International Red Cross (whose flag is the inverse of the Swiss flag) and the International Olympic Committee are also based in Geneva. Swiss neutrality has encouraged the growth of the Swiss banking industry, whose stability has encouraged numerous foreign deposits.

CONTEMPORARY ISSUES

With minor exceptions, Switzerland's boundaries have remained stable since the end of the Napoleonic Wars. Its neutrality, which is also guaranteed by the Congress of Vienna, has kept Switzerland out of the conflicts that engulfed Europe during the 19th and early 20th centuries. With the admission of Austria to the European Union in 1994, Switzerland and its tiny neighbor, Liechtenstein, came to be surrounded completely by European Union members. Since then, Switzerland has worked to coordinate its trade, economic, and other policies to conform with those of the European Union although it has yet to consider joining the European Union. Switzerland remains neutral in global affairs, although it joined the United Nations in 2002.

See also   Austria, France, Germany, Italy, Liechtenstein

Further Reading

Jessica Dacey. "Swiss seek multilingual equilibrium." *Guardian Weekly*, August 7, 2009, http://www.unige.ch/traduction-interpretation/recherches/groupes/elf/medias/GuardianWeekly-SwissMultilingualism.pdf.

Swissworld.org. "Neutrality and isolationism." 2001, http://www.globalstudies.gu.se/digitalAssets/1269/1269811_perspectives12.pdf.

UKRAINE

OVERVIEW

Ukraine is a former Soviet republic located in Eastern Europe. Its land area is 233,090 square miles, slightly smaller than Texas. Ukraine's population is about 46 million. About three-quarters of Ukraine's people are ethnic Ukrainians, and nearly 20 percent are ethnic Russians. Most of

Ukraine consists of low, flat land that is farmed intensively.

Ukraine shares boundaries with Moldova and Romania to the southwest, Hungary, Slovakia, and Poland to the west, Belarus to the north, and Russia to the north and east. Ukraine has a lengthy coast on the Black Sea to the south. Ukraine has two borders with Romania, and these borders are separated from each other by the boundary between Ukraine and Moldova. From the Black Sea, the Danube River forms the boundary between Ukraine and Romania westward and upstream to the confluence with the Danube and its tributary, the Prut River. The southern tripoint between Ukraine, Romania, and Moldova is located near this confluence. The boundary between Ukraine and Moldova extends northward from this tripoint to the Dniester River. It follows the Dniester upstream and northwestwards to a point near the Moldovan town of Ocnita. From this point, the boundary turns westward to the northern tripoint between Ukraine, Moldova, and Romania on the Prut River.

The boundary between Ukraine and Romania continues westward to the tripoint between Ukraine, Romania, and Slovakia. Much of this boundary follows short straight-line segments, but the western portion of the boundary follows the Tisza River. The Tisza also forms most of the short boundary between Ukraine and Hungary, although a small section of Hungarian territory is located north of the Tisza. The tripoint between Ukraine, Hungary, and Slovakia is located on the Tisza near the Ukrainian village of Solomonovo. From that tripoint, the boundary between Ukraine and Slovakia follows short straight-line segments north-northeastward

to the tripoint between Ukraine and Poland. The boundary between Ukraine and Poland continues in a northeasterly direction, passing just west of the historically significant Ukrainian city of L'viv, to the tripoint between Ukraine, Poland, and Belarus near the edge of Ukraine's Sackij National Park.

At this tripoint, Ukraine's border with Belarus extends in a generally eastward direction. It follows a large number of short straight-line segments, and it was drawn with the intention of separating Ukrainian-majority communities to the south and Belarusian-majority communities to the north. This boundary passes a few miles north of Chernobyl, which was the scene of the worst nuclear accident in world history in 1986.

Ukraine's longest boundary is its boundary with Russia. This boundary is also a cultural boundary, separating ethnic Ukrainians and ethnic Russians. From the tripoint between Ukraine, Russia, and Belarus, it extends eastward to a point north of the village of Seredyna-Buda. It then turns in a southeasterly direction, passing a few miles northeast of Ukraine's second-largest city of Kharkiv. Near the city of Luhansk, it turns southwestward to the Sea of Azov, which is an arm of the Black Sea. Ukrainian territory includes the Crimean Peninsula, which extends southward into the Black Sea. The eastern portion of the Crimean Peninsula is only three miles west of Russian territory, nearly enclosing the Sea of Azov and nearly separating it from the Black Sea.

HISTORICAL CONTEXT

Archaeologists have found evidence of human habitation in present-day Ukraine dating back about 30,000 years. The Black Sea coast of Ukraine was settled and governed by various tribes until the ninth century AD, when the Kievan Rus culture arose. The Kievan Rus state was centered on Ukraine's modern capital city of Kiev, and at its height it included much of present-day Ukraine, Belarus, and western Russia. The Kievan Rus Empire was toppled by Mongol invasions during the 13th century.

After the Mongols were expelled, present-day Ukraine was contested among various foreign powers. It became part of the Grand Duchy of Lithuania in the late 14th century. In 1569, the Grand Duchy was merged with Poland to become the Polish-Lithuanian Commonwealth. In the late 18th century, Poland was partitioned among the major European powers. Western Ukraine became part of the Austro-Hungarian Empire while eastern Ukraine became absorbed into the Russian Empire. This division of Ukraine between the two empires continues to affect Ukrainian politics.

After World War I and the Russian Revolution, eastern Ukraine became part of the Soviet Union while western Ukraine was attached to Poland. Eastern Ukraine became the Ukrainian Soviet Socialist Republic, which was one of the founding republics of the Soviet Union in 1922. Forced collectivization of agriculture in the 1930s resulted in the deaths of several million Ukrainian nationals. In 1939, a secret agreement between the Soviet Union and Nazi Germany divided Poland and Ukraine into Soviet and German spheres of influence. Western Ukraine was part of the Soviet sphere of influence, and the Soviets incorporated it into the Ukrainian

Soviet Socialist Republic. During nearly seven decades of communist rule, the government of the Soviet Union encouraged ethnic Russians to move to Ukraine

In 1990, Ukraine's parliament adopted a Declaration of State Sovereignty of Ukraine. The declaration included provisions calling for economic independence and the priority of Ukrainian law over Soviet law within Ukraine. The government of the Soviet Union rejected the declaration. However, the Soviet Union collapsed in 1991, and Ukraine declared its independence. A large majority of Ukraine's voters expressed support for Ukrainian independence in a referendum held in December 1991. After several years of economic decline associated with the transition from a planned economy to a market economy, Ukraine became more prosperous and has seen steady economic growth.

The historical division of Ukraine between its western and eastern components has affected Ukraine's politics since independence. Many western Ukrainians, who live in areas connected historically with Austria-Hungary and Poland, have favored closer ties with Central and Western Europe. On the other hand, eastern Ukrainians favored closer ties with Russia and the former Soviet Union. These differences have also affected the extent to which Ukraine should form closer ties with the European Union.

This division has been reflected in presidential elections in Ukraine, especially in the election of 2004. The leading candidates were the current prime minister, Viktor Yanukovych, and former prime minister and opposition leader Viktor Yushchenko. Yanukovych, who favored closer ties with Russia, was supported by Russian president

Vladimir Putin, whereas the pro-Western Yushchenko was supported by the European Union and the United States. On November 21, the government announced that Yanukovych won the election by a margin of 49.46 to 46.69 percent of the vote. However, international observers identified election fraud, including ballot box stuffing and unexplained large increases in voter turnout in areas supporting Yanukovych. After the government announced that Yanukovych had been elected, concerns about the legitimacy of the outcome led to protests, strikes, and acts of civil disobedience. These protests became known as the "Orange Revolution" because Yushchenko's supporters had used the color orange in the campaign. In early December, the Ukrainian Supreme Court ordered a repeat of the runoff election. The second runoff took place on December 26, and Yushchenko won with 52 percent of the vote to 44 percent for Yanukovych.

The distribution of votes within Ukraine showed not only the geographic divisions between pro-Western supporters of Yushchenko and pro-Russian supporters of Yanukovych, but it also illustrated long-standing, historical divisions within Ukraine. Yushchenko's candidacy was strongest in northern and western Ukraine. A majority of people in this region are Ukrainian Orthodox or Roman Catholics, and the area has close historical ties to Poland. Yanukovych ran best in southern and eastern Ukraine. In this part of the country, the percentage of people of Russian ancestry is higher, and more people adhere to the Russian Orthodox Church. A similar pattern prevailed in the 2009 election, in which Yanukovych was returned to the presidency.

CONTEMPORARY ISSUES

Ukraine's boundaries are stable. However, Ukraine in recent years has dealt with some issues involving nearby countries. Ukraine and Romania have disagreed about the status of the Danube River, which forms their boundary west of the Black Sea. Historically, the lower reaches of the Danube north of its main channel were navigable through what is now southwestern Ukraine. However, the channel silted, and by the 1960s the northern channel was no longer navigable. A canal allowing navigation from the Danube directly into the Black Sea through Ukraine was proposed by Ukraine's government in 2004. However, the United States and other countries opposed the construction of the proposed Bystroye Canal on the grounds that its construction would cause substantial environmental degradation in the ecologically sensitive region near the Black Sea coast. Romania has proposed to divert the waters of the Danube southward, making navigation on the lower Danube through Ukraine impossible even if the Bystroye Canal was to be completed and opened.

Elsewhere, Ukraine and Russia had disagreed over the location of the maritime boundary between them in the Sea of Azov. However, the two countries agreed on this maritime boundary in 2007. The boundary between Ukraine and Belarus, parts of which had not been delineated precisely, was agreed upon by an agreement signed between the two countries in 2009.

See also Belarus, Hungary, Moldova, Poland, Romania, Russia, Slovakia

Further Reading

Adrian Karatnycky. "Ukraine's Orange Revolution." *Foreign Affairs*, 84 (2005), pp. 35–52.

Serhiy Solodky. "The European Union may help Ukraine by providing a membership perspective." *Eastern Partnership Community*, June 17, 2012, http://www.easternpartnership.org/community/debate/european-union-may-help-ukraine-providing-membership-perspective.

World Wildlife Federation. "WWF initiates dialogue with Ukrainian authorities on Bystroye Canal." December 18, 2009, http://wwf.panda.org/what_we_do/where_we_work/black_sea_basin/danube_carpathian/news/?184821/WWF-initiates-dialogue-with-Ukrainian-authorities-on-Bystroye-Canal.

UNITED KINGDOM

OVERVIEW

The United Kingdom of Great Britain and Northern Island occupies the island of Great Britain, the northeastern part of the island of Ireland, and smaller nearby islands off the northwestern coast of mainland Europe. The islands are located in the northeastern Atlantic Ocean, with the North Sea to the east, the Irish Sea separating Great Britain and Ireland, and the English Channel to the south. The total land area of the United Kingdom is 94,060 square miles, slightly smaller than Michigan. Its total population is about 64 million.

The United Kingdom consists of four provinces. England, which occupies most of the southern part of the island of Great Britain, is about 50,000 square miles in land area. It has a population of about 52 million, more than 80 percent of the country's total population. Scotland, which occupies the northern third of Great Britain and about 800 offshore islands, has a land area of about 30,000 square miles and a population of about 5.5 million. Wales, which is located along the west coast of the island, has a land area of about 8,000 square miles and a population of 3 million. The fourth component, Northern Ireland, is located on the island of Ireland with a land area of approximately 5,000 square miles and about 1.8 million people.

The United Kingdom's only land border is with the Republic of Ireland. This boundary separates 6 of the 32 traditional counties of historic Ireland from the other 26 that belong to the Republic of Ireland. The boundaries dividing the traditional counties of Ireland from one another date back to the Middle Ages. Many of the boundaries separating Northern Ireland from the Republic of Ireland follow rivers or lakes. The boundary begins at Lough Foyle, which is an inlet of the Atlantic Ocean at the northern end of the island. From the southern shore of Lough Foyle, it follows the River Foyle southwestward for part of its length. Near the shore of Lower Lough Erne, the boundary turns eastward. It is complex but extends in a generally eastward direction to the Carlingford Lough, which is an arm of the Irish Sea. By water, the United Kingdom is separated from France on the European mainland by the English Channel, which is about 20 miles wide at its narrowest point.

HISTORICAL CONTEXT

The British Isles have been settled for at least 30,000 years. Throughout recorded

UNITED KINGDOM

North Atlantic
Ocean

ORKNEY ISLANDS
Mainland

Lewis with Harris

North Uist

South Uist

Skye

HEBRIDES

Mull

Islay

•Inverness

Aberdeen•

SCOTLAND

•Saint Andrews

•Edinburgh

Glasgow

Arran

North
Sea

U.K.

NORTHERN Belfast
IRELAND *Isle of Man (U.K.)*

IRELAND

•Middlesbrough

York•

•Preston

Liverpool•

•Grimsby

•Nottingham

Stafford•

ENGLAND

•Norwich

Aberystwyth•

Northampton•

•Cambridge

WALES

•Oxford

London★

•Bristol

Dover•

•Winchester

BELGIUM

Southampton•

*Celtic
Sea*

Exeter•

•Plymouth

English Channel

Alderney
(U.K.)

FRANCE

N

0   50   100 km
0   50   100 mi

history, the islands have seen successive waves of migration from continental Europe. All of these migrant populations have influenced the contemporary English language and the culture of the United Kingdom.

Celtic peoples occupied Great Britain when the Roman Empire conquered much of the southern and eastern portions of the island in AD 43. The Romans remained in control of this area, which they named Britannia, until the fifth century AD. During the sixth and seventh centuries, the Angles, Saxons, and Jutes from present-day Germany and Denmark moved across the North Sea into Great Britain, and the original Celtic inhabitants of the island were driven westward into Wales. The Angles, Saxons, and Jutes formed several kingdoms in what is now southern and eastern England. Viking raiders began to plunder the coasts of northern England in AD 793 and established several kingdoms along the northeastern coast. Viking raids continued intermittently over the next two centuries.

Southern Great Britain was first unified politically by the Kingdom of England, which traces its history to AD 927 and included much of present-day England and Wales. In 1066, Norman invaders from Normandy in present-day northern France invaded England and gained control of the island, initiating political unity within England that has been maintained ever since. Wales was formally incorporated into the English state in 1535.

Scotland was settled originally by Celtic tribes. The two largest tribes were the Picts, who are believed to have moved to Scotland from Ireland during and after the Roman occupation of Great Britain, and the Gaels. These peoples became

amalgamated into the Scottish nation before the 10th century AD. During the early Middle Ages, the Kingdom of the Picts governed much of Scotland. The Kingdom of the Picts evolved eventually into the Kingdom of Alba and eventually into the Kingdom of Scotland. England and Scotland fought numerous wars and battles over the next thousand years. The crowns of England and Scotland were united in 1603 with the accession of James VI to the English throne as James I. The two kingdoms were united formally via the Act of Union in 1707.

During the Protestant Reformation, the Church of England (today's Episcopalian, or Anglican, Church) became the established church in England, while Ireland remained predominantly Roman Catholic. King Henry VIII of England, a Protestant, attempted to conquer Ireland in the 16th century. The conquest was completed in 1603. After Irish Catholics recaptured Ireland in 1641, the English government under the Puritan Oliver Cromwell reconquered Ireland between 1649 and 1653. Thus Ireland became part of the United Kingdom and the British Empire. The British government encouraged Protestants to move from Scotland and England into Ireland. Most of the migrants from Great Britain settled in the province of Ulster in northeastern Ireland. As a result, most of Ulster had a Protestant majority by the 18th century.

The British Parliament enacted the Act of Union in 1801, creating the United Kingdom of Great Britain and Ireland. The Irish Parliament ratified the Act of Union. However, at that time Roman Catholics in Ireland were disenfranchised, and the Irish Parliament had no Roman Catholic members. Many Roman

Catholic Irish agitated for Irish independence throughout the 19th century. Civil war broke out between 1916 and 1921. In 1922, Ireland was separated into the Catholic-majority Irish Free State, which eventually became the Republic of Ireland, and Protestant-majority Northern Ireland.

CONTEMPORARY ISSUES

The status of Northern Ireland remains a major issue of contention between the United Kingdom and Ireland. During the 19th and early 20th centuries, supporters of Irish independence advocated independence for the entire island. Many Protestants in Northern Ireland supported remaining part of the United Kingdom, and the Protestant-majority counties of Ulster remained part of the United Kingdom. Ireland continued to claim sovereignty over Northern Ireland until it dropped this claim as a part of the Belfast Agreement between the United Kingdom and the Republic of Ireland in 1998. According to the Belfast Agreement, Northern Ireland could become part of the Republic of Ireland if union between Northern Ireland and the Republic of Ireland was supported by a majority of voters in Northern Ireland.

The status of Scotland has also been contested. Since the 1970s, the Scottish Nationalist Party (SNP) has gained increasing influence in Scotland's politics. Some members of the SNP have argued for outright independence. They have argued that an independent Scotland would prosper as a member of the European Union, noting that Denmark, Finland, and other EU members had been successful members of the EU despite lower populations and fewer resources than Scotland itself.

In 1997, the government of the United Kingdom granted Scotland and Wales increased autonomy over local affairs. However, the SNP continues to promote independence. The SNP obtained a majority of seats in the Scottish Parliament in 2011, and the new SNP government has promised to hold a referendum on Scottish independence.

Extraterritorial claims on the part of the United Kingdom in Gibraltar and the Falkland Islands have been disputed by Spain and Argentina, respectively. In 1982, war occurred between the United Kingdom and Argentina after Argentina invaded the Falkland Islands, which are located in the South Atlantic Ocean about 300 miles east of the Argentine mainland. British forces retook the islands and reasserted sovereignty over the Falklands, but Argentina continues to claim sovereignty over the islands.

See also   Ireland

Further Reading

Rebecca Fraser. *The story of Britain: From the Romans to the present.* New York: W. W. Norton, 2003.

Christopher Harvie. *Scotland and nationalism.* London: Routledge, 2004.

William Mulligan and Brendan Simms (eds.). *The primacy of foreign policy in British history, 1660–2000: How strategic concerns shaped modern Britain.* New York: Palgrave Macmillan, 2010.

VATICAN CITY

OVERVIEW

Vatican City is the world's smallest independent country. Vatican City is an enclave

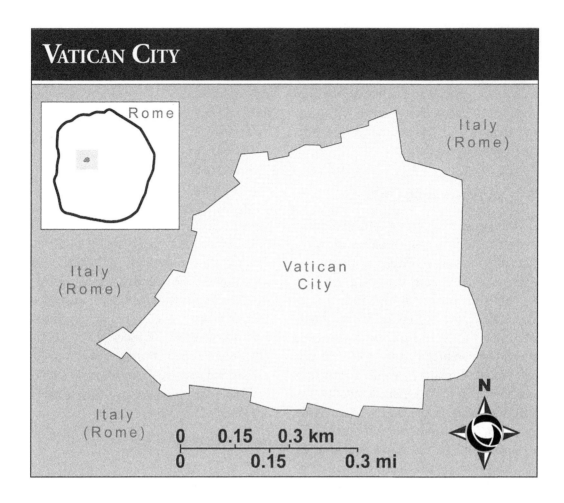

of about 110 acres, or 0.17 square miles, within the city of Rome, Italy. Its permanent population is about 800. Vatican City includes the headquarters of the Roman Catholic Church. The pope is sovereign over Vatican City. It includes St. Peter's Basilica, the Sistine Chapel, and the Apostolic Palace, which serves as the pope's official residence.

HISTORICAL CONTEXT

In AD 325, the Roman emperor Constantine made Christianity the official religion of the Roman Empire. Rome became the seat of the papacy and has held this distinction ever since, except for a period in the 14th century when the pope's seat was moved to Avignon in present-day France.

In 791, Charlemagne granted the pope secular political authority over Rome and other areas of present-day central Italy. This territory came to be known as the Papal States. The Papal States became part of reunified Italy in the 1860s. Italy took control of Rome in 1870, and Rome became the capital of the reunified Italian state. The Roman Catholic Church continued to claim temporal authority over

Rome and the Papal States into the 20th century, although such claims were only symbolic.

The question of temporal sovereignty over Rome and the Papal States continued until Italy and the Vatican signed the Lateran Accords in 1929. Under terms of the Lateran Accords, Italy recognized the temporal sovereignty of the Church over Vatican City. The Church formally relinquished temporal control over the rest of Rome and the Papal States. In exchange, Italy agreed to recognize the primacy of the Roman Catholic Church throughout the country.

See also Italy

Further Reading

Michael Collins. *The Vatican.* London: DK Adult, 2011.

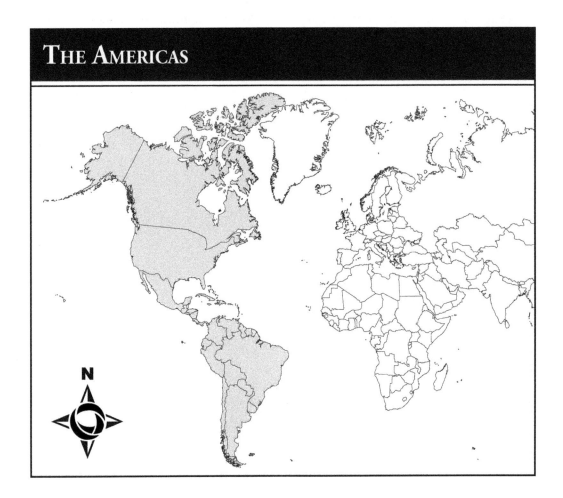

CHAPTER 2

THE AMERICAS

This chapter includes vignettes on those states located in and near the continents of North America and South America. These are the only continents located in the Western Hemisphere; the other inhabited continents of the world comprise the Eastern Hemisphere. The physical environments, economies, cultures, and political systems of the Americas are highly diverse. The landmass of North America and South America, which are connected by the narrow Isthmus of Panama, extends from north of the Arctic Circle to the southernmost inhabited places in the world. The region includes the longest and second-highest mountain range in the world, its largest tropical rainforest, virtually rainless deserts, and some of the wettest places on earth. The United States has dominated the global economy for the past century, whereas the Americas also include some of the poorest and least developed areas in the world.

Despite this diversity, the Americas have some important communalities. Before 1500, both continents were inhabited by indigenous peoples whose ancestors migrated from Asia at least 10,000 years ago. Europeans began to explore, colonize, and settle North and South America in the 16th century. The arrival of Europeans devastated the Native American population.

Millions died from European diseases or from famine and starvation. Many others were sold into slavery or were displaced from their ancestral lands by Europeans anxious to obtain land and/or access to mineral resources. Despite the wholesale slaughter and displacement of these Native American nations, many people of full or partial Native American ancestry continue to live in North, Central, and South America. Native Americans make up the majority of the populations of several countries today.

All of the now-independent countries of the Americas were European colonies at various times between the 16th and the 19th centuries. European colonizers were anxious to obtain access to mineral resources and to grow crops for export to Europe. Many of these crops were grown on plantations. Mining and plantation agriculture required large labor forces. At first, Europeans attempted to force Native Americans into slavery to provide this labor, but many died from overwork or exposure and others fled to avoid enslavement. The Europeans then turned to Africa as a source of slave labor, and over more than 200 years, millions of Africans were captured, transported to the Americas, and sold into slavery. Their descendants form a population majority in some countries, especially in the Caribbean, and significant population minorities in many other countries.

In contrast to Africa and Asia, most countries on the mainlands of North, Central, and South America became independent states before 1900. Some countries, especially small islands in the Caribbean, remained under European colonial rule until after World War II. A few places within the Western Hemisphere, including Puerto Rico, Guadeloupe, Martinique, and French Guiana, remain under colonial rule today.

Frequently, geographers divide the Americas between Latin America, the Caribbean region, and North America. Latin America refers to those countries in mainland South America and Central America that have a history of Spanish or Portuguese colonial rule. This region extends from Mexico southward to Argentina and Chile. It does not include the countries of Guyana, Suriname, and Belize. These countries were not Spanish or Portuguese colonies and have long had important trading links with the Caribbean islands, so they are generally included into the Caribbean region rather than with the other mainland countries. North America includes only two countries, the United States and Canada.

Latin America extends from the U.S.-Mexico border south to Tierra del Fuego. Given this large land area, and given its considerable extent from north to south, it is not surprising that the environment of Latin America is very diverse. The human population of the Americas before the voyages of Columbus has been estimated at between 10 million and 100 million. However, most anthropologists agree that about 90 percent of the pre-Colombian population of the Americas lived in present-day Latin

America and the Caribbean; only about 10 percent are believed to have lived in what is now the United States and Canada.

Before the Spanish and Portuguese conquest, Latin America was the home of several advanced civilizations, including the Maya, Aztec, and Inca. These cultural traditions remain influential in present-day Latin America. The Mayan civilization was centered in the Yucatan Peninsula and nearby portions of present-day southeastern Mexico and northern Central America. Between AD 250 and 900, the Mayans ruled this area while trading with other cultures in the Caribbean islands and on the mainland. The Mayans were well-known for their intellectual and artistic achievements, including accurate predictions of the dates of eclipses and other astronomical observations. The classic Maya civilization collapsed approximately AD 900, for unknown reasons. Some anthropologists have speculated that the collapse of the Mayan civilization was due to a long-term drought that made it impossible to grow enough food to feed the population.

Today, an estimated 8 million descendants of the Maya live in southern Mexico, Guatemala, Belize, El Salvador, and Honduras. Many of these people speak a Mayan language as their first language, learning Spanish as a second language. During the period of Spanish rule, and into the 20th century, the use of Mayan and other indigenous languages was discouraged or forbidden in these countries and in many other parts of Latin America. Today, these languages are being recognized and revived.

The Aztecs were the dominant civilization in present-day central and southern Mexico at the time of Spanish conquest in the early 16th century. The Aztec capital,

Tenochtitlan, was located near the site of Mexico City today. The population of the Valley of Mexico, which was the center of the Aztec empire, is believed to have declined by as much as 80 to 90 percent after the Spanish arrived. The Inca Empire dominated northwestern South America at the time of Spanish conquest. The Incas controlled much of present-day Ecuador, Peru, Bolivia, and northern Chile. Like the Aztecs, many people in Inca-controlled territory died of exposure to smallpox and other European diseases shortly after the Spanish conquered the area.

During the late 15th century, Portuguese explorers sailed down the African coast in an effort to reach India. In 1492, Christopher Columbus attempted to sail west to reach East Asia, and in doing so he "discovered" North and South America. Recognition that there were new lands to explore and conquer excited Europeans and their rulers.

Spain and Portugal negotiated the Treaty of Tordesillas in 1494. The Treaty of Tordesillas, which was negotiated under the supervision of Pope Alexander VI, was an agreement between Spain and Portugal over control of "newly discovered" territories. Spain and Portugal agreed to divide "newly discovered" lands along a line 370 leagues west of the Cape Verde Islands. This line became known as the Line of Demarcation. Newly discovered lands west of the Line of Demarcation would belong to Spain, and those lands east of the Line of Demarcation would belong to Portugal. Not surprisingly, the Treaty of Tordesillas was not accepted by other European powers such as France, the Netherlands, or Britain. However, the treaty paved the way for Spain to become the dominant colonial power in Latin America. The exception was Brazil, part of which is located east of the Line of Demarcation and which became a Portuguese colony.

Spanish and Portuguese explorers quickly established settlements in what would become Latin America. The Spanish and Portuguese were motivated by a search for gold, silver, and other precious metals. They believed that wealth was determined on the basis of how much gold and silver one possessed. Because they were successful in developing gold and silver mines in Latin America and exporting these metals to Europe, they claimed to be the wealthiest countries in the world. By 1600, many of the cities of Latin America were already well established and thriving. Cities located near mines, such as Mexico City, and port cities such as Veracruz, Mexico, and Cartagena, Colombia, from which gold and silver were transported by sea to Europe, were especially large and prosperous.

The Caribbean islands can be divided into two major groups, the Greater Antilles and the Lesser Antilles. The Greater Antilles are the largest and most populous islands in the region, and they include Cuba, Hispaniola, Puerto Rico, and Jamaica. The Lesser Antilles include several groups of smaller islands. The Leeward and Windward Islands are located to the east of the Greater Antilles. The Lesser Antilles also include several islands located near the coast of South America, including Aruba and Curacao. The population of the Caribbean comes from a wide variety of origins including North and South America, Africa, Europe, and Asia. The cultures of the various Caribbean islands and countries reflect this very diverse population history.

Population densities vary considerably throughout the region. Some areas of the Caribbean have dense populations; others, including the inland areas of countries on the mainland, are very sparsely populated.

Anthropologists believe that the first human inhabitants of the Caribbean islands were Arawaks who moved northward from South America by boat between 1,500 and 2,000 years ago. The Arawaks fished, hunted, and grew corn, cassava, and vegetables. An estimated 100,000 to 1 million Arawaks are believed to have lived in Hispaniola, with many others in Jamaica and Puerto Rico, when the Spanish arrived in the late 15th century. Within 30 years, as many as 90 percent of the Arawaks had died, primarily from exposure to European diseases to which they had no immunity.

Centuries after the Arawaks arrived, but before the arrival of Europeans, the Caribs also moved northward from the South American mainland. By the time of Spanish conquest, the more warlike Caribs had displaced the Arawaks from the Lesser Antilles. Large numbers of Caribs were also killed by the Spanish or died from European diseases. However, a few people of primarily Carib ancestry still live in the Lesser Antilles, particularly on the island of Dominica.

European colonists quickly recognized that the tropical climate and fertile soils of many areas in the Caribbean region were highly suitable for the cultivation of sugarcane and other lucrative tropical crops. For several centuries, slaves provided the labor whereas European colonists owned the land. Initially, Europeans attempted to enslave the indigenous Arawaks and Caribs. After most of the indigenous people died, they began to import slaves from

Africa to provide labor for sugar plantations and other agricultural enterprises. Descendants of African slaves make up a majority of the population in several Caribbean countries, notably those such as Jamaica and Barbados with long histories of sugar production on slave-worked plantations.

Slavery was abolished throughout Europe and its colonies in the 19th century. In order to ensure themselves of a continued labor supply, Caribbean planters and colonial leaders began importing workers from various parts of South Asia as agricultural laborers. Many workers from India, which was then a British colony, moved to British colonies in the Caribbean, including Trinidad and Guyana. The Dutch imported workers from present-day Java to their colony of Surinam (present-day Suriname). Today, Asians make up a substantial percentage of the population of these now-independent countries.

Over the past hundred years, many people from various parts of the Caribbean have left the islands. Most have moved to the United States, Canada, or Europe in search of jobs and economic opportunities. Others, including Cubans and Haitians, left the Caribbean as political refugees. The out-migration of Caribbean natives to other parts of the world has been called the "Caribbean diaspora." Many Caribbean natives who have left their home countries move to their homelands' current or former colonial powers. For example, large numbers of Jamaicans now live in the United Kingdom, while many natives of Suriname live in the Netherlands. Many of those leaving the Caribbean are well educated. It has been estimated that as many as 80 percent of persons born in Jamaica and Haiti who hold college degrees live abroad.

In the 20th century, North America emerged as the most prosperous region in the entire world, supplanting Europe. In contrast to Renaissance and post-Renaissance Europe, North America contained vast quantities of productive agriculture and abundant natural resources. The United States was the first former British colony to become an independent state when it declared independence in 1776. Over the course of the 19th century, the United States expanded to take control of its current territory.

After most of the countries of mainland South and Central America became independent of Spain and Portugal in the early 19th century, the United States announced the Monroe Doctrine in 1823. The purpose of the Monroe Doctrine was to make clear to European powers that the Americas were no longer open to further European colonization. U.S. policy would guarantee independence to independent countries in North, Central, and South America. In effect, the Monroe Doctrine was a statement that the United States was the strongest power in the Western Hemisphere. Monroe went on to declare that any effort on the part of European powers to threaten the independence of newly independent countries in the Western Hemisphere would be regarded as a threat to the United States, thereby justifying U.S. intervention as necessary. The Monroe Doctrine has undergirded U.S. policy toward Latin America and the Caribbean countries ever since.

ANTIGUA AND BARBUDA

OVERVIEW

Antigua and Barbuda is located in the northern Leeward Islands in the Caribbean Sea. The country consists of the main island of Antigua and several smaller islands, including the island of Barbuda. The total land area of Antigua and Barbuda is 170 square miles, slightly more than twice the size of the District of Columbia. The population is about 82,000. More than 95 percent of the country's people live on Antigua, which contains about two-thirds of the country's land area.

Antigua and Barbuda's closest island neighbors are the French colonies of Montserrat to the southwest and Guadeloupe to the south. The closest independent country is St. Kitts and Nevis, which is located about 50 miles west of the island of Antigua. Antigua is about 400 miles east of Puerto Rico and about 600 miles north of the coast of Venezuela.

HISTORICAL CONTEXT

Columbus sighted Antigua during his second voyage to the Americas in 1493. The first permanent European settlement was established by the English in 1632. Sugar production quickly became the mainstay of Antigua's economy. Thousands of slaves from West Africa were imported to work on sugar plantations. Today, about 90 percent of the residents of Antigua and Barbuda are of African origin. The islands remained under British colonial rule until 1981, when they became an independent country and a part of the British Commonwealth.

Given its location close to Puerto Rico and the U.S. Virgin Islands, some concerns have been raised about narcotics trafficking and money laundering in Antigua and Barbuda. Antigua and Barbuda and the United States have signed several agreements intended to address these ongoing issues. Another recent

ANTIGUA AND BARBUDA

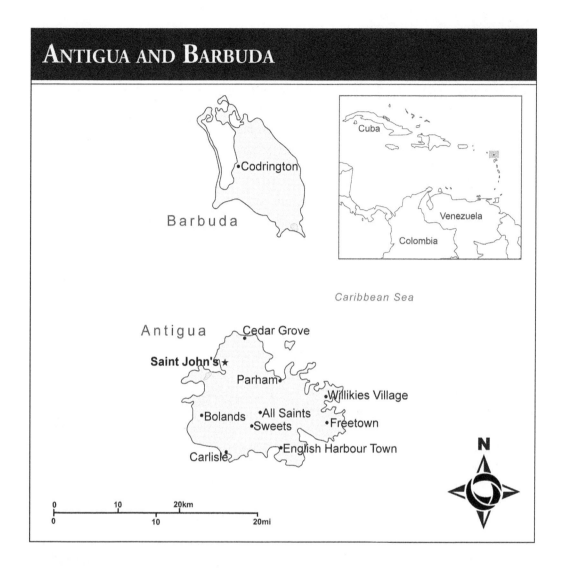

issue has involved online betting sites. The United States banned U.S. banks and credit card firms from making payments to online betting sites outside the United States, and Antigua and Barbuda claimed that this ban violated international trade norms as promoted by the World Trade Organization.

Further Reading

BBC News. "Antigua hits back at US on gaming." June 21, 2007, http://news.bbc.co.uk/2/hi/business/6226930.stm.

ARGENTINA

OVERVIEW

The Argentine Republic is located in southeastern South America. It is the second-largest country by land area in South America, the eighth-largest country by land area in the world, and the third-largest Spanish-speaking country by land area in the world. Argentina has a land area of 1,068,302 square miles, making it almost as twice as large as Alaska. Its population

ARGENTINA

Bolivia

Paraguay

Salta•

San Miguel
de Tucuman•

Formosa•

Resistencia•

•Posadas

Santo Tome•

Catamarca•

La Ribja•

Brazil

Pacific
Ocean

Rio
Parana

Cordoba• Santa Fe•

San Juan•

•Parana

Mendoza•

•Resario

Uruguay

Mercedes• Venado•
Tuerto

Buenos Aires

San Rafael•

Realico•

La Plata•

Rio de la Plata

Santa Rosa• Argentina

Chile

Bahia
•Blanca

•Mar del Plata

Zapala•   •Neuquen

Viedma

•San Carlos de Bariloche

Rawson•

Atlantic
Ocean

•Comodoro Rivadavia

Las Heras

•Puerto Deseado

•Puerto Santa Cruz

•Rio Gallegos

Falkland
Islands

N

0   200   400km
0   200   400mi

•Ushuaia

Tierra del
Fuego

is about 40 million. Argentina and Chile, along sometimes with other parts of southern South America, are referred to often as the "Southern Cone" given their shape on the map.

Argentina's neighbors are Chile to the west and south, Bolivia and Paraguay to the north, and Brazil and Uruguay to the northeast. Argentina has a long coastline on the Atlantic Ocean to the east. The boundary between Argentina and Chile follows the crest of the Andes Mountains. Mount Aconcagua, the highest mountain in South America, is located along this boundary. The Andes represent the boundary between the two countries southward to the 52nd parallel of south latitude, which becomes part of the southern boundary until it extends southeastward to the Atlantic. The boundary between Argentina and Chile also divides the island of Tierra del Fuego along the 68° 34′ meridian of west longitude.

To the north, the tripoint between Argentina, Chile, and Bolivia is located at the summit of Cerro Zapaleri in the Andes. From this tripoint, the boundary between Argentina and Bolivia follows a complex series of straight lines northeastwards through the Andes. Near the Bolivian town of Entre Rios, the boundary begins to trend eastward and slightly southward along the Porongal and Bermejo rivers to the 22nd parallel of south latitude. The boundary continues along the 22nd parallel to the Pilcomayo River, which forms the boundary between the two countries westward to the tripoint between Argentina, Bolivia, and Paraguay. The boundary between Argentina and Paraguay continues along the Pilcomayo River to its confluence with the Paraguay River, and hence along the Paraguay River to its confluence with the

Rio Parana. The boundary follows the Rio Parana upstream to its confluence with its tributary, the Iguazu River. This confluence is the tripoint between Argentina, Paraguay, and Brazil.

The Iguazu River forms the western portion of the boundary between Argentina and Brazil. The boundary includes a short series of geometric lines between the Iguazu and the drainage basin of the Uruguay River. The boundary then reaches the Pepiri-Guazu River and follows the Pepiri-Guazu southward to its confluence with the Uruguay River. The boundary then follows the Uruguay past its confluence with the Quaraí River. This confluence is the tripoint between Argentina, Brazil, and Uruguay. From this confluence the boundary between Argentina and Uruguay follows the Uruguay River southward until its mouth into the Rio de la Plata.

HISTORICAL BACKGROUND

Anthropologists believe that present-day Argentina was settled relatively sparsely by indigenous people, relative to other parts of South America, at the time the Spanish arrived. Spanish explorers sighted present-day Argentina in 1502. Buenos Aires was founded in 1536, although this settlement was abandoned in light of attacks by local Native Americans five years later. A permanent Spanish settlement was established on the same site in 1580. Given its location near the mouth of the Rio de la Plata, Buenos Aires soon became developed as a port and trading center.

In 1776, Spain established the Viceroyalty de la Plata, with its administrative headquarters at Buenos Aires. The Viceroyalty included the northern two-thirds of present-day Argentina, all of present-day Paraguay and Uruguay, and parts of present-day Bolivia and Chile. Independence efforts occurred throughout South America beginning in 1810, and the Viceroyalty declared its independence in 1816. Argentina and Brazil went to war with each other in 1825 and 1826. The peace agreement following the war finalized the separation of Uruguay from Argentina and confirmed Uruguay's status as an independent sovereign state.

The political status of present-day Argentina remained uncertain during the middle of the 19th century. Most of the provinces of what is now northern Argentina united as the Argentine Confederation beginning in 1829. In 1853, Buenos Aires seceded from the Confederation and attempted to establish itself as an independent state. After nine years of civil war, Buenos Aires rejoined the Confederation in 1862. In the late 19th century, united Argentina extended its control southward into Patagonia in which is now the southern portion of the country.

The boundaries between Argentina and its neighbors were delineated during the 19th century. Argentina and Chile signed a treaty in 1881 through which they agreed upon their boundary. The main point of contention between the two countries was control of the Straits of Magellan along with Tierra del Fuego and other neighboring land areas. Chile, which traded extensively with Europe, sought guaranteed access to the Straits of Magellan. Both countries also claimed all of Tierra del Fuego. Under the terms of the treaty, the Straits of Magellan were neutralized, and Tierra del Fuego was divided between the two countries. Argentina and Bolivia agreed upon their boundary in 1865, with various modifications agreed upon by the two countries in several subsequent treaties.

Argentina and Paraguay experienced a series of ongoing boundary disputes during the 19th century. Both had belonged to the Viceroyalty de la Plata, and the boundaries within the Viceroyalty had not been identified clearly after it achieved independence. Argentina hoped to expand into what is now Paraguay, but the two countries agreed initially upon their boundary in 1856. In 1865, however, Argentina allied with Brazil and Uruguay against Paraguay in the War of the Triple Alliance. After Paraguay was defeated in the war, Argentina proposed to divide defeated Paraguay between itself and Brazil. Brazil did not agree to this proposal. After several years of negotiation, the two countries agreed upon their boundary in 1876.

The boundary between Argentina and Brazil was delineated by a treaty signed by the two countries in 1857. However, territory between the Iguazu and the Pepiri-Guazu rivers remained in dispute until the late 19th century. During the 1880s, the two countries agreed to have their dispute arbitrated by the United States. In 1895, U.S. President Grover Cleveland issued a decision establishing the Pepiri-Guazu as the boundary and demarcating the boundary between the drainage basins of the two rivers. The Uruguay River was recognized as the boundary between Argentina and Uruguay following Uruguay's independence in 1826.

CONTEMPORARY ISSUES

The boundaries between Argentina and its neighbors have been largely stable since the late 19th century. However, several issues regarding Argentina's boundaries remain.

For nearly 200 years, Argentina and Britain have disputed control of the Falkland Islands, which are known in Argentina as the Islas Malvinas. The Falkland Islands are an archipelago consisting of two main islands and over 700 smaller islands. They are located in the South Atlantic Ocean about 300 miles east of the Argentine mainland. The islands were uninhabited when first sighted by Europeans in the late 16th century. Over the next two centuries, the islands were claimed at various times by Britain, Spain, France, and Portugal. Britain asserted control of the islands in 1833 and established a permanent settlement at the capital city of Stanley in 1840. However, Argentina also claimed sovereignty over the islands.

On April 2, 1982, Argentina invaded the Falkland Islands and the nearby British territory of South Georgia. Britain dispatched a naval expedition to recapture the islands, and the recapture was completed on June 14. Approximately 250 British military personnel and 650 Argentine military personnel were killed during the Falklands War. Since the end of the Falklands War, Britain has retained sovereignty over the archipelago, but Argentina continues to claim the islands as Argentine territory. The dispute remains unresolved, and the discovery of oil deposits off the coast of the Falkland Islands has encouraged both countries to pursue their currently unresolved territorial claims.

Argentina and its neighbor, Chile, are also involved in a long-standing dispute over Antarctica. In the early 20th century, Argentina claimed the territory between the 25th and 74th meridians of west longitude, the 60th parallel of south latitude, and the South Pole. This territory includes the Antarctic Peninsula. Argentina constructed a base on the Antarctic mainland in 1904 and today maintains six permanent bases with a combined year-round population of about 230 people. Argentina has justified its claims on their maintenance of these bases, the relative proximity of the Antarctic Peninsula to the Argentine mainland, and the fact that the peninsula's landforms show affinities with the Andes Mountains. However, the area between the 53rd and 74th meridians of west longitude has also been claimed by Chile.

In 1959, the Antarctic Treaty was signed by 12 countries with interests in Antarctica, including Argentina, Chile, and five other countries that had claimed parts of Antarctica as part of their territories. The treaty stipulated that territorial claims south of the 60th parallel would not be recognized by the international community. However, Argentina continues to claim its Antarctic territory although it has not pressed its claim in recent years.

A third dispute has involved relationships between Argentina and Uruguay along the Uruguay River, which forms the boundary between the two countries. In 2003, Uruguay authorized a Spanish country to construct a paper mill on the shore of the river. Construction of another paper mill was authorized by the Uruguayan government in 2005. The boundary agreement between Uruguay and Argentina stipulates that each country must inform the other of any plans to undertake projects that might affect the river. After plans to build the mills were announced, Argentina argued that their construction was authorized without informing

Argentina. The Argentine government saw this as violating the terms of the treaty in that the mills were likely to pollute the river once in operation.

In late 2005, protests against Uruguay's actions began. The protest actions included a blockade of the General de San Martin Bridge connecting the two countries across the Uruguay River. Argentine officials lent tacit support to the protestors, inflaming the dispute. In 2006, Argentina requested an injunction from the International Court of Justice against construction of the paper mills, but the court declined to order a halt to construction. The dispute was resolved, at least temporarily, in 2011, when the two countries agreed to establish a bilateral commission to monitor pollution on the river.

See also   Bolivia, Brazil, Chile, Paraguay, Uruguay

Further Reading

Gabriel Kessler. *On Argentina and the Southern Cone: Neoliberalism and national imaginations.* London: Rutledge, 2005.

Robert Looney. "Argentina's dubious boom." *Foreign Policy*, March 14, 2012, http://www.foreignpolicy.com/articles/2012/03/14/argentinas_dubious_boom.

Martin Middlebrook. *Argentine fight for the Falklands.* Barnsley, South Yorkshire, UK: Pen and Sword, 2009.

BAHAMAS

OVERVIEW

The Commonwealth of the Bahamas is an island country located in the western Atlantic Ocean. The country includes about 700 islands, cays, and atolls, of which 30 are inhabited. The overall land area of the country is 5,382 square miles, with a population of approximately 355,000.

As an island country, the Bahamas has no land neighbors. The closest countries by water are the United States, which is 50 miles west of the island of Grand Bahama, and Cuba, which is 60 miles southwest of the island of Great Inagua.

HISTORICAL BACKGROUND

The Bahamas were first inhabited by Lucayans, whose ancestors are believed to have moved northward from Cuba and Hispaniola between about AD 500 and 1000. Anthropologists believe that 30,000 to 40,000 Lucayans lived on the islands by 1492, when Christopher Columbus initially made landfall. Many scholars believe that this landfall occurred on Watling Island, while others believe that he first landed on Samana Cay. Both of these small islands are located in the southeastern part of the present-day Bahamas. Within a century of initial contact, the Lucayan population was wiped out. Many of the Lucayans died from exposure to European diseases to which they had no immunity, and others were captured and sold into slavery in Cuba or Hispaniola.

In 1648, English Puritans from Bermuda established the first permanent European settlement in the Bahamas on the island of Eleuthera. British control of the islands was contested by France and Spain during the late 17th and early 18th centuries. Located near the Gulf Stream, the Bahamas were close to the main shipping routes between the Caribbean islands and Europe. The islands became a haven for English privateers and pirates while remaining under

BAHAMAS

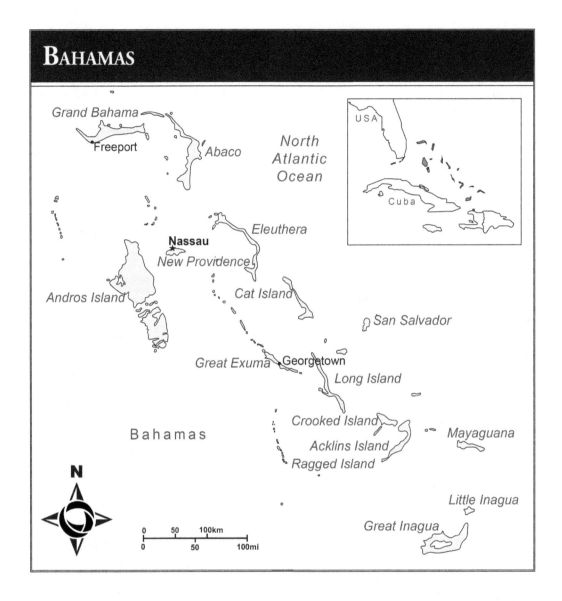

English control. After the American Revolution, the British government encouraged American Loyalists, who had opposed the Revolution, to move to the Bahamas and granted them land. Many of these Loyalists who moved to the Bahamas were slave owners who brought their slaves with them before slavery was abolished throughout the British Empire in 1834. The population of people of African descent increased rap-

idly. Today, about 85 percent of Bahamians claim African ancestry.

During the 20th century, the Bahamas became an increasingly popular destination for American tourists. Tourism from the United States to the Bahamas increased rapidly after 1959, when Fidel Castro took over the government of Cuba. The Bahamas became a self-governing colony within the British Empire in 1964 and became a fully independent state in 1973. The Bahamas and Cuba have disputed the maritime boundary between themselves, but the two countries negotiated a settlement to this dispute in 2011.

Further Reading

Michael Craton and Gail Saunders. *Islanders in the stream: A history of the Bahamian people.* Vol. 1, *From ending of slavery to the twenty-first century.* Athens: University of Georgia Press.

Timothy M. Shaw, Gordon Mace, and Andrew F. Cooper. *Inter-American cooperation at a crossroads.* London: Palgrave Macmillan, 2011.

BARBADOS

OVERVIEW

Barbados is an island country located east of the main arc of the Windward Islands just east of the Caribbean Sea. Barbados is densely populated, with about 280,000 people living in an area of about 179 square miles, or about 2.5 times the size of the District of Columbia. Barbados's nearest neighbors are St. Lucia and St. Vincent and the Grenadines, both of which are located about 150 miles to the west. Barbados is located about 200 miles northeast of the island of Trinidad and

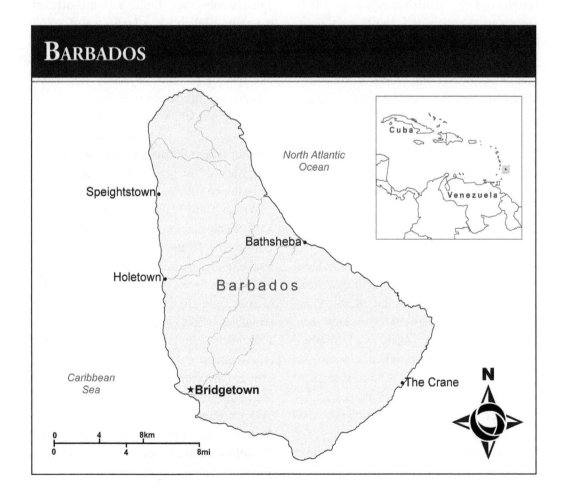

250 miles northeast of the coast of mainland Venezuela.

HISTORICAL CONTEXT

Barbados was first settled by the British in 1627. During the 1640s, sugar cultivation was introduced to the island. Barbados became one of the leading sugar production areas in the world. The heavy labor requirement associated with sugar production resulted in the importation of thousands of African slaves, giving Barbados an African-majority population.

Slavery was abolished in Barbados and throughout the British Empire in 1834, However, emancipated slaves and their descendants had few political rights. The government continued to be dominated by plantation owners and others of European ancestry, in part because the law specified a minimum-income qualification for voting. In the 1930s, people of African ancestry began demanding a greater voice in politics. In 1958, Barbados became independent as part of the West Indian Federation, which also included Jamaica, Trinidad and Tobago, and several smaller islands. The federation collapsed in 1962 following internal conflicts, which were exacerbated by the fact that the largest island, Jamaica, is located so distant from the others. After the federation collapsed, Barbados became a self-governing territory of the British Empire until 1966, when it achieved complete independence. With tourism as a mainstay of its economy, Barbados is the wealthiest country in the Caribbean, and it ranks third behind the United States and Canada in per capita income in the Western Hemisphere.

Further Reading

Hillary McD. Beckles. *A history of Barbados from Amerindian settlement to Caribbean single market.* New York: Cambridge University Press, 2007.

Sir John Mordecai. *Federation of the West Indies.* Evanston, IL: Northwestern University Press, 1968.

BELIZE

OVERVIEW

Belize is located in northeastern Central America. It is the only Central American country with a long history of English colonial rule, and English is the official language. Belize has a land area of 8,867 square miles, the size of New Jersey. Its population is about 340,000, making Belize one of the most sparsely populated countries of the Western Hemisphere.

Belize borders Mexico to the north and Guatemala to the west and south. The Caribbean Sea is located to the east of Belize. Most of the boundary between Belize and Mexico follows the Rio Hondo, which flows eastward between the two countries until it empties into Chetumal Bay in the Caribbean. To the west, a short straight-line segment extends southward from the Rio Hondo to the tripoint between Belize, Mexico, and Guatemala. Belize's western boundary with Guatemala includes two straight-line segments. The more northerly segment extends due south from the tripoint between Belize, Guatemala, and Mexico. Further south, a second segment extends slightly west of south. At the southern end of this segment, the boundary follows the Sarstun River eastward to its mouth in the Caribbean Sea.

BELIZE

Mexico

•Corozul

0   20   40km
0   20   40mi

Orange Walk•

New

Belize

⚬ Ambergris Cays

Belize City•

Turneffe Islands

★ **Belmopan**

•San Ignacio

Banque Viejo
del Carmen

Guatemala

Belize

•Dangrige

*Caribbean
Sea*

•Punta Gorda

N

Honduras

HISTORICAL CONTEXT

Belize was part of the Mayan Empire before the empire collapsed during the 10th and 11th. The area was still occupied by Mayan people in the early 16th century, when the eastern coast of Central America was first sighted by Spanish explorers and was claimed by Spain. Most of the local Mayan people died from exposure to European diseases, while others were enslaved or forced to move elsewhere. However, present-day Belize was remote from the centers of Spanish power in the Western Hemisphere, and Spain's control over the area was only nominal. The main resource of the area was logwood, which was used by Europeans to extract dye. Mahogany was also an important timber product.

Beginning in the mid-17th century, British buccaneers and pirates began to use the sparsely populated coast of present-day Belize as a base of operations. Pirates attacked Spanish ships, and later some British settlers began to cut and export logwood themselves. During the 18th century, Spain attacked the British settlements on several occasions, but the Spanish were unsuccessful in their efforts to expel the British from the region. The Treaty of Paris, which ended the Seven Years' War in 1763, awarded Spain sovereignty over present-day Belize but affirmed the right of British settlers to continue cutting and exporting logwood and mahogany. In 1796, a Spanish military expedition tried unsuccessfully to remove the British settlers, but they were defeated in what came to be known as the Battle of St. George's Cay. During the 18th and 19th centuries, many African slaves were brought to the area to work in timber cutting and production. The area became a British colony formally in 1862 and was named British Honduras.

In 1859, Guatemala and Britain signed a treaty in which Guatemala agreed to recognize Britain as sovereign over British Honduras. The British agreed to construct a railroad from Guatemala to the port of Punta Gorda on the Caribbean, but the railroad was never built. In 1940, Guatemala claimed sovereignty over British Honduras on the grounds that Britain had not honored its obligations under the 1859 treaty. The dispute over sovereignty continued after British Honduras became independent and was renamed Belize in 1981. Belize argued that the 1859 treaty was null and void because Belize was not a signatory to the treaty. Guatemala recognized Belize in 1991, and diplomatic relations between the two countries were established. However, Guatemala continues to claim the southern half of Belize.

CONTEMPORARY ISSUES

The territorial dispute between Guatemala and Belize regarding sovereignty over southern Belize remains unresolved. After diplomatic relations between the two countries were established in 1991, the two countries began to negotiate the dispute. However, the dispute remains unsettled after two decades of negotiation. In 2008, leaders of the two countries agreed in principle that referenda be held in both countries about whether to refer the ongoing dispute to the International Court of Justice. In 2012, the two countries agreed that the referenda would be held simultaneously in 2013.

See also   Guatemala, Mexico

Further Reading

Anne Sutherland. *The making of Belize: Globalization in the margins.* Santa Barbara, CA: Praeger, 1998.

Peter Thomson. *Belize: A concise history.* London: Macmillan, 2005.

BOLIVIA

OVERVIEW

The Plurinational State of Bolivia is a landlocked South American country. Most of the country is located in the Andes Mountains, although eastern Bolivia extends into the lowland Amazon Basin. The country's administrative capital city of La Paz, at an altitude of 12,000 feet above sea level, has the highest altitude of any national capital city in the world. Bolivia's land area is 424,163 square miles, making it nearly twice as large as Texas. It has a population of approximately 11 million. Bolivia and neighboring Paraguay are the only landlocked countries in Latin America.

Bolivia consists of two very distinctive geographic regions, including the very high peaks of the Andes to the west and tropical lowlands to the east. Bolivia's neighbors are Brazil to the north and east, Paraguay to the southeast, Argentina to the south, Chile to the southwest, and Peru to the east. The boundaries between Bolivia and Brazil, Paraguay, and Argentina are located in lowland areas, whereas the boundaries between Bolivia and Chile and Peru are located in the high elevations of the Andes.

Most of the boundary between Bolivia and Brazil follows rivers or drainage basins. The tripoint between Bolivia, Brazil, and Peru is located near the Brazilian town of Assis Brasil and the adjacent Peruvian town of Inapari, both of which are located within a mile of this tripoint. The boundary follows the Rio Acre eastward and downstream for about five miles and then becomes a complex series of short straight-line segments extending in a generally northeastward direction. These segments are north of and roughly parallel to the Madre de Dios River. They continue toward the villages of Manoa and Nuevo Manoa along the Guapore River, into which the Madre de Dios River empties. The Guapore, which is known in Bolivia as the Itenez River, is a major tributary of the Amazon and forms much of the boundary between northeastern Bolivia and neighboring south-central Brazil. At the edge of Bolivia's Parque Nacionale Noel Kempff, it follows straight-line segments southward, eastward, and southward again to the tripoint between Bolivia, Brazil, and Paraguay.

From this tripoint, the boundary between Bolivia and Paraguay follows numerous straight-line segments extending in a generally circular direction through the arid and sparsely populated Gran Chaco region to the tripoint between Bolivia, Paraguay, and Argentina. The circular pattern places Bolivia at the concave side of the boundary, while Paraguay's shape as viewed from the southeast is convex. The boundary between Bolivia and Argentina is primarily geometric. However, from the tripoint between Bolivia, Argentina, and Paraguay the boundary follows the Pilcomayo River upstream to the 22nd parallel of south latitude. It follows the 22nd parallel westward to the Bermejo River and then upstream in a southwesterly direction to the mouth of its tributary, the Porongal River. From the town of Entre Rios on the Porongal, it follows geometric lines southwestward into

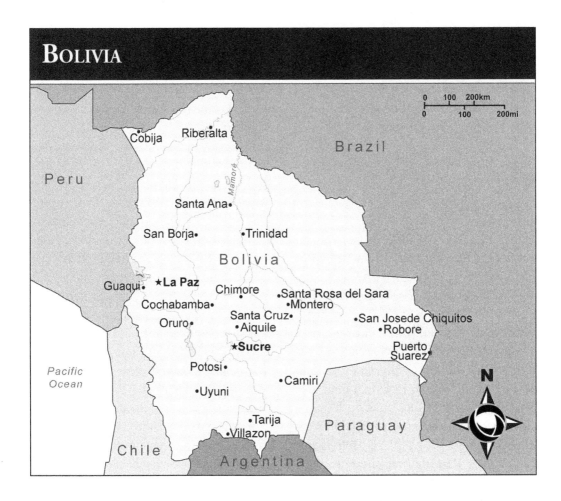

BOLIVIA

the Andes toward the tripoint between Bolivia, Argentina, and Chile. This tripoint is located at the summit of Cerro Zapaleri, an extinct volcano at an elevation of nearly 18,500 feet above sea level.

From the summit of Cerro Zapaleri, the boundary between Bolivia and Chile follows a series of geometric lines northward through the Andes. Many of these segments separate high mountain peaks on either side of the boundary. The boundary between Bolivia and Peru continues in a generally northward and northeastward direction from the tripoint between Bolivia, Peru, and Chile to Lake Titicaca, which at 12,500 feet above sea level is one of the highest lakes by elevation in the world and is also the largest freshwater lake in South America. From Lake Titicaca, the boundary continues northward, generally following straight-line segments to the Rio Heath, which forms the boundary northward to its confluence with the Madre de Dios. From there it follows a straight geometric line northwestward to the tripoint between Bolivia, Peru, and Brazil.

HISTORICAL CONTEXT

The original inhabitants of the Andes portion of present-day Bolivia were the Aymara people, who established an empire in the region centered on Lake Titicaca between approximately AD 600 and 1000. The region was conquered and added to the Inca Empire in the early 15th century. Spanish conquistadors topped the Inca Empire beginning in the 1520s. A large deposit of silver was discovered near Cerro de Potosi, located southeast of Lake Titicaca toward the present-day boundary between Brazil and Argentina. Spaniards founded the city of Potosi, which by 1600 had become the largest city in South America with more than 100,000 residents. The great wealth of Potosi depended greatly on slave labor. Slaves working in the mines included indigenous South Americans and Africans brought to the area via the trans-Atlantic slave trade. Death rates from overwork and disease among these slaves were very high. By 1800, most of the silver mines had become depleted although some silver mining continues to take place in the area today.

Bolivia, then known as Upper Peru, was made part of the Viceroyalty de la Plata, centered on Buenos Aires, in 1776. Agitation for independence began in the early 19th century. Upper Peru declared its independence in 1825 and was renamed Bolivia in honor of Simon Bolivar, the leader of independence movements throughout South America. Bolivia and Peru united as the Peru-Bolivian Confederation in 1836, but the union lasted only three years before it was dissolved. War between Bolivia and Peru broke out after the dissolution of the Confederation, and armed conflict ended with a peace treaty signed by both countries in 1842.

War broke out between Bolivia, Peru, and Chile in 1879 in what became known as the War of the Pacific. Conflict involved control over the Bolivian province of Antofagasta and three provinces in southern Peru. All of these provinces are highly rich in nitrates and other minerals. The war began after Chile occupied the city of Antofagasta, which was Bolivia's only port on the Pacific Ocean. After armed hostilities began, Chilean forces defeated the armies of Bolivia and Peru. A truce between Bolivia and Chile was signed by both countries in 1884. Under terms of this agreement, control of Antofagasta was transferred from Bolivia to Chile. Thus Bolivia lost its only access to the Pacific and became landlocked. The boundary agreement between the two countries was reaffirmed by the Treaty of Peace and Friendship, which was signed in 1904 and established definite boundaries between them. Under terms of this agreement, Chile also agreed to construct a railroad between La Paz and Antofagasta, and it agreed to grant Bolivia free and unrestricted commercial access through Chilean territory.

Bolivia's boundaries with its other neighbors were established during the early 20th century. The boundary between Bolivia and Brazil began to be demarcated in 1904. At that time, the area near the present-day boundary had been visited infrequently by people of European ancestry and was inhabited only by indigenous tribes. The boundary was demarcated more precisely once the area had been explored by officials acting on behalf of both countries. An ongoing boundary dispute between Bolivia and Peru was settled after the dispute was referred to the government of Argentina for mediation during the first decade of the 20th century. Bolivia also lost territory to Paraguay after the Gran Chaco War, which was fought between the two countries between 1932 and 1935 and ended with the signing of a peace agreement in 1938.

CONTEMPORARY ISSUES

Although Bolivia disputed its boundaries with its neighbors during the first century after it became independent, the country's boundaries have been stable and uncontested since the end of the Gran Chaco War. However, Bolivia has reasserted its claim over the Antofagasta region of northern Chile. Chile has offered unrestricted access to its port facilities at the city of Antofagasta in accordance with the Treaty of Peace and Friendship. However, Chile has not considered offering Bolivia sovereignty over the area and does not support restoring Bolivian access to the Pacific.

Bolivia's considerable natural resource base has also resulted in conflicts with neighboring countries and with large corporations elsewhere. Bolivia contains the world's largest known deposits of lithium, a mineral used to produce batteries and of increasing value in the 21st-century world economy. Currently, Bolivia's indigenous populations are in conflict with multinational corporations over profits associated with lithium extraction and production. Bolivia has also been a center for production of illegal drugs, causing conflicts with the United States, Brazil, and other countries.

See also Argentina, Brazil, Chile, Paraguay, Peru

Further Reading

Rachel Glickhouse. "Bolivia inks anti-drug accord with Brazil and the United States." *Americas/Society*, January 24, 2012, http://www.as-coa.org/article.php?id=3913.

Herbert S. Klein. *A concise history of Bolivia.* New York: Cambridge University Press, 2011.

Simon Romero. "In Bolivia, untapped bounty meets nationalism. *New York Times*, February 2, 2009, http://www.nytimes.com/2009/02/03/world/americas/03lithium.html?pagewanted=all.

Steven Topik, Zephyr Frank, and Carlos Marichal (eds.). *From silver to cocaine: Latin American commodity chains and the building of the world economy, 1950–2000.* Durham, NC: Duke University Press, 2006.

BRAZIL

OVERVIEW

The Federative Republic of Brazil occupies eastern South America, and its land area encompasses nearly half of the South American continent. Brazil is the fifth-largest country in the world by land area (behind Russia, Canada, the United States, and China) and the fifth-largest country in the world by population (behind China, India, the United States, and Indonesia). Its land area is 3,287,597 square miles, slightly smaller than that of the United States. Its population is about 195 million.

Brazil has boundaries with every country in South America except for Ecuador and Chile. Its neighbors are French Guiana, Suriname, Guyana, and Venezuela to the north; Colombia, Peru, Bolivia, and Paraguay to the west; and Argentina and Uruguay to the southwest. Brazil has a lengthy coastline on the Atlantic Ocean to the northeast and to the southeast. Most of

BRAZIL

the drainage basin of the Amazon River, which is by far the largest river in the world by volume of water, is located in Brazil.

Brazil's boundary with the small French colony of French Guiana extends southwestward from the Atlantic coast inland along the Oiapoque River. The boundary continues along the course of the river westward near Guiana Amazonian National Park in French Guiana. Tumucumaque National

Park in Brazil adjoins Guiana Amazonian National Park. Together, these parks form one of the largest areas of protected tropical rainforest in the world. The tripoint between Brazil, French Guiana, and Suriname is adjacent to the southwest corner of Guiana Amazonian National Park.

From this tripoint, the boundary between Brazil and Suriname follows drainage divides to the tripoint between Brazil,

Suriname, and Guyana. Streams south of this boundary in Brazil are part of the Amazon drainage basin, while those that are located north of the boundary in Suriname flow northward into the Caribbean Sea. This drainage divide continues as the boundary between Brazil and Guyana across the Serra Acarai mountain range to the Tacutu River. This boundary then turns northward and downstream along the Tacutu, which despite its northward flow along the boundary is actually a tributary to the Amazon. At the downstream confluence between the Tacutu and the Ireng River, the Tacutu turns southwestward into Brazil. The boundary between Brazil and Guyana continues northward, generally separating the drainage basin of the Amazon from those of northward-flowing streams, to the tripoint between Brazil, Guyana, and Venezuela at the summit of Mount Roraima, which is the highest mountain in northeastern South America.

The boundary between Brazil and Venezuela extends westward from Mount Roraima. Much of this boundary follows the drainage divide between the Amazon in Brazil and the Orinoco River in Venezuela. This section of the boundary extends in a generally westerly direction to a point at the border of Jaue-Sarisaranama National Park in Venezuela. From here it turns southward, and then westward again. All of this territory is part of the Amazon rainforest and is virtually uninhabited. Further west, a small section of the Amazon Basin extends across the boundary into Venezuela to the Rio Negro, which is one of the largest and longest tributaries of the Amazon. The tripoint between Brazil, Venezuela, and Colombia is located on the Rio Negro near the town of La Guadalupe in Colombia.

From this tripoint, the boundary between Brazil and Colombia follows a short straight-line segment south-southwestward for about 20 miles. The boundary then turns northward, and then westward again. The boundary consists of a large number of very short straight-line segments. It continues generally along the drainage divide between the Amazon and the Orinoco. The boundary continues westward along a straight-line segment to a point south of Puinawai National Park in Colombia. West of the park, it turns southward again, following straight lines, and then goes south-southwestward to the tripoint between Brazil, Colombia, and Peru on the Amazon itself near the town of Benjamin Constant. An exception to this general trend is a small section of Colombian territory that extends eastward to the Uaupes River, known in Colombia as the Vaupes River.

The entire boundary between Brazil and Peru is located within the Amazon drainage basin south of the Amazon itself. From Benjamin Constant, the boundary follows the Javari River upstream from the confluence between the Javari and the Amazon. This boundary follows the Javari westward and then turns southward and the southeastward. It leaves the Javari and then crosses eastward to Purus River. After following the Purus briefly eastward, it follows a straight line south to the Acre River, following the Acre downstream and eastward to the tripoint between Brazil, Peru, and Bolivia. This tripoint is located near the Brazilian town of Assis Brasil and the adjacent Peruvian town of Inapari.

From the tripoint between Brazil, Bolivia, and Peru, the boundary between Brazil and Bolivia follows the Acre downstream and eastward for about five miles.

It then follows a complex series of straight-line segments eastward. These segments parallel the course of the Madre de Dios River in Bolivia. They continue eastward to the Madeira River. The boundary then turns southward, following the Madeira upstream to its source at the confluence between the Madre de Dios and the Guapore rivers. The boundary then follows the Guapore upstream and southeastward to Noel Kempff National Park in Bolivia. From this park, the boundary follows straight lines south. It then turns eastward again and then turns southward once again to the tripoint between Bolivia, Brazil, and Paraguay in the Gran Chaco region.

The boundary between Brazil and Paraguay extends southward from this tripoint to the Paraguay River, which it follows southward to a point south of the town of Porto Murtinho in Brazil. It then leaves the river, extending east, and then south, and then east again to the Rio Parana near the town of Guaira. From Guaira, the boundary follows the Rio Parana southward and downstream to the tripoint between Brazil, Paraguay, and Argentina on the Rio Parana. This tripoint is located at the confluence of the Iguazu River and the Rio Parana near the Paraguayan city of Ciudad del Este.

From this tripoint, the Rio Parana continues southward and eastward as the boundary between Paraguay and Argentina. However, the boundary between Brazil and Argentina follows the Iguazu upstream for a short distance and then follows a series of short-line segments to the Pepiri-Guazu River. It then follows the Pepiri-Guazu downstream and southward to its confluence with the Uruguay River and then continues along the Uruguay southward

to the tripoint between Brazil, Argentina, and Uruguay at the confluence between the Uruguay and the Quaraí River. From this confluence, the boundary between Brazil follows the Quaraí upstream to the Jaguarão River, follows the Jaguarão further upstream, and then crosses to the estuarine lake of Laguna Mirim. The boundary continues southward through Laguna Mirim and then extends southward and southeastward to the Atlantic Ocean.

HISTORICAL CONTEXT

During the age of exploration, Portugal and Spain signed the Treaty of Tordesillas dividing spheres of influence over the non-European world between themselves. The Line of Demarcation associated with the treaty was to be drawn 370 leagues, or about 1,100 miles, west of the Cape Verde Islands off the coast of Africa. Although the line dividing these spheres of influence was not delineated clearly, Portugal claimed that this line cut across eastern South America. On this basis, Portugal claimed the Atlantic coast of Brazil in 1500.

The Portuguese began establishing settlements along the coast of present-day Brazil in 1532. The city of Rio de Janeiro, which would become the capital city of independent Brazil, was founded by Portugal in 1565. Over the next two centuries, Portugal expanded its control over the territory. Tropical crop production and mining became the mainstays of colonial Brazil's economy. Millions of slaves were imported from Africa in order to provide a labor force, adding to the diversity of Brazil's population that remains a hallmark of the country today.

Portugal and Spain contested some of their boundaries in Latin America during the 17th and 18th centuries. In 1777, the two countries signed the Treaty of San Ildefonso. This agreement clarified the general contours of the boundaries between Portuguese and Spanish possessions in South America. Under terms of the treaty, Portugal ceded control over present-day Uruguay to Spain, and Spain ceded some territory in the Amazon River basin to Portugal. Thus, the treaty established most of the present-day boundaries between Brazil and those countries in South America that were then under Spanish control. Brazil's boundaries with Guyana, Suriname, and French Guiana were ascertained by agreements between independent Brazil and Britain, the Netherlands, and France respectively in the late 19th and early 20th centuries. In 1900, Swiss diplomats helped to resolve a dispute between Brazil and France over the location of the boundary between Brazil and French Guiana. Under terms of this agreement, the two countries agreed that the name Oiapoque would be as the official name of the river separating Brazil from French Guiana.

Brazil became an independent monarchy in 1822. The first emperor was Dom Pedro I, who was the son of Portugal's King Joao VI. Independent Brazil reasserted its claim over Uruguay, which it called Cisplatania. However, Brazil relinquished this claim and recognized Uruguay as an independent state in 1828. The monarchy was overthrown in 1889 and a republic was declared, although the country was ruled by dictators for much of the next 50 years. Democracy was restored after World War II, although the Brazilian military ruled the country between 1964 and 1985. Brazil has maintained a multiparty democracy since that time. In recent years, Brazil's economy has boomed. According to United Nations statistics, by early 2012 Brazil had surpassed Britain as the sixth-largest economic power in the world.

CONTEMPORARY ISSUES

Brazil and its neighbors have experienced several conflicts with one another in recent years. One of the most significant conflicts involves the boundary region near Brazil, Paraguay, and Argentina. Brazil and Paraguay first considered the possibility of damming the Rio Parana in the late 19th century. In 1973, work began on a dam across the Rio Parana. The Itaipu Dam was completed and opened 1984. The Itaipu Dam was the largest in the world, with the greatest hydroelectric power generating capacity in the world, until the Three Gorges Dam in China was completed and opened in 2009.

The Itaipu project caused concern in both Argentina and Paraguay. Argentina's government became concerned that the dam's operation would cause flooding on the downstream reaches of the Parana, which flows from the border region into Argentina. Meanwhile, Brazil and Paraguay signed a treaty in which each agreed to sell excess electric capacity to each other. Because Brazil uses much more electricity than much smaller Paraguay, the treaty forced Paraguay to sell this excess capacity to Brazil at rates far less than market value. Thus Paraguay argued that the terms of the treaty favored Brazil at its own expense. However, the two countries renegotiated the treaty in 2009. The area around the dam has boomed economically in all three countries, with rapid increases in population. Brazil has regarded this boundary region as a haven for smuggling and drug running and has expressed concern that Paraguay has been unable to control these illegal activities.

Brazil has also been addressing issues involving its northern and western neighbors in the Amazon River basin. The Amazon basin is the largest area of tropical rainforest in the world, but development pressures have resulted in substantial deforestation in recent years. It has been estimated that 25,000 square miles of rainforest, or an area the size of West Virginia, is lost to deforestation each year. Ongoing conflicts between the Brazilian government and indigenous peoples in the area have occurred. Many of these conflicts involve tensions over development and its potential impacts on local indigenous peoples as well as on the natural environment.

The experience of the state of Rondonia in western Brazil illustrates these issues. Rondonia contains about 90,000 square miles (somewhat bigger than Oklahoma) and about 1.6 million people (roughly half the population of Oklahoma). It has been estimated that about 60 percent of Rondonia's rainforest land has been depleted since 1970. Depletion has been encouraged by the production of cattle and soybeans for export. The state of Mato Grosso, which is adjacent to Rondonia, has become Brazil's leading producer of corn and soybeans. Construction of highways has encouraged depletion because these highways have made more rainforest lands accessible to transportation networks. In particular, the governments of Brazil and Peru have discussed the possibility of constructing a highway through Rondonia that would cross the Andes and connect Rio de Janeiro and Sao Paulo with Lima. Environmentalists have expressed concern that the construction and opening of this highway would accelerate the pace of deforestation in an already fragile environment.

See also   Argentina, Bolivia, Colombia, Guyana, Paraguay, Peru, Suriname, Uruguay, Venezuela

Further Reading

BBC News. "Why Brazil gave way on Itaipu Dam." July 26, 2009, http://news.bbc.co.uk/2/hi/8169139.stm.

Lael Brainard and Leonardo Martinez-Dias (eds.). *Brazil as an economic superpower? Understanding Brazil's changing role in the global economy.* Washington, DC: Brookings Institution Press, 2009.

Simon Romero. "Brazil sending more troops to guard Amazon borders." *New York Times*, May 4, 2012, http://www.nytimes.com/2012/05/04/world/americas/brazil-sending-more-troops-to-guard-amazon-borders.html?_r=1&partner=rss&emc=rss.

Julia E. Sweig. "A new global player: Brazil's far-flung agenda." *Foreign Affairs*, November/December 2010.

CANADA

OVERVIEW

Canada occupies the northern portion of North America between the United States and the Arctic Ocean. With a land area of 3,854,085 square miles, Canada is the second-largest country in the world by land area behind only Russia. It is one of three countries, along with the United States and Russia, that border on three oceans. Canada's population is approximately

35 million. The large majority of Canadians live in the southern part of Canada near the United States border, while most of northern Canada is very sparsely populated. Canada includes 10 provinces and also 3 territories located north of the 60th parallel of north latitude.

Canada's only land neighbor is the United States. The boundary between Canada and the United States is the longest land boundary in the world, extending from the Atlantic Ocean on the east to the Pacific Ocean on the west and from the Pacific north to the Arctic Ocean. Northwestern

Canada borders the U.S. state of Alaska, which is separated from the rest of United States territory by the Canadian province of British Columbia and Yukon Territory. Canada also includes many islands, including Newfoundland and Prince Edward Island off the Atlantic coast, Vancouver Island off the Pacific coast, and numerous islands in the Arctic Ocean. Baffin Island, Victoria Island, and Ellesmere Island in the Arctic are 3 of the 10 largest islands by land area in the world.

On the east, the boundary between Canada and the United States extends inland

from Passamaquoddy Bay in the Bay of Fundy, which is an arm of the Atlantic. It begins at the mouth of the St. Croix River and extends upstream to the river's headwaters at Spednic Lake. From Spednic Lake it extends northward directly to the St. John River. The boundary then follows the St. John upstream in a northwesterly direction to the city of Edmundston, New Brunswick, where the St. John bends from a northeasterly flow to a southeasterly flow. The boundary continues southwestward and upstream along the St. John to its confluence with the St. Francis River at the town of Saint-Francois-de-Madawaska and then follows the St. Francis in a northwesterly direction. Hence it extends along a straight line running north-northeast to south-southwest until it reaches the drainage divide between the St. Lawrence River on the Canadian side of the boundary and the rivers flowing into the Atlantic directly on the United States side of the boundary. It continues along this drainage divide to Hall's Stream, a tributary of the Connecticut River, and follows this stream to the 45th parallel of north latitude. The boundary then follows the 45th parallel westward to the St. Lawrence near Cornwall, Ontario, and then follows the St. Lawrence upstream to its source in Lake Ontario.

West of the St. Lawrence, the boundary follows Lake Ontario, Lake Erie, Lake Huron, and Lake Superior. Between Lake Ontario and Lake Erie, the Niagara River forms the boundary. Between Lake Erie and Lake Huron, the boundary follows the Detroit River northward from Lake Erie upstream to Lake St. Clair. Here the boundary separates the Canadian city of Windsor from the American city of Detroit. From

Lake St. Clair, it continues northward and upstream along the St. Clair River to Lake Huron. It continues northward and then westward through Lake Huron and Lake Superior. The St. Marys River forms the boundary between Lake Huron and Lake Superior, separating the Canadian city of Sault Ste. Marie, Ontario, and the American city of the same name in Michigan.

From western Lake Superior, the boundary extends westward and upstream along the Pigeon River to its headwaters at the Height of Land Portage. The Height of Land Portage is located at the drainage divide between the Atlantic and Arctic oceans and separates the Canadian province of Ontario from the U.S. state of Minnesota. The boundary crosses a narrow isthmus and then follows the Rainy River westward to Lake of the Woods. From Lake of the Woods, the boundary follows the 49th parallel for more than 1,000 miles westward to the Pacific Ocean. Off the Pacific coast, part of Vancouver Island including the city of Victoria is located south of the 49th parallel. However, all of Vancouver Island along with several smaller nearby islands is part of Canada.

The Canadian coast on the Pacific Ocean, adjacent to the province of British Columbia, extends from the 49th parallel northward to the 54° 40′ parallel, or the southernmost point in the U.S. state of Alaska. The Coast Mountains, which include Canada's highest peaks, are located very close to the Pacific coast of British Columbia. From this point northward to the Arctic Ocean, Canada and Alaska share a boundary. The boundary follows the crest of the Coast Mountains, paralleling the Pacific coast northward and then westward to the 141st meridian of west longitude. It then follows the 141st meridian northward to the Arctic.

HISTORICAL CONTEXT

The first Europeans known to have visited present-day Canada were Norse seafarers from Iceland and Greenland, who visited the Canadian Atlantic coast approximately AD 1000. Ruins of a Norse settlement have been excavated by archaeologists at L'Anse-aux-Meadows near the northern tip of the island of Newfoundland. However, the Norse abandoned this settlement after a few years.

The first permanent European activity in present-day Canada took place in the 16th century. In 1534, the French explorer Jacques Cartier visited the St. Lawrence River and claimed the territory for France. In 1608, Samuel de Champlain founded the city of Quebec on the St. Lawrence River. Champlain sent several parties upstream along the St. Lawrence to explore the interior of North America. These explorers and French traders explored the area as far west as the Great Lakes, and the city of Montreal was founded at the head of navigation on the St. Lawrence in 1642. The French also settled present-day Nova Scotia, New Brunswick, and Prince Edward Island. Collectively, the name New France was given to these French colonies.

The British also became interested in what is now eastern Canada. Britain claimed the island of Newfoundland, which was also claimed by France. Other British settlers moved northeastward along the Atlantic coast from New England, establishing settlements in what is now the state of Maine. By the early 18th century, British settlers throughout North America and their descendants vastly outnumbered French settlers and their descendants in North America.

In 1756, Britain and France fought the Seven Years' War, which was actually a set of wars fought in different parts of the world between the two powers. In North America, the conflict became known as the French and Indian War. The Seven Years' War ended with the signing of the Treaty of Paris in 1763. Under terms of the Treaty of Paris, France ceded all of its territorial claims in North America to the British, with the exception of the small islands of St. Pierre and Miquelon off the coast of Newfoundland. Britain guaranteed the right of the French settlers in Quebec to maintain their French language and Roman Catholic faith.

After 1763, numerous British settlers moved to what is now Canadian territory along the Great Lakes. During and after the American Revolution, they were joined by many "Loyalists" from the Thirteen Colonies who opposed American independence. Britain recognized the independence of the United States in 1783, but what is now Canada remained under British rule. As more and more people moved into the area from Britain and the United States, the British divided the area into two colonies—Lower Canada along the St. Lawrence and Upper Canada further upstream and along the Great Lakes.

In 1867, the two colonies along with New Brunswick and Nova Scotia formed the Dominion of Canada. Lower Canada and Upper Canada became the provinces of Quebec and Ontario respectively. Quebec remained overwhelmingly French speaking, while the large majority of residents of Ontario, New Brunswick, and

Nova Scotia spoke English. Canada became an officially bilingual country, and tensions over language and language rights have been prevalent in Canada ever since. Between 1867 and 1905, the provinces of Prince Edward Island, British Columbia, Alberta, Saskatchewan, and Manitoba joined the Dominion. The 10th province, Newfoundland, retained separate colonial status within the British Empire until it joined Canada in 1949. The province includes the mainland territory of Labrador and was renamed Newfoundland and Labrador in 2001.

The boundary between Canada and the United States was first established in 1783 as part of the Treaty of Paris (not to be confused with the 1763 treaty of the same name), in which Britain recognized the United States's independent status. This treaty established the 45th parallel as the boundary between Lower Canada and the United States and the St. Lawrence and the Great Lakes as the boundary between Upper Canada and the United States. In 1818, an agreement between Britain and the United States established the 49th parallel as the boundary from Lake of the Woods westward to the Rocky Mountains.

The 1818 agreement was modified by the Webster-Ashburton Treaty of 1842. The Webster-Ashburton Treaty resolved an ongoing dispute over the eastern boundary between New Brunswick and Maine. It also established the boundary between Minnesota and Ontario from Lake Superior westward to Lake of the Woods.

Britain and the United States also disputed the boundary between the Rockies and the Pacific Ocean. The Americans claimed the territory between the Rockies

and the southern boundary of Alaska at 54° 40′ north latitude. However, the British wanted to extend the boundary as far south as the 42nd parallel (the present-day boundary between the U.S. states of Oregon and California). Britain was interested especially in controlling the area north of the Columbia River, which today separates the U.S. states of Washington and Oregon. Using the slogan "Fifty-Four Forty or Fight," some Americans agitated for war with Britain if Britain did not accept the United States's territorial claim. In 1846, however, the two countries negotiated an agreement by which the 49th parallel was extended as the boundary westward to the Pacific, with the exception that Britain would maintain control of Vancouver Island.

The boundary between western Canada and Alaska was contested throughout the 19th and early 20th centuries. In 1821, Britain (which then controlled Canada) and Russia (which then controlled Alaska) agreed to the general principle that the southern portion of the boundary between their colonies should extend along the high peaks of the mountains along the coast. However, the agreement did not provide specific guidance as to the precise location of the boundary. Canada and the United States inherited this dispute after Canada became independent and the United States purchased Alaska from Russia. The discovery of gold in the Klondike region of Canada's Yukon Territory heightened tensions between the two countries. In 1903, the countries agreed to establish an international tribunal to determine the boundary. The boundary as determined by this tribunal remains the boundary between the two countries today.

CONTEMPORARY ISSUES

Reflecting a long history of friendship and close relationships between Canada and the United States, the boundary separating the two countries is the longest undefended boundary in the world. However, a few issues of contention remain. Canada is also in dispute with some other countries over the Arctic Ocean.

The maritime boundaries between Canada and the United States in both the Pacific and the Atlantic oceans have been disputed for many years. On the Pacific coast, the dispute involves maritime boundaries west of the mouth of the Strait of Juan de Fuca, which separates Vancouver Island to the north from the U.S. mainland to the south. The two countries disagree as to where the mouth of the strait ends. This disagreement in turn affects interpretation of the principle of equidistance, via which the boundary is drawn such that it is equidistant from the nearest land area belonging to each country. A similar situation prevails in the Bay of Fundy and the Atlantic coast. Although the maritime boundary in this area was determined in general in a ruling by the International Court of Justice in 1984, the specific boundary remains unclear and has not been marked definitively.

To the north, Canada and the United States have disagreed as to whether the waters separating the islands in the Arctic Ocean north of the Canadian mainland should be considered internal or international waters. The Canadian Arctic Archipelago consists of over 36,000 islands. In addition to Baffin, Victoria, and Ellesmere, the archipelago includes 91 additional islands with land areas of more than 50 square miles each. During the 18th and

19th centuries, numerous European explorers attempted to find the Northwest Passage, or a sea route through the archipelago connecting the Atlantic and Pacific oceans. The Northwest Passage was navigated finally between 1903 and 1906 by Roald Amundsen, who is best known today as the first explorer to reach the South Pole.

Pack ice persisting in the area throughout the year has made the Northwest Passage generally useless for commercial shipping. However, increased sea surface temperatures associated with warming temperatures throughout the world have reduced the amount of ice in the Northwest Passage. The Passage may become increasingly accessible to ships if the volume of ice continues to decrease.

The potential navigability of the Northwest Passage has intensified competing claims over its legal status. Canada claims that the waters of the Northwest Passage are internal waters, in which case Canada would have the right to close the Passage to foreign shipping. This implies that foreign ships must secure the Canadian government's permission to traverse the Passage. However, the United States and some European countries regard the waters of the Passage as international waters. Under international law, a sovereign country cannot restrict access to international waters, and permission to traverse these waters is not required. Reinforcing its claim that the Northwest Passage is internal rather than international, in 2006 the Canadian government declared that the Canadian armed forces would henceforth refer to the Passage as the Canadian Internal Waters.

The legal status of the territory between the Canadian Arctic Archipelago and the North Pole has also been disputed among

Canada and other countries that border the Arctic Ocean. In 2011, Denmark claimed jurisdiction over that portion of the Arctic Ocean between Greenland, whose foreign policy is administered by Denmark, and the North Pole. Canada and Russia have responded by making similar claims over those sections of the Arctic north of their own land territories. The issue has become more controversial because continued reduction in the volume of pack ice in the Arctic Ocean could make the ocean navigable in the summer and because potentially lucrative deposits of oil and other minerals have been discovered on the Arctic seabed. The status of these territorial claims is under review by the International Court of Justice.

The status of the Canadian province of Quebec also remains contested. Present-day Quebec along the valley of the St. Lawrence River was home to thousands of French-speaking *habitants* at the time the Treaty of Paris was signed between Britain and France in 1763. Quebec was ceded to Britain, but the population of Quebec continued to be dominated by French-speaking descendants of the early French settlers who had arrived during the 17th and early 18th centuries. The large majority of Quebecois have been Francophones ever since. After Canada became an independent country, a debate about the extent to which Quebec, as a primarily French-speaking province, should have "special status" relative to the other provinces has been ongoing.

By the 1960s, many Quebecois had begun to advocate for increased autonomy or outright independence from Canada. The Parti Quebecois, a political party favoring Quebec's independence, won control of the provincial government in 1976. In 1980, the Parti Quebecois sponsored a referendum on the future status of Quebec. According to the text of the referendum, the government of Quebec would seek to negotiate an agreement that "would enable Quebec to acquire the exclusive power to make its laws, levy its taxes and establish relations abroad—in other words, sovereignty." However, a majority voted against the referendum. A second referendum was rejected narrowly by the voters in 1995. In 2006, the Canadian House of Commons passed a resolution recognizing "that the Quebecois form a nation within a united Canada." However, this resolution was symbolic rather than substantive, and its meaning with respect to the legal status of Quebec within Canada remains uncertain.

See also   United States

Further Reading

Robert Bothwell. *Canada and Quebec: One nation, two histories.* Vancouver: UBC Press, 2006.

Zachary Fillingham. "Arctic ownership claims." *Geopolitical Monitor*, April 8, 2009, http://www.geopoliticalmonitor. com/arctic-ownership-claims.

John Kirton. *Canadian foreign policy in a changing world.* Scarborough, Ontario, Canada: Nelson, 2006.

CHILE

OVERVIEW

The Republic of Chile occupies a long, narrow strip of land in South America between the Andes Mountains and the Pacific Ocean. It is more than 2,700 miles from north to south, but it is less than 250 miles

CHILE

wide at its widest point and has an average width of only 110 miles. Chile's total land area is about 292,000 square miles, making it somewhat larger than the U.S. state of Texas. Its population is about 17.3 million.

Chile's neighbors are Peru to the north, Bolivia to the northeast, and Argentina to the east. The boundary with Peru consists of a series of geometric lines that trend in a generally northeasterly direction from the Pacific Ocean. This boundary crosses the extremely arid and very sparsely populated Atacama Desert. From the tripoint between Chile, Peru, and Bolivia, the boundary between Chile and Bolivia follows a series of geometric lines extending in a generally southward direction through the Andes Mountains. Most of these lines are located between high mountains on either side of the boundary, and the boundary crosses the Parinacota volcano at more than 20,000 feet above sea level. Cerro Zapaleri, an extinct volcano more than 18,500 feet in elevation, is the tripoint between Chile, Bolivia, and Argentina.

Most of Chile's boundary with Argentina runs along the crest of the Andes Mountains. The highest peak in South America, Aconcagua, is located along this boundary. In southern Chile, the boundary turns eastward. The 52nd parallel of south latitude forms the boundary, which turns southeastward before reaching the Atlantic Ocean. The island of Tierra del Fuego is divided between Chile to the west and Argentina to the east at the 68° 34′ meridian of west longitude.

HISTORICAL CONTEXT

Chile became a Spanish colony after its current capital city of Santiago was founded in 1541. In 1810, the War of Chilean Independence began. Many Chileans opposed independence, and the conflict between pro-independence forces and anti-independence forces, which were supported by Spain, continued for more than a decade. The last Spanish troops were expelled from mainland Chile in 1821. In 1840, Spain recognized Chilean independence, and full diplomatic relations were established.

Most of the Atacama Desert in what is now northern Chile was controlled by Bolivia and Peru for much of the 19th century. Boundary tensions among these countries intensified after valuable deposits of nitrates and other minerals were discovered in the Atacama near the borders. In 1866, Bolivia and Chile agreed to the 24th parallel of south latitude as their boundary. The two countries agreed to share revenues associated with taxing mineral extraction occurring between the 23rd and 25th parallels. Chilean entrepreneurs, often with the help of foreign capital, invested heavily in mining operations in the boundary region. Bolivian investment in the area was hindered by the fact that the Andes Mountains separated it from the rest of the country. Chile objected to having to continue to share revenues with Bolivia, which invested far less capital into the mining operations than Chile did. Continued tensions eventually led to the War of the Pacific, which broke out between Chile and Bolivia in 1879. Peru entered the war on the side of Bolivia, but Chile gained the upper hand in most battles.

The War of the Pacific ended in 1883. After the war, peace agreements between Chile and Peru and between Chile and Bolivia ended armed hostilities. The Treaty of Ancun between Chile and Peru specified that Peru's two southernmost provinces, Tacna and Arica, would be occupied by Chile. The treaty specified that a plebiscite would take place to determine whether Tacna and Arica would be Peruvian or Chilean. However, this plebiscite was never held. Finally, in 1929 the two countries agreed that Chile would keep Arica and Peru would keep Tacna, with the boundary between these two provinces becoming the international boundary. In 1884, Bolivia and Chile signed a truce agreement that gave Chile control over the province of Antofagasta along the Pacific Ocean. Chilean sovereignty over Antofagasta was confirmed in a 1904 treaty between the two countries.

The boundary between Chile and Argentina was established via a treaty between the two countries signed in 1881. The major issues resolved through this treaty were the boundaries in southern Chile, along with access to the Straits of Magellan. Chile, which maintained extensive trade with Europe, wanted control of the Straits of Magellan in order to ensure access to the Atlantic Ocean. Both countries also claimed all of Tierra del Fuego. According to the treaty, the Straits of Magellan were neutralized, and Tierra del Fuego was divided between the two countries.

CONTEMPORARY ISSUES

Chile's boundaries with its neighbors have been uncontested since the 19th century. More recently, Chile was involved in the question of sovereignty over Antarctica. Chile claimed all of the area from between longitude 53° west and 90° west from the 60th parallel of south latitude southward to the South Pole. The Antarctic Treaty, which went into effect in 1961, prohibited military activity in Antarctica and set aside the continent as an international scientific preserve. However, it did not set aside fully the claims of Chile and other countries to sovereignty over their territorial claims in Antarctica.

See also   Argentina, Bolivia, Peru

Further Reading

Ricardo Lagos, Blake Hounshell, and Elizabeth Dickinson. *The southern tiger: Chile's fight for a democratic and prosperous future*. New York: Palgrave Macmillan, 2011.

Luis S. Merico. *Antarctica: Chile's claim*. Honolulu, HI: University Press of the Pacific, 2004.

Rossana Castiglioni Nunez. *The politics of social policy change in Chile and Uruguay: Retrenchment versus maintenances, 1973–1998*. New York: Routledge, 2006.

John L. Rector. *The history of Chile*. New York: Palgrave Macmillan, 2005.

Southern Affairs. "Chile's foreign policy: 2008." April 22, 2008, http://www.south ernaffairs.org/2008/04/chilean-foreign-policy-2008.html.

COLOMBIA

OVERVIEW

The Republic of Colombia is located in northwestern South America. With a land area of 440,831 square miles, Colombia is nearly twice the size of Texas and is the fourth-largest country by land area in South America, following Brazil, Argentina, and Peru. Its population is approximately 46 million.

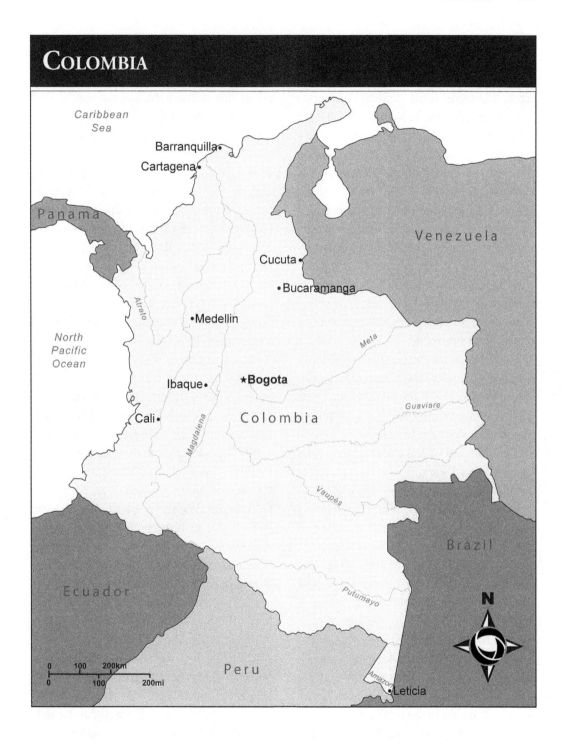

COLOMBIA

Caribbean
Sea

Barranquilla•
Cartagena•

Panama

North
Pacific
Ocean

Atrato

•Medellin

Cucuta •
• Bucaramanga

Venezuela

Meta

Ibaque•   ★Bogota

Cali•   Colombia

Magdalena

Guaviare

Vaupés

Brazil

Ecuador

Putumayo

Peru

Amazon

Leticia

N

0   100   200km
0   100   200mi

Colombia has boundaries with Panama to the northwest, Venezuela and Brazil to the east, and Peru and Ecuador to the south. It has coastlines on the Pacific Ocean to the west and the Caribbean Sea to the north, making Colombia the only country in South America to border both the Pacific and the Caribbean. The boundary between

Colombia and Panama extends in a generally northerly direction from the Pacific to the south to the Caribbean to the north, separating the isthmus of Central America from the South American mainland. To the south, the boundary straddles the heavily forested and sparsely populated Darien Gap region. The northern portion of the boundary follows the crest of the Sierra del Darien mountain range. The entire region on both sides of the boundary is rugged, very sparsely populated, and densely forested. The Darien Gap is the only place between Canada and Alaska in northern North America and Chile and Argentina in southern South America that is not traversed by paved roads.

From the Caribbean coast, the boundary between Colombia and Venezuela begins at a point west of Venezuela's Lake Maracaibo in a generally southerly direction. It enters the drainage basin of the Orinoco River southwest of Lake Maracaibo. Near Tama National Park, it turns westward to the Meta River and follows this river eastward to its confluence with the Orinoco. From there it follows the main channel of the Orinoco southward and upstream. At the confluence of the Guaviare River and the Orinoco, it turns southward and crosses from the Orinoco to the Amazon drainage basin. The boundary continues southward to the Rio Negro, the largest northern tributary of the Amazon River. It follows the Rio Negro to the tripoint between Colombia, Venezuela, and Brazil near the Colombian town of La Guadalupe.

The boundary between Colombia and Brazil extends first in a generally westward direction from La Guadalupe and then northward and again westward. In general, the boundary follows the drainage divide between the Orinoco River basin on the Colombian side of the border to the north and the Amazon River basin on the Brazilian side of the border to the south. This boundary continues until a point about 50 miles east of Colombia's Puinawai Nature Reserve. At this point, the drainage divide is crossed and the rest of eastern and southeastern Colombia is located in the Amazon basin. From this point it extends along straight lines in a westerly direction and along the southern boundary of the reserve. It continues eastward past the reserve to a point northeast of the small village of Minu. It then turns southward, generally following straight-line segments, to the Amazon River.

An exception to this southward trend is the inclusion of territory along and south of the Vaupes River, which is known in Brazil as the Uaupes River, within Colombian territory east of the general boundary trend. This section, which is part of the Colombian department of Yavarate, is about 600 square miles in land area. In Brazil, the Uaupes flows into the Rio Negro. The Rio Negro, in turn, flows into the Amazon River. All of the boundary region between Colombia and Brazil consists of hot, humid tropical rainforest land and is very sparsely inhabited. To the south of the section of Colombia located in the Vaupes drainage basin, the boundary follows several straight-line segments southward to a point adjacent to the Brazilian town of Vila Bittencourt. From Vila Bittencourt, the boundary follows a single straight-line segment that extends in a south-southwesterly direction to the Amazon itself near the small Colombian city of Leticia, near which the tripoint between Colombia, Brazil, and Peru is located.

The boundary between Colombia and Peru continues upstream along the Amazon for about 80 miles. Near the Colombian village of Atacuran, which is located 10 miles north of the main channel of the Amazon, the boundary follows a straight line about 80 miles long northeastward to the Putumayo River, which is a tributary of the Amazon River. The boundary then follows the Putumayo upstream to the tripoint between Colombia, Peru, and Ecuador. From this tripoint, the boundary between Colombia and Ecuador continues along the source of the Putumayo westward into the Andes Mountains. From a point downstream from the source of the Putumayo, the boundary crosses the Andes to the westward-flowing Guepi River. It follows the Guepi westward to the confluence of the Guepi River and the Mataje River, into which the Guepi empties. From this confluence it continues in a generally westward position along the Mataje until the Mataje empties into the Pacific Ocean.

HISTORICAL CONTEXT

Present-day Colombia has been occupied for at least 10,000 years by indigenous Native Americans. Spanish exploration of the region began in 1499, and Christopher Columbus, after whom the country of Colombia was named, visited the Caribbean coast of present-day northern Colombia in 1502. The city of Santa Marta was founded in 1523, and Cartagena was founded in 1533.

In 1538, a Spanish expedition into the interior of Colombia established a settlement that they named Santa Fe de Bogota, which became the modern Colombian capital of Bogota. The region became part of the Viceroyalty of Peru. However, most of Colombia was located far from the Viceroyalty of Peru's capital city of Lima. In 1549, the Spanish government elevated Colombia and neighboring areas to the status of an *audiencia*, giving this area considerable administrative autonomy from the Viceroyalty of Peru. Santa Fe de Bogota became the capital of the *audiencia*, which was named New Granada. In 1717, the *audiencia* became the Viceroyalty of New Granada, which also included present-day Venezuela, Ecuador, and Panama.

In 1819, rebels in New Granada under the leadership of Simon Bolivar declared independence for New Granada under the name of Gran Colombia. Gran Colombia included present-day Colombia, Venezuela, Ecuador, and Peru. The federation dissolved after Venezuela became independent in 1829 and Ecuador became independent in 1830. The remaining territory, consisting of present-day Colombia and Panama, retained the name Nueva Granada, or New Granada, until 1856, when its present name was adopted. What is now Panama was a province, or department, of Colombia.

Panama remained an integral part of Colombia until 1903. The separation of Panama from the rest of Colombia was triggered by the construction of the Panama Canal in the late 19th and early 20th centuries. In 1903, the United States, which took charge of completing the canal after France suspended its work on the project, proposed a treaty with Colombia giving the United States the right to complete the canal through Colombian territory. However, the Senate of Colombia refused to ratify the treaty. After Colombia rejected the treaty, the United States began active support of Panamanian rebels who had already been pressing for independence and had initiated a rebellion that became known as the Thousand Days' War. Panama declared its independence from Colombia in November 1903, and Colombia recognized Panamanian independence in 1921 after the United States agreed to pay Colombia $25 million in redress of the U.S. role in separating Panama from Colombia. The boundary between what had been the department of Panama and the rest of Colombia was recognized as the boundary between the two independent states when Colombia recognized the independence of Panama.

The boundary between Colombia and Peru was contested for many years after the two countries became independent from Spain. The dispute involved control of territory in the Amazon basin east of the tripoint between Colombia, Peru, and Ecuador. Although Colombia was part of the Viceroyalty of New Granada after 1717 and Peru was part of the Viceroyalty of Peru, the boundary between them had never been defined clearly because Spain saw both colonies as subject to the Spanish crown and because what became the disputed region was inaccessible and sparsely populated. However, the discovery and extraction of wild rubber in the Amazon basin became a highly lucrative activity in the late 19th century. Thus both countries attempted to secure control of rubber-producing territory, and both desired access to the Amazon. The city of Leticia, which became Colombia's only port on the Amazon, was founded in 1867.

In 1922, Colombia and Peru signed the Salomon-Torres Agreement, which was intended to resolve the dispute. Under terms of the Agreement, Peru recognized Colombian sovereignty over Leticia, thus recognizing Colombia's right of access to the Amazon. In return, Colombia recognized Peru's sovereignty over the territory south of the Putumayo River. However, Leticia was attacked by Peruvian troops in 1932. Combat between Colombian and Peruvian soldiers continued into 1933. In 1934, the League of Nations awarded sovereignty over Leticia to Colombia.

CONTEMPORARY ISSUES

Despite the long history of conflict, the boundaries between Colombia and its neighbors remain settled. However, ongoing conflicts occur in the boundary regions between Colombia and its neighbors. The absence of paved roads near the boundary between Colombia and Panama in the Darien Gap region has made this area attractive for smugglers and drug traffickers. Colombia is a major source of illegal narcotics, whose production and distribution have been controlled by powerful drug cartels. Illegal drugs from South American are smuggled through the Darien Gap into Central America, Mexico, and eventually the United States.

A larger question is whether paved roads should be constructed in this region at all. The Darien Gap is the only place along the Pan-American Highway, which extends for more than 20,000 miles from northern Alaska to the southern tip of Chile, that has not been constructed and paved. Proponents of constructing paved roads have argued that completing the paved Pan-American Highway will expedite transportation, reduce travel costs, and make the region more easily accessible to tourists. However, environmentalists have expressed concern that the road will cause significant damage to the previously undisturbed natural environment. Paving the road could also make smuggling, drug running, and illegal trading more convenient and make it more difficult for governments to regulate these activities.

Colombia's recent history of political instability has also resulted in issues in its border regions. For more than three decades, a Marxist-Leninist guerilla organization known as the Revolutionary Armed Forces of Colombia (FARC) became active in efforts to take over the government of Colombia. By early in the 21st century, FARC was believed to control as much as a third of Colombia's land area. The group has been financed in part by illegal drug trafficking and through kidnappings for ransom. FARC's strength was concentrated particularly in southern Colombia near its boundaries with Ecuador and Peru. Ongoing guerilla warfare has driven thousands of refugees out of Colombia, particularly into Ecuador. In 2009, the government of Ecuador estimated that more than 200,000 Colombian refugees were living legally in Ecuador. Many more refugees have moved across the boundary illegally.

See also   Brazil, Ecuador, Panama, Peru, Venezuela

Further Reading

James J. Brittain. *Revolutionary social change in Colombia: The origin and direction of the FARC-EP.* London: Pluto Press, 2010.

Robin Kirk. *More terrible than death: Drugs, violence, and America's war in Colombia.* New York: PublicAffairs, 2004.

Michael J. LaRosa and German R. Mejia. *Colombia: A concise contemporary history.* Lanham, MD: Rowman and Littlefield.

COSTA RICA

OVERVIEW

The Republic of Costa Rica is located in the southeastern portion of the isthmus of Central America. Costa Rica has a land area of 19,653 square miles (about twice the size of Maryland) and a population of 4.4 million. Costa Rica is the wealthiest country in Central America, with a per capita gross domestic product of nearly $14,000. Costa Rica is known for its biodiversity, its national parks, and its commitment to the environment. About one-quarter of Costa Rica's land area is protected in its national park system, which is known as its Protected Areas Program. Costa Rica's economy has emphasized the production of coffee, bananas, and other tropical crops. Tourism has become increasingly important to the economy of Costa Rica. Much of this tourism is oriented to the environment and to the Protected Areas Program.

Costa Rica's neighbors are Nicaragua to the north and Panama to the east. The Caribbean Sea is located along the northeast coast of Costa Rica, with the Pacific Ocean to the south and west. The eastern portion of the boundary between Costa Rica and Nicaragua follows the Rio San Juan, which flows eastward out of Lake Nicaragua to the Caribbean Sea. All of Lake Nicaragua is located in Nicaragua, and the upper reaches of the Rio San Juan are located within Nicaragua. West of the river, the boundary follows straight-line segments parallel to but south of the lake. Near the Nicaraguan town of Sapoa, the border is a straight-line segment perpendicular to the lake. This line proceeds for about 12 miles southwestward to the Bahia de Salinas,

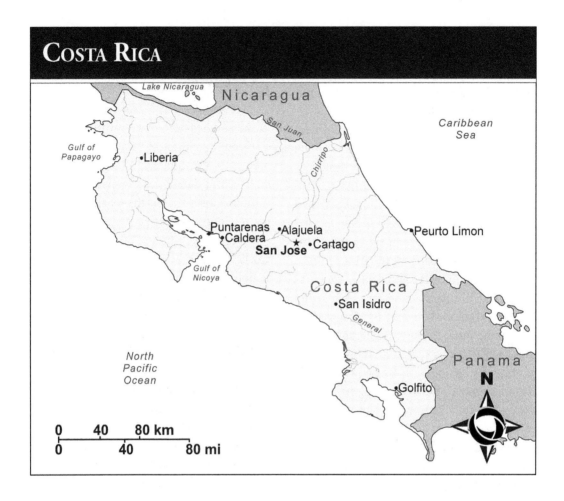

COSTA RICA

which is part of the Pacific Ocean. The boundary between Costa Rica and Panama trends in a north-south direction. Most of it is irregular, although it follows the 83rd meridian of west longitude for part of its length in the center of the country. The central portion of the boundary is traversed by the Parque Nacional la Amistad, which includes territory in both countries.

HISTORICAL CONTEXT

Christopher Columbus first visited the east coast of present-day Costa Rica in 1502, and the first permanent Spanish settlement in what is now Costa Rica was established in 1524. For the next 300 years, Costa Rica was part of the Captaincy General of Guatemala, which was part of the Spanish-ruled Viceroyalty of New Spain. In 1821, Costa Rica and the other Spanish possessions in Central America declared independence, and two years later it became part of the United Provinces of Central America. Costa Rica, which was the poorest and most isolated of the United Provinces, declared its independence from the federation in 1838.

The boundary between Nicaragua and Costa Rica was first delineated via the Canas-Jerez Treaty, signed in 1858. The treaty established that Nicaragua was sovereign over the Rio San Juan but that Costa Rica retained the right of navigation along the river. Sovereignty over the river and navigation rights on the river have been issues of conflict between the two countries ever since. During the 19th century, a route along the Rio San Juan and through Lake Nicaragua was considered seriously as a route for a canal across Central America, adding to ongoing tension between the two neighbors. The Canas-Jerez Treaty was arbitrated by the United States in 1888 and by the Central American Court of Justice in litigation culminating in a 1916 decision.

The boundary between Costa Rica and Panama was also in dispute for many years. Before 1821, Panama was part of Colombia. Thus, the frontier between present-day Costa Rica and present-day Panama was the frontier between two of Spain's major administrative units in the Americas—the Viceroyalty of New Spain, which included Mexico and Central America from Costa Rica northward, and the Viceroyalty of New Grenada, which included present-day Panama, Colombia, Venezuela, and Ecuador. After Costa Rica and Colombia became independent, Colombia claimed the territory between the coast of the Caribbean Sea and the crest of the Cordillera of Central America, which separates that area of Costa Rica drained by the Caribbean from that area drained by the Pacific Ocean. Panama inherited the dispute after it became independent of Colombia in 1903. In 1910, the two sides agreed to arbitration by the chief justice of the United States. Chief Justice Edward D. White issued a decision awarding the disputed territory to Costa Rica in 1914, establishing the current boundary.

CONTEMPORARY ISSUES

Disputes over navigation rights on the Rio San Juan have been ongoing. In 1998, Nicaragua imposed a tax on Costa Rican nationals and tourists who entered the Rio San Juan. In 2009, the International Court of Justice ruled on this case. The court ruled that Nicaragua had the right to require Costa Rican nationals entering or traveling on watercraft in the Rio San Juan to carry identification and to require Costa Rican vessels to register at Nicaraguan ports along the river. However, Nicaragua was denied the right to require Costa Ricans using the river to obtain visas or to pay taxes to use it.

See also   Nicaragua, Panama

Further Reading
Elsa Arsimendi. "Fear and voting in Costa Rica." *Foreign Policy in Focus*, October 24, 2007, http://www.fpif.org/articles/fear_and_voting_in_costa_rica.

Joshua Keating. "Nicaragua cites Google Earth to justify 'invading' Costa Rica." *Foreign Policy*, November 5, 2010, http://blog.foreignpolicy.com/posts/2010/11/05/nicaragua_cites_google_earth_to_justify_invading_costa_rica.

Steven Palmer and Ivan Molina. *The Costa Rica reader: History, culture, politics.* Durham, NC: Duke University Press, 2004.

CUBA

OVERVIEW

The Republic of Cuba is an island country in the Caribbean Sea. The country includes the island of Cuba, which is the largest island by land area in the Caribbean, and several smaller islands. The largest of these is the Isla de la Juventud, previously known as the Isle of Pines, located south of the main island. The total land area of the country is 42,426 square miles, making Cuba approximately the size of Tennessee. Cuba has a population of about 11.2 million.

As an island country, Cuba has no land neighbors. Its closest neighbors by sea are the United States, the Bahamas, Mexico, Jamaica, and Haiti. At its closest point, Cuba is approximately 90 miles south of Key West, Florida, and the distance between Cuba's capital of Havana and Miami, Florida, is 227 miles. The minimum distance from Cuba to Haiti is about 50 miles; the minimum distance from Cuba to the Bahamas is about 60 miles; the minimum distance from Cuba to Jamaica is about 110 miles; and the minimum distance from Cuba to Cancun on the Yucatan Peninsula of Mexico is about 120 miles.

HISTORICAL CONTEXT

Anthropologists estimate that approximately 100,000 indigenous Taino and Ciboney people were living on the island of Cuba at the time of Columbus. The Spanish claimed Cuba, established their first settlement on the island in 1511, and founded the Cuban capital city of Havana in 1515. Within a century after the Spanish arrived, most of the indigenous people of Cuba had died out, primarily from exposure to smallpox and other European diseases.

During the 19th century, various groups agitated for Cuban independence from Spain. In 1892, Jose Marti founded the Cuban Revolutionary Party, which was dedicated to securing Cuban independence. Armed insurrections against the

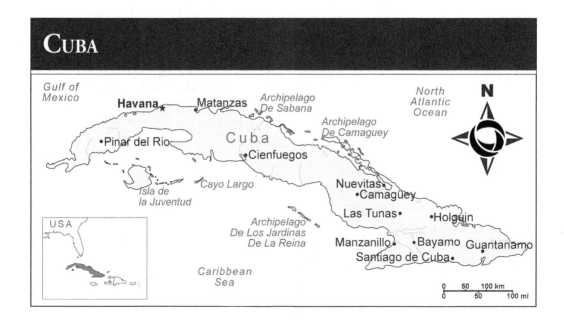

Spanish government of Cuba broke out in 1895, leading to the Cuban War for Independence. Marti was killed in battle in 1895, but his followers continued to fight against Spanish rule for the next three years. In 1898, the United States entered the conflict on the side of the Cuban revolutionaries against Spain in what came to be known as the Spanish-American War. The war ended later that year, and sovereignty over Cuba was transferred to the United States

Cuba achieved formal independence in 1902, but between 1902 and 1959, its economy was controlled closely by the United States. The 1902 independence agreement specified that the United States retained the right to intervene in Cuban domestic affairs and to control Cuba's foreign policy. The United States also claimed what became the Guantanamo Bay Naval Base on the southeastern coast of the island of Cuba. U.S. sovereignty over Guantanamo was established by a treaty between Cuba and the United States signed in 1903. A 1934 treaty reaffirmed U.S. sovereignty over the Guantanamo Bay base but renounced the United States's right to intervene in Cuban domestic affairs. This treaty stipulated that U.S. sovereignty over Guantanamo will continue unless both countries agree to terminate the lease agreement or the United States decides to abandon the base. Today nearly 10,000 American military personnel are stationed at the base.

The close relations between Cuba and the United States ended abruptly in 1959, when Fidel Castro assumed control of Cuba's government. Castro aligned Cuba with the Soviet Union during the Cold War. U.S.-backed forces tried unsuccessfully to overthrow Castro's government, most notably during the failed Bay of Pigs Invasion in 1961. The close relationship between Cuba and the Soviet Union culminated in the Cuban Missile Crisis of 1962, during which the Soviets placed missiles aimed at the United States on Cuban soil. After U.S. president John F. Kennedy ordered a U.S. naval blockade of Cuba, the Soviets agreed to dismantle their missiles in Cuba while the United States ended the blockade. However, the United States suspended economic relations with Cuba. The United States had been Cuba's leading trade partner before Castro assumed power.

During the 1960s, the United States imposed a trade embargo on Cuba. Tourism has been a mainstay of the Cuban economy since the early 20th century. Tourist traffic from the United States to Cuba ended abruptly after Castro assumed power; however, large numbers of European and Canadian tourists continued to visit Cuba each year. In order to prevent Cubans from escaping Cuba by crossing into U.S. territory at Guantanamo Bay, Castro's government built a fence around the perimeter of the base. Both sides planted numerous mines near the border between the base and Cuba. The United States removed its mines from the border area in the late 1990s, but those on the Cuban side of the border are still in place.

During the 1960s and 1970s, Cuba provided weapons and financial support to pro-communist insurgency movements in less developed countries in various areas of the world. Hundreds of thousands of Cubans, including many professionals and business owners, left Cuba after Castro's takeover. Many of these refugees moved to the Miami area, where they remain an influential political and economic bloc to the present day. Cuba relied heavily on trade with the Soviet Union. The Soviet government's collapse worsened already deteriorating economic conditions in Cuba.

Castro has remained in power since taking over the Cuban government in 1959. Because of his advanced age and declining health, Castro formally resigned as Cuba's president and ceded his duties as head of state to his brother, Raul Castro, in 2008.

CONTEMPORARY ISSUES

Cuba's relationships with its neighbors are dominated by ongoing tensions between Cuba and the United States. The United States and Cuba do not maintain diplomatic relations with each other. The American trade embargo with Cuba, which had been imposed in the 1960s, remains in effect. During the first decade of the 20th century, the United States gave support to anti-Castro organizations within the United States and to efforts to promote democracy in Cuba. After Barack Obama was inaugurated as president of the United States in 2009, however, the new administration began tentative efforts to reduce tensions between the two countries. These efforts included easing restrictions on travel and a reduction in long-standing economic sanctions that had been imposed on Cuba.

The status of the American military base at Guantanamo Bay has been a particular point of contention between the two countries. Controversy intensified, both between the two countries and within the United States, when U.S. officials began to use Guantanamo as a detention camp to house enemy fighters and suspected Al Qaeda terrorists after the 9/11 attacks on the United States by Al Qaeda in 2001. An ongoing dispute between Cuba and the Bahamas over the maritime boundary between the two countries was resolved by a treaty signed by both countries in 2011.

Further Reading

Julia E. Sweig. "Fidel's final victory." *Foreign Affairs*, January/February 2007.

Michele Zebich-Knox and Heather N. Nicol. *Foreign policy toward Cuba: Isolation or engagement?* Lanham, MD: Lexington Press, 2005.

DOMINICA

OVERVIEW

The Commonwealth of Dominica is an island country in the Caribbean Sea. It occupies the island of Dominica in the Lesser Antilles. Dominica's land area is 290 square miles, or about four times the size of the District of Columbia. Its population is approximately 73,000. The northernmost part of Dominica is about 30 miles south of the French colony of Guadeloupe, and its southernmost part is about 30 miles north of the French colony of Martinique. The closest independent country is St. Lucia, about 100 miles to the south of Dominica. Tourism and agriculture are Dominica's major sources of income.

HISTORICAL CONTEXT

Columbus sighted Dominica in 1493 and named it for Sunday, the day of the week on which he first saw the island. France claimed the island in 1635, but in 1660 France and Britain agreed to set aside the

DOMINICA

island as a home for indigenous Carib people who had been displaced from other Caribbean islands. However, in 1715 France established settlements on the island, and in 1727 it became formally a colony of France. Sovereignty was transferred from France to Britain in 1763 in accordance with the 1763 Treaty of Paris that ended the Seven Years' War. France occupied the island from 1778 to 1783, when Britain was preoccupied with the American Revolution. The 1783 Treaty of Paris, which ended the Revolutionary War, reaffirmed British control of Dominica. French forces attempted unsuccessfully to regain control of Dominica in 1795 and 1805. Dominica became independent in 1978.

CONTEMPORARY ISSUES

Dominica and Venezuela have disputed control over Aves Island in the Caribbean. Aves is a tiny island located about 100 miles west of Dominica and 340 miles north of Venezuela. Venezuela claims Aves as part of its exclusive economic zone under terms of the United Nations Law of the Sea treaty. This claim would grant Venezuela the right to control maritime resources, including minerals that may be discovered underneath the continental shelf, within 200 miles of Aves. However, Dominica argues that the island is too small for permanent human habitation and therefore that Venezuela's claim should be limited to within 12 miles of the island.

Further Reading

Patrick L. Baker. *Centring the periphery: Chaos, order, and the ethnohistory of Dominica.* Montreal, Quebec, Canada: McGill-Queens University Press, 1994.

Peter Clegg. "The development of the Windward Islands banana export trade: Commercial opportunity and colonial necessity." Society for Caribbean Studies Annual Conference Papers, 2000, http://www.caribbeanstudies.org.uk/papers/2000/olv1p4.pdf.

DOMINICAN REPUBLIC

OVERVIEW

The Dominican Republic includes the eastern two-thirds of the Caribbean island of Hispaniola, which is the second largest island in the Greater Antilles. The Dominican Republic's land area is 18,704 square miles, the size of Vermont and New Hampshire combined. Its population is about 10 million.

The Dominican Republic shares Hispaniola with Haiti, its neighbor to the west. The boundary between the two countries extends from the Atlantic Ocean to the north to the Caribbean Sea to the south. The northern portion of the boundary follows the Dajabón River from its mouth on the Atlantic upstream to the mouth of the Capotillo River (which is also known as the Bernard River). The boundary continues upstream along the Capotillo to its source in the interior mountains of Hispaniola. From there it extends across the crests of mountains in a generally southward direction. The southern portion of the boundary follows the Pedernales from the mountains southward and downstream to its mouth in the Caribbean.

HISTORICAL CONTEXT

Hispaniola was populated by Taino people prior to the arrival of the Spaniards in the late 15th century. Columbus landed on Hispaniola in December 1492 and claimed the island for Spain. Four years later, Columbus's brother Bartholomew founded what would become the first permanent European settlement in the Western Hemisphere at Santo Domingo. Santo Domingo became the administrative center of the colony, which was given the same name, and it remains the capital and largest city of the Dominican Republic today. Within 50 years of Columbus's arrival, the indigenous Taino population was decimated and nearly wiped out by exposure to European diseases, enslavement, and war.

French settlers occupied western Hispaniola in the late 17th century. France claimed the western part of Hispaniola and established the colony of Saint-Domingue. The Treaty of Ryswick, signed by France and Spain in 1697, formalized the division of Hispaniola into an area of French control to the west and an area of Spanish control to the east and was recognized by both countries. In 1777, France and Spain signed a treaty reaffirming the division of the island between Spanish and French spheres of influence. However, the boundary was not delineated precisely until the 20th century. Spain ceded its portion of Hispaniola

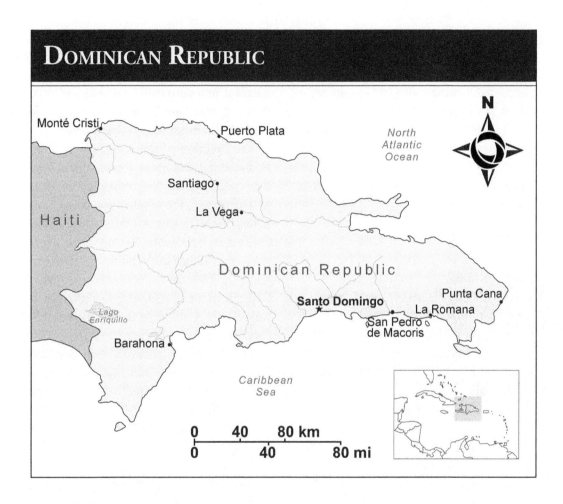

DOMINICAN REPUBLIC

Monté Cristi
Puerto Plata
North Atlantic Ocean
N
Santiago
La Vega
Haiti
Dominican Republic
Punta Cana
Santo Domingo
La Romana
Lago Enriquillo
San Pedro de Macoris
Barahona
Caribbean Sea

0   40   80 km
0   40   80 mi

to France in 1795, but Spain regained control of this area in 1808.

In 1821, Santo Domingo declared independence. However, newly independent Haiti invaded the present-day Dominican Republic and occupied the territory. The Dominican Republic declared its independence in 1844. The next 125 years were characterized by considerable political instability, including U.S. occupation of the country between 1916 and 1922.

In 1929, the Dominican Republic and Haiti signed an agreement formalizing the boundary between the two countries. A commission surveyed and demarcated the exact boundary. A few discrepancies between the treaty and the boundary on the ground were identified, and these differences were resolved through a second agreement between the two countries in 1935.

CONTEMPORARY ISSUES

The boundary between the Dominican Republic and Haiti has been undisputed since the 1935 agreement was signed. However, migration from Haiti to the Dominican Republic remains an issue of contention today. As many as 2 million Haitians are believed to have crossed the boundary into the much wealthier Dominican Republic.

Many work as laborers, peddlers, or domestic servants, and many others are unemployed. Some Dominican officials are concerned that the influx of Haitian immigrants has impeded the delivery of public services and has contributed to environmental degradation. Migration from Haiti to the Dominican Republic has increased since the earthquake that devastated Haiti in February 2010.

See also   Haiti

Further Reading

Randal C. Archibold. "As refugees from Haiti linger, Dominicans' good will fades." *New York Times*, August 30, 2011, http://www.nytimes.com/2011/08/31/world/americas/31haitians.html?page wanted=all.

Steven Gregory. *The devil behind the mirror: Globalization and politics in the Dominican Republic.* Berkeley: University of California Press, 2006.

Frank Moya Pons. *The Dominican Republic: A national history.* Princeton, NJ: Markus Wiener, 2010.

ECUADOR

OVERVIEW

The Republic of Ecuador is located along the Pacific Ocean in northwestern South America. Its name comes from the fact that the equator bisects the country. Ecuador has a land area of 109,483 square miles, approximately the size of Nevada. Its population is about 15 million. Ecuador is also sovereign over the Galapagos Islands, which are located in the Pacific Ocean about 600 miles west of Ecuador's Pacific coast.

Ecuador has borders with Colombia to the north and Peru to the east and south. To the west, mainland Ecuador has a coastline about 1,400 miles long on the Pacific. The western portion of the boundary between Ecuador and Colombia follows the Guepi River westward to its confluence with the Mataje River. From there the Mataje remains the boundary as its flows westward until emptying into the Pacific Ocean. Near the source of the Guepi in the Andes Mountains, the boundary reaches the Putumayo River, a tributary of the Amazon River. It follows the Putumayo to the tripoint between Ecuador, Peru, and Colombia.

The boundary between Ecuador and Peru has been contested since both countries became independent of Spain in the early 19th century. This boundary extends southward and southeastward from the tripoint between Ecuador, Colombia, and Peru, which is located near the eastern end of Ecuador's Cuyabeno National Park. From the tripoint, the boundary extends through the Amazon basin and then moves into the Andes. Near the Tabaconas Namballe National Sanctuary in the Andes Mountains of Peru, the boundary trends northwestward toward the Pacific Ocean following the Chinchipe, Canchis, and Espindola rivers. It shifts to the northeast near the Peruvian Zona Reservade Tumbes before proceeding northward to the Gulf of Guayaquil in the Pacific Ocean. The two countries have fought several wars over control of territory near their boundary. Disputes have focused on the portions of those countries located in the Amazon basin east of the Andes.

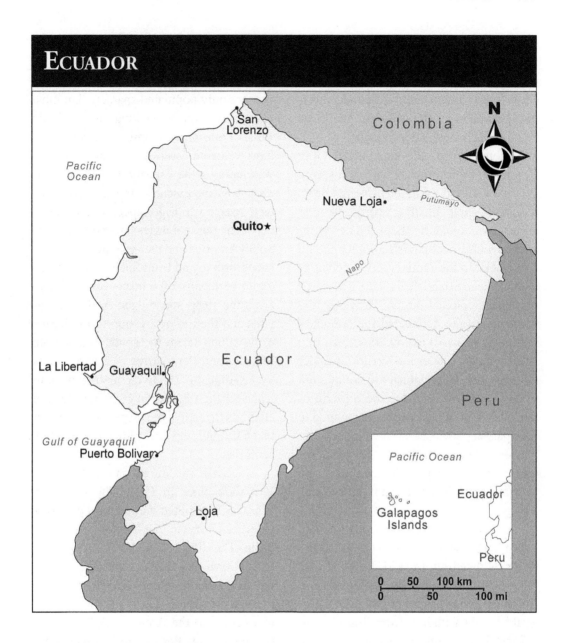

ECUADOR

HISTORICAL CONTEXT

Most of present-day Ecuador was part of the Inca Empire before the Inca regime was deposed by Spanish conquistadors in the early 16th century. After the Spanish assumed control of the territory, present-day Ecuador became part of the Spanish Viceroyalty of Peru until 1717, when it was transferred to the new Viceroyalty of New Grenada. The Viceroyalty of New Grenada also included present-day Venezuela, Colombia, and Panama, with its capital at Bogota. When Ecuador was transferred from the Viceroyalty of Peru to the Viceroyalty of New Grenada, the boundaries of the two viceroyalties were not demarcated. That they were not demarcated was an eventual cause of the long-standing boundary dispute between Ecuador and Peru after both countries achieved independence.

Simon Bolivar, the founder of Gran Colombia, argued that boundary disputes should be settled using the principle of *uti possitedis juris*. In other words, Bolivar argued that boundaries between newly independent former Spanish colonies should correspond to the administrative divisions that had been established by the Spaniards during the colonial period. However, the Spanish had not delineated the boundary between the two viceroyalties, resulting in disagreement over the territories under their control. The Spanish did not attempt to demarcate the boundary because all of the lands in both viceroyalties belonged to the Spanish Crown. Moreover, the frontier between New Grenada and Peru crossed areas that were sparsely inhabited and in some cases had not been explored by Europeans.

The city of Guayaquil declared independence from Spain in 1820. The rest of Ecuador followed suit in 1822. It joined with the newly independent Republic of Gran Colombia along with Venezuela and Colombia until it withdrew from Gran Colombia and became an independent republic in 1830. Border disputes with Peru began even before Ecuador achieved full independence. In 1828 and 1829, Gran Colombia and Peru went to war over control of what is now northeastern Peru and southeastern Ecuador. A peace treaty signed in 1829 stipulated the establishment of a binational boundary commission charged with determining the border precisely, but

this effort ended with dissolution of Gran Colombia in the following year.

The frontier region east of the Andes was not only populated sparsely, but most of it was seen as lacking in economic value. From an economic standpoint, the most valuable asset of the frontier region was access to the Amazon River. The Amazon was an essential transportation artery, used to transport people and goods between the countries of northwestern South America and the Atlantic Ocean and henceforth to and from Spain. The only alternative means of transportation was to cross the steep and rugged Andes Mountains and then to go by ship to the Straits of Magellan far to the south. Hence both Ecuador and Peru strove to ensure access to the Amazon. The two countries went to war over their border in 1859, and several attempts to resolve the dispute were undertaken through the late 19th and early 20th centuries.

A second war known as the Zarumilla War took place in 1941. The Zarumilla War was associated with control over disputed territory in the Amazon drainage basin. The disputed land was located east of the Cordillera del Condor range extending to the Rio Santiago and its tributary, the Rio Maranon. These rivers have direct access to the Amazon. After hostilities broke out, Peru's much larger army overwhelmed Ecuador's forces, and Peru occupied much of the disputed territory as well as territory within Ecuador that was not in dispute between the two countries. In 1942, Ecuador and Peru signed the Rio de Janeiro Protocol of Peace, Friendship, and Boundaries. Negotiations leading to the signing of the protocol were observed by Argentina, Chile, Brazil, and the United

States. The protocol divided the disputed territory roughly in half. It guaranteed Ecuador's access to the river but denied Ecuador's claim of a boundary directly on the river.

Legally, the signing of the protocol ended the boundary dispute that had been ongoing since 1830. However, aerial surveys revealed that boundary demarcation had been undertaken without accurate knowledge of the local terrain. In 1960, Ecuador's president attempted to nullify the protocol on the grounds that Ecuador was forced to agree to it under coercion. Peru and the observer countries rejected this argument. Armed hostilities broke out in 1981 and again in 1995. The dispute was resolved finally with the signing of a new comprehensive peace treaty in 1998.

CONTEMPORARY ISSUES

Although the 1998 treaty formally ended the ongoing dispute over the land boundaries between Ecuador and Peru, the maritime boundary between the two countries remained contested. The Pacific waters off the coasts of the two countries are among the richest fishing grounds in the world, and both countries had a strong interest in drawing boundaries to claim access to as much of the disputed offshore territory as possible. In 2011, Ecuador and Peru signed an agreement resolving the dispute by establishing the line of latitude at which the boundary intersects the Gulf of Guayaquil as the maritime boundary. The agreement also specified that the Gulf of Guayaquil was recognized as internal Ecuadorian waters, as opposed to international waters.

See also   Colombia, Peru

Further Reading

Monica Herz and João Nogueira. *Ecuador vs. Peru: Peacemaking amid rivalry.* Boulder, CO: Lynne Rienner, 2002.

Osvaldo Hurtado. *Portrait of a nation: Culture and politics in Ecuador.* Translated by Barbara Sipe. Toronto: Madison, 2010.

Phil Locker. "Peru accepts Ecuador maritime borders, much to Chile's chagrin." MercoPress, May 4, 2011, http://en.mercopress.com/2011/05/04/peru-accepts-ecuador-maritime-borders-much-to-chile-s-chagrin.

EL SALVADOR

OVERVIEW

The Republic of El Salvador is the smallest and most densely populated country in Central America, and it is the only Central American country that does not have a Caribbean seacoast. It has a land area of 8,124 square miles, about the size of Massachusetts, and a population of about 6.2 million.

El Salvador borders Guatemala to the west and Honduras to the north and east, with the Pacific Ocean to the south. Most of the boundary between El Salvador and Guatemala follows the Rio Paz, which rises in the highlands of southern Guatemala and flows southwestward into the Pacific.

The western portion of the boundary between El Salvador and Honduras also follows rivers. From the tripoint between El Salvador, Honduras, and Guatemala, the boundary extends eastward to the Rio Sumpul. It follows the Rio Sumpul eastward to its confluence with the Rio Lempa, which is the longest river in Central America. The eastern portion of the boundary trends

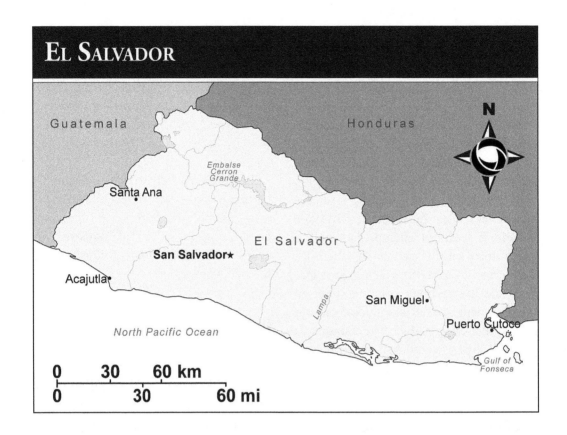

EL SALVADOR

Guatemala

Honduras

N

Embalse
Cerron
Grande

Santa Ana

El Salvador

San Salvador★

Acajutla

Lampa

San Miguel•

Puerto Cutoco

North Pacific Ocean

Gulf of
Fonseca

0   30   60 km

0   30   60 mi

from west-northwest to east-southeast, following a combination of straight-line segments and other rivers. The boundary then turns southward, following the Rio Goascorán to its mouth at the Gulf of Fonseca and the Pacific Ocean.

HISTORICAL CONTEXT

El Salvador became a colony of Spain in 1525 and remained under Spanish rule until it declared its independence, along with other Spanish possessions in Central America, in 1821. In 1823, El Salvador became part of the United Provinces of Central America. Beginning in 1838, civil war resulted in the dissolution of the United Provinces. El Salvador declared its independence in 1840. Efforts were made to

reunite some or all of the United Provinces in 1842, 1852, 1896, and 1921, but none of these efforts were successful. The longest-lived of these reunions was the Greater Republic of Central America, which included El Salvador, Honduras, and Nicaragua. This union lasted only two years before collapsing in 1898.

The boundaries between the United Provinces were not defined well before and during its establishment. Not until after the United Provinces split into the independent countries of Central America were the boundaries among them delineated clearly. The boundary between El Salvador and Guatemala was delineated formally by agreement between the two countries in 1938.

El Salvador and Honduras resolved a long-standing border dispute that dated back to the period of Spanish rule in the late 18th century. The dispute involved sovereignty over about 200 square miles of territory along the boundary, over three islands in the Gulf of Fonseca, and over Honduran access to the Pacific Ocean via the Gulf. The disputed boundary was an underlying cause of the Football War, known as the Soccer War in the United States. Armed hostilities broke out briefly between the two countries after a dispute over an international football (soccer) match in 1969. In 1980, the two countries agreed to turn the dispute over to the International Court of Justice if they could not resolve it between themselves. After five years of negotiation, the issue was referred to the court, which handed down its decision in 1992. The decision gave Honduras about two-thirds of the disputed territory and sovereignty over one of the islands. El Salvador was granted sovereignty over the other two islands, Conchaquita and Meanguera. The agreement also assured Honduran access to the Pacific.

Between 1980 and 1992, El Salvador experienced civil war between its military government and left-wing revolutionaries comprising the Farabundo Marti National Liberation Front (FMLN). An underlying cause of the war was the division of wealth between the rich minority and the poor majority. During the 20th century, coffee was El Salvador's main export. However, the coffee plantations of El Salvador, along with the profits associated with coffee exports, were controlled by a small number of very wealthy landowners while the large majority of Salvadorians lived in poverty. Efforts to promote economic and social reforms were suppressed by the government, and armed conflict broke out in 1980. The United States supported the government and claimed that the revolutionaries were supported by communist Cuba, although American claims that the Salvadorian government was respecting human rights in suppressing the rebellion were undermined by the murders of several Salvadorian and American Roman Catholic priests, bishops, and nuns.

A peace agreement ending the Salvadorian Civil War was signed by both sides in 1992. During 12 years of conflict, however, the war resulted in about 75,000 deaths. Hundreds of thousands of refugees left the country, and even after 1992, many other Salvadorians moved away in search of economic opportunities elsewhere. Estimates suggest that as many as 3 million Salvadorians live elsewhere, with about 2 million in the United States. Remittances from these Salvadorian refugees back to El Salvador have become a significant contributor to the contemporary Salvadorian economy. It has been estimated that remittance payments represent more than 10 percent of El Salvador's national income.

CONTEMPORARY ISSUES

The most significant boundary-related issue facing El Salvador today is the question of its maritime boundaries, specifically in the Gulf of Fonseca. The Gulf of Fonseca is about 1,200 square miles in size. El Salvador, Honduras, and Nicaragua all have coastlines along the coast of the Gulf. The Gulf represents Honduras's only access to the Pacific. In resolving the boundary dispute between El Salvador and Nicaragua in 1992, the International Court of Justice ruled that all three countries would share access to the Gulf and its resources.

See also   Guatemala, Honduras

Further Reading

Jorge H. Dominguez (ed.). *Boundary disputes in Latin America.* Washington, DC: United States Institute of Peace, 2003, http://www.glin.gov/view.action?glinID=205255.

William H. Durham. *Scarcity and survival in Latin America: Ecological origins of the Football War.* Palo Alto, CA: Stanford University Press, 1979.

Diana Villiers Negroponte. *Seeking peace in El Salvador: The struggle to reconstruct a nation at the end of the Cold War.* London: Palgrave Macmillan, 2012.

GRENADA

OVERVIEW

Grenada is a small island country in the Windward Islands in the Caribbean Sea. It includes the main island of Grenada and several nearby islands. The main island of Grenada contains about three-quarters of the country's land and about 95 percent of its population. The total land area of Grenada is 133 square miles, or about twice the size of the District of Columbia. Its population is approximately 110,000. The Martinique Channel separates Grenada from St. Vincent and the Grenadines, the nearest sovereign country to the north. Grenada is located about 100 miles north of Trinidad and about 120 miles northwest of the coast of Venezuela on the South American mainland.

HISTORICAL CONTEXT

Grenada was inhabited by Caribs when it was first sighted by Spanish explorers during Columbus's third voyage in 1498. The first permanent European settlement in present-day Grenada was established by France in 1649. Britain captured Grenada in 1762, and sovereignty over Grenada was transferred formally from France to Britain under terms of the Treaty of Paris, which ended the Seven Years' War in 1763. Both the French and the British brought numerous African slaves to the island, and today more than 80 percent of Grenadians are of African descent. Grenada became a Crown Colony in 1877. Internal autonomy was granted to Grenada in 1967, and the country became fully independent in 1974.

A pro-communist government seized power in Grenada in a coup d'état in 1983. Cuban engineers began construction of an airstrip on the island. Concerned about the possibility that Cuba, backed by the Soviet Union, would use the airstrip to supply communist governments and rebels in Central and South America, the United States invaded Grenada in October 1983 with the support of several Caribbean countries. Although the United Nations condemned the action, the invaders ousted the pro-communist regime and restored the previous government to power. Since then, Grenada has maintained cordial relations with neighboring countries, and there are no ongoing controversies involving Grenada.

Further Reading

Peter Clegg. "The development of the Windward Islands banana export trade: Commercial opportunity and colonial necessity." Society for Caribbean Studies Annual Conference Papers, 2000, http://www.caribbeanstudies.org.uk/papers/2000/olv1p4.pdf.

GRENADA

Petit
Martinique

Hillsborough•
Carriacou   •Grand Bay

Caribbean
Sea

N

Ronde Island

North
Atlantic
Ocean

Sauteurs•

•Victoria

Gouyave•   Tivoli•

Grenada

•Grand Roy
              •Grenville

Marquis•

★St.George's •Saint Davids
•Belmont

Calivigny•

Cuba

Venezuela

0	5	10 km
0	5	10 mi

GUATEMALA

OVERVIEW

Guatemala is the northernmost country of Central America. It has a land area of approximately 42,000 square miles, the size of Kentucky. Its population of 13.5 million makes it the largest country by population in Central America. About 1.5 million Guatemalans live outside Guatemala, primarily in the United States and Mexico.

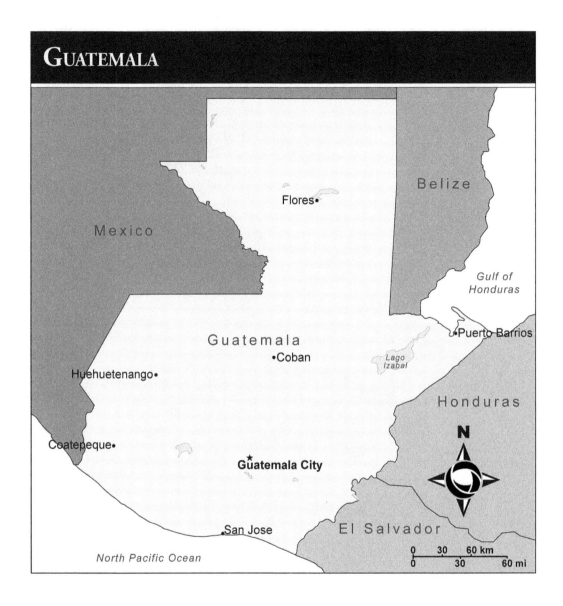

GUATEMALA

Guatemala is bordered by Mexico to the west and north, Belize to the northeast, Honduras to the east and southeast, and El Salvador to the south. It has seacoasts on the Caribbean Sea to the east and the Pacific Ocean to the west. The border between Guatemala and Mexico combines physical and cultural boundaries. The Rio Suchiate forms the southwesternmost portion of this border as far inland as Tacana, a volcano that is the second-highest mountain in Central America. From Tacana, it extends in a straight-line segment northeastward and then due eastward to the Rio Usamacinta. It then follows the Usamacinta northwestward until it turns eastward. It then follows geometric lines to the tripoint with Belize, with the eastern portion of this boundary following the 17° 49′ parallel of north latitude.

Most of the boundary between Guatemala and Belize consists of two straight-line segments. The more northerly segment extends due south from the tripoint with Mexico. The second segment trends slightly west of south. At the southern end of this segment, the boundary turns eastward and follows the Sarstun River to its mouth in the Caribbean Sea. The boundary between Guatemala and Honduras includes a combination of rivers, drainage divides, and straight-line segments. It trends generally from northeast on the Caribbean to southwest at the tripoint between Guatemala, Honduras, and El Salvador. Most of the boundary between Guatemala and El Salvador follows the Rio Paz, which rises in the highlands of Guatemala and then flows southwestward into the Pacific.

HISTORICAL CONTEXT

Present-day Guatemala was part of the Mayan Empire several centuries before the arrival of Spanish conquistadors in the late 15th century. Today, many Guatemalans speak Mayan languages as their first languages. Spain conquered the areas during the 1520s, and Guatemala remained part of the Spanish colonial empire until it became independent in 1821.

In 1822 and 1823, Guatemala and other former Spanish colonies in Central America were part of Mexico. The union between Mexico and Central America was dissolved in 1823, when Guatemala became part of the United Provinces of Central America. It remained part of the United Provinces until the United Provinces dissolved in 1840. During the 19th century, Guatemala claimed the neighboring Mexican state of Chiapas. In 1882, Guatemala renounced its claim to Chiapas, and the two countries agreed to their present boundary.

Guatemala's boundary with Honduras was disputed between the two countries after the dissolution of the United Provinces of Central America. After several unsuccessful attempts to resolve the dispute, the two countries agreed to arbitration by the United States, which issued its decision in 1933. Guatemala and El Salvador agreed to its boundary in 1938.

Throughout its history, Guatemala claimed sovereignty over Belize. Guatemala based its claim on the Treaty of Tordesillas, which divided the Western Hemisphere between Spain and Portugal in 1493. Britain, of course, did not recognize the Treaty of Tordesillas and established the colony of British Honduras, which would become Belize after Belize achieved its independence in 1981. In 1859, Guatemala agreed to recognize British sovereignty over British Honduras in exchange for Britain's agreement to finance construction of a railroad connecting Guatemala with the Caribbean coast of British Honduras. The railroad was never constructed, and in 1940 Guatemala withdrew its recognition of British sovereignty over Belize on the grounds that Britain had not lived up to its treaty obligations. The dispute continued after Belize's independence. Guatemala finally recognized Belize in 1991, but the boundary issue remains unresolved.

CONTEMPORARY ISSUES

The most important issue facing contemporary Guatemala's boundaries is the conflict with Belize. Although Guatemala now recognizes Belize's sovereignty, it continues to claim some of Belize's territory. Negotiations to resolve the dispute continued throughout the 1990s and into the first decade of the 21st century. In 2008, leaders of the two countries agreed in principle that referenda be held in both countries about whether to refer the ongoing dispute to the International Court of Justice. The referenda have been scheduled for 2013.

See also   Belize, El Salvador, Honduras, Mexico

Further Reading

Steven S. Dudley. "How Mexico's drug war is killing Guatemala." *Foreign Policy*, July 20, 2010, http://www.foreignpolicy.com/articles/2010/07/20/How_Mexicos_Drug_War_Is_Killing_Guatemala?showcomments=yes.

Strategic Media Group. "Guatemala: Times of change." 2010, http://www.foreignaffairs.com/files/attachments/guatemala.pdf/.

Steven Topik, Zephyr Frank, and Carlos Marichal (eds.). *From silver to cocaine: Latin American commodity chains and the building of the world economy, 1950–2000*. Durham, NC: Duke University Press, 2006.

GUYANA

OVERVIEW

The Co-Operative Republic of Guyana is located on the northern coast of South America. Guyana is the only former British colony in South America and the only South American country whose official language is English. Guyana has a land area of 83,000 square miles, about the size of Idaho. Its population is approximately 760,000. Most Guyanese residents live near the coast, and inland areas of Guyana are very sparsely populated.

Guyana's neighbors are Suriname to the east, Brazil to the south and southwest, and Venezuela to the west, with the Atlantic Ocean adjoining Guyana to the north. The Courantyne River represents the boundary between Guyana and Suriname. To the south, the boundary between Guyana and Brazil follows the drainage basin between the Amazon River in Brazil and the northward-flowing rivers of Guyana through the Serra Icaria mountain range. To the west, the Tacutu River forms part of the boundary. Although the Tacutu flows northward along the boundary, it is a tributary of the Amazon.

The Tacutu turns southwestward into Brazil at its confluence with the Ireng River, which flows southward and becomes the boundary extending northward. Near the source of the Ireng, the boundary turns westward over land to the tripoint between Guyana, Brazil, and Venezuela. This tripoint is located at the summit of Mount Roraima, the highest peak in the Guyana Highlands. From this tripoint, the boundary between Venezuela and Guyana extends along a straight-line segment extending northwestward to the Wenama River and hence downstream to the Cuyuni River. It continues along the Cuyuni northward, then crosses the Imataca Mountains to the source of the Amakura River. From there it follows the Amakura as it joins other rivers, reaching the Barima River to the Atlantic Ocean coast.

HISTORICAL CONTEXT

Guyana was inhabited by Arawak and Carib peoples prior to the arrival

GUYANA

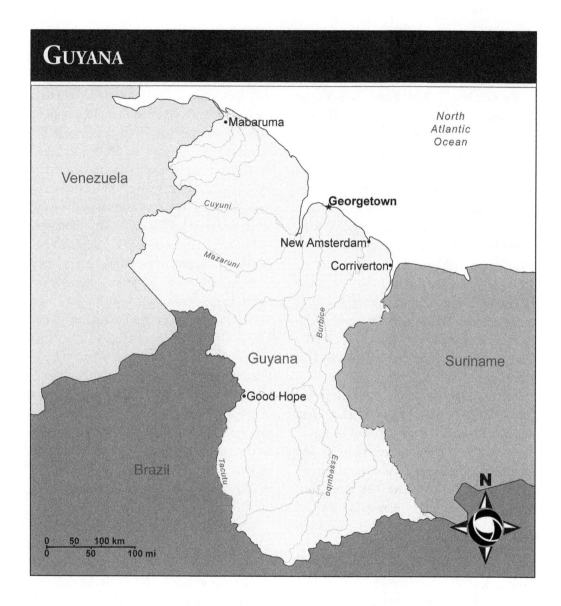

of European settlers. The Dutch began to establish trading posts on the rivers of present-day Guyana in the 17th and 18th centuries. The first such trading post was established near the mouth of the Essequibo River in 1616. Two additional settlements were established on the Berbice River in 1627 and on the Demerara River in 1752. The Dutch administered each of these settlements as separate colonies.

Dutch settlers also established plantations to produce sugar, tobacco, and other tropical crops. At first the fields were worked by indigenous people who had been enslaved by the Dutch. After most of these slaves died from overwork and from European diseases, the Dutch began to import slaves from Africa. By the 18th century, a majority of Guyana's people were of African descent.

In the 1740s, the Dutch began to encourage British settlers to move to the area. Many moved from British colonies in the Caribbean, where land was scarce and soils had become depleted. By the 1780s, British settlers in present-day Guyana outnumbered the Dutch settlers in the region. During the French Revolution, France occupied the Netherlands in 1795. Britain declared war on France and sent an expeditionary force to seize control of the Dutch-administered settlements. The British retained de facto control of present-day Guyana until 1814, when the Netherlands formally relinquished control of the colony. The area became part of the British Empire and was known as British Guiana. Guyana became independent in 1966.

After slavery was abolished throughout the British Empire in 1834, many former slaves refused to continue working on the plantations. Some moved to cities and towns, and others established small farms in the countryside. Faced with a continuing shortage of labor, plantation owners turned to Asia as a source of plantation workers. Thousands of indentured servants were brought to Guyana from India. Today, nearly half of Guyana's people are of Asian Indian origin and about a third are of African origin. About 17 percent claim mixed-race ancestry. The boundaries between Guyana and its neighbors were established prior to Guyanese independence. Britain and the Netherlands, which was sovereign over Suriname, agreed to the Courantyne River as the boundary between the two colonies. However, at that time the upper reaches of the river had yet to be explored by Europeans. Eventual European exploration of the river led to the discovery of two tributaries, either of which could be regarded as the source of the river. Britain claimed that the Kutari River to the east was the source of the Courantyne, whereas the Netherlands claimed that the source of the river was the New River to the west. An agreement negotiated in 1895 identified the Kutari River to the east as the source of the Courantyne. However, Suriname continues to claim the area known as the New River Triangle between the two tributaries.

The boundary between Guyana and Venezuela has been contested since the early 19th century. Since Venezuela became independent, it has claimed sovereignty over the territory west of the Essequibo River, which bisects Guyana. In 1840, the British authorized a survey after which the entire drainage basin of the Cuyuni, which is a western tributary of the Essequibo, was claimed by Britain. Venezuela continued to claim all of the land in present-day Guyana west of the Essequibo. The dispute intensified with the discovery in the late 19th century of gold on lands located between the Essequibo and the Cuyuni.

Under the auspices of the Monroe Doctrine, the two countries agreed to the Treaty of Arbitration between Great Britain and Venezuela in 1897. The Treaty of Arbitration authorized the establishment of an international tribunal to resolve the dispute. In 1899, the tribunal issued its decision that gave sovereignty over most of the disputed territory to Britain. However, it awarded sovereignty over the entire delta of the Orinoco River to Venezuela.

CONTEMPORARY ISSUES

Although the 1899 decision established the present-day boundary between Guyana and Venezuela, Venezuela continues to claim the territory west of the Essequibo. Venezuela refers to the area as the Guayana Esequiba or the Zona en Reclamacion (Reclamation Zone). The Guayana Esequiba includes more than half of the territory of Guyana. When Guyana became independent in 1966, a conference concerning the boundary was held in Geneva. The Treaty of Geneva, which resulted from this conference, stipulated that the two countries would attempt to determine a "practical, peaceful, and satisfactory" solution to their ongoing dispute, although the issue has yet to be resolved fully. In 2012, the United Nations began to take an active role in facilitating negotiations to resolve the dispute. Because the area along the Atlantic coast west of the mouth of the Essequibo remains in dispute, Guyana and Venezuela have yet to establish maritime boundaries in the Atlantic. The maritime boundary between Guyana and Suriname remains contested, with the presence of potentially valuable undersea oil deposits intensifying this dispute.

See also   Brazil, Suriname, Venezuela

Further Reading

Jacqueline Anne Braveboy-Wagner. *The Venezuela-Guyana border dispute: Britain's colonial legacy in Latin America.* Boulder, CO: Westview Press, 1984.

Brian Ellsworth. "Guyana oil exploration stirs up Venezuela border dispute." *Reuters*, June 6, 2012, http://www.reuters.com/article/2012/06/06/us-venezuela-guyana-idUSBRE8551E720120606.

Frank Senauth. *The making of Guyana: From a wilderness to a nation.* Bloomington, IN: AuthorHouse, 2009.

HAITI

OVERVIEW

The Republic of Haiti occupies the western third of the island of Hispaniola. Haiti has a land area of 10,714 square miles, the size of Maryland. Its population is about 9.7 million. Haiti is the poorest country in the Western Hemisphere. More than 60 percent of Haitians work as subsistence farmers, and nearly half of Haiti's adults are illiterate. Tourism has been a major source of income, but tourism into Haiti has suffered because of high crime rates and well-publicized kidnappings and robberies of American, Canadian, and European tourists.

Haiti's only land neighbor is the Dominican Republic, which occupies the eastern two-thirds of Hispaniola. Nearly all of the boundary between the two countries follows physical features. It trends in a north-south direction from the Atlantic Ocean to the north to the Caribbean Sea to the south. The Dajabón River, which empties into the Atlantic, serves as the northern part of the boundary. The boundary follows the Dajabón upstream to its confluence with its tributary, the Capotillo River (which is also known as the Bernard River). The boundary continues upstream along the Capotillo to its source in the interior mountains of Hispaniola. From there it extends across the crests of mountains in a generally southward direction. The southern portion of the boundary follows the Pedernales River southward to its mouth, from which the Pedernales empties into the Caribbean.

HISTORICAL CONTEXT

Prior to the arrival of Europeans, Hispaniola was occupied by indigenous Taino

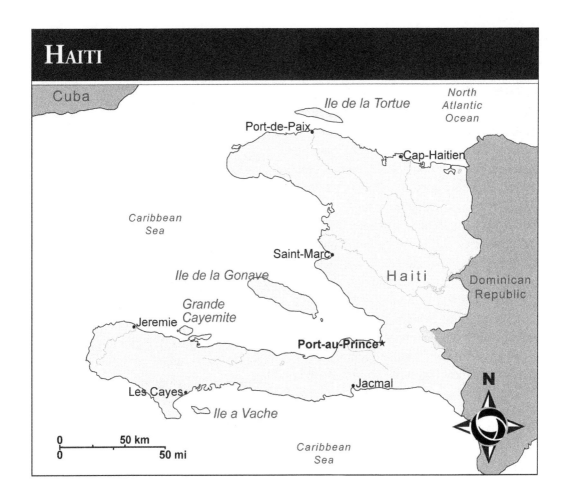

HAITI

Cuba

Ile de la Tortue

North Atlantic Ocean

Port-de-Paix

Cap-Haitien

Caribbean Sea

Saint-Marc

Ile de la Gonave

Haiti

Dominican Republic

Grande Cayemite

Jeremie

Port-au-Prince

Les Cayes

Jacmal

Ile a Vache

0   50 km

0   50 mi

Caribbean Sea

N

peoples. Columbus visited Hispaniola and established a settlement in 1492. Within 50 years of the arrival of the Spanish, nearly all of the Taino of Hispaniola had died, probably because of exposure to European diseases.

Spain lost interest in Hispaniola in the 16th century, instead turning its attention to the American mainland, where lucrative gold and silver deposits had been discovered and mined. In the early 17th century, French buccaneers and pirates established settlements and posts on the island of Tortuga in the Atlantic off the coast of western Hispaniola. From its base on Tortuga,

France claimed the western part of Hispaniola and established the colony of Saint-Domingue on the island. The Treaty of Ryswick, signed by France and Spain in 1697, formalized the division of Hispaniola into an area of French control to the west and an area of Spanish control to the east and was recognized by both countries.

At the time that the Treaty of Ryswick was signed, the interior regions of Hispaniola were sparsely populated. The division of the island between French and Spanish spheres of influence was recognized by both countries, but the boundary between the two colonies was defined only vaguely. In 1777, France and Spain signed a treaty reaffirming the division of the island. However, the boundary was not delineated precisely until 1929 following an agreement between the two countries.

The economy of Saint-Domingue was based on the export of sugar and coffee, which were produced on large French-owned plantations. Thousands of slaves, primarily from Africa, were brought to Saint-Domingue to provide a labor force for the plantations. By the late 18th century, a large majority of Haiti's people were of African ancestry. Slave revolts became common and many people of African ancestry, whether or not enslaved, opposed the French government and its policies of racial discrimination.

Inspired by the American and French revolutions, slaves and former slaves sought independence from France. Independence was declared on January 1, 1804, and the new country was given its original Taino name of Haiti. Having sold the Louisiana territory to the United States the previous year, Napoleon Bonaparte did not attempt to reassert French control over Haiti. France did not formally recognize Haiti until 1826, however. In large part because the Haitian government was controlled by former slaves, the United States did not recognize Haiti until 1862. Invoking the Monroe Doctrine, the United States occupied Haiti from 1915 until 1934.

During the 20th century, Haiti was ruled by a series of corrupt and brutal dictators. Between 1957 and 1986, Haiti was ruled by the particularly repressive regime of Francois "Papa Doc" Duvalier (1907–1971) and his son, Jean-Claude "Baby Doc" Duvalier (1951–), before Baby Doc was ousted in a coup d'état. Since that time, Haiti has struggled with the legacies of corruption, mismanagement, poverty, and environmental problems.

On January 12, 2010, an earthquake measuring 7.0 on the Richter scale occurred not far from Haiti's capital city of Port au Prince. More than 300,000persons lost their lives, and hundreds of thousands of others were injured or became homeless. The tragedy was exacerbated and relief efforts were hampered by Haiti's inadequate infrastructure, poor transportation, and shoddy building construction.

Because of Haiti's long history of poverty and repressive government, many Haitian natives live abroad. It is believed that at least a million people born in Haiti live in the United States, Canada, or France. Emigration from Haiti has been especially prevalent among the educated. An estimated 80 percent of Haitians who hold college degrees live outside of Haiti.

CONTEMPORARY ISSUES

Haiti's boundary with the Dominican Republic has been settled since the early 20th century. Today, three major issues faced by Haiti include migration to the Dominican Republic, deforestation, and water rights. As many as 2 million Haitians are believed to be living in the Dominican Republic, whose per capita income is about six times higher than in Haiti. Many work as laborers or domestic servants. Some Dominican officials have expressed concern that large-scale immigration from Haiti to the Dominican Republic is straining public services and accelerating environmental degradation.

Deforestation is an especially significant problem in Haiti. In 1925, about

60 percent of Haiti was forested. Most of these forests were cut down during the 20th century. By 2006, only about 2 percent of Haiti remained in forest cover whereas about 30 percent of the Dominican Republic remained under forest cover. Haiti's forests were cleared for subsistence farming, and lumber companies cleared other forests. As Haiti's population increased and as more forests were cut down, wood became more and more valuable as a source of fuel and charcoal, accelerating the deforestation process. Deforestation has contributed to soil erosion in Haiti. It has been estimated that as many as 15,000 acres of topsoil are lost to erosion every year. The loss of topsoil not only has an impact on agriculture but also contributes to flooding, mudslides, and landslides during and after the hurricanes and tropical storms that often affect Hispaniola. Dominican officials have expressed concern that continuing deforestation in Haiti could cause environmental degradation on both sides of the boundary.

See also   Dominican Republic

Further Reading

Randal C. Archibold. "As refugees from Haiti linger, Dominicans' good will fades." *New York Times*, August 30, 2011, http://www.nytimes.com/2011/08/31/world/americas/31haitians.html?pagewanted=all.

Laurent Dubois. *Haiti: The aftershocks of history.* New York: Metropolitan Books, 2012.

Paul Farmer. *Haiti after the earthquake.* New York: PublicAffairs, 2012.

Charles Kenny. "The Haitian migration." *Foreign Policy*, January 9, 2012, http://www.foreignpolicy.com/articles/2012/01/09/the_haitian_migration.

HONDURAS

OVERVIEW

The Republic of Honduras is located on the Central American isthmus, and it also includes several small islands in the Caribbean Sea off the coast of the Honduran mainland. Its land area is 43,278 square miles, about the size of Kentucky. Its population is approximately 8.3 million.

Honduras has land borders with Guatemala to the west, El Salvador to the south, and Nicaragua to the southeast. To the north, Honduras has a long coastline on the Caribbean. To the east of El Salvador and to the west of Nicaragua, Honduras has a short coastline on the Gulf of Fonseca, which is an arm of the Pacific Ocean. Honduras also has sovereignty over several small islands in the Caribbean.

Most of Honduras's boundaries follow natural features. The boundary between Honduras and Guatemala trends in a generally southwesterly direction from the Caribbean coast. Near Guatemala's Rio Motagua Cerro Azul National Park, the boundary follows rivers and drainage divides southward to the tripoint between Honduras, Guatemala, and El Salvador.

The western portion of the boundary between El Salvador and Honduras follows the Rio Lempa, the longest river in Central America. From the tripoint between Honduras, El Salvador, and Guatemala, it follows the Rio Sumpui until its confluence with the Rio Lempa. The eastern portion of the boundary follows straight-line segments and other rivers eastward from the

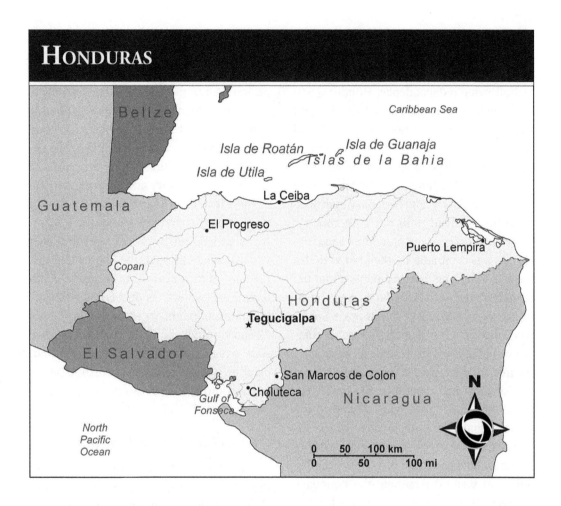

HONDURAS

Rio Lempa to the Rio Goascorán. This river forms the southwestern portion of the boundary to its mouth at the Gulf of Fonseca and the Pacific Ocean.

The boundary between Honduras and Nicaragua extends in a generally southwestwardly direction between the Caribbean and the Gulf of Fonseca. Most of the boundary follows the Rio Coco, which flows from the highlands near the Pacific coast in a northeasterly direction. The Rio Coco is the boundary from the Honduran town of San Marcos de Colon to its mouth in the Caribbean. From San Marcos de Colon, the boundary follows the Rio Coco's tributary, the Rio Poteca, to its

mountain headwaters. It then trends southward following straight-line segments and drainage divides southward across the mountains. The southernmost segment of the boundary follows the Rio Goascorán to the Gulf of Fonseca.

HISTORICAL CONTEXT

Columbus visited the Bay Islands off the coast of the present-day Honduran mainland in 1502. Spanish forces from Mexico invaded the mainland of Honduras in 1524, and Honduras was incorporated formally into the Spanish Empire in 1526. Honduras was governed as part of the Spanish colony of Guatemala until Spain's possessions in Central America became independent in 1821.

Following independence, Honduras and its neighbors became part of the Federal Republic of Central America in 1823 until it seceded from the Federal Republic and became an independent country in 1838. However, at that time the boundaries were not defined clearly, and boundary questions were not resolved until the 20th century. The boundary between Honduras and Guatemala was arbitrated by the United States in 1933. Ongoing disagreements about the boundary between Honduras and Nicaragua were referred to the king of Spain, who ruled in 1906 that the current boundary would take effect. However, Nicaragua regarded the king's decision as favorable to Honduras and continued to contest the boundary. The matter was referred to the International Court of Justice, which affirmed the king of Spain's decision in 1960.

Since the dissolution of the Federal Republic of Central America, the boundary between Honduras and El Salvador has been contested. The main issue of contention between the two countries included control of about 200 square miles of territory on the mainland, control over three islands in the Gulf of Fonseca, and guarantees of Honduran access to the Pacific Ocean through the gulf. Hostilities broke into open warfare in 1969 during the Football War, or Soccer War, which was named because tensions were heightened during a bitterly fought soccer match between the two countries' national teams.

In 1980, the two countries signed the General Peace Treaty. Under terms of this treaty, they agreed to negotiate the boundary dispute with the understanding that the International Court of Justice would hear the case if the two countries could not come to agreement within a five-year period. After the two countries failed to reach agreement on the dispute, the case was referred to the court in 1985. The court handed down its decision in 1992. The decision gave Honduras about two-thirds of the disputed territory and sovereignty over of the island of El Tigre, while El Salvador was granted sovereignty over the remaining mainland territory and over the other two islands. Although the court ruled that the Gulf of Fonseca was not considered international waters, its decision guaranteed Honduras the right of passage to the Pacific Ocean through the Gulf. The Court ruled also that Honduras, El Salvador, and Nicaragua, which also has a coastline on the gulf, would share its resources.

CONTEMPORARY ISSUES

Although the General Peace Treaty and the subsequent decision of the International Court of Justice resolved the long-standing boundary dispute between Honduras and El Salvador, the decision allowed for the possibility that Honduras, El Salvador, and Nicaragua could divide the waters at a later date if they wished to do so.

See also   El Salvador, Guatemala, Nicaragua

Further Reading

William H. Durham. *Scarcity and survival in Latin America: Ecological origins of the Football War.* Palo Alto, CA: Stanford University Press, 1979.

Matthew W. King. *Political ecology of mangroves in southern Honduras:*

Emergence and evolution of environmental conflict in the Gulf of Fonseca 1973–2006. Saarbrücken, Germany: VDM Verlag, 2009.

Steven Topik, Zephyr Frank, and Carlos Marichal (eds.). *From silver to cocaine: Latin American commodity chains and the building of the world economy, 1950–2000*. Durham, NC: Duke University Press, 2006.

JAMAICA

OVERVIEW

Jamaica is an island country in the Caribbean Sea. The country occupies all of the island of Jamaica, which is one of the four islands included in the Greater Antilles along with Cuba, Hispaniola, and Puerto Rico. Jamaica is also sovereign over several small islands off the coast of the main island. With a land area of 4,244 square miles, Jamaica is about 20 percent smaller than the state of Connecticut. Its population is about 2.9 million.

As an island country, Jamaica has no land boundaries. Its nearest maritime neighbors are Cuba and Haiti, which occupies the western third of Hispaniola. At their closest points, Cuba is about 90 miles to the north of Jamaica, and Haiti is about 120 miles to the east.

HISTORICAL CONTEXT

Jamaica was occupied by Arawak and Taino peoples before the arrival of Europeans in the late 15th century. Columbus sighted Jamaica and claimed the island for Spain in 1494. In 1655, Britain captured Jamaica. Spain formally relinquished its territorial claim to Jamaica in 1870. Over the next two centuries, Britain developed Jamaica as a center for sugar production. Large numbers of African slaves were

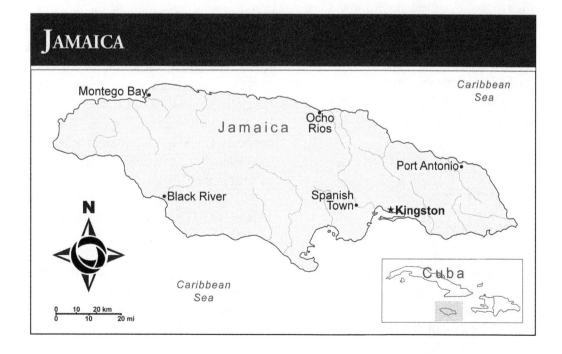

brought to Jamaica to work on sugar plantations until Britain abolished the slave trade in 1807. Slavery was abolished in Jamaica and throughout the British Empire in 1834. Today, about 90 percent of Jamaica's people are of African ancestry.

In 1958, Britain granted independence to Jamaica as part of the Federation of the West Indies, which also included Barbados, Trinidad, and other former British colonies in the Caribbean. The federation proved unwieldy. Jamaica was by far the largest island in the federation by both population and land area and is located far to the northwest of the other members of the federation. These geographic factors contributed to dissension among the federation's members. The federation dissolved in 1962, and Jamaica became an independent sovereign state. Currently Jamaica is involved in no territorial disputes.

Further Reading

Sir John Mordecai. *Federation of the West Indies*. Evanston, IL: Northwestern University Press, 1968.

John Rapley. "Letter from Jamaica: The fall of the modern-day barons." *Foreign Affairs*, June 29, 2010.

Ian Thomson. *The dead yard: A story of modern Jamaica*. New York: Nation Books, 2011.

MEXICO

OVERVIEW

The United Mexican States occupies the southern portion of North America, between the United States to the north and Central America to the south. Mexico has a total land area of 761,606 square miles,

making it three times the size of Texas. Its population is approximately 115 million. Thus Mexico is the 14th-largest country in the world by land area and the 11th-largest country in the world by population.

Mexico is bordered on the north by the United States and on the south by Guatemala and Belize. Eastern Mexico adjoins the Gulf of Mexico, and it also has a short seacoast on the Caribbean Sea east of the Yucatan Peninsula. To the west and south, Mexico has a long coastline on the Pacific Ocean. The boundary between Mexico and the United States crosses North America from the Gulf of Mexico to the east to the Pacific Ocean to the west. The Rio Grande, which is known in Mexico as the Rio Bravo del Norte, forms the boundary between northeastern Mexico and the U.S. state of Texas. Near the twin cities of Juarez, Mexico, and El Paso, Texas, the boundary becomes geometric. It follows the 32° 22′ parallel of north latitude, turns to the south at the 107° 40′ meridian of west longitude, and then turns again to the west at the 31° 20′ parallel of north latitude. A diagonal line extending from southeast to northwest forms the boundary between Mexico and the U.S. state of Arizona northwestward to the Colorado River. The Colorado forms a brief section of the boundary, and then the boundary continues as a straight line from the Colorado in a direction slightly south of west to the Pacific.

To the south, the boundary between Mexico and Guatemala extends from the mouth of the Rio Suchiate inland from the river's mouth on the Pacific Ocean. The boundary follows the Rio Suchiate to the mountain peak of Tacana. From Tacana, it follows straight-line segments northeastward and then eastward to the Rio

MEXICO

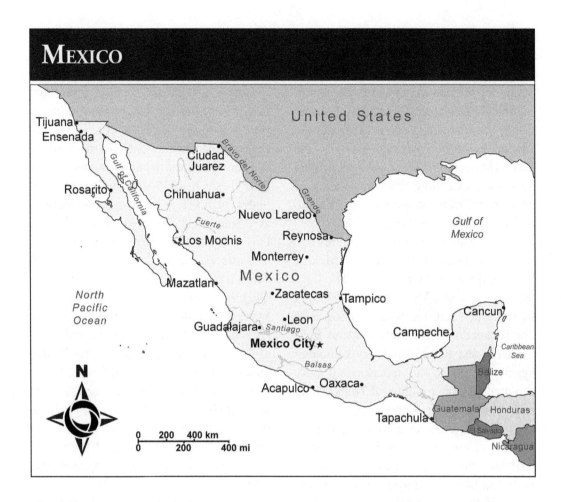

Usamacinta. It follows the Usamacinta northwestward, and then follows geometric lines to the tripoint between Mexico, Guatemala, and Belize. From this tripoint, the boundary between Mexico and Belize follows a short straight-line segment northward until it reaches the Rio Hondo. It follows the Rio Hondo in a generally eastward direction to the Rio Hondo's mouth in the Caribbean Sea.

HISTORICAL CONTEXT

Present-day Mexico was the home of several important Native American civilizations prior to its conquest by Spaniards in the early 16th century. The Olmec

civilization arose about 1500 BC in what is now the state of Tabasco along the Gulf of Mexico. Starting around AD 200, the Mayan civilization dominated the Yucatan Peninsula and nearby areas of present-day southeastern Mexico, Guatemala, and Belize. The Mayans were the first North American civilization to practice writing and were highly skilled astronomers. After ruling a large territory in southeastern Mexico for several hundred years, the Mayan empire collapsed between AD 900 and 1000. The reasons for the collapse of the Mayan empire are unknown. However, many descendants of the Mayan civilization who speak the Mayan language continue to live on and near the Yucatan Peninsula today.

Later, the Aztec civilization arose in the Valley of Mexico in the country's central highlands. The largest Aztec city, Tenochtitlan, was founded in about 1325 near the site of present-day Mexico City. By the early 16th century, the Aztecs controlled an empire extending from the Valley of Mexico eastward to the Gulf of Mexico and westward to the Pacific Ocean.

Spain began to establish port cities and trading posts along the Gulf of Mexico coast in the early 16th century. The largest of these ports, Veracruz, was founded in 1518. In 1519, the Spanish conquistador Hernando Cortes moved inland from Veracruz and began a military campaign against the Aztec Empire. Cortes's army captured the Aztec capital of Tenochtitlan and overthrew the Aztec rulers. Present-day Mexico became a Spanish colony known as New Spain. New Spain included territory from the current states of Guatemala and Belize northward to encompass much of the contemporary southwestern United States from Texas westward to California. Mexico was governed by the Spanish as part of the Viceroyalty of New Spain, which also included Cuba, Puerto Rico, and most of Central America.

In 1810, rebels within Mexico who supported Mexican independence began what would be known as the Mexican War for Independence. After 11 years of intermittent warfare, Mexico became independent in 1821. During the U.S. Civil War, France invaded Mexico and attempted to replace Mexico's republican government with a monarchy. A European Hapsburg prince, Ferdinand Maximilian of Austria, was installed as the Emperor Maximilian

I. However, the monarchy was deposed in 1867, and Maximilian was captured and executed.

Between 1821 and 1853, the northern portions of newly independent Mexico were lost to the United States. The northeasternmost portion of Mexico north of the Rio Bravo became the independent Republic of Texas in 1836 and joined the United States in 1845. The Mexican-American War was fought between 1846 and 1848. Following the military defeat of Mexico's armies, the Treaty of Guadalupe Hidalgo was signed in 1848. Under terms of this treaty, sovereignty over northwestern Mexico, including what is now California, Arizona, New Mexico, Nevada, and much of Utah, was transferred to the United States. Five years later, the United States purchased what is now southern Arizona and southern New Mexico via the Gadsden Purchase. After the Gadsden Purchase, the boundary between the United States and Mexico was delineated formally, and it remains in place today.

The boundary between Mexico and Guatemala was contested between the two countries for much of the 19th century. The main point of contention was sovereignty over the southeastern Mexican state of Chiapas, which is located along the Pacific coast west of the present-day boundary between the two countries. Both countries claimed Chiapas after both became independent of Spain in 1821. The territorial dispute was unresolved until 1882, when Mexico and Guatemala signed a treaty in which Guatemala renounced its rights to Chiapas. A protocol to this treaty, signed the following year, established a commission charged with delineating the boundary precisely.

The delineation process was completed in 1899. The boundary between Mexico and Belize, and then the British colony of British Honduras, was agreed upon in principle in 1893 by Mexico and Britain and delineated formally in 1897.

CONTEMPORARY ISSUES

Mexico and the United States have experienced ongoing issues involving their long boundary. Both sides of the boundary contain large and dense populations. Numerous pairs of cities are located astride the international boundary. From west to east, the largest of these pairs of cities include Tijuana and San Diego, Calexico and Mexicali, Juarez and El Paso, Nuevo Laredo and Laredo, and Matamoras and Brownsville. Tijuana and Matamoras are located on the Pacific and Gulf of Mexico coasts, respectively. The boundary between the United States and Mexico is the second-most frequently crossed boundary in the world, following only the boundary between the United States and Canada. It is crossed by more than 5 million motor vehicles annually.

Three major issues involving the boundary between the United States and Mexico include illegal immigration, drug trafficking and smuggling, and water rights. Over many years, numerous Mexicans have crossed the border illegally into the United States. U.S. government estimates suggest that between 6 and 8 million Mexicans live illegally in the United States. In 2006, the United States began to construct a border fence intended to curtail the flood of illegal immigrants. Currently, the fence extends along about a third of the boundary. Thousands of U.S. Border Patrol agents are also stationed along the boundary in order to deter illegal immigration.

Both countries have also become concerned with the smuggling of illegal narcotics from Mexico into the United States. Mexico supplies well over half of the heroin, marijuana, and illegal prescription drugs used in the United States. The street value of these drugs has been estimated at more than $15 million each year. Many of these drugs are supplied by Mexican drug cartels, which control drug trafficking in various parts of Mexico and remain in ongoing conflict with the Mexican government. Mexico has also become a transshipment point for other illegal drugs, including cocaine, that are produced in South America. Both countries have worked to reduce the flow of illegal drugs across the international boundary, but with only limited success.

Water rights have also become an issue of concern. For most of its length, the boundary between Mexico and the United States extends across deserts or semiarid territory. The Rio Bravo is the only permanent stream in the boundary region separating northeastern Mexico from Texas. In recent years, overuse of the river by farmers, industrialists, and residents of cities and towns, along with ongoing drought, has caused a continuing decline in the amount of water flowing through the Rio Bravo. The flow has been reduced further by the construction and operation of dams along tributaries of the Rio Bravo on both sides of the border. At times, the Rio Bravo is now so dry that it fails to flow continuously into the Gulf of Mexico. Most experts on climate predict that the boundary region will become hotter and drier in the years ahead. Given this climate shift and given the continuing rapid increase in the region's population, it is often predicted that water-related conflicts will increase in intensity in the future.

See also Belize, Guatemala, United States

Further Reading

Patrick Corcoran. "Release of Mexican murder stats reveals shifting landscape." *Insight.com*, October 23, 2011, http://www.insightcrime.org/insight-latest-news/item/1744-release-of-mexico-government-info-reveals-shifting-landscape.

Rodolfo O. de la Garza and Jesus Velasco. *Bridging the border: Transforming Mexico-U.S. border relations.* Lanham, MD: Rowman and Littlefield, 1997.

Robert Lee Maril. *The fence: National security, public safety, and illegal immigration along the U.S.-Mexico border.* Lubbock: Texas Tech University Press, 2011.

NICARAGUA

OVERVIEW

Nicaragua is located on the Central American isthmus. It has a land area of 50,193 square miles, the size of Mississippi. Nicaragua's population is approximately 6 million.

Nicaragua's neighbors are Honduras to the north and Costa Rica to the south. The Caribbean Sea is located to the east of Nicaragua, and the Pacific Ocean, including the Gulf of Fonseca, is located to the west. The boundary between Nicaragua and Honduras extends in a northeasterly direction from the Pacific to the Caribbean. The drainage divide between the Caribbean and the Pacific is located in a mountainous area much closer to the Pacific than to the Caribbean coast. On the Pacific side of the mountains, the boundary follows straight-line segments from the drainage divide to the Rio Goascorán, which flows into the Gulf of Fonseca. East of the drainage divide, the boundary follows the Rio Poteca from its headwaters to its confluence with the Rio Coco, and then it follows the Rio Coco to its mouth on the Caribbean.

The eastern portion of the boundary between Nicaragua and Costa Rica follows the Rio San Juan from its mouth on the Caribbean to a point just south of where the river rises in Lake Nicaragua. All of Lake Nicaragua and the upper portion of the Rio San Juan are located within Nicaragua. To the west, the boundary consists of straight-line segments parallel to the southern shore of the lake. From a point near the town of Sapoa near the southwest corner of Lake Nicaragua, the boundary extends southwestward along a straight-line segment that extends to the Bahia de Salinas, which is part of the Pacific.

HISTORICAL CONTEXT

Present-day Nicaragua is located south of the areas controlled by the Mayan civilization and northwest of the areas controlled by the Incas and other South American peoples. Thus, preconquest Nicaragua was inhabited by a substantial variety of indigenous peoples. Columbus explored Nicaragua's Caribbean coast, which is known as the Miskito Coast, during his fourth voyage to the Western Hemisphere in 1502. Spain established its first settlements in present-day Nicaragua in 1524. In 1536,

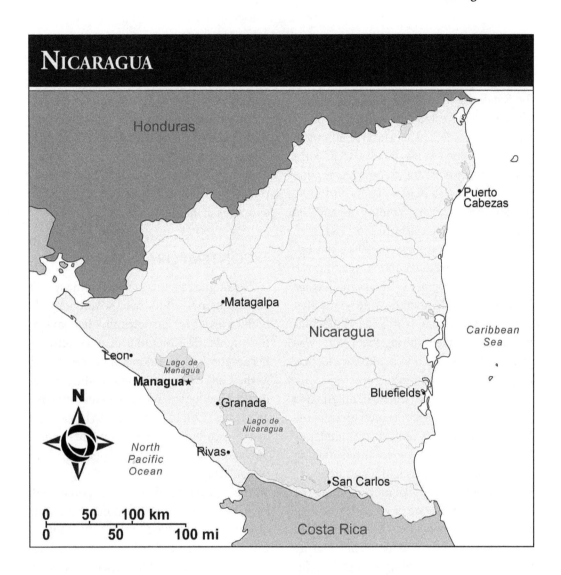

these settlements became part of the Vice-royalty of New Spain.

In the early 19th century, Spanish rule was overthrown, and Nicaragua became part of the United Provinces of Central America in 1821. After the United Provinces dissolved in 1838, Nicaragua became an independent state. However, Britain maintained interest in the Miskito Coast. This area was a British protectorate between 1655 and 1850. Sovereignty over the former British protectorate on the Miskito Coast was transferred to Nicaragua in 1860. Nicaragua was occupied by the United States beginning in 1909 until U.S. troops were withdrawn in 1933.

In 1936, Anatasio Somoza Garcia established a dictatorship in Nicaragua. Somoza died in 1956 and power was transferred to his two sons. Beginning in 1972, opposition forces known as the Sandinistas, named after the Nicaraguan leader who had led protests against the U.S. occupation in the 1920s, began guerilla action against the Somoza government. After nearly a decade of civil war, the Somoza dictatorship was overthrown in 1979, and the Sandinistas assumed power. The Sandinista regime established close ties with Cuba and professed a Marxist approach to governance. With covert U.S. support, opponents of the Sandinista regime known as contras began efforts to topple the government. The Sandinistas and the contras agreed to a cease-fire in 1988, with free elections to follow. In 1990, the opposition won these elections, ousting the Sandinista government. Nicaragua has remained under democratic rule since that time. Daniel Ortega, who had led the Sandinista government during the 1980s, was elected president in a free and fair election in 2006.

The boundaries between Nicaragua and its neighbors were delineated during the 19th and early 20th centuries. Boundaries between the present-day countries making up the United Provinces of Central America were defined only vaguely, forcing the countries to delineate boundaries among themselves after each of the former United Provinces became independent. During the 19th century, Nicaragua and Honduras experienced ongoing dispute over their boundary. Eventually, the two countries agreed to refer their dispute to the king of Spain. In 1906, the king determined that the two countries would be separated by their current boundary. However, Nicaragua regarded the king's decision as favorable to Honduras and continued to contest the boundary. The matter was referred to the International Court of Justice, which affirmed the king's decision in 1960.

The boundary between Nicaragua and Costa Rica was first delineated via the Canas-Jerez Treaty, which was signed in 1858. The treaty established the San Juan as the boundary between Lake Nicaragua and the Caribbean. It also stipulated that Nicaragua was sovereign over the Rio San Juan, but that Costa Rica retained the right of navigation along the river. Sovereignty over the river and navigation rights on the river have been contested between the two countries ever since.

CONTEMPORARY ISSUES

Nicaragua remains in disagreement with both of its neighbors over sovereignty. In both cases, these disputes involve navigation rights. The ongoing dispute between Nicaragua and Honduras involves access to the Gulf of Fonseca, upon which Nicaragua, Honduras, and El Salvador all have coastlines. Dispute over access to the Gulf of Fonseca has involved Honduras and El Salvador primarily. The dispute involved not only navigation rights on the gulf, but control of several islands in the gulf as well as on the Central American mainland. The dispute was resolved by the International Court of Justice in 1992. The court's decision divided the disputed territory between Honduras and El Salvador. The court also ruled that the Gulf of Fonseca would not be considered international waters. Although the decision guaranteed free access to the gulf and the Pacific to all three countries, it left open the possibility that the gulf could be blockaded in the future. The decision also provided for sharing of natural resources among the three countries.

To the south, Nicaragua and Costa Rica have contested access to the Rio San Juan. The disputes have arisen in response to interpretation of the Canas-Jemez Treaty, which gave Nicaragua sovereignty over the river. Although the treaty guaranteed Costa Rican access to the river, it left open the issue of the extent to which Nicaragua could regulate this access given its sovereignty over the river. In 1998, Nicaragua began to tax Costa Rican nationals and foreign tourists traveling on ships and boats that entered the Rio San Juan. In 2009, the International Court of Justice ruled that Nicaragua had the right to require Costa Rican nationals entering or traveling on watercraft in the Rio San Juan to carry identification and the right to require Costa Rican vessels to register at Nicaraguan ports along the river. However, the decision forbade Nicaragua from taxing Costa Rican vessels or their passengers using the river.

Some residents of eastern Nicaragua along the Miskito Coast have agitated for independence from Nicaragua. In contrast to the rest of Nicaragua, the large majority of residents of the Miskito Coast are of combined Spanish, English, African, and indigenous ancestry, reflecting this area's unique history relative to the rest of Nicaragua. The Miskito people have a long history of opposition to the Nicaraguan government, and many supported the contra opposition to the Sandinista regime in the 1980s.

The dispute intensified in the late 20th century when the government imposed restrictions on the hunting of endangered green sea turtles, upon which the Miskito had long depended for their livelihood. In 2007, eastern Nicaragua was struck by Hurricane Felix, a Category 5 hurricane that caused 133 fatalities and left 40,000 people homeless. Most of the victims were Miskitos, many of whom criticized the Ortega government for slow response to the storm.

Some Miskito activists proposed making the Miskito-dominated area of eastern Nicaragua an independent country to be called the Communitarian Nation of Moskitia. The territory would include nearly half of Nicaragua's land area and about 11 percent of its population. A unilateral declaration of independence was announced in 2009, but Moskitia's independence and sovereignty have not been recognized by the international community.

See also   Costa Rica, Honduras

Further Reading

Maria Cristina Garcia. *Seeking refuge: Central American migration to Mexico, the United States, and Canada.* Berkeley: University of California Press, 2009.

Dennis Gilbert. *Sandinistas: The party and the revolution.* New York: Blackwell, 1988.

Indigenous People Issues and Resources. "Miskitos declare independent nation of Moskitia in Nicaragua." June 10, 2009, http://indigenouspeoplesissues.com/index.php?option=com_content&view=article&id=827:miskitos-declare-independent-nation-of-moskitia-in-nicaragua&catid=30&Itemid=63.

Joshua Keating. "Nicaragua cites Google Earth to justify 'invading' Costa Rica." *Foreign Policy*, November 5, 2010, http://blog.foreignpolicy.com/posts/2010/11/05/nicaragua_cites_google_earth_to_justify_invading_costa_rica.

PANAMA

OVERVIEW

The Republic of Panama is the southernmost and easternmost country in Central

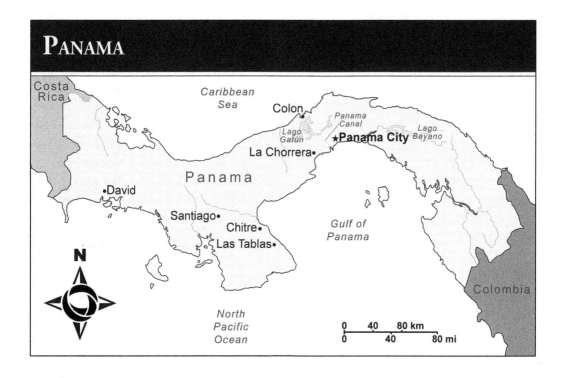

PANAMA

America. It has a land area of 29,157 square miles (slightly larger than West Virginia) and a population of approximately 3.4 million. Its neighbors are Costa Rica to the west and Colombia to the east. The Caribbean Sea is located to the north of the long, narrow country, with the Pacific Ocean to the south.

Panama's land boundaries with Colombia and Costa Rica extend across the Central American isthmus between the Caribbean and the Pacific. The boundary with Colombia is highly irregular but trends in a north-south direction. It crosses the Darien Gap, which is a sparsely populated, densely forested region between the Central American isthmus and the South American mainland. The northern portion of the Panama-Colombia boundary follows the crest of the Sierra del Darien mountain range. The eastern boundary of Darien National Park,

the largest national park in Panama, follows the international border for most of that border's length. The border with Costa Rica also trends in a north-south direction. Most of it is irregular, although it follows the 83rd meridian of west longitude for part of its length in the center of the country. The central portion of the boundary is traversed by the Parque Nacional la Amistad, which includes territory in both countries.

HISTORICAL CONTEXT

The Isthmus of Panama was first traversed by a Spanish expedition under the command of Vasco Nunez de Balboa in 1513. Balboa claimed the territory for Spain, and Panama's capital city of Panama City was founded by the Spanish on the shores of the Pacific Ocean in 1519. Panama remained a Spanish colonial possession for the next 300 years.

In 1713, the Spanish government established the Viceroyalty of New Granada, which included present-day Colombia, Venezuela, and Ecuador. In 1739, present-day Panama was added to the Viceroyalty.

The Viceroyalty of New Granada declared its independence in 1819 and became the Republic of Colombia. It was also known as Gran Colombia, or "Great Colombia." The Republic of Colombia dissolved in 1830, when Venezuela and Ecuador become independent states. The remaining territories of Colombia and Panama remained united as the Republic of Colombia. On several occasions during the 19th century, some Panamanians tried unsuccessfully to secede from Colombia. Panama's location along the narrowest part of the Central American isthmus made the region an important center for trade and commercial activity. During the 19th century, various European powers along with the United States pursued interests in constructing a canal across Central America. At that time, any ship on its way from the Atlantic to the Pacific had to circumnavigate South America.

In 1878, the Colombian government granted a French-based international company the right to construct a canal across present-day Panama. Construction began in 1881. However, difficulties in dealing with the rugged and mountainous terrain and with tropical diseases such as malaria and yellow fever impeded construction. Unable to surmount these problems, the French suspended work on the canal in 1889.

After the French suspended their work, the United States became the chief proponent of the canal project. In 1903, a treaty giving the United States the right to complete the canal was signed by American and Colombian diplomats, but the Colombian senate refused to ratify the treaty. In response, the United States threw its weight behind Panamanian separatists, who had agitated for independence since 1899. With U.S. support, Panama declared its independence from Colombia on November 3, 1903. Colombia recognized Panama as an independent state in 1921. The boundary between Panama and Colombia that had existed since the days of Spanish colonialism remained unchanged.

The boundary between Panama and neighboring Costa Rica had been in dispute since the United States of Central America, including Costa Rica, and Gran Colombia both became independent of Spain in the early 19th century. Newly independent Panama inherited the boundary dispute. Panama claimed sovereignty over the Caribbean Sea coast of Costa Rica and the territory between that coast and the crest of Cordillera of Central America, which divides the area drained by the Caribbean from that drained by the Pacific Ocean. In 1910, the two sides agreed to arbitration by the chief justice of the United States. Chief Justice Edward D. White issued a decision establishing the current boundary in 1914.

In February 1904, the newly independent government of Panama granted the United States control of the Panama Canal Zone, which was a strip of land 10 miles wide stretching across the isthmus. Construction of the canal resumed, and the project was completed in 1914. In 1978, the United States and Panama signed the Torrijos-Carter Treaties, which provided for eventual Panamanian control of the canal. The Canal Zone reverted to Panamanian sovereignty in 1979. In 1999, Panama took over full operation of the canal, which remains a vital component of Panama's economy.

CONTEMPORARY ISSUES

Panama's two land boundaries are clearly delineated and have remained stable since the border dispute between Panama and Costa Rica was resolved in 1914. Both boundaries extend across rugged, densely forested, and sparsely populated terrain.

The isolation of these regions has created problems for Panama, particularly in the Darien Gap. There are no paved road connections between Panama and Colombia, and therefore there are no road links between North America and South America. The border region has been a haven for smugglers, particularly those smuggling illegal drugs from South America into Central America and eventually to Mexico and the United States. Kidnappings, both of local residents and of tourists, and the poaching of wild animals and birds are not unusual occurrences.

A related issue is whether a road connection between Panama and Colombia should be constructed. The Pan-American Highway extends for more than 20,000 miles from northern Alaska to the southern tip of Chile. The Darien Gap is the only place along the Pan-American Highway route in which a road has not been built. The question of whether to build this road remains controversial. While proponents point to reduced travel costs, opponents argue that the completion of the Pan-American Highway would cause irreparable harm to the pristine environment and would expedite smuggling and other illegal trading activities.

See also   Colombia, Costa Rica

Further Reading

Robert C. Harding. *The history of Panama.* Santa Barbara, CA: Greenwood Press, 2006.

David McCullough. *The path between the seas: The creation of the Panama Canal, 1870–1914.* New York: Simon and Schuster, 1978.

PARAGUAY

OVERVIEW

The Republic of Paraguay is located in south-central South America. Paraguay is one of two landlocked South American countries, the other being Bolivia. It has a total land area of 157,048 square miles, slightly smaller than California, and a population of about 6.5 million. Paraguay is bisected by the Paraguay River, which divides the country into two distinct regions. The large majority of the people live in eastern Paraguay, which has a temperate climate and fertile soil for agriculture. The sparsely populated and semiarid Gran Chaco region occupies the western half of the country. This region contains more than half of the country's land area but only about 2 percent of its population.

Paraguay is landlocked. It is bordered by Argentina to the southwest, south, and southeast, Brazil to the east, and Bolivia to the north and west. Most of the boundary between Paraguay and Argentina follows rivers. The Pilcomayo River forms the boundary between Paraguay and Argentina eastward from the tripoint between Paraguay, Argentina, and Bolivia to its confluence with the Paraguay River.

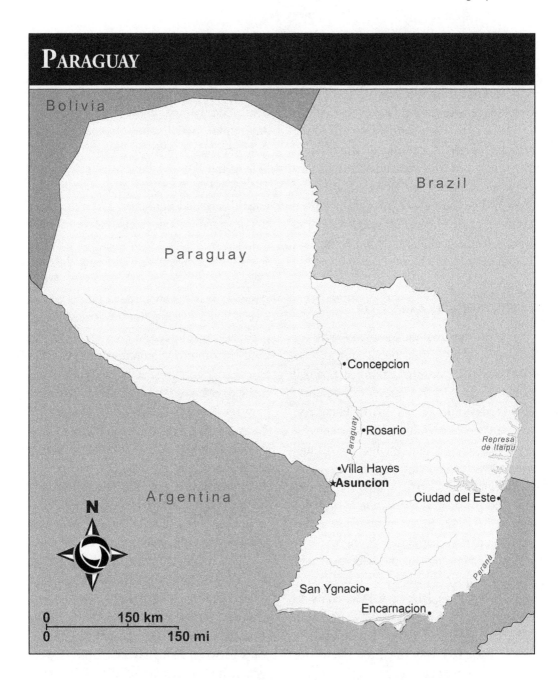

From there it follows the Paraguay River to its confluence with southern South America's longest river, the Rio Parana. The boundary then follows the Rio Parana upstream to its confluence with its tributary, the Iguazu River. The confluence between the Rio Parana and the Iguazu is the tripoint between Paraguay, Argentina, and Brazil.

The Rio Parana continues northward as the boundary between Paraguay and Brazil to a point near the Brazilian town of Guaira. From that point, the boundary trends westward, and then northward, and then westward again along straight-line segments to the Paraguay River. The boundary then follows the Paraguay upstream and northward until it reaches the river's confluence with the Apa River. It then follows the Apa River northwestward to the tripoint between Paraguay, Brazil, and Bolivia. From this tripoint, the boundary between Paraguay and Bolivia consists of straight-line segments extending in a generally circular direction through the Gran Chaco to the tripoint between Paraguay, Bolivia, and Argentina.

HISTORICAL CONTEXT

Present-day eastern Paraguay was occupied by the Guarani people for at least 1,000 years before the arrival of Spanish conquistadors in the early 16th century. Even today, a large majority of Paraguayans have both Guarani and Spanish ancestry. Both Guaraní and Spanish are official languages of Paraguay.

Beginning in 1516, Spanish explorers traveled by boat along Paraguay's major rivers. In 1542, Spain established a formal colony in what is now Paraguay. The colony became part of the Viceroyalty of Peru, which was headquartered in Lima in present-day Peru. Paraguay declared its independence from the Viceroyalty and from Spain in 1811. For most of the next 170 years, Paraguay was ruled by a series of dictators whose authoritarian regimes generally kept Paraguay isolated from much of the outside world.

In the early 1860s, Paraguayan dictator Francisco Solano Lopez began to pursue a policy of aggressive expansion of Paraguay by attempting to annex territory belonging to Paraguay's neighbors. Landlocked

Paraguay was especially interested in obtaining territory on the Atlantic Ocean so that Paraguayan ships could trade with Europe without having to sail through waters controlled by other countries. Neighboring Argentina, Brazil, and Uruguay resisted this expansion actively, resulting in the War of the Triple Alliance that lasted from 1864 to 1870. The War of the Triple Alliance devastated Paraguay. More than half of Paraguay's people, including a very large majority of its adult males, died in battle or from disease or starvation during the war. On a per capita basis, the War of the Triple Alliance was the most devastating war in world history. After the war ended, Paraguay was also forced to give up territory to both Brazil and Argentina. However, both Brazil and Argentina supported the continued existence of Paraguay as a buffer state between these two much larger countries. Paraguay and Argentina agreed upon their current boundary in 1876, and an agreement confirming the Apa River as part of the boundary between Paraguay and Brazil was signed by the two countries in 1927.

In the early 20th century, Paraguay and Bolivia contested control of the Gran Chaco. Hostilities intensified in the 1930s, and in 1932 armed hostilities broke out. After three years of fighting, Paraguayan troops controlled about two-thirds of the disputed territory. The present-day boundaries between Paraguay and Bolivia were established as a part of the 1938 peace agreement that ended the Gran Chaco War.

CONTEMPORARY ISSUES

Paraguay's boundaries with its neighbors are uncontested. However, conflict between Paraguay, Brazil, and Argentina continues in the region where the three countries converge at the confluence of the Iguazu River and the Rio Parana. The discord stems from the construction and operation of the Itaipu Dam along the Rio Parana. Brazil and Paraguay first agreed in 1876 to dam the Rio Parana in order to provide hydroelectric power to both countries. Construction of the dam began in 1973, and the dam was completed in 1984. Upon completion, the Itaipu Dam became the largest hydroelectric power generating dam in the world until its capacity was surpassed by the completion of the Three Gorges Dam in China in 2009.

In 1979, the governments of Paraguay, Brazil, and Argentina signed an agreement concerning levels of the Rio Parana and the charges associated with the use of hydroelectric power from the dam. Downstream Argentina expressed concern that Brazil could open the dam's floodgates and inundate northeastern Argentina as far downstream as Buenos Aires. Today, the Dam supplies over 90 percent of Paraguay's electricity, and it supplies almost 20 percent of that used in Brazil. After the dam opened, Paraguayan officials became concerned that the terms of the 1979 treaty favored Brazil at the expense of Paraguay. The original 1979 agreement stipulated that each would sell excess electric capacity to the other. Much smaller Paraguay uses far less electricity than Brazil, so Paraguay had to sell excess capacity to Brazil at rates far below market value. In the revised agreement, Brazil agreed to triple its annual payment to Paraguay. The 2009 revision also allows Paraguay to sell excess capacity to Brazilian companies at market rates rather than at fixed rates. The boundary region is growing rapidly, especially on the Paraguayan side of the Rio Parana, where the Paraguayan city of Ciudad del Este is the fastest-growing city in Paraguay. The Ciudad del Este area has been regarded, especially in Brazil, as a haven for smuggling and illegal narcotics trafficking across the boundary.

See also   Argentina, Bolivia, Brazil

Further Reading

Alexei Barrionuevo. "Energy deal with Brazil gives boost to Paraguay." *New York Times*, July 26, 2009, http://www.nytimes.com/2009/07/27/world/americas/27paraguay.html?_r=1.

Belen Bogado. "Paraguay: The chaotic Ciudad del Este." *Global Voices Online*, January 19, 2010, http://globalvoices online.org/2010/01/19/paraguay-the-chaotic-ciudad-del-este/.

Kregg Hetherington. *Guerilla auditors: The politics of transparency in neoliberal Paraguay*. Durham, NC: Duke University Press, 2011.

PERU

OVERVIEW

The Republic of Peru is located in western South America. With a land area of 496,225 square miles, Peru is roughly twice the size of Texas. Its population is about 30 million. Peru straddles three distinct geographic environments: the arid coastal plain along the Pacific Ocean coast, the high plateau and peaks of the central Andes Mountains, and the interior rainforest lowlands of the South American continent.

Peru has boundaries with Ecuador and Colombia to the north, Brazil to the east,

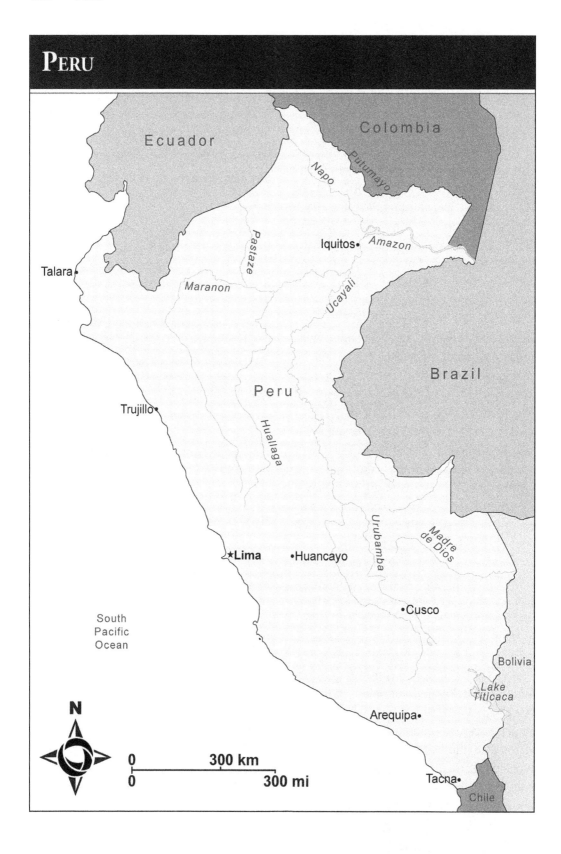

Bolivia to the southeast, and Chile to the south. The Pacific Ocean adjoins the west coast of Peru. The boundary between Peru and Ecuador extends southward and then southeastward inland from the Gulf of Guayaquil in the Pacific Ocean. This section of the boundary follows the Zarumilla and Tumbes rivers inland. Near the Peruvian town of Cazaderos, the boundary reaches the Chira River and then turns northeastward. This section of the boundary passes through the Andes Mountains into the Amazon basin and continues in a northeasterly direction to the tripoint between Peru, Ecuador, and Colombia. This tripoint is located on the Putumayo River near the border between the Zona Reservada Gueppi in Peru and Cuyabeno National Park in Ecuador.

The boundary between Peru and Colombia follows the Putumayo, which is a tributary of the Amazon River, in an east-southeasterly direction for most of this boundary's length. It continues to follow the Putumayo downstream to a point east of Zona Reservades Yagues. It then turns southwestward, following a straight-line segment to the main channel of the Amazon. From this point, it follows the Amazon downstream and eastward to a point near the Colombian city of Leticia. The tripoint between Peru, Colombia, and Brazil is located in the Amazon off the shore from Leticia.

All of the boundary between Peru and Brazil is located within the Amazon drainage basin. From near the tripoint between Peru, Brazil, and Colombia, the boundary extends along the Javari River. The boundary follows the Javari upstream in a semicircle, going from west to south and then back to the southeast. It then turns eastward to the Purus River and then turns southward to the Acre River. The boundary turns westward again, following the Acre downstream to the tripoint between Peru, Brazil, and Bolivia.

From this tripoint, the boundary between Peru and Bolivia follows a straight diagonal line that extends south-southeastward. This segment connects the Acre with the Rio Madre de Dios at its confluence with the Rio Heath. The boundary follows the Rio Heath southward and upstream into the Andes Mountains. It continues high into the mountains to Lake Titicaca at 12,500 feet above sea level. After crossing the lake, the boundary continues southwestward and then southward through the Andes to the tripoint between Peru, Bolivia, and Chile. From this tripoint, the boundary between Peru and Chile follows two diagonal segments southwestward to Laguna Blanca and then follows straight-lines segments westward and then southward to the Pacific Ocean. This boundary descends from the Andes into the almost rainless Atacama Desert.

HISTORICAL CONTEXT

During the 15th and early 16th centuries, much of present-day Peru was ruled by the Inca Empire from the Inca's capital city of Cuzco in the Andes Mountains. Spanish conquistadors led by Francisco Pizarro first made contact with the Incas in 1526. In 1532, Pizarro led Spanish troops into the heartland of the Inca Empire. Emperor Atahualpa was captured and executed in 1533. Over the next 40 years, the Spanish eliminated Inca resistance and incorporated the former Inca territory into the Spanish Empire. Pizarro founded the city of Lima in 1535, and Peru was made the center of the Viceroyalty of Peru in 1542.

Peru, like other Spanish colonies in South America, became independent in the early 19th century. The Peruvian War for Independence began in 1809. Although many in Lima opposed the independence movement, General Jose de San Martin proclaimed Peru's independence in 1821. Spanish resistance to Peruvian independence continued for the next three years, and Spain did not recognize Peru as an independent country until 1879. In 1836, Peru and Bolivia formed a confederation, but this union dissolved in 1839.

In 1879, Peruvian and Bolivian forces fought against Chilean troops in the War of the Pacific. A major issue in the war was control over mineral-rich regions of the Atacama Desert, some of which was then controlled by Bolivia. Armed hostilities ended in 1883, after which Bolivia gave up its territory on the Pacific coast. This territory was divided between Peru and Chile. The two countries failed to agree on their boundary, however, until the boundary dispute was settled in 1929.

CONTEMPORARY ISSUES

The boundary between Peru and Ecuador was disputed from the time that both countries became independent in the early 19th century. Much of the conflict involved the status of sparsely populated areas in the Amazon basin lowlands east of the Andes. The disagreement arose in response to conflicting interpretations of the territorial extent of the Viceroyalty of Peru, including Peru, and the Viceroyalty of New Grenada, including Ecuador. During colonial days, much of the boundary region was unsettled by people of European ancestry, and the boundary was defined only loosely. After independence, both countries claimed territories along the frontiers between the two countries. Wars between the two countries broke out between 1857 and 1860 and again in 1941. Another armed skirmish took place along the border in the valley of the Cenepa River on the Andes in 1995. The dispute was settled finally with the 1898 signing of a comprehensive peace agreement between the two countries.

While this agreement ended the dispute over the location of land boundaries between Peru and Ecuador, the two countries remain in disagreement about their maritime boundaries in the Pacific Ocean and its arm, the Gulf of Guayaquil. The delineation of these boundaries has been of great concern to both countries because the Pacific waters off the coasts of the two countries include some of the richest and most lucrative fishing grounds in the world. The two countries agreed to resolve the dispute in 2011 by recognizing the line of latitude at which their common boundary enters the Gulf of Guayaquil as their maritime boundary.

See also   Bolivia, Brazil, Chile, Colombia, Ecuador

Further Reading

Lisa M. Glidden. *Mobilizing ethnic identity in the Andes: A study of Ecuador and Peru.* Lanham, MD: Lexington Books, 2011.

Monica Herz and João Noguiera. *Ecuador vs. Peru: Peacemaking amid rivalry.* Boulder, CO: Lynne Rienner, 2002.

Arno Kopecky. "A proxy war in Peru." *Foreign Policy*, May 19, 2010, http://www.foreignpolicy.com/articles/2010/05/19/a_proxy_war_in_peru.

Phil Locker. "Peru accepts Ecuador maritime borders, much to Chile's chagrin." MercoPress, May 4, 2011, http://en.mercopress.com/2011/05/04/peru-accepts-ecuador-maritime-borders-much-to-chiles-chagrin.

ST. KITTS AND NEVIS

OVERVIEW

The Federation of St. Christopher and Nevis, also known as the Federation of St. Kitts and Nevis, consists of the islands of St. Christopher (St. Kitts) and Nevis in the Leeward Islands. The total land area of the federation is 104 square miles, or roughly

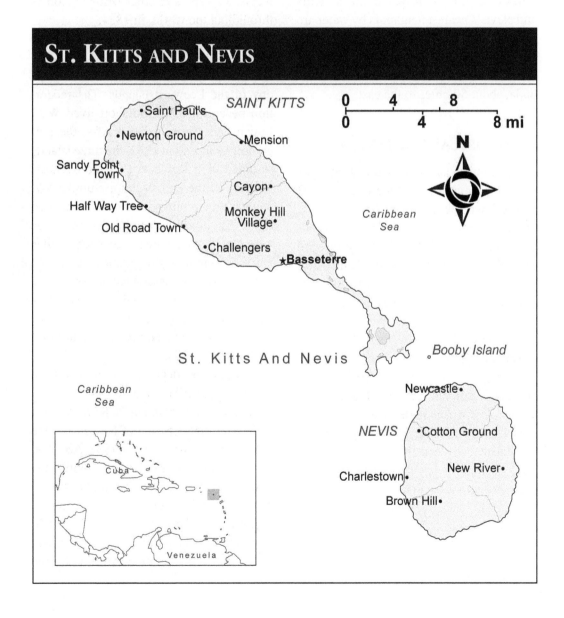

one and a half times the land area of the District of Columbia. The population is about 53,000. St. Kitts and Nevis is the smallest independent country by land area and by population in the Western Hemisphere.

St. Kitts is the larger of the two islands, with about 60 percent of the land area of the country and two-thirds of the population. The islands are separated by a strait known as The Narrows, which is about two miles wide at its narrowest point. St. Kitts and Nevis's nearest neighbors by water are the French territory of Montserrat, about 50 miles to the south-southeast, and the independent country of Antigua and Barbuda, about 50 miles to the east.

HISTORICAL CONTEXT

Columbus visited St. Kitts during his second voyage to the Americas in 1493 and claimed the island for Spain. At that time, St. Kitts was inhabited by Carib people whose ancestors had moved northward through the Leeward Islands from mainland South America. The Caribs had displaced the island's earlier Arawak people, many of whom are believed to have moved northwestward to the Greater Antilles to escape the warlike and aggressive Caribs.

During the 17th century, St. Kitts was contested among Britain, France, and Spain. A British settlement was established on St. Kitts in 1623, and a French settlement was established in 1625. In 1629, a Spanish navy attempted to drive these British and French settlers away from St. Kitts, but an agreement signed by Britain and Spain in 1630 reaffirmed the British right to settle the island. Between 1630 and 1763, the British and the French continued to struggle for control of St. Kitts.

The issue was resolved in 1763, when the Treaty of Paris reaffirmed British control of the island. Nevis was also contested between Britain and France from the early 17th century until 1713, when sovereignty was awarded to Britain via the Treaty of Utrecht. Sugar production dominated the economies of both islands, and labor was provided by slaves imported from Africa. Slavery was abolished in St. Kitts and Nevis, as well as in other British colonies throughout the world, in 1834.

In 1833, Britain united St. Kitts, Nevis, and the island of Anguilla to the north as a single colony known as the Federated Colony of the Leeward Islands. The federation became part of the short-lived West Indian Federation in 1958. After the federation collapsed in 1962, the three islands resumed their status as a single overseas territory of the British Empire until 1967, when it became an independent Associated State. Anguilla, the smallest of the three islands with a land area of 35 square miles and a contemporary population of 14,000, seceded from the Associated States in 1971 and reverted to its original status as a British overseas colony, a status that it retains today. St. Kitts and Nevis became fully independent in 1983.

Since independence, many on Nevis have felt that the distribution of revenues and political power favors larger St. Kitts. A referendum on the secession of Nevis from the country was held in Nevis in 1998. About 60 percent of the voters of Nevis supported the referendum, but it fell short of the two-thirds majority required for approval. In light of falling sugar prices, the sugar industry in St. Kitts and Nevis has collapsed, and tourism is now the main source of revenue for the country.

Further Reading

Stanford Conway. "St. Kitts-Nevis to improve food security." *SKNVibes*, June 6, 2012, http://www.sknvibes.com/news/newsdetails.cfm/58869.

Vincent K. Hubbard. *A history of St. Kitts: The sweet trade.* Northampton, MA: Interlink, 2002.

ST. LUCIA

OVERVIEW

St. Lucia is an island country in the Caribbean Sea. The island is part of the Windward Islands that separate the Caribbean from the Atlantic Ocean. The island has a land area of 238 square miles, a little more than three times the land area of the District of Columbia. Its population is about 175,000. St. Lucia's closest neighbors by water are St. Vincent and the Grenadines, 30 miles to the south, and the French territory of Martinique, 30 miles to the north.

HISTORICAL CONTEXT

As elsewhere in the Leeward and Windward Islands, St. Lucia was inhabited by

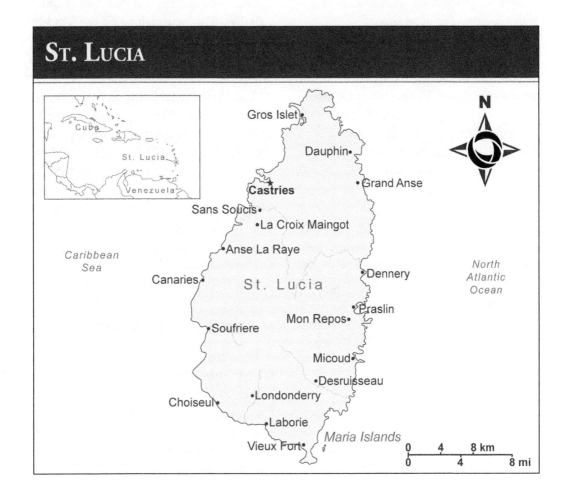

Arawak and later Carib peoples when it was first visited by Europeans. During the 16th and early 17th centuries, the Caribs resisted early European attempts to establish trading posts on the island.

France claimed St. Lucia in 1635 and established the first permanent European settlement on St. Lucia in 1643. Britain claimed sovereignty over St. Lucia in 1664, and for the next century the island was contested between France and Britain. The island was developed as a source of sugarcane. Indigenous Caribs were enslaved to work on sugar plantations. However, most died from overwork and disease, and Africans were imported to provide slave labor. About 82 percent of St. Lucia's people today are of African ancestry.

In 1763, sovereignty over St. Lucia was transferred from France to Britain in conjunction with the Treaty of Paris, which ended the Seven Years' War. However, France continued to contest control of St. Lucia until 1814, when British sovereignty over the island was confirmed and France agreed to drop its claims to St. Lucia permanently. In 1838, Britain included St. Lucia as part of its British Windward Islands colony, which was administered first from Barbados and later from Grenada. Britain continued to administer St. Lucia as a colony until it became part of the West Indian Federation in 1958. After the federation was dissolved in 1962, Britain once again administered St. Lucia until it became fully independent in 1979.

Further Reading

Tennyson S.D. Joseph. *Decolonization in St. Lucia: Politics and global neo-* *liberalism, 1945–2010.* Jackson: University Press of Mississippi, 2011.

ST. VINCENT AND THE GRENADINES

OVERVIEW

St. Vincent and the Grenadines is an island country that is part of the Windward Islands in the Caribbean Sea. The country consists of the island of St. Vincent and several smaller islands that extend southward toward the country of Grenada. The total land area is about 150 square miles, or about twice the size of the District of Columbia. The country's population is about 120,000. The main island of St. Vincent contains 90 percent of the country's land area and the large majority of the country's population.

The closest neighbor to St. Vincent and the Grenadines is Grenada, whose northernmost islands are directly south of the southernmost islands of the Grenadines. The Martinique Channel, which is less than half a mile wide, separates the island of Petit St. Vincent in St. Vincent and the Grenadines from the island of Petite Martinique in Grenada. The main islands of St. Vincent and Grenada are about 60 miles apart. St. Vincent is 150 miles west of Barbados.

HISTORICAL CONTEXT

St. Vincent, like the other Windward Islands, was inhabited by Carib peoples before the arrival of European mariners. Columbus is believed to have sighted St. Vincent in 1502, although the hostility of the indigenous Carib population delayed European occupation of the island. During

St. Vincent and the Grenadines

the 17th and 18th centuries, escaped African slaves from other islands settled in St. Vincent, and many intermarried with the local Carib population, reinforcing hostility to European settlement. Their descendants became known as Black Caribs.

Britain claimed the island in 1627, but the French established the first European settlement on St. Vincent in 1719. Sovereignty over the island was awarded to Britain under terms of the Treaty of Paris ending the Seven Years' War in 1763. In 1779, a French naval force attacked and captured St. Vincent, with the support of many of the Black Caribs. British sovereignty over St. Vincent was restored with the 1783 Treaty of Paris. Both the French and the British imported African slaves, who worked as agricultural laborers, to the island. In 1795, Black Carib leaders backed a rebellion against British rule. The British put down this rebellion and exiled several thousand Black Caribs from St. Vincent to the island of Roatan in present-day Honduras.

St. Vincent continued to be administered by Britain until 1958, when it joined with other former British colonies in the West Indies to become the West Indies Federation. The West Indies Federation dissolved in 1962, after which St. Vincent resumed its colonial status. Britain granted St. Vincent internal autonomy in 1969, and the country achieved full independence in 1979.

Further Reading

Lawrence S. Grossman. *The political ecology of bananas: Contract farming, peasants, and agrarian change in the Eastern Caribbean.* Chapel Hill: University of North Carolina Press, 1998.

SURINAME

OVERVIEW

The Republic of Suriname is the smallest country in mainland South America by land area, population, and population density. Suriname has a land area of about 64,000 square miles, the size of Wisconsin, with a population of about 500,000.

Suriname's neighbors are Guyana to the west, Brazil to the south, and the French colony of French Guiana to the east. To the north, Suriname has a coastline along the Atlantic Ocean. The majority of Suriname's people live within 10 miles of the Atlantic coast.

Suriname's boundaries follow physical features. The Marowijne River separates Suriname from French Guiana. The boundary between Suriname and Brazil follows the drainage divide between rivers flowing northward into the Atlantic Ocean on the Suriname side and the Amazon River drainage basin on the Brazilian side. The Courantyne River is the boundary between Suriname and Guyana.

HISTORICAL CONTEXT

British settlers tried unsuccessfully to cultivate tobacco along the Atlantic coast of present-day Suriname in 1630. The British attempted again to settle the area in 1650, but this settlement was attacked by Dutch forces in 1667. Later that year, Britain and the Netherlands agreed to the Treaty of Breda, which recognized Dutch sovereignty over Suriname and British sovereignty over New Amsterdam, or present-day New York City. The British occupied Suriname again between 1799 and 1816, when peace agreements following the Napoleonic Wars restored Dutch sovereignty.

Suriname's resident population is characterized by substantial ethnic diversity. During the 17th, 18th, and early 19th centuries, African slaves were imported to work in Suriname's tobacco and sugar plantations. After the Netherlands abolished

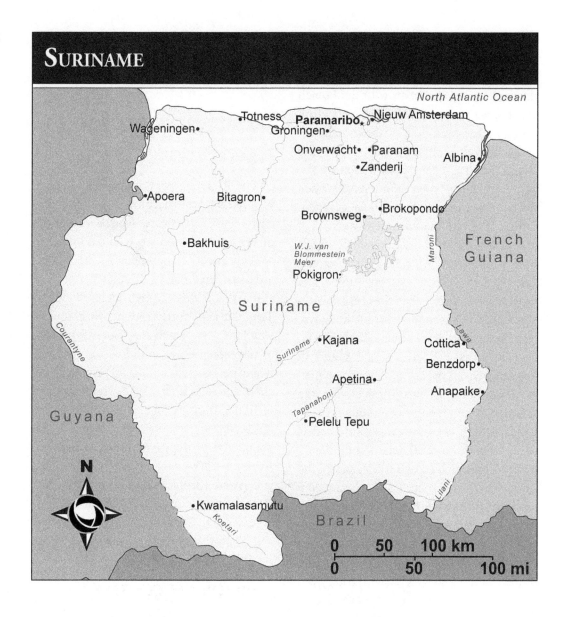

SURINAME

slavery in 1863, many people from India moved to Suriname as contract agricultural laborers. During the 20th century, other contract agricultural labors came from the Indonesian island of Java, which was also under Dutch rule at the time. Today about 37 percent of Suriname's citizens are of Indian origin, with 31 percent of African or mixed African and European origin and 15 percent of Javanese origin. There are also substantial communities of Chinese, Amerindians, Brazilians, and American expatriates.

The Netherlands granted Suriname partial independence in 1954, when Suriname received internal autonomy but the Netherlands retained control over Suriname's defense and foreign policy. Suriname received complete independence in 1975.

The Dutch and Brazil agreed upon the southern boundary of Suriname in 1906. The eastern and western boundaries of Suriname were agreed upon with the French and British, respectively, during the 19th century. However, both of these boundaries have long been contested because the rivers that had been agreed upon as the boundary had not been explored fully when the boundary agreements were negotiated. To the east, the question involved which of two tributaries is the true source of the Marowijne River, with the Dutch arguing that the Lawa River was the source and the French arguing that the Tapanahony River, somewhat to the west of the Lawa, was the source. An international commission identified the Lawa as the source in 1861. However, the question was reopened in 1885 after gold was discovered in the region between the Lawa and the Tapanahony. In 1888, the Lawa was reinforced as the boundary; however, a new controversy arose as to which of two tributaries of the Lawa was its true source. This controversy remains unresolved. A similar controversy arose between Suriname and what is now Guyana in the 19th century after two separate tributaries were identified as the source of the Courantyne River. The territory between the two tributaries was awarded to the British in 1895.

See also   Brazil, Guyana

Further Reading

Rosemarijn Hoefte. *In place of slavery: A social history of British Indian and Javanese laborers in Suriname.* Gainesville: University Press of Florida, 1998.

Simon Romero. "With aid and migrants, China expands its presence in a South American nation." *New York Times*, April 10, 2011, http://www.nytimes.com/2011/04/11/world/americas/11suriname.html.

TRINIDAD AND TOBAGO

OVERVIEW

The Republic of Trinidad and Tobago is a former British colony located southeast of the Windward Islands and north of the South American mainland country of Venezuela. Geographically the islands are considered part of South America. The country contains the two main islands of Trinidad and Tobago along with several small nearby islands. About 95 percent of the republic's people live on Trinidad, which contains more than 90 percent of the country's land area. The overall land area of Trinidad and Tobago is 1,981 square miles, slightly smaller than Delaware. The population is approximately 1.3 million. At its closest points, the island of Trinidad is separated from Venezuela by less than 20 miles by sea from Trinidadian peninsulas extending westward from the northwest and southwest corners of the island.

HISTORICAL CONTEXT

As was the case with most of the islands of the Caribbean, the islands of Trinidad and Tobago were first settled by Native Americans from the South American mainland. Archaeologists believe that the islands were first settled at least 7,000 years ago. In 1498, Columbus visited the islands during his third voyage and claimed the islands for Spain. Spain remained in control of Trinidad and Tobago until the islands were ceded to Britain in 1797.

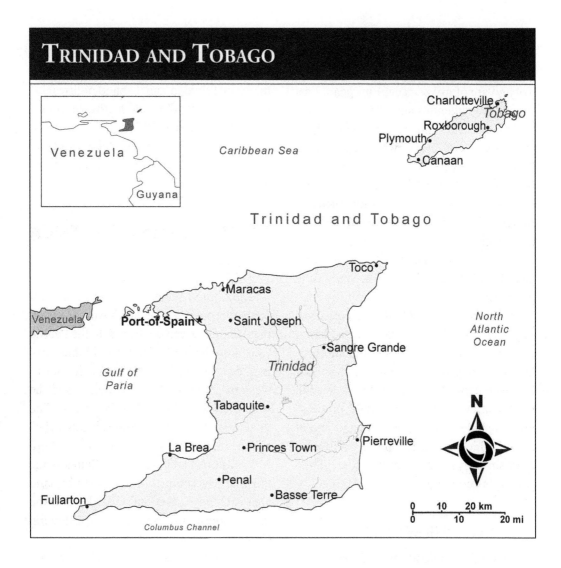

TRINIDAD AND TOBAGO

The British encouraged the development of plantations upon which tropical crops were produced. Some slaves were brought to Trinidad, but after Britain abolished the slave trade in 1807, British plantation owners brought contract laborers to the island to work on the plantations. Many of these contract laborers were of African descent, and some were freed slaves from the United States or from other British colonies in the Western Hemisphere. Later in the 19th century, plantation owners relied on Asia, and especially India, as a source of contract labor.

The history of importing labor from elsewhere has influenced the ethnic distribution of Trinidad and Tobago. Today, about 40 percent of Trinidadians are of African origin. Another 40 percent of the people are of East Indian origin. Indo-Trinidadians are descended from contract laborers who were brought to Trinidad to work on sugar plantations during the 19th century after slavery was abolished in the British Empire. Most other residents of Trinidad and Tobago are of mixed-race, European, East Asian, or indigenous ancestry.

Trinidad and Tobago remained a British colony until 1958, when the Federation of the West Indies was established with British support. In addition to Trinidad and Tobago, the federation included Jamaica, Barbados, and several other former British colonies in the West Indies. The unwieldy federation collapsed in 1962, and Trinidad and Tobago became fully independent.

In contrast to most Caribbean countries, Trinidad and Tobago has an industrial economy emphasizing petroleum production and petrochemicals. Oil was first discovered on Trinidad in 1857. Wealth from petroleum production and processing has made Trinidad and Tobago one of the wealthiest countries in the Caribbean. Tourism plays only a minor role in the country's economy.

CONTEMPORARY ISSUES

Although Trinidad and Tobago has no land boundaries, maritime boundary controversies between Trinidad and Tobago and nearby countries have occurred in recent years. Under the auspices of the United Nations Convention on the Law of the Sea, Trinidad and Tobago has signed maritime boundary agreements with Venezuela, Barbados, and Grenada. All of these countries have remained very interested in locating these maritime boundaries because of potentially lucrative oil deposits under Caribbean waters separating the countries from one another.

Further Reading

Kirk Meighoo. "Ethnic mobilisation vs. ethnic politics: Understanding ethnicity in Trinidad and Tobago politics." *Commonwealth & Comparative Politics*, 46 (2008), pp. 101–127.

Eric Williams. *History of the people of Trinidad and Tobago.* New York: Praeger, 1962.

UNITED STATES OF AMERICA

OVERVIEW

The United States of America extends across the continent of North America from the Atlantic Ocean on the east to the Pacific Ocean on the west. The United States also includes the state of Alaska in the northwestern corner of North America and the state of Hawaii in the Pacific Ocean. The total area of the United States is 3,678,190 square miles, and its population is about 315 million. Thus the United States is the third-largest country in the world by land area (behind Russia and Canada) and the third largest by population (following China and India).

The United States's land neighbors are Canada to the north and Mexico to the south. To the northwest, Little Diomede Island off the coast of the Alaskan mainland is separated from Big Diomede Island in Russia by only three miles of water. The eastern end of the boundary between the United States and Canada is located at the mouth of the St. Croix River in the Bay of Fundy, which is an arm of the Atlantic. The boundary continues upstream and northwestward to the river's headwaters at Spednic Lake. From there it extends directly northward in a straight line to the St. John River. It follows the St. John upstream, trending northwesterly and then southwesterly to its confluence with the St. Francis River in northwestern Maine. From there it extends southwestward to the drainage divide between rivers flowing into the Atlantic on the American side of the boundary and the St. Lawrence River drainage basin on the Canadian side. It follows this drainage divide until reaching Hall's Stream, which is a tributary of the Connecticut River, and then extends along the Connecticut to the 45th parallel of north latitude. From this point, the boundary then follows the 45th parallel westward to the St. Lawrence near Cornwall, Ontario. Then it follows the St.

Lawrence upstream to its source in Lake Ontario.

The boundary extends through Lake Ontario, Lake Erie, Lake Huron, and Lake Superior, with the rivers and straits connecting these Great Lakes serving as the boundary also. The Niagara River, including Niagara Falls, is the international boundary from Lake Ontario to Lake Erie. The Detroit River and the St. Clair River form the boundary from Lake Erie to Lake Huron. The Detroit River separates the U.S. city of Detroit from the Canadian city of Windsor, Ontario. Detroit is the largest American city located directly on the boundary. From Lake Huron to Lake

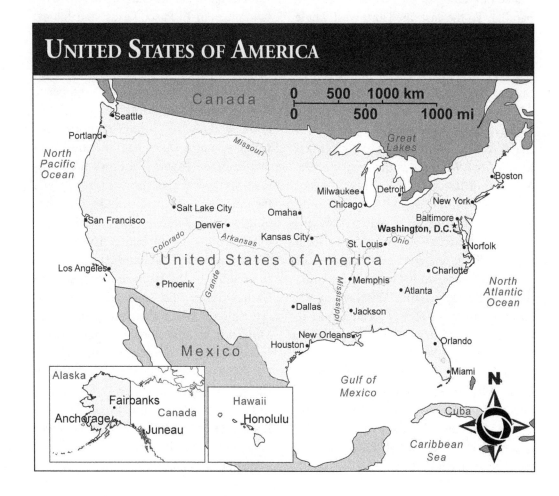

Superior, the boundary is the St. Marys River.

West of Lake Superior, the boundary follows the Pigeon River upstream to the Height of Land Portage. After crossing the portage, the boundary follows the Rainy River westward to its mouth in Lake of the Woods. The 49th parallel, which is the longest geometric boundary in the world, forms the border from Lake of the Woods westward to the Pacific Ocean. However, all of Vancouver Island, part of which extends south of the 49th parallel, is Canadian territory.

Two small areas that are unconnected to the United States by land but connected to Canada by land are located near the 49th parallel. To the east, the Northwest Angle in Minnesota on the northwestern shore of Lake of the Woods is located north of the 49th parallel but belongs to the United States. The Northwest Angle is an area of 123 square miles but has only 152 permanent residents. Its inclusion in the United States resulted from a mistaken belief that Lake of the Woods was the source of the Mississippi River. At the western end of the boundary, the community of Point Roberts, Washington, is also a U.S. exclave that is accessible by land only from Canada. Point Roberts has a land area of about six square miles and a population of approximately 1,400. The town of Alburgh, Vermont, which is located in Lake Champlain, is also accessible by land only from Canada. Alburgh has a land area of 29 square miles and a population of about 2,000. All of these exclaves can be reached directly from U.S. territory only by water.

The U.S. state of Alaska borders the Canadian province of British Columbia and the Canadian Yukon Territory. From south to north, the boundary begins at the 54° 40′ parallel and follows the crest of the mountain range along the Pacific coast. It continues along this crest until reaching the 141st meridian of west longitude, which it follows northward to the Arctic Ocean. Thus the United States is one of only three countries (along with Canada and Russia) that have coastlines on three oceans.

The boundary between the United States and Mexico also extends across the North American continent, from the Gulf of Mexico to the east to the Pacific Ocean to the west. The Rio Grande, known also as the Rio Bravo, forms the boundary between the U.S. state of Texas and Mexico from its mouth in the Gulf of Mexico to the twin cities of El Paso, Texas, and Juarez, Chihuahua. From El Paso, it extends westward following the 32° 22′ parallel of north latitude. It turns south at the 107° 40′ meridian of west longitude and hence westward again at the 31° 20′ parallel of north latitude. It continues northwestward, separating Arizona from Mexico, to the Colorado River. It follows the Colorado northward and upstream briefly and then extends along a straight line running slightly south of west until reaching the Pacific Ocean between San Diego, California, and Tijuana, Baja California. In contrast to the boundary between the United States and Canada, the boundary region between the United States and Mexico is heavily populated and crosses several pairs of cities along the border. The largest pairs of border cities are San Diego and Tijuana; Mexicali, California, and Calexico, Baja California; El Paso and Juarez; Laredo, Texas, and Nuevo Laredo, Tamaulipas; and Brownsville, Texas, and Matamoras, Tamaulipas.

HISTORICAL CONTEXT

Anthropologists have estimated that between 1 and 4 million Native Americans lived in what is now the United States at the time of Columbus. The first places in the present-day United States to be settled by Europeans were St. Augustine, Florida, and several settlements along the Rio Grande in New Mexico. Both of these areas were settled by Spaniards in the 16th century.

North of St. Augustine, several European powers had interests in the territories along the Atlantic coast in what is now the eastern seaboard region of the United States. The first British settlement was the "Lost Colony" on Roanoke Island near the Outer Banks of present-day North Carolina. The settlement was founded in 1585 but disappeared without a trace between 1587 and 1590. The first permanent British settlements were established at Jamestown, Virginia, in 1607 and at Plymouth Rock, Massachusetts, in 1620. Meanwhile, Swedes settled the area near present-day Wilmington, Delaware. The Dutch claimed the area between the Connecticut and Delaware rivers, which they called the North and South rivers respectively. The Dutch established a settlement, which they named New Amsterdam, at the mouth of the Hudson River. New Amsterdam eventually became the city of New York. In 1664, the Netherlands relinquished its claims to eastern North America to Britain in exchange for recognition of Dutch sovereignty over present-day Suriname. Thus what is now the eastern seaboard of the United States between Georgia and present-day Maine was under British control by the end of the 17th century.

The British established 13 colonies, from New Hampshire in the north to Georgia in the south. During the 18th century, the Thirteen Colonies grew rapidly in population, and independence sentiment increased. Support for independence grew until the American Revolution broke out in 1775. The Revolutionary War ended in 1781, and the Treaty of Paris, signed in 1783, guaranteed U.S. independence. The terms of the Treaty of Paris recognized U.S. sovereignty over the territory between the Atlantic Ocean to the east, the border with Spanish Florida to the south, the Mississippi River to the west, and the border with British possessions in what is now Canada to the north.

During the 19th century, the United States expanded to its current configuration. In 1803, U.S. president Thomas Jefferson pushed to obtain the city of New Orleans, which controlled trade on the lower Mississippi River. At that time, New Orleans was in French hands, and Jefferson feared that a hostile French government could close the port or establish a blockade to prevent American shipping. Jefferson sent two envoys, Robert Livingston and future president James Monroe, to Paris to negotiate the purchase of New Orleans from the French ruler Napoleon Bonaparte. Napoleon offered to sell not only New Orleans but also all of France's territory in central North America. This territory, known as the Louisiana Territory, included all of the drainage basin of the Mississippi west of the Mississippi itself, except for those areas along the Red River that were controlled by Spain and eventually became part of the state of Texas. Livingston and Monroe agreed, and after the U.S. Senate ratified the purchase agreement the Louisiana Purchase became part of the United States.

After the Louisiana Purchase was completed, the United States obtained the Florida territory from Spain in 1819. The Florida territory included not only the present-day state of Florida, but also a strip of land along and near the Gulf Coast on the Gulf of Mexico as far west as Baton Rouge, Louisiana. In 1818, the United States and Britain agreed to the border separating the United States from what is now Canada. The 1818 agreement was modified by the Webster-Ashburton Treaty of 1842. The Webster-Ashburton Treaty resolved an ongoing dispute over the eastern boundary between New Brunswick and Maine. It also established the boundary between Minnesota and Ontario from Lake Superior westward to Lake of the Woods.

After 1842, Britain continued to dispute the location of the boundary in the area between the crest of the Rocky Mountains westward to the Pacific Ocean. The United States claimed what is now the southern boundary of Alaska at 54° 40′ north latitude. Using the slogan "Fifty-Four Forty or Fight," some Americans agitated for war with Britain if Britain did not accept the United States's territorial claim. In 1846, however, the two countries negotiated an agreement by which the 49th parallel, which was already the boundary between Lake of the Woods and the Rockies, would be extended as the boundary westward to the Pacific Ocean. However, Britain retained sovereignty over Vancouver Island, some of which extends south of the 49th parallel.

Meanwhile, the United States obtained control of Texas and the Southwest during the 1840s and early 1850s. In 1836, Texas

declared its independence from Mexico, which had become independent of Spain in 1821. It remained an independent country until 1845, when it joined the United States. Hostilities between the United States and Mexico erupted into open warfare in 1846, and one of the causes of the war was a dispute between the two countries over control of the Texas territory between the Nueces River to the north and the Rio Grande. The war ended with the signing of the Treaty of Guadalupe Hidalgo in 1848. Under terms of the Treaty of Guadalupe Hidalgo, most of what is now the southwestern United States was transferred to the United States. The lands ceded by Mexico included all of California and Nevada and much of the land area of several other U.S. states. In 1853, the United States purchased southern New Mexico and southern Arizona via the Gadsden Purchase. The terms of the Treaty of Guadalupe Hidalgo and the Gadsden Purchase established the boundary between the United States and Mexico. This boundary remains in place today, although it has been adjusted slightly on a few occasions because the Rio Grande has changed course.

The territories acquired by the United States between 1783 and 1853 eventually became the 48 conterminous states of the United States. The two remaining states, Alaska and Hawaii, were obtained after the U.S. Civil War. The United States purchased Alaska from Russia in 1867. The boundary between Alaska and what is now Canada had been established in principle in an 1882 agreement between Russia and Britain. The agreement provided that the high peaks of the Coast Range should be the boundary, but it offered no specific guidance about where the boundary would be located. The discovery of gold in Canada's Yukon Territory, and the gold rush that followed this discovery, resulted in heightened tensions. In 1903, the countries agreed that an international tribunal should be established and charged with drawing the boundary. The tribunal delineated the boundary, which remains the border today. Hawaii, an archipelago in the Pacific Ocean about 2,500 miles west-southwest of the coast of California, became a U.S. possession in 1898.

CONTEMPORARY ISSUES

The United States's long borders with Canada and Mexico have been retained amicably since the late 19th century. The two boundaries are the most frequently crossed international boundaries in the world. However, tensions remain along the boundaries between the United States and both of its neighbors.

The primary issue of concern between the United States and Canada has been the maritime boundaries between the two countries in both the Atlantic and the Pacific oceans. The issue involves interpretation of how the offshore boundaries should be determined relative to the nearest land area. In 1984, the International Court of Justice issued an opinion concerning the location of the maritime boundary on the Atlantic coast in general. However, the boundary has not been delineated specifically. The tiny and uninhabited Machias Seal Island, about 10 miles off the coast of the State of Maine and about 10 miles off the coast of the Canadian province of New Brunswick, remains in dispute. At the west end of the boundary, disagreement involves the maritime boundary west of the mouth of

the Strait of Juan de Fuca, which separates the state of Washington's Olympic Peninsula on the U.S. mainland from Canada's Vancouver Island. The dispute involves interpretation of the location of the strait.

The location of the boundary between the United States and Mexico is generally undisputed. However, ongoing tensions characterize the region along the boundary, which is crossed by more than 5 million motor vehicles each year. The major issues include illegal immigration into the United States from Mexico, along with the smuggling of drugs and other contraband into the United States. In 2011, the U.S. government estimated that between 11 and 14 million undocumented illegal immigrants were living in the United States. About 60 percent of these immigrants were believed to have come from Mexico, with most crossing the international boundary in motor vehicles or on foot. Some illegal immigrants are smuggled into the United States by paid smugglers known locally as "coyotes." About half of the United States's illegal immigrant population lives in the border states of California, Arizona, New Mexico, and Texas.

In 2006, the U.S. government began constructing a fence along the boundary in order to stem the flow of illegal immigrants. Steel and concrete were used to deter cross-border movements. About 640 miles of border fence were constructed, at a cost of nearly $3 million per mile of fence, until the project was halted in 2010. The fence covers about a third of the entire boundary. However, it is absent in cities along the river. It is also unconstructed in some rural desert areas, notably those south of Arizona. In this rough and hot desert environment, several hundred Mexican nationals who have tried to cross the border have died from exhaustion, thirst, heatstroke, and other causes each year.

The smuggling of illegal narcotics has also become a major issue of concern between the United States and Mexico. Millions of dollars' worth of illegal drugs are smuggled into the United States from Mexico each year. Many of these drugs are supplied by Mexican drug cartels, which control drug trafficking in various parts of Mexico and remain in ongoing conflict with the Mexican government. The cartels' activities are financed in large part by profits made from smuggling these drugs into the United States, where they are sold. It has been estimated that as much as 70 percent of the heroin and much of the marijuana used in the United States are imported illegally from Mexico. The value of illegal drugs moving from Mexico into the United States has been estimated at between $15 and $50 million annually. Mexico has also become a transshipment point for illegal drugs, including cocaine, that are produced in South America. Ongoing efforts by U.S. and Mexican government officials to combat the drug trafficking and smuggling problem have resulted in several hundred fatalities in recent years.

Another issue associated with the boundary between the United States and Mexico has involved water rights. Most of the boundary region is arid or semiarid, and the Rio Grande is the only permanent stream flowing through the area. The area along the Rio Grande downstream from Laredo, Texas, and Nuevo Laredo, Tamaulipas, is heavily populated on both sides of the boundary, and the population of the region is increasing rapidly. Demand for water for drinking, agriculture, and industry continues to increase. Given that most climatic projections predict warmer and drier weather in the U.S.-Mexico border region, it is expected that disputes over water rights and water usages in the Rio Grande will intensify in the years ahead.

See also   Canada, Mexico

Further Reading

Harm de Blij. *Why geography matters: Three challenges facing America.* New York: Oxford University Press.

Frederick S. Weaver. *The United States and the global economy: From Bretton Woods to the current crisis.* Lanham, MD: Rowman and Littlefield, 2011.

Fareed Zakaria. *The post-American world.* New York: W. W. Norton, 2009.

URUGUAY

OVERVIEW

The Oriental Republic of Uruguay is located in southeastern South America. Uruguay has a land area of 68,037 square miles, approximately the size of Missouri. Its population is about 3.3 million. More than half of Uruguay's people live in the capital city of Montevideo or its suburbs.

Uruguay's neighbors are Brazil to the north and Argentina to the west, with the Atlantic Ocean bordering Uruguay to the east and south. Most of Uruguay's boundaries follow rivers. The boundary between Uruguay and Brazil extends in a generally southeast to northwest direction from the Atlantic Ocean inland. From the coast, the boundary follows a tidal channel known

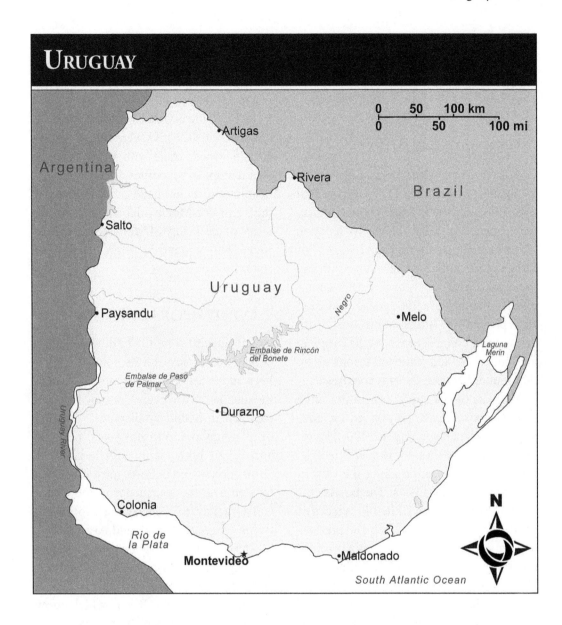

as the Arroyo Chuy inland to the town of Chuy. The boundary between Chuy and the neighboring Brazilian town of Chui is located along a street. From Chuy, the boundary trends northwestward to the estuarine lagoon of Laguna Merin, which is known as Lago Mirim in Portuguese.

Further inland, the boundary follows the Jaguarão River northwestward to the cities of Rio Branco in Uruguay and Jaguarão in Brazil. Rio Branco and Jaguarão are connected by an international bridge. The western portion of the boundary follows the Quaraí River, which flows northwestward to its confluence with the Uruguay River. This confluence represents the tripoint between Uruguay, Brazil, and Argentina. From this tripoint, the boundary between Uruguay and Argentina follows the Uruguay River southward to its mouth into the Rio de la Plata. The estuary of the Rio de la Plata separates southeastern Uruguay from the city of Buenos Aires in Argentina.

HISTORICAL CONTEXT

Present-day Uruguay was first visited by Spanish explorers in 1516, and the first Spanish settlement in what is now Uruguay was founded in 1624. Given its location along the boundary with Brazil, control of Uruguay was contested between Spain and Portugal during the 17th and 18th centuries. In order to resist Portuguese expansion from present-day Brazil southwards, Spain encouraged colonists to move to Uruguay and built forts and stationed troops along the frontier between the two countries.

What is now Uruguay was administered from Buenos Aires as part of the Viceroyalty de la Plata beginning in 1776. The region became known as the Banda Orientale, referring to its location along the eastern bank of the Rio de la Plata. The Banda Orientale was part of the United Provinces of the Rio de la Plata, which included present-day Paraguay, northern Argentina, southern Bolivia, and a small portion of northern Chile in addition to Uruguay. The United Provinces became independent in 1810.

Following independence, the United Provinces and Portugal, which remained in control of Brazil, contested control of what is now Uruguay. In 1816, Portuguese forces moved southward from the southern Brazilian state of Rio Grande del Sul into what is now Uruguay and annexed the area. In 1825, leaders of the Banda Orientale declared independence from Brazil. The independence movement led to the Argentina-Brazil War, also known as the Cisplatine War. Neither side was able to establish military superiority during the war.

In 1827, the two sides entered peace negotiations. Peace talks were encouraged by Britain, whose trade with South America was disrupted by military hostilities. The negotiations culminated in the signing of the Treaty of Montevideo in 1828. Under terms of the Treaty of Montevideo, the territory was recognized as an independent state.

CONTEMPORARY ISSUES

The general contours of the boundaries between Uruguay and its neighbors have been uncontested since Uruguay became independent. However, Uruguay has been engaged in boundary disputes with both of its neighbors in recent years. Uruguay and Brazil both claim Brazileria Island (Brasileria Island in Portuguese), which is located near the confluence of the Quaraí and Uruguay rivers near the tripoint between Uruguay, Brazil, and Argentina.

The current dispute between Uruguay and Argentina is associated with a plan to construct paper mills on the Uruguayan side of the Uruguay River, which forms the boundary between the two countries. In 2003, a Spanish company received permission from the government of Uruguay to build one of the mills. Uruguay authorized a Finnish company to build a second mill in 2005. The boundary agreement between Uruguay and Argentina stipulates that each country must inform the other of any plans to undertake projects that might affect the river.

After plans to construct the paper mills were announced, Argentina expressed concern about the likelihood that the mills, once constructed and operated, would discharge pollutants into the river. Argentina claimed that Uruguay had not asked permission to build the mills, and Uruguay responded that the terms of the treaty did not require Uruguay to notify Argentina of its plans. In late 2005 and early 2006, several protest rallies and demonstrations against the planned paper mills took place. Protest actions included an ongoing blockade of the General de San Martin Bridge connecting the two countries across the Uruguay River. The protesters were supported by national and international environmental groups as well as by local Argentine officials. In 2006, Argentina sued Uruguay in the International Court of Justice on the grounds that Uruguay had violated its obligations under terms of the treaty. Argentina requested an injunction against construction of the paper mills, but the court declined to order a halt to construction. In 2011, the two countries agreed to establish a bilateral commission to monitor pollution on the river, and blockades were suspended.

See also   Argentina, Brazil

Further Reading

BBC News. "Argentine in pulp mill protest." November 11, 2007, http://news.bbc.co.uk/2/hi/americas/7089226.stm.

Rossana Castiglioni Nunez. *The politics of social policy change in Chile and Uruguay: Retrenchment versus maintenances, 1973–1998.* New York: Routledge, 2006.

VENEZUELA

OVERVIEW

The Bolivarian Republic of Venezuela is located in northern South America along the coast of the Caribbean Sea. Venezuela's land area is 353,841 square miles, about the size of Texas and Oklahoma combined. Its population is about 30 million. Much of Venezuela is located within the drainage basin of the Orinoco River, and some of its boundaries separate the Orinoco drainage basin from the drainage basin of the Amazon River.

Venezuela's neighbors are Colombia to the west, Brazil to the south, and Guyana to the east. Trinidad and Tobago in the Caribbean Sea is less than 20 miles from the Venezuelan coast at its closest point. It has a long coast on the Caribbean Sea to the north and a shorter coast on the Atlantic Ocean east of Trinidad to the northeast.

The boundary between Venezuela and Colombia extends southward from the Caribbean Sea west of Venezuela's Lake Maracaibo. It continues southward to a point near Venezuela's El Tama National Park and then turns westward to the Meta River, which is a tributary of the Orinoco. It follows the Meta eastward and downstream to its confluence with the main channel of the Orinoco itself. The boundary then turns southward, following the Orinoco upstream to its confluence with the Guaviare River. From this confluence, the boundary continues southward and enters the Amazon basin, continuing to the Rio Negro. It then follows the Rio Negro to the tripoint between Venezuela, Colombia, and Brazil.

VENEZUELA

From that tripoint the Rio Negro continues into Brazil and eventually flows into the Amazon.

Most of the boundary between Venezuela and Brazil is located through dense rainforest that is sparsely populated and in some places virtually uninhabited. From the Rio Negro, the boundary extends eastward to Panmo-Tapirapeco National Park. The rest of the boundary follows the drainage divide between the Orinoco and the Amazon. From Panmo-Tapirapeco National Park, it extends northward to Jaue-Sarisaranama National Park. These parks along with nearby parks in Brazil preserve one of the largest areas of tropical rainforest in the world. The area is also home to the Yanomami people, one of the most isolated nations in the world with a population of about 20,000 on both sides of the border. The boundary then continues westward along the Orinoco-Amazon drainage divide to Mount Roraima, which is the tripoint between Venezuela, Brazil, and Guyana and is the highest mountain outside the Andes in northern South America.

The boundary between Venezuela and Guyana follows physical features. It extends northward from Mount Roraima. It follows a diagonal line northwest to the Wenama River, and then follows the Wenama downstream to its confluence with the Cuyuni River. It continues downstream along the Cuyuni, then crosses into the Imataca Mountains to the source of the Amakura River. It follows the Amakura River northward to the Haiowa River, and then northward to the Mururuma River, and then further northward to the Barima River and hence to the Atlantic Ocean. This boundary has been contested for many years because Venezuela claims part of Guyanese territory eastward to the Essequibo River in central Guyana.

HISTORICAL CONTEXT

Columbus visited the coast of present-day Venezuela in 1498, and Spanish colonization of the coast began in the early 16th century. The Spanish moved inland gradually and expanded control over local indigenous cultures over the course of the 16th century. The present-day Venezuelan capital of Caracas was established by the Spanish in 1567. By the late 18th century, Spanish influence had spread southward to the Orinoco River. In the 16th century, Venezuela was administered from Santo Domingo in what is now the Dominican Republic. In 1713, it became part of the Viceroyalty of New Granada along with present-day Colombia, Ecuador, and Panama.

Venezuela first declared independence from Spain and from the Viceroyalty of New Granada in 1811. The independence claim was rejected by Spain, and the new republic collapsed. A similar unsuccessful effort was made in 1813. In 1821, the Viceroyalty became independent under the name of Gran Colombia. Venezuela seceded from Gran Colombia and became fully independent in 1830. The newly independent country was ruled by dictators throughout most of the 19th century. During that period, Venezuela claimed the territory between its current boundary with Guyana and the Essequibo River in what was then British Guiana. This area was known as the as the Guayana Esequiba or the Zona en Reclamacion (Reclamation Zone). In 1899, a tribunal gave sovereignty over most of the Guayana Esequiba to the British. Oil was discovered in Lake Maracaibo in the early 20th century, and exploitation of these oil deposits over many years has helped Venezuela to become one of the most prosperous countries in South America.

CONTEMPORARY ISSUES

Despite the 1899 ruling concerning the boundary between Venezuela and Guyana over the status of the Guayana Esequiba, Venezuela continues to maintain a claim over the region. It renewed this claim after Guyana became independent in 1966. The United Nations has taken a more active interest in the dispute. The issue involves not only the territory between the Barima and Essequibo rivers but also the maritime boundaries between the two countries. The maritime boundary is important to both countries because of oil deposits and other mineral resources off the coast of the two countries.

The area near the boundary between Venezuela and Brazil had been a point of contention between these two states. Gold has been discovered in the region, and gold miners have moved into the area, in some places disrupting local indigenous cultures as well as the tropical rainforest environment. Because this border is located in sparsely inhabited territory and is not well patrolled, smuggling of weapons and illegal drugs across the boundary has occurred on many occasions. In addition, Venezuela has disputed its maritime boundaries in the Caribbean Sea with both Trinidad and Tobago and Colombia. As is the case with Guyana, this area of the Caribbean is located above valuable offshore oil and natural gas deposits.

See also   Brazil, Colombia, Guyana

Further Reading

Jacqueline Anne Braveboy-Wagner. *The Venezuela-Guyana border dispute: Britain's colonial legacy in Latin America.* Boulder, CO: Westview Press, 1984.

Jonathan di John. *From windfall to curse: Oil and industrialization in Venezuela, 1920 to the present.* University Park: Pennsylvania State University Press, 2009.

Humberto Marquez. "Gold mine pits jobs against environment in Venezuela." *Venezuelaanalysis.com*, September 29, 2005, http://venezuelanalysis.com/analysis/1391.

Tinker Salas. *The enduring legacy: Oil, culture, and society in Venezuela.* Durham, NC: Duke University Press, 2009.

SUB-SAHARAN AFRICA

N

CHAPTER 3

SUB-SAHARAN AFRICA

Africa is the second-largest continent in the world by land area, and it contains a wide variety of physical environments. The world's largest desert, the Sahara Desert, crosses northern Africa from the Atlantic Ocean to the west to the Red Sea to the east. The Sahara separates the countries of Africa into two groups. Those African countries whose population centers are located along the Mediterranean Sea north of the Sahara have strong historical and cultural communalities with the countries of Southwest Asia. The countries of Southwest Asia and North Africa are discussed together in chapter 5. This chapter focuses on Sub-Saharan Africa, which consists of Africa south of the Sahara Desert.

Sub-Saharan Africa is one of the fastest-growing areas of the world. Some sub-Saharan countries have among the highest birth rates in the world. High birth rates are associated with high total fertility rates, or average numbers of children born to women over the course of their lifetimes. As a result, most African countries have very young populations. The median age in Burkina Faso is 16.7 years; in other words, more than half of Burkina Faso's people are less than 17 years old.

Sub-Saharan Africa's population remains predominantly rural. In some countries, as much as 80 percent of the workforce consists of farmers. However, rural population densities vary considerably from place to place within sub-Saharan Africa. Rural areas in Nigeria, Kenya, Malawi, Tanzania, and Ethiopia are densely populated. Other areas, such as Gabon and Botswana, are sparsely populated. In general, population densities are lower in deserts and in tropical rainforests relative to other areas of the continent.

Despite the fact that many Africans continue to live in rural areas, African cities are growing very rapidly. Most African cities are growing at faster rates than rural areas because of the large number of people moving to urban areas in search of employment. Some African cities such as Mombasa, Kenya, and Timbuktu, Mali, were major urban centers centuries before the arrival of Europeans. Others, including Lagos, Nigeria, and Cape Town, South Africa, were established by the Europeans. Many of Africa's major cities are ports, reflecting the importance of sea trade in the relationships between African colonies and the European colonial powers.

During the 19th century, most of Africa was carved up into colonies of the various European powers. Britain, France, Spain, Portugal, Belgium, Germany, the Netherlands, and Italy all maintained colonies in Africa during the late 19th or early 20th century. In 1910, only three present-day sub-Saharan

African countries were independent—Liberia, Ethiopia, and South Africa. Between 1957 and 1975, most of the former European colonies in sub-Saharan Africa became independent countries. Most of Africa's boundaries were drawn by European diplomats in the late 19th century. At that time, Europeans had very little knowledge of the African interior, and they did not know what people, natural resources, or physical features were located on either side of the boundaries that were drawn.

Many African boundaries are drawn perpendicular to the coast. This was done because each European colonial power focused its attention on port cities, through which trade between Africa and Europe took place. Many of the boundaries were drawn around port cities that had already been established by various European powers. After most African countries became independent during the 1950s and 1960s, the boundaries drawn by the European colonial powers continued to be used. Today, many African states face conflicts among various ethnic and tribal groups living within their boundaries. In other cases, boundaries separated ethnic groups. For example, many people living in eastern Ethiopia are ethnic Somalis who would prefer that their home territory be attached to Somalia, rather than remain part of Ethiopia. The lack of correspondence between nations and states has led to many conflicts, including shooting wars, between African countries both before and after independence.

ANGOLA

OVERVIEW

The Republic of Angola is located in southwestern Africa. This former Portuguese colony has a land area of about 481,000 square miles, making it nearly twice the size of Texas. Angola's population is about 18.5 million.

Angola's neighbors are the Democratic Republic of the Congo to the north and east, Zambia to the east, and Namibia to the south. To the west, Angola has a long seacoast on the Atlantic Ocean. Angola also includes the exclave of Cabinda, which is north of the main territory of the country and borders the Democratic Republic of the Congo and the Republic of the Congo.

Some of Angola's boundaries are geometric, and some follow natural features. The boundary between Angola and the Democratic Republic of the Congo follows the lower reaches of the Congo River from its mouth on the Atlantic Ocean. The head of navigation on the Congo River is located near the city of Matadi on the Congolese side of the border. Near this point, the course of the Congo turns northeastward, eventually becoming the boundary between the Democratic Republic of the Congo and the Republic of the Congo. The boundary between Angola and the Democratic Republic of the Congo continues from a few miles southwest of Matadi in an easterly direction to the Cuango River, which is called the Kwango River in the Democratic Republic of the Congo. Near Angola's Reserva Especial do Milando, the boundary leaves the Cuango and turns eastward along straight-line segments. It goes northward briefly and then turns eastward again to the Kasai River. It then follows the Kasai River southward and upstream. It then turns eastward once again, following the drainage divide between the Zambezi River in Angola and the Congo River in the Democratic Republic of the

ANGOLA

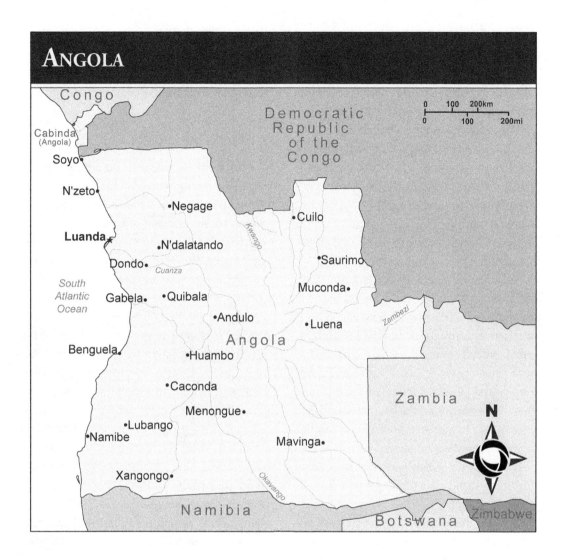

Congo. The boundary between Angola and Zambia is geometric. The northern portion of this boundary consists of numerous short, straight lines. It then extends westward along the 13th parallel of south latitude and then turns southward again along the 22nd meridian of east longitude. The southern end of this boundary consists of straight-line segments that follow in general the floodplain of the eastern side of the Kwando River. The boundary between Angola and Namibia from east to west includes a southwest-trending diagonal line, the course of the Okavango River, another straight line following the 17° 23′ 25″ parallel of south latitude, and the lower course of the Kunene River before this river empties into the Atlantic Ocean.

HISTORICAL CONTEXT

The city of Luanda, which is Angola's capital city today, was founded by the Portuguese explorer Paulo Dias de Novais in 1565. Portugal remained in control of the Angolan coast throughout the 17th, 18th, and 19th centuries. Portuguese slave traders captured hundreds of thousands of indigenous Angolan people, transporting many of them to Brazil.

Portugal annexed Angola formally in 1884 as Portuguese West Africa. Frontiers between colonies of Portugal and Belgium, Britain, and Germany (which controlled the present-day Democratic Republic of the Congo, Zambia, and Namibia, respectively) were disputed, but these disputes were resolved and Angola's boundaries were delineated by agreements among these countries between 1886 and 1905. The boundaries remain in place today.

Angola became independent in 1975. After independence, Angola was the scene of many years of civil war between various factions fighting for control of the government. After 27 years of warfare, a cease-fire was agreed upon in 2002. Angola remains impoverished and decimated by the long war. However, Angola has an abundance of natural resources, whose extraction has helped Angola's economy develop rapidly. By 2012, Angola was experiencing the most rapid economic growth in sub-Saharan Africa.

Angola also includes the exclave of Cabinda, which is located along the Atlantic coast between the Republic of the Congo to the north and the Democratic Republic of the Congo to the south. Its land area is bout 3,000 square miles, about half the size of Connecticut. About half of its 150,000 residents are believed to be refugees from the Democratic Republic of the Congo. The southern boundary between Cabinda and the Democratic Republic of the Congo is about 20 miles north of the main portion of Angola. Like the rest of Angola, Cabinda was a Portuguese colony. It was formally annexed as a colony by Portugal in 1885 and was known as Portuguese Congo.

Despite substantial local opposition, Cabinda was incorporated into Angola in 1975 though the Treaty of Alvor, which provided for Angolan independence.

CONTEMPORARY ISSUES

The most significant boundary issue currently facing Angola is the status of Cabinda. In the 1960s, the Front for the Liberation of the Enclave of Cabinda (FLEC) was founded. The Treaty of Alvor, which was signed by Portugal and by the various factions that would grapple for control of Angola for the next three decades, was not signed by FLEC. Shortly after independence, Angolan troops invaded Cabinda and incorporated the exclave forcibly into Angola. Conflict between the government and Cabindan rebels has continued since then, with each side accusing the other of human rights violations. Conflict escalated with the discovery of proven oil reserves, and Cabinda now produces about 60 percent of Angola's petroleum. A cease-fire was negotiated in 2006 in exchange for Angolan recognition of special status for Cabinda, but sporadic violence continues.

Angola and the Democratic Republic of the Congo have also been involved in a boundary dispute. The area along the boundary is rich in diamond mines and has considerable oil deposits. Angola has been concerned about illegal migration of miners across the boundary, and Angolan security forces expelled 25,000 Congolese miners from what it considered Angolan territory in 2004. In 2007, the two countries agreed to empower a boundary commission consisting of representatives from the two colonial powers, Portugal and

Belgium, to delineate this boundary precisely subject to ratification by the African Union.

See also Democratic Republic of the Congo, Namibia, Zambia

Further Reading

Patrick Chabal and Nuno Vidal. *Angola: The weight of history.* New York: Columbia University Press, 2007.

Joao Gomes Porto. "Cabinda: Notes on a soon-to-be-forgotten war." Institute for Security Studies, Paper 77, 2003, http://dspace.cigilibrary.org/jspui/bitstream/123456789/31255/1/PAPER77.pdf?1.

Nicholas Shaxson. *Poisoned wells: The dirty politics of African oil.* London: Palgrave Macmillan, 2008.

Stephen L. Weigert. *Angola: A modern military history, 1961–2002.* New York: Palgrave Macmillan, 2011.

BENIN

OVERVIEW

The Republic of Benin is located in West Africa on the Gulf of Guinea. Benin's land area is 43,484 square miles, about the size of Virginia. Its population is about 10 million.

Benin's neighbors are Togo to the west, Burkina Faso and Niger to the north, and Nigeria to the east. The boundary between Benin and Togo extends northward and inland from the Gulf of Guinea. Some of the southern portion of this boundary follows the Mono River, which has been dammed in order to provide hydroelectric power to both countries. A few miles east of the village of Bimi in Benin, the boundary trends northwestward. It follows a geometric, diagonal line northwestward for about 50 miles to a point near the village of Datori and then trends northward again to the tripoint between Benin, Togo, and Burkina Faso.

Most of the boundary between Benin and Burkina Faso trends in a northeasterly direction and follows rivers. From the tripoint between Benin, Burkina Faso, and Togo, the boundary follows the Pendjari River, which flows eventually into Lake Volta in Ghana. The northeastern portion of the boundary between Benin and Burkina Faso follows the Mekrou River. The Mekrou flows northeastward and empties into West Africa's largest river, the Niger River. Between the Pendjari and the Mekrou, the boundary between Benin and Burkina Faso is a straight-line segment extending from southwest to northeast. This segment crosses a mountainous area known as the chaine de l'Atacora.

From the tripoint between Benin, Burkina Faso, and Niger, the Mekrou River continues downstream as the boundary between Benin and Niger until it empties into the Niger River. The boundary continues downstream and southeastward along the Niger River until it reaches the tripoint between Benin, Niger, and Nigeria. The boundary between Benin and Nigeria extends in a generally southward direction to the Bight of Benin, which is itself part of the Gulf of Guinea. Part of this boundary follows the Okpara River, which rises in central Benin and flows eastward and southward into the Bight.

HISTORICAL CONTEXT

Much of the southern part of present-day Benin was part of the African kingdom of Dahomey during the 17th, 18th,

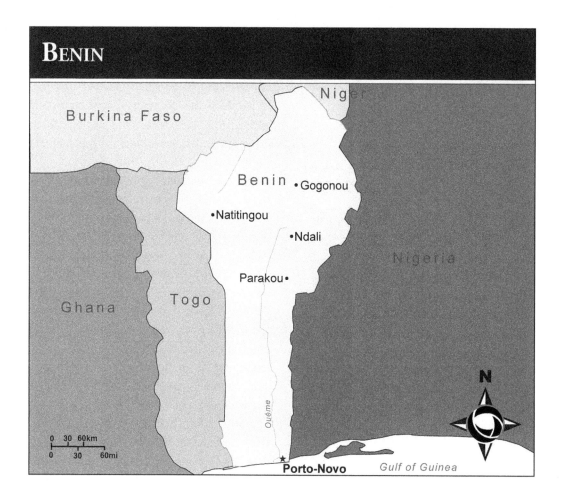

BENIN

and early 19th centuries. Dahomey became a major regional power in West Africa, and its rulers were notorious for their participation in the trans-Atlantic slave trade. France became increasingly influential in present-day Benin in the late 19th century. French forces toppled the monarchy of Dahomey in 1894. The French incorporated Dahomey into French West Africa, which also included present-day Senegal, Mali, Niger, Burkina Faso, Guinea, Cote d'Ivoire, and Mauritania, in 1904.

French Dahomey became a self-governing colony within the French Community in 1958. In 1960, the country became fully independent under the name of Da-homey. The newly independent country suffered from ongoing ethnic tensions during its early years of independence. A Marxist-Leninist government took power in 1972. In 1975, the government changed the name of the country from Dahomey to the People's Republic of Benin. This change was made because the original Kingdom of Dahomey ruled only the southern portion of the country. The Marxist-Leninist government was deposed in 1990, and the name was changed to the Republic of Benin. Since that time, Benin has remained a democracy in which defeated candidates for the presidency have not contested election results.

Benin's boundaries were delineated during colonial times. The boundary between Benin and Togo was first agreed upon by France and Germany, which controlled present-day Togo, in 1885. This boundary was modified by a subsequent agreement in 1897. The boundary between Benin and Burkina Faso, both of which were part of French West Africa, was delineated by France beginning in 1909. France also designated the Mekrou and Niger rivers as the boundary between Benin and Niger. However, after independence the two countries disputed sovereignty over several islands in the Niger River. In 2001, both countries agreed to submit this dispute to the International Court of Justice, which resolved the dispute in a ruling issued in 2005. France and Britain agreed to what would become the boundary between Benin and Nigeria in 1906. The boundary was adjusted slightly by agreement between the two colonial powers in 1912.

CONTEMPORARY ISSUES

Benin and Togo have experienced a boundary dispute that stems from the fact that the boundary, although agreed upon between France and Germany in 1897, was not marked fully. In 2001, the government of Benin accused Togo of relocating some existing boundary markers eastward. A joint boundary commission was established in order to delineate the boundary precisely.

See also Burkina Faso, Niger, Nigeria, Togo

Further Reading

Tony Chafer. *The end of empire in French West Africa: France's success-ful decolonization?* London: Berg, 2002.

Jennifer Seely. *The legacies of transition governments in Africa: The cases of Benin and Togo.* New York: Palgrave Macmillan, 2009.

BOTSWANA

OVERVIEW

The Republic of Botswana is located in southern Africa. It has a land area of 224,610 square miles, making it slightly smaller than Texas. Botswana's population is about 2.2 million, and hence it is one of the most sparsely populated countries in Africa. The western two-thirds of Botswana are located within the Kalahari Desert, and drought remains an ongoing problem in the country.

Landlocked Botswana has boundaries with Namibia to the west and north, Zimbabwe to the east, and South Africa to the south. It also has a very short boundary, less than a mile long, with Zambia to the northeast. Much of the boundary between Botswana and Namibia is geometric. From the tripoint between Botswana, Namibia, and South Africa in Kgalagadi Transnational Park, the boundary extends northward along the 20th meridian of east longitude to the 22° 30′ parallel of south latitude north of the town of Mamuno. It follows the 22° 30′ parallel eastward to the 21st meridian of east longitude and then follows the 21st meridian northward to the western end of Namibia's Caprivi Strip. From this point the boundary turns eastward again, following a long diagonal line extending in an east-northeasterly direction to the Kwando River, which it follows

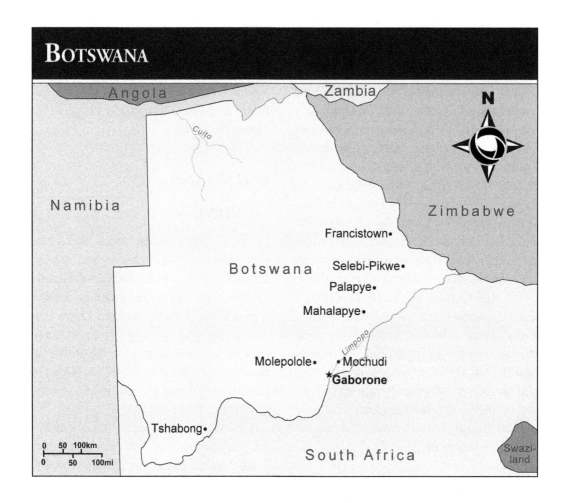

southeastward to its confluence with the Linyanti. It follows the Linyanti eastward to the Chobe River, which empties into the main channel of the Zambezi River. The Chobe empties into the Zambezi at the tripoint between Botswana, Namibia, and Zambia.

The tripoint between Botswana, Zambia, and Zimbabwe is located on the Zambezi a few yards downstream from the confluence of the Chobe and the Zambezi. From this tripoint, the boundary follows roads and short-line segments to the source of the Ramaquaban River. It follows the Ramaquaban southeastward and downstream to its confluence with the Shashe River and then follows the Shashe south-

eastward to its confluence with the Limpopo River at the tripoint between Botswana, Zimbabwe, and South Africa.

Most of the boundary between Botswana and South Africa also follows rivers. From the tripoint between Botswana, Zimbabwe, and South Africa, the boundary follows the Limpopo upstream to the confluence with its tributary, the Notwane River. A few miles east of Botswana's capital city of Gaborone, the boundary leaves the Notwane and extends westward and then southwestward to the Molopo River. It follows the Molopo southwestward and downstream to its confluence with the Nossob River and then turns northwestward and follows the Nossob to the tripoint between Botswana, South African, and Namibia at the 20th meridian.

HISTORICAL CONTEXT

Modern-day Botswana was settled by Bantu tribes moving southward and westward from present-day Zambia, Angola, and Zimbabwe around AD 1000. Internal conflicts among Bantu kingdoms induced some local leaders to request British protection. The British established the Protectorate of Bechuanaland in 1885. The seat of administration of Bechuanaland was the South African city of Mafeking, which is located outside of Botswana itself.

After South Africa became independent in 1910, Britain considered turning administration of the Protectorate over to South Africa. However, the British ended consideration of this possibility after South Africa elected its Nationalist government, which instituted the apartheid policy, in 1948. In 1965, the seat of administration was moved to the newly established city of Gaborone, which became Botswana's capital. Botswana became fully independent in 1966. Since that time, Botswana has been one of few African countries to have had an unbroken history of parliamentary democracy characterized by free, fair, multiparty elections. Today Botswana retains strong relationships with its neighbors. The country has one of Africa's higher per capita incomes but has been hit very hard by the HIV/AIDS pandemic, and life expectancy has declined by more than 10 years in the past two decades.

CONTEMPORARY ISSUES

After Botswana became independent, Botswana and Namibia became embroiled in a territorial dispute that centered on control of Sedudu Island, which is known in Namibia as Kasikile Island, in the Chobe River. The island has a land area of only two square miles, is subject to seasonal flooding, and is uninhabited. The dispute arose as a result of ambiguity in the agreements made by Britain and Germany, as the colonial powers governing Botswana and Namibia respectively, in an 1890 treaty. The treaty specified that the boundary would follow the "main channel" of the Chobe, but it was unclear whether the main channel flowed north or south of the islands. In 1992, the International Court of Justice ruled that the main channel flowed to the north of Sedudu Island and therefore that the island belonged to Botswana. However, the decision affirmed that both countries would have free right of navigation in both channels around the island.

See also   Namibia, South Africa, Zimbabwe

Further Reading

Kenneth Good. *Diamonds, dispossession, and democracy in Botswana.* Woodbridge, Surrey, UK: James Currey, 2008.

Abdi Ismail Samatar. *An African miracle: State and class leadership and colonial legacy in Botswana development.* London: Heinemann, 1999.

BURKINA FASO

OVERVIEW

Burkina Faso is located in West Africa. Burkina Faso has a land area of 105,869 square miles, the size of Colorado. Its population is about 16 million.

Burkina Faso is landlocked. Its neighbors are Mali to the northwest, Niger to the northeast, Benin to the east and southeast,

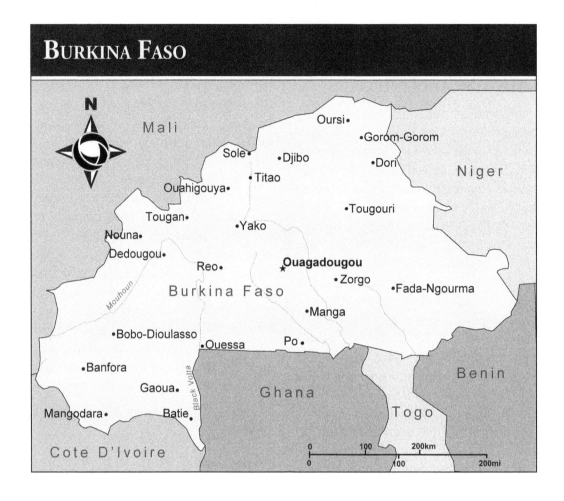

BURKINA FASO

and Togo, Ghana, and Cote d'Ivoire to the south. Most of the boundary between Burkina Faso and Mali follows short straight-line segments that extend northeast and then east from the tripoint between Burkina Faso, Mali, and Cote d'Ivoire. This boundary roughly parallels the drainage divide between streams flowing southward into the Volta River in Burkina Faso from those flowing northward into the Niger River in Mali. However, the central portion of the boundary is located south of the Volta-Niger drainage divide. To the east, the boundary follows straight-line segments that extend eastward to the tripoint between Burkina Faso, Mali, and Niger.

This tripoint is located at the edge of the Sahel Reserve in northern Burkina Faso. The boundary between Burkina Faso and Niger follows many straight-line segments that extend in a generally southeastward direction to the tripoint between Burkina Faso, Niger, and Benin.

From the tripoint between Burkina Faso, Niger, and Benin, the boundary between Burkina Faso and Benin follows the Mekrou River, which is a tributary of the Niger, upstream and southwestward. It then crosses a hilly area known as the chaine de l'Atacora before reaching the Pendjari River, which is part of the drainage basin of the Volta. From the tripoint between Burkina Faso, Benin, and Togo on the Pendjari, the boundary between Burkina Faso and Togo consists primarily of straight lines along and near the 11th parallel of north latitude. Much of the boundary between Burkina Faso and Ghana also follows straight-line segments near the 11th parallel, extending eastward from the tripoint between Burkina Faso, Ghana, and Togo to the Black Volta River, which is one of the three major tributaries of the Volta itself. Here the boundary turns southward and follows the Black Volta downstream to the tripoint between Burkina Faso, Ghana, and Cote d'Ivoire. From this tripoint the boundary between Burkina Faso and Cote d'Ivoire follows small streams and short straight-line segments to the Leraba River, also known as the Coroe or Koroe River. It then follows the Leraba and its tributary, the Leraba Occidentale River, westward to the tripoint between Burkina Faso, Cote d'Ivoire, and Mali. This tripoint is located where the Danboro and Zagoundouba rivers join to form the Leraba Occidentale River.

HISTORICAL CONTEXT

Much of present-day Burkina Faso was ruled by the Mossi Empire beginning in the 15th century. The Mossi remained in power until the late 19th century, when French incursions into the area began. The French captured the Mossi capital city of Ouagadougou in 1896, ending Mossi resistance to French colonization although local resistance to the French continued for the next several years. The area became part of the colony of Upper Senegal and Niger, including present-day Senegal, Mali, and Niger, in 1904. Upper Senegal and Niger

became part of the larger French colony of French West Africa.

In 1919, the French separated present-day Burkina Faso from Upper Senegal and Niger and established it as a separate colony. The new colony was named French Upper Volta, referring to the Volta River that drains much of the area. French Upper Volta was partitioned among present-day Cote d'Ivoire, Mali, and Niger in 1932, but the colony was reconstituted in 1947. The country became independent as the Republic of Upper Volta in 1960, and the name of the country was changed to Burkina Faso in 1984.

CONTEMPORARY ISSUES

Since independence, Burkina Faso has experienced tensions and conflicts with several of its neighbors. A boundary dispute between Burkina Faso and Mali erupted into a shooting war in 1985. This dispute involved control of a region known as the Agacher Strip, which is located along the current boundary between the two countries. Both Burkina Faso and Mali claimed the Agacher Strip, which was believed to be rich in mineral resources. After war broke out in 1985, the dispute was referred to the International Court of Justice. In 1986, the court divided the Agacher Strip between the two countries.

The boundary between Burkina Faso and Niger remains uncertain also. This boundary was originally delineated by France in 1927, but the delineation was ambiguous and left sovereignty over some places along the boundary unclear. In 2010, the two countries asked the International Court of Justice to delineate the boundary clearly. Tensions escalated along the boundary in late 2010 and early 2011 while the court was working on this issue.

Burkina Faso and its neighbors have also experienced tension over the status of migrants and refugees. Burkina Faso is one of the poorest and least developed countries in the world, with a long history of autocratic government and abuses of human rights. Poverty and repression have induced many residents of Burkina Faso to leave the country. Many fled to the much wealthier neighboring country of Cote d'Ivoire, where some have been victims of discrimination and ethnic violence. However, current political crises in Cote d'Ivoire and in Mali have pushed many refugees into Burkina Faso. As of early 2012, more than 60,000 Malian refugees have relocated into Burkina Faso, where many of these refugees have faced malnutrition resulting from severe shortages of food.

See also   Benin, Cote d'Ivoire, Ghana, Mali, Niger, Togo

Further Reading

Pierre Englebert. *Burkina Faso: Unsteady statehood in West Africa.* Boulder, CO: Westview Press, 1999.

Jane Labous. "The forgotten crisis: Refugees in Burkina Faso glimpse hope despite the conditions, as the U.N.'s Valerie Amos pays a visit." *Huffington Post*, May 23, 2012, http://www.huffingtonpost. co.uk/jane-labous/the-forgotten-crisis-refu_b_1539584.html.

BURUNDI

OVERVIEW

The Republic of Burundi is located in east-central Africa. Its land area is 10,745 square miles, the size of Maryland. Its population is 10.5 million.

Burundi has boundaries with the Democratic Republic of the Congo to the west, Rwanda to the north, and Tanzania to the east and south. Most of these boundaries are located along rivers and lakes. The tripoint between Burundi, the Democratic Republic of the Congo, and Tanzania is located in Lake Tanganyika, a long, narrow lake that extends in a north-south direction. The lake forms the southern portion of the boundary between Burundi and the Democratic Republic of the Congo. To the north, the boundary between Burundi and the Democratic Republic of the Congo follows the Ruzizi River from its mouth at the north end of Lake Tanganyika upstream to the confluence between the Ruzizi and the Ruwa, or Luhwa, River. The tripoint between Burundi, the Democratic Republic of the Congo, and Rwanda is located at this confluence.

From this tripoint, the boundary between Burundi and Rwanda extends eastward along the Ruwa to its tributary, the Kanyaru River. It extends across additional streams and short-line segments eastward and then northward to Lake Cyohoha and the larger Lake Rweru, both of which are located along the boundary. From Lake Rweru, the boundary follows the Nyabarongo River, which flows from Lake Rweru into the Kagera River to the tripoint between Burundi, Rwanda, and Tanzania at the confluence between the Kagera and the Mwibu River.

The boundary between Burundi and Tanzania extends in a southwesterly direction from this tripoint to Lake Tanganyika. The northernmost section follows the Mwibu southward and upstream along the

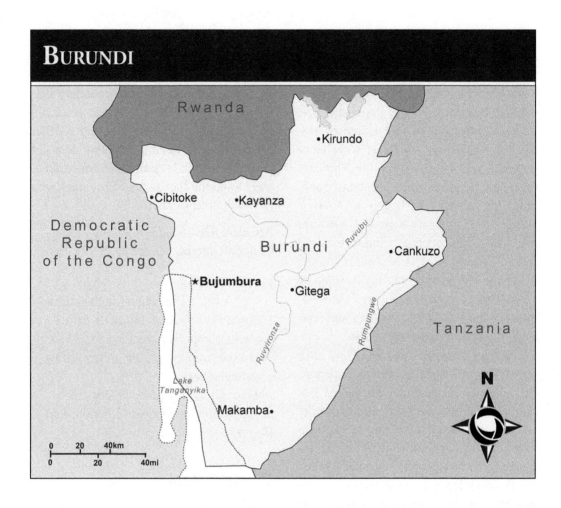

BURUNDI

Mwibu. The boundary then follows short straight-line segments and portions of streams to the tripoint between Burundi, Tanzania, and the Democratic Republic of the Congo in Lake Tanganyika.

HISTORICAL CONTEXT

Most of present-day Burundi along with neighboring territories was part of the Kingdom of Burundi, which arose in the 16th century and remained in power through the 19th century. The Burundi monarchy resisted European incursions in the late 19th century. However, the last king of Burundi was forced to accept German

sovereignty over the kingdom in 1899. Burundi was attached to German East Africa along with present-day Rwanda and Tanganyika, which is today the mainland portion of Tanzania. After Germany was stripped of its colonies following World War I, the League of Nations divided German East Africa into Belgian and British mandates. Burundi and Rwanda were awarded to Belgium as a single entity known as Ruanda-Urundi, while Tanganyika was assigned to the British. In 1924, Britain and Belgium agreed upon the boundary between these mandates. Belgium administered Ruanda-Urundi as a United Nations Trust Territory after World War II.

Most people in Ruanda-Urundi belonged to one of two major ethnic groups, the Tutsi and the Hutu. The two nations have been in ongoing and often violent conflict before and since independence. Today, 85 percent of the people of Burundi are Hutu, but the Tutsi were more powerful politically. During the 20th century, the Belgians ruled Ruanda-Urundi indirectly through Tutsi chiefs. As Belgium began to prepare Ruanda-Urundi for eventual independence, ethnic tensions flared. Thousands of Tutsi were murdered in the late 1950s in present-day Rwanda by Hutu. This genocide encouraged the separation of the colony into two counties. Burundi became independent in 1962.

Tensions between Tutsi and Hutu have characterized Burundi since independence. In 1972, the Tutsi-dominated Burundian army was accused of mass murder of Hutu civilians. In 1992 and 1993, thousands of Tutsi were killed by Hutu. An estimated 250,000 people have been killed in ethnic violence since Burundi became independent, and hundreds of thousands more have left the country as refugees. Efforts to resolve the conflict are ongoing, but the country's economy is in shambles as a result of the conflict, and Burundi is one of the poorest countries in the world.

CONTEMPORARY ISSUES

Burundi's boundaries are generally stable. However, Burundi and Rwanda have disputed sovereignty over territory along the courses of the Kanyara and Kageru rivers. These disputes have arisen because the rivers have changed course since the boundary along these rivers was agreed upon before Burundi became independent. The status of refugees living in Burundi also remains problematic. Thousands of refugees from civil war in the neighboring Democratic Republic of the Congo have fled across the international boundary into Burundi. As one of the poorest countries in the world, and facing ongoing conflict between Tutsi and Hutu, Burundi does not have the financial resources to house, feed, and clothe the thousands of refugees who now live in Burundi.

See also Democratic Republic of the Congo, Rwanda, Tanzania

Further Reading

Josh Kron. "The country in the mirror." *Foreign Policy*, June 14, 2010, http://www.foreignpolicy.com/articles/2010/06/14/the_country_in_the_mirror?show comments=yes.

Peter Uvin. *Life after violence: A people's story of Burundi.* London: Zed Books, 2009.

CAMEROON

OVERVIEW

The Republic of Cameroon is located in west-central Africa slightly north of the equator. Cameroon's land area is 183,568 square miles, approximately the size of Colorado and Utah combined. Its population is about 21 million.

Cameroon is shaped roughly like a triangle. Its shares boundaries with Nigeria to the northwest, Chad and the Central African Republic to the east, and the Republic of the Congo, Gabon, and Equatorial Guinea to the south. To the southwest, Cameroon has a coastline on the Gulf of Guinea. The island of Bioko, which is part of Equatorial Guinea, lies about 20 miles southwest of the coast of Cameroon.

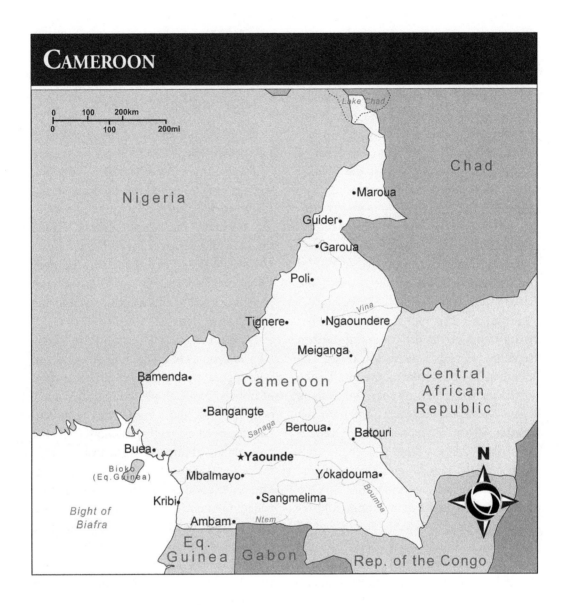

CAMEROON

The boundary between Cameroon and Nigeria extends in a generally northeasterly direction from the Gulf of Guinea in the southwest to Lake Chad in the north. From the Gulf of Guinea, the boundary extends northeastward to the Donga River, which flows into the Benue River in Nigeria. The boundary follows the Donga southeastward and upstream and then turns northeastward again to the Faro River, which is another tributary of the Benue. It then continues northeastward along the course of the Faro to its confluence with the Benue. From this confluence, the border continues along straight-line segments and short streams in a north-northeasterly direction to Lake Chad. The northernmost section of Cameroon, south of Lake Chad, is long and narrow and is only about 20 miles wide near Chad's capital city of N'Djamena. The tripoint between Cameroon, Nigeria, and Chad is located in Lake Chad.

From Lake Chad, the boundary between Cameroon and Chad follows the Chari River southward to its confluence with the Logone River, a tributary that joins the Chari near N'Djamena. From that point, the boundary follows the Logone upstream and southward. Near the town of Bongor, the boundary leaves the Logone and extends westward. It turns southeastward near the town of Guidei and continues following short straight-line segments and roads to the tripoint between Cameroon, Chad, and the Central African Republic. This tripoint is located along the Mbéré River.

From this tripoint, the boundary between Cameroon and the Central African Republic extends southward along the Mbéré and some of its tributaries. To the south, the boundary reaches the Sangha River. The tripoint between Cameroon, the Central African Republic, and the Republic of the Congo is located near the confluence of the Sangha and Ngoko rivers. The boundary between Cameroon and the Democratic Republic of the Congo follows the Ngoko upstream to the south end of Cameroon's Nki National Park. From the park, it extends westward along and near the 2nd parallel of north latitude to the tripoint between Cameroon, the Republic of the Congo, and Gabon, which is located at the junction of the 11° 20' meridian of east longitude and the Aïna River.

The boundary between Cameroon and Gabon extends westward and upstream along the Aïna. It then crosses to the Kom River and follows the Kom downstream to its confluence with the Ntem River. Much of the boundary between Cameroon and Equatorial Guinea continues westward along the 2nd parallel. The westernmost section of this boundary follows the Ntem to its mouth in the Gulf of Guinea.

HISTORICAL CONTEXT

Bantu tribes are believed to have moved into present-day Cameroon approximately 2,000 years ago. Over the next 1,500 years, various kingdoms and chiefdoms rose and fell in various parts of Cameroon's modern territory. Portuguese sailors visited the Gulf of Guinea coast of Cameroon in 1472. The Portuguese and other Europeans established trading centers but did not penetrate into the interior until well into the 19th century.

During the late 19th century, two German companies began trading activities and other operations, including the cultivation of tropical crops on plantations, in Cameroon. In 1884, these companies requested and received formal protection from the government of Imperial Germany. The protectorate was known as German Cameroon. French and British forces occupied and invaded German Cameroon during World War I. After Germany was stripped of its overseas colonies after the war, the United Nations divided Cameroon between French and British mandates. Most of the colony was placed under a French mandate, while a long, narrow strip of territory along the boundary between the colony and present-day Nigeria was placed under a British mandate. The two mandates were known as Cameroun and the British Cameroons respectively. Although Cameroun's land area was much larger, the two mandates had approximately equal populations.

French Cameroun became independent under the name of the Republic of Cameroon in 1960. In 1961, residents of the British

Cameroons were given the choice to unite with the Republic of Cameroon or with Nigeria. A majority of voters in the southern part of the British Cameroons, or Southern Cameroons, chose to unite with Cameroon, while those in the northern part of the British Cameroons elected to join Nigeria. Religion was an important factor in this decision in that the majority of people in the southern British Cameroons were Christians whereas the majority of people in the northern British Cameroons were Muslims.

CONTEMPORARY ISSUES

Beginning in the 1960s, Cameroon and Nigeria experienced a border dispute. The dispute was focused on the control of the Bakassi Peninsula, which extends southwestward into the Gulf of Guinea. The Bakassi region is one of the richest fishing grounds in the world, and it is also believed to contain valuable oil deposits. In 1993, Nigerian troops occupied the peninsula, and armed skirmishes broke out. The dispute over Bakassi was referred to the International Court of Justice in 1994. In 2002, the court ruled in favor of Cameroon. Sovereignty over Bakassi was granted to Cameroon, but Cameroon was required to protect the rights of Nigerian people living on the peninsula. A border commission was established and charged with delineating the entire boundary between the two countries precisely.

Secessionist activities have taken place in the former southern portion of the British Cameroons, which had voted to unite with Cameroon in 1961. In 1999, an organization known as the Southern Cameroons National Council declared that the former Southern Cameroons was the independent Republic of Ambazonia, whose population is about 6 million. However, Ambazonian independence has not been recognized by the Republic of Cameroon or by the international community.

Cameroon and Equatorial Guinea have also contested sovereignty over three very small islands in the Gulf of Guinea. These islands are located near valuable oil deposits, and both Cameroon and Equatorial Guinea have pressed their claims over the islands because control over the islands would have a considerable impact on the eventual delineation of maritime boundaries and therefore over access to these oil deposits.

See also   Central African Republic, Chad, Equatorial Guinea, Gabon, Nigeria, Republic of the Congo

Further Reading

Carlson Anyangwe. *Imperialistic politics in Cameroun: Resistance and the inception of the statehood of Southern Cameroons.* Oxford, UK: African Books Collective, 2008.

Foreign Affairs. "Cameroon: At the crossroads." July/August 2008, http://www.foreignaffairs.com/about-us/sponsors/cameroon-at-the-crossroads.

UN News Centre. "Ban praises Cameroon, Nigeria for carrying out border demarcation ruling." November 22, 2011, http://www.un.org/apps/news/story.asp?NewsID=40486&Cr=cameroon&Cr1.

CAPE VERDE

OVERVIEW

The Republic of Cape Verde is an island country in the Atlantic Ocean off the

CAPE VERDE

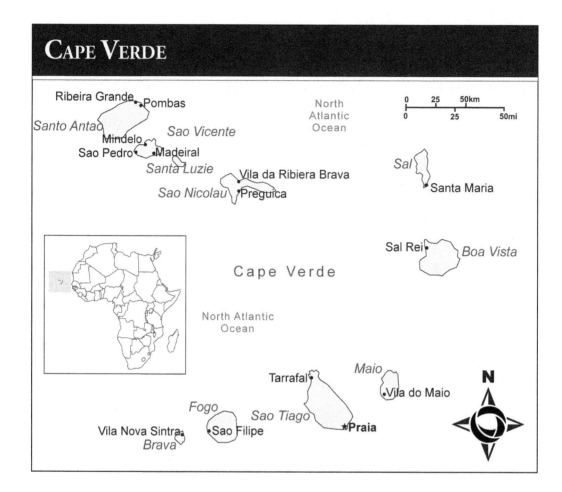

coast of northwest Africa. The Cape Verde Islands archipelago consists of 10 islands, 9 of which are inhabited. The total land area of Cape Verde is 1,557 square miles, the size of Rhode Island. The population of Cape Verde is about 600,000. The islands are located about 400 miles west of the coasts of Mauritania and Senegal.

HISTORICAL CONTEXT

The Cape Verde Islands may have been visited by Phoenician, Arab, or African sailors before the 15th century, but the islands were uninhabited until they were visited by Portuguese mariners in the 1450s.

The first permanent settlement on the islands, established in 1462, was Cidade Velha on the island of Sao Tiago. The islands became an important trading center as well as a resupply point for ships traversing the Atlantic.

The Cape Verde Islands remained a Portuguese colony into the 20th century. Portugal changed the status of the islands from a colony to an overseas province in 1951. The struggle for complete independence continued and intensified after most other European colonial powers granted independence to their African colonies in the late 1950s and early 1960s. After the Portuguese dictatorship was overthrown in 1974 and democracy was restored, Portugal granted independence to the islands in 1975. Cape Verde was a one-party state until 1990, when multiparty democracy was implemented.

Further Reading

Richard A. Lobban. *Cape Verde: Crioulo colony to independent nation.* Boulder, CO: Westview Press, 1998.

CENTRAL AFRICAN REPUBLIC

OVERVIEW

The Central African Republic is a landlocked country located in north-central Africa. It has a land area of about 240,000 square miles, making it slightly smaller than Texas. Its population is about 4.6 million. The Central African Republic is one of the poorest and least developed countries in the world.

The Central African Republic's neighbors are Chad to the north, Sudan to the northeast, South Sudan to the east, the Democratic Republic of the Congo to the south, the Republic of the Congo to the southwest, and Cameroon to the west. Many of the Central African Republic's boundaries are physical boundaries. Most of the boundary between the Central African Republic and Chad follows rivers. From the tripoint between the Central African Republic, Chad, and Cameroon on the Mbéré River, this boundary follows the Mbéré eastward and continues along its tributary, the Lebe River.

From the source of the Lebe River, it crosses a short drainage divide to the Taibo River and follows this river eastward to its source. It then follows a short straight line to the source of the Bokola River, following this river to its confluence with the Nana Barya River and hence to its confluence with the Ouham River. From the Ouham, it crosses to the Chari River and follows the Chari and its tributaries to their headwaters at the tripoint between the Central African Republic, Chad, and Sudan. Most of the boundary between the Central African Republic and Sudan and the boundary between the Central African Republic and South Sudan follow the drainage divide between the Congo River to the west and the Nile River to the east.

The tripoint between the Central African Republic, South Sudan, and the Democratic Republic of the Congo is located on the Mbomou River. From this tripoint, the boundary follows the Mbomou River westward to its confluence with the Ubangi River, which is one of the major tributaries of the Congo. It then follows the Ubangi westward and then southward past the Central African Republic's capital city of Bangui. It continues southward and downstream along the Ubangi to its confluence with the Lobaye River. This confluence marks the tripoint between the Central African Republic, the Democratic Republic of the Congo, and the Republic of the Congo.

The boundary between the Central African Republic and the Republic of the Congo follows the Lobaye upstream and then turns southward to the Dzanga-Sangha National Park, where the tripoint between the Central African Republic, the Republic of the Congo, and Cameroon is located. From there, the boundary between the Central African Republic and Chad follows the Sangha River, another tributary

CENTRAL AFRICAN REPUBLIC

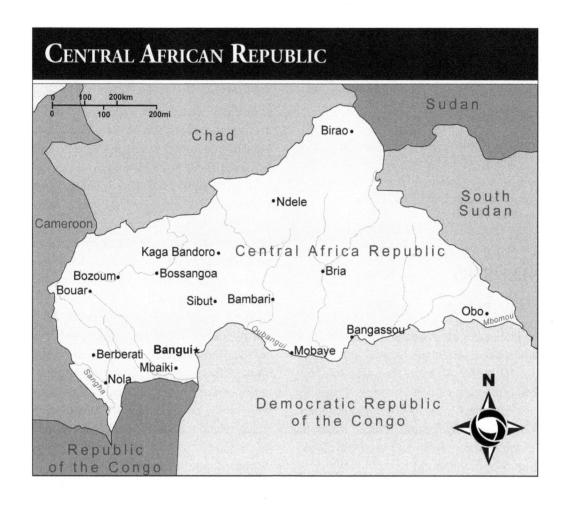

of the Congo, to the north along the edge of the park. It continues northward from the Sangha to the drainage basin of the Mbéré River, following tributaries of the Mbéré northward to the tripoint between the Central African Republic, Cameroon, and Chad.

HISTORICAL CONTEXT

What is now the Central African Republic was colonized by France beginning in the 1880s. The French established a settlement on the Ubangi River at Bangui, which is now the capital city of the Central African Republic. In 1894, France named the territory Ubangi-Chari after the rivers that

formed its southern and northern borders, respectively. Ubangi-Chari became part of the French colony of French Equatorial Africa along with Chad, Gabon, and Middle Congo (present-day Congo) in 1904. Ubangi-Chari was administered jointly with Chad until the two units were separated in 1920. The Central African Republic became an autonomous unit within the French Community in 1958 and achieved full independence in 1960.

For much of its history, the Central African Republic has been ruled by dictators. Perhaps the most notorious was Jean-Bédel Bokassa, who ruled the Central African Republic in the 1970s, renamed the country the "Central African Empire," and declared himself emperor for life before he was deposed in a coup d'état in 1979. Democratic elections were held in 1993, but freely elected governments have been deposed since then in additional coups d'état.

The Central African Republic's boundaries with its neighbors were established by agreements in the late 19th and early 20th centuries between France and other European colonial powers that controlled neighboring territories. The boundary between the present-day Central African Republic and present-day Sudan and South Sudan was agreed upon by France and Britain in 1924. France and Belgium agreed upon the Ubangi River as the boundary between French Equatorial Africa and what was then the Belgian Congo in 1885. The boundary between the Central African Republic and Cameroon, which was a German colony before World War I, was agreed upon by France and Germany in 1908. France delineated the boundaries between the Central African Republic and Chad and the Central African Republic and Congo after all three of these present-day countries had become part of French Equatorial Africa.

CONTEMPORARY ISSUES

The boundaries of the Central African Republic have remained uncontested since the country became independent. By the early 21st century, the Central African Republic had become more stable politically than its unstable neighbors. By 2009, an estimated 200,000 refugees from Sudan and from the Democratic Republic of the Congo had moved across the borders from these countries into the Central African Republic. Providing basic services

for these refugees has strained the already limited financial resources of the impoverished country.

See also   Cameroon, Chad, Democratic Republic of the Congo, Republic of the Congo, South Sudan, Sudan

Further Reading

Irin News. "DRC-Central African Republic: Refugees not ready to return." January 15, 2010, http://www.irinnews.org/Report/87743/DRC-CENTRAL-AFRICAN-REPUBLIC-Refugees-not-ready-to-return.

Brian Titley. *Dark age: The political odyssey of Emperor Bokassa.* Montreal, Quebec, Canada: McGill-Queens University Press, 1997.

CHAD

OVERVIEW

The Republic of Chad is located in north-central Africa. Chad's land area is 495,753 square miles, or almost twice the size of Texas. Its population is approximately 11 million.

Chad is landlocked, and its territory stretches from the Sahara Desert to the north through the semiarid Sahel region into the savannas of central Africa to the south. Chad's neighbors are Libya to the north, Sudan to the east, the Central African Republic to the south, and Cameroon, Nigeria, and Niger to the west. The boundary between Chad and Libya includes two diagonal segments. The longer segment extends from the point at which the Tropic of Cancer intersects the 16th meridian of east longitude southwestward to the tripoint between Chad, Libya, and Sudan at

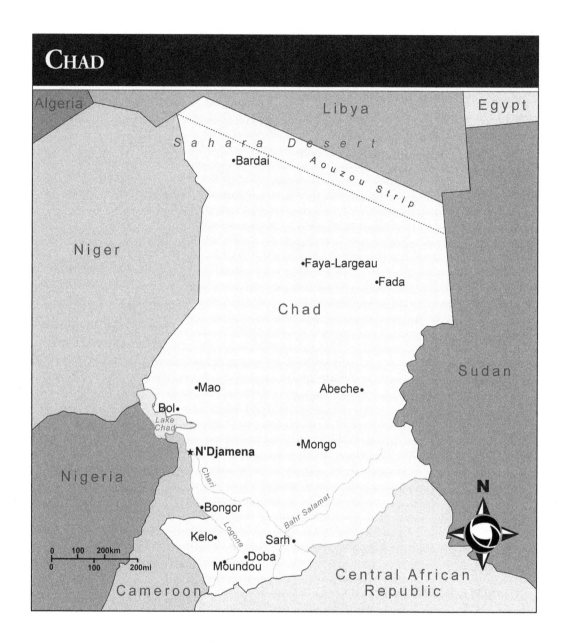

latitude 19° 30′ North, longitude 24° East. West of the 16th meridian, the rest of the boundary is a short diagonal segment extending southwestward to the tripoint between Chad, Libya, and Niger. Both of these segments cross uninhabited territory in the Sahara Desert.

From the tripoint between Chad, Sudan, and Libya, the boundary between Libya and Sudan follows the 24th meridian southward to the Wadi Howa, an intermittent stream that meets the 24th meridian at approximately latitude 15° 43′ North. From there it continues in a generally southwesterly direction to separate Sudan's territory of Darfur from Chad.

The tripoint between Chad, Sudan, and the Central African Republic is located on the Mare de Tizi River. From this tripoint, the boundary between Chad and the Central African Republic follows the Mare de Tizi southwestwards and downstream to its confluence with the Aoukalé River. It continues down the Aoukalé until this river flows into the Bahr Aouk River, which in turn flows into the Chari River. At the confluence of the Bahr Aouk and the Chari Rivers, the Chari flows northward into Chad, and the boundary between Chad and the Central African Republic continues in a southwesterly direction, following several small streams and straight-line segments, to the tripoint between Chad, the Central African Republic, and Cameroon.

From this tripoint, the boundary between Chad and Cameroon follows roads, short straight-line segments, and streams in a generally northwesterly direction until it reaches a point near the Chadian village of Lere. It then follows straight-line segments northeastward and then turns eastward until it reaches the Logone River. The boundary then follows the Logone River downstream and northwestward to the confluence between the Logone and the Chari near Chad's capital city of N'Djamena. From N'Djamena the boundary follows the Chari into Lake Chad, which contains the tripoint between Chad, Cameroon, and Nigeria. The boundary between Chad and Nigeria is located entirely within Lake Chad. From the tripoint between Chad, Nigeria, and Niger in Lake Chad, the boundary between Chad and Niger extends northward toward the tripoint between Chad, Niger, and Libya. Most of the boundary follows geometric segments. It cuts across uninhabited desert territory and is crossed by no paved highways or railroads.

HISTORICAL CONTEXT

Scientists believe that the climate of north-central Africa was much wetter several thousand years ago than is the case today, and therefore that Lake Chad covered much more area than it does now. Various kingdoms governed portions of the territory north and east of Lake Chad during the first millennium AD. During the eighth and ninth centuries AD, the Kanem peoples, who controlled trade routes from Lake Chad through the Sahara Desert, came to dominate what is now northern and central Chad.

The Kanem Empire, ruled by the Islamic Sayfawa dynasty, came to power in AD 1068. By the 13th century, the Kanem Empire controlled much of north-central Africa, including most of present-day Chad and its neighbors. After the Sayfawas lost considerable territory in the late 13th and 14th centuries, the Kanem Empire became reconstituted as the Bornu Empire in the 15th century. The Bornu Empire continued to dominate the region into the 19th century, but the Sayfawa dynasty died out in 1846. The empire itself came to an end in 1893.

In the late 19th century, the French began to penetrate into Chad. Chad became a French colony in 1900, and it was made part of French Equatorial Africa along with Cameroon, the Central African Republic, the Republic of the Congo, and Gabon. The French delineated boundaries among these components of French Equatorial Africa and between French Equatorial Africa and its other neighbors that were not under French administration. Chad became independent in 1960. Ethnic conflict and political instability have plagued Chad ever since, and Chad remains one of the poorest countries in the world. However, Chad has substantial mineral resources whose extraction could provide the country with a springboard for eventual development.

CONTEMPORARY ISSUES

Chad's boundaries, which were delineated by the European colonial powers during the late 19th and early 20th centuries, are generally uncontested. However, Chad and Libya have contested control of the Aouzou Strip. The Aouzou Strip is a sparsely inhabited territory about 500 miles long and 60 miles wide in the Sahara Desert south of the boundary between Libya and Chad. In 1935, France and Italy agreed that the Aouzou Strip should be ceded from French Equatorial Africa to Libya. The agreement was voided two years later after Italy allied itself with Nazi Germany. However, Libya as the successor state to Italy continued to claim the Aouzou Strip after both Chad and Libya became independent. Libya claimed also that the few inhabitants of the Aouzou Strip were linked culturally and historically to Libya rather than to Chad or French Equatorial Africa. Armed conflict over the Aouzou Strip broke out in 1978 and continued through the 1980s. The dispute was referred eventually to the International Court of Justice, which awarded sovereignty over the strip to Chad in 1994.

Hundreds of thousands of refugees fleeing conflict in neighboring countries have moved to Chad, including more than 200,000 who moved across the boundary from Sudan to Chad during the conflict with Darfur in the first decade of the 21st century. The large numbers of destitute refugees have strained Chad's already very limited economic resources, with accusations of abuse of refugees particularly in eastern Chad near the international boundary.

See also   Cameroon, Central African Republic, Libya, Niger, Nigeria, Sudan

Further Reading

Louise Arbour. "No exit?" *Foreign Policy*, September 4, 2009, http://www.foreignpolicy.com/articles/2009/09/04/no_exit.

Mario J. Azevedo. *Roots of violence: A history of war in Chad.* London: Routledge, 1998.

Frank Jacobs. "The world's largest sandbox." *New York Times*, November 7, 2011, http://opinionator.blogs.nytimes.com/2011/11/07/the-worlds-largest-sandbox/.

COMOROS

OVERVIEW

The Union of the Comoros is located in the western Indian Ocean off the east coast of Africa. The country includes three main islands in the Comoros archipelago, Njazidja (Grand Comoro), Mwali, and Nzwani, and several smaller islands. A fourth main island in the archipelago, Mayotte, is not part of the Union of the Comoros but instead remains under French administration. The overall land area of the country (excluding Mayotte) is 719 square miles, slightly more than half the size of Rhode Island. The country's population is about 800,000. The Comoros's nearest neighbors by water are Mozambique, about 175 miles to the west, and Madagascar, about 225 miles to the southeast.

COMOROS

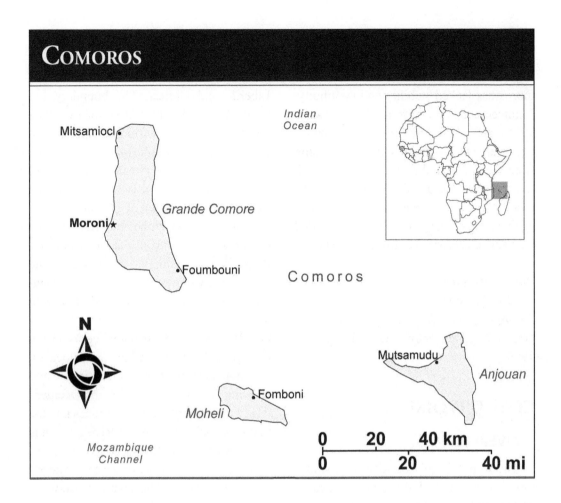

Mitsamiocl

Indian Ocean

Grande Comore

Moroni

Foumbouni

Comoros

N

Mutsamudu

Anjouan

Fomboni

Moheli

Mozambique Channel

0   20   40 km

0   20   40 mi

HISTORICAL CONTEXT

Mariners from mainland Africa and from present-day Indonesia are believed to have settled the Comoros archipelago beginning about 2,000 years ago. The islands became a trading hub for merchants from India, Persia, the Arab world, and mainland Africa. The Comoros was one of the first places outside the Arab world in which Islam took hold shortly after the death of the Prophet Mohammed in the seventh century. Portuguese and Dutch traders arrived in the late 15th and 16th centuries, but an Omani-based sultanate based on Zanzibar seized control of the Comoros in the late

18th century. The islands became a French protectorate in 1886 and became a formal French colony in 1912.

In 1973, the French government began to work with local officials to transition the Comoro Islands toward eventual independence. Referenda on the independence question were held on each of the four main islands in 1974. While majorities in Njazidja, Mwali, and Nzwani supported independence, a majority of Mayotte's voters cast ballots against independence. Mayotte was separated politically from the other islands and remained a French colony. The other three islands became the independent Union of the Comoros in 1975.

Since 1975, the government of the Comoros has lacked stability and continuity. Eighteen coups d'état took place between 1975 and 2000. In 1997, the smaller islands of Mwali and Nzwani attempted secession from the Union and requested that French rule be restored, but France declined the request. Nzwani declared independence again in 2007, but a Comoros force invaded Nzwani and secured control of the island.

Further Reading

M.D.D. Newitt. *The Comoro Islands: Struggle against dependency in the Indian Ocean.* Farnham, Surrey, UK: Gower, 1984.

COTE D'IVOIRE

OVERVIEW

The Republic of Cote d'Ivoire, sometimes referred to as Ivory Coast, is located on the southern coast of West Africa. Cote d'Ivoire has a land area of 124,502 square miles, slightly larger than New Mexico. Its population is about 22 million.

Cote d'Ivoire's neighbors are Liberia and Guinea to the west, Mali and Burkina Faso to the north, and Ghana to the east. To the south, Cote d'Ivoire has a coastline on the Gulf of Guinea in the Atlantic Ocean. Most of the boundary between Cote d'Ivoire and Liberia follows rivers. The Cavalla River forms the southern two-thirds of the boundary, extending upstream and northward and then northwestward inland from its mouth in the Atlantic Ocean. The northern third of the boundary follows the Cestos River, which empties into the

Atlantic in Liberia, upstream and northeastward from a point near the village of Touleplou to the tripoint between Cote d'Ivoire, Liberia, and Guinea. The boundary between Cote d'Ivoire and Guinea extends northward from this tripoint, following a combination of straight-line segments and short passages along streams northward to the trip between Cote d'Ivoire, Guinea, and Mali north of the town of Odienne.

From this tripoint, the boundary between Cote d'Ivoire and Mali extends eastward. It follows both straight-line segments and drainage divides until reaching the Danboro River, which it follows downstream to its confluence with the Leraba Occidentale River, where the tripoint between Cote d'Ivoire, Mali, and Burkina Faso is located. The boundary between Cote d'Ivoire and Burkina Faso follows the Leraba Occidentale eastward until this river empties into the main channel of the Leraba River, which is also known as the Coroe or Koroe River. To the east, the Leraba flows into northeastern Cote d'Ivoire. The boundary between Cote d'Ivoire and Burkina Faso continues eastward to the tripoint between Cote d'Ivoire, Burkina Faso, and Ghana on the Volta Noire, or Black Volta, River, which is one of the three major tributaries of the Volta River. The boundary between Cote d'Ivoire and Ghana follows the Volta Noire southward and downstream to the northern edge of Bui National Park on the Ghanaian side of the border. From there, it continues southward along straight-line segments and small streams to the Gulf of Guinea.

HISTORICAL CONTEXT

Various kingdoms ruled parts of present-day Cote d'Ivoire for centuries before Eu-

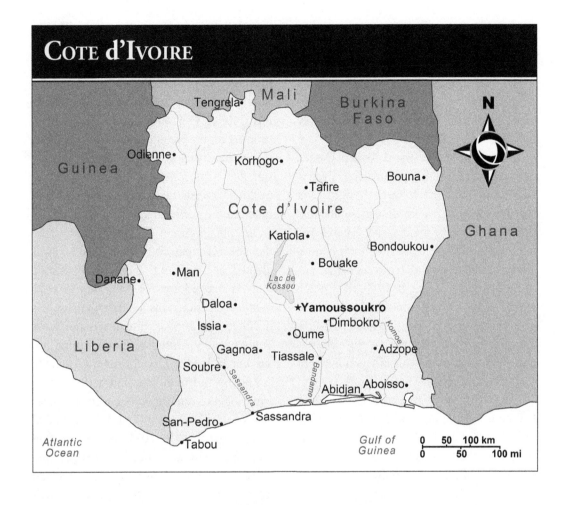

COTE D'IVOIRE

ropeans began to visit the coasts of the Gulf of Guinea during the 15th and 16th centuries. European traders established lucrative trade linkages with Europe. Spices, precious metals, and elephant ivory, from which the Ivory Coast got its name, were exported to European ports. Beginning in the 16th century, the Gulf of Guinea became a center for the trans-Atlantic slave trade. However, present-day Cote d'Ivoire, unlike other points along the Gulf of Guinea and Atlantic coasts to the east and west, lacked good harbors and therefore played only a minor role in the slave trade. Exports of ivory declined in the 18th century after widespread overhunting caused

a severe depletion in local elephant populations.

In the early 19th century, the Agni and Baoule kingdoms ruled what are now southern and central Cote d'Ivoire respectively. France signed treaties with the kings of both monarchies in 1843 and 1844. The treaties established them as French protectorates. Under the terms of the treaties, France was authorized to establish trading centers, and in exchange France agreed to make annual payments to the kingdoms in exchange for the use of their lands. In 1885, French sovereignty over the coastal regions of Cote d'Ivoire was recognized by the European powers by the Congress of

Berlin. However, the Congress of Berlin only recognized territorial claims associated with "effective control" of these territories. France moved to establish effective control of the interior, and Britain recognized French sovereignty over inland Cote d'Ivoire.

Cote d'Ivoire became a formal French colony in 1893. Shortly thereafter, France negotiated agreements with Britain over the boundary between Cote d'Ivoire and the Gold Coast, or present-day Ghana, and with independent Liberia over their boundaries. In 1904, Cote d'Ivoire became part of French West Africa. In 1958, the French authorized a referendum in Cote d'Ivoire on the question of independence. After a majority of voters supported the referendum, France granted full independence to Cote d'Ivoire in 1960.

Cote d'Ivoire's first president, Felix Houphouet-Boigny, continued in office until he died in 1993. After Houphouet-Boigny's death, tensions between ethnic groups simmered and political instability ensued. Religious tensions between the predominantly Muslim north and the predominantly Christian south also festered. Between the 1960s and the 1990s, Cote d'Ivoire became one of the most prosperous countries in West Africa. Cote d'Ivoire's prosperity attracted millions of migrants and refugees from other parts of West Africa. Estimates have suggested that by 2000, as many as a quarter of Cote d'Ivoire's people were immigrants from other countries.

In 2000, a majority of voters approved a constitutional change requiring both parents of Cote d'Ivoire's president to have been born within Cote d'Ivoire. The new procedure prevented candidates whose parents were foreign-born Cote d'Ivoire citizens from running for the presidency. One excluded candidate was Alassane Ouattara, who was highly popular among immigrants from nearby Mali and Burkina Faso. After Ouattara was excluded from running for the presidency of Cote d'Ivoire, troops deserting the Cote d'Ivoire's army initiated armed attacks on several cities in 2002. Rebels quickly seized control of much of the northern half of Cote d'Ivoire.

In 2000, Laurent Gbagbo, who is from the southern part of Cote d'Ivoire, was elected as president. Gbagbo suspended elections scheduled for 2005, but in 2010 another election was held. Ouattara was declared the winner, and his majority of votes was confirmed by international observers. However, Gbagbo claimed that the election was fraudulent, and he refused to leave office. Each side accused the other side of murdering political opponents and other atrocities. In 2011, armed conflict arose between supporters of Ouattara and those of Gbagbo. Gbagbo was arrested and taken to The Hague, where he was scheduled to be tried by the International Criminal Court for crimes against humanity. At least 100,000 refugees have left Cote d'Ivoire, with many moving across the borders into Liberia or Ghana, and many migrants from neighboring states have also left the country in light of political violence and a deteriorating economy.

CONTEMPORARY ISSUES

Cote d'Ivoire's boundaries are uncontested. However, the status of refugees moving in and out of Cote d'Ivoire from neighboring countries remains problematic. Large numbers of refugees from nearby countries have moved into Cote d'Ivoire, which for much of the postindependence period has been more stable and prosperous than its neighbors, in order to escape political persecution, poverty, and violence. Refugees have been victims of discrimination and prejudice on many occasions. More recently, however, Ivorians have left Cote d'Ivoire in order to get away from ongoing political tension associated with ethnic conflict. Cote d'Ivoire is the largest producer of cacao, which is used to make chocolate, in the world. However, plantation owners in Cote d'Ivoire have been accused of relying on child slaves to provide labor on these cacao plantations. Many of these slaves are believed to have been kidnapped or enticed with false promises into Cote d'Ivoire from other African countries.

See also Burkina Faso, Ghana, Guinea, Liberia, Mali

Further Reading

Liz Ford. "Burkina Faso and Mali brace for migrants escaping Ivorian conflict." *Guardian*, April 18, 2011, http://www.guardian.co.uk/global-development/2011/apr/18/burkina-faso-and-mali-brace-for-ivory-coast-refugees.

Lowell J. Satre. *Chocolate on trial: Slavery, politics & the ethics of business.* Athens: Ohio University Press, 2005.

DEMOCRATIC REPUBLIC OF THE CONGO

OVERVIEW

The Democratic Republic of the Congo is located in central Africa. The country is sometimes referred to as Congo-Kinshasa, after its capital city, to distinguish it from the Republic of the Congo, or Congo-Brazzaville. The Democratic Republic of the Congo is the largest country in Africa by land area and the 11th-largest country by land area in the world. With a land area of 905,355 square miles, the Democratic Republic of the Congo is more than three times the size of Texas. Its population is about 75 million. Most of the country is included within the drainage basin of the Congo River, from which the country was named.

The Democratic Republic of the Congo has boundaries with Angola to the southwest, Zambia to the south, Tanzania, Burundi, Rwanda, and Uganda to the east, South Sudan to the northeast, the Central African Republic to the north, and the Republic of the Congo and the Angolan exclave of Cabinda to the northwest. To the west, the Democratic Republic has a very short coastline on the Atlantic Ocean near the mouth of the Congo River. The Congo's territory near the Atlantic separates the main territory of Angola from its exclave of Cabinda. Most of these boundaries follow rivers or drainage divides.

The boundary between the Democratic Republic of the Congo and the main territory of Angola follows the Congo River briefly from its mouth upstream to a point near the Congolese city of Matadi. From Matadi, the boundary follows straight-line segments eastward to the Kwango River, which is called the Cuango River in Angola. It follows the Kwango southward and then follows straight-line segments eastward to the Kasai River. Both the Kwango and the Kasai are tributaries of the Congo. The boundary follows the Kwango southward before turning eastward once again.

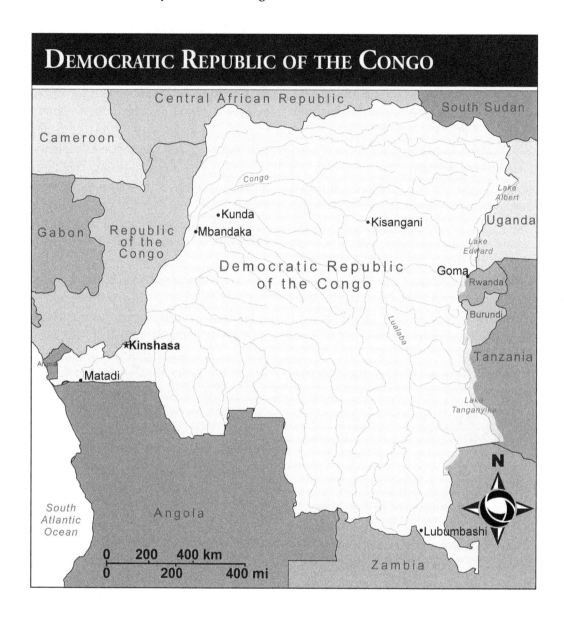

DEMOCRATIC REPUBLIC OF THE CONGO

It follows the drainage divide between the Congo River drainage basin in the Democratic Republic of the Congo and the Zambezi River drainage basin in Angola eastward to the tripoint between the Democratic Republic of the Congo, Angola, and Zambia.

From this tripoint, the boundary between the Democratic Republic of the Congo and Zambia extends in an easterly direction. It

continues to follow the drainage divide between the Congo and Zambezi basins. The extreme southeastern portion of the Democratic Republic of the Congo is a long, narrow strip of territory known as the Congo Pedicle, which extends well into Zambia's main territory and separates the northwestern and northeastern sections of that country. At the eastern end of the Congo Pedicle, the boundary turns northward at the eastern end of the Demarques de Leshwe nature reserve. The boundary continues northward to the Luapula River and then follows the Luapula downstream to Lake Mweru. From Lake Mweru, the boundary follows a straight line east-northeastward to Lake Tanganyika, in which the tripoint between the Democratic Republic of the Congo, Zambia, and Tanzania is located.

Lake Tanganyika forms the entire boundary between the Democratic Republic of the Congo and Tanzania. The boundary between the Democratic Republic of the Congo and Burundi continues along Lake Tanganyika to its northern end, where the Ruzizi River empties into the lake. This boundary continues northward along the Ruzizi upstream to its confluence with the Ruwa River, where the tripoint between the Democratic Republic of the Congo, Burundi, and Rwanda is located. The boundary between the Democratic Republic of the Congo and Rwanda continues northward along the Ruzizi to its source in Lake Kivu. North of this lake, the boundary continues in a northeasterly direction through mountainous terrain to Mount Sabyinyo, which is a peak nearly 12,000 feet in altitude in the Virunga Mountains.

From Mount Sabyinyo, the boundary between the Democratic Republic of the Congo and Uganda continues in a northerly direction to the Ishasha River. It continues northward along the Ishasha to its mouth in Lake Edward. From Lake Edward, it continues northward to Lake Albert. From there, it follows the drainage divide between the Congo in the Democratic Republic of the Congo and the Nile River in Uganda to the tripoint between the Democratic Republic of the Congo, Uganda, and South Sudan. This drainage divide turns west-northwestward and forms the entire boundary between the Democratic Republic of the Congo and South Sudan. The tripoint between the Democratic Republic of the Congo, South Sudan, and the Central African Republic is located on the Mbomou River along this drainage divide near the Bengangai Game Reserve in South Sudan.

From this tripoint, the boundary between the Democratic Republic of the Congo and the Central African Republic follows the Mbomou downstream and westward to its confluence with the Ubangi River. It follows the Ubangi westward and then southward to the tripoint between the Democratic Republic of the Congo, the Central African Republic, and the Republic of the Congo at the confluence between the Ubangi and the Lobaye River. The boundary between the Democratic Republic of the Congo and the Republic of the Congo follows the Ubangi southward and southwestward from this confluence to the confluence between the Ubangi and the Congo River itself. It then follows the Congo itself, passing between the Democratic Republic of the Congo's capital city of Kinshasa and the Republic of the Congo's capital city of Brazzaville. About 50 miles downstream from Kinshasa, the boundary leaves the river and turns northward. It then turns westward again to the Democratic Republic of the Congo's Mangroves National Park. The western boundary of the park forms most of the boundary between the Democratic Republic of the Congo and the Angolan exclave of Cabinda. A strip of Democratic Republic of the Congo coastline about 30 miles in length from the Congo River in the south to the boundary between the Democratic Republic of the Congo and

Angola in the north separates Cabinda from the rest of Angola.

HISTORICAL CONTEXT

Unlike most of the other other large rivers of the world, the Congo River is not navigable by oceangoing ships for much of its length because navigability is blocked by the Livingstone Falls downstream from Kinshasa. That oceangoing ships cannot access the inland sections of the Congo discouraged Europeans from exploring the Congo basin. European exploration was discouraged also by dense forests, tropical diseases, hostile indigenous peoples, and the lack of readily accessible natural resources. Thus the present-day Democratic Republic of the Congo was one of the last parts of Africa to be visited or settled by Europeans in the 19th century.

As the interior of Africa was divided among European colonial powers during the late 19th century, Congo became a Belgian colony in 1885. The present-day Democratic Republic of the Congo became the personal property of Belgium's King Leopold II, who named his colony the Congo Free State. Leopold established the capital city of Kinshasa, which he named Leopoldville after himself. He promoted the establishment of lucrative rubber plantations. Many indigenous Africans were forced to work on these plantations, and labor exploitation was widespread. Estimates suggest that as many as 10 million Congolese, or half of the indigenous Congolese population, died during the first two decades of Leopold's rule because of overwork, forced labor, displacement from their lands, and exposure to European diseases.

In 1908, the Belgian government transferred control of the Congo Free State from the monarchy to the elected government. The colony was renamed Belgian Congo. After World War I, authority over the former German colony of Ruanda-Urundi was transferred to Belgium by the League of Nations. Belgium governed Ruanda-Urundi separately from the Belgian Congo and established the boundary between these colonies. Ruanda-Urundi would later become the independent countries of Rwanda and Burundi.

The Belgian Congo became independent in 1960. After independence, the province of Katanga in southeastern Congo north of Zambia, northeast of Angola, and west of Lake Tanganyika attempted to secede from the newly independent Democratic Republic of the Congo. Katanga is rich in copper, uranium, and other mineral resources, and Belgian-based companies with financial interests in these resources supported the independence movement. Several thousand Belgian troops were sent to Katanga in support of the independence movement, which the Congolese government opposed in part because of Katanga's wealth relative to the rest of the country. The United Nations Security Council called on Belgium to withdraw its troops from Katanga and sent a peacekeeping force into the area although the UN refused to authorize these peacekeepers to make efforts to forcibly reunite Katanga with the rest of the country. Efforts to resolve the conflict were hampered after the UN's secretary-general, Dag Hammerskjold, was killed in an airplane crash while on his way to attempt to mediate the dispute. Eventually, the UN peacekeeping force was given the authority to disarm secessionist fighters. In 1962, the UN authorized an invasion of Katanga that ended the rebellion.

During these early years of Congolese independence, various political factions from throughout the Democratic Republic of the Congo competed for control of the government. In 1965, power was seized by Joseph Mobutu, a young Congolese military officer. Mobutu consolidated power throughout the country quickly and established an authoritarian regime. Mobutu changed the name of the country to Zaire in 1971 and renamed himself Mobutu Sese Seko in the following year. Mobutu's power was enhanced by his close relationship with Western countries, whose leaders saw Mobutu as an important ally against communism during the Cold War. However, Mobutu's government was regarded as highly corrupt, with Mobutu and his associates amassing vast personal fortunes while the standards of living across the country were very low. Western support for the increasingly brutal and corrupt Mobutu regime waned after the collapse of the Soviet Union. With the support of Rwanda and Uganda, Mobutu's regime was overthrown in 1997. Both Rwanda and Uganda accused the Mobutu government of harboring and abetting revolutionaries who were intent on overthrowing the governments of their respective countries. Mobutu fled the country and died in exile in Morocco a few months later.

After the overthrow of Mobutu, the new regime dropped the name Zaire, and the country's name reverted to its original name of the Democratic Republic of the Congo. Over the next six years, civil war broke out. Governments of neighboring countries intervened in support of both sides: the government and rebel factions.

A UN peacekeeping force was sent to the northeastern Democratic Republic of the Congo in 1999 in an effort to reduce the violence and restore order. As many as 5 million Congolese military personnel and civilians are believed to have lost their lives during the conflict. Many, including large numbers of young children, died because of famine and disease. A peace agreement was reached in 2003, and a transitional government was established, with the first democratic election in more than 30 years taking place in 2006. However, various rebel factions continue to operate in various parts of the country, particularly in the east and northeast near the boundaries of Burundi, Rwanda, Uganda, and South Sudan. International estimates have suggested that nearly 3 million additional Congolese have died during these continuing conflicts since 2004, and many others have left the country as refugees. Nevertheless, abundant natural resources in Katanga and other parts of the country are seen as an opportunity for the economic development of the impoverished state.

CONTEMPORARY ISSUES

The war-torn Democratic Republic of the Congo continues to be affected by conflict with neighboring countries as it struggles to develop as a functioning multiparty democracy. However, conflicts involving neighbors of the Democratic Republic of the Congo directly have abated. Relations between the Democratic Republic of the Congo and Rwanda have improved since the 1990s, when each country accused the other of helping rebel forces and contributing to genocide and human rights violations. In 2009, the two countries resumed diplomatic relations after 13 years, and Rwanda's president agreed not to allow Congolese rebels to use Rwandan territory as their base of operations.

The northeastern part of the Democratic Republic of the Congo has also been affected by the operations of the Lord's Resistance Army (LRA). The LRA is a terrorist organization that has operated primarily in neighboring Uganda but whose activities have spilled across the international boundary into the Democratic Republic of the Congo. The LRA has been accused of abducting or killing thousands of Congolese civilian, displacing thousands of other Congolese from their homes. LRA activity in the Democratic Republic of the Congo increased after the Ugandan government stepped up efforts to eliminate the organization.

See also   Angola, Burundi, Central African Republic, Republic of the Congo, Rwanda, South Sudan, Tanzania, Uganda, Zambia

Further Reading

Tim Allen and Koen Vlassenroot. *The Lord's Resistance Army: Myth and reality.* London: Zed Books, 2010.

BBC News. "New era for DR Congo and Rwanda." August 22, 2009, http://news.bbc.co.uk/2/hi/africa/8188715.stm.

Mvemba Phezo Dizolele. "A crisis in the Congo." *Foreign Policy*, December 14, 2011, http://www.foreignpolicy.com/articles/2011/12/13/a_crisis_in_the_congo.

John Prendergast. "A light at the end of the tunnel in Congo." *Foreign Policy*, February 26, 2010, http://www.foreignpolicy.com/articles/2010/02/26/a_light_at_the_end_of_the_tunnel_in_congo.

Xan Rice. "Lord's Resistance Army terrorizes Congo after Uganda crackdown." *Guardian*, September 14, 2009, http://www.guardian.co.uk/world/2009/sep/14/lords-resistance-army-terrorises-congo.

Jason K. Stearns. *Dancing in the glory of monsters: The collapse of Congo and the Great War of Africa.* Madison: University of Wisconsin Press, 2012.

DJIBOUTI

OVERVIEW

The Republic of Djibouti is located in the Horn of Africa. It has a land area of 8,958 square miles, about the size of New Jersey. Its population is approximately 920,000.

Djibouti is bordered by Eritrea to the north, Ethiopia to the west and south, and Somalia to the southeast. Eastern Djibouti has a coast on the Gulf of Aden and the Bab el Mandab, a strait that connects the Gulf of Aden with the Red Sea. The Bab el Mandab separates the coast of Djibouti from the coast of Yemen on the Arabian Peninsula, and it is about 25 miles wide at its narrowest point. Historically, present-day Djibouti has had many cultural and economic ties with Arabia as well as with other parts of East Africa.

Djibouti's boundary with Eritrea extends diagonally southwestward from the Ras Doumeira, a peninsula on the Bab el Mandab, to the Oued We'ima, an intermittent stream that continues in a generally southwesterly direction inland. The section of the boundary on and near the Ras Doumeira near the coast is contested between the two countries. The boundary follows

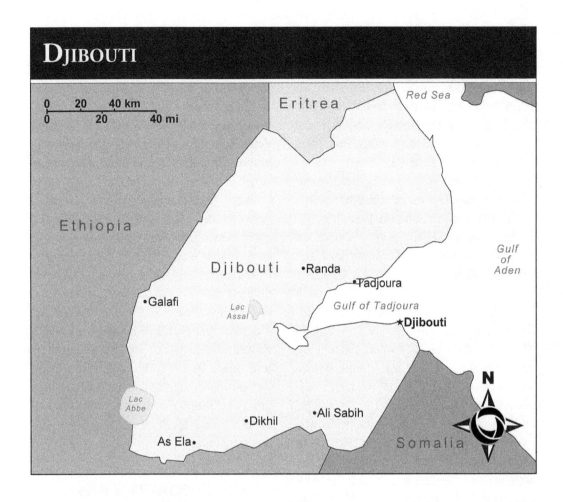

DJIBOUTI

the Oued We'ima, and then turns north-westward along straight-line segments be-fore turning southwestward once again to the tripoint between Djibouti, Eritrea, and Ethiopia. The inland section of the bound-ary between Djibouti and Eritrea is a rocky desert region with very few inhabitants.

The boundary between Djibouti and Ethiopia continues in a generally south-erly direction along straight-line segments through Lake Abhe, a natural salt lake that straddles the border between the two coun-tries. About 10 miles south of Lake Abhe, the boundary between Djibouti and Ethio-pia turns eastward, following straight-line segments to the tripoint between Djibouti,

Ethiopia, and Somalia. From that tripoint, the boundary between Djibouti and Soma-lia is a single geometric line running from southwest to northeast to the Gulf of Aden near the village of Loyada on the coast.

HISTORICAL CONTEXT

Given its strategic location on the Bab el Mandab, the Djibouti area has been a center for trade between Africa and the Arabian Peninsula for thousands of years. Trade from Djibouti is believed to have taken place as far eastward as India and perhaps East Asia via the Gulf of Aden and the In-dian Ocean. The major national groups in present-day Djibouti are the Afar, who live in northern Djibouti and neighboring Eritrea and eastern Ethiopia, and the Issa, who live in southern and southeastern Djibouti and across the boundary in Somalia. The Issa speak the Somali language and have close cultural and ethnic affinities with residents of Somalia.

France began to take an active interest in present-day Djibouti during the middle of the 19th century, and the French established control over the port of Obock on the northeastern coast of Djibouti in 1862. French interest intensified after the Suez Canal was opened in 1869. The French were intent to prevent Britain, which controlled the Arabian coast of the Bab el Mandab and the Gulf of Aden, from being able to close access to the Mediterranean via the canal. During the 1880s, the French government signed treaties with local Afar and Issa rulers to extend French protection over the region. France made the city of Djibouti its administrative center for the area, giving it the name of French Somaliland in 1894. Before and during World War II, French forces based in Djibouti experienced several armed skirmishes with Italian forces that controlled present-day Eritrea, Ethiopia, and Somalia.

In 1958, a referendum on independence was held in French Somaliland. Voters were given the choice of joining the newly independent Somali Republic or remaining in association with France. A majority of voters supported continuing association with France. The electorate was divided sharply. Union with Somalia was supported by a majority of Issas, whereas the majority of Afars voted to remain associated with France. A second referendum was held in 1967, and again the majority of voters cast ballots against independence. After this referendum, France renamed the colony the French Territory of the Afars and Issas. Another referendum on independence for the French Territory took place in 1977, and this time independence was supported by a large majority of voters. Djibouti became fully independent in 1977.

After independence, ethnic conflicts between the Afar and Issa populations continued. The first postindependence government was dominated by Issas, and in the 1980s a guerilla movement known as the Front for the Restoration of Unity and Democracy (FRUD) became active. Civil war between FRUD, most of whose supporters were Afars, and the government took place in 1991. The two sides negotiated a peace agreement in 2000, ending nearly a decade of civil war. However, tensions between the Afar and Issa communities remain.

CONTEMPORARY ISSUES

Djibouti and Eritrea contest the portion of their boundary near the Bab el Mandab. The conflict has centered on control of the Ras Doumeira peninsula. Conflict arose as a result of varying interpretations of boundary agreements that had been negotiated between France and Italy when Djibouti and Eritrea were French and Italian colonies, respectively. In 1897, France and Italy agreed that the boundary between Djibouti and Eritrea in the Ras Doumeira should follow a drainage divide. This agreement stipulated also that several islands located off the coast would belong to neither France nor Italy. In 1935, however, France and Italy agreed to move the boundary southeastward and to assign the offshore islands to Italy. After both Djibouti and Eritrea became independent, the two countries disputed the boundary. Djibouti claimed that the 1935 agreement was null and void and that the boundary should follow the earlier 1897 agreement. In the first decade of the 21st century, both countries stationed troops along the disputed frontier, and a brief shooting war broke out in 2008. In 2010, however, the two countries agreed to allow Qatar to mediate the dispute.

See also Eritrea, Ethiopia, Somalia

Further Reading

BBC News. "Eritrea denies Djibouti war claim." May 8, 2008, http://news.bbc.co.uk/2/hi/africa/7390945.stm.

Samson Bezabah. "Citizenship and the logic of sovereignty in Djibouti." *African Affairs*, 110 (2011), pp. 587–606.

Hassan Darar Houffaneh. "The role of Djibouti to foster security in the Horn of Africa." *Somaliland Sun*, June 17, 2012, http://somalilandsun.com/index.php?option=com_content&view=article&id=926:the-role-of-djibouti-to-foster-security-in-the-horn-of-africa&catid=25:international.

EQUATORIAL GUINEA

OVERVIEW

The Republic of Equatorial Guinea is one of the smallest countries in Africa. The country consists of two parts: a rectangular territory on the African mainland known as Rio Muni and several offshore islands in the Gulf of Guinea, which is part of the Atlantic Ocean. Despite the country's name,

nearly all of Equatorial Guinea is located north of the equator; only the southernmost island of Annobon is south of the equator. The country's capital of Malabo is located on the offshore island of Bioko, which was previously known as Fernando Po. Equatorial Guinea has a land area of about 11,000 square miles, making it about the size of Maryland. Its population is approximately 650,000. The population is divided approximately equally between Rio Muni and the offshore islands.

Rio Muni's neighbors are Cameroon to the north and Gabon to the east and south, along with seacoast along the Atlantic Ocean to the west. The border with Cameroon runs along the 2° 10′ parallel of latitude for most of its length. To the west, this boundary trends northwestward along the Ntem River to the Atlantic. At the eastern end of the boundary between Equatorial Guinea and Cameroon, the town of Ebebiyin is located adjacent to the tripoint between Equatorial Guinea, Cameroon, and Gabon. From this point, the boundary with Gabon follows the 11° 20′ meridian of east longitude southward to the first parallel of north latitude. It then follows the first parallel westward to the Utamboni River, which is also known as the Mitimele River. It follows this river westward until it empties into the Gulf of Guinea.

HISTORICAL CONTEXT

In 1471, the Portuguese explorer Fernando do Po became the first European to visit Bioko Island, which was then named for him. Portuguese settlers began arriving in Fernando Po and Annobon three years later. Portugal claimed the islands along with Rio Muni until 1778, when sovereignty

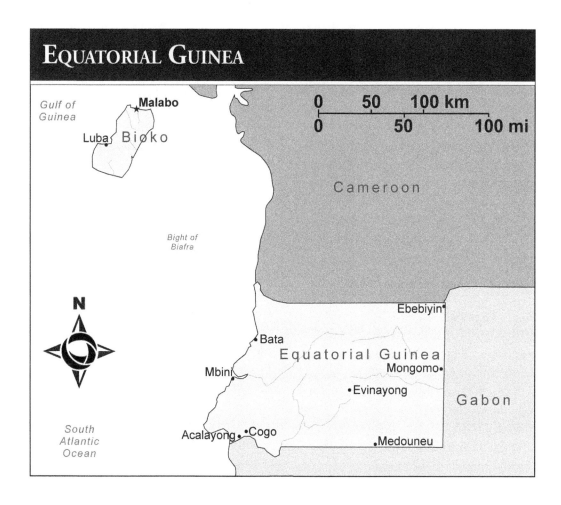

EQUATORIAL GUINEA

over the area was transferred to Spain in exchange for territorial rights in South America via the Treaty of El Pardo. During the 19th century, Britain established a base on Bioko and claimed rights to part of Rio Muni. In 1900, the Treaty of Paris resolved these conflict claims, and sovereignty over both the islands and Rio Muni was granted to Spain. Spain granted independence to Equatorial Guinea in 1968. The country has been ruled by dictators ever since, and the United Nations has identified Equatorial Guinea as a country with one of the worst human rights records in the world.

CONTEMPORARY ISSUES

Equatorial Guinea and Gabon have disputed control of Mbanie, Cocotiers, and Congas islands. These islands are located in Corsico Bay in the Gulf of Guinea. These islands are very small and have few permanent residents. However, they are located near valuable offshore deposits. Because sovereignty over the islands would affect the eventual delineation of maritime boundaries between the two countries, both countries have continued to press their claims. Regardless of how this dispute is resolved, Equatorial Guinea has promising oil supplies that when exploited could increase its development potential considerably.

See also Cameroon, Gabon

Further Reading

Foreign Affairs. "Equatorial Guinea: The future vision." May/June 2011.

Menas Borders. "UN to mediate on Corsico Bay dispute." February 22, 2011, http://menasborders.blogspot.com/2011/02/un-to-mediate-on-corisco-bay-dispute.html.

Nicholas Shaxson. *Poisoned wells: The dirty politics of African oil.* London: Palgrave Macmillan, 2008.

ERITREA

OVERVIEW

The State of Eritrea is located in northeastern Africa. Its land area is 45,406 square miles, about the size of Pennsylvania. Eritrea's population is about 6.1 million.

Eritrea shares boundaries with Sudan to the west, Ethiopia to the south, and Djibouti to the southeast. To the east and northeast, Eritrea has a long coastline on the Red Sea. The southern tip of coastal Eritrea is located along the Bab el Mandab, which is a strait connecting the Red Sea with the Gulf of Aden and hence with the Indian Ocean. The port of Assab in southeastern Eritrea is about 40 miles from Yemen on the Arabian Peninsula across the Bab el Mandab. Eritrea also includes numerous islands in the Red Sea. These include the Dahlak Islands, an archipelago of about 125 islands of which the four largest are inhabited permanently. Eritrea is also sovereign over some of the Hanish Islands, an archipelago located midway between the mainland coasts of Eritrea and Yemen. These islands were contested between Eritrea and Yemen for many years.

Most of Eritrea's land area is contained within an area roughly triangular in shape, with a long, narrow strip of territory extending southeastward along the Red Sea. This coastal strip is about 300 miles long and averages about 50 miles in width. The boundary between Eritrea and Sudan extends from the Red Sea along straight-line segments that extend in a generally southwesterly direction. Southwest of the Yob Wildlife Reserve on the Eritrean side of the border, the boundary turns more directly southward following straight-line segments to a point southwest of the village of Meneb. The boundary then follows a single straight-line segment that extends in a south-southeasterly direction to the tripoint between Eritrea, Sudan, and Ethiopia near the Ethiopian village of Himora on the Tekezé River, which is also known as the Takkaze River.

From Himora, the boundary between Eritrea and Ethiopia extends eastward following the course of the Tekezé upstream to its confluence with the Tomsa River. From that tripoint, the boundary turns northeastward, following a diagonal line to the Mareb River, which is also called the Gash River. The Mareb is an intermittent stream whose course runs westward but that dries up during periods of drought. The boundary follows the line of the Mareb to a point south of Eritrea's capital city of Asmara. From that point the boundary trends southeastward. Here it follows straight-line segments extending in a southeasterly direction parallel to the Red Sea coast until it reaches the tripoint

ERITREA

Sudan

Saudi Arabia

Red
Sea

Eritrea

Keren•
Ak'ordat•   Massawa•

Asmara★

Adi Kwala   •Senafe

N

Ethiopia

Yemen

0   50   100 km
0   50   100 mi

Djibouti

between Eritrea, Ethiopia, and Djibouti. Eritrea's boundary with Djibouti extends in a northeasterly direction between this tripoint and the Red Sea. It follows straight-line segments to the Oued We'ima, which is another intermittent stream that flows in a generally westerly direction. It follows the Oued We'ima upstream and then follows a diagonal line running northeastward to a point near the Red Sea coast. The Ras Doumeira, a peninsula on the coast in the border area, has been disputed between Eritrea and Djibouti since the two countries became independent.

HISTORICAL CONTEXT

Present-day Eritrea and the nearby coast of the Red Sea were known to the ancient Egyptians as the Land of Punt as much as 4,500 years ago. During the first millennium AD, Eritrea and northern Ethiopia were part of the Kingdom of Aksum. Aksum was involved strongly in land and oceanic trade with the Roman Empire and with Persia and India. The Aksum rulers were converted to Christianity in the fourth century AD. However, Aksum fell into decline after the seventh century AD.

Muslim rulers from present-day Sudan and the Arabian Peninsula became dominant in Eritrea until the Ottoman Empire took control of the coastal portions of the area in the 16th century.

In 1869, Italy purchased the port of Assab. Over the next two decades, Italy extended its control inland to encompass much of the present-day area of Eritrea. Eritrea became an Italian protectorate in 1882. During the late 19th century, boundaries between Italian Eritrea and its neighbors were agreed upon. After Italy invaded and took over Ethiopia in the mid-1930s, the Italian government merged Eritrea, Ethiopia, and Italian Somalia into Italian East Africa as part of the Italian Empire in 1936.

During World War II, British troops defeated the Italian army during the Battle of Keren. Eritrea was then placed under British administration. After World War II, Eritrea was contested between Ethiopia and Sudan. The British proposed to divide Eritrea on religious lines, with predominantly Muslim areas going to Sudan and predominantly Christian areas going to Ethiopia. However, the Ethiopian emperor Haile Selassie I claimed most of Eritrea, and the former Italian colony was transferred to Ethiopia by the United Nations in 1952. Eritrea was to have autonomy except in matters of defense and foreign policy. However, Haile Selassie's Ethiopian government rejected efforts to promote autonomy in Eritrea. The federation agreement was abrogated in 1962, and Eritrea became absorbed into Ethiopia.

After the absorption of Eritrea into Ethiopia, the Eritrean Liberation Front became active in promoting Eritrean independence. The Eritrean Liberation Front merged into a more militant secessionist organization,

the Eritrean People's Liberation Front (EPLF). Civil war broke out between the EPLF and the Ethiopian army. The Soviet Union supported Ethiopia, where Haile Selassie's regime had been toppled and replaced by a Marxist government in the early 1970s. With Soviet support, Ethiopia repulsed the rebel forces. As the Soviet Union began to disintegrate in the late 1980s, however, the Soviets withdrew their support of the Ethiopian regime. By 1991, the EPLF had seized control of most of the territory that is now part of Eritrea, and Eritrea declared its independence on April 27, 1991. The United Nations sponsored a referendum in Eritrea in 1993. A large majority of Eritrean voters supported independence, and the new Eritrean government was recognized by the international community.

CONTEMPORARY ISSUES

Since independence, Eritrea has been involved in border conflicts with neighboring Ethiopia and Djibouti. After Eritrea became independent in 1991, Eritrean and Ethiopian officials worked to delineate their boundary. Negotiations were unsuccessful, with both countries claiming sovereignty over communities in the border region. War between the two countries broke out in 1998 and lasted for the next two years. Between 70,000 and 100,000 Eritrean and Ethiopian soldiers were killed during the war. A cease-fire agreement was negotiated in 2000, and the two countries agreed to establish a demilitarized zone 15 miles wide, and a UN peacekeeping force was brought in to maintain order. The agreement stipulated that a boundary commission would be established and charged with delineating the boundary precisely. The commission issued its report in 2002, with disputed territory divided between the two countries. However, neither country was fully satisfied with the commission's decisions. The UN peacekeeping mission was terminated in 2008, after which both countries once again stationed troops near their boundary.

Eritrea and Djibouti have contested control of the Ras Doumeira, a peninsula along the Bab el Mandab along the border between the two countries. Dispute over control of the Ras Doumeira stemmed from the history of boundaries as drawn by the colonial powers of Italy and France. Italy and France agreed initially that the Ras Doumeira should be split between Eritrea and Djibouti following drainage divides. Several small islands in the Red Sea off the coast were assigned to neither colonial power. In 1935, Italy and France agreed to shift the boundary southeastward, with the Ras Doumeira and the offshore islands going to Italy. While Djibouti regards the 1935 agreement as null and void, Eritrea uses it to justify its claim to the Ras Doumeira. Both countries have stationed troops in the border region. In 2010, however, the two countries agreed to allow Qatar to mediate their ongoing dispute.

The Hamish Islands in the Red Sea have also been disputed between Eritrea and Yemen. These islands are located about halfway between the Eritrean and Yemeni coasts. In 1998, the two countries agreed to resolve their dispute. Sovereignty over the larger islands was granted to Yemen, but Eritrean retained control of some smaller islands closer to the Eritrean coast.

See also   Djibouti, Ethiopia, Sudan

Further Reading

BBC News. "New Ethiopia-Eritrea border revealed." April 13, 2002, http://news.bbc.co.uk/2/hi/africa/1927986.stm.

Daniel J. Dzurek. "Eritrea-Yemen dispute over the Hanish Islands." Durham University, International Boundaries Research Unit, 1996, http://www.dur.ac.uk/resources/ibru/publications/full/bsb4-1_dzurek.pdf.

Tricia Redeker Hepner. *Soldiers, martyrs, traitors, and exiles: Political conflict in Eritrea and the diaspora.* Philadelphia: University of Pennsylvania Press, 2011.

ETHIOPIA

OVERVIEW

The Federal Democratic Republic of Ethiopia is located in northeastern Africa at the edge of the Horn of Africa. Ethiopia has a land area of 426,371 square miles, nearly twice the size of Texas. With a population of 84 million, it is the second-largest country by population in Africa behind Nigeria. Ethiopia's capital city of Addis Ababa is the headquarters of the African Union.

Ethiopia was once united with Eritrea, which has a coast on the Red Sea. Since Ethiopia and Eritrea became separate countries, Ethiopia has been landlocked. Ethiopia's neighbors are Eritrea to the north, Djibouti to the northeast, Somalia to the east, Kenya to the south, and South Sudan and Sudan to the west. The tripoint between Ethiopia, Eritrea, and Sudan is located west of the village of Himora on the Tekezé River, a tributary of the Nile River. The boundary between Ethiopia and Eritrea follows the Tekezé upstream and eastward to its confluence with its tributary, the Tomsa

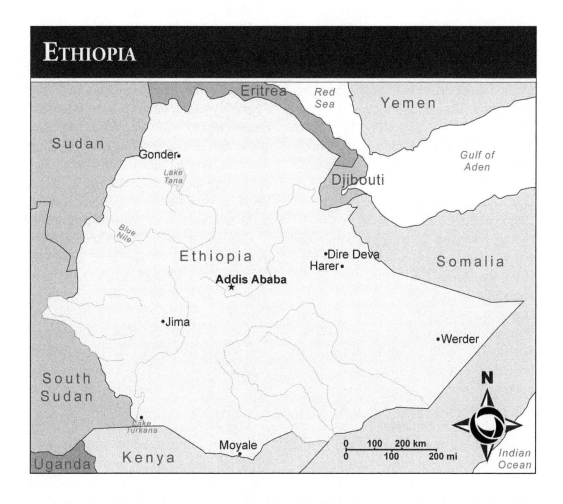

ETHIOPIA

River. At this juncture, the boundary turns northeastward along a diagonal line to the Mareb River, which unlike the Tekezé is an intermittent stream that will dry up under drought conditions. The boundary continues in an eastward direction, following generally the line of the Mareb. It then turns southeastward, following straight-line segments and paralleling the Red Sea coast to the tripoint between Ethiopia, Ethiopia, and Djibouti. This section of the boundary crosses dry, rocky desert territory with a very sparse population.

From this tripoint, the boundary between Ethiopia and Djibouti follows straight-line segments to Lake Abhe. It continues southward from Lake Abhe and then turns eastward to the tripoint between Ethiopia, Djibouti, and Somalia. The boundary between Ethiopia and Somalia extends southwestward along straight-line segments from that tripoint and then turns southeastward. South of the Somali town of Hargeisa, the boundary follows a long segment extending east-southeastward and then a shorter segment directly eastward to a point about 40 miles south of the town of Garoowe in Somalia. From here the boundary turns southwestward, following a single diagonal line about 250 miles in length to a point near the Somali village of Beledweyne. It then turns in a more westerly direction to the village of Dolo on the Dawa River. The boundary turns southwestward, following the Dawa upstream to the tripoint between Ethiopia, Somalia, and Kenya. This eastern section of Ethiopia, east of a line connecting the tripoint between Ethiopia, Somalia, and Djibouti with the tripoint between Ethiopia, Somalia, and Kenya, is known as Ogaden. The Ogaden region has been disputed between Ethiopia and Somalia for many years.

The boundary between Ethiopia and Kenya continues westward and upstream along the Dawa. Leaving the Dawa, the boundary follows numerous straight-line segments westward to Lake Turkana, in which the tripoint between Ethiopia, Kenya, and South Sudan is located. The boundary between Ethiopia and South Sudan follows short straight-line segments northwestward to a point west of Gambela National Park in Ethiopia. The boundary turns northeastward, passing north of this park, the turns northward to the tripoint between Ethiopia, South Sudan, and Sudan. From there the boundary between Ethiopia and Sudan follows many short segments that extend northeastward to the tripoint between Ethiopia, Sudan, and Eritrea on the Tekezé River.

HISTORICAL CONTEXT

Most anthropologists and paleontologists believe that present-day Ethiopia and Kenya were the places in which *Homo sapiens* originated several hundred thousand years ago. Present-day Ethiopia was known to the ancient Egyptians 5,000 years ago. About 2,000 years ago, the Axumite Kingdom took control of the Ethiopian highlands, retaining control of the area for the next 600 years. Christianity was introduced into the Axumite Kingdom in the fourth century AD. The Axumites were succeeded by other kingdoms until the Zagwe dynasty established the Ethiopian Empire in 1137. The Solomonic dynasty, whose rulers claimed descent from King Solomon and the Queen of Sheba, succeeded the Zagwe dynasty in 1270. At its height, the empire controlled the Ethiopian highlands, Eritrea, and neighboring areas.

Ethiopia retained its independence throughout most of the 19th and early 20th centuries. In 1889, Ethiopia and Italy signed a treaty in which Italy recognized Ethiopia's sovereignty over its present-day territory in return for Italian sovereignty over present-day Eritrea. Italy attempted to expand its influence from Eritrea into Ethiopia, but Italian forces were defeated by Ethiopian forces in the First Italo-Abyssinian War in 1896. A second war broke out in 1935, when Italian troops invaded Ethiopia. Although both countries were members of the League of Nations, the league made no effort to stop the invasion despite Haile Selassie's appeal to the League. Italy obtained military control of Ethiopia in 1936, and its sovereignty over Ethiopia was recognized by France and Britain in 1938. Italy then merged Ethiopia, Eritrea, and Italian Somaliland (much of today's Somalia) into a single colony known as Italian East Africa. Allied forces ousted the Italians in 1941, and Britain and Ethiopia signed an agreement reaffirming Ethiopia's independence in 1944. Haile Selassie's government resumed power, and it remained in power until it was toppled by a Marxist military junta, backed by the Soviet Union, which overthrew the regime, deposed Haile Selassie, and seized power in a coup d'état in 1974. The regime relaxed its grip on the country in the 1990s, and multiparty elections were held for the first time in 1998 and again in 2005. However, international observers claimed that fraud affected the election results.

During the second half of the 20th century, Ethiopia experienced ongoing conflicts with neighboring Eritrea and Somalia. Religion was an important factor in both cases in that a majority of Ethiopians are Christians and most Somalis and Eritreans are Muslims. In the 1980s, Eritrean secessionists rebelled against Ethiopia's Marxist government. An Eritrean force under the leadership of the Eritrean People's Liberation Front (EPLF) assumed de facto control of Eritrea. A referendum on independence was held in Eritrea in 1993, and Eritrea became independent after most Eritreans supported independence.

After Eritrea became independent, however, the two countries disagreed on the location of their boundary. War between Ethiopia and Eritrea began in 1998, and over the next two years more than 70,000 Ethiopian and Eritrean soldiers were killed. In 2000, a cease-fire agreement was negotiated, and a UN peacekeeping force was dispatched to the border region. A boundary commission was created and charged with determining the exact location of the border between the two countries. In 2002, the commission reported its findings and divided the disputed territory between Ethiopia and Eritrea. Despite this effort to settle the dispute, both sides continue to claim additional territory. Both stationed troops along the boundary after the UN peacekeeping force was withdrawn in 2008.

Territorial disputes also broke out in Ogaden, many of whose residents are ethnic Somalis. After the overthrow of the Haile Selassie regime, a separatist organization known as the Western Somali Liberation Front became active in promoting independence for Ogaden. The separatists were supported by the government of Somalia, and war broke out in 1977. Somalia captured much of Ogaden briefly, but Ethiopian troops backed by the Soviet Union and some of its allies recaptured Ogaden in 1978.

CONTEMPORARY ISSUES

Ethiopia's relationships with its neighbors remain unsettled. Neither Ethiopia nor Eritrea has been satisfied with the results of the United Nations–sponsored efforts to resolve their boundary dispute. Both countries continue to station troops along their boundary, and each has accused the other of harboring and abetting rebel groups intent on overthrowing the governments of the two countries. Ethiopian forces attacked Eritrean military installations on the border in early 2010, renewing concerns that war will break out once again.

Tensions also continue in and near Ogaden. In 2006, Ethiopian forces moved into Baidoa, the third-largest city in Somalia located in the southern part of the country near the Ethiopian boundary. Somalia lacks a functioning central government and was unable to resist the Ethiopian invasion. However, the Somali militant group al-Shabaab, which many international observers link with Al Qaeda and which maintains de facto military control of southern Somalia, regained control of the city in 2009. Baidoa and neighboring areas have been contested by Ethiopia and al-Shabaab ever since.

See also   Djibouti, Eritrea, Kenya, Somalia, South Sudan, Sudan

Further Reading

BBC News. "New Ethiopia-Eritrea border revealed." April 13, 2002, http://news.bbc.co.uk/2/hi/africa/1927986.stm.

William Davison. "Ethiopian Army at tacks Eritrean military post in retaliation for rebel violence." *Christian Science Monitor*, March 15, 2012, http://www.csmonitor.com/World/Africa/2012/0315/Ethiopian-Army-attacks-Eritrean-military-post-in-retaliation-for-rebel-violence.

Damien McClory and Rosa Prince. "Ethiopian troops seize important town from Al Shabaab." *Telegraph*, February 22, 2012, http://www.telegraph.co.uk/news/worldnews/africaandindianocean/somalia/9098735/Ethiopian-troops-seize-important-town-from-al-Shabaab.html.

Nathaniel Myers. "Ethiopia's democratic sham." *Foreign Policy*, May 21, 2010, http://www.foreignpolicy.com/articles/2010/05/21/ethiopias_democratic_sham.

Gebru Tereke. *The Ethiopian revolution: War in the Horn of Africa*. New Haven, CT: Yale University Press, 2009.

GABON

OVERVIEW

The Gabonese Republic is located along the Atlantic coast of west-central Africa, where it straddles the equator. Gabon has a land area of 103,347 square miles, the size of Colorado. With a population of about 1.5 million, Gabon is one of the most sparsely populated countries in Africa. Gabon has an abundance of mineral resources, including substantial oil reserves, and its per capita income is among the highest on the African continent.

Gabon's neighbors are Equatorial Guinea and Cameroon to the north and the Republic of the Congo to the east and south. To the west, Gabon has a coastline on the Atlantic Ocean. The boundary between Gabon and Equatorial Guinea follows the Utamboni River eastward and inland from its mouth on the Atlantic. West of Gabon's Crystal Mountain National Park, the boundary follows the first parallel of north latitude eastward to its intersection with the 11° 20′ meridian of east longitude. The boundary then turns northward, following this meridian to the tripoint between Gabon, Equatorial Guinea, and Cameroon.

Most of the boundary between Gabon and Cameroon follows rivers. From the tripoint between Gabon, Equatorial Guinea, and Cameroon, it follows the Ntem River and its tributary, the Kom River, upstream and eastward. The boundary then follows the 2° 15′ parallel of north latitude briefly to the Aïna River. The Aïna forms the boundary as it flows eastward toward the tripoint between Gabon, Cameroon, and the Republic of the Congo.

Near this tripoint, the Aïna turns southward, where it forms the boundary between Gabon and the Republic of the Congo to its confluence with the Djoua River. The confluence between the Aïna and the Djoua forms the Ivindo River. The Ivindo is a principal tributary of the Ogowe River, whose basin drains much of Gabon as it flows westward into the Atlantic Ocean. The boundary between Gabon and the Republic of the Congo follows the Djoua eastward and upstream. It then turns to the south, following short segments to a point south of Gabon's Bateke Plateau National Park. All of this boundary region is heavily

GABON

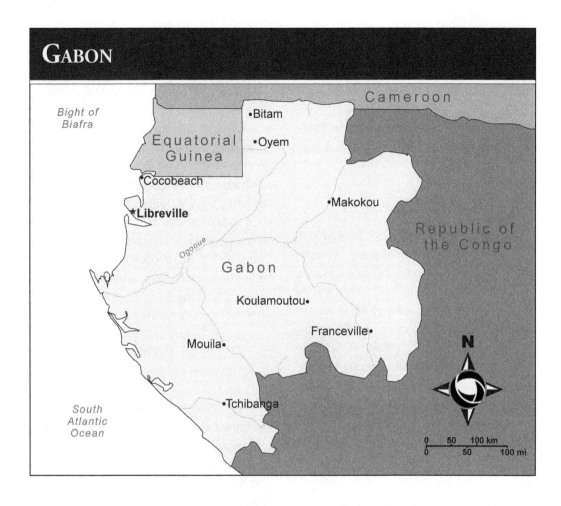

forested and sparsely populated, with very few all-weather roads. The boundary turns westward at the park and extends westward to a point near the village of Mongoungou. Here the boundary turns southward again, following short straight-line segments and various streams, until it reaches the Atlantic northwest of the Conkouati Reserve on the Congo side of the border.

HISTORICAL CONTEXT

The earliest inhabitants of present-day Gabon were Twa, or Pygmy, peoples who lived in the rainforests of the region. During the 14th and 15th centuries, Bantu peoples moved into the area. Portuguese mariners are believed to have been the first Europeans to visit the coast of Gabon. During the 16th and 17th centuries, Gabon became an important base for the trans-Atlantic slave trade.

France established control of the Gabonese coast during the 1830s and 1840s. Freed slaves founded the settlement of Libreville in 1849. Today, Libreville is the capital city of Gabon, and about half of Gabon's people live in the city and its surrounding metropolitan area. Gabon became a formal French colony in 1903. In 1910, Gabon became part of French Equatorial Africa along with the present-day Republic of the Congo, Chad, and the Central

African Republic. Gabon became independent in 1960. In 1967, power was seized by Omar Bongo, who remained in office until he died in 2009. Bongo was the ruler of a one-party state until multiparty elections were held for the first time in 1991. He was elected in 1991 and reelected in 1998 and 2005.

CONTEMPORARY ISSUES

Gabon and Equatorial Guinea have disputed sovereignty over Mbanie, Cocotiers, and Congas islands in Corsico Bay in the Gulf of Guinea. These islands are very small, with the land area of Mbanie less than one-tenth of a square mile. However, the islands are located above potentially very lucrative oil deposits, and both countries have continued to press their claims over them. In 2011, Gabon and Equatorial Guinea agreed that the dispute should be mediated by the United Nations.

See also   Cameroon, Equatorial Guinea, Republic of the Congo

Further Reading

John Ghazvinian. *Untapped: The struggle for Africa's oil*. Orlando, FL: Harcourt, 2006.

Menas Borders. "UN to mediate on Corsico Bay dispute." February 22, 2011, http://menasborders.blogspot.com/2011/02/un-to-mediate-on-corisco-bay-dispute.html.

GHANA

OVERVIEW

Ghana is located in West Africa on the coast of the Gulf of Guinea. It has a land area of 92,098 square miles, slightly smaller than Michigan. Its population is about 25 million.

Ghana's neighbors are Cote d'Ivoire to the west, Burkina Faso to the west and north, and Togo to the east. The Gulf of Guinea coast is located to the south. The boundary between Ghana and Cote d'Ivoire extends northward from the Gulf of Guinea along straight-line segments and small streams until it reaches the Volta Noire, or Black Volta, River at Ghana's Bui National Park. The Volta Noire is one of the three major tributaries of the Volta, which empties into the Gulf of Guinea in Ghana. The northernmost section of the boundary between Ghana and Cote d'Ivoire follows the Volta Noire upstream and northward to the tripoint between Ghana, Cote d'Ivoire, and Burkina Faso.

The boundary between Ghana and Burkina Faso continues northward from this tripoint along the Volta Noire. West of the village of Bangwon along the border, this boundary leaves the Volta Noire, following straight-line segments eastward for most of its remaining length. These segments are located near the 11th parallel of north latitude. The easternmost section of the boundary is more irregular, following straight-line segments and streams in a generally easterly and northeasterly direction to a point near the village of Kulungugu. The boundary then follows a longer straight-line segment extending in an east-southeasterly direction to the tripoint between Ghana, Burkina Faso, and Togo. From this tripoint, the boundary between Ghana and Togo extends southward following a combination of short segments, streams, and drainage divides, passing just east of Lake Volta in Ghana, and then

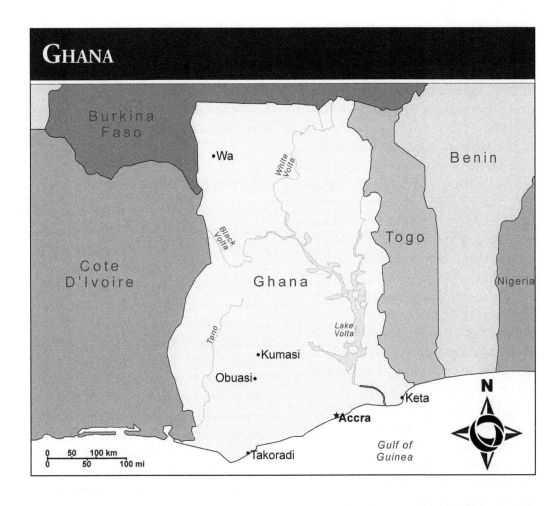

GHANA

Burkina
Faso

•Wa

White Volta

Benin

Black Volta

Togo

Cote
D'Ivoire

Ghana

Nigeria

Tano

Lake
Volta

•Kumasi

Obuasi•

Keta

N

★Accra

Gulf of
Guinea

0   50   100 km
0   50   100 mi

•Takoradi

continues to the Gulf of Guinea just west of the Togolese capital of Lome.

HISTORICAL CONTEXT

Ghana's name comes from the Ghana Empire, which was a powerful West African kingdom during the Middle Ages. However, the Ghana Empire's realm was centered in parts of modern-day Mali and Mauritania, several hundred miles northwest of the modern state of Ghana. Anthropologists believe that a majority of people living in present-day Ghana by AD 1000 were members of the Akan nation. Several Akan groups competed for influence in precolonial Ghana over the next several hundred years. In the early 18th century, the Ashanti Empire took control of the area. At its height, the Ashanti Empire controlled most of present-day Ghana and parts of several neighboring countries.

European contact with present-day Ghana began in the late 15th century, when Portuguese sailors established forts and trading posts along the coast. During the 16th and 17th centuries, other settlements were established by the Dutch, British, and Spanish. The Europeans named the region the Gold Coast because of the availability of gold that they obtained in trade with local groups. Britain became the dominant colonial power in the Gold Coast region during the 19th century, subduing the Ashanti Empire in a series of conflicts. In 1874, the area became a British protectorate. It became a formal British colony in 1897.

The German colony of Togoland adjoined Gold Coast to the east. After World War I, Germany was stripped of its colonies, and Togoland was divided between British and French mandates by the League of Nations. The British section of the former German colony became British Togoland. This area included the eastern portion of present-day Ghana east of Lake Volta north to the boundary with present-day Burkina Faso. Britain administered British Togoland under the auspices of the League of Nations and then under a United Nations trusteeship after World War II.

In 1947, local activists established the United Gold Coast Convention to promote independence of the Gold Coast colony. The Convention People's Party (CPP) was established as a formal political movement in 1949. The CPP had strong popular support. In 1957, the Gold Coast became the first colony in sub-Saharan Africa to become independent from a European colonial power. The CPP's leader, Kwame Nkrumah, became the newly independent country's first president, and the country adopted its present name.

Nkrumah was ousted in 1966, and Ghana experienced a series of coups d'état over the next 15 years. In 1981, power was seized by the military officer Flight-Lieutenant Jerry Rawlings. Rawlings ruled as an autocrat over the next decade, and during the 1980s many Ghanaians, including large numbers of business owners and professionals, left the country. However, a new constitution was drafted in 1992, restoring multiparty rule, and Rawlings was elected president in 1992. Since then, stable democracy has taken root, and power has been transferred peacefully between opposing political parties.

CONTEMPORARY ISSUES

Ghana has become one of the more prosperous countries in sub-Saharan Africa. Its prosperity stems from its political stability along with its agricultural productivity and valuable natural resources, including gold. Ghana's prosperity has allowed it to avoid the civil wars and ethnic violence that have plagued other African countries in recent years. Many refugees from less stable West African countries such as Cote d'Ivoire and Liberia have moved to Ghana in response to ongoing wars and conflicts in these countries. Oil production in Ghana is increasing, leading observers to consider whether dependence on oil exports will corrupt its currently successful economy.

See also   Burkina Faso, Cote d'Ivoire, Togo

Further Reading

Michael Bratton and Nicholas van de Walle. *Democratic experiments in Africa: Regime transitions in comparative perspective.* New York: Cambridge University Press, 1997.

Roger S. Gocking. *The history of Ghana.* Westport, CT: Greenwood Press, 2005.

Todd Moss. "Saving Ghana from itself." *Foreign Policy*, September 4, 2009, http://www.foreignpolicy.com/articles/2009/09/04/saving_ghana_from_itself.

Paul Nugent. *Smugglers, secession-ists, and loyal citizens on the Ghana-Togo frontier.* Athens: Ohio University Press, 2002.

Dana Sherne. "Refugees in Ghana double since Cote d'Ivoire crisis." *Graphic.com.gh*, June 21, 2011, http://www.graphic.com.gh/news/page.php?news=13686.

GUINEA

OVERVIEW

Guinea is a former French colony in West Africa with a land area of about 95,000 square miles, slightly larger than Kansas, and a population of 10 million. Guinea's neighbors are Guinea-Bissau to the northwest, Senegal to the north, Mali to the northeast, Cote d'Ivoire to the southeast, and Liberia and Sierra Leone to the south. Western Guinea has a seacoast on the Atlantic Ocean. The country is sometimes known as Guinea-Conakry, after its capital city, in order to distinguish it from neighboring Guinea-Bissau. The country is shaped like a crescent, with the western end on the Atlantic and the eastern end along the boundaries between Guinea and Liberia and between Guinea and Cote d'Ivoire. From southeastern Guinea, travel

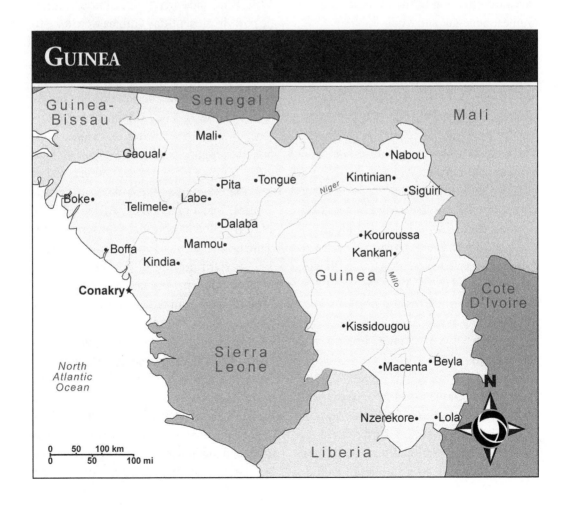

in a straight line to the capital of Conakry on the Atlantic Ocean requires crossing Sierra Leone.

Guinea's boundary with Guinea-Bissau extends in a generally northeasterly direction inland from the Atlantic Ocean. The tripoint between Guinea, Guinea-Bissau, and Senegal is located at the intersection of the 12° 40′ 30″ parallel of north latitude and the 16th meridian of west longitude. From this tripoint, the boundary between Guinea and Senegal follows the 12° 40′ 30″ parallel to the intersection of this parallel and the Tanague River. From there, it follows a complex series of straight lines and short river segments in a generally eastward direction to the tripoint between Guinea, Senegal, and Mali.

The boundary between Guinea and Mali continues in an easterly direction and turns southward near the Guinean village of Fontine. Like the boundary between Guinea and Senegal, this boundary consists of a series of straight-line segments. The boundaries between Guinea and Cote d'Ivoire and between Guinea and Liberia include both straight-line segments and rivers. The tripoint between Guinea, Cote d'Ivoire, and Liberia is located along the St. John River. The boundary Guinea and Liberia follows the St. John, the Niandi, and the Magoni rivers. The Magoni, or Makona, River represents the northwestern-most section of this boundary, ending at the tripoint between Guinea, Liberia, and Sierra Leone.

Most of the boundary between Sierra Leone and Guinea follows rivers and other physical features. From the Atlantic Ocean, it trends northeastward toward the Outamba Kilimi National Park in Guinea. It then follows the 10th parallel of latitude

eastward to a point northwest of the village of Kaliere. From there the boundary trends southeastward and then southward following a complex series of short segments to a point near the village of Kelama in Sierra Leone. It then trends northeastward for about 20 miles to the tripoint between Guinea, Sierra Leone, and Liberia. A small strip of territory about 20 miles long and less than two miles wide is located in Guinea west of the Moa River.

HISTORICAL CONTEXT

France maintained control of the Atlantic coast of what is now Guinea during the 17th, 18th, and early 19th centuries. Atlantic ports in present-day Guinea were used to transport captured slaves across the Atlantic to North, Central, and South America. However, the French did not show interest in what is now the interior of Guinea until the 1880s. They established the colony of Rivieres-du-Sud in 1882, with boundaries approximating those of Guinea today. France incorporated Guinea, which was then known as the Colony of French Guinea, into French West Africa in 1891 and cemented its control of the territory by defeating an army of local forces in 1898. The western portion of French West Africa, including present-day Senegal, Benin, Cote d'Ivoire, and Niger, was governed by a French governor-general based in Dakar, the capital of present-day Senegal.

In 1957, France gave residents of its colonies in French West Africa a choice between retaining colonial status within the French Community and outright independence. Guinea chose the latter and became independent in 1958. Since then, Guinea has been ruled by dictators throughout most of its history. Guinea's long history of autocratic rule has contributed to the country's poverty, which has been exacerbated by rapid population growth, lack of infrastructure, and environmental degradation.

The boundaries between Guinea and its neighbors outside French West Africa were established by agreements between France and other colonial powers. The French negotiated boundary agreements with Britain, which controlled Sierra Leone, in 1882 and with Portugal, which controlled Guinea-Bissau, in 1886. The boundary between Guinea and Liberia was agreed upon originally by France and Liberia in 1892. At that time, the boundary agreed upon consisted of two straight-line segments. Beginning in 1915, the boundary was modified in accordance with physical features and the distribution of settlements. The boundaries between Guinea and other colonies comprising French West Africa were delineated initially as administrative divisions by the French in the late 19th and early 20th centuries.

CONTEMPORARY ISSUES

Guinea's boundaries, established in the late 19th and early 20th centuries by France, have remained largely intact since that time. However, a border dispute between Guinea and Sierra Leone has taken place in recent years. The dispute has centered on the village of Yenga, which is located along the border about 25 miles northwest of the tripoint between Guinea, Sierra Leone, and Liberia. Both countries claim Yenga, which was first occupied by Guinean troops during Sierra Leone's civil war in 1999. Although this civil war ended in 2001, Guinea continues to occupy the

area. Because of Yenga's location along the major road connecting Guinea with the interior of Sierra Leone and the interior of Liberia, Guinea has held onto Yenga in order to control the border and reduce smuggling and other cross-boundary movements of people and goods. In early 2012, Guinea agreed to hand Yenga over to Sierra Leone. The Yenga occupation illustrates that the porous boundaries in West Africa may be contributing to the political destabilization of West Africa.

See also   Cote d'Ivoire, Guinea-Bissau, Liberia, Mali, Senegal, Sierra Leone

Further Reading

Mohamed Massaquoi. "Sierra Leone: Guinea not ready to give up Yenga." *Allafrica.com*, June 14, 2012, http://allaf rica.com/stories/201206150538.html.

David Zounmenou. "Guinea: Hopes for reform dashed again." *Allafrica.com*, January 2, 2009, http://allafrica.com/sto ries/200901020524.html.

GUINEA-BISSAU

OVERVIEW

The Republic of Guinea-Bissau is located on the Atlantic Ocean coast of West Africa. Its name refers to its capital city of Bissau and is used in order to avoid confusion with nearby Guinea (sometimes called Guinea-Conakry after its capital city) and Equatorial Guinea. Guinea-Bissau has a land area of 13,948 square miles, or slightly smaller than Massachusetts and Connecticut combined. Its population is approximately 1.8 million.

Guinea-Bissau has boundaries with Senegal to the north and Guinea to the east

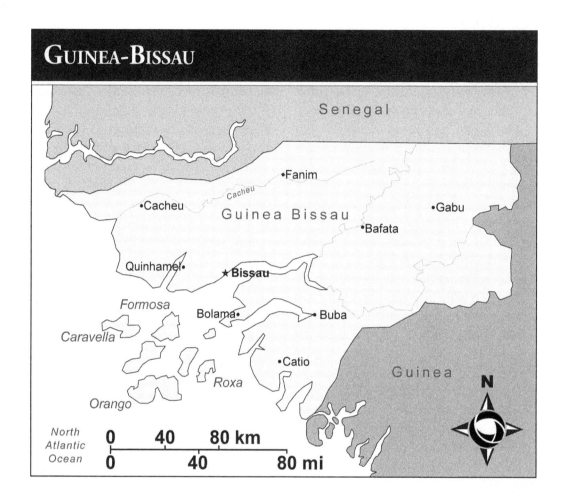

GUINEA-BISSAU

Senegal

•Fanim

Cacheu

•Cacheu

Guinea Bissau

•Gabu

•Bafata

Quinhamel•

★Bissau

Formosa

Bolama•

• Buba

Caravella

•Catio

Guinea

Roxa

Orango

North
Atlantic
Ocean

0   40   80 km

0   40   80 mi

N

and south. To the west, Guinea-Bissau has a coastline on the Atlantic. Guinea-Bissau also includes the Bissagos Islands, which are located in the Atlantic southwest of the country's capital city of Bissau. This archipelago includes more than 80 islands, of which 20 are inhabited with a combined population of about 30,000.

From the Atlantic coast, the boundary between Guinea-Bissau and Senegal extends inland in a generally north-northeasterly direction along a series of short straight-line segments. These segments are located roughly halfway between the Rio Cachou, which drains the northwestern part of Guinea-Bissau, and the Casamance River in southern Senegal. In general, the boundary is located an average of 20 to 30 miles north of the main channel of the Rio Cachou. Northeast of the town of Sare Mancama, the boundary reaches the 12° 40′ 30″ parallel of north latitude. The boundary follows this parallel eastward to the tripoint between Guinea-Bissau, Senegal, and Guinea-Conakry at its intersection with the 16th meridian of west longitude.

From this tripoint, the boundary between Guinea-Bissau and Guinea-Conakry follows straight-line segments southward. It reaches the Rio Corubal, the major river of southeastern Guinea-Bissau. The Rio Corubal forms the boundary briefly. To the south, the Rio Corubal flows into Guinea-Bissau, and the boundary between Guinea-Bissau and Guinea continues southward before turning westward. Here it separates two sections of Guinea-Bissau's Dulombi-Boe National Forest from Guinea. The boundary region is heavily forested and sparsely populated. Southwest of the forest, the boundary turns southwestward and continues along straight-line segments to the Atlantic Ocean.

HISTORICAL CONTEXT

Present-day Guinea-Bissau was part of the Mali Empire, which controlled much of West Africa during the 14th, 15th, and 16th centuries. Portugal claimed the territory along the coast of Guinea-Bissau in 1446. The port of Cachou at the mouth of the Cachou River became an important center for the trans-Atlantic slave trade between the 16th and the 18th centuries. Although Portugal claimed all of present-day Guinea-Bissau, in practice it controlled only the area immediately along the coast until the 19th century. The area was administered from the Portuguese-controlled Cape Verde Islands until the mainland colony was separated from the islands in 1879. What is now Guinea-Bissau became the Overseas Province of Guinea.

Nationalist movements sprung up throughout Africa in the 1950s. Support for independence in Guinea-Bissau intensified after 1960, when nearby former British and French colonies became independent. In the 1960s, the African Party for the Independence of Guinea and Cape Verde (PAIGC) began a series of guerilla campaigns against the Portuguese administration of Portuguese Guinea. By the early 1970s, the PAIGC had achieved control of most of the rural areas of Portuguese Guinea, although the Portuguese government remained in control of the capital city of Bissau and nearby areas. PAIGC's leaders declared independence in 1973. Portugal recognized Guinea-Bissau's independence in 1974. The country has experienced considerable political turmoil, including several coups d'état, since independence.

CONTEMPORARY ISSUES

Although Guinea-Bissau's boundaries are uncontested, Guinea-Bissau is involved indirectly in a secessionist movement in the Casamance region of neighboring Senegal. Activists in Casamance, which is Senegalese territory located between Guinea-Bissau and the Gambia, have been pressuring for independence from Senegal for the past three decades. Occasional armed skirmishes between Casamance rebels and the government of Senegal have displaced many residents of Casamance, some of whom have crossed the border into Guinea-Bissau. It is estimated that between 10,000 and 50,000 refugees from Casamance are now living in Guinea-Bissau.

See also Guinea, Senegal

Further Reading

Wagane Faye. "The Casamance separatism: From independence claim to resource logic." M.S. thesis, Naval Postgraduate School, 2006, http://calhoun. nps.edu/public/bitstream/handle/10945/ 2750/06Jun_Faye.pdf?sequence=1.

Joshua B. Forrest. *Lineages of state fragility: Rural civil society in*

Guinea-Bissau. Athens: Ohio University Press, 2003.

KENYA

OVERVIEW

The Republic of Kenya is located along the Indian Ocean coast of East Africa. It is slightly smaller than Texas, with a land area of 224,000 square miles. Its population is about 41 million.

Kenya's neighbors include Tanzania to the south, Uganda to the west, South Sudan to the northwest, Ethiopia to the north, and Somalia to the east. Southeastern Kenya has a seacoast along the Indian Ocean. Kenya's boundaries were delineated initially by European colonial powers. A few remain disputed or uncertain.

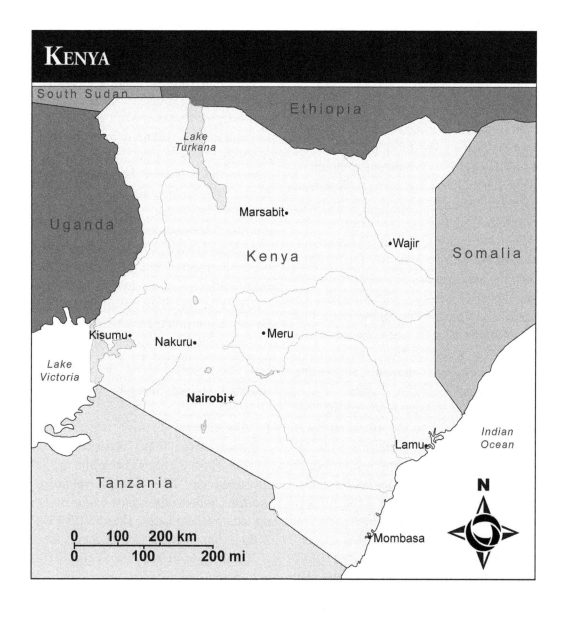

Most of Kenya's boundary with Tanzania consists of two long, straight segments that extend southeastward from the tripoint between Kenya, Tanzania, and Uganda in Lake Victoria to the Indian Ocean. In between the two segments is a shorter boundary consisting of several segments that trend north to south. Within this boundary region, Lake Jipe is part of the boundary. Lake Victoria represents the southern portion of the boundary between Kenya and its western neighbor, Nigeria. From the tripoint between Kenya, Tanzania, and Uganda, the boundary between Kenya and Uganda follows the Sio River and its tributary, the Sango River, northward from the mouth of the Sio River to the summit of Mount Elgon. From there, the boundary follows a long and complex series of short, straight lines trending in a general direction to the tripoint between Kenya, Uganda, and South Sudan.

East of this tripoint, the boundary between Kenya and South Sudan consists of straight-line segments extending toward the tripoint between Kenya, South Sudan, and Ethiopia. This tripoint is located in Lake Turkana, which was once known as Lake Rudolf. An area of land about the size of Massachusetts known as the Ilemi Triangle has long been in dispute between Kenya and South Sudan. The easternmost point of the Ilemi Triangle is the Kenya–South Sudan–Ethiopia tripoint. From Lake Turkana, the boundary between Kenya and Ethiopia follows numerous short straight-line segments that extend generally in an eastward direction to the Dawa River, which it follows eastward and downstream to the tripoint with Somalia. The boundary between Kenya and Somalia is geometric. Most of it follows the 41st meridian of east longitude, with a southwest-to-northeast segment in the north and two northwest-to-southeast segments that extend from slightly south of the equator to the Indian Ocean.

HISTORICAL CONTEXT

Present-day Kenya has been a crossroads of various civilizations for thousands of years. For nearly 2,000 years, Arab traders have traveled to and from Kenya. The port of Mombasa, which is located on Mombasa Island off the mainland coast, is believed to have been established more than 1,000 years ago, and trade linkages were maintained from Mombasa throughout East Africa, the Middle East, India, and East Asia. The Portuguese navigator Vasco de Gama visited Mombasa in 1498. Swahili, which has become an important lingua franca in eastern Africa, was developed in this area in order to facilitate trade among people speaking different languages. Swahili's vocabulary includes words derived from Arabic as well as from various African languages. Today, most Kenyans speak Swahili and English along with their ancestral languages.

In 1895, Britain established the East African Protectorate, which was also known as British East Africa. The area of the East African Protectorate corresponded roughly with the area occupied by the Republic of Kenya today. The Protectorate became the Colony of Kenya in 1920. Numerous white residents of Britain, many of whom were military officers or veterans, moved to Kenya after World War I. These British-born settlers owned much of the farmland, controlled the colony's government, and dominated the Colony of Kenya's economy and political system. Especially after World War II, African nationalist movements arose in opposition to European dominance of the Kenyan government and the Kenyan economy. In 1963, the Kenya Colony became independent. In recent years, Kenya has maintained a democratic government although recent elections have been marked by violence and accusations of corruption and electoral fraud.

The boundaries between Kenya and its neighbors were delineated formally during the period of British rule. The boundary between Kenya and Tanzania was delimited originally beginning in 1886, when the mainland portion of Tanzania was part of the German colony of Tanganyika. What is now Uganda was known as the Kingdom of Buganda until the late 19th century, when Britain extended its East African protectorate to include the kingdom. In 1905, Britain considered uniting Kenya and Uganda as a single colony but eventually decided against doing so.

CONTEMPORARY ISSUES

Kenya's boundary issues include the need to clarify its boundary with South Sudan, a dispute with Uganda over islands in Lake Victoria, and the status of refugees. The dispute between Kenya and South Sudan involves control of the Ilemi Triangle, an area of about 5,000 square miles southeast of South Sudan, north of Kenya, and southwest of Ethiopia. Kenya occupies the area currently. Both Kenya and South Sudan, which inherited Sudan's claim over the area after becoming independent in 2011, claim the Ilemi Triangle.

Kenya and Uganda are contesting control over several islands in Lake Victoria, which is located between the two countries. The dispute also involves fishing rights in the lake. In October 2008, Ugandan police arrested 15 Kenyan fishermen near Migingo Island and charged them with fishing illegally in Ugandan waters. The tiny island, less than an acre in size, was claimed by both countries. A survey of the lake showed that the island is located on the Kenyan side of the boundary. Uganda has recognized Kenya's claim but continues to charge Kenyan fishermen with violating territorial fishing rights.

The status of refugees in Kenya remains an issue. As a stable and relatively prosperous democracy, Kenya has received numerous refugees fleeing its less stable neighbors. More than 250,000 refugees are believed to be living in Kenya. Most have moved to Kenya from South Sudan, following the conflict between preindependence South Sudan and Sudan. Others have come from Uganda, escaping Uganda's corruption and autocratic rule as well as the atrocities of Joseph Kony's Lord's Resistance Army. Kenya has also made efforts to forestall the large-scale inmigration of refugees from Somalia, which lacks a functioning central government.

See also Ethiopia, Somalia, South Sudan, Tanzania, Uganda

Further Reading

Joel D. Barkan and Makau Mutna. "Turning the corner in Kenya: A new constitution for Nairobi." *Foreign Affairs*, August 10, 2010, http://www.foreign affairs.com/articles/66510/joel-d-barkan-and-makau-mutua/turning-the-corner-in-kenya.

Robert H. Bates. *Beyond the miracle of the market: The political economy of agrarian development in Kenya.* New York: Cambridge University Press, 2005.

UN News Centre. "UN-run camps for Somali refugees in Kenya enter 20th year of existence." February 21, 2012, http://www.un.org/apps/news/story.asp?NewsID=41307&Cr=somali&Cr1=.

LESOTHO

OVERVIEW

The landlocked southern African country of Lesotho has a land area of about 11,600 square miles, slightly larger than Maryland. Its population is about 1.9 million. Lesotho is an elevated plateau, most of which lies at more than 5,000 feet above sea level.

Lesotho is surrounded completely by South Africa. Most of the boundary between South Africa and Lesotho follows physical features. The Mohokare and Caledon rivers form the northwestern boundary between Lesotho and South Africa. The Mohokare and the Caledon are tributaries of the Orange River, which flows westward to the Atlantic Ocean. The northeastern and southeastern boundary follows the crest of the Drakensberg Mountains, separating the drainage basin of the Orange

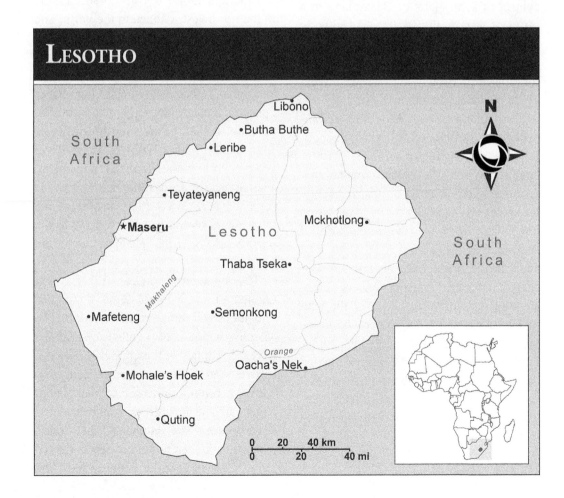

River from those of eastward-flowing rivers. The southern and southwestern boundary consists of a combination of short geometric lines and river segments.

HISTORICAL CONTEXT

Present-day Lesotho was established as the Kingdom of Basutoland in 1822. Basutoland is located between Britain's Cape Colony (today the Eastern Cape Province of South Africa) and the Orange Free State (today the Free State), which was controlled by Boers of Dutch ancestry. Basutoland's boundaries were not defined clearly, and Boers from the Orange Free State took control of some parts of Basutoland in a series of wars in the 1850s and 1860s. In order to prevent further Boer incursions, Basutoland's king appealed to the British for protection. Britain established a protectorate over Basutoland in 1868.

The Union of South Africa became independent in 1910. With British support, South Africa attempted to annex Basutoland. However, Basutoland resisted annexation and remained a British colony. Basutoland's opposition to annexation intensified following the imposition of apartheid in South Africa in 1948, and annexation efforts were abandoned. Basutoland became independent in 1966, adopting its current name. Over the next two decades, South Africa accused Lesotho repeatedly of harboring and encouraging the African National Congress, which was committed to overthrowing South Africa's apartheid regime. Nevertheless, Lesotho's economy remains tied closely to that of South Africa.

See also   South Africa

Further Reading

Glenn Ashton. "Southern Africa: A case for greater interaction between South Africa, Lesotho, and Swaziland?" *Allafrica.com*, June 18, 2012, http://allafrica.com/stories/201206180027.html.

LIBERIA

OVERVIEW

The Republic of Liberia is located along the Atlantic coast of West Africa. Liberia has a land area of about 43,000 square miles, the size of Virginia. Its population is about 4 million.

Liberia's neighbors are Sierra Leone to the northwest, Guinea to the north, and Cote d'Ivoire to the east. To the southwest, Liberia has a coastline on the Atlantic Ocean. The boundary between Liberia and Sierra Leone follows the Mano River upstream and northeasterly inland from the Atlantic. It then follows the Morro River from its confluence with the Mano River and then follows the Mano River upstream. The boundary then follows straight-line segments northeastward to the Mauwa and the Magoni rivers, which it follows to the tripoint between Liberia, Sierra Leone, and Guinea.

The boundary between Liberia and Guinea follows a combination of straight-line segments and portions of rivers. The Magoni, which is also called the Makona River, continues as the boundary between Liberia and Guinea upstream and eastward. It turns southward to the Niandi River, which it follows southward and downstream. The boundary then turns eastward and then northeastward to the tripoint between Liberia, Guinea, and Cote

LIBERIA

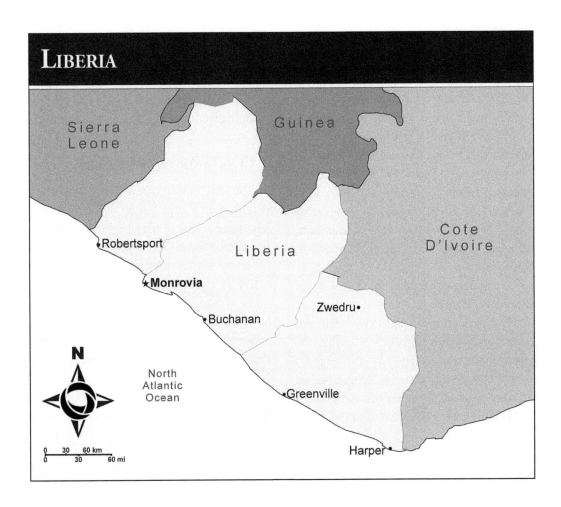

d'Ivoire on the St. John River. All of these streams flow southwestward through Liberia into the Atlantic Ocean. The boundary between Liberia and Cote d'Ivoire follows the Cestos River southward and then turns eastward briefly before following the Cavalla River southward to its mouth in the Atlantic. The Cavalla forms the southern two-thirds of the boundary between Liberia and Cote d'Ivoire.

HISTORICAL CONTEXT

The Atlantic coast of present-day Liberia was named the Pepper Coast by Portuguese sailors who first visited it in the 15th century. Britain established a trading port on the coast in 1663.

In the early 19th century, some Americans proposed to create a colony in Africa for freed slaves in the United States. The American Colonization Society was founded in 1816. Its supporters included abolitionists as well as slave owners who regarded freed slaves as a labor force whose presence would undercut the slave-based plantation economy. In 1821, the society purchased Cape Mesurado on the Atlantic coast, and the first shiploads of freed slaves arrived. They founded the city of Monrovia, which was named for U.S. president James Monroe and became Liberia's capital city.

Over the next 25 years, additional settlers arrived. In 1847, Liberia declared its independence. Liberia and Ethiopia are the only African states today that have never been formal colonies of European states.

The repatriated freed slaves and their descendants were known as Americo-Liberians. At the time of independence, Americo-Liberians made up less than 5 percent of Liberia's population whereas more than 95 percent were indigenous Africans. However, Americo-Liberians, whose culture was modeled on that of the United States, dominated the government and the economy.

The dominance of Liberia by Americo-Liberians ended abruptly in 1980, when the government was overthrown in a violent coup d'état led by Samuel K. Doe. Conflict between national groups within Liberia developed, and by 1989 it had erupted into a full-scale civil war.

A rebel organization known as the National Patriotic Front of Liberia (NPFL) invaded Liberia. Over the next year, the NPFL seized control of most of the country, and Doe was captured and executed. However, rival factions contested control of the government with the NPFL over the next several years.

In 1997, NPFL leader Charles Taylor was elected president of Liberia. Taylor's government was accused of atrocities, including selling weapons to revolutionaries in Sierra Leone in exchange for blood diamonds. Insurrections against Taylor's government began in 1999, initiating a second civil war. Under international pressure, Taylor resigned in 2003. A transitional government was appointed, and a United Nations peacekeeping force was brought in to restore orders. Free elections took place in 2005. Ellen Johnson Sirleaf, a Harvard-educated economist of mixed indigenous and Americo-Liberian ancestry, was elected president and become the first woman elected as an African head of state.

CONTEMPORARY ISSUES

The civil war within Liberia affected neighboring Sierra Leone, which also experienced civil war at the same time. During the 1980s, the NPFL supported the Revolutionary United Front (RUF), which was active in trying to overthrow the government of Sierra Leone. Supporters of both governments accused the RUF of selling and trading diamonds in order to finance the rebel groups in both countries. The NPFL was accused of buying these blood diamonds and providing the RUF with weapons. During the Liberian civil wars, thousands of refugees crossed the international boundary into Sierra Leone. Others have moved to Guinea, Cote d'Ivoire, and other African countries.

See also   Cote d'Ivoire, Guinea, Sierra Leone

Further Reading

Robert H. Bates. *When things fell apart: State failure in late-century Africa.* New York: Cambridge University Press, 2008.

Dino Mahtani. "Tarnishing the Iron Lady of Africa." *Foreign Policy*, May 28, 2010, http://www.foreignpolicy.com/articles/2010/05/28/tarnishing_the_iron_lady_of_africa.

Colin M. Waugh. *Charles Taylor and Liberia: Ambition and atrocity in Africa's Lone Star state.* London: Zed Books, 2011.

MADAGASCAR

OVERVIEW

The Republic of Madagascar is located on the island of Madagascar, which is located in the Indian Ocean off the southeast coast of mainland Africa. Madagascar is the fourth-largest island in the world. It is one of the most biodiverse places in the world, and a large majority of its plant and animal species are endemic. Development and increasing population have caused considerable threat to Madagascar's fragile ecosystem.

The Republic of Madagascar includes the island of Madagascar along with several smaller nearby islands. The total area of the Republic is 226,597 square miles, or

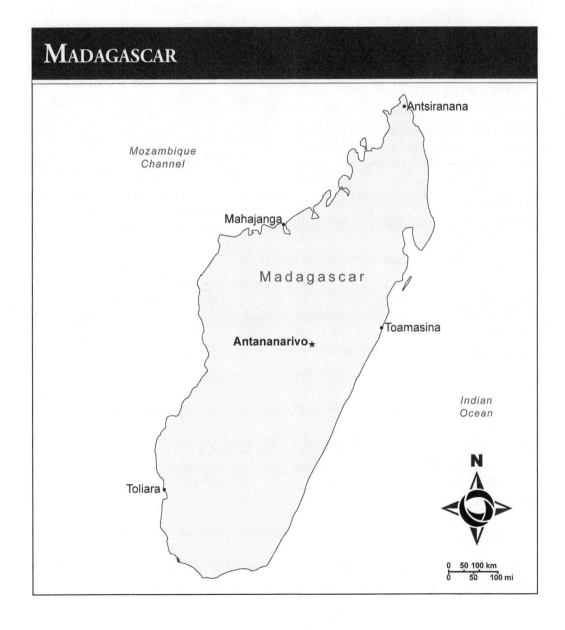

slightly smaller than Texas. Its population is 26 million. As an island country, Madagascar has no immediate neighbors. The main island is separated from the African mainland by the Mozambique Channel. At its closest point, Madagascar is about 280 miles east of the Mozambique coast on the mainland.

HISTORICAL CONTEXT

Most anthropologists believe that Madagascar was settled by migrants from present-day Indonesia who arrived by outrigger canoe about 2,000 years ago. In the seventh century AD, Arabs from southwest Asia and northwest Africa established trading posts along the northern coasts of the island. About 1,000 years ago, Bantu-speaking migrants from East Africa arrived. European explorers first visited the island in the early 16th century, and Britain and France established trading posts along the island's east coast.

Before 1800, Madagascar was divided into numerous kingdoms and principalities. The Merina kingdom, which was based in the central highlands of the island, succeeded in establishing control over the entire island in the early 19th century. In 1883, France began efforts to colonize the island. The Merina royal family was deposed in 1896, and Madagascar became a French colony. Madagascar became an independent state in 1960, and after independence it was known as the Malagasy Republic. The country's present name was adopted in 1975.

CONTEMPORARY ISSUES

As a former French colony, Madagascar retains close links and trade relationships with France. The United States, Germany, and Japan are also major trading partners of Madagascar. Madagascar is a member of the African Union but has not been involved heavily with African politics and international relations. In 2004, Madagascar joined the Southern African Development Community, which is headquartered in Botswana and includes all of the African countries from Angola, Congo, and Tanzania southward to South Africa.

Although agriculture has long been a mainstay of Madagascar's economy, tourism and mining are increasingly important. In light of Madagascar's unique natural history and biogeography, Madagascar has become an increasingly popular destination for ecotourists. Madagascar's mineral resources include nickel and oil and gas. Efforts to extract and export these resources continue, although many environmentalists have expressed concern that these activities will place additional stress on Madagascar's unique ecology.

Further Reading

Solofo Randrianja and Stephen Ellis. *Madagascar: A short history.* Chicago: University of Chicago Press, 2009.

Genese Marie Sodikoff. *Forest and labor in Madagascar: From colonial concession to global biosphere.* Bloomington: Indiana University Press, 2012.

MALAWI

OVERVIEW

The Republic of Malawi is a landlocked country located in east-central Africa. Its land area is 45,747 square miles, approximately the size of Pennsylvania. Its population is about 16 million.

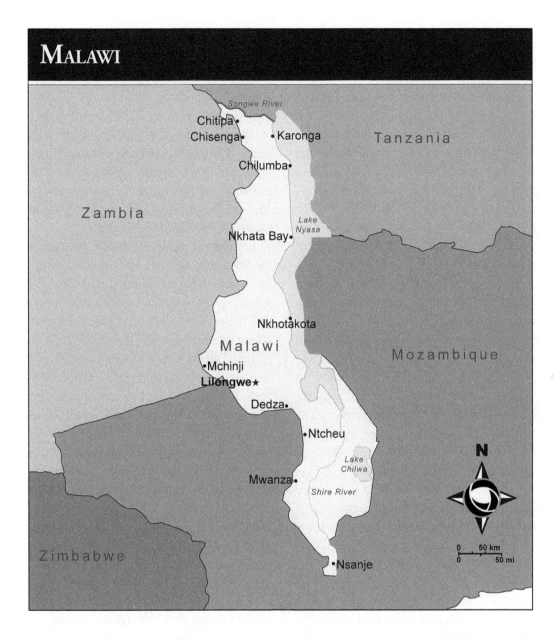

MALAWI

Malawi is bordered by Tanzania to the north, Zambia to the west, and Mozambique to the southwest, south, southeast, and east. To the northeast, Malawi has a long coastline on Lake Malawi, which is known also as Lake Nyasa. On the opposite shore of this long, narrow lake are Tanzania east of the northern half of the lake and Mozambique east of the southern half. Most of the boundary between Malawi and Tanzania is located within Lake Malawi, which is the eighth-largest and second-deepest lake in the world. From the northwestern shore of the lake, this boundary extends northwestward to the tripoint between Malawi, Tanzania, and Zambia. This section of the boundary follows the course of the Songwe River. However, the Songwe is subject to frequent flooding and has changed its course repeatedly, so the precise location of the boundary is uncertain.

Most of the boundary between Malawi and Zambia follows drainage divides. On the Malawian side of the boundary, streams flow eastward into Lake Malawi. On the Zambian side of the boundary, streams are tributaries of the Zambezi River. However, Lake Malawi drains southward via the Shire River into the Zambezi in Mozambique, and thus all of Malawi is part of the Zambezi drainage basin.

The tripoint between Malawi, Zambia, and Mozambique is located about 40 miles west of Malawi's capital city of Lilongwe. From this tripoint, it continues southward along the drainage divide between Lake Nyasa and the Shire River in Malawi to the east and the Zambezi itself in Mozambique to the west. Malawian territory extends into Mozambique's territory on both sides, with the result that western Mozambique is separated from northeastern Mozambique. The Malawian strip of territory continues southward to a point west of the village of Mbisa. The boundary turns eastward, following straight-line segments to the Shire River. From this point, the boundary follows the Shire River and its tributaries, the Ruo River and the Malosa River, upstream and northward. From the Malosa, the boundary continues northward along straight-line segments to the tripoint between Malawi, Mozambique, and Tanzania in Lake Malawi.

HISTORICAL CONTEXT

According to archaeological evidence, present-day Malawi has been inhabited by humans for several hundred thousand years. Bantu tribes moved into Malawi around the 10th century AD, establishing kingdoms that ruled various parts of the country over the next several hundred years. Beginning in the 15th century, modern Malawi was ruled by the Maravi Empire, from which present-day Malawi derives its name. The Maravi Empire's center of administration was located on the southwestern shore of Lake Malawi in present-day Malawi, but it also ruled parts of what is today Zambia and Mozambique.

Portuguese explores visited Malawi in the 16th century and established trade relationships with the Maravi, including the sale of slaves to the Portuguese, who resettled these slaves in Mozambique or transported them across the Atlantic Ocean to Brazil. During the 19th century, Maravi territory was invaded by other tribes from both the north and the south, and the Maravi Empire disintegrated. At the same time, traders from the Arab world moving inland from Zanzibar established trading centers along Lake Malawi, trading with the successors to the Maravi Empire.

The British explorer David Livingstone visited the shore of Lake Malawi in 1859. British traders and missionaries began to settle the area in the late 19th century, ending the slave trade. At that time, both Britain and Portugal claimed what is now Malawi. In 1890, Britain issued an ultimatum to Portugal, demanding Portuguese withdrawal from Malawi. Portugal acquiesced to the ultimatum and withdrew from the area. Malawi became the Shire Highlands Protectorate in 1891. The name was changed to the British Central Africa Protectorate in 1893 and to Nyasaland Protectorate in 1907. The British established plantations that produced coffee and other tropical crops, displacing native small farmers. During this period, the

British delineated Nyasaland's boundaries with Zambia, which was also a British colony. Britain and Portugal agreed in principle on the boundary between Nyasaland and Mozambique in 1891, with boundary adjustments agreed upon via several subsequent treaties between 1893 and 1952. The boundary between Malawi and Tanzania was agreed upon by Britain and Germany, which then controlled Tanganyika on the mainland of Tanzania, in 1914.

In 1953, the British joined Nyasaland with Northern Rhodesia (present-day Zambia) and Southern Rhodesia (present-day Zimbabwe) to form the Federation of Rhodesia and Nyasaland. The federation was seen as a potential dominion of the British Empire, with power to be shared between the indigenous majority and the white minority, who controlled much of the land and dominated the economy. However, indigenous Africans demanded a greater share of power. Nyasaland became a self-governing colony in 1963 and a fully independent state within the British Commonwealth in 1964 under its present name.

Independence leader Hastings Banda became Malawi's first president after independence. In 1966, he declared Malawi to be a one-party state. Banda made himself president for life in 1970, in effect becoming the country's dictator who ran one of Africa's most repressive regimes. Following protests within Malawi and facing international pressure, Malawi held a referendum choosing between maintaining Banda's one-party regime and multiparty democracy. After a large majority of voters preferred multiparty democracy. Banda, who by this time was in his 90s, ran for the presidency in the first multiparty election in 1994 but was defeated. Malawi has maintained multiparty democracy since that time.

CONTEMPORARY ISSUES

Malawi and Tanzania have disputed control of the northeastern quadrant of Lake Malawi. Malawi claims all of the lake north of the tripoint between Malawi, Tanzania, and Mozambique. However, Tanzania claims that the boundary should be the middle of the lake, equidistant from both shores. The disagreement stems from conflicting interpretations of treaties and agreements negotiated in colonial times. Tanzania bases its claim on the original agreement between Britain and Germany negotiated in 1914. However, Malawi claims that all of Lake Malawi except for that portion under Mozambique's administration was assigned to Nyasaland rather than Tanganyika (present-day Tanzania) after the League of Nations assigned Tanganyika to Britain after World War I. Although Malawi has not pursued its claim actively, on various occasions it has detained Tanzanian fishermen who it has accused of fishing illegally in Malawian waters.

See also Mozambique, Tanzania, Zambia

Further Reading

Archibald Kasakura. "Malawi's foreign policy under microscope." *Malawi News*, May 19, 2012, http://www.bnltimes.com/index.php/malawi-news/headlines/national/6491-malawis-foreign-policy-under-microscope.

Reuters. "Malawi sees troubled economy slowly growing." June 8, 2012, http://af.reuters.com/article/investingNews/idAFJOE85708D20120608.

MALI

OVERVIEW

The Republic of Mali is located in West Africa. Its land area is 478,839 square miles, nearly twice as large as Texas. Mali's population is about 16 million. Geographically, Mali extends from the Sahara Desert in the north into the Sahel region, which occupies most of the central and southern portions of the country. Average annual rainfall increases steadily from north to south. The country is divided into two broad sections. The northeastern section is arid, with the northern portion of this sector extending well into the Sahara. The other section is located to the southwest of the northern section. This region is semiarid with more dependable rainfall. The large majority of Malians live in the southern part of Mali, which is drained largely by the Niger River.

Mali is landlocked. It has boundaries with Mauritania to the west, Algeria to the northeast, Niger and Burkina Faso to the east and southeast, Cote d'Ivoire to the south, and Guinea and Senegal to the southwest. The tripoint between Mali, Mauritania, and

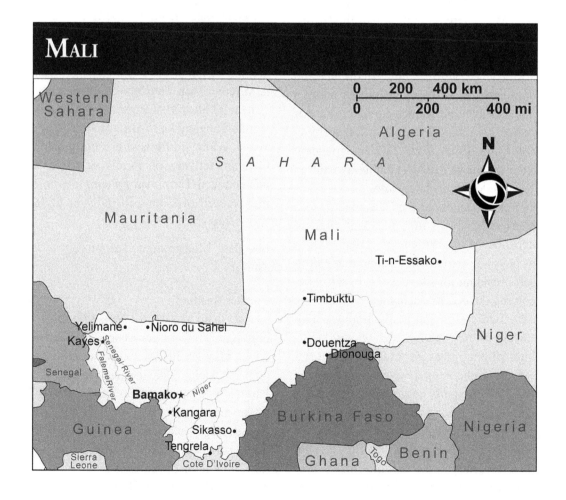

Senegal is located near the confluence of the Senegal River and the Falémé River. From this tripoint, the boundary between Mali and Mauritania extends eastward along streams and drainage divides to the 15° 30′ parallel of north latitude. It follows this parallel eastward for about 200 miles to the point at which it intersects the 5° 30′ meridian of west longitude. At this point, the boundary turns northward. Most of this section of the boundary follows a long, straight line that runs in a north-northwesterly direction northward to the 25th parallel of north latitude. It then turns eastward again, following the 25th parallel eastward to the tripoint between Mauritania, Mali, and Algeria. The boundary region north of the 15° 30′ parallel is primarily desert and is very sparsely populated.

The boundary between Mali and Algeria follows a long, diagonal segment that extends southeastward from the tripoint between Mali, Algeria, and Mauritania to a point near the source of the Tin-in-Zouatene Wadi and then continues to the course of the I-n-Akantarer Wadi. These wadis are intermittent streams that contain water only during rainy seasons and dry up in the dry seasons and during droughts. From the tripoint between Mali, Algeria, and Niger, the boundary between Mali and Niger extends southward and then abruptly westward, following straight lines to the tripoint between Mali, Niger, and Burkina Faso.

Most of Mali's boundary with Burkina Faso follows short geometric lines that extend in a westerly and then southwesterly direction to the tripoint between Mali, Burkina Faso, and Cote d'Ivoire. For most of its length, this boundary parallels the drainage divide between the Niger River basin to the north in Mali and the Volta River basin to the south in Burkina Faso. However, a small portion of the Volta drainage basin is located in Mali. The tripoint between Mali, Burkina Faso, and Cote d'Ivoire is located where the Danboro and Zagoundouba rivers join to form the Leraba Occidentale River. The boundary between Mali and Cote d'Ivoire extends westward along the Danboro and then follows several other streams and drainage divides westward. The boundary between Mali and Guinea extends northward from the tripoint between Mali, Guinea, and Cote d'Ivoire along straight-line segments. After crossing the Niger River, it turns westward to the tripoint between Mali, Guinea, and Senegal on the Falémé River. The Falémé forms much of the boundary between Mali and Senegal, but a small area of Senegal is located east of the river near the north-central portion of this boundary. To the north, the Falémé becomes the boundary once again until it flows into the Senegal River near the tripoint between Mali, Senegal, and Mauritania.

HISTORICAL CONTEXT

Present-day Mali was located near the center of three of West Africa's major empires—the Ghanaian Empire, the Malian Empire after which the present-day country was named, and the Songhai Empire. The Ghanaian Empire dominated the region from the 9th to the 13th centuries, until it was supplanted by the Malian Empire from which the current country of Mali derives its name in the 13th century. The city of Timbuktu, located on the north bank of the Niger River in the central portion of present-day Mali, was a well-known center for Islamic learning and scholarship. In the 14th century, the Songhai Empire arose and took over the eastern portion of the Malian Empire. All of these empires profited from trading across the Sahara Desert, but the economic importance of this trade declined as European mariners developed sea routes between the African coast and the Mediterranean basin.

France assumed control of present-day Mali in the late 19th century. The area became a French colony known as French Sudan in 1890. French Sudan became part of French West Africa along with Senegal, Mauritania, Niger, Benin, Cote d'Ivoire, Burkina Faso, and Guinea. What is now Mali was parceled out among these other colonies in 1899, but in 1920 the colony was reunited under the name of French Sudan with its current boundaries.

In 1959, the colonies of French Sudan and Senegal were merged with each other as the Federation of Mali. The federation became independent in 1960, but after only two months the federation collapsed and Mali and Senegal became separate, independent countries. Mali experienced political instability, including several periods of autocratic military or dictatorial rule over the next three decades. However, a free and fair democratic election for the presidency of Mali took place in 1992. Since that time, Mali has been marked by successful democratic governance. In March 2012, however, soldiers stormed Mali's presidential palace and claimed to overthrow Mali's president. The coup was condemned by the international community, and economic sanctions were placed on Mali by its neighbors. A few weeks later, the rebel leaders agreed to transfer power back to a transitional civilian government.

CONTEMPORARY ISSUES

Secessionists are currently attempting to separate northern Mali from the rest of the country. Most of the inhabitants of northern Mali are Tuaregs, whose cultural affinities are associated more with North Africa and the Middle East as opposed to sub-Saharan Africa. The Tuareg language is related closely to the Berber language spoken in parts of North Africa. The Tuareg population of North Africa has been estimated at about 6 million, of whom more than half live in Mali and neighboring Niger.

Ever since Mali became independent, some Tuareg have felt that they have been ignored by the Malian government, which is centered in the southwestern part of the country. Since the 1990s, a separatist organization known as Ansar Dine has been active in promoting independence for northern Mali, which is sometimes called as Azawad. Ansar Dine is an Islamist organization and is believed to have ties with Al Qaeda. Another organization known as the National Movement for the Liberation of Azawad (MNLA) was founded in 2011. Both organizations are made up primarily of Tuareg fighters, some of whom are believed to have served in the Libyan armed forces.

In early 2012, the rebels seized control of much of the northern section of Mali north of the Niger River, including the city of Timbuktu. Dissatisfaction with the Malian government's efforts to thwart the rebels' efforts was a cause of Mali's short-lived coup d'état in March. In April 2012, rebels declared this region to be the independent state of Azawad. However, the sovereignty of Azawad has yet to be recognized by the Malian government or by the international community which is concerned about linkages between the rebels and extremist Islamic fundamentalist groups abroad. In May, the Islamist Ansar Dine and the secular MNLA announced plans to merge, with the goal of establishing Azawad as a fully recognized Islamic Republic of Azawad. Although Azawad's independence has yet to be recognized, Ansar Dine and MNLA retain de facto control of northern Azawad.

During the 1970s and 1980s, Mali and Burkina Faso experienced conflict over the Agacher Strip region along the frontier between the two countries. Both countries claimed the Agacher Strip, in part because the region was believed to contain substantial mineral deposits. War between Mali and Burkina Faso broke out in 1985, with about 200 casualties. The boundary dispute was referred to the International Court of Justice. In 1986, the court issued a ruling that divided the Agacher Strip region roughly equally between the two countries.

See also   Algeria, Burkina Faso, Cote d'Ivoire, Guinea, Mauritania, Niger, Senegal

Further Reading

Michael Bratton and Nicholas van de Walle. *Democratic experiments in Africa: Regime transitions in comparative perspective.* New York: Cambridge University Press, 1997.

James Traub. "Two cheers for Malian democracy." *Foreign Policy*, April 13, 2012, http://www.foreignpolicy.com/articles/2012/04/13/two_cheers_for_malian_democracy.

Susanna Wing. "The coup in Mali is only the beginning." *Foreign Affairs*, April 11, 2012.

MAURITANIA

OVERVIEW

The Islamic Republic of Mauritania is located in northwestern Africa and is part of the Sahel region, whose climate and environment are transitional between the Sahara Desert to the north and the savannas of north-central Africa to the south. Mauritania's land area is 397,954 square miles, slightly larger than Texas and New Mexico combined. Mauritania is one of the most sparsely populated countries in Africa, with a population of 3.2 million. For most of its postindependence history, Mauritania has been ruled by autocrats, and it is one of the poorest countries in the world.

Mauritania is bordered by Algeria to the northeast, Mali to the east, and Senegal to the south. Northern Mauritania borders Western Sahara, which is recognized by Mauritania as an independent country but is also claimed by Morocco. Western Mauritania has a long coastline on the Atlantic Ocean. The northern portion of Mauritania is located in the Sahara Desert, and the boundaries between Mauritania and Western Sahara, Algeria, and Mali are geometric. The western portion of the boundary between Mauritania and Western Sahara extends eastward from the Atlantic, north of the Mauritanian town of Nouadhibou, along the 21° 20′ parallel of north latitude. This parallel is the boundary for about 200 miles inland before turning northward and northeastward along a series of shorter straight-line segments to the 12th meridian of west longitude. From there it extends northward to the 26th parallel of north latitude, eastward to the 8° 40′ meridian of west longitude, and northward

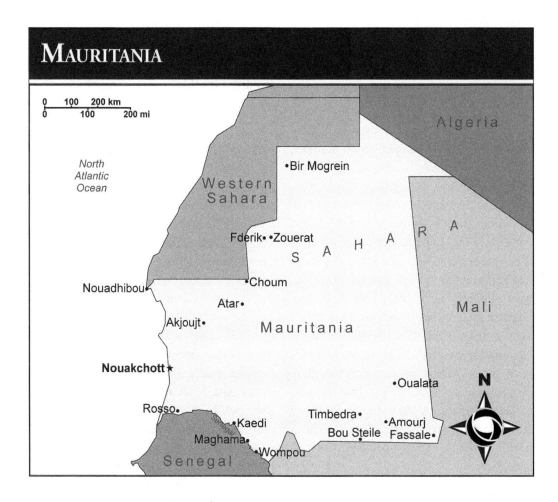

MAURITANIA

to the tripoint between Mauritania, Western Sahara, and Algeria at latitude 27° 17′ 40″ north and longitude 8° 40′ west. The boundary between Mauritania and Algeria is a geometric line extending southeastward from this tripoint to the tripoint between Mauritania, Algeria, and Mali at latitude 25° north, longitude 4° 50′ west.

The boundary between Mauritania and Mali extends westward from this tripoint along the 25th parallel for about 100 miles. It then turns southward and becomes a long, straight line extending in a south-southeastward direction. Two shorter straight-line segments continue the boundary until it turns westward at latitude 15°

30′ north, longitude 5° 30′ west. It follows the 15° 30′ parallel westward for about 200 miles and then follows permanent streams in a westward direction to the tripoint between Mauritania, Mali, and Senegal on the Senegal River. The boundary between Mauritania and Senegal follows the Senegal River to the river's mouth in the Atlantic.

HISTORICAL CONTEXT

Many of modern Mauritania's early inhabitants were Berbers. During the late Middle Ages, Arabs moving southward from present-day Morocco and Algeria took control of the area, converting the local population to Islam. France took control of present-day Mauritania in the late 19th and early 20th centuries. In 1920, the colony became part of French West Africa. Mauritania became independent in 1960.

With the exception of Western Sahara, Mauritania's neighbors are also former French colonies. The boundaries between these colonies were determined by France. The boundary between Mauritania and Senegal was established in 1904; the boundary between Mauritania and Algeria was established in 1909; and the boundary between Mauritania and Mali, which was then known as French Soudan, was established in 1913 and modified by French colonial administrators in 1944. France and Spain, which controlled the present-day Western Sahara, agreed to the boundary between the two colonies in 1900.

CONTEMPORARY ISSUES

The major issue involving Mauritania and its neighbors since Mauritania become independent has been the status of Western Sahara, located along the Atlantic coast north of Mauritania and south of Morocco. For most of the 20th century, Western Sahara was a Spanish colony known as Spanish Sahara. Spain relinquished its claim to Spanish Sahara in 1975. At that time, Spain, Mauritania, and Morocco negotiated an agreement that specified that Morocco would administer the northern two-thirds of the territory, with the southern third to be administered by Mauritania. Morocco invaded the southern part of Western Sahara and claimed all of it as Moroccan territory. Meanwhile, guerilla forces known as the Polisario agitated for full independence for Western Sahara. In 1979, Mauritania withdrew its forces from Western Sahara, and in 1984 it recognized Western Sahara as an independent state with the name of Sahrawi Arab Democratic Republic. However, Morocco continues to claim all of Western Sahara and it maintains de facto control of the territory. Thus the Polisario government is a government in exile.

In the late 1990s, parties to the dispute invited former U.S. secretary of state James Baker to serve as a mediator. Baker proposed that a referendum be held in which voters in Western Sahara would be able to choose among three options: the status quo or continued autonomy within Morocco, full integration with Morocco, and full independence. However, Morocco rejected Baker's proposal, and it continues to control administer much of Western Sahara.

Mauritania is also involved in border-control negotiations with the European Union. The negotiations have been aimed at reducing migration from Mauritania to the Canary Islands, a Spanish possession in the Atlantic Ocean off the coast of Western Sahara. Given the Canary Islands' status as part of Spain, people moving to the islands have easy access to mainland Spain and the rest of the European Union. Spain has provided Mauritania with personnel and equipment to aid Mauritanian officials in controlling the country's borders.

See also   Algeria, Mali, Senegal

Further Reading

Noel Foster. *Mauritania: The struggle for democracy.* Boulder, CO: Lynne Rienner, 2010.

Erik Jensen. *Western Sahara: Anatomy of a stalemate.* Boulder, CO: Lynne Rienner, 2005.

Toby Shelley. *Endgame in the Western Sahara: What future for Africa's last colony?* London: Zed Books, 2004.

MAURITIUS

OVERVIEW

The Republic of Mauritius is an island country located in the western Indian Ocean. To many people, Mauritius is best known as the home of the extinct dodo. Mauritius has a land area of 787 square miles and a population of about 1.3 mil-

lion. Mauritius's closest neighbor by water is the French possession of La Reunion, which is located about 100 miles to the southwest. The closest sovereign country to Mauritius is Madagascar, which is 500 miles to the west.

HISTORICAL CONTEXT

Mauritius may have been visited by Arab sailors during the Middle Ages, but it was uninhabited when it was first visited by Portuguese mariners in 1507. The Dutch established the first European settlement on Mauritius in 1638, but this settlement and subsequent Dutch efforts to colonize the island were unsuccessful and

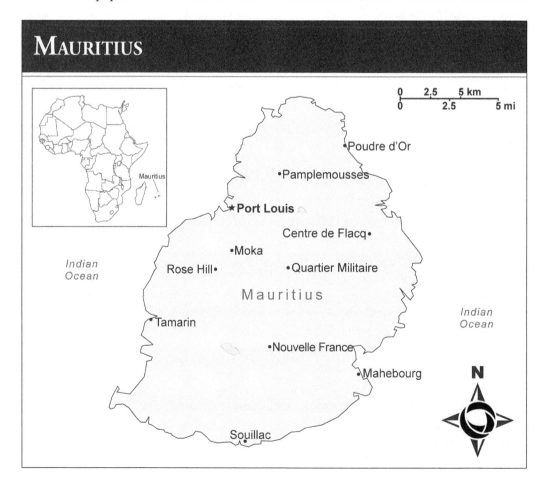

MAURITIUS

were abandoned finally in 1710. France then took control of the island in 1715, colonized it successfully, and established a naval base at the present-day capital city of Port Louis. The economy was based on supplying ships plying the Indian Ocean, felling and export of lumber from ebony trees, and cultivation of sugar on plantations. To provide labor, France imported slaves from Madagascar and the mainland of Africa.

In 1810, a British naval force captured Mauritius. British sovereignty over Mauritius was confirmed via the Treaty of Paris, which ended the Napoleonic Wars, in 1814. Under terms of this treaty, the British agreed to respect local customs and traditions including the use of the French language and a legal system based on the Napoleonic Code. After slavery was abolished throughout the British Empire in 1834, sugar plantation owners brought thousands of contract labors from India, China, and other Asian origins to provide labor. Today, the population of Mauritius is highly diverse and includes many people of European, African, and Asian origin. Mauritius became independent in 1968. Mauritius retains close economic ties with Britain and France. In recent years, it has become aligned increasingly with Africa, and it is a member of the African Union and the Southern Africa Development Community. It is also a member of the Indian Ocean Rim Association for Regional Cooperation, whose members include countries with seacoasts on the Indian Ocean from South Africa east to Indonesia and Australia.

CONTEMPORARY ISSUES

Mauritius claims sovereignty over the Chagos Archipelago, which includes the island of Diego Garcia. Diego Garcia is located about 1,350 miles northeast of Mauritius and about 800 miles south-southwest of the mainland of India, and it is the only inhabited island in the archipelago. In 1967, Britain and the United States began plans to build a joint naval base on Diego Garcia. Over the next six years, all of the roughly 2,000 inhabitants of Diego Garcia were forced to leave the island and were moved to Mauritius or the Seychelles. These islanders and their dependents have petitioned for the right to return to the Chagos Archipelago. Mauritius has objected also to the decision of the British government to put the marine territories surrounding the Chagos Archipelago off limits from oil and natural gas exploration.

Further Reading

Andrew Bomford. "Diego Garcia: Remembering paradise lost." *BBC News*, January 10, 2001, http://news.bbc.co.uk/2/hi/uk_news/835963.stm.

MOZAMBIQUE

OVERVIEW

The Republic of Mozambique is located in southeastern Africa. It has a land area of 309,496 square miles, about the size of Texas and Oklahoma combined. Its population is approximately 24 million.

Mozambique's neighbors are Tanzania to the north, Malawi and Zambia to the northwest, Zimbabwe to the west, South Africa to the west and south, and Swaziland to the south. Eastern Mozambique has a long coastline on the Indian Ocean. The Mozambique Channel separates Mozambique from the island country of Madagascar.

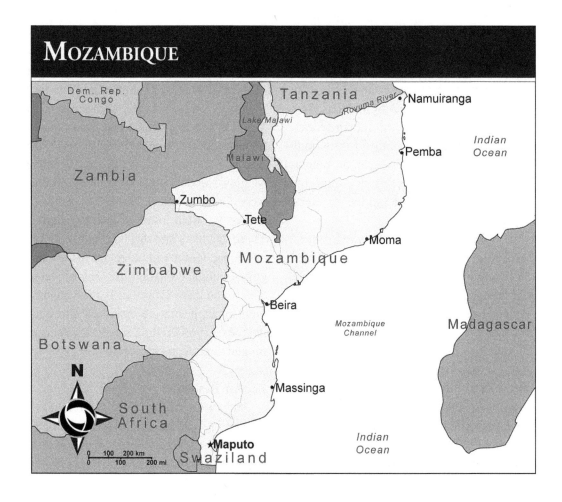

Mozambique

Mozambique's boundary with Tanzania follows the Rovuma River inland from its mouth on the Indian Ocean westward to the confluence with its tributary, the Msinje River. The Rovuma formed a significant barrier to commerce and interaction between the two countries until the Unity Bridge connecting the two countries by road was opened in 2010. The boundary extends inland along the course of the Msinje to Lake Nyasa, which is also known as Lake Malawi. Lake Nyasa is the eighth-largest lake in the world and the second-deepest lake in Africa. Mozambique, Tanzania, and Malawi all have coastlines on Lake Nyasa.

Malawi's territory extends southward from Lake Nyasa toward the center of Mozambique, separating northeastern and northwestern Mozambique from each other. From Lake Nyasa, the boundary extends southeastward and then southward along straight-line segments until reaching the Malosa River. It then follows the Malosa, Ruo, and Shire rivers, which flow into the Zambezi River. It turns northwestward where the main drainage basin of the Zambezi meets the drainage basin of the Shire, which is an outlet of Lake Nyasa. Thus Malawi contains the western portion of the Shire's drainage basin. The boundary between these drainage divides continues in a northwesterly direction to the tripoint between Mozambique, Malawi, and Zambia.

From this tripoint, the boundary between Mozambique and Zambia extends in a west-southwesterly direction along straight-line segments for approximately 200 miles. A few miles north of the village of Unhumbue, it turns southward following both natural features and straight-line segments to a point at the southeastern corner of Lower Zambezi National Park in Zambia. At this point, it turns straight eastward and then turns southward again following a combination of straight-line segments and small rivers. The boundary between Mozambique and Zimbabwe continues in this southerly direction to the tripoint between Mozambique, Zimbabwe, and South Africa. This tripoint is located where the boundary reaches the Limpopo River.

There are two boundaries between Mozambique and South Africa. From the tripoint between Mozambique, South Africa, and Zimbabwe, the boundary is a series of straight-line segments extending in a south-southeasterly direction. This boundary separates Limpopo National Park in Mozambique from Kruger National Park in South Africa. It continues southward to the northern tripoint between Mozambique, South Africa, and Swaziland. The boundary between Mozambique and Swaziland continues southward to the southern tripoint between these countries. From there it follows straight-line segments eastward to the Indian Ocean. Mozambique's capital city of Maputo is located on the Indian Ocean in the far southern portion of the country, less than 50 miles north of the boundary between Mozambique and South Africa.

HISTORICAL CONTEXT

Settlers of Bantu origin are believed to have moved into present-day Mozambique along the lower reaches of the Zambezi and Limpopo Rivers between 1,500 and 2,000 years ago. Arabs and native Africans established ports and trading posts along the Indian Ocean more than 1,000 years ago. From these ports, a thriving trade was maintained throughout the Indian Ocean as far away as the Arabian Peninsula, the Indian subcontinent, and Southeast Asia. During the 16th century, these ports and the trans–Indian Ocean trade was taken over by the Portuguese. Portugal established a colony in present-day Mozambique known as Portuguese East Africa, but its influence was limited largely to the regions along the coast of the Indian Ocean and the Mozambique Channel until the 20th century. Throughout most of its history, Portuguese East Africa was governed by private companies. In 1942, however, the private companies were dissolved and Portuguese East Africa was administered by the Portuguese government as an overseas province of Portugal.

As many countries in sub-Saharan Africa became independent in the late 1950s and early 1960s, independence sentiment increased in Mozambique. A guerilla movement known as the Front for the Liberation of Mozambique (FRELIMO) became active, trying to put an end to Portuguese rule. As FRELIMO gained control of more and more territory within Mozambique, many Portuguese left the colony. Mozambique became independent in 1975.

The boundaries between Mozambique and its neighbors were established during its period of colonial rules by agreement between Portugal and other colonial powers. The boundary between Mozambique and Tanzania was established by agreement between Portugal and Germany in 1886. Mozambique's other neighbors are former British colonies. The boundary between Mozambique and these British colonies was first established through an agreement between Portugal and Britain in 1891. These boundaries were modified and clarified through a further series of agreements negotiated and signed in the 1890s and the early 20th century.

CONTEMPORARY ISSUES

Mozambique's relationships with its neighbors are stable. After Mozambique became independent, South Africa accused Mozambique of harboring and abetting opponents of the white-minority South African government. These tensions eased after South African's white-minority government left office and the policy of apartheid was eliminated. Mozambique has extensive deposits of natural resources and may face conflicts with foreign powers and corporations that wish to become involved in their extraction and export.

See also Malawi, South Africa, Swaziland, Tanzania, Zambia, Zimbabwe

Further Reading

William Finnegan. *A complicated war: The harrowing of Mozambique.* Berkeley: University of California Press, 1993.

William Minter. *Apartheid's Contras: An inquiry into the roots of war in Angola and Mozambique.* Charleston, SC: BookSurge, 2008

NAMIBIA

OVERVIEW

The Republic of Namibia is located in southwestern Africa along the coast of the Atlantic Ocean. Namibia's land area is 318,696 square miles, or the size of Texas and Louisiana combined. Its population is approximately 2.2 million, and with only about seven people per square mile, it is one of Africa's most sparsely countries. Most of Namibia is arid, and much of its land area is located within the coastal Namib Desert, from which the country's name is derived, and the inland Kalahari Desert. Namibian territory includes the Caprivi Strip, which extends eastward from northeastern Namibia to a point near the confluence between the Chobe and Zambezi rivers. The Caprivi Strip is nearly 300 miles long, but much of it is only about 25 miles wide.

Namibia's neighbors are Angola and Zambia to the north, Botswana to the east, and South Africa to the south. The west coast of Namibia is situated on the Atlantic Ocean. From the coast, the boundary between Namibia and Angola follows the Kunene River upstream and eastward from its mouth in the Atlantic. It then follows the 17° 23′ 25″ parallel of south latitude inland to the Okavango River and then follows the Okavango downstream and eastward. From the Okavango, it follows a long diagonal-line segment that extends east-northeast to the tripoint between Namibia, Angola, and Zambia at the north of the Caprivi Strip.

All of the boundary between Namibia and Zambia separates Zambia from the Caprivi Strip. The straight line separating Namibia and Angola continues east-

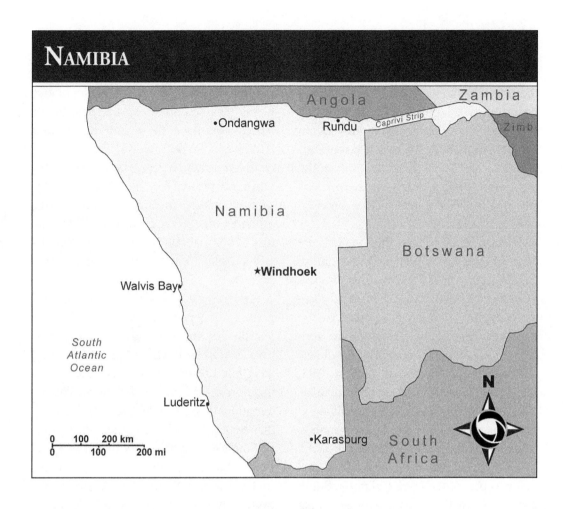

NAMIBIA

northeastward as the boundary between Namibia and Zambia to the Zambezi River. It then follows the Zambezi downstream and southeastward to the tripoint between Namibia, Zambia, and Botswana at the confluence of the Zambezi and the Chobe River. From this tripoint, Namibia and Zimbabwe are separated by less than a mile along the Zambezi.

The tripoint between Namibia and Botswana follows the Chobe upstream to its confluence with the Linyanti River and then follows the Linyanti upstream to its confluence with the Kwando River. The boundary continues up the Kwando to a diagonal line that parallels the northern boundary of the Caprivi Strip that separates Namibia and Angola. At the western end of the Caprivi Strip, the boundary follows the 21st meridian of east longitude southward to the 22° 30′ parallel of south latitude. It follows this parallel to the 20th meridian of east longitude and then turns southward along the 20th meridian to the tripoint between Namibia, Botswana, and South Africa in Kgalagadi Transnational Park. The 20th meridian continues southward as the boundary between Namibia and South Africa until it intersects the Orange River. From this intersection, the boundary follows the Orange downstream and westward to its mouth on the Atlantic Ocean.

HISTORICAL CONTEXT

The San people, or Bushmen, were the first inhabitants of Namibia. The San were nomads who survived by hunting and gathering. Various other tribes moved into Namibia from the north, east, and south beginning about 2,000 years ago. Given the dry desert climate, many of these tribes survived by herding livestock as opposed to crop agriculture.

Portuguese mariners first visited the coast of Namibia in the late 15th century. In the 18th and 19th centuries, traders from the Netherlands, Britain, and Germany established trading centers along the Namibian coast. However, given the very dry climate, none of these European settlers penetrated very far inland. In 1793, the Netherlands established a port at Walvis Bay, which is located on the only good deep-water harbor in present-day Namibia. Walvis Bay was ceded to Britain in 1797. In 1878, Britain annexed Walvis Bay formally as part of the Cape Colony in South Africa. Walvis Bay remained under British control and was later a part of South Africa until South Africa ceded it to independent Namibia in 1994.

In 1884, Germany claimed present-day Namibia with the exception of the Walvis Bay exclave under the name of German Southwest Africa. In 1890, a treaty between Germany and Britain gave control of the Caprivi Strip to German Southwest Africa. Control of the Caprivi Strip gave Germany access to the Zambezi River and hence gave it river access to the Indian Ocean.

Troops from South Africa, a former British colony and a member of the British Commonwealth, occupied German Southwest Africa during World War I. After the war, German Southwest Africa was placed under a South African mandate by the League of Nations, and it was renamed South-west Africa. South Africa continued to govern South-west Africa after World War II. White farmers from South Africa, who had begun to move into present-day Namibia in the 19th century, moved in larger numbers north of the Orange River in the early 20th century. Today about 20 percent of Namibia's people are of white or mixed-race ancestry.

After South Africa refused to consider granting independence to Namibia during the 1960s, South Africa's mandate over South-west Africa was revoked by the United Nations as the successor organization to the League of Nations. The International Court of Justice ruled in 1971 that South Africa's continued occupation of South-west Africa was illegal and that South Africa was obligated to withdraw its troops from South-west Africa. However, South Africa ignored this directive. The colonial government was dominated by Namibia's white minority.

In the 1970s, a proindependence organization known as the South-west Africa People's Organisation (SWAPO) began guerilla attacks on South African troops in South-west Africa. SWAPO's guerilla activities were launched from bases in Zambia and Angola. International efforts to settle the question of Namibia's status began in the 1970s and continued into the 1980s. A formal transition period began in 1989, and South Africa granted independence to Namibia in 1990. Since that time, Namibia has functioned successfully as a multiparty democracy.

CONTEMPORARY ISSUES

Since independence, secessionists in the Caprivi Strip have pushed for independence. Most of the Caprivi Strip's residents are members of the Lozi nation, which has more cultural, ethnic, and linguistic affinities with people in nearby Angola, Zambia, and Zimbabwe than with other nations in the rest of Namibia. In 1994, a paramilitary organization known as the Caprivi Liberation Front began to launch guerilla attacks against Namibians in the Caprivi Strip. Guerilla attacks continued intermittently for the next five years. In 1999, a brief civil war ended in the defeat of the Caprivi Liberation Front by Namibia's armed forces. Secessionists in the Caprivi Strip declared independence as the Free State of Caprivi in 2002, but the free state has not been recognized by Namibia or by the international community.

Namibia and Botswana have also disputed access to water on the Okavango River, which rises in Angola, forms a portion of the boundary between Namibia and Angola, and then flows across the Caprivi Strip into Botswana. Namibia has proposed to build a canal to divert water from the Okavango into Namibia. However, Botswana has opposed this plan on the grounds that enough water would be diverted into Namibia that little or no water would continue to flow downstream into Namibia. Efforts to address this issue are ongoing. In 1994, Namibia, Botswana, and Angola established the Okavango Basin Steering Committee, which is charged with managing this water resource that remains of great importance to all three arid countries.

See also   Angola, Botswana, South Africa, Zambia

Further Reading

Martin W. Lewis. "Problems in the panhandle: Namibia's Caprivi Strip." *Geocurrents*, September 13, 2011, http://geocurrents.info/geopolitics/problems-in-the-panhandle-namibia%E2%80%99s-caprivi-strip.

Emmanuel Ike Odugu. *Liberating Namibia: The long diplomatic struggle between the United Nations and South Africa.* Jefferson, NC: Mcfarland, 2011.

NIGER

OVERVIEW

The Republic of Niger is a former French colony in north-central Africa. Niger has a land area of about 490,000 square miles, making it about twice as large as Texas. The Sahara Desert covers the northern three-quarters of Niger. Most of its 15 million people live in the rainier southern part of the country. The country's name is taken from the Niger River, which is the largest river in West Africa; it flows through southwestern Niger and forms part of the country's boundary.

Niger's neighbors include Algeria and Libya to the north, Chad to the east, Nigeria to the south, Benin and Burkina Faso to the southwest, and Mali to the west. Niger's northern boundaries with Algeria and Libya cross very sparsely populated areas of the Sahara Desert. These boundaries are geometric, with the border between Niger and Algeria extending from southwest to northeast and the border between Niger and Libya trending from northwest to southeast. Both boundaries consist of straight lines connecting locally prominent physical landscape features. Only

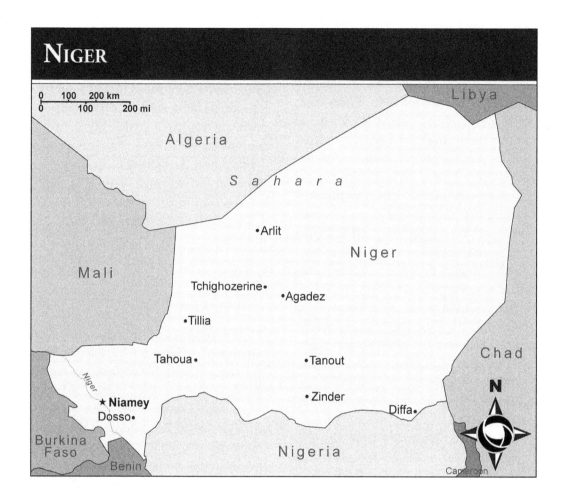

one paved road crosses the boundary with Algeria, and none cross the Niger-Libya boundary.

To the east, the boundary between Niger and Chad trends from north to south. Most of this boundary, which is also geometric, also crosses uninhabited territory. Lake Chad is located at the southern end of this boundary. The tripoint between Niger, Chad, and Nigeria is located in Lake Chad, where it intersects the boundary between Niger and Nigeria.

Niger's boundary with Nigeria is a complex geometric boundary that trends east to west from Lake Chad. To the west,

this boundary turns sharply southward at a point east of the city of Dosso. The Niger River forms much of the boundary between Niger and Benin. The Mekrou River, a tributary of the Niger, forms the southwestern portion of the Niger-Benin boundary. The boundary between Niger and Burkina Faso is more irregular but trends in a generally northwestward direction toward the boundary between Niger and Mali. The boundary between Niger and Mali is geometric, trending from west to east and then turning northward to intersect the boundary between these two countries and Algeria.

HISTORICAL CONTEXT

As is the case in much of sub-Saharan Africa, most of Niger's boundaries result from decisions made by European colonial powers. The boundaries cut across territories inhabited by various ethnic and cultural groups, increasing the potential for conflict.

The European colonial powers recognized French sovereignty over what is now Niger in the late 19th century. It was administered from Dakar in present-day Senegal. During the early 20th century, what is now Niger was part of the colony of Upper Senegal and Niger, which included present-day Niger, Mali, and Burkina Faso. Niger became a separate colony and a member of the French West Africa federation of colonies in 1922. The boundary between French West Africa and the other major federation of French colonies in Africa, French Equatorial Africa, became the boundary between Niger and Chad after the two countries became independent. Niger achieved independence in 1960.

With the exception of Libya and Nigeria, all of Niger's neighbors were also French colonies. The boundary between Libya and Niger was established by agreement between France and Italy in 1919. France and Britain agreed upon the boundary between present-day Niger and present-day Nigeria in 1890, with the boundaries modified by additional agreements in 1894, 1900, and 1910.

CONTEMPORARY ISSUES

Most of Niger's boundaries have been demarcated clearly. However, the boundary between Niger and Burkina Faso remains unclear. The original boundary was established by the French in 1927. However, after independence it became recognized that the boundary specified by the French had been delineated imprecisely and ambiguously. In 2010, the two countries requested that the International Court of Justice resolve the issue and demarcate the boundary clearly. In late 2010 and early 2011, however, tensions escalated, and each country accused the other's security forces of harassing local residents on the other side of the border. A demilitarized buffer zone was proposed within the border region pending resolution of the boundary dispute.

Controversy along the boundary between Niger and Mali may be more problematic. The boundary was demarcated fully in 1939, and the two countries ratified this boundary in 1962 after both had become independent from France. However, the boundary between Niger and Mali cuts across the traditional homeland of the Tuareg culture. About 6 million Tuareg live in northern Niger, northern Mali, and neighboring Libya and Algeria. The Tuareg are closely related to the Berber of North Africa, speak a language similar to the Berber language, and are related only distantly to the other cultures of Niger. The Tuareg homeland is populated sparsely relative to the rest of Niger. The province of Agadez, which extends northward into the Sahara Desert and in which most of Niger's Tuareg people live, contains more than half of Niger's land area but only about 3 percent of its populations.

Since Niger became an independent country, many Tuaregs have demanded more autonomy if not outright independence. These demands have intensified following the discovery of uranium in the

Tuareg-dominated areas of northern Niger. Uranium now accounts for more than 40 percent of Niger's export income. However, Tuareg activists have become concerned that they will see little benefit from uranium mining because the profits are controlled by the government, which is based in the south. On the other hand, the Tuareg have lost grazing rights, and their lands in Agadez have suffered environmental damage associated with mining activities. Clashes between guerillas representing a Tuareg-led separatist organization, the Niger Movement for Justice, and the government of Niger have been ongoing.

See also   Algeria, Benin, Burkina Faso, Chad, Libya, Mali, Nigeria

Further Reading

Steven Emerson. "Desert insurgency: Lessons from the third Tuareg rebellion." *Small Wars and Rebellions*, 22 (2011), pp. 669–687.

Cordula Meyer. "Tuareg activist takes on French nuclear company." *Spiegel.de Online*, April 2, 2010, http://www.spiegel.de/international/world/uranium-mining-in-niger-tuareg-activist-takes-on-french-nuclear-company-a-686774.html.

Nathalie Prevost. "Tuareg uprising in Mali threatens Niger." msnbc.com, May 3, 2012, http://www.msnbc.msn.com/id/47274703/ns/world_news/t/analysis-tuareg-uprising-mali-threatens-neighbor-niger/#.T-ckOPLDuSo.

NIGERIA

OVERVIEW

The Federal Republic of Nigeria is located on the coast of the Gulf of Guinea in west-central Africa. Its land area is 356,667 square miles, slightly larger than Texas and Oklahoma combined. With a population of about 175 million, Nigeria is by far the largest country in Africa by population and the sixth-largest country by population in the world. Northern Nigeria is located at the edge of the semiarid Sahel region, whereas southern Nigeria has a rainy climate and has been heavily forested. Its population is highly diverse, with numerous nations living within its boundaries. Nigeria has been plagued in recent years by conflict between residents of the predominantly Muslim north and the predominantly Christian south.

Nigeria's neighbors are Benin to the east, Niger to the north, Chad to the northeast, and Cameroon to the east and southeast. To the south, Nigeria has a coast on the Gulf of Guinea. The western portion of this coast is on the Bight of Benin, which is part of the Gulf. The boundary between Nigeria and Benin extends northward from the Bight of Benin. From the coast west of Nigeria's largest city and former capital city of Lagos, the boundary extends northward to the Okpara River, whose lower reaches and mouth are in Benin. The boundary follows the Okpara upstream and northward. South of the town of Parakou in Benin, the boundary leaves the Okpara and turns to the northeast. It then turns northward again until it reaches the tripoint between Nigeria, Benin, and Niger on the Niger River.

The boundary between Nigeria and Niger is geometric. From the tripoint between Nigeria, Niger, and Benin, this boundary continues northward following straight-line segments. Near the village of Dogondoutchi in Niger, the boundary turns eastward. It continues along numerous

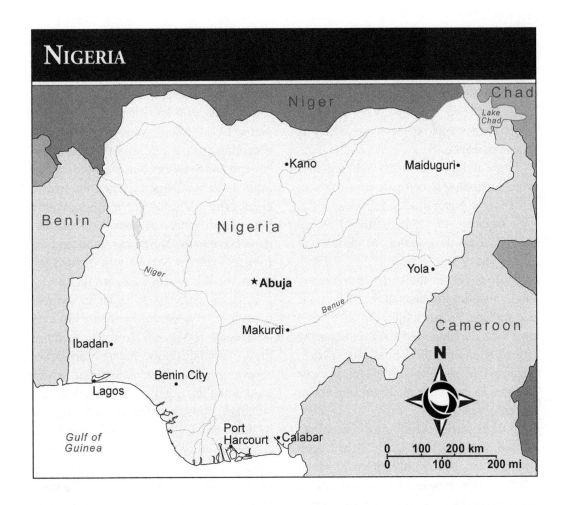

NIGERIA

straight-line segments eastward to Lake Chad. Lake Chad is shared between Nigeria, Niger, Chad, and Cameroon, and the entire boundary between Nigeria and Chad is located in the lake. The tripoint between Nigeria, Niger, and Chad and the tripoint between Nigeria, Chad, and Cameroon are located in Lake Chad.

From Lake Chad, the boundary between Nigeria and Cameroon extends in a generally southwesterly direction to the Gulf of Guinea. The northern part of the boundary follows straight-line segments to the confluence between the Benue River and the Faro River. From that confluence, the boundary follows the Faro River upstream and southwestward to a point near its source. The boundary then continues southwestward through the Cameroon Hills to the Donga River, which is another tributary of the Benue. The boundary follows the Donga upstream and northwestward. It then turns southwestward again, following straight-line segments to the gulf.

HISTORICAL CONTEXT

Present-day Nigeria has been governed by numerous kingdoms and city-states for thousands of years. The Oyo Empire ruled what is now southwestern Nigeria beginning in the 14th century. To the west, the

Benin Empire (not to be confused with the modern state of Benin) arose and took control of the area west of the Oyo Empire, continuing westward into present-day Benin and Togo. Present-day northwestern Nigeria became part of the Songhai Empire in around 1500.

These and other empires and kingdoms were continuing to compete for control of what is now Nigeria when European influence began in the 18th century. Present-day Nigeria was a center for the capture and export of slaves prior to the 19th century. However, in the early 19th century the British Empire banned the slave trade and forbade British subjects to participate in it. With the support of abolitionists in the United Kingdom, the British Royal Navy began to blockade the Gulf of Guinea coast in order to prevent the illegal exports of slaves.

In 1851, Britain began to concentrate its operations at Lagos, which had been founded by the Benin Empire in about 1700. Britain annexed Lagos and nearby areas along the coast as the Lagos Colony in 1861. In 1891, Britain established the Niger Coast Protectorate, which included the territory included in the Niger River delta along the Nigerian coast east of the Lagos Colony. Meanwhile, the Royal Niger Company took control of areas further upstream along the river. This area was added to the Niger Coast Protectorate in 1900. In 1906, the Lagos Colony was added to the protectorate, which became the Colony and Protectorate of Southern Nigeria.

The northern part of present-day Nigeria was placed under a British sphere of influence via the Treaty of Berlin, which established European spheres of influence throughout Africa. In order to counteract the increasing influence of France and Germany in nearby colonies, the British worked to consolidate their control over this region now known as Northern Nigeria. Local rulers were pressured into accepting British rule. In 1914, Northern Nigeria and Southern Nigeria were unified as the colony of Nigeria. Later, the British created three administrative regions within the colony. What had been Northern Nigeria became the Northern region, and the former Southern Nigeria was divided between the Western and Eastern regions.

African nationalists began to express opposition to continued British rule over the colony of Nigeria. However, many of these nationalist movements were associated with particular nations and ethnic groups within Nigeria. The creation of a Nigerian nationalist identity was hampered by the cultural, ethnic, and religious diversity of the colony. Nevertheless, efforts to create an independent and unified Nigeria intensified in the 1950s. Each of the three regions was given formal self-governing status in 1957 and 1958. Nigeria became independent within the British Commonwealth in 1960.

Following World War I, the former German colony of Cameroon was divided between British and French mandates by the League of Nations. The British mandate included two sections of territory along the eastern boundary of the Colony of Nigeria. The two sections were known as Southern Cameroons and Northern Cameroons, and the two were separated by the larger French mandate called Cameroun. As Cameroun prepared for independence as the state of Cameroon, residents of each British mandate were given the opportunity to vote on whether to join with Cameroon or Nigeria. A majority in Northern Cameroons voted for unification with Nigeria, and this territory was added to the Northern Region of Nigeria in 1961. The majority of voters in Southern Cameroons voted for unification with Cameroon.

Nigeria was constituted as a federal state, with power divided formally between Nigeria's federal government and those of its regions. The regions were later subdivided into the states that comprise Nigeria today. Conflicts between different nations soon arose. The dominant ethnic groups in the Northern Region were the Muslim Hausa and Fulani. The Yoruba were dominant in the Western Region, and the Igbo dominated the Eastern Region. The Yoruba are divided about evenly between Christians and Muslims, and the majority of Igbo are Christians. The Northern Region, which contained more than half of Nigeria's population and about three-quarters of its land area, had the most seats in Nigeria's parliament and dominated the government. The elected government was toppled by a military-backed coup d'état in 1966.

In 1967, the Eastern Region attempted to secede from the Federal Republic and to create an independent state known as Biafra. Some states recognized Biafra's independence, but the United States, Britain, and the Soviet Union did not do so, and they supported the Nigerian government's efforts to suppress Biafra's secession attempt. Civil war soon broke out. Over the next three years, an estimated 2 to 3 million Biafrans died from starvation, famine, disease, and in combat. A majority of the casualties were children. Biafra surrendered in 1970 and was reabsorbed into Nigeria.

After the Biafran war ended, Nigeria went through successive periods of civilian and military rule. Democracy was restored in 1999 after 16 years of military rule. Nigeria has significant oil deposits, and by the 1970s it had become a significant oil producer. Thus Nigeria's per capita income is higher than average for sub-Saharan Africa. Nigeria is Africa's leading oil producer and oil exporter. Some economists have criticized Nigeria for ignoring or neglecting other sectors of its economy, including agriculture and manufacturing, while focusing on oil production. For this reason, and because of the country's rapid population growth, Nigeria is now a net importer of food and agricultural products.

Conflicts between the north and the south have been commonplace. For example, conflicts and riots have emerged in Nigeria over the instituting of Sharia law. Some states in Muslim-majority northern Nigeria have adopted Sharia legal principles. For example, some require children to attend single-sex schools, ban alcohol and gambling, and ban women from playing soccer. The federal government of Nigeria is officially secular, and state laws in some Muslim-majority states are sometimes in conflict with Nigerian federal law. Another issue is whether non-Muslims who live in Muslim-majority states should be required to adhere to Sharia law.

After Nigeria became independent, Nigerian leaders decided to move the capital city of the country from Lagos, which is located on the coast of the Gulf of Guinea in the southwestern part of the country, to a more centralized location. As in some other countries, the decision to move the capital was based also on a conscious decision to separate economic power, which is heavily concentrated in Lagos, from political power. The central location was also selected in response to Nigeria's cultural, linguistic, and religious diversity. It was considered a neutral site relative to both the heavily Muslim north and the predominantly Christian south. Construction on the new capital of Abuja, which is located in the approximate geographic center of the country, began in the early 1980s. The seat of government was moved from Lagos to Abuja in 1991. About 800,000 people currently live in Abuja.

CONTEMPORARY ISSUES

Nigeria continues to address various disputes with its neighbors. Nigeria and Cameroon have disputed control of the Bakassi Peninsula since both countries became independent in the early 1960s. The Bakassi Peninsula extends from the mainland along the boundary between the two countries into the Gulf of Guinea. Both countries regard the Peninsula as important because it is believed to contain very lucrative petroleum and natural gas deposits and because the offshore waters are among the world's richest fishing grounds. Nigerian troops occupied the peninsula in 1993, but a cease-fire was negotiated and the dispute was referred to the International Court of Justice. The court granted sovereignty over the peninsula to Cameroon but ordered Cameroon to protect the rights of Nigerian residents of the area.

Nigeria's boundaries with Niger, Chad, and Cameroon in Lake Chad have yet to be delineated precisely. This issue is also important in that Lake Chad also contains valuable oil deposits. Northern Nigeria also faces the possibility of water shortages given very rapid population growth and ongoing droughts. The two major sources of water for northern Nigeria are the Niger River and Lake Chad, both of which are shared with neighboring countries. Nigeria has joined with eight other countries that include parts of the Niger drainage basin to form the Niger Basin Authority in order to manage the river and its water resources.

See also   Benin, Cameroon, Chad, Niger

Further Reading

Adekeye Adebajo and Abdul Raufu Mustapha. *Gulliver's troubles: Nigeria's foreign policy after the Cold War*. Durban, South Africa: University of KwaZula-Natal Press, 2008.

BBC News. "Border disputes an African colonial legacy." October 10, 2002, http://news.bbc.co.uk/2/hi/africa/2316 645.stm.

John Campbell. *Nigeria: Dancing on the brink*. Lanham, MD: Rowman and Littlefield, 2010.

Adedoyin J. Omede. "Nigeria's relations with her neighbours." *Studies of Tribes and Tribals*, 4 (2006), pp. 7–17.

Atah Pine. "Nigerian foreign policy, 1960–2011: Fifty-one years of conceptual confusion." *Modernghana.com*, October 4, 2011, http://www.modernghana.com/news/354264/1/nigeria-foreign-policy-1960–2011-fifty-one-years-o.html.

REPUBLIC OF THE CONGO

OVERVIEW

The Republic of the Congo is located in west-central Africa. It is often called Congo-Brazzaville after its capital city in order to avoid confusion with its larger neighbor,

REPUBLIC OF THE CONGO

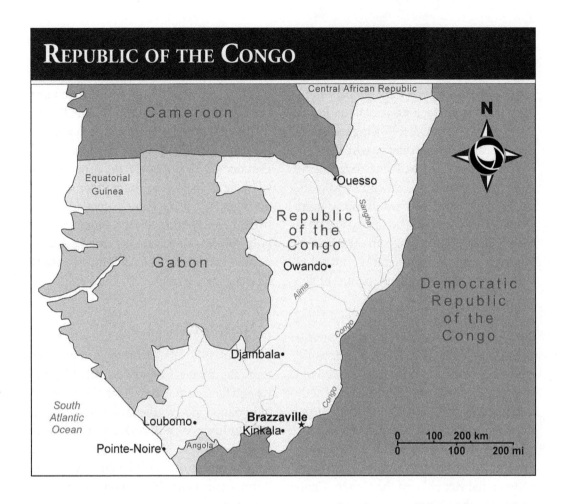

the Democratic Republic of the Congo, or Congo-Kinshasa. The Republic of the Congo has a land area of 132,047 square miles, slightly smaller than Montana. Its population is about 4 million.

The Republic of the Congo has boundaries with Gabon to the west, Cameroon to the northwest, the Central African Republic to the north, the Democratic Republic of the Congo to the east and south, and the Angolan exclave of Cabinda to the southwest. The Republic of the Congo also has a short coastline on the Atlantic Ocean to the southwest. The boundary between the Republic of the Congo and Gabon extends in a generally northeasterly direction inland from the Conkouati Nature Reserve on the Atlantic coast. The territory on both sides of the boundary is heavily forested and sparsely populated. Much of this boundary is highly irregular, following numerous short straight-line segments. The general trend of the boundary is northeastward around the reserve. From there it trends northward past another reserved area in the Republic of the Congo known as the Domaine du Chasse de Mont Marvoumbou.

North and east of this reserved area, the boundary generally follows a drainage divide separating the waters of the Ivindo River in Gabon from streams flowing eastward into the Republic of the Congo. The boundary turns eastward north of this reserve and trends in a generally easterly direction to Bateke Plateau National Park in Gabon. From the park, the boundary turns northward until reaching the Djoua River. It then turns westward, following the Djoua downstream to its confluence with the Aïna River. The confluence of the Djoua and the Aïna forms the Ivindo, which flows downstream and southwestward to the Atlantic Ocean. However, the boundary between the Republic of the Congo and Gabon follows the Aïna upstream and northward to the tripoint between the Republic of the Congo, Gabon, and Cameroon.

The boundary between the Republic of the Congo and Cameroon extends eastward from this tripoint. It extends eastward along straight-line segments located on and near the 2nd parallel of north latitude to a point near the town of Ouesso in the Republic of the Congo. From Ouesso, the boundary turns northward and follows the Ngoko River upstream to the tripoint between the Republic of the Congo, Cameroon, and the Central African Republic.

The boundary between the Republic of the Congo and the Central African Republic continues in a northeasterly direction from this tripoint. At Dzangai-Sangha National Park in the Central African Republic, the boundary turns eastward to the Lobaye River, which it follows eastward to its confluence with the Ubangi River. The tripoint between the Republic of the Congo, the Central African Republic, and the Democratic Republic is located at this confluence.

The boundary between the Republic of the Congo and the Democratic Republic of the Congo follows the Ubangi downstream and southward to its confluence with the Congo River. From there, it continues downstream along the Congo past the Republic of the Congo's capital city of Brazzaville. Downstream from Brazzaville, the boundary leaves the Congo River and turns northward to Mangroves National Park in Republic of the Congo. The boundary between the Republic of the Congo, the Democratic Republic of the Congo, and Cabinda is located at the northern end of the boundary. From there the boundary between the Republic of the Congo and Angola follows short straight-line segments northwestward and then southwestward to the Atlantic seacoast.

HISTORICAL CONTEXT

About 1400, much of what is now the Republic of the Congo was ruled by the Kongo Kingdom, from which the river and the country derive their names. In 1482, the Portuguese sailor Diogo Cao made contact with the Kongo Kingdom on the lower reaches of the Congo River. The Portuguese made this region a center for the trans-Atlantic slave trade, which continued for the next three centuries.

In the 19th century, the Portuguese competed with France and Belgium for influence in the Congo River basin. After the Berlin Conference divided Africa into European spheres of influence in 1884, the region was divided among Portugal, Belgium, and France. Portugal obtained Cabinda, and the Congo River became the boundary between Belgian territory, which would become the Democratic Republic of the Congo, to the south and east and French territory, which would become the Republic of the Congo, to the north and west. The French colony was established formally in 1886 and was known originally as the

Colony of Gabon and Congo. Its name was changed to French Congo in 1891. In 1910, French Congo became part of French Equatorial Africa along with present-day Gabon, the Central African Republic, and Chad. After World War I, Cameroon was added to French Equatorial Africa after administration of Cameroon was transferred from Germany to France by the League of Nations.

French colonial rule continued until 1960, when French Equatorial Africa was dissolved and each of its component units became an independent sovereign state. In 1968, the Republic of the Congo's president was deposed in a military coup d'état led by a military officer, Captain Marien Ngouabi. Ngouabi assumed dictatorial powers and began to govern the Republic of the Congo as a Marxist-Leninist communist state. Ngouabi was assassinated in 1977, but his successors maintained the Republic of the Congo as a Marxist state until the early 1990s. During that period the Republic of the Congo maintained close relationships with the Soviet Union and its allies. The first multiparty election since the 1968 coup was held in 1992. However, civil war between rival political factions broke out in 1997, causing thousands of deaths and displacing hundreds of thousands of people. The war ended in 1999, but multiparty democracy has yet to return to the Republic of the Congo. The Republic of the Congo has substantial oil reserves, and today about two-thirds of its export income comes from petroleum products.

CONTEMPORARY ISSUES

The Republic of the Congo's boundaries were drawn during the late 19th century by the European colonial powers. The general outline of the boundaries between the Republic of the Congo and Cabinda and between the Republic of the Congo and the Democratic Republic of the Congo were determined via the Treaty of Berlin. The Republic of the Congo's other neighbors were fellow components of French Equatorial Africa. The boundaries of the Republic of the Congo are stable and uncontested. Like many other sub-Saharan countries, the Republic of the Congo continues to struggle with poverty and lack of economic development while concerns about whether multiparty democracy will succeed continue.

See also Cameroon, Central African Republic, Democratic Republic of the Congo, Gabon

Further Reading

Africa News Update. "Congo-Brazzaville: Post-election crackdown on opposition." October 12, 2009, http://www.afrika.no/Detailed/18800.html.

Nicholas Shaxson. *Poisoned wells: The dirty politics of African oil.* London: Palgrave Macmillan, 2008.

RWANDA

OVERVIEW

The Republic of Rwanda is a landlocked state located in east-central Africa. It has a land area of 10,169 square miles, about the size of Maryland. Its population is about 12 million.

Rwanda shares boundaries with Uganda to the north, Tanzania to the east, Burundi to the south, and the Democratic Republic of the Congo to the west. The tripoint

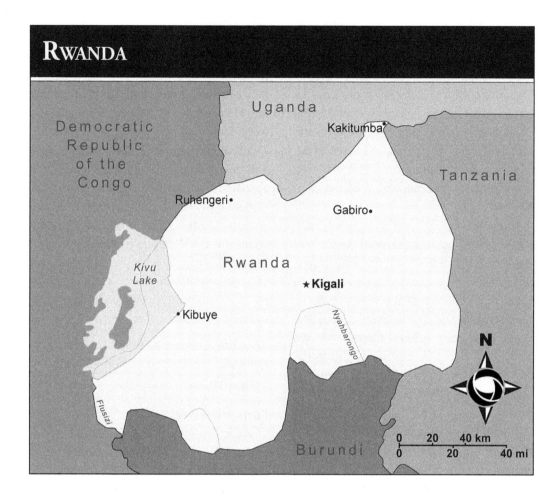

RWANDA

between Rwanda, Uganda, and the Democratic Republic of the Congo is at Mount Sabyinyo. From Mount Sabyinyo, the boundary between Rwanda and Uganda extends eastward. It follows short straight-line segments and drainage divides to the Lubirizi River. It then follows the Lubirizi River downstream to its confluence with the Tshinzinga River and the Tshinzinga downstream to its confluence with the Kagitumba. The tripoint between Rwanda, Uganda, and Tanzania is located at the confluence between the Kagitumba and the Kagera River, which at this point turns from flowing north to flowing east into Lake Victoria.

From the tripoint between Rwanda, Uganda, and Tanzania, the Kagera forms the entire boundary between Rwanda and Tanzania. This boundary follows the Kagera upstream and southward. Near Tanzania's Bungi Game Reserve, the boundary turns westward, still following the Kagera upstream, to the tripoint between Rwanda, Tanzania, and Burundi at the confluence of the Kagera and its tributary, the Mwibu River. The boundary between Rwanda and Burundi follows the Kagera upstream to another tributary, the Nyabarongo River. It continues along the Nyabarongo upstream and westward to Lake Rweru and then extends westward following streams and short-line segments to the Mabono River. From that point, the boundary follows the Mabono southward, westward, and downstream to its confluence with the Ruwa River, which it follows to the tripoint between Rwanda, Burundi, and the Democratic Republic of the Congo where the Ruwa empties into the Ruzizi River.

The boundary between Rwanda and the Democratic Republic of the Congo follows the Ruzizi upstream and northwards to Lake Kivu, where the Ruzizi originates. Lake Kivu is one of the African Great Lakes, and it forms the central section of the boundary between Rwanda and the Democratic Republic of the Congo. At the north end of Lake Kivu, the boundary extends northeastward from a point between the city of Gisenyi and the adjacent city of Goma in the Democratic Republic of the Congo. With a combined population of nearly half a million, the Gisenyi-Goma conurbation is one of the largest cross-border urbanized areas in Africa. From Gisenyi, the boundary between Rwanda and the Democratic Republic of the Congo extends northeastward across mountains to Mount Sabyinyo. Many of these mountains are volcanoes, and the border region experiences more volcanic activity than does anywhere else in Africa.

HISTORICAL CONTEXT

For hundreds of years, the territory now occupied by Rwanda has been plagued by ethnic violence between the majority Hutu and minority Tutsi populations. Today, about 85 percent of Rwandans are Hutu. In the 15th century, the Kingdom of Rwanda took control of most of the territory included within present-day Rwanda. The kingdom's rulers were Tutsi, who also controlled most of the kingdom's wealth. Later kings dispossessed the Hutu of much of their lands, which were given to Tutsi landowners while the Hutu provided most of the manual labor on the land.

Europeans had little contact with the Kingdom of Rwanda until the late 19th century. In 1890, an agreement between Germany, Britain, and Belgium divided central Africa into spheres of influence associated with each country. Rwanda and present-day Burundi became part of the German Empire, while what is now the Democratic Republic of the Congo became a Belgian colony, and Uganda became a British protectorate. Rwanda and Burundi were administered jointly as the colony of Ruanda-Urundi.

After World War I, Ruanda-Urundi was assigned to Belgium as a League of Nations mandate. The Belgians continued to favor Tutsi interests at the expense of the majority Hutu population. All residents of the colony were required to carry identity cards that identified each resident as a Hutu or a Tutsi. The United Nations reaffirmed the Belgian mandate over Ruanda-Urundi after World War II.

In the 1950s, independence sentiment in Ruanda-Urundi increased. Demands for independence in present-day Rwanda were coupled with ethnic conflict, reflecting Hutu resentment of the Tutsi who continued to control the monarchy and much of the country's wealth. Armed conflict between the Hutu and the Tutsi began in 1959. As many as 100,000 Tutsi were killed, and at least 150,000 Tutsi, including the last king of Rwanda, fled to neighboring countries. In 1961, Belgium decided to divide Ruanda-Urundi into what would become the separate states of Rwanda and Burundi. The following year, a referendum was held, and an overwhelming majority of Rwandans voted to abolish the monarchy and establish a republic. Rwanda became independent in 1962.

After independence, the government of newly independent Rwanda was dominated by the Hutu. Many Tutsi fled to neighboring Burundi or Uganda. A Tutsi-dominated group known as the Rwandan Patriotic Front (RPF) became active in Uganda in the late 1980s. The Rwandan Patriotic Front's military wing, the Rwandan Patriotic Army, invaded northern Rwanda in 1990. The invasion triggered the Rwandan Civil War, which continued until a cease-fire agreement was negotiated in 1993.

In 1994, an airplane carrying President Juvenal Habyarimana, a Hutu, was shot down, and Habyarimana was killed. The crash triggered the Rwandan Genocide, in which Hutu massacred thousands of Tutsi. As many as 1 million Tutsi were killed during the Rwandan Genocide. Another 2 million Rwandans left the country as refugees. The RPF seized control of the government in 1994, and many of the refugees were Hutu who feared that the Tutsi-dominated RPF would initiate reprisals against the Hutu in response to the Rwandan Genocide. However, the RPF eliminated the practice of forcing Rwandans to carry ethnic identification papers and attempted to promote reconciliation between the Tutsi and the Hutu. Many Rwandan refugees returned to the country. Rwanda's government has promoted economic development and integration into the world economy but has been criticized widely by the international community for human rights violations.

CONTEMPORARY ISSUES

Today, Rwanda's foreign relations continue to be affected by the aftermath of the Rwandan Civil War and the Rwandan Genocide. Although most of the Tutsi and Hutu refugees who left the country during the early 1990s have returned to Rwanda, thousands of refugees continue to live outside Rwanda. The current government has endeavored to ease tensions between the Hutu and the Tutsi, although tensions between the two ethnic groups continue. Rwanda's relationships with the Democratic Republic of the Congo were strained during the 1990s. Rwanda's government accused the government of the Democratic Republic of the Congo of supporting opponents of the RPF intent on toppling their government. However, in 2009 the two countries resumed diplomatic relations.

See also Burundi, Democratic Republic of the Congo, Tanzania, Uganda

Further Reading

BBC News. "New era for DR Congo and Rwanda." August 22, 2009, http://news.bbc.co.uk/2/hi/africa/8188715.stm.

Mark Doyle. "Rewriting Rwanda." *Foreign Policy*, April 25, 2006, http://www.foreignpolicy.com/articles/2006/04/25/rewriting_rwanda.

Gerard Prunier. *Africa's world war: Congo, the Rwandan genocide, and the making of a continental catastrophe.* New York: Oxford University Press, 2011.

Scott Straus and Lars Waldorf (eds.). *Remaking Rwanda: State building and human rights after mass violence.* Madison: University of Wisconsin Press, 2011.

SAO TOME AND PRINCIPE

OVERVIEW

The Democratic Republic of Sao Tome and Principe is an island country located in the Gulf of Guinea off the west coast of Africa. The larger island, Sao Tome, is located just north of the equator. Both islands are volcanic and are part of an ancient volcanic mountain range that extends northeastward from Sao Tome and Principe to the island of Bioko in Equatorial Guinea and onto the mainland of Cameroon. The overall land area of Sao Tome and Principe is 372 square miles, smaller than Guam and about five times the size of the District of Columbia. The population is about 165,000. Sao Tome is the larger of the two islands, with about 90 percent of the country's land area and 97 percent of its population. The nearest land neighbor of Sao Tome and Principe is Gabon, whose west coast is about 140 miles to the east across the Gulf of Guinea.

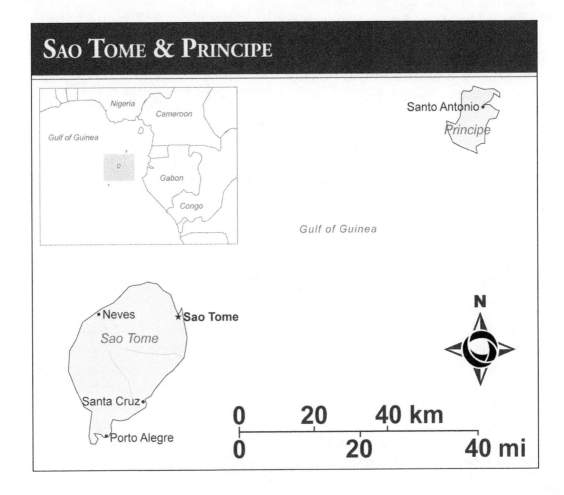

HISTORICAL CONTEXT

The islands of Sao Tome and Principe were uninhabited until they were discovered by Portuguese mariners in the 1470s. The first permanent settlement was established on Sao Tome in 1493. In the 16th century, the Portuguese developed large sugar plantations on Sao Tome, with labor provided by slaves imported from the African mainland. However, Sao Tome's sugar production on Sao Tome could not compete with production from European colonies in the Caribbean, and the industry languished. In the 19th century, coffee and cacao were introduced and began to be cultivated for export. Slavery was abolished legally in 1876, but concerns over forced labor and unsafe working conditions for former slaves continued well into the 20th century. Sao Tome became independent in 1975 and has maintained itself as a multiparty democracy ever since.

Further Reading

Gerhard Seibert. *Comrades, clients, and cousins: Socialism and democratization in Sao Tome and Principe.* Leiden, Netherlands: Brill.

SENEGAL

OVERVIEW

The Republic of Senegal is located in West Africa along the Atlantic Ocean. Its capital city of Dakar is the westernmost point on the mainland of Africa. Senegal's land area is 76,000 square miles, the size of South Dakota. Its population is about 13 million.

Senegal's neighbors are Mauritania to the north, Mali to the east, and Guinea and Guinea-Bissau to the south. Senegal also surrounds the Gambia, which extends from its short coast on the Atlantic inland along the Gambia River. Senegal itself has a longer, discontinuous coast on the Atlantic. The boundary between Senegal and Mauritania follows the Senegal River from the river's mouth in the Atlantic eastward and upstream to the tripoint between Senegal, Mauritania, and Mali near the Senegalese town of Bakel. This tripoint is located near the confluence of the Senegal and the Falémé River. Much of the boundary between Senegal and Mali follows the Falémé upstream and southward. However, Senegalese territory includes a small strip of land east of the Falémé. Further upstream, the Falémé forms the boundary once again, continuing southward to the tripoint between Senegal, Mali, and Guinea.

The Falémé forms a brief portion of the boundary between Senegal and Guinea. From the Falémé, it then follows straight-line segments and short river segments westward to the Tanague River, and then down the Tanague to the 12° 40′ 30″ parallel of north latitude, which it then follows westward to the tripoint between Senegal, Guinea, and Guinea-Bissau. The boundary between Senegal and Guinea-Bissau continues along this parallel and then follows other straight-line segments extending in a west-southwesterly direction to the Atlantic coast. The western portion of this border is roughly equidistant between the Casamance River in Senegal and the Rio Cachou in Guinea-Bissau. It is located generally 20 to 30 miles south of the Casamance, which flows westward into the Atlantic and drains this southwestern portion of Senegal. The Gambia includes a strip of land 20 to 30 miles wide along the

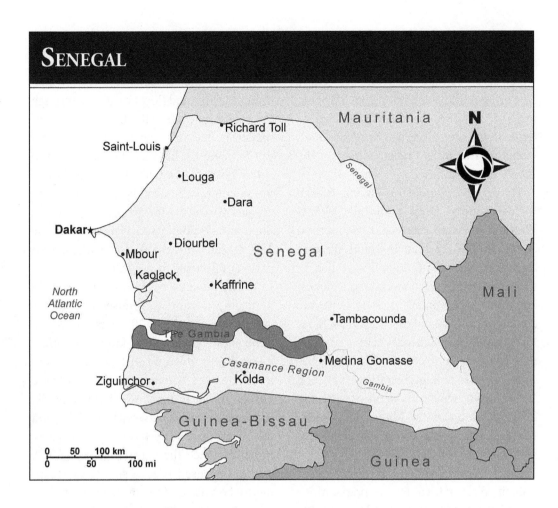

SENEGAL

Gambia River, which flows from east to west through the Gambia. The Gambia is about 150 miles long and is about 30 miles wide at its widest point, including territory both north and south of the main channel of the river.

HISTORICAL CONTEXT

Present-day Senegal was ruled by various West African empires for hundreds of years before it was settled by Europeans. Eastern Senegal was on the western periphery of the Ghanaian Empire, which dominated portions of inland West Africa from the 9th to the 13th century AD. The

Mali Empire became dominant in the valleys of the Gambia, Senegal, and upper Niger River between the 13th and the 17th centuries.

Beginning in the 15th century, European powers competed with one another for control of trade along the coast of present-day Senegal. France established the port city of Saint Louis near the mouth of the Senegal River in 1659. Saint Louis became an important center for the trans-Atlantic slave trade. Over several centuries, millions of people from Senegal and other portions of West Africa were captured, enslaved, and transported across the Atlantic Ocean to North, Central, and South

America. Meanwhile, France took over the island of Goree in present-day Dakar, which had been administered previously by Portugal, the Netherlands, and Britain, in 1677. In 1783, Britain relinquished its rights to the area along the Senegal River, including Dakar, to France as part of the Treaty of Versailles.

During the Napoleonic Wars, British forces captured Saint Louis and Goree. These ports were returned to France on condition that the French would agree to abolish the slave trade from these cities. In the 19th century, French traders, officials, and military personnel began to penetrate the interior of Senegal eastward from Saint Louis and Dakar. Senegal became an overseas colony of France in 1895. Dakar became the seat of administration of French West Africa, which included present-day Senegal along with Mauritania, Mali, Niger, Benin, Cote d'Ivoire, Burkina Faso, and Guinea.

After World War II, the colonies of French West Africa began preparations for independence. Senegal and present-day Mali, then known as French Sudan, united to form the Mali Federation in 1959. The Mali Federation became independent in 1960 but split apart to form the independent countries of Senegal and Mali only two months later. During the 1980s, Senegal and the Gambia formed a loose confederation known as Senegambia. However, efforts to unify the two countries further were abandoned in 1989.

CONTEMPORARY ISSUES

A separatist movement has arisen in Casamance, which is located in southwestern Senegal between Senegal's boundaries with the Gambia to the north and Guinea-Bissau to the south. The region derives its name from the Casamance River, which drains the area and flows westward through the region into the Atlantic Ocean. Casamance is cut off from Dakar and northern Senegal by land by the Gambia, and it has historic ties with the former Portuguese colony of Portuguese Guinea (now Guinea-Bissau). Moreover, Casamance's population is dominated by members of the Jola nation, while the Wolof are the largest nation of Senegal as a whole.

When Senegal became independent in 1960, its government promised Casamance independence within 20 years. After the Senegalese government failed to follow up on that promise, a resistance movement known as the Movement of Democratic Forces of Casamance (MDFC) arose. Armed skirmishes between the MDFC and the Senegalese army have occurred intermittently since the early 1980s. In 2010, Senegal accused Iran of supplying weapons to the MDFC. The conflict over the status of Casamance has displaced thousands of people, many of whom have crossed the borders into the Gambia or Guinea-Bissau.

See also   Guinea, Guinea-Bissau, Mali, Mauritania, the Gambia

Further Reading

Daily Observer. "Senegambia revisited." April 7, 2008, http://observer.gm/af rica/gambia/article/2008/4/7/ senegambia-revisited.

Wagane Faye. "The Casamance separatism: From independence claim to resource logic." M.S. thesis, Naval Postgraduate School, 2006, http://calhoun.nps. edu/public/bitstream/handle/10945/2750/ 06Jun_Faye.pdf?sequence=1.

David Lewis. "Casamance conflict is unhealed sore for Senegal." *Reuters*, February 25, 2012, http://www.reuters.com/article/2012/02/25/us-senegal-casamance-idUSTRE81O09C20120225.

Charles Piot. *Nostalgia for the future: West Africa after the Cold War*. Chicago: University of Chicago Press, 2010.

SEYCHELLES

OVERVIEW

The Republic of Seychelles is an island state located in the western Pacific Ocean. The Seychelles archipelago consists of about 155 islands, most of which are small and uninhabited. The overall land area of Seychelles is 174 square miles, slightly more than twice as large as the District of Columbia. The population is about 87,000. About 90 percent of the people of Seychelles live on the largest island of Mahe, which contains about a third of the country's land area.

Seychelles is about 950 miles north-northeast of Madagascar, about 1,100 miles east of the coast of Kenya on the mainland of Africa, and over 1,500 miles southwest of the mainland of India.

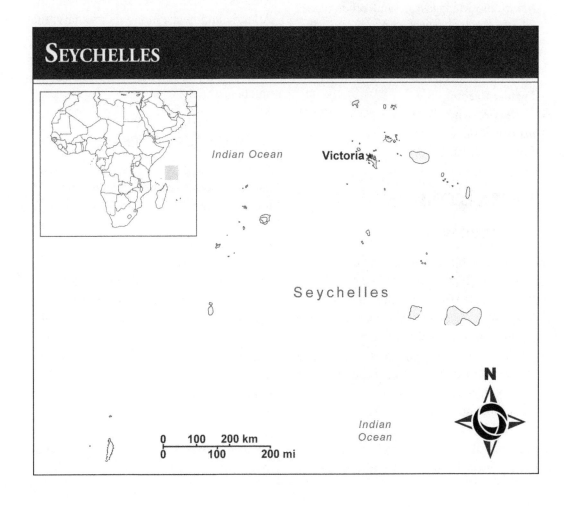

SEYCHELLES

Indian Ocean

Victoria

Seychelles

Indian Ocean

N

0   100   200 km
0   100   200 mi

HISTORICAL CONTEXT

The Seychelles were probably visited by Indonesian, Indian, and Arab seafarers before and during the Middle Ages. The first European known to have visited the Seychelles was the Portuguese mariner Vasco de Gama, who sighted them in 1502. France claimed sovereignty over the Seychelles in 1754 and developed the islands as centers for production of spices and tropical crops. Slaves from Africa were imported to provide a labor force.

Britain took over the Seychelles in 1811. After the abolition of slavery throughout the British Empire, the local labor force was augmented by former slaves from Mauritius, Madagascar, and other places who worked as contract laborers for plantation owners. Seychelles became independent from Britain in 1976.

Further Reading

Deryck Scarr. *Seychelles since 1770: A history of slave and post-slavery society.* London: Hurst, 2000.

SIERRA LEONE

OVERVIEW

The Republic of Sierra Leone is located along the Atlantic coast of West Africa. It has a land area of 27,699, making it slightly larger than West Virginia. Sierra Leone's population is about 6.5 million.

Sierra Leone's neighbors are Guinea to the north and east and Liberia to the southeast. Southwestern Sierra Leone has a coastline on the Atlantic Ocean. Most of the boundary between Sierra Leone and Guinea follows rivers and other physical features. From the Atlantic Ocean, it trends northeastward toward the Outamba Kilimi National Park. Northeast of the park, the boundary follows the 10th parallel of latitude eastward to a point northeast of the village of Damsodia. From there the boundary trends southeastward and then southward following a complex series of short segments to a point near the village of Kelama. It then trends northeastward for about 20 miles to the tripoint between Sierra Leone, Guinea, and Liberia.

The boundary between Sierra Leone and Liberia extends in a southwesterly direction from the tripoint between Sierra Leone, Liberia, and Guinea to the Atlantic Ocean. The southwestern portion of the boundary follows the Mano River upstream from the Atlantic and hence along its tributary, the Morro River. Further inland, it follows a complex series of geometric lines northeastward to the Mauwa and Magoni rivers and hence to the tripoint.

HISTORICAL OVERVIEW

Beginning in 1787, the British established present-day Sierra Leone as a haven for descendants of Africans who had been captured and sold into slavery. People from England, present-day Canada, and the West Indies settled in what is now Sierra Leone. Some of Sierra Leone's settlers were escaped slaves from the southern United States who had fought with the British Army during the American Revolution. These settlers and their descendants became known as Creoles or Krios. The Krios dominated the local economy and were often resented by indigenous people living in the colony. Sierra Leone remained a British colony until becoming independent in 1961.

SIERRA LEONE

For much of its history as an independent country, Sierra Leone has experienced ethnic conflict, civil war, and one-party governance. The country remains poor although mineral resources, especially diamonds, are leading contributors to Sierra Leone's economy. Sierra Leone also has one of the world's largest deposits of rutile, which is a titanium ore used in welding and in making paint.

Sierra Leone's boundaries were established in the 19th century. The boundary between Sierra Leone and Guinea was established by an agreement between Britain and France, which controlled the two colonies respectively, in 1882. Britain and Liberia agreed to the Mano River as the boundary between Sierra Leone and Liberia in 1885. The inland portion of the boundary was agreed upon by treaty in 1911.

CONTEMPORARY ISSUES

Although Sierra Leone's boundaries are not contested, boundary issues between Sierra Leone and its neighbors remain. During the 1990s, both Liberia and Sierra Leone experienced civil wars. A rebel army known as the Revolutionary United Front (RUF) attempted to seize control of Sierra Leone's government beginning in

1991. The RUF was supported by the National Patriotic Front of Liberia, which was attempting to seize power in Liberia at the same time. The RUF assumed control of parts of eastern and southern Sierra Leone adjacent to the boundary with Liberia. Supporters of both governments accused the RUF of selling diamonds in order to finance the rebel groups in both countries. The sale of these blood diamonds, some of which were smuggled illegally across the boundary into Liberia, allowed the RUF to purchase weapons and armaments. Meanwhile, thousands of Liberian refugees fled across the international boundary into Sierra Leone, where many were forced to join the RUF's military forces. The war ended in 2002 with the signing of the Lome Peace Accord, and an estimated 50,000 Sierra Leone citizens are believed to have lost their lives. The conflict provided a background to the 2006 movie *Blood Diamond*, starring Leonardo DiCaprio.

Sierra Leone has also been involved in an ongoing boundary dispute with Guinea. This dispute involves control of the village of Yenga, northwest of the tripoint between Sierra Leone, Guinea, and Liberia. Yenga was first occupied by Guinean troops during Sierra Leone's civil war in 1999, and Guinea continued to occupy the village after the war ended in 2001. Although only about 100 people live in Yenga, it is located along the major road connecting the interior of Sierra Leone with the interior of Guinea. Hence Yenga is important to control of the boundary.

See also   Guinea, Liberia

Further Reading

Greg Campbell. *Blood diamonds: Tracing the deadly path of the world's most precious stones.* New York: Basic Books, 2005.

Mohamed Massaquoi. "Sierra Leone: Guinea not ready to give up Yenga." *Allafrica.com*, June 14, 2012, http://allafrica.com/stories/201206150538.html.

Marda Mustapha and Joseph J. Bangura. *Sierra Leone beyond the Lome Peace Accord.* New York: Palgrave Macmillan, 2010.

SOMALIA

OVERVIEW

The Somali Republic occupies the eastern portion of the Horn of Africa along the coasts of the Arabian Gulf and the Indian Ocean. It has a land area of 246,200 square miles, slightly smaller than Texas. Somalia's population is approximately 11 million. The large majority of Somalia's people are ethnic Somalis. Despite the fact that Somalia is more ethnically homogeneous than most states in sub-Saharan Africa, Somalia is generally recognized as a failed state. It has lacked a fully functional central government since the early 1990s and remains embroiled in civil war.

Somalia's neighbors are Djibouti to the northwest, Ethiopia to the west, and Kenya to the south. It has a coastline on the Gulf of Aden, which separates Somalia from the Arabian Peninsula, to the north. Somalia has a longer coastline on the Indian Ocean to the southeast. Somalia's boundaries are geometric, and many cross sparsely populated deserts with few permanent settlements. The boundary between Somalia and Djibouti is a single long line segment that extends southwestward from the Gulf of Aden coast inland for about 40 miles to

SOMALIA

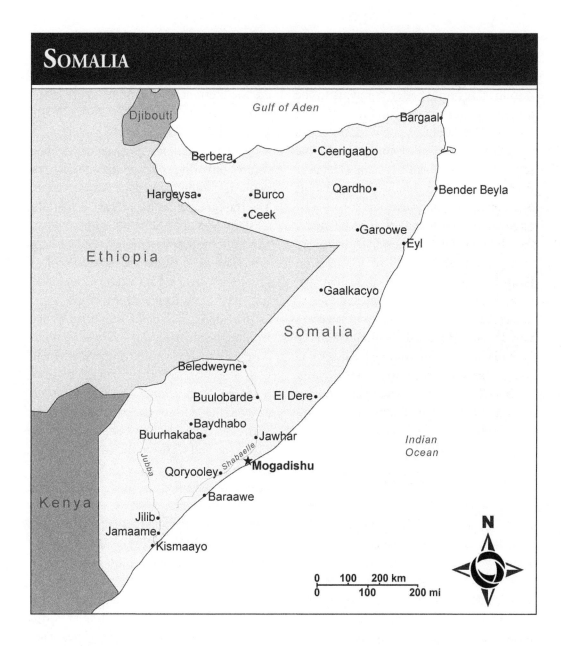

the tripoint between Somalia, Djibouti, and Ethiopia. From there, the same segment continues briefly as the boundary between Somalia and Ethiopia. It continues southwestward along straight-line segments and then turns southeastward at a point about 50 miles northwest of the Somali town of Boorama, which is the only significant settlement in this boundary region.

The boundary between Somalia and Ethiopia continues southeastward along straight-line segments past Boorama, reaching a longer diagonal line that extends in an east-southeastward direction. South of the village of Laascaanood, the boundary turns to the east, following another long, straight segment. The boundary turns abruptly to the southwest, following another diagonal straight-line segment that extends for more than 100 miles to a point near the town of Beledwayne. From there it follows several shorter segments to the tripoint between Somalia, Ethiopia, and Kenya. The boundary between Somalia and Kenya consists of four straight-line segments. A diagonal segment extending from northeast to southwest represents this boundary southwestward to the 41st meridian of east longitude. The boundary then follows the 41st meridian southward to a point slightly south of the equator. From there it follows a straight-line segment that extends in a southeasterly direction toward the Indian Ocean and separates Lag Badana-Bushbush National Park in Somalia from Boni National Reserve in Kenya. Between these two national parks, the boundary turns southward and follows a short line segment southward to the Indian Ocean.

HISTORICAL CONTEXT

Archaeologists have discovered cave paintings in northern Somalia that are believed to have been produced more than 10,000 years ago. Somalis are believed to have been the first culture to domesticate camels and use them as beasts of burden. By the first millennium BC, trade networks between present-day Somalia and the cultures of the Mediterranean Sea region, including the Roman Empire, were developed. Trade was conducted over land using camels and by water using the Red Sea. Overseas trade with Arab merchants from the Arabian Peninsula was also developed. Indian traders also visited the Indian Ocean coast of present-day Somalia and conducted trade with local inhabitants

of the coastal regions. By the Middle Ages Somalia had emerged as a major center for trade with the Arab world, the countries of the Mediterranean, and South Asia. In the seventh century AD, Arab traders brought Islam to present-day Somalia.

Several kingdoms and sultanates took control of various parts of present-day Somalia during and after the Middle Ages. The Ifat Sultanate ruled present-day northwestern Somalia, Djibouti, and some of eastern Ethiopia beginning in the 13th century. The Adal Sultanate took control of this region in the 15th century, supplanting the Ifat Sultanate. Meanwhile, what is now southern Somalia was ruled by the Ajuuraan Sultanate. All of these regimes promoted trade along the Indian Ocean and Gulf of Aden coasts. Trade continued from ports on the Somali coast to ports as far away as the Mediterranean Sea lands to the north and to the Indian Peninsula, Southeast Asia, and China to the east.

Having circumnavigated Africa, Portuguese mariners became the first Europeans to visit the Somali coast by sea in the late 15th century. Portugal attempted to overthrow the local Somali sultanates and seize control of their valuable ports on the Indian Ocean. However, Somali resistance prevented the Portuguese from achieving this goal. In their resistance to potential Portuguese conquest, the Somali regimes were aided by the Ottoman Empire, which by this time had become an active participant in Somali trade.

During the scramble for Africa, Britain claimed present-day northern Somalia. However, Somali sultanates resisted British efforts to establish control of this region. The Somali resistance was aided by the Ottomans and, during World War I, by the

German Empire. The British established a protectorate over this area, which became British Somaliland, in 1920. Meanwhile, Italy had established a sphere of influence over what would become the southern portion of Somalia along the Indian Ocean coast. Italian military efforts to establish colonial control of this area began in 1925. By 1927, Italy had obtained effective control of the region, which came to be known as Italian Somaliland or Italian East Africa.

During the early days of World War II, Italy conquered British Somaliland and added this territory along with Ethiopia and Eritrea to Italian East Africa. However, British forces ousted the Italians from British Somaliland in 1941, and this territory resumed its status as a British protectorate. British forces also drove Italy from Italian Somaliland. In 1949, the United Nations awarded limited control of Italian Somaliland back to Italy on condition that Somalia would become an independent state within 10 years. British Somaliland and Italian Somaliland were united as the single state of Somalia, which became independent in 1960.

Democratic elections were held in Somalia for the first time shortly after independence. However, Somalia's second president, Abdirashid Ali Shermarke, was assassinated in 1969. Shortly after Shermarke's assassination, the Somali army under the supervision of General Mohamed Siad Barre seized power in a bloodless coup d'état. Barre put Somalia under one-party dictatorial rule. He established close linkages with the Soviet Union and other communist regimes and renamed the country the Somali Democratic Republic. In 1977, the Somali military attempted to take control of Ogaden, whose population was largely Somali, from Ethiopia. Somalia's army succeeded in taking over much of Ogaden, but the Soviets decided to intervene on the side of Ethiopia, and Ethiopia regained control of the area. Thus Somalia was largely abandoned by the Soviets. In 1991, Barre's totalitarian government was ousted and Barre was exiled to Nigeria, where he died in 1995.

After the Barre regime was removed from power, civil war broke out in Somalia. Armed groups competed with one another to fill the power vacuum created by Barre's ouster. In 1992, the United Nations authorized the placement of a peacekeeping force to maintain order and to provide humanitarian assistance to Somalis displaced by the conflict. The peacekeeping force was withdrawn in 1995. Since that time, competition for government control has continued although no government has been successful in taking control of the entire government. An ongoing issue has been the extent to which Somali law should be governed by Islamic principles. Some factions competing for control have pushed for the implementation of Sharia law throughout Somalia. A new government that took power in 2010 has attempted to regain control against opposition from the radical Islamist al-Shabaab organization and from local warlords. Ongoing civil war and worsening drought conditions has contributed to widespread famine in Somalia.

CONTEMPORARY ISSUES

Conflict over control of Somalia's government continues. In particular, al-Shabaab remains a threat to Somalia's fragile central government. Al-Shabaab became established in 2005 and 2006 as a militant offshoot of the Islamic Courts Union, which took control of parts of southern Somalia during the Somali Civil War. Al-Shabaab has been associated with Al Qaeda, has implemented a harsh and strict interpretation of Sharia law and is regarded by the United States as a terrorist organization. By 2010, al-Shabaab had taken control of most of southern Somalia including the capital city of Mogadishu.

Above and beyond its ongoing internal conflicts and civil wars, Somalia is experiencing several issues involving its neighbors and international relations. The status of Ogaden and those areas of Somalia adjacent to Ogaden remains unresolved. During the first decade of the 20th century, Ethiopian troops invaded southern Somalia. Areas of this region, including Somalia's third-largest city of Baidoa, have been contested between al-Shabaab and Ethiopian forces since 2006. Ethiopia took control of Baidoa in 2006, but al-Shabaab regained control of the city in 2009.

Somalia has also become notorious as a center for attacks by pirates operating in the Gulf of Aden and the Indian Ocean. The lack of an effective government, especially in the northern part of Somalia, has allowed pirates to operate with impunity off the Somali coast. Worldwide, pirate activities today are concentrated off the coasts of Africa and Asia, including Somalia. The International Maritime Bureau has estimated that about 300 pirate attacks per year have occurred worldwide since 2000, with the largest number taking place in the Gulf of Aden and the Indian Ocean near the Somali coast. Losses associated with piracy have been estimated at between $13 and $16 billion annually. Somali pirates have seized numerous ships on the high seas. Ships' captains and crew members have been captured and held for ransom. Pirates have also stolen crew members' identity papers as well as high-value, low-bulk cargo such as software and CDs.

Many of the pirate ship crew members are young Somali men who regard association with pirates and pirate activities as a way out of poverty. Some of the pirates were once local fishermen whose knowledge of seafaring and of the local coastlines is valuable to their operations. Some pirates use global positioning systems and other sophisticated technologies in their efforts. Residents of ports in which the pirates operate have mixed reactions to the pirates' activities. Piracy is seen by some as an economic boon, promoting trade. Others see pirates as disruptive to local communities. UN estimates suggest that between 3,000 and 5,000 pirates are currently active in Somalia. Many of these pirates are active in the Puntland region of northeastern Somalia, which has coasts on both the Gulf of Aden and the Indian Ocean and is outside the control of the Somali government.

In 2008, there were 111 attacks on ships by Somali-based pirates, and 42 of these attacks were successful. There were 21 more successful attacks on ships in the first four months of 2009. The increased number of attacks has induced the international community to begin coordinated efforts to combat piracy off Somali waters. In 2008, the United Nations passed a resolution to strengthen sanctions against Somalia for its failure to prevent increased piracy. The UN also authorized international land and sea efforts to pursue pirates. Thousands of sailors from the United States, the United

Kingdom, France, Germany, China, Japan, and other countries are actively patrolling the Indian Ocean against pirate attacks. Their efforts have met with mixed success, although the International Maritime Bureau has estimated that the number of successful pirate attacks on ships in international waters has been declining.

See also Djibouti, Ethiopia, Kenya

Further Reading

Afyare Abdi Elmi and Abdi Aynte. "Negotiating an end to Somalia's war with al Shabaab." *Foreign Affairs*, February 7, 2012.

BBC News. "Somalia famine: UN warns of 750,000 deaths." September 5, 2011, http://www.bbc.co.uk/news/world-africa-14785304.

BBC News. "Somali piracy 'boosts Puntland economy.' " January 12, 2012, http://www.bbc.co.uk/news/world-africa-16534293.

Economist. "A bloody border: The war intensifies, especially near the border with Kenya." March 31, 2011, http://www.economist.com/node/18491682.

Frank Gardner. "Seeking Somali pirates, from the air." *BBC News*, February 21, 2012, http://www.bbc.co.uk/news/world-middle-east-17095887.

Martin N. Murphy. *Somalia: The new Barbary?* New York: Columbia University Press, 2011.

SOUTH AFRICA

OVERVIEW

The Republic of South Africa is located at the southern tip of the continent of Africa, between the Atlantic Ocean to the west and the Indian Ocean to the east. Its land area is 471,443 square miles, nearly twice the size of Texas. Its population is about 50 million. Today about 80 percent of South Africa's people are of African ancestry, 10 percent are white, and 10 percent are "coloured" people of mixed-race ancestry or Asian.

South Africa has boundaries with Namibia to the northwest, Botswana and Zimbabwe to the north, and Mozambique and Swaziland to the northeast. In addition, the country of Lesotho is surrounded completely by South Africa. The boundary between South Africa and Namibia follows the Orange River eastward and upstream from its mouth in the Atlantic Ocean. The Orange continues as the boundary eastward to the 20th meridian of east longitude. It then follows the 20th meridian northward to the tripoint between South Africa, Namibia, and Botswana in Kgalagadi Transfrontier Park, which is shared between South Africa and Botswana.

From this tripoint, the boundary between South Africa and Botswana follows the Nossob River eastward and upstream to its tributary, the Molopo River. Near the headwaters of the Molopo, the boundary continues eastward across a drainage divide to the Notwane River. It follows the Notwane downstream and northeastward to its confluence with the Limpopo River. The Limpopo, which empties eventually into the Indian Ocean, forms the eastern portion of the boundary between South Africa and Botswana and continues as the boundary between South Africa and Zimbabwe to the tripoint between South Africa, Zimbabwe, and Mozambique.

The boundary between South Africa and Mozambique extends southward from

SOUTH AFRICA

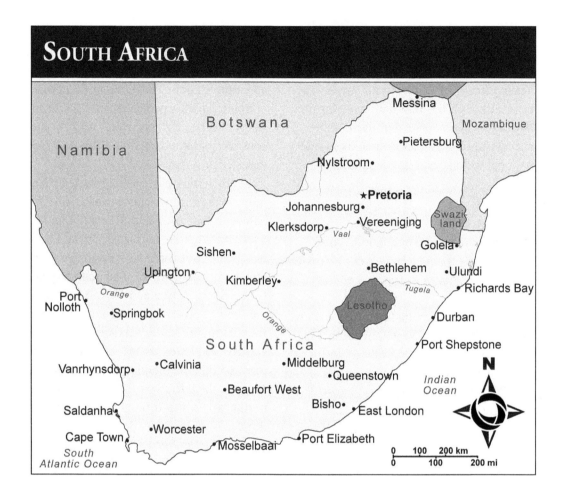

this tripoint along the Limpopo, following short straight-line segments to the northern tripoint between South Africa, Mozambique, and Swaziland. From there the boundary between South Africa and Mozambique extends west, and then south, and then east following straight-line segments in an irregular semicircle to the more southerly tripoint between the three countries. This tripoint is located by the Ndumo Game Reserve. From there the boundary between South Africa and Mozambique extends directly eastward to the Indian Ocean at the northern end of South Africa's Isimangaliso National Park.

HISTORICAL CONTEXT

Archaeologists have demonstrated that humans have occupied the southern portion of the African continent for at least 150,000 years. Ancestors of today's San, or Bushmen, were hunters and gatherers who were probably the earliest inhabitants of the region. Bantu-speaking peoples from central Africa first crossed the Limpopo into present-day eastern South Africa about 1,500 years ago, and they absorbed earlier populations or drove them to less hospitable, drier lands in what is now Botswana and Namibia.

In 1488, the Portuguese mariner Bartolomeu Dias became the first European to sight the Cape of Good Hope near the present-day city of Cape Town. However, the area remained unoccupied by European settlers until the 17th century, when the Dutch landed at the Cape of Good Hope. They established a refreshment station at which Dutch ships sailing between the Netherlands and Dutch colonies in East Asia could replenish their stores of provisions. Dutch farmers known as Boers settled the area, growing crops that were used to replenish the ships' food supplies. Slaves from East Asia and from Madagascar were imported to provide labor for these agricultural operations.

During the 18th century, Dutch settlement expanded slowly eastward. At the same time, Xhosa people of Bantu ancestry moved westward. As the two waves of movement intersected, armed conflict broke out, primarily over land rights. Meanwhile, valuable deposits of diamonds, gold, and minerals were discovered in South Africa. Britain seized control of Cape Town in 1795 in order to keep it out of French hands and in order to replenish British ships on their way to and from India and Australia. The British then established control over what was then known as the Cape Colony, which included the area south of the Orange River southward to the Indian and Atlantic coasts of present-day South Africa.

The British abolished the slave trade in 1807 and abolished slavery throughout the British Empire in 1834. In response to the British ban on slaveholding, thousands of Boers moved northward and eastward and established the Boer republics of Transvaal and the Orange Free State in the South African interior. Diamonds were discovered in the Boer republics beginning in 1867. These discoveries triggered a large-scale migration of British miners and settlers into the Boer republics. Animosities between the British and the Boers, and between both groups of Europeans and indigenous Africans, led to open warfare. The British attempted unsuccessfully to annex the Boer republics in 1880.

Gold was discovered the Transvaal region near the present-day city of Johannesburg in 1886. A subsequent gold rush brought thousands of miners from the Cape Colony, the British Isles, and elsewhere in Europe. These settlers were known as *uitlanders*, or "outlanders." Fearful of losing political and economic control over the Boer Republics, leaders of Transvaal tried to curb *uitlander* influence by imposing heavy taxes and establishing long residency requirements for voting and political participation. However, the British reasserted their efforts to take over Transvaal and the Orange Free State. In 1899, the Boer War began. After three years, the Boers, or Afrikaaners, were defeated, and Britain assumed control of the Republics.

In 1910, Transvaal and the Orange Free State were united with the Cape Colony and the province of Natal along the Indian Ocean to form the Union of South Africa. The Union of South Africa was made a dominion of the British Empire. At this time, people of European ancestry were a small minority of the population but controlled most of the land and much of the union's wealth. The union became an independent country within the British Commonwealth in 1931.

The National Party assumed control of the South African government in 1948.

Soon thereafter, South Africa's apartheid policies were enacted. All South Africans were required to identify themselves as white, black, Asian, or "coloured" or people of mixed ancestry. Strict laws prohibited integration among these communities, and nonwhites, who represented a large majority of South Africa's population, had no voice in government. In 1961, a referendum on South Africa's status was held in which only whites could vote. A majority of these white voters voted to end South Africa's status as a member of the British Commonwealth and make South Africa an independent republic. After South Africa became an independent republic, its name was changed from the Union of South Africa to the Republic of South Africa.

The South African government's apartheid policies met with fierce resistance from many people of African ancestry and were condemned vigorously by the international community. Many opponents of the apartheid regime were associated with the African National Congress (ANC). The regime banned the ANC in the early 1960s. Nelson Mandela, one of the leaders of the ANC, was jailed in 1962 and remained in prison for the next 27 years.

Facing increased pressure from the international community as well as increased opposition by whites as well as nonwhites within South Africa, the government began to soften its apartheid policies in the late 1980s. The government removed the ban on the ANC and released Mandela from prison in 1990. The apartheid policies were repealed. In 1994 South Africa's first multiracial elections were held, and Mandela was elected president. Since then, South Africa has prospered although it has been affected significantly by the global HIV/AIDS crisis. South Africa became the first African country to host a major global international sporting event when it hosted the World Cup in 2010.

CONTEMPORARY ISSUES

South Africa's borders are stable and uncontested. However, the League of Nations gave South Africa a mandate over the former German colony of South-west Africa (today's Namibia) after World War I. The mandate was reasserted by the United Nations as the successor organization to the league after World War II. However, South Africa refused to consider granting independence to Namibia in the 1960s. South Africa's failure to grant independence, along with its racially discriminatory policy of apartheid, induced the United Nations to revoke the mandate. In 1971, the International Court of Justice ruled that South Africa's continuing occupation of present-day Namibia was illegal. South-west Africa's government, along with that of South Africa itself, was run by a white minority. In 1990, however, South Africa granted independence to Namibia.

As a peaceful and relatively prosperous country in an unstable region, South Africa has attracted a substantial number of refugees. As many as 200,000 refugees from neighboring Zimbabwe fleeing the repressive regime of Zimbabwe's president Robert Mugabe are believed to be living in South Africa. Other refugees have moved to South Africa from other war-torn African countries, including Burundi and the Democratic Republic of the Congo.

See also   Botswana, Lesotho, Mozambique, Namibia, Swaziland, Zimbabwe

Further Reading

Nancy L. Clark and William Werger. *South Africa: The rise and fall of apartheid.* London: Longman, 2011.

Eve Fairbanks. "South Africa's awkward teenage years." *Foreign Policy*, January/February 2012, http://www.foreignpolicy.com/articles/2012/01/03/south_africa_s_awkward_teenage_years.

Martin Meredith. *Diamonds, gold, and war: The British, the Boers, and the making of South Africa.* New York: 2007.

SOUTH SUDAN

OVERVIEW

The Republic of South Sudan is located in east-central Africa. South Sudan includes the southern quarter of previously unified Sudan and upon becoming independent in 2011 became the world's newest independent state. South Sudan has a land area of 239,285 square miles, approximately the size of Texas. Its population is about 9 million.

South Sudan is landlocked. It has boundaries with Sudan to the north, the Central African Republic to the west, the Democratic Republic of the Congo, Uganda, and Kenya to the south, and Ethiopia to the east. The boundary between South Sudan and Sudan extends in a generally eastward direction from the tripoint between South Sudan, Sudan, and Ethiopia to the east to the tripoint between South Sudan, Sudan, and the Central African Republic to the west. The entire boundary follows short straight-line segments. These segments trend northward just east of the Ethiopian tripoint. It trends southward again and then turns westward crossing the White Nile, eventually

reaching the Central African Republic tripoint on the drainage divide between the drainage basin of the Nile in South Sudan and the drainage basin of the Congo River in the Central African Republic.

The boundary between South Sudan and the Central African Republic follows this drainage divide in a southeasterly direction to the tripoint between South Sudan, the Central African Republic, and the Democratic Republic of the Congo. This tripoint is located near the edge of the Bengaigai Game Reserve in South Sudan. The boundary between South Sudan and the Democratic Republic of the Congo continues to the southeast, also following the drainage divide between the Nile and the Congo drainage basins. The tripoint between South Sudan, the Democratic Republic of the Congo, and Uganda is located near the village of Kuluba on the border between the Democratic Republic of the Congo and Uganda.

From this tripoint, the boundary between South Sudan and Uganda extends northeastward briefly to Uganda's Mt. Kei White Rhino Sanctuary. East of the sanctuary, it follows a longer diagonal line from northwest to southeast. It then trends eastward, crosses the White Nile again, and continues to follow short straight-line segments to the Kidepo Valley Game Reserve in South Sudan and the adjacent Kidepo Valley National Park in Uganda. From these parks it follows a diagonal segment northeastward to the tripoint between South Sudan, Uganda, and Kenya.

The diagonal segment continues in a northeasterly direction as the boundary between South Sudan and Kenya. It then turns to the east-northeast along a single segment before following several shorter segments to the tripoint between South

SOUTH SUDAN

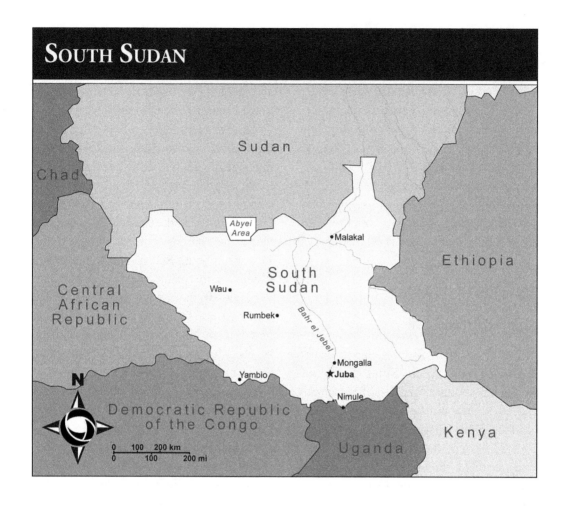

Sudan, Kenya, and Ethiopia at the edge of Lake Turkana. The boundary between South Sudan and Ethiopia follows straight-line segments northwestward to a point near the northwestern edge of Boma National Park in South Sudan and near Gambela National Park in Ethiopia. From there the boundary turns northeastward, following many short straight-line segments to the tripoint between South Sudan, Ethiopia, and Sudan.

HISTORICAL CONTEXT

Present-day South Sudan has been oc-cupied by various sub-Saharan African cultures for thousands of years. During the 16th, 17th, and 18th centuries, most of mod-ern Sudan was controlled by the Sultanate of Sennar. The sultanate was deposed by Egyptian forces in 1821. After overthrow-ing the sultanate, Egyptian forces attempted to extend their control southward along the White Nile into modern South Sudan. In 1870, a few British settlers established the outpost of Equatoria, which includes what is today the southern part of South Sudan and northern Uganda. Egypt took control of Equatoria and the rest of South Sudan in 1889. In 1899, Equatoria along with the rest of present-day South Sudan and present-day Sudan were united as the colony of Anglo-Egyptian Sudan. Within Anglo-Egyptian Sudan, South Sudan was administered separately from present-day Sudan.

During the 20th century, Egypt attempted to incorporate Anglo-Egyptian Sudan into the Egyptian state. However, Britain opposed this unification effort. In 1947, representatives from Britain and Anglo-Egyptian Sudan met in Juba, the present-day capital of South Sudan, to consider the question of preparing for eventual independence. At the Juba Conference, a proposal to unite South Sudan and Uganda was rejected, and it was decided to unite South Sudan with northern Sudan as a single country. Independence was granted to Sudan by Britain and Egypt in 1956.

The decision to unite southern and northern Sudan resulted in ethnic, cultural, and religious tensions from the outset. The majority of people in South Sudan consist of people of sub-Saharan African ancestry who are Christians. On the other hand, most people in present-day Sudan are Arabic-speaking Muslims whose cultural affinities are closer to Arabia and North Africa than to sub-Saharan Africa.

Various Sudanese governments attempted to impose Islamic values, including Sharia law, on the entire country. In 1969, Colonel Jaafar al Nimeiri led a military coup d'état deposing Sudan's civilian government. In 1983, Nimeiri decreed that Sharia law would be the basis of civil law throughout the country. This decree and its enforcement by the Sudanese government triggered an outbreak of civil war between southern secessionists and government forces. Between 1983 and 2005, an estimated 2 million people in South Sudan died and 3 or 4 million others were displaced.

During the early 21st century, peace negotiators made progress toward ending the Sudanese civil war. In 2005, negotiators from both sides signed the Comprehensive Peace Agreement. Under terms of the agreement, the Autonomous Government of Southern Sudan was established. The Autonomous Government was given autonomy over its internal affairs for six years. A referendum on independence would be held after this six-year period. The agreement stipulated also that Sharia law would be not be used as the basis of civil law in South Sudan.

The promised referendum took place in January 2011. More than 98 percent of the voters supported independence. South Sudan achieved independence on July 9, 2011. Its independence was recognized immediately by Sudan and soon thereafter by the international community, and South Sudan then joined the United Nations. Although it is one of the poorest and least developed states in the world, extensive natural resources have given South Sudan promise for eventual development. The independence agreement freed South Sudan from any obligation to honor agreements that had been made by the Sudan government with other countries or corporations over natural resource extraction. Rather, the new government of South Sudan was given the freedom to renegotiate these agreements.

CONTEMPORARY ISSUES

South Sudan's border with Sudan has not been settled completely. The population of the border region is more evenly divided between Christians and Muslims than are populations further to the south in South Sudan or to the north in Sudan. Moreover, the border region is rich in oil and natural resources. Thus the location of the boundary could have a considerable impact on the economies of the two countries, both of which depend heavily on mineral extraction for much of their export incomes.

The Abyei district along the boundary, with a land area of about 4,000 square miles, is in dispute between South Sudan and Sudan. Abyei has been a center for trade and interaction between present-day South Sudan and Sudanese people of the north for centuries. Both South Sudan and Sudan claim the district. In 2011, Sudan sent 5,000 troops to occupy Abyei, but Sudan agreed to withdraw its troops in 2012 pending resolution of the boundary dispute. A referendum in which residents of the Abyei district would vote whether to be part of South Sudan or part of Sudan is under consideration.

See also Central African Republic, Democratic Republic of the Congo, Ethiopia, Kenya, Sudan, Uganda

Further Reading

Brookings Institute, Africa Growth Initiative. "South Sudan one year after independence: Opportunities and obstacles for Africa's newest country." June 2012, http://www.brookings.edu/~/media/re search/files/reports/2012/6/south%20sudan/ 06%20south%20sudan.pdf.

Howard W. French. "Smothering love: How the West's South Sudan obsession hurts the country." *Atlantic*, June 22, 2012, http://www.theatlantic.com/interna tional/archive/2012/06/smothering-love-how-the-wests-south-sudan-obsession-hurts-the-country/258858/.

International Boundaries Research Unit. "Sudan and South Sudan hold talks following conflict in disputed border region." April 4, 2012, http://www.dur.ac. uk/ibru/news/boundary_news/?itemno=14 302&rehref=%2Fibru%2F&resubj=Boun dary+news+Headlines.

SUDAN

OVERVIEW

The Republic of the Sudan is located in northeastern Africa and extends between the Sahara Desert into the Sahel region and south to rainier territory. Sudan was the largest country in Africa prior to 2011, when South Sudan seceded to become an independent country. Even without South Sudan, Sudan has a land area of 728,215 square miles, about three times the size of Texas. It is the second-largest country in sub-Saharan Africa by land area behind the Democratic Republic of the Congo. Its population is about 33 million.

Sudan's neighbors are Egypt to the north, Libya to the northwest, Chad to the west, the Central African Republic to the southwest, South Sudan to the south, and Ethiopia and Eritrea to the southeast. To the northeast, Sudan has a coast on the Red Sea. The boundary between Sudan and Egypt extends westward from the Red Sea along the 22th parallel of north latitude. It continues along this parallel, crossing the Nile River, to the 25th meridian of east longitude. The intersection of the 22nd parallel and the 25th meridian represents the tripoint between Sudan, Egypt, and Libya. Except near the valley of the Nile, the boundary region is located within the Sahara Desert and is uninhabited. From the

SUDAN

tripoint between Sudan, Libya, and Egypt, the boundary between Sudan and Libya continues southward along the 25th meridian to the 20th parallel of north latitude. It then follows the 20th parallel west to the 24th meridian of longitude and then turns southward along the 24th meridian to the tripoint between Sudan, Libya, and Chad at latitude 19° 30′ north.

From this tripoint, the boundary between Sudan and Chad continues southward along the 24th meridian for more than 200 miles to the intermittent stream of Wadi Howa.

It then turns westward and then southwestward and then turns in a more south-southeasterly direction. Some of this boundary follows straight-line segments, whereas other portions of the boundary follow other wadis or follow drainage divides between these intermittent streams. This boundary continues to the tripoint between Sudan, Chad, and the Central African Republic. This tripoint is located along the drainage divide between the Nile River drainage basin in Sudan and the Congo River drainage basin in the Central African

Republic. The entire boundary between Sudan and the Central African Republic follows this drainage divide in a southeasterly direction to the tripoint between Sudan, the Central African Republic, and South Sudan south of Radom National Park in Sudan.

The boundary between Sudan and South Sudan extends eastward from the eastern end of the park. It follows short straight-line segments in a generally eastward direction, crossing the Nile once again. It then turns to the north and then turns south-southeast again before turning eastward along a short segment to the boundary between Sudan, South Sudan, and Ethiopia. The boundary between Sudan and South Sudan has not been delineated completely and in some places remains contested between the two countries.

From the tripoint between Sudan, South Sudan, and Ethiopia, the boundary between Sudan and Ethiopia follows numerous straight-line segments. These extend in a northeasterly direction to the edge of Dinder National Park in Sudan, and then they continue northeastward to the tripoint between Sudan, Ethiopia, and Eritrea on the Tekezé River. The boundary between Eritrea and Sudan continues along straight-line segments northward and then northeastward to the Red Sea. The coastal region is uninhabited, and the entire boundary is crossed by only one paved road.

HISTORICAL CONTEXT

The Nile River valley has been settled for thousands of years. During the second millennium BC, it was tributary to Egyptian rulers further downstream. Approximately 1100 BC, the independent Kingdom of Kush arose in the region near the confluence between the White Nile and the Blue Nile. The Sudanese capital city of Khartoum is located at this confluence today. The Kingdom of Kush took control of all of Egypt for more than 100 years in the eighth and ninth centuries BC before being pushed back into present-day Sudan by the Assyrians. Nevertheless, the Kingdom of Kush and its successor kingdoms continued to rule the upper Nile valley over hundreds of years into the Middle Ages. Islam became the dominant religion of present-day Sudan during the seventh and eighth centuries AD.

The Sultanate of Sennar took control of the Nile valley between Khartoum and what is now southern Egypt in 1504. At its height in the late 16th and early 17th centuries, the sultanate governed most of present-day northern Sudan along with parts of present-day Ethiopia and Eritrea. In 1821, Egypt invaded and conquered southern Egypt and northern Sudan. At that time, Egypt was under the nominal control of the Ottoman Empire but functioned effectively as an independent kingdom.

In the late 19th century, Britain succeeded the Ottomans as the dominant European power in Egypt. Britain and Egypt agreed to joint control of Sudan in 1899. The area was named Anglo-Egyptian Sudan, but Britain was the dominant power in this arrangement. The British took an active interest in the region in order to influence trade on the Nile and also in response to Ottoman, German, and Italian efforts to establish colonies in northeastern Africa. In the early 20th century, Egyptian activists sought to incorporate Sudan into Egypt. However, these efforts were opposed by the British, who continued to administer

Sudan separately from Egypt. However, the British administered Muslim-majority northern Sudan and Christian-majority southern Sudan separately. After World War II, Egypt abandoned its efforts to unite Egypt and Sudan, and in 1954, Egypt and Britain signed an agreement recognizing the eventual independence of Sudan as a single independent state including both Muslim-majority and Christian-majority areas. Independence was granted formally in 1956.

The population of newly independent Sudan included a Muslim, Arabic-speaking majority in the north and a Christian minority of sub-Saharan African ancestry in the south. After independence, the government of Sudan came to be dominated by Muslims from the northern portion of the country, including the capital of Khartoum. The predominantly Christian southern portion of Sudan called for more autonomy. However, the original democratically elected government of Sudan was overthrown in a military coup d'état in 1958. Since then, Sudan has been governed by military leaders for much of the time. Successive Sudanese governments worked to impose Arabic culture, the Arabic language, and Islamic law on the entire country. These efforts were resisted by the non-Arab, non-Muslim south and led eventually to the independence of South Sudan.

A second secessionist movement arose in Darfur in western Sudan in the late 1990s. The Sudanese provinces comprising Darfur are located along Sudan's boundaries with Chad and the Central African Republic. The name "Darfur" means "Land of the Fur." The Fur people are Muslims, but not Arabs. Their language is unrelated to Arabic, although many speak Arabic as a second language. Darfur was an independent sultanate from the 15th century until 1875, when it came under British jurisdiction. The British incorporated Darfur into Sudan in 1916, in part to maintain control of the Khartoum area and the Nile valley against possible efforts on the part of other European colonial powers to control the region.

After Sudanese independence in 1956, many residents of Darfur felt neglected by the Arab-dominated government in Khartoum. Hostilities between Fur leaders and the Sudanese government escalated into armed conflict in the late 1990s. Over the next decade, an estimated 100,000 residents of Darfur were killed and as many as 200,000 other people died as a result of disease, famine, and starvation as the Sudanese government was accused of genocide. More than 2 million Darfur residents were displaced. Many left the country, moving to neighboring Chad or other countries as refugees.

The United Nations sent a peacekeeping force to Darfur in 2006. However, Sudan's government regarded the Darfur conflict as an internal issue and identified the peacekeepers as "foreign invaders." During this period, China gave strong support to the Sudanese government's effort to suppress the rebellion in Darfur. China, which is the largest consumer of oil from Sudan, was accused of supplying the Sudanese government with weapons that were used against the Darfur rebels in exchange for access to Sudanese oil and natural resources. In 2006, an agreement to end armed hostilities was signed by the Sudanese government and the largest separatist organization in Darfur, the Sudan Liberation Movement. Under the terms of this agreement, the

Sudan government agreed to grant more autonomy to Darfur, to increase Darfur's representation in the national government, and to work with the United Nations to provide humanitarian assistance to those displaced by the war. A second agreement, reinforcing the first, was signed by the Sudanese government and other Darfur separatist organizations in 2011.

Tensions between the central government, which continued to be dominated by Arab Muslims, and the South continued throughout Sudan's history as an independent state. Southerners continued to resist the government's efforts to impose Islamic law and Arabic culture on the entire country. After more than two decades of civil war, a peace agreement between the Sudanese government and rebels in southern Sudan was signed in 2005. The agreement called for southern autonomy for six years, followed by a referendum on South Sudanese independence. This referendum took place in 2011. A large majority of South Sudan's voters supported independence. The southern portion of Sudan became the independent country of South Sudan in July 2011.

CONTEMPORARY ISSUES

Although agreement between the government of Sudan and rebels in Darfur and South Sudan led to autonomy for Darfur and independence for South Sudan, Sudan continues to face tensions with neighboring countries. Although South Sudan became independent in 2011, the boundary between Sudan and South Sudan has not been delineated precisely. The boundary dispute involves two key issues. The population in the border region is divided between Muslims and Christians. Delineating a boundary in such a way as to place as many Muslims in Sudan and Christians in South Sudan as possible has been problematic. As well, the border region contains valuable oil deposits that both countries wish to control and exploit. Both countries claim the Abyei region, an area of about 4,000 square miles along the boundary halfway between Chad and Ethiopia. Sudanese troops occupied Abyei in May 2011, but in May 2012 Sudan agreed to withdraw its forces from Abyei. The two countries have agreed in principle to hold a referendum within Abyei over whether it should join Sudan or South Sudan.

Sudan and Egypt have disputed control of a region known as the Hala'ib Triangle. The Hala'ib Triangle is located north of the 22nd parallel and along the Red Sea coast but is claimed by both countries. It has a land area of about 8,000 square miles, and its population has been estimated at about 30,000. Sudan bases its claim to the Hala'ib Triangle in part on the grounds that its inhabitants have historical and cultural ties to the Sudanese, rather than to the Egyptians. The Hala'ib region, including the Red Sea offshore, contains valuable oil deposits. On the basis of its claim to the Hala'ib Triangle, Sudan granted oil exploration rights in the Red Sea off the coast of the triangle to a Canadian company in 1992. In response, Egypt sent troops into the triangle and blockaded the area from Sudan. Negotiations to resolve the conflict continue, including the possibility of a referendum in which residents of the Hala'ib Triangle would be given the opportunity to vote whether to be part of Sudan or Egypt.

Ongoing conflicts in Darfur and South Sudan have displaced millions of people from Sudan and South Sudan. In 2011, the United Nations estimated that more than a million Sudanese refugees were living outside Sudan, including more than 200,000 in Chad. Refugees in neighboring countries have struggled with food shortages, violence, disease, discrimination, and unemployment. International organizations are working to provide humanitarian assistance to these refugees. However, the eventual fate of the refugees, including the possibility of repatriation, remains uncertain.

See also Central African Republic, Chad, Egypt, Eritrea, Ethiopia, Libya, South Sudan

Further Reading

Robert H. Bates. *When things fell apart: State failure in late-century Africa.* New York: Cambridge University Press, 2008.

BBC News. "Abyei crisis: UN confirms Sudan troop pullout." May 30, 2012, http://www.bbc.co.uk/news/world-africa-18260082.

Richard Cockett. *Sudan: Darfur and the failure of an African state.* New Haven, CT: Yale University Press, 2010.

M. W. Daly. *Darfur's sorrow: A history of destruction and genocide.* New York: Cambridge University Press, 2007.

Andrew Natsios. "Beyond Darfur: Sudan's slide towards civil war." *Foreign Affairs*, May/June 2008.

SWAZILAND

OVERVIEW

The Kingdom of Swaziland is located in southern Africa. Its land area is 6,704 square miles, slightly smaller than Connecticut and Rhode Island combined. The population of Swaziland is about 1.3 million.

Swaziland is landlocked. It is nearly surrounded by South Africa, with a boundary with Mozambique to the east. There are two tripoints between Swaziland, South Africa, and Mozambique. The northern tripoint is located north of Shewula Nature Reserve in northeastern Swaziland and south of the South African town of Mbuzini. From that tripoint, the boundary forms a semicircle to the southern tripoint between the three countries. Much of it follows straight-line segments, including a diagonal segment running from southeast to northwest about 60 miles in length. It then turns to the south and then to the west to the reservoir formed by the Pongolapoort Dam on the Pongola River. From this reservoir the boundary follows straight lines northward to the Maputo River. It follows the Maputo River eastward and downstream to the southern tripoint between Swaziland, South Africa, and Mozambique. The two tripoints are connected by the boundary between Swaziland and Mozambique, which follows straight-line segments extending in a north-to-south direction.

HISTORICAL CONTEXT

Archaeologists have discovered human artifacts in contemporary Swaziland that are believed to be as much as 200,000 years old. Bantu tribes moved into the area between 1,500 and 2,000 years ago. The Swazi king Mswati II consolidated power over the area in the mid-19th century. Meanwhile, Boers of Dutch descent began to move into Swaziland around the same

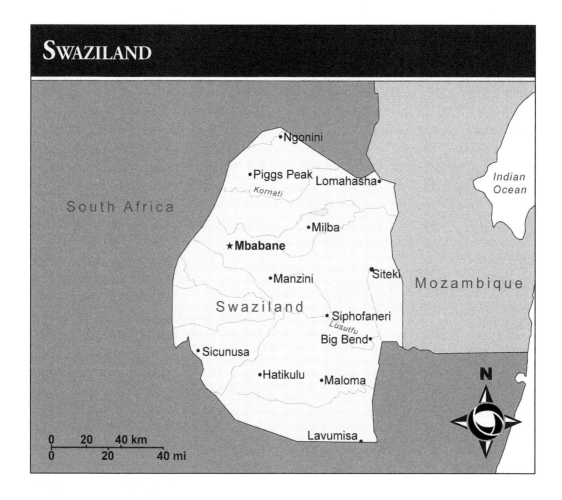

time. Under pressure from the Boers as well as neighboring Zulu warriors, Mswati asked for British protection against neighboring tribes in exchange for British guarantees of independence.

After the Anglo-Boer War of 1899–1902 ended in the defeat of the Boers, Britain claimed jurisdiction over Swaziland in 1903. Swaziland was administered originally as part of the Province of Transvaal, but the two were separated administratively in 2006, and the British administrators worked with the Swazi monarchy to govern the colony. During the early years of British rule, British administrators considered the possibility of turning over control

of Swaziland eventually to South Africa. However, this option was dropped from consideration after South Africa implemented its apartheid policies. Swaziland achieved independence from Britain as a constitutional monarchy in 1968. However, in 1973 King Sobhuza II abolished the Swazi constitution and made himself an absolute ruler. Sobhuza died in 1982 and was succeeded by his son Mswati III, who is one of the last absolute monarchs remaining in the world today. Swaziland has one of the highest rates of HIV/AIDS infection in the world.

See also   Mozambique, South Africa

Further Reading

Glenn Ashton. "Southern Africa: A case for greater interaction between South Africa, Lesotho, and Swaziland?" *Allafrica.com*, June 18, 2012, http://allafrica.com/stories/201206180027.html.

TANZANIA

OVERVIEW

The United Republic of Tanzania is located in east-central Africa along the Indian Ocean. Tanzania's overall land area is 364,898 square miles, about as large as Texas and New Mexico combined. Its population is about 45 million.

Tanzania consists of Tanganyika on the African mainland and the islands of Zanzibar off the coast. The country's name is an amalgamation of the names of the two once-separate territories. Nearly 98 percent of Tanzania's land area and about 98 percent of the country's population are on the mainland. Zanzibar consists of two main islands, Unjuga (which is often called Zanzibar) and Pemba. Together, these islands are about 1,020 square miles in land area,

or the size of Rhode Island, with a population of about 1.1 million.

On the mainland, Tanzania shares boundaries with Kenya and Uganda to the north, Rwanda, Burundi, and the Democratic Republic of the Congo to the west, and Zambia, Malawi, and Mozambique to the south. Eastern mainland Tanzania has a coastline on the Indian Ocean. Most of the boundary between Tanzania and Kenya consists of two long, geometric lines that run from southeast to northwest. One extends northwestward from the Indian Ocean inland to Lake Jife. The boundary continues to the west and then to the north around the town of Taveta near the north end of the lake. It follows short segments northeastward to Lake Chala, follows another segment in a north-northwesterly direction, and then follows the other long diagonal segment northwestward to the tripoint between Tanzania, Kenya, and Uganda in Lake Victoria. This boundary passes just north of Mt. Kilimanjaro on the Tanzanian side the boundary.

From Lake Victoria, the boundary between Tanzania and Uganda follows the 1st parallel of south latitude westward to the Kagera River. It then follows the Kagera upstream and southwestward to the tripoint between Tanzania, Uganda, and Rwanda. The Kagera also forms the boundary between Tanzania and Rwanda. The boundary between Tanzania, Rwanda, and Burundi is located at the confluence between the Kagera and its tributary, the Mwibu River. The boundary between Tanzania and Burundi follows the Mwibu southward and upstream. From the Mwibu, it trends southwestward following streams and straight-line segments to the tripoint between Tanzania, Burundi, and

the Democratic Republic of the Congo in Lake Tanganyika. Lake Tanganyika separates Tanzania and the Democratic Republic of the Congo with Tanzanian territory on the east bank and the Democratic Republic of the Congo on the west bank. The boundary is located through the center of the lake, which is about 50 miles wide near the tripoint.

From Lake Tanganyika, the boundary between Tanzania and Zambia extends southeastward following a combination of straight-line segments and streams. The boundary between Tanzania and Malawi continues southeastward along the Songwe River, which empties into Lake Malawi. However, the Songwe has changed course on numerous occasions because of flooding, and therefore the precise boundary between the two countries has yet to be agreed upon. Near the mouth of the Songwe, the boundary then extends southward within Lake Malawi to the tripoint between Tanzania, Malawi, and Mozambique near the center of the lake. The boundary between Tanzania and Mozambique extends eastward from Lake Malawi and reaches the Rovuma River, which it follows downstream to its mouth in the Indian Ocean.

HISTORICAL CONTEXT

Present-day Tanganyika has been settled by a variety of peoples over thousands of years. Bantu-speaking tribes are believed to have moved into the area from the west about 2,000 years ago. Later, pastoralists from the upper Nile valley moved into the area from the north. The Tanganyikan coast has long been a center for trade. Traders from India and the Persian Gulf region established trade links with

East Africa at least 1,500 years ago, with coastal ports dominating trade between these overseas regions and the East African interior.

In 1498, the Portuguese mariner Vasco de Gama became the first European to visit the East Indian coast of present-day Tanzania. Portugal controlled the coastal region of mainland Tanzania until the early 18th century, when Arabs from present-day Oman drove the Portuguese out and established the Sultanate of Zanzibar, which also controlled coastal regions on the mainland north of the Ruvuma River. The Arabs continued to control the region into the 19th century.

After the European powers divided Africa into spheres of influence at the Congress of Berlin in 1885, Tanganyika became part of German East Africa in 1891. After World War I, administration of Tanganyika was transferred from Germany to Britain via the League of Nations. Most of Tanzania's boundaries were delineated following agreements between Germany or Britain and the European powers that controlled neighboring colonies during the late 19th and early 20th centuries.

Zanzibar has been an important trading center for hundreds of years. After two centuries of Portuguese administration, control of Zanzibar passed to the Sultanate of Zanzibar. Zanzibar became a center for the slave trade. In the early 19th century, Britain developed both commercial and humanitarian interests in Zanzibar. The British pressured the Sultanate of Zanzibar to outlaw the slave trade, but it was not abolished formally until 1876. The British Empire took over Zanzibar. In 1890, Germany agreed not to interfere with British domination of the islands, and Zanzibar became a British protectorate ruled locally by the sultanate's royal family. Tanganyika became independent from Britain in 1962, and Zanzibar became independent in 1963. Shortly after independence, the last ruling sultan of Zanzibar was overthrown in a coup d'état. The two countries were united as Tanzania in April 1964, although Zanzibar retains a considerable degree of local autonomy.

CONTEMPORARY ISSUES

Tanzania's boundaries with its neighbors are stable, although the specific location of the boundary between Tanzania and Malawi within Lake Malawi has been disputed. However, some political leaders on Zanzibar have expressed support for secession from Tanzania. Secessionists have argued that Zanzibar, with its thriving port, was the wealthiest place in Tanzania at the time that Zanzibar was merged with Tanganyika but has become a poor and isolated backwater in the 50 years since the merger. As a relatively stable and thriving democracy, Tanzania hosts hundreds of thousands of refugees, many of whom have fled from political violence and civil war in Burundi and the Democratic Republic of the Congo. Some estimates have suggested that Tanzania has the largest refugee population in Africa.

See also   Burundi, Democratic Republic of the Congo, Kenya, Malawi, Mozambique, Rwanda, Uganda, Zambia

Further Reading

Laura Edmonson. *Performance and politics in Tanzania: The nation on stage.* Bloomington: Indiana University Press, 2007.

IRIN News. "Burundi-Tanzania: Refugees face mounting pressure to go home." February 24, 2012, http://www.irinnews.org/Report/94945/BURUNDI-TANZANIA-Refugees-face-mounting-pressure-to-go-home.

Siri Lange. "Gold and governance: Legal injustices and lost opportunities in Tanzania." *African Affairs*, 110 (2011), pp. 233–252.

James Mwakisyala. "Tanzania: Zanzibar renews call for independence." *East African Business Week*, August 16, 2010, http://allafrica.com/stories/20100816 1469.html.

THE GAMBIA

OVERVIEW

The Republic of the Gambia is located in West Africa along the banks of the Gambia River. It is a long, narrow country whose land area extends from east to west. It is only 30 miles wide at its widest point but extends inland from the Atlantic for more than 150 miles in a west-to-east direction. Its total land area is 4,007 square miles, slightly smaller than Connecticut, and the Gambia is the smallest country by land area in Africa. The population is about 1.8 million. The Gambia is best known to many Americans as the place from which author Alex Haley's ancestor, Kunta Kinte, was captured and sold into slavery in the United States. Haley reconstructed Kunta Kinte's experiences in his book *Roots*, which later became a television miniseries.

The Gambia's land territory is surrounded completely by Senegal, with the exception of a 50-mile coastline on the Atlantic on either side of the Gambia River. From the Atlantic, both the northern and southern boundaries of the Gambia are latitudinal and located north of the 13th and south of the 14th parallel of latitudes. Eastward of these parallels, the boundary consists of a series of arcs on both sides of the river. These arcs are located approximately 10 miles north and south of the river. The

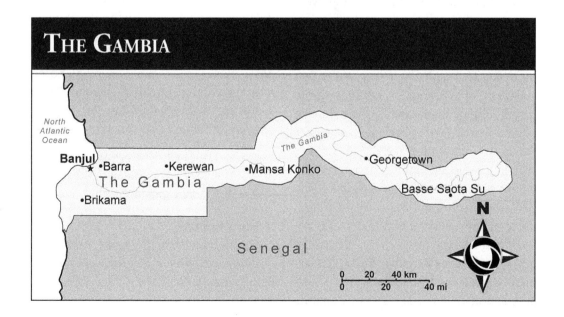

village of Juffure, in which Kunta Kinte is believed to have been born and raised, is located on the northern side of the river about 20 miles east of the Atlantic coast.

HISTORICAL CONTEXT

Present-day The Gambia was a center for slave trading during and after the Middle Ages. As many as 3 million slaves are believed to have been shipped from ports on the mouth of the Gambia River to the Americas during the 16th, 17th, 18th, and early 19th centuries. During that time, the Gambia River was contested among European powers, especially Britain and France. A 1783 treaty gave Britain control of the lower reaches of the river and territory on both sides. In 1807, Britain abolished the trans-Atlantic slave trade. The British established the settlement of Bathurst at the mouth of the Gambia River in 1816 in order to enforce the abolition of the slave trade. Bathurst eventually grew into the Gambia's capital and largest city of Banjui. The Gambia, which was then known simply as Gambia, became a colony of Britain in 1888, and the borders between Gambia and Senegal were established by an agreement between Britain and France in 1889.

The Gambia became independent as a constitutional monarchy in 1965 and became a republic in 1970. In 1982, the Gambia and Senegal signed an agreement to unite their armed forces, defense, economies, and currencies. This agreement created what became known as the Senegambia Confederation, but the confederation dissolved in 1989. The two countries remain closely associated with one another, and the idea of confederation remains.

CONTEMPORARY ISSUES

The Gambia's boundary with Senegal has been stable since it was first agreed upon by Britain and France in 1889, and the two countries agreed to their maritime boundaries in 1975. However, tension remains between the Gambia, Senegal, and other countries in West Africa. As a stable and relatively prosperous democracy, the Gambia has seen an influx of refugees from poorer and more unstable countries nearby.

Many of these refugees have moved into the Gambia from the Senegalese province of Casamance, which is located in southwestern Senegal south of the Gambia and north of nearby Guinea-Bissau. Leaders of Casamance have pushed for independence from Senegal since the early 1980s, and the conflict between Casamance and the Senegalese government has escalated into violence on several occasions. The conflict has displaced thousands of refugees, many of whom have moved northward across the boundary into the Gambia. In addition, the Gambia's location at the mouth of the Gambia River and its long history of oceanic trade have made the country an attractive target for smugglers and others who are engaged in illegal trading activities.

See also   Senegal

Further Reading

Daily Observer. "Senegambia revisited." April 7, 2008, http://observer.gm/africa/gambia/article/2008/4/7/senegambia-revisited.

Donald R. Wright. *The world and a very small place in Africa: A history of globalization in Niumi, the Gambia.* London: M. E. Sharpe, 2004.

TOGO

OVERVIEW

The West African country of Togo has a land area of about 22,000 square miles (slightly smaller than West Virginia) with a population of about 6.6 million. The long, narrow country borders Ghana to the west, Burkina Faso to the north, and Benin to the east. To the south, Togo has a short coastline on the Gulf of Guinea.

The boundary between Togo and Ghana is complex but oriented from south to north. It includes straight-line segments, rivers, and drainage divides. It originates less than five miles west of Togo's capital city of Lome and then extends northward. Most of the boundary between Togo and Burkina Faso follows straight lines at or near the 11th parallel of north latitude. The Sansargou River forms a six-mile portion of the eastern portion of this boundary. To the east, the boundary is a straight line connecting the Sansargou with the tripoint where Togo, Burkina Faso, and Benin meet. The boundary between Togo and Benin extends southward from that tripoint to the Gulf of Guinea. It includes numerous short straight-line segments and also follows several streams. Much of the southern portion of this boundary follows the Mora River, which has been dammed in order to provide hydroelectric power to both countries.

HISTORICAL CONTEXT

Togo was part of a German colony known as Togoland from 1884 until 1916. Togoland included present-day Togo along with what is now eastern Ghana. The contemporary boundaries between Togo and its neighbors generally follow boundaries agreed upon by Germany, Britain, and France during the late 19th and early 20th centuries.

Britain and France assumed control of Togoland after World War I broke out in 1914. In 1916, the colony was divided into zones of French occupation to the east and British occupation to the west. These zones were known as French Togoland and British Togoland respectively. British Togoland eventually became part of Ghana, whereas French Togoland became the present-day country of Togo. After ratification of the Treaty of Versailles, French Togoland became a League of Nations mandate with control assigned to France by the League of Nations in 1920. Togo remained a French colony until it became independent in 1960.

The boundary between present-day Togo and present-day Ghana was established initially in 1916 as the boundary between French Togoland and British Togoland. This boundary was delineated formally by agreement between France and Britain in 1929. British Togoland voted to become part of Ghana in 1956, and hence the 1929 boundary became the boundary between Togo and Ghana after both became independent. The boundary between Togoland and Burkina Faso was established in a series of agreements between Germany and France between 1898 and 1902. The Togo-Benin border was agreed upon initially by Germany and France in 1885, and the agreement was modified in 1897.

CONTEMPORARY ISSUES

Togo and Benin have faced minor boundary disputes in recent years. The boundary

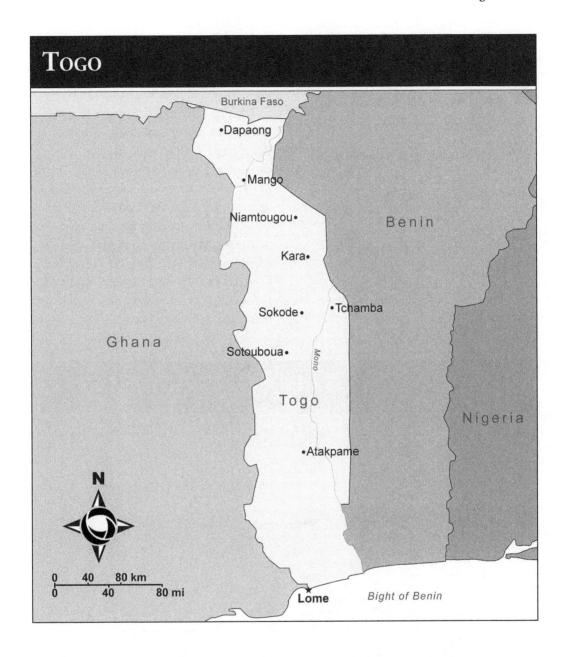

TOGO

between Togo and Benin has been in place since 1897, but in some areas the boundary has not been marked on the ground completely. In 2001, Benin accused Togo of relocating some existing boundary markers eastward in order to expand Togolese territory at the expense of Benin. A joint boundary commission was established in order to delineate the boundary precisely. Both countries agree that the dam on the lower reaches of the Mora River has been successful in providing power and promoting economic development in both Togo and Benin. A second dam has been proposed but has not yet been funded or constructed.

See also   Benin, Burkina Faso, Ghana

Further Reading

Paul Nugent. *Smugglers, secessionists, and loyal citizens on the Ghana-Togo frontier.* Athens: Ohio University Press, 2002.

Charles Piot. *Nostalgia for the future: West Africa after the Cold War.* Chicago: University of Chicago Press.

UGANDA

OVERVIEW

The Republic of Uganda is located in east-central Africa along the north shore of Lake Victoria, which is the largest lake in Africa. Uganda has a land area of 91,136 square miles, slightly larger than Minnesota. Its population is about 37 million.

Uganda is landlocked, and it has boundaries with the Democratic Republic of the Congo to the west, South Sudan to the north, Kenya to the east, and Tanzania and Rwanda to the south. The tripoint between Uganda, the Democratic Republic of the Congo, and Rwanda is located at the southwestern corner of Uganda's Mgahinga National Park on Mount Saby-inyo, an extinct volcano whose summit is nearly 12,000 feet above sea level. From there, the boundary between Uganda and

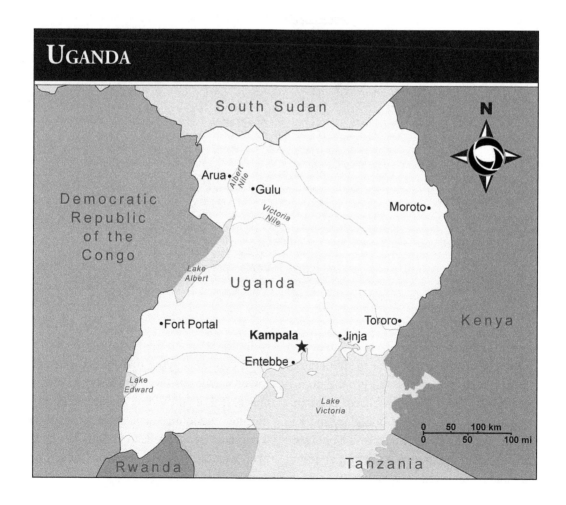

the Democratic Republic of the Congo extends northward to the Ishasha. It follows the Ishasha to its mouth in Lake Edward, which is the smallest of East Africa's Great Lakes. From Lake Edward, the boundary extends northeastward through the Rwenzori Mountains to Lake Albert. North from Lake Albert, the boundary between Uganda and the Democratic Republic of the Congo follows the drainage divide between the Nile River basin in Uganda and the Congo River basin in the Democratic Republic of the Congo. It follows this divide to the tripoint between Uganda, the Democratic Republic of the Congo, and South Sudan near the village of Koluba.

From the tripoint between Uganda, South Sudan, and the Democratic Republic of the Congo, the boundary between Uganda and South Sudan extends eastward. Most of this boundary follows straight-line segments. The longest of these segments extends northeastward from Uganda's Kidepo Valley National Park to the tripoint between Uganda, South Sudan, and Kenya. The boundary between Uganda and Kenya extends southward from this tripoint. It follows a series of short straight-line segments to Mount Elgon. From Mount Elgon, the boundary follows the Sango River southward until it empties into the Sio River, and then it follows the Sio southward until it empties into Lake Victoria.

The tripoint between Uganda, Kenya, and Tanzania is located in Lake Victoria. From that tripoint, the boundary between Uganda and Tanzania follows the 1st parallel of south latitude across the lake and westward on land to the Kagera River. It then follows the Kagera River upstream and westward to the tripoint between Uganda, Tanzania, and Rwanda at

the confluence of the Kagera and its tributary, the Kagitumba River. The Kagitumba forms the eastern portion of the boundary between Uganda and Rwanda. The boundary follows the Kagitumba and its tributaries, the Tshinzingi and Lubirizi rivers, upstream and westward, and then follows short streams and straight-line segments to the peak of Mount Sabyinyo.

HISTORICAL CONTEXT

Present-day Uganda was occupied for many thousands of years by various hunting and gathering cultures before Bantu farmers from central Africa began to move into the country around 2,000 years ago. By the 18th century, the Bunyoro and Buganda kingdoms had become the dominant powers in what is now Uganda. The Bunyoro kingdom was based in the west near Lake Albert, and the Buganda kingdom was centered on the northern shores of Lake Victoria. The country's current name of Uganda comes from the name of the Buganda kingdom.

Uganda's local rulers and populations had little interaction with Europeans until the mid-19th century. Arab and European traders, many of whom were interested in obtaining elephant ivory, began to establish trade linkages with Buganda's rulers and other Ugandan populations in the 1840s. Britain established the British Protectorate of Uganda in 1892. The British negotiated boundary agreements with European colonial powers that controlled neighboring colonies during the late 19th and early 20th centuries.

Britain began preparing Uganda for eventual independence after World War II. In contrast to many other African colonies, there was little organized agitation for independence in part because of Uganda's great national, ethnic, religious, and linguistic diversity. After independence was granted in 1962, these divisions made it difficult for newly independent Uganda to establish political stability.

In 1971, Idi Amin seized power in a military coup d'état. Amin became a notorious and brutal dictator. As many as half a million Ugandans are believed to have been murdered during Amin's rule, and many more left Uganda as refugees. In 1978, Amin initiated an effort to seize the Kagera Province in northwestern Tanzania. This effort led to a brief war between the two countries. Uganda's efforts to obtain Kagera were unsuccessful, and Amin was ousted from power and exiled in 1979. Amin's predecessor, Milton Obote, was elected to the presidency once again in 1981, but Obote was deposed in a military coup d'état in 1985. Multiparty politics were banned in 1986, but the ban was lifted in 2005.

CONTEMPORARY ISSUES

Uganda has been embroiled in a variety of issues involving its African neighbors. As a country that has largely avoided internal armed conflict since the overthrow of the Amin regime, Uganda has attracted numerous refugees from nearby countries. During a civil war in the Democratic Republic of the Congo between 1998 and 2003, thousands of refugees moved across the border from the Democratic Republic into Uganda. Additional refugees have moved across the border in response to the violence that arose as an aftermath of the disputed Congolese elections in late 2011.

In addition, thousands of refugees have moved into Uganda to escape ongoing conflict between Sudan and newly independent South Sudan. As of early 2012, the United Nations estimated that there were between 150,000 and 200,000 refugees from other countries living in Uganda.

Northern Uganda is also the base of operations for the Lord's Resistance Army (LRA), which operates also in neighboring countries. The LRA originated in the late 1980s as an outgrowth of efforts on the part of nations in the northern part of Uganda to oppose the Ugandan central government, which they believed was dominated by Bugandans and other nations in the southern part of the country. The LRA is responsible for numerous atrocities, including the murder of civilians and soldiers and the abduction of thousands of children, some of whom have been conscripted forcibly into the LRA's armed forces. At least a million persons in northern Uganda have been displaced by the LRA. The LRA operates also across Uganda's boundaries in the Democratic Republic of the Congo, South Sudan, and the Central African Republic.

See also   Democratic Republic of the Congo, Kenya, Rwanda, South Sudan, Tanzania

Further Reading

Tim Allen and Koen Vlassenroot. *The Lord's Resistance Army: Myth and reality.* London: Zed Book, 2010.

Cindy McCain. "The plight of Congolese refugees in Uganda." *Huffington Post*, June 8, 2012, http://www.huffing tonpost.com/cindy-mccain/the-plight-of-congolese-r_1_b_1580644.html.

Abraham McLaughlin. "The end of Uganda's mystic rebel?" *Christian*

Science Monitor, December 31, 2004, http://www.globalpolicy.org/component/content/article/165/29547.html.

Thomas P. Ofcansky. *Uganda: Tarnished pearl of Africa.* Boulder, CO: Westview Press, 1999.

ZAMBIA

OVERVIEW

The Republic of Zambia is located in south-central Africa. Its land area is 290,587 square miles, or slightly larger than Texas. Its population is about 14 million. The country derives its name from the Zambezi River, which drains most of the country.

Zambia is landlocked. Its neighbors include Angola to the west, the Democratic Republic of the Congo to the north, Tanzania to the northeast, Malawi to the east, Mozambique to the southeast, and Zimbabwe to the south. To the southwest, Zambia has a very brief boundary with Botswana and a boundary with Namibia's Caprivi Strip. The tripoint between Zambia, Angola, and Namibia is located at the edge of Sioma Ngezi National Park. From that tripoint, it extends northwestward following the drainage divide between the Chobe River on the Angolan side to the southwest

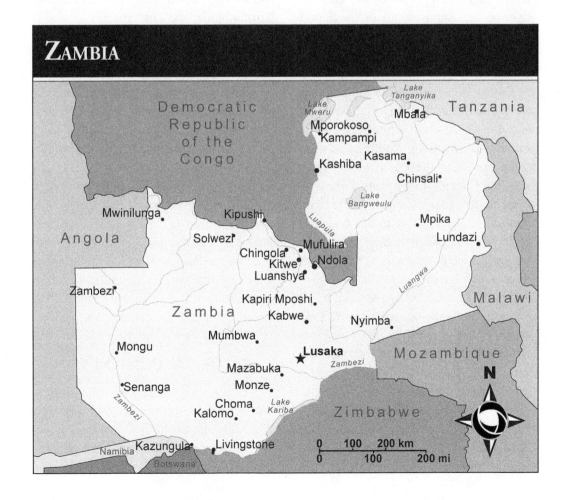

and streams flowing eastward and north-ward into Zambia to the northeast. The boundary continues in this northwesterly direction to the 22nd meridian of east longitude. It then extends northward along the 22nd meridian to the 13th parallel of south longitude. From this intersection the boundary turns eastward along the 13th parallel and then turns northward again following straight-line segments and rivers to the tripoint between Zambia, Angola, and the Democratic Republic of the Congo.

The boundary between Zambia and the Democratic Republic of the Congo extends in an eastward to southeastward direction from this tripoint. In general, it follows the drainage divide between the Zambezi River on the Zambian side of the boundary to the south and the Congo River on the Congolese side of the boundary to the north. Here a Congolese region known as the Congo Pedicle separates northwestern and northeastern Zambia. The boundary then turns northward abruptly, following a meridian separating Zambian territory to the east from the Democratic Republic of the Congo's Demarques de Leshwe nature reserve in the Congo Pedicle to the west. All of the territory in this boundary region is in the Congo drainage basin. The boundary extends northward to the Luapula River, which is a tributary of the Congo. It follows the Luapula to Lake Mweru, which is located along the boundary. From Lake Mweru it follows a straight line that extends east-northeastward to the tripoint between Zambia, the Democratic Republic of the Congo, and Tanzania in Lake Tanganyika.

From Lake Tanganyika, the boundary between Zambia and Tanzania extends in a generally southeasterly direction to the tripoint between Zambia, Tanzania, and

Malawi. From that tripoint, the boundary between Zambia and Malawi extends southward. It generally follows the drainage divide between the main channel of the Zambezi in Zambia and the Shire River, a major tributary of the Zambezi, in Malawi. It continues along this drainage divide to the tripoint between Zambia, Malawi, and Mozambique. The boundary between Zambia and Mozambique extends south-southwestward along straight-line segment to a point east of the Lower Zambezi National Park. It continues southward east of the park to the western end of Lake Cahora Bassa, an artificial lake that was formed by damming the Zambezi in Mozambique. The tripoint between Zambia, Mozambique, and Zimbabwe is located at the western end of the lake.

The entire boundary between Zambia and Zimbabwe is formed by the Zambezi. The boundary extends westward and upstream to the tripoint between Zambia, Zimbabwe, and Botswana. The boundary between Zambia and Zimbabwe includes Victoria Falls, one of the largest waterfalls in the world. A brief boundary between Zambia and Botswana, less than a mile long, also follows the Zambezi. The Zambezi continues as the boundary between Zambia and Namibia, which then follows a straight-line segment from the Zambezi west-southwestward to the tripoint between Zambia, Namibia, and Angola.

HISTORICAL CONTEXT

The original inhabitants of present-day Zambia were hunters and gatherers who were displaced by Bantu farmers by the 12th century AD. Various kingdoms controlled parts of Zambia over the next several hundred years. Europeans began to explore what is now Zambia in the late 18th and early 19th centuries. The British explorer David Livingstone visited Victoria Falls in 1855, and British influence over the area increased.

In 1888, Zambia and Zimbabwe came under British protection, and the colony of Northern Rhodesia was established by the British in 1911. British interest in the area increased after copper was discovered in the northern part of Northern Rhodesia in the 1920s and 1930s. In 1953, Britain joined Northern Rhodesia with Southern Rhodesia (today's Zimbabwe) and Nyasaland (present-day Malawi) to form the Federation of Rhodesia and Nyasaland. The federation continued until 1963, when the three colonies were separated. Northern Rhodesia became an independent country with its present name in 1964.

Zambia became a one-party state in the mid-1960s. Its first president, Kenneth Kaunda, remained president through the 1980s. Global copper prices declined in the 1970s and 1980s, causing considerable economic turmoil in Zambia, whose economy was based largely on copper exports. In 1991, Kaunda agreed to remove the long-standing ban on political parties. The first multiparty election took place that year, and Kaunda was defeated and retired from politics. Multiparty democracy has been retained since then. However, Zambia's economy remains heavily dependent on the copper industry, much of which is controlled by foreign investors.

CONTEMPORARY ISSUES

Zambia's boundaries are stable, and throughout its history it has played an important role in resolving conflicts between African countries. For example, it took a leadership role in mediating civil wars within Angola and with the Democratic Republic of the Congo during the 1990s. Numerous refugees from Angola, the Democratic Republic of the Congo, and other African countries have moved into Zambia. Although many of these refugees have been repatriated, as of 2012 more than 100,000 Angolan and Congolese refugees continued to live in Zambia.

The status of the Congo Pedicle, which extends from the Democratic Republic of the Congo deep into the heart of Zambian territory, is also problematic. Zambia has supported in general the maintenance of boundaries drawn during colonial times, including its own boundaries. However, the Congo Pedicle has affected Zambia's development by cutting off transportation between northeastern and northwestern Zambia. During civil wars in the Democratic Republic of the Congo, Zambians could not cross the Congo Pedicle. With peace having returned to both countries, construction of a road giving unrestricted access to Zambians across the Congo Pedicle is under serious consideration.

See also Angola, Democratic Republic of the Congo, Malawi, Mozambique, Tanzania, Zimbabwe

Further Reading

William Grant. *Zambia then and now: Colonial rulers and their African successors.* London: Routledge, 2009.

Martin W. Lewis. "The Congo Pedicle and its challenges to Zambian development." *Geocurrents*, September 20, 2011, http://geocurrents.info/econo

mic-geography/the-congo-pedicle-and-its-challenges-to-zambian-development.

Denine Waters. "Examining Zambia's copper industry." *Consultancy Africa Intelligence*, August 2, 2010, http://www.consultancyafrica.com/index.php?option=com_content&view=article&id=499:examining-zambias-copper-industry-&catid=82:african-industry-a-business&Itemid=266.

ZIMBABWE

OVERVIEW

The Republic of Zimbabwe is located south of the Zambezi River in south-central Africa. The landlocked country has a land area of 150,871 square miles, slightly larger than Montana. Its population is about 14 million.

Zimbabwe is roughly circular in shape and lies between southern Africa's two major rivers, the Zambezi River and the Limpopo River. Zimbabwe's neighbors are Zambia to the north, Mozambique to the east, South Africa to the south, and Botswana to the southwest. The tripoint between Zimbabwe, Zambia, and Botswana is located on the Zambezi River. This tripoint is located less than a mile downstream from the tripoint between Zambia, Botswana, and the Caprivi Strip of Namibia. From the tripoint between Zimbabwe, Zambia, and Mozambique, the Zambezi flows eastward, forming the entire boundary between Zimbabwe and Zambia. The tripoint between Zimbabwe, Zambia, and Mozambique is located on the Zambezi at the extreme western end of Lake Cahora Bassa, an artificial lake that was created by damming the Zambezi in Mozambique.

From the tripoint on Lake Cahora Bassa, the boundary between Zimbabwe and Mozambique follows short straight-line segments primarily. It forms a rough semicircle eastward, southward, and then westward to the tripoint between Zimbabwe, Mozambique, and South Africa on the Limpopo River. The boundary between Zimbabwe and South Africa follows the Limpopo upstream to the tripoint between Zimbabwe, South Africa, and Botswana at the confluence between the Limpopo and its tributary, the Shashe River. From this tripoint, the boundary follows the Shashe upstream to its confluence with the Ramaquaban River, and then up the Ramaquaban to its source. It continues northwestward past Zimbabwe's Hwange National Park to the Zambezi.

HISTORICAL CONTEXT

The precolonial history of present-day Zimbabwe begins with the migration of Bantu tribes from the north around 1,000 years ago. Between the 13th and 15th centuries, much of what is now Zimbabwe was governed by the Kingdom of Zimbabwe, from which the present-day state derives its name. The Kingdom of Mutapa supplanted the Kingdom of Zimbabwe in the 15th century. Both kingdoms established thriving trade linkages with Arab traders on the Indian Ocean. In the 17th century, Portuguese forces invaded the area but were repulsed by local rulers.

The British South Africa Company, headed by Cecil Rhodes, began taking interest in present-day Zimbabwe in the late 19th century. In 1888, Rhodes negotiated mining rights in the area via treaties with local leaders. These treaties were followed

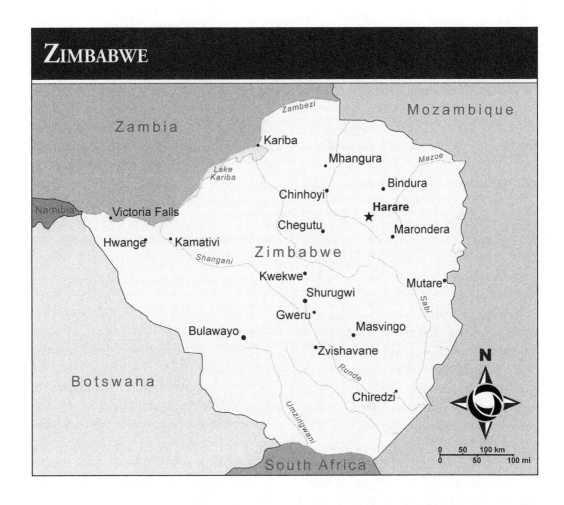

ZIMBABWE

by two wars in which British troops asserted control of the region and deposed the local rulers and chiefs. The area was named Southern Rhodesia in 1898, with the name Northern Rhodesia given to what is now Zambia. The Zambezi River became the boundary between Southern Rhodesia and Northern Rhodesia, and it remains the boundary between Zambia and Zimbabwe today.

In contrast to many other European colonies in Africa, Southern Rhodesia was settled by substantial numbers of European farmers, planters, and miners. The white population of present-day Zimbabwe has been estimated at more than 300,000 by 1970 and increased rapidly in the 1970s as many people of European ancestry moved into Southern Rhodesia from other parts of Africa.

In 1953, Britain merged Southern Rhodesia, Northern Rhodesia, and Nyasaland (present-day Malawi) into the Federation of Rhodesia and Nyasaland. As elsewhere in Africa, the economy of the federation was dominated by the European minority, who owned a large share of land and other resources. The federation was dissolved in 1964, and Zambia and Malawi became independent countries. However, Southern Rhodesia remained a British colony and changed its name to Rhodesia after the former Northern Rhodesia became independent.

In 1965, white leaders in Rhodesia led by Ian Smith issued a Unilateral Declaration of Independence. Under terms of the Unilateral Declaration, the white minority-dominated government of Rhodesia remained in power. The Unilateral Declaration was condemned quickly by the United Nations on the grounds that it was an illegal seizure of power by a "racist minority" of the population. The British Commonwealth also condemned the Unilateral Declaration as illegal. In the 1970s, civil war broke out between guerillas associated with the Zimbabwe African National Union (ZANU) and the Rhodesian government. ZANU was aided by Zambia and Mozambique in its efforts to topple the Smith government. The government was supported by South Africa's white-minority apartheid government.

By the late 1970s, many Rhodesians of European ancestry had left the country, and the population included approximately 20 Africans to every European. ZANU and other guerilla organizations were supported more strongly by the international community. The United States imposed economic sanctions on Rhodesia, and in 1976 South Africa withdrew its support for Smith's regime. Multiracial elections were held in 1979, and ZANU won a majority of legislative seats.

In 1980, the country became the independent state of Zimbabwe. Robert Mugabe, a ZANU leader, became Zimbabwe's first prime minister. Mugabe dissolved the office of prime minister in 1987, becoming president. Since then, Mugabe

has remained in power and has functioned in effect as a dictator. He has been re-elected in several elections since 1987, but the elections have been condemned by the international community as rigged and unfair. Mugabe's regime has been criticized vigorously by the international community for numerous human rights violations. In recent years, Zimbabwe has been plagued not only by these human rights violations but by famine, the HIV/AIDS pandemic, and outbreaks of other diseases.

CONTEMPORARY ISSUES

The abuses of Mugabe's regime have enhanced tensions between Zimbabwe and many other countries. After Mugabe's reelection in 2008, Zambia condemned the Mugabe government, including its refusal to hold free elections, as a "regional embarrassment." Kenya's president advocated Zimbabwe's expulsion from the African Union. In 2009, Mugabe agreed to a power-sharing arrangement with his principal rivals. During the Mugabe regime, thousands of Zimbabweans have left the country as refugees.

See also Botswana, Mozambique, South Africa, Zambia

Further Reading

Ian Bremmer. "Zimbabwe is set for more uncertainty." *Foreign Policy*, September 30, 2011, http://eurasia.foreignpolicy.com/posts/2011/09/30/zimbabwe_is_set_for_more_uncertainty.

Martin Meredith. *Power, plunder, and the struggle for Zimbabwe's future.* New York: PublicAffairs, 2007.

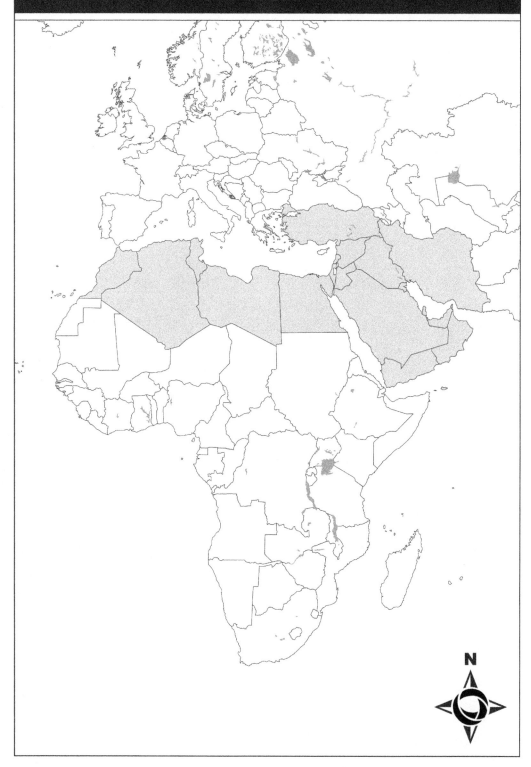

CHAPTER 4

SOUTHWEST ASIA AND NORTH AFRICA

Southwest Asia and North Africa, which is often called the Middle East, includes the Asian countries of Turkey, Syria, Lebanon, Israel, Jordan, Saudi Arabia, Yemen, the United Arab Emirates, Qatar, Bahrain, Oman, Kuwait, Iraq, and Iran. In North Africa, the region includes the countries of Morocco, Algeria, Tunisia, Libya, and Egypt.

The region is defined by many common characteristics. Much of the region has a dry climate, and the region includes the Sahara, which is the world's largest desert. The region is the area of origin for Islam, and a large majority of current residents are Muslims. Many residents of the region are of Arabic ancestry, although many non-Arabs reside in Southwest Asia and North Africa. Many, but by no means all, of the countries in the region have significant petroleum reserves.

Of course, these general characteristics do not apply to the entire region. Areas of countries such as Morocco, Algeria, Tunisia, and Turkey receive plentiful rainfall, allowing for productive agriculture. In other areas such as the Nile valley of Egypt and the Fertile Crescent of Mesopotamia, major rivers have provided enough water to permit productive agriculture for thousands of years. Substantial non-Muslim populations are found throughout the region. A majority of Israel's people are Jewish, and there are substantial Christian majorities in Lebanon and other countries. Most people in the Arabian Peninsula and North Africa are Arabs, but two of the largest and most influential countries in the region, Turkey and Iran, are non-Arab.

Given its location near the intersection of Europe, Asia, and Africa, it is not surprising that Southwest Asia and North Africa has been an important trading and cultural crossroads for several thousand years. The region has experienced numerous conflicts over territorial control and governance throughout history. As the events of the Arab Spring of 2011 indicated, the area remains a region whose sovereignty and boundaries are highly contested.

Throughout recorded history, parts of Southwest Asia and North Africa have been controlled by various kingdoms and dynasties, many of which originated outside the region. Ancient Egypt was ruled by various dynasties, whose histories have been recorded, for several thousand years. Portions of Mesopotamia were ruled by the Assyrians, Babylonians, and Persians between 2,000 and 3,000 years ago. At other times, parts of the region were ruled by empires based outside of the region.

Alexander the Great conquered much of the area about 330 BC, and after his death much of his empire was ruled by Hellenistic kingdoms centered in present-day Greece. The Hellenistic Empire was displaced by the Romans, who ruled over most of Southwest Asia and North Africa for several centuries until they themselves lost their grip on the region.

Other empires controlled the region after the expulsion of the Romans. Following the death of the Prophet Muhammad in AD 632, his successors established the Umayyad Caliphate. At its zenith, the Umayyad Caliphate controlled all of the Arabian Peninsula along with territories as far east as modern-day Pakistan, as far north as modern Armenia and Azerbaijan, and as far west as present-day Morocco, Spain, and Portugal. Beginning in the 16th century, the Ottoman Empire included all of present-day Turkey along with Mesopotamia, Iran, Egypt, and coastal regions of North Africa as well as southeastern Europe.

Although control of Southwest Asia and North Africa was contested, often violently, between these and other ruling dynasties, until recently boundaries between various kingdoms and dynasties were defined only loosely and vaguely. That boundaries were not defined clearly prior to the modern era is due in part to the region's highly uneven population distribution. For example, over a period of 5,000 years, Egypt was controlled by various Egyptian-based dynasties, the Roman Empire, the Umayyad Caliphate, and the Ottoman Empire. However, this control was concentrated in the Nile valley in which the very large majority of Egyptians live. Areas located more than a few miles from the Nile valley were uninhabited and therefore uncontested.

Today, almost all boundaries in Southwest Asia and North Africa are defined completely, and many are contested. Boundary delineation has occurred not only because the European system of states diffused into Southwest Asia and North Africa, but also because of conflict between nations and because of the discovery of valuable natural resources. For example, Saudi Arabia's boundaries with Qatar, the United Arab Emirates, and Oman were not delineated formally until oil reserves were discovered in the region during the 20th century. Once oil was discovered, its value encouraged countries to define their boundaries accurately in order for each country to get what it regarded as its fair share of oil resources. Territorial conflicts have also arisen over control of transportation corridors and, increasingly, water resources given the area's rapid population growth and dry climate.

ALGERIA

OVERVIEW

The People's Democratic Republic of Algeria is part of the Maghreb region that includes Morocco, Tunisia, and Libya and extends across North Africa from Egypt to the Atlantic Ocean. Algeria has a land area of 920,000 square miles, making it nearly twice as large as Alaska. With South Sudan having split from Sudan to become an independent country, Algeria is now the largest country by land area on the continent of Africa.

Algeria has a population of about 35 million. Much of Algeria's land is located

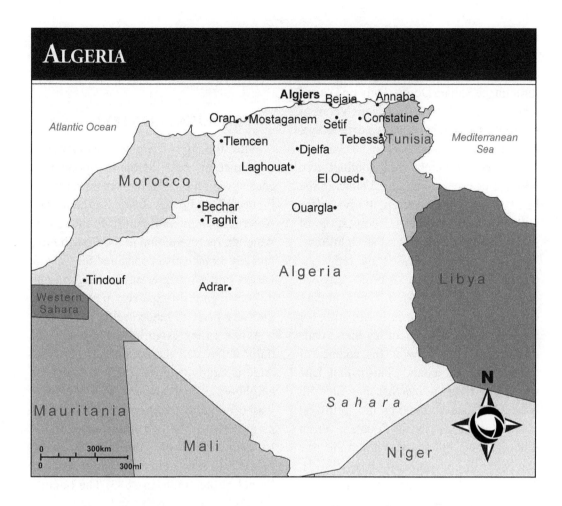

ALGERIA

Algiers Bejaia   Annaba
Atlantic Ocean
Oran Mostaganem Setif Constatine
Tlemcen   Tebessa Tunisia   Mediterranean
Djelfa   Sea
Laghouat•
El Oued•
Morocco
•Bechar   Ouargla•
•Taghit

Algeria

•Tindouf   Adrar•   Libya
Western
Sahara

Mauritania   Sahara

0   300km
0   300mi   Mali   Niger

N

in the sparsely populated Sahara Desert. More than 70 percent of Algeria's people live in the coastal strip between the Atlas Mountains and the Mediterranean Sea. More than 97 percent of the people are Arabs or Berbers, and more than 98 percent are Muslims.

Algeria's neighbors are Tunisia and Libya to the east, Niger to the southeast, Mali to the south, and Mauritania and Morocco to the west. The Mediterranean Sea adjoins Algeria to the north. Algeria's borders with Tunisia and Libya follow straight-line segments. The boundary between Algeria and

Tunisia extends southward from the Mediterranean coast and then turns westward to a point south of the Algerian town of Ain el-Assel. From there, the boundary turns southward and southwestward to El-Kala National Park. It then extends southward to the Chott el-Gharsa. The Chott el-Gharsa is a salt lake that is filled with water only during the winter and dries up during the hot, dry summers. South of the Chott el-Gharsa, the boundary continues southward following straight-line segments through very sparsely populated territory to the tripoint between Algeria, Tunisia, and Libya near the village of Ghudamis in Libya. The boundary between Algeria and Libya continues southward and southeastward through the Sahara Desert. Only one paved road crosses this boundary, which continues to the tripoint between Algeria, Libya, and Niger.

Algeria's southern and southwestern boundaries cross uninhabited areas in the heart of the Sahara Desert. Its boundary with Niger is geometric, consisting of several northeast-southwest straight lines. This boundary is crossed by only one paved road. From the tripoint between Algeria, Niger, and Mali, the boundary continues in a southwesterly direction for about 63 miles. The boundary then trends northwestward, following the courses of the I-n-Akantarer and Tin-in-Zouatene wadis (dry river valleys that may fill with water after heavy rains) as far northwest at the source of the Tin-in-Zouatene. From this point, the boundary is a straight line extending from southeast to northwest. This line continues northwestward to become the boundary between Algeria and Mauritania.

The boundary between Algeria and Morocco includes a short segment along the 8° 40′ meridian extending northward from the tripoint between these countries and Mauritania. This meridian includes the boundary between Algeria and the disputed territory of Western Sahara. At 27° 40′ north latitude, the Algeria-Morocco boundary trends northeastward, remaining south of the Atlas Mountains. Much of this boundary follows the Draa River. Near the Algerian town of Beni Ounif, the boundary turns northward, crosses the mountains, and extends through thickly populated territory to the Mediterranean. To the north, the boundary passes just west of the Moroccan city of Oujda.

HISTORICAL CONTEXT

After the city of Algiers was captured by France in 1830, the densely populated coastal region of Algeria was annexed by France. The French treated present-day Algeria as an integral part of France, with Algerian representation in the French Parliament. France also controlled the Sahara Desert portion of present-day Algeria but did not regard this sparsely populated region as a part of France itself.

While ruling Algeria, the French initially delineated the boundaries between Algeria and its eastern and western neighbors. The boundary with Morocco was originally determined by an agreement between the two countries in 1845. Its boundaries with Tunisia were established by France after Tunisia became a French protectorate in 1883. The boundary between Algeria and Libya was agreed upon by a treaty between France and Italy in 1919. This treaty was modified by an agreement between France and independent Libya in 1956. The revised agreement clarified the boundary between Algeria and Libya.

France continued to treat Algeria as part of France after World War II, but many Algerians began to oppose continued French rule over Algeria. Representation in the Algerian Parliament was an issue, because Muslims were entitled to only half of the seats, whereas Europeans and other non-Muslim residents were entitled to the other half. Opposition escalated into open rebellion in 1954. In a referendum held in 1958, a large majority of Algeria's people voted for independence. After eight years of warfare, Algeria became an independent country with its present boundaries in 1962.

CONTEMPORARY ISSUES

Algeria's major conflict involves its western neighbor, Morocco. The issue involves control of the former Spanish colony of Western Sahara. Western Sahara was a Spanish colony known as Spanish Sahara from the 1880s until 1975. At that time, Spain relinquished control of Spanish Sahara, and the region was administered jointly by its neighbors, Morocco and Mauritania. However, Morocco claimed sovereignty over the entire territory.

Today, Morocco maintains effective control over most of the region. However, an Algerian-backed insurgent movement known as the Polisario has agitated for independence for Western Sahara. The Polisario is associated with the Sahwari Arab Democratic Republic (SADR), which also claims sovereignty over Western Sahara. Although Algeria has made no territorial claims in Western Sahara, it strongly supports the Polisario and SADR in part because it opposes Moroccan expansion.

See also Libya, Mali, Mauritania, Morocco, Niger, Tunisia

Further Reading

Erik Jensen. *Western Sahara: Anatomy of a stalemate.* Boulder, CO: Lynne Rienner, 2005.

Azzedine Layachi. "Meanwhile in the Maghreb." *Foreign Affairs,*March 31, 2011.

John Phillips and Martin Evans. *Algeria: Anger of the dispossessed.* New Haven, CT: Yale University Press, 2011.

John Ruedy. *Modern Algeria: The origins and development of a nation.* 2nd ed. Bloomington: Indiana University Press, 2005.

BAHRAIN

OVERVIEW

The Kingdom of Bahrain consists of an archipelago of 33 islands in the Persian Gulf. The country's total land area is about 290 square miles, or four times as large as the District of Columbia. The population is about 1.2 million. The main island, known as Bahrain Island, contains about three-quarters of the country's land area and a majority of the population.

As an island state, Bahrain has no land boundaries. Its closest neighbors are Saudi Arabia, across the Persian Gulf to the west, and Qatar, across the Persian Gulf to the south. The Saudi coast is about 8 miles west of the Bahraini island of Umm an Nasan and 12 miles west of the main island. The coast of Qatar is about 20 miles from Bahrain Island. Bahrain's Hawar Islands are located only a mile from the Qatari mainland. The King Faud Causeway connects Bahrain Island with Saudi Arabia, and a longer bridge connecting the island with Qatar is under construction.

BAHRAIN

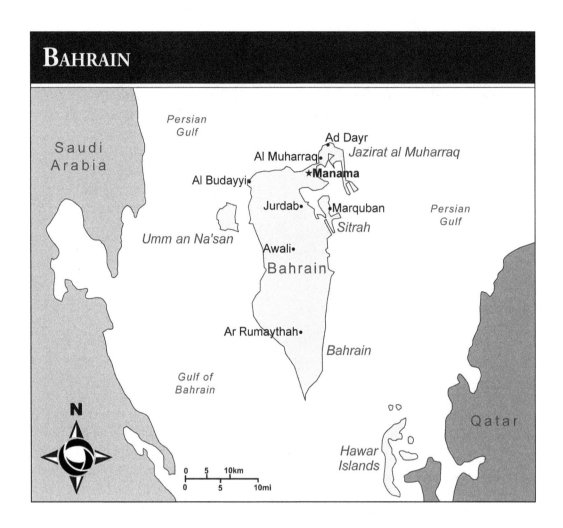

HISTORICAL CONTEXT

Since the Middle Ages, Bahrain has been controlled at various times by kingdoms from present-day Iran, Iraq, and Saudi Arabia. Portugal claimed Bahrain in 1521, but the Portuguese were expelled by the Persian-based Safavid dynasty in 1602. The Safavids ruled Bahrain until 1722, when they were ousted from present-day Iran. Iranian rulers continued to control Bahrain until the early 19th century.

In 1820, the Al-Khalifa family, which originated in present-day Kuwait, became the ruling dynasty of Bahrain. During the 19th century, the British achieved major influence in Bahrain and throughout the Persian Gulf region. In 1868, the Al-Khalifa rulers and the British signed a treaty placing Bahrain under British protection. Bahrain became an important trading center, and the discovery of oil in 1932 added to Bahrain's prosperity. Iran claimed sovereignty over Bahrain beginning in 1923, and in 1957 the shah of Iran declared that Bahrain was an Iranian province. In 1970, Britain and Iran agreed to hold a referendum through which Bahraini residents would express their views on Bahrain's sovereignty. A large majority of voters supported complete independence, and Bahrain was recognized as an independent state.

CONTEMPORARY ISSUES

The major issue facing contemporary Bahrain involves conflict between Shi'ite and Sunni Muslims. The conflict is associated with Bahrain's location between the Sunni-dominated Arabian mainland and Shi'ite-dominated Iran. The various dynasties that ruled Bahrain were associated with both branches of Islam.

Today, about three-quarters of Bahrain's people practice Shi'ite Islam. However, the ruling Al-Khalifa family is Sunni. The Shi'ite majority has accused the royal family and other Bahraini leaders of giving preferential treatment to Sunni Muslims. The royal family has also been accused of encouraging immigration by Sunni Muslims from other countries in order to decrease the size of the country's Shi'ite majority.

During the Arab Spring demonstrations throughout the Middle East, tensions rose in Bahrain. In February 2011, protestors took to the streets demanding democracy and recognition of Shi'ite rights. The protestors were supported by Iran, while Saudi Arabia and other Sunni-majority states on the Arabian Peninsula supported the government. The government quickly cracked down on the protestors, with hundreds of protestors detained or arrested. At least 36 Bahrainis are known to have lost their lives during the protests.

Bahrain and Qatar have experienced ongoing conflict over control of the Hawar Islands, which are located in the Bay of Bahrain between Bahrain Island and the mainland. The largest island, Hawar, contains more than 80 percent of the disputed territory. The islands were settled by people from Bahrain in the 19th century. In 2001, the International Court of Justice resolved the dispute in favor of Bahrain. Currently, efforts are under way to construct a causeway to be known as the Qatar-Bahrain Friendship Bridge. This bridge would connect Bahrain Island with the mainland of Qatar. A Bahraini newspaper reported in early 2011 that the bridge has been scheduled for opening in 2015.

Further Reading

Ian Black. "Bahrain: A special case among the Arab Spring uprisings." *Guardian*, June 19, 2012, http://www.guardian.co.uk/world/2012/jun/19/bahrain-special-case-arab-spring.

Krista E. Wiegand. "Bahrain, Qatar, and the Hawar Islands: Resolution of a Gulf territorial dispute." *Middle East Journal*, 66 (2012), pp. 79–96.

EGYPT

OVERVIEW

The Arab Republic of Egypt is located in the northeastern corner of Africa and includes the Sinai Peninsula of Asia. With a land area of approximately 390,000 square miles, Egypt is larger than Texas and New Mexico combined. More than 90 percent of Egypt's land is in Africa, with the Sinai Peninsula in Asia having a land

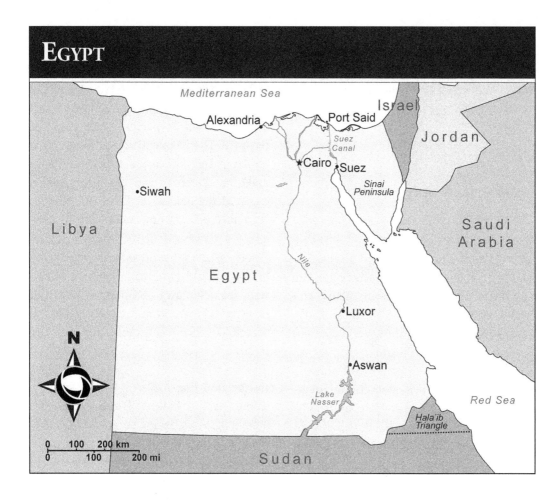

EGYPT

area of about 23,000 square miles. Egypt is by far the largest country in North Africa by population, with nearly 85 million people.

The entire African portion of Egypt is located in the Sahara Desert. A large majority of Egyptians live in the valley of the Nile River, which is the only permanent river to cross the desert. Most areas more than 10 miles from the river are sparsely populated or uninhabited. Egypt's capital city of Cairo is the largest city on the African continent. About 17 million people live in Cairo or its suburbs.

Egypt's neighbors are Libya to the west, Sudan to the south, and Israel to the northeast. Northeastern Egypt also faces Jordan and Saudi Arabia across the long, narrow Gulf of Aqaba. Northern Egypt has a long coastline on the Mediterranean Sea, and eastern Egypt has a long coastline on the Red Sea. The Mediterranean and Red seas are connected by the Suez Canal.

The boundary between Egypt and Libya is entirely geometric. The northern portion of the boundary includes numerous short straight-line segments. The southern three-quarters of the boundary follows the 25th meridian of east longitude. This section of the boundary crosses uninhabited desert territory and has never been demarcated clearly.

The tripoint between Egypt, Libya, and Sudan is located at the intersection of the 25th meridian and the 22nd parallel of north latitude. From this tripoint, the 22nd parallel forms most of the boundary between Egypt and Sudan. An area known as the Hala'ib Triangle is located along the Red Sea north of the 22nd parallel in southeastern Egypt. The Hala'ib Triangle includes about 8,000 square miles of territory with a population of about 30,000. It has been administered by Sudan since the early 20th century but is also claimed by Egypt.

The current boundary between Egypt and Israel is also geometric. It crosses the Negev Desert in a south-southeasterly direction from the Mediterranean Sea near the Egyptian town of Rafah to the Gulf of Aqaba just west of the Israeli city of Eilat. This boundary has been contested between the two countries since Israel became independent in 1948.

HISTORICAL CONTEXT

Egypt is one of the world's oldest civilizations. People have lived along the banks of the Nile River for more than 5,000 years, relying on annual floods along the Nile to irrigate crops. Egypt was first unified about 3150 BC. Over the next 3,000 years, it was ruled by a series of dynasties until 323 BC, when the Ptolemaic dynasty was established. Ptolemy I, the founder of the Ptolemaic dynasty, was a contemporary of Alexander the Great and was Egypt's first foreign-born ruler. Rome conquered Egypt in 30 BC, and Egypt became part of the Roman Empire.

In the seventh century, Egypt became part of the Islamic Caliphate, and most of its people were converted to Islam. Rulers associated with the caliphate continued to govern Egypt until it was incorporated into the Ottoman Empire in 1517. The Ottomans were expelled in 1801 and Kavalali Mehmed Ali Pasha became the sultan of Egypt in 1805. Ali Pasha, who took the name Muhammad Ali, established a dynasty that ruled Egypt until the monarchy was toppled in 1952.

European powers began to take an interest in Egypt beginning in the late 18th century. By the early 19th century, the British had become the dominant European power in Egypt. Although Egypt remained nominally independent, the British were the effective rulers of the country, and Egypt became a British protectorate. The 22nd parallel was established as the boundary between Egypt and Sudan in 1899. The boundaries between Egypt and Libya, then an Italian colony, were agreed upon in 1925.

European powers constructed the Suez Canal, which is located at the west of the Sinai Peninsula and connects the Mediterranean Sea and the Red Sea, in the late 19th century. The opening of the canal reduced the cost of trade between Europe and Asia dramatically. No longer did ships have to circumnavigate Africa to travel between European and Asiatic ports. The canal was built originally by French engineers. It was opened to shipping in 1869. Britain took control of the canal in 1882 and administered it until 1952. The Suez Canal is 119 miles long. Because of the flat terrain, there are no locks on the canal.

In 1952, Egyptian army officers overthrew the monarchy and established the Egyptian Republic. In 1956, Egypt under its new ruler, Gamal Abdul Nasser, nationalized the Suez Canal. In response, Britain, France, and Israel invaded Egypt. After the United States declined to intervene, the Suez Crisis eased, and the British and French troops withdrew. The canal was reopened to shipping in 1957. In 1958, Egypt and Syria unified under the name of the United Arab Republic. Syria withdrew from this confederation in 1961, but Egypt continued to be known as the United Arab Republic until 1969.

Egypt and Israel maintained an antagonistic relationship from 1948 through 1979. The two countries went to war in 1948, 1956, 1967, and 1973. The 1967 conflict, known as the Six-Day War, resulted in a decisive victory for Israeli forces. After the war, Israel occupied the Sinai Peninsula and the neighboring Gaza Strip, which is located northeast of the peninsula along the southeast coast of the Mediterranean. In response, Egypt closed the Suez Canal. The canal remained closed until Egypt reopened it in 1975.

In 1977, Egyptian president Anwar Sadat became the first ruler in the Arab world to visit Israel. His visit led to the Camp David Accords, which resulted in the signing of a peace treaty between Egypt and Israel in 1979. Under the terms of this treaty, Egypt recognized Israel and guaranteed access to the canal to Israeli ships. Israel removed its troops from the Sinai Peninsula, and full control over the peninsula was returned to Egypt. Sadat was assassinated by fundamentalist Egyptian officers in 1981, but Egypt and Israel have maintained diplomatic relations since 1980.

After Sadat's assassination, Hosni Mubarak succeeded to the presidency of Egypt. Mubarak pursued a moderate foreign policy and retained cordial relations with Israel, but his rule within Egypt came to be perceived as increasing autocratic and corrupt. Widespread protests against Mubarak's regime began in January 2011. Mubarak resigned on February 11. The Supreme Council of the Armed Forces assumed power temporarily with the promise of free elections, which were held later in 2011. Candidates supported by Islamic fundamentalist parties won a majority of seats in the first post-Mubarak Parliament. In June of 2012, Mohammed Morsi was elected president of Egypt. Morsi was supported strongly by Islamic fundamentalists. After his election, Morsi declared that his government would honor Egypt's long-standing treaties and agreements with Israel. However, some have expressed concern that Morsi's government will abrogate the agreements eventually.

CONTEMPORARY ISSUES

Aside from ongoing conflict with Israel, the main boundary-related issue facing Egypt today is the resolution of the dispute with Sudan over the Hala'ib Triangle. In 1992, Sudan granted oil exploration rights in the Red Sea off the coast of the Hala'ib Triangle to a Canadian-based oil company. Egypt objected and sent troops into the area. The possibility of valuable resources in and off the coast of the Hala'ib Triangle resulted in intensification of the boundary dispute. In 1995, Sudan asked Egypt to submit the dispute for arbitration by the Organization of African Unity (OAU). Egypt refused this request. Tensions increased after an assassination attempt on Mubarak at an OAU meeting in Addis Ababa, Ethiopia, later in 1995. Egypt accused Sudan of complicity in the attack on Mubarak's life and sent additional troops into the triangle region.

Sudan withdrew its forces from the triangle in 2000, giving de facto control of the region to Egypt. However, Sudan continued to claim sovereignty over the triangle and pointed out the historical and ethnic ties between the region's residents and Sudan. Egypt has blockaded the region and restricted movement of Sudanese people and goods in the area. A referendum in which residents of the Hala'ib Triangle would be given the opportunity to vote on their political status as part of Egypt or Sudan has been proposed.

See also   Israel, Libya, Sudan

Further Reading

Ian Black. "Egypt protests: Israel fears unrest may threaten peace treaty." *Guardian*, January 31, 2011, http://www.guardian.co.uk/world/2011/jan/31/israel-egypt-mubarak-peace-treaty-fears.

Daniel Brumberg. "Can Egypt unite?" *Foreign Policy*, June 25, 2012, http://mideast.foreignpolicy.com/posts/2012/06/25/can_egypt_unite.

Steven A. Cook. *The struggle for Egypt: From Nasser to Tahrir Square*. New York: Oxford University Press, 2011.

David H. Shinn. "Nile Basin relations: Egypt, Sudan, and Ethiopia." George Washington University, Elliott School of International Affairs, July 2006, http://elliott.gwu.edu/news/speeches/shinn0706_nilebasin.cfm.

IRAN

OVERVIEW

The Islamic Republic of Iran is located in southwestern Asia. Iran's land area is 636,372 square miles, or slightly larger than Alaska. Its population is approximately 80 million.

Iran's neighbors are Iraq to the west, Turkey to the northwest, Armenia and Azerbaijan to the north, Turkmenistan to the northeast, and Afghanistan and Pakistan to the east. The Caspian Sea borders Iran to the north, between its borders with Azerbaijan and Turkmenistan. Iran has coastlines on the Persian Gulf to the west and south and the Gulf of Oman to the south. The Strait of Hormuz, which connects the Persian Gulf and the Gulf of Oman, separates Iran from Oman and the United Arab Emirates. At its narrowest point, the strait is only 21 miles wide.

From the Persian Gulf, the boundary between Iran and Iraq begins at the mouth of the Shatt al-Arab, or the combined delta of the Tigris and Euphrates rivers. It follows straight-line segments that parallel the course of the Shatt al-Arab inland and northwestward. It then turns northward, leaving the Mesopotamian plain into the Zagros Mountains. It continues through the Zagros Mountains, following drainage divides and some short streams, to the tripoint between Iran, Iraq, and Turkey. From this point, the boundary between Iran and Turkey continues along straight-line segments northward to a point near the village of Siru Ma'qui. Here it turns sharply

IRAN

westward to a point near Mount Ararat in Turkey, and from there it follows the Qareh Su River to the tripoint between Iran, Turkey, and the enclave of Nakhchivan in Azerbaijan.

The boundary between Iran and Nakhchivan follows the Aras River southeastward and downstream from this tripoint. The Aras forms the boundary between Iran and Nakhchivan and the short boundary between Iran and Armenia. From the tripoint between Iran, Armenia, and the main portion of Azerbaijan, the Aras turns northeastward. The river remains the boundary between Iran and Armenia to a point south

of the Azeri village of Bahramtepe. Here the boundary turns eastward, while the course of the Aras continues northeastward until it empties into the Caspian Sea in Azerbaijan. The boundary then follows a diagonal straight line southeastward for about 35 miles, then turns southward and eventually eastward into the Caspian Sea.

The western end of the boundary between Iran and Turkmenistan is located on the eastern shore of the Caspian Sea near the mouth of the Atrek River. Most of the boundary follows the channel of the Atrek River eastward and then southeastward. The Atrek flows through desert and semidesert regions, and its waters are used heavily for irrigation. Thus the lower reaches of the river are often dry except in the event of flooding or unusually heavy rainfall. From the Atrek, the boundary then follows straight lines eastward and southward to the Harirud River, which it follows southward to the tripoint between Iran, Turkmenistan, and Afghanistan. The Harirud is known in Turkmenistan as the Tedzhen River and, like the Atrek, is subject to overuse and dries up under drought conditions.

The Harirud forms the northern portion of the boundary between Iran and Afghanistan. To the south, the course upstream of the Harirud turns eastward, and the boundary between Iran and Afghanistan continues in a generally southward direction to the tripoint between Iran, Afghanistan, and Pakistan. Most of this boundary follows straight-line segments, but a small portion of it follows the course of the Helmand River, which is a major source of irrigation water for both countries. From this tripoint, the boundary between Iran and Pakistan continues in a southerly direction following a combination of drainage divides, straight-line segments, and short stretches along rivers. The southernmost section of this boundary is a straight-line segment that extends in a south-southwesterly direction just east of Iran's Bahukalat Protected Area to the Gulf of Oman.

HISTORICAL CONTEXT

Agricultural communities developed in present-day Iran in the fourth millennium BC. Most of what is now northern and central Iran was united into a single political unit by the Medes in the seventh century BC. The Medean Empire was conquered in 550 BC by Persian forces under Cyrus the Great, who established the Achaemenid, or Persian, Empire. For the next two centuries, the Persian Empire was the largest and most powerful empire in the world. At its height, it included much of Turkey, the Nile delta of Egypt and the coastline of the Mediterranean between the Nile delta and the Anatolian peninsula, and present-day western Afghanistan and western Pakistan as well as most of Iran itself.

The Achaemenid Empire was overthrown by Alexander the Great in 333 BC. The next major empire to arise in present-day Iran was the Parthian Empire, which ruled Iran between 238 BC and AD 226. Roman forces under the command of Marc Antony tried unsuccessfully to overthrow the Parthians about 30 BC. The Roman and Parthian empires continued to contest the areas along their frontier, which extended from the Black Sea through present-day eastern Turkey into central Syria. The Parthians were overthrown by the Sassanid Empire, which ruled most of Iran into the seventh century AD.

Muslim invaders attacked the Sassanid Empire beginning about AD 642. By AD 651, the Sassanids had been overthrown, and most of present-day Iran came under Muslim rule. Disagreement about leadership of the Islamic community after the death of Mohammed led eventually to a schism within Islam between Shi'ite and Sunni Muslims. The schism was complete by about AD 680. Worldwide, the large majority of Muslims are Sunnis. However, most Iranians are Shi'ite Muslims. Tension between the Shi'ite and Sunni interpretations of Islam affected relationships between Iran and its Muslim neighbors and continues to do so today.

Unlike most of its neighbors, Iran remained independent throughout its history and was never incorporated into a European colonial empire. In 1925, the Qajars were overthrown by the Pahlavi dynasty. Reza Khan ruled as the first shah until he was forced to abdicate by Britain and the Soviet Union during World War II. His son, Mohammad Reza Shah Pahlavi, became shah. In 1979, he was ousted and exiled during the Iranian Revolution, and the country was given its present name of the Islamic Republic of Iran. The new government, led by Ayatollah Ruhollah Khomeini, established a theocratic state based on the principles of Shi'ite Islam. Iran and Iraq went to war during the 1980s, with a major issue being control of the oil-rich province of Khuzestan in western Iran along the Iraqi border. War between Iran and Iraq continued until 1988, when the two countries agreed to a cease-fire after as many as half a million Iranian and Iraqi soldiers had been killed during the war. Under terms of the cease-fire agreement, the boundary between Iran and Iraq remained intact.

Most of Iran's boundaries predate World War II. The frontier between the Ottoman Empire, which controlled present-day Turkey and Iraq before World War I, and Persia was recognized by the two empires in 1639. It was delineated more precisely beginning in 1911. In 1913, the Constantinople Agreement established the boundary between Iran, then known as Persia, and the Ottoman Empire, including present-day Iraq. However, control of the delta of the Shatt al-Arab was disputed, with

the Ottomans and later the British claiming control of the entire delta. The current boundary, which gives Iran access to the east bank of the lowest reaches of the Shatt al-Arab, was agreed upon in 1937. The 1639 agreement also became the basis of the boundary between Iran and Turkey. This boundary was reaffirmed via the Constantinople Agreement and was adjusted slightly through a treaty signed by both countries in 1937.

Present-day Azerbaijan, Armenia, and Turkmenistan were part of the Russian Empire during the 19th century, and they became part of the Soviet Union following the Russian Revolution after World War I. The Russian Empire began to encroach on Persia, then ruled by the Qajar dynasty, during the 19th century. Following a series of wars, Persia was forced to give up territory to the Russian Empire. The Treaty of Gulistan, signed by Persia and Russia in 1813, transferred territory in what is now Azerbaijan and Georgia to the Russian Empire. Lands east of the Caspian Sea were transferred from Persia to the Russian Empire in subsequent treaties signed in 1828 and 1881. This territory is now part of Turkmenistan and Uzbekistan.

The boundaries established between Persia and the Russian Empire as part of the 1881 agreement remained in place, with minor adjustments, through World War II. In 1954, Iran and the Soviet Union signed an agreement to establish a binational commission to delineate their common boundary precisely. This boundary as delineated by the commission became the current boundaries between Iran and Azerbaijan, Armenia, and Turkmenistan, all of which were part of the Soviet Union prior to 1991.

The boundaries between Iran and Afghanistan and between Iran and Pakistan were agreed upon by Persia and the British Empire during the late 19th and early 20th centuries. The boundary between Persia and Afghanistan was agreed upon in 1872 and was modified in 1935. Baluchistan, which is now part of Pakistan, had been under Persian influence prior to the colonization of India by the British in the 18th and 19th centuries. In 1871, Persia and Britain agreed to divide Baluchistan with the understanding that territories inhabited largely by Persians would remain part of Persia whereas the rest of the area would become part of British India. The 1871 agreement was modified in 1895 and 1905. In 1958, after Pakistan had become an independent country, Iran and Pakistan reiterated their boundary while correcting a few ambiguities in its delineation.

CONTEMPORARY ISSUES

In general, the boundaries between Iran and its neighbors have remained stable since the middle of the 20th century. However, several issues of contention between Iran and nearby states remain unresolved.

Relationships between Iran and Azerbaijan have deteriorated since Azerbaijan became fully independent following the 1991 collapse of the Soviet Union. Tensions in the relationships between the two countries have long been associated with ethnic differences between Persian-speaking Iranians and Azeris, whose language is related to Turkish. In recent years, Iran has accused Azerbaijan of harboring and abetting opponents of the current Iranian regime. Both countries have accused each other of meddling in their respective internal affairs.

Iran and Azerbaijan also dispute access to the Caspian Sea, which contains valuable oil deposits and other natural resources. In addition to Iran and Azerbaijan, the countries of Russia, Kazakhstan, and Turkmenistan have coastlines on the Caspian Sea. Iran has argued that the Caspian Sea should be divided into five parts. However, other countries that border the Caspian Sea have not agreed to this proposal. Iran has accused Azerbaijan of polluting the Caspian in conjunction with Azerbaijan's oil industry.

The status of the Helmand River remains in dispute between Iran and Afghanistan. The Helmand rises in the Hindu Kush Mountains in Afghanistan and flows through Afghanistan for much of its length. However, the downstream portion of the river forms part of the boundary between Iran and Afghanistan. In this dry environment, the river is an important source of water for irrigation and is subject to heavy use by both countries. Iran has accused Afghanistan of overusing the river, reducing the availability of water to Iran. Thousands of Afghan refugees have crossed the boundary into Iran over the past two decades, straining Iran's limited resources to provide them with basic needs and services.

The boundary between Iran and Iraq on the lower reaches of the Shatt al-Arab remains a point of contention. The current boundary gives Iran a short border extending inland from the mouth of the Shatt al-Arab on the Persian Gulf. However, the two countries have long disputed navigation rights along the Shatt al-Arab. This issue is especially significant because of the international importance of overseas shipping of petroleum, and the Shatt al-Arab is the only navigable waterway that extends inland from the Persian Gulf in either country.

Iran and the United Arab Emirates (UAE) have disputed control over the island of Abu Musa, which is located at the southeastern end of the Persian Gulf near the entrance to the strategically important Strait of Hormuz. Abu Musa is about 4.6 miles in land area with a permanent population of about 2,000. The island is equidistant between the southern coast of Iran and the northeastern coast of the United Arab Emirates, and the main shipping lanes connecting the Persian Gulf and the Strait of Hormuz pass between Abu Musa and the Iranian coast. Conflict over the island extends to control of shipping lanes, airspace, and resources located underneath the offshore continental shelf.

The dispute over control of Abu Musa and the nearby small Tunb Islands dates back to the early 20th century. Historically, Abu Musa was controlled by Persia. In 1908, however, Britain claimed Abu Musa and the other islands in the Persian Gulf. Sovereignty over Abu Musa was given to the sheikdom of Sharjah, which became part of the United Arab Emirates in 1971. British forces withdrew from the island in 1971, when Iran and the newly independent UAE signed a memorandum of understanding that the islands would be administered jointly by the two countries. After the United Arab Emirates became independent, however, Iran took control of the islands, justifying its claim on the basis of Persia's historical sovereignty over them. The UAE claimed that Iranian occupation of Abu Musa and the Tunb Islands was illegal and took its case to United Nations

Security Council, which ruled against the UAE in 1980. Subsequently, the dispute was referred to the International Court of Justice, which has yet to rule definitively on the issue. In April 2012, Iran announced a threat to use force against the UAE to back up its claims to the islands. The Iranian threat was denounced by the Gulf Cooperation Council (GCC), which includes Bahrain, Kuwait, Oman, Qatar, Saudi Arabia, and the UAE. Religious tensions as well as economic concerns underlie the ongoing dispute in that the GCC states are all ruled by Sunni regimes as opposed to the Shi'ite regime in Iran.

Finally, Iran has experienced calls for increased autonomy or independence on the part of its Kurdish population. A substantial minority of Kurds live in Iran as well as in nearby Turkey, Iraq, and Syria. An estimated 7 million Kurds live in northwestern Iran, and Kurds comprise about 8 to 10 percent of Iran's total population. As boundaries between Iran and its neighbors were delineated, the Kurdish homeland came to be divided between these countries, leaving the Kurds as a minority in each state. Efforts to create an independent Kurdish state after World War I were rejected, and the Kurds remain divided politically today. In 2005, Amnesty International documented ongoing discrimination against Kurds on the part of the Iranian government. In the report's words, "social, political and cultural rights have been repressed, as have their economic aspirations." In 2009 and 2010, six Kurdish activists in Iran were tortured and executed. Guerilla activity and other protests against the Iranian government in Kurdish-dominated areas of northwestern Iran continue.

See also   Afghanistan, Armenia, Azerbaijan, Iraq, Pakistan, Turkey, Turkmenistan

Further Reading

Eurasianet.org. "Tensions growing between Azerbaijan and Iran?" March 14, 2011, http://www.eurasianet.org/node/63070.

Robert Johnson. *The Iran-Iraq War.* New York: Palgrave Macmillan, 2010.

Denise Natali. *The Kurds and the state: Evolving national identity in Iraq, Turkey, and Iran.* Syracuse, NY: Syracuse University Press, 2005.

IRAQ

OVERVIEW

The Republic of Iraq is located in southwestern Asia north of the Arabian Gulf. Much of Iraq's land area is part of the Fertile Crescent, which contains nearly all of Iraq's population. Iraq has a land area of 169,234 square miles, about the size of California. Its population is about 32 million.

Iraq's neighbors are Iran to the east, Turkey to the north, Syria to the northwest, Jordan to the west, Saudi Arabia to the southwest, and Kuwait to the south. To the southeast, Iraq has a very short coast on the Arabian Gulf at the Shatt al-Arab, which is the combined delta of the Tigris and Euphrates rivers. From the Shatt al-Arab, the boundary between Iraq and Iran follows the line of the Tigris inland and northwestward along the northeastern edge of the Mesopotamian plain. East of Iraq's capital city of Baghdad, the boundary leaves the plain and turns northward into the Zagros Mountains. This section

of the boundary follows drainage divides and short streams. The boundary continues through the Zagros Mountains in a northerly direction to the tripoint between Iraq, Iran, and Turkey. This area of the Zagros Mountains is rugged, steep, and sparsely populated.

From the tripoint between Iraq, Iran, and Turkey, the boundary between Iraq and Turkey extends to the west. It continues along the Zagros and then continues back into the Mesopotamian floodplain west of the Tigris. This section of the boundary follows straight-line segments across this portion of Mesopotamia to the Nahr al Khabur River. It then follows the Nahr al Khabur downstream to its confluence with the Tigris near the tripoint between Iraq, Turkey, and Syria.

From this tripoint, the boundary between Iraq and Syria trends in a southwesterly direction, following straight-line segments across Mesopotamia to the Euphrates River. South of the Euphrates, the boundary follows one long segment that extends from northeast to southwest to the tripoint between Iraq, Syria, and Jordan. The region southwest of the Euphrates is dry and sparsely populated desert.

The boundary between Iraq and Jordan extends in a south-southeasterly direction from that tripoint, following one long segment and several shorter segments, to the tripoint between Iraq, Jordan, and Saudi Arabia. From there the boundary between Iraq and Saudi Arabia follows longer straight-line segments in a southwesterly direction. The boundary turns eastward north of the Saudi town of Hafar al Batin to the tripoint between Iraq, Saudi Arabia, and Kuwait. Most of the region through which the boundaries between Iraq and

IRAQ

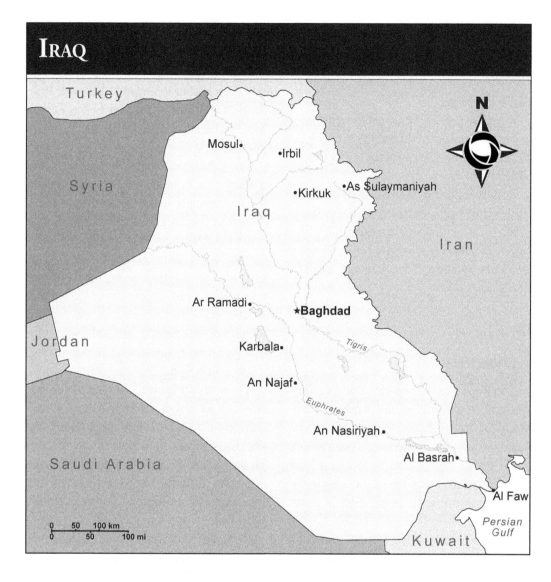

Jordan and between Iraq and Saudi Arabia extend is uninhabited, and these boundaries were not delineated precisely until well into the 20th century. From the tripoint between Iraq, Saudi Arabia, and Kuwait, the boundary between Iraq and Kuwait follows short straight-line segments northeastward and then eastward. A final segment extends in a southeasterly direction to the Khor Abdullah waterway, which empties into the Persian Gulf. The Khor Abdullah waterway separates the Iraqi mainland from the islands of Warbah and Bubiyan in Kuwait.

HISTORICAL CONTEXT

Mesopotamia, or the plains drained by the Tigris and Euphrates rivers, has been an important crossroads of civilization for several thousand years. During the first and second millennia BC, Mesopotamia was controlled by the Assyrian and Babylonian empires. The Babylonians fell to the Persian Empire, which in turn lost control of Mesopotamia to the Greeks under Alexander the Great in the fourth century BC. The region was contested between the Roman Empire and later Persian dynasties until AD 224, when it was conquered by the Sassanid Persian Empire. It remained under Sassanid control until it was taken over by Islamic conquerors from the Arabian Peninsula during the seventh century AD.

After Islam came to present-day Iraq, the Abbasid Caliphate took power in about AD 750. The Abbasids established the city of Baghdad in AD 762. At its greatest extent, the Abbasid Caliphate included present-day Iran, the Arabian Peninsula, and lands along the Mediterranean coast westward to present-day Egypt and Libya. The Abbasids lost control of much of their empire in the 10th and 11th centuries AD but regained power in the 12th century. After a brief interregnum following invasions by Mongols, the Abbasids remained in power until they were toppled by the Ottoman Empire in the early 16th century. Iraq remained part of the Ottoman Empire until the empire was dismembered after World War I.

Following the war, the League of Nations granted control of Mesopotamia to the United Kingdom as the British Mandate of Mesopotamia. The boundaries of the British Mandate were worked out by Britain along with Turkey, Iran, and France as the colonial power in charge of Syria. These boundaries approximate Iraq's boundaries today. The boundaries were drawn without regard for the distribution of national groups across the country. Thus, the population of the British Mandate included a primarily Kurdish population to the north, a majority Shi'ite Muslim population in the central part of the country, and a predominantly Sunni Muslim population to the south. These distinctions have caused considerable turmoil within Iraq ever since.

The British placed Faisal I on the throne as king of Iraq in 1921. Britain's mandate over Iraq ended in 1932, and Iraq became independent. In 1958, Iraq's King Faisal II and Jordan's King Hussein proposed to unify the two kingdoms as the Arab Federation of Iraq and Jordan. However, Faisal II was deposed in a coup d'état, and the plan to unify Iraq and Jordan was abandoned. Iraq was proclaimed a republic. In 1968, the Arab Socialist Ba'ath Party seized power in another coup d'état. Saddam Hussein, a leader of the Ba'ath Party, became president of Iraq in 1979. The one-party Ba'athist government was officially secular but in fact was dominated by Sunni Muslims.

Conflict between Iraq and Iran ensued after the shah of Iran was deposed in the Iranian Revolution in 1979. The revolution's Shi'ite leader, Ayatollah Ruhollah Khomeini, called upon Iraq Shi'ites to rebel against the Sunni-dominated Ba'athist government. Hussein's government regarded Iran as an increasing threat to its own regime. As well, Iraq wished to obtain control over the oil-rich and Sunni-majority province of Khuzestan and wanted full control over the Shatt al-Arab waterway. The Iran-Iraq War broke out in 1980 and continued for eight years. As many as half a million Iraqi and Iranian soldiers were killed before a cease-fire agreement was reached in 1988. Under this agreement, the boundary between the two countries reverted to the pre-1980 boundary.

In 1990, Iraq invaded and claimed sovereignty over Kuwait. Iraq justified its claim to Kuwait on the grounds that it was the successor state to the Ottoman Empire, which had controlled both Iraq and Kuwait prior to World War I. The Iraqi annexation of Kuwait was condemned by the United Nations, the United States, and many other countries. In 1991, a UN-sponsored military force led by American troops attacked Iraq and restored Kuwait's independence. The United Nations imposed economic sanctions on Iraq, offering to lift these sanctions in exchange for disarmament. In 2003, the United States led an invasion of Iraq with the goal of removing possible weapons of mass destruction and restoring democracy. The Hussein regime was overthrown, and Hussein himself was executed in 2006. An elected government took power in 2005, and the final U.S. troops were pulled out of Iraq in 2011.

CONTEMPORARY ISSUES

Iraq continues to face a variety of issues and conflicts involving nearby conflicts. Many of these conflicts stem from the fact that the boundaries drawn by the British in the 1920s have combined three distinct populations—Shi'ites, Sunnis, and Kurds—into a single country.

The boundary between Iraq and Iran, which had been delineated after World War I, was left unaltered after the Iran-Iraq War ended in 1988. However, the two countries continue to contest their boundary, especially near the mouth of the Shatt al-Arab in the Persian Gulf. Currently, the Shatt al-Arab is under Iraqi sovereignty although Iranian territory extends to the edge of the Shatt al-Arab near its mouth. Navigation rights on the Shatt al-Arab have long been in dispute, with Iran anxious to preserve its right to use the Shatt al-Arab for shipping. Iraq is one of the largest oil exporters in the world, and the Shatt al-Arab is the only outlet from either Iraq or Iran to the Persian Gulf and thereby to international waters.

Iraq and Kuwait also dispute control of territory and shipping in the Persian Gulf. The status of Warbah Island and Bubiyan Island remains a matter of concern. These islands are located near the mouth of the Euphrates River. Both islands are controlled by Kuwait, and both are uninhabited. However, Iraq claims that Kuwaiti control of the islands can interfere with shipping from the Iraqi mainland to the Persian Gulf. In 2011, Kuwait announced a plan to build a port facility on Bubiyan Island. Iraq has asked Kuwait to desist from this project on the grounds that its construction and operation will interfere with Iraqi commerce. Kuwait has responded that the Bubiyan is dry land under Kuwaiti sovereignty and that Iraq has no right to interfere.

The status of Iraq's Kurdish population remains problematic. The Kurdish homeland is located in northern Iraq and neighboring areas of Turkey, Iran, and Syria. About 5 million Kurds live in Iraq, where they comprise about 15 percent of Iraq's overall population. When democracy was restored to Iraq in 2005, the new constitution guaranteed Iraq's Kurdistan Region autonomy within Iraq. However, separatist movements continue to operate, and some Iraqi Kurds would prefer political union with Kurds in nearby countries.

See also Iran, Jordan, Kuwait, Saudi Arabia, Syria, Turkey

Further Reading

Camilla Hall and James Drummond. "Port rivalry tests Iraq-Kuwait relations." *FT.com*, September 14, 2011, http://www.ft.com/intl/cms/s/0/13e087f4-dc4e-11e0-8654-00144feabdc0.html#axzz1z8qEJOsl.

Robert Johnson. *The Iran-Iraq War.* New York: Palgrave Macmillan, 2010.

Brendan O'Leary, John McGarry, and Khaled Saleh. *The future of Kurdistan in Iraq.* Philadelphia: University of Pennsylvania Press, 2005.

William R. Polk. *Understanding Iraq: The whole sweep of Iraqi history, from Genghis Khan's Mongols to the Ottoman Turks to the British Mandate to the American occupation.* New York: Harper Perennial, 2006.

Stephen M. Walt. "Top 10 lessons from the Iraq War." *Foreign Policy*, March 20, 2012, http://www.foreignpolicy.com/articles/2012/03/20/top_ten_lessons_of_the_iraq_war?page =0,6&hidecomments=yes.

ISRAEL

OVERVIEW

The State of Israel is located on the Mediterranean seacoast of southwestern Asia. Its land area is approximately 8,000 square miles, although frequent boundary adjustments have affected its exact land area over the past 60 years. Israel is slightly smaller by land area than New Jersey. It has a population of about 8 million. About 75 percent of Israel's people are Jewish, making Israel the only Jewish-majority state in the world. About 20 percent of Israel's citizens are Arabs.

Israel's neighbors are Lebanon to the north, Syria to the northeast, Jordan to the east, and Egypt to the southwest. It borders the Palestine Occupied Territories in two places, with the West Bank to the east of Israel and the Gaza Strip to the southwest. Israel has two seacoasts. These include a long coast on the Mediterranean Sea to the west and a much shorter coast on the Gulf of Aqaba to the south. Thus Israel and Egypt are the only countries in the world that have direct access by sea to the Atlantic Ocean via the Mediterranean Sea and to the Indian Ocean via the Gulf of Aqaba and the Red Sea.

All of Israel's boundaries have been contested since Israel became independent in 1948. Its boundary with Lebanon extends eastward from the Mediterranean, following short straight-line segments eastward to a point near the town of Malkiya. From Malkiya, the boundary turns to the north. It parallels the western edge of the Golan Heights to a point near the town of Makula, then turns westward again to the tripoint between Israel, Lebanon, and Syria. This boundary was delineated by the United Nations in 2000 and is known as the Blue Line. However, several armed skirmishes including a five-week war in 2006 have occurred along the boundary since the Blue Line was established as the border.

The Jordan River formed the original boundary between Israel and Syria. The Jordan flows from north to south through the Sea of Galilee into the Dead Sea on the boundary between Israel and Jordan. However, in 1967 Israeli forces occupied the Golan Heights region in southwestern Syria. Israel continues to occupy the Golan Heights today. Israeli-occupied territory

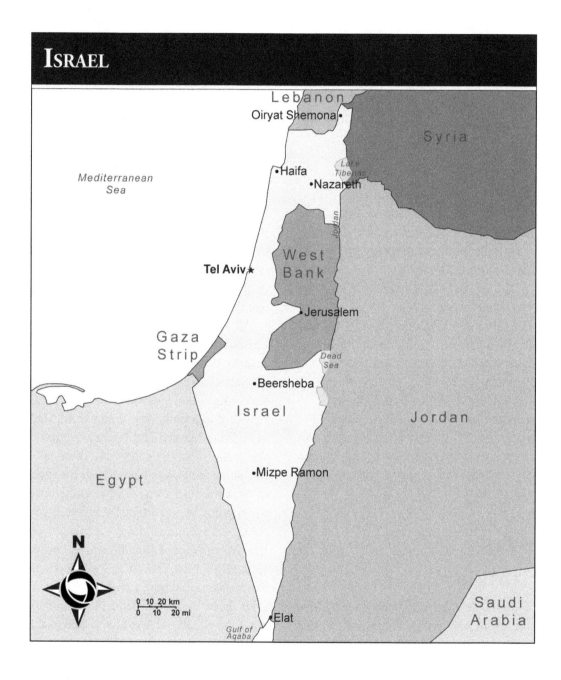

ISRAEL

in the Golan Heights is located east of the Jordan River. The current line of demarcation between the Israeli-occupied Golan Heights extends southward to the Yarmouk River.

The boundary between Israel and Jordan follows the Yarmouk downstream and westward to its confluence with the Jordan River. Originally, the Jordan served as the boundary between Israel and Jordan southward to the Dead Sea. However, the West Bank region is now part of the Palestine Occupied Territories. The West Bank is comprised of territory west of the Jordan, hence its name, and extends westward to include part of the city of Jerusalem. The West Bank is shaped like a rectangle. Its boundary with Israel extends westward from the Jordan River to a point near the town of Katsir-Harish and then southward and eastward to include the eastern part of Jerusalem. From there it extends westward and southward once again to a point near the Israeli town of Meitar, and then it extends eastward to the Dead Sea.

From the Dead Sea, the boundary between Israel and Jordan continues southward along straight-line segments through the sparsely populated Arabah region to the Gulf of Aqaba. The boundary reaches the Gulf of Aqaba at a point between the Israeli city of Eilat to the west and the Jordanian city of Aqaba to the east. The Israeli coast on the Gulf of Aqaba is less than 10 miles long.

The boundary between Israel and Egypt crosses the Sinai Peninsula and connects the Gulf of Aqaba and the Mediterranean Sea. It follows straight-line segments that extend in a north-northwesterly direction between the Gulf and the Mediterranean. The Gaza Strip, which is the other portion of the Palestine Occupied Territories, extends along the Mediterranean coast north of the boundary between Israel and Egypt. The boundary between Israel and the Gaza Strip parallels the Mediterranean coast 5 to 10 miles inland. This boundary extends in a northeasterly direction to a point near the town of Sderot and then turns northwestward to the Mediterranean.

HISTORICAL CONTEXT

Present-day Israel has been ruled by a variety of kingdoms and empires for the past 4,000 years. The Kingdom of Israel, discussed in the Old Testament of the Bible, became the dominant power in the region in around the 11th century BC. The kingdom was divided eventually into the Kingdom of Israel to the north and the Kingdom of Judah to the south. Israel fell to Assyria in 722 BC, while Judah remained independent until it was taken over by the Babylonians in the fourth century BC.

During the first century BC, the region along the east coast of the Mediterranean was conquered by the Roman Empire and was made a Roman province. Many of the region's Jewish people were killed or expelled by the Romans in the Diaspora during the first century AD. The region was conquered by the Arabs in AD 635 and became known as Palestine. Palestine was taken over by the Ottomans in 1516. By this time, most of the region's Jews had left, and the large majority of the people of Palestine were Muslim Arabs.

In the late 19th century, Jewish leaders in Europe began promoting the resettlement of European Jews, who were often victims of persecution throughout Europe, in Palestine. The idea of encouraging European Jews to move to Israel and to establish an independent Jewish state became known as Zionism. Many Jews moved to Palestine after World War I, by which time Palestine and Jordan had become a British mandate awarded by the League of Nations. As many as 250,000 more Jews moved to Palestine to escape persecution and genocide by the Nazis in Germany. About a third of

Palestine's people at the outset of World War II were Jewish.

Jewish migration to Palestine intensified after the war, when hundreds of thousands of Jewish survivors of the Holocaust from throughout Europe relocated to the region. In 1947, the United Nations proposed to terminate the British mandate and to replace it with an independent Jewish state and an independent Arab state. The city of Jerusalem, which is sacred to Jews, Muslims, and Christians, was to be a free city accessible to people of all faiths. However, the plan was rejected by neighboring Arab-majority countries. Israel declared its independence in 1948. Shortly thereafter, troops from Egypt, Iraq, Syria, and Transjordan (present-day Jordan) attacked Israel. During the ensuing Arab-Israeli War, Egypt took control of the Gaza Strip, and Jordan took control of the West Bank. More than half a million Palestinians left Israel and relocated to the Gaza Strip, the West Bank, or other countries.

After the Arab-Israeli War, hostile relations between Israel and its neighbors continued. In 1967, Israel attacked Egypt, Iraq, Syria, and Jordan in the Six-Day War. Israel seized control over the Golan Heights in Syria, the West Bank, the Gaza Strip, and the Sinai Peninsula in Egypt. During the Yom Kippur War of 1973, Egyptian and Syrian forces attacked Israel but were repulsed by the Israeli military. In 1979, Egypt's president Anwar Sadat visited Israel. His visit prompted peace negotiations and led to the signing of the Camp David Accords in 1978 and a peace treaty in 1979. Israel withdrew subsequently from the Sinai Peninsula, and the two countries agreed to work toward autonomy for the Palestinian-dominated West Bank and Gaza Strip. In 1994, Jordan became the second Arab country to recognize Israel. After years of armed hostilities, the boundary between Israel and Lebanon known as the Blue Line was delimited by the United Nations in 2000. Israel continues to occupy the Golan Heights while the West Bank and the Gaza Strip comprise the Palestine Occupied Territories.

CONTEMPORARY ISSUES

Israel has faced hostility from many of its Arab neighbors since it became independent in 1948. Many of these Arab governments have objected to the Zionist movement of the early 20th century and the influx of Jewish settlers, while many Palestinians gave up their lands and left Israel. Israel's relationships with Jordan and Egypt have been generally friendly in recent years, whereas relationships with Syria and Lebanon have been more hostile.

Relations between Israel and Egypt were normalized in 1979, and relations between Israel and Jordan were normalized in 1994. The peace treaty signed by Israel and Jordan in 1994 clarified the question of what would happen to the boundary were the Jordan River to change course. The countries agreed that the Jordan would remain the boundary if its course were to change. The agreement also opened border crossings between the two countries and provided opportunities for the two countries to work toward solutions to common problems such as water shortages in this dry and drought-prone area of the world. Meanwhile, Israel and Lebanon have been involved in several skirmishes over their Blue Line boundary since 2000, and Syria continues to object to Israeli occupation of the Golan Heights.

The rise of Islamism in the Middle East has been a matter of concern to Israelis. In Egypt, Sadat was assassinated in 1981. His successor, Hosni Mubarak, assumed dictatorial power with the support of Egypt's armed forces. However, the Mubarak regime was toppled following a wave of protests in what became known as Arab Spring in early 2011. In 2012, voters of Egypt elected as their president a candidate supported by the previously banned Islamic political faction known as the Muslim Brotherhood. Concerns have been raised whether the new president, Mohammed Morsi, would honor the Camp David Accords and maintain Egypt's longstanding relationship with Israel. Meanwhile, Iran is believed to have developed nuclear weapons and has threatened to use them against Israel.

See also Egypt, Jordan, Lebanon, Palestine Occupied Territories, Syria

Further Reading

Amos Harel, Avi Issacharoff, and Ora Cummings. *34 Days: Israel, Hezbollah, and the war in Lebanon.* Translated by Moshe Tlamim. New York: Palgrave Macmillan, 2008.

Yaakov Katz and Yoaz Hendel. *Israel vs. Iran: The shadow war.* Dulles, VA: Potomac Books, 2012.

Zeev Maoz. *Defending the Holy Land: A critical analysis of Israel's security and foreign policy.* Ann Arbor: University of Michigan Press, 2009.

Mark Tessler. *A history of the Israeli-Palestinian conflict.* Bloomington: Indiana University Press, 2009.

JORDAN

OVERVIEW

The Hashemite Kingdom of Jordan is located in southwestern Asia north of the Arabian Peninsula. Jordan has a land area of 35,637 square miles, approximately the size of Indiana. Its population is about 7 million.

Jordan has boundaries with Israel and the West Bank, which is part of the Palestine Territory, to the west, Syria to the north, Iraq to the northeast, and Saudi Arabia to the east and southeast. To the south, Jordan has a very short coastline on the Gulf of Aqaba, which empties into the Red Sea. From the city of Aqaba along the Gulf of Aqaba, the boundary between Jordan and Israel extends through the Arabah northward to the Dead Sea. The Arabah region crosses hot, dry desert terrain and is very lightly populated except along the Gulf of Aqaba coast. From the Dead Sea, the boundary between Jordan and Israel follows the Jordan River northward and upstream. The Jordan River also forms the boundary between Jordan and the Autonomous Region of Palestine, which was known as the West Bank. North of the Autonomous Region of Palestine, the Jordan River continues as the boundary between Jordan and Israel upstream to its confluence with the Yarmouk River at the southern end of the Golan Heights. The boundary follows the Yarmouk upstream and northeastward to the tripoint between Jordan, Israel, and Syria.

From this tripoint, the boundary between Jordan and Syria continues along the Yarmouk upstream and eastward. Near the source of the Yarmouk, the boundary follows numerous short straight-line

JORDAN

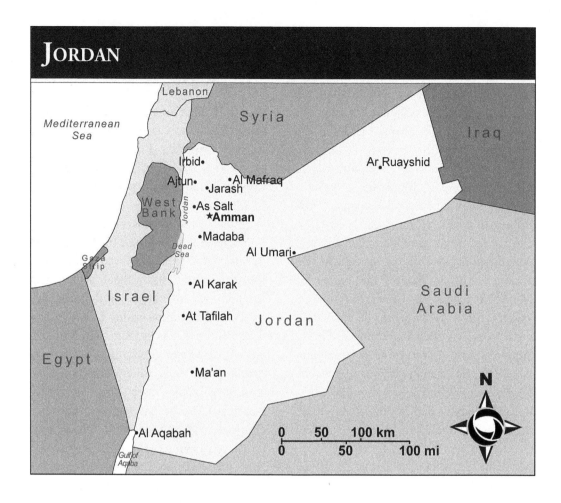

segments extending in a southeasterly direction. Near the Syrian village of Al Qar'a, the boundary turns northeastward. Nearly all of this boundary is a straight diagonal line extending from southwest to northeast to the tripoint between Jordan, Syria, and Iraq. The boundary between Jordan and Iraq is also geometric, following one long segment and several short segments extending in a south-southeasterly direction to the tripoint between Jordan, Iraq, and Saudi Arabia. The region containing the eastern section of the boundary between Jordan and Syria and the boundary

between Jordan and Iraq is virtually uninhabited desert. No roads cross the boundary between Jordan and Syria east of Al Qar'a, and the boundary between Jordan and Iraq is crossed by only one road.

The boundary between Jordan and Saudi Arabia is geometric. From the tripoint between Jordan, Iraq, and Saudi Arabia, the boundary between Jordan and Saudi Arabia extends west-southwestward. Most of this boundary is located on a single diagonal segment. The boundary turns southeastward, then back to the southwest along several straight-line segments. The southernmost portion of the boundary is a segment about 40 miles in length extending west-northwestward to the Gulf of Aqaba. Only two roads cross the entire boundary between Jordan and Saudi Arabia. Jordan's coast on the Gulf of Aqaba is about 15 miles long and is Jordan's only outlet to the sea.

HISTORICAL CONTEXT

Present-day Jordan has been a crossroads of civilizations and cultures for thousands of years. During Roman times, the area was governed by the Nabatean Kingdom, which was a client state of the Roman Empire. Other small city-states ruled portions of modern Jordan until it was conquered by the Arabic Umayyad Empire in the seventh century AD. Jordan became part of the Abbasid Empire, based in Baghdad in modern Iraq, in AD 750 and remained under Abbasid control for the next five centuries. Jordan was contested among various kingdoms for the next 300 years until it became part of the Ottoman Empire in 1517.

The Ottoman Empire broke up after World War I. Present-day Jordan became part of the British Mandate for Palestine, which also included present-day Israel and the Palestine Autonomous Region. The portion of the mandate that was to become Jordan was known as Transjordan, recognizing the area's location east of the Jordan River. Transjordan became independent as the Hashemite Kingdom of Trans-Jordan in 1946. In 1948, Jordan, along with other Arab-dominated states, participated in an invasion of newly independent Israel. It claimed sovereignty over the West Bank region, including part of the city of Jerusalem, in 1949. It then changed its name to the Hashemite Kingdom of Jordan in recognition of its claim over territory on both sides of the Jordan River. Jordan and Saudi Arabia negotiated a boundary adjustment agreement in 1965. This agreement extended the length of Jordan's coast on the Gulf of Aqaba and provided Jordan with the opportunity to construct a deep-water port.

In 1967, Jordanian forces fought alongside troops from Syria, Iraq, and Egypt in what would become known as the Six-Day War. During the war, Israel captured and began to occupy the West Bank, including all of Jerusalem. Numerous Palestinian refugees crossed the Jordan River from the West Bank, and some remain in Jordan. Jordan continued to claim the West Bank until 1988, when it renounced its claims and announced support for the Palestine Liberation Organization's claim over the West Bank as the "sole representative" of the Palestinian people.

CONTEMPORARY ISSUES

Despite a long history of turmoil and conflict, relationships between Jordan and Israel have remained amicable. Jordan and Israel signed a peace agreement in 1994. This treaty normalized relations between the two countries and resolved remaining boundary disputes, including a stipulation that the Jordan River would remain the boundary between Jordan and Israel even if its course were to change. The agreement also provided opportunities for international cooperation between the two countries over issues such as water rights and water shortages, and it opened previously closed border crossings.

See also   Iraq, Israel, Palestine Occupied Territories, Saudi Arabia, Syria

Further Reading

Yoav Alon. *The making of Jordan: Tribes, colonialism, and the modern state.* London: I. B. Tauris, 2009.

Yitzhak Gil-Har. "Boundaries delimitation: Palestine and Trans-Jordan." *Middle Eastern Studies*, 36 (2000), pp. 68–81.

Abdul Majali, Jawad A. Anani, and Munther J. Haddadin. *Peace-making: The inside story of the 1994 Jordanian-Israeli Treaty.* Norman: University of Oklahoma Press, 2006.

KUWAIT

OVERVIEW

The State of Kuwait occupies the northeastern corner of the Arabian Peninsula on the coast of the Persian Gulf. It has a land area of 6,880 square miles, about the size of New Jersey. Its population is about 3.6 million.

Kuwait is one of the leading oil-producing countries in the world, and because of its oil reserves it is a wealthy country. As is the case with other oil-rich countries of Southwest Asia and North Africa, only a minority of Kuwait's people are natives of Kuwait. Estimates suggest that only about a third of Kuwait's residents were born there. About 45 percent are of Arabic ancestry but from outside of Kuwait. Nearly 15 percent of the population come from Pakistan, India, or Bangladesh. These people and other expatriates have moved to Kuwait and other oil-producing countries in search of employment opportunities.

Kuwait's neighbors are Iraq to the north and west and Saudi Arabia to the south. The Persian Gulf is located to the east. Much of Kuwait's Persian Gulf coastline adjoins the Kuwait Bay, which provides an important harbor for the country. Kuwait's territory also includes several islands in the gulf.

Except near the coast, Kuwait's boundaries cross uninhabited territory. The Khor Abdullah waterway, which empties into the Persian Gulf, separates Iraq and Kuwait along the coast of the Gulf. The waterway separates Iraqi territory from Warbah Island and the larger Bubiyan Island, which are part of Kuwait. Bubiyan Island is connected to the Kuwaiti mainland by a bridge that was destroyed during the Persian Gulf War in 1991 but has since been rebuilt. Inland from the Khor Abdullah waterway, the boundary follows short straight-line segments that trend westward and then southwestward to the tripoint between Kuwait, Iraq, and Saudi Arabia. From that tripoint, the boundary between Kuwait and Saudi Arabia consists of two long, east-west segments at the western and eastern ends, with a more complex series of straight lines running from north-northwest to south-southeast in between these segments. As is the case with the Iraqi border, this boundary crosses uninhabited territory except near the Persian Gulf coast.

HISTORICAL CONTEXT

Kuwait was founded in 1705 by the Bani Utbah, a confederation of Arabic tribes who originated in the Arabian Peninsula.

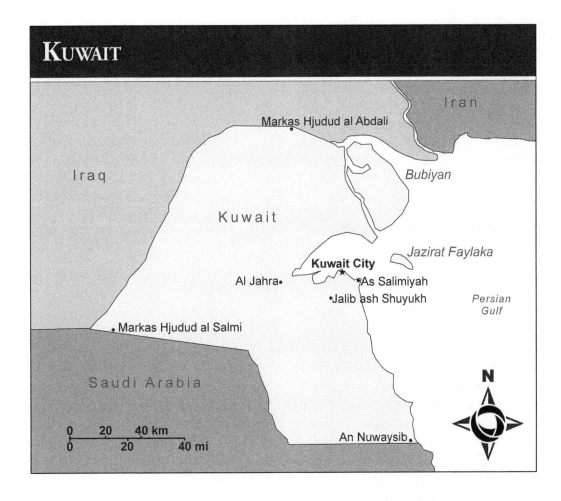

The Bani Utbah built a fort near the natural harbor of Kuwait Bay. This fort eventually became Kuwait City, which soon became an important port and commercial center. Kuwait City and its surrounding territory became an autonomous city-state under the protection of the Ottoman Empire in the late 19th century. After the dissolution of the Ottoman Empire in 1918, Kuwait became an "independent sheikdom" under the protection of the British Empire.

The boundary between Kuwait and Saudi Arabia was established by the Treaty of Al Uqayr in 1922. The treaty established a Neutral Zone between the two countries.

The Neutral Zone remained in effect until 1966, when the two countries agreed to divide the territory between them. The division took effect in 1969. However, Kuwait and Saudi Arabia agreed to share revenues associated with oil production in the former Neutral Zone equally.

Kuwait became fully independent in 1961. However, Iraq claimed sovereignty over Kuwait on the grounds that the Iraqi state was the legal successor state to the Ottoman Empire, which had ruled present-day Iraq and provided protection to Kuwait. In 1963, Iraq relinquished its claim to sovereignty over Kuwait and the two countries agreed upon their current boundaries, although Iraq continued to claim Warbah and Bubiyan islands. In 1990, Iraq reaffirmed its claim to Kuwait, and it invaded and annexed Kuwait. A United Nations coalition led by the United States expelled Iraq from Kuwait in 1991, and the UN reaffirmed Kuwait's sovereignty over its territory.

CONTEMPORARY ISSUES

The status of Kuwait relative to Iraq remains a matter of controversy. Much of this conflict involves the status of Warbah and Bubiyan islands, which are located in the Persian Gulf off the coast of the Kuwaiti mainland. Both islands are uninhabited, and the bridge between Bubiyan and the Kuwaiti mainland is used only for military purposes. However, the islands' location just west of the mouth of the Euphrates River in Iraq has given them considerable strategic and commercial importance. Iraq has claimed that Kuwaiti control of the islands interferes with Iraqi commerce, in particular with the movement of oil tankers from the Iraqi port of Al-Basra.

In 2011, the government of Kuwait announced plans to build a port facility on Bubiyan Island to be known as the Mubarak Al Kabeer Port. A contract to build the port facility was signed with a South Korean company, which intended to complete the project in time for the port to open in 2016. Iraq asked Kuwait to stop work on the port, claiming that its operation would interfere with Iraqi navigation and shipping. However, Kuwaiti officials stressed that the port would be built on land under Kuwaiti sovereignty and thus would have no impact on Iraq's commerce.

See also   Iraq, Saudi Arabia

Further Reading

Michael S. Casey. *The history of Kuwait*. New York: Greenwood Press, 2007.

Camilla Hall and James Drummond. "Port rivalry tests Iraq-Kuwait relations." *FT.com*, September 14, 2011, http://www.ft.com/intl/cms/s/0/13e087f4-dc4e-11e0-8654-00144feabdc0.html#axzz1z8qEJOsl.

LEBANON

OVERVIEW

The Lebanese Republic is located in southwestern Asia along the coast of the Mediterranean Sea. Lebanon's land area is 4,036 square miles, almost twice the size of Delaware. Its population is about 4.4 million. In contrast to most of the countries of Southwest Asia, Lebanon has a substantial population of Christians as well as Muslims. Today about 60 percent of Lebanon's residents are Muslims. The population of Muslims relative to Christians continues to increase because of higher Muslim birth rates, an influx of Muslim refugees, and out-migration by Christians.

Lebanon's neighbors are Syria to the north and east and Israel to the south. To the west is Lebanon's coast on the Mediterranean Sea. From the Mediterranean Sea, the boundary between Lebanon and Syria extends eastward and upstream along the Nahr el-Kebir River into the Jabal Al-Sharqi mountain range. Near the village of Karha, the boundary turns southward and follows the higher peaks in the Jabal Al-Sharqi range separating Lebanon from

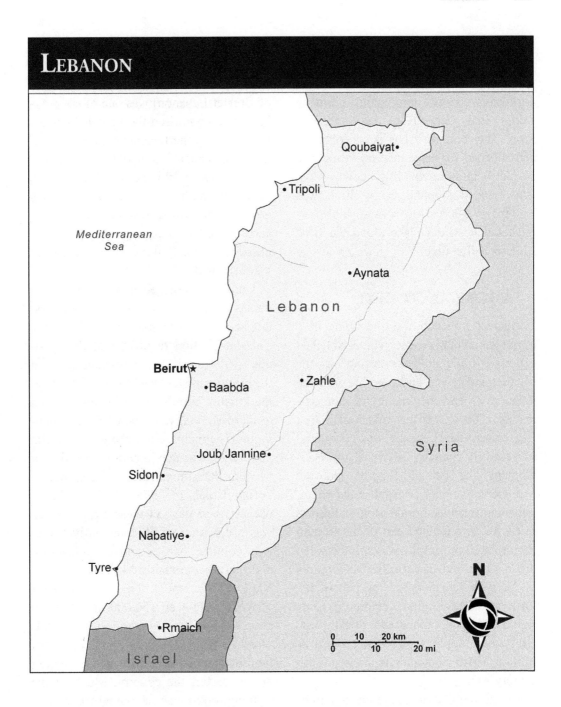

LEBANON

Qoubaiyat•

• Tripoli

Mediterranean Sea

•Aynata

L e b a n o n

Beirut★

•Baabda   • Zahle

S y r i a

Joub Jannine•

Sidon•

Nabatiye•

Tyre◄

•Rmaich

I s r a e l

```
0    10    20 km
0         10    20 mi
```

N

Syria. This boundary continues southward into the northern portion of the contested Golan Heights, which extend southward from southeastern Lebanon to the border region separating Israel and Syria. The tripoint between Lebanon, Syria, and Israel is located near the Lebanese village of Ouazzani.

From this tripoint, the boundary between Lebanon and Israel extends westward to a point near the Israel village of Makula. From this point, it then turns southward following straight-line segments along the western edge of the Golan Heights. Near the Israeli town of Malkiya, the boundary turns westward once again, following straight-line segments to the Mediterranean. This boundary has been contested and adjusted for more than 60 years. The current boundary, which is known as the Blue Line, was delineated by the United Nations in 2000. However, several skirmishes have taken place along the Blue Line since that time.

HISTORICAL CONTEXT

Ancient Lebanon was the home base of the Phoenician people, who established extensive trade linkages throughout the Mediterranean Sea and possibly into the Atlantic Ocean beginning in approximately 1500 BC. In the first millennium BC, present-day Lebanon was conquered successively by the Assyrians, the Babylonians, the Persian Empire, and the Macedonians under Alexander the Great. Lebanon was added to the Roman Empire in 64 BC. It remained part of the Roman Empire until the empire was split between the Western and Eastern Roman Empires in AD 395. Lebanon became part of the Eastern Roman Empire, centered in Constantinople. It remained part of the Eastern Roman Empire until it was taken over by Arab Muslim conquerors in the seventh century AD.

During the Crusades, present-day Lebanon was fought over by Muslim and Christian kingdoms. It became part of the Ottoman Empire in the late 15th century and remained under Ottoman sovereignty until the Ottoman Empire was dismembered after World War I. In 1920,

the League of Nations awarded a mandate over Lebanon and neighboring Syria to France. Lebanon (then known as the State of Greater Lebanon) was one of six provinces that comprised the French Mandate for Syria and the Lebanons. France maintained its mandate until 1943, when Lebanon along with Syria became independent under the authority of the Free French government. Allied troops occupied Lebanon in order to protect Lebanon from possible German attacks until the end of World War II.

Under terms of Lebanon's constitution, quotas of seats in the parliament were established for Christians and Muslims. The constitution required that the president of Lebanon be a Christian and that the prime minister be a Muslim. However, the Muslim population of Lebanon began to increase relative to the Christian population. The increase in Lebanon's Muslim population was due in part to an influx of Muslim Palestinian refugees from neighboring Israel. In 1975, civil war broke out between the Lebanese Front, which was a coalition of predominantly Christian political parties and organizations, and the predominantly Muslim Lebanese National Movement. The war lasted for 15 years. Between 150,000 and 250,000 people were killed, hundreds of thousands were wounded or injured, and hundreds of thousands more were displaced from their homes or left the country. Much of the fighting took place in southern Lebanon, near the Israeli boundary. This area was controlled by the Palestine Liberation Organization and contained a large number of Palestinian refugees.

The civil war ended officially in 1990, when the belligerents signed the Taif

Agreement. Under terms of the Taif Agreement, named for the Saudi Arabian city in which it was negotiated, the religious requirement for executive offices was abandoned. During the war, Syrian troops were sent into Lebanon. Syria occupied portions of Lebanon and continued to do so until 2005. Israel sent troops into southern Lebanon in 1982. Israeli troops remained in Lebanon until 2000, when the United Nations established the Blue Line as the boundary between the two countries. With a few minor exceptions, the Blue Line followed the original boundary between Lebanon and Israel as had been established in 1949 after both countries became independent. After the Blue Line was delineated, Israel withdrew its forces from Lebanon.

CONTEMPORARY ISSUES

Lebanon's boundary with Israel has been contested since the Blue Line was established in 2000. In 2006, war broke out between Lebanon's Hezbollah militia and the Israeli army. Hezbollah militants fired missiles across the boundary. After several Israeli soldiers were killed in these attacks, Israel sent ground troops across the boundary into Lebanon, and its navy blockaded Lebanese ports. Several thousand Lebanese and Israeli soldiers and civilians were killed during the war. After five weeks of warfare, the United Nations negotiated a cease-fire agreement, and Israel withdrew its forces and lifted the naval blockade. Border clashes also took place in 2010 and 2011. On several occasions, Lebanon has accused the Israeli air force of violating Lebanese airspace.

Lebanon has also been affected by civil war in neighboring Syria. Fighting between supporters of Syrian president Bashar al-Assad's government and rebels seeking to topple al-Assad's regime has taken place in the city of Tripoli (not to be confused with the capital city of Libya), which is located in northern Lebanon near the boundary between Lebanon and Syria.

See also   Israel, Syria

Further Reading

Amos Harel, Avi Issacharoff, and Ora Cummings. *34 days: Israel, Hezbollah, and the war in Lebanon.* Translated by Moshe Tlamim. New York: Palgrave Macmillan, 2008.

Dilip Hiro. *Lebanon: Fire and embers: A history of the Lebanese civil war.* New York: St. Martin's Press, 1993.

Emile Hokayem. "Lebanon's little Syria." *Foreign Policy*, May 15, 2012, http://www.foreignpolicy.com/articles/2012/05/15/lebanon_s_little_syria?page=full.

Sandra Mackey. *Lebanon: A house divided.* New York: W. W. Norton, 2006.

LIBYA

OVERVIEW

The Libyan Arab Jamahiriya is located in northeastern Africa. Its neighbors include Egypt to the east, Sudan to the southeast, Chad and Niger to the south, and Algeria and Tunisia to the west. Northern Libya has a long coastline on the Mediterranean Sea. Libya's land area is 679,359 square miles, making it slightly larger in land area than Alaska.

More than 90 percent of Libya's land area is part of the Sahara Desert, and most of this land is uninhabited. Many areas

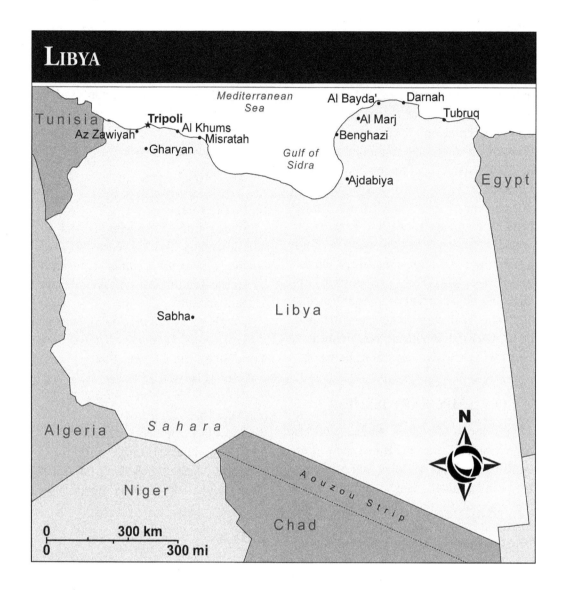

within this region are virtually rainless and lacking in vegetation. Settlement is restricted to oases. Most of Libya's 5.7 million people live in cities, which are concentrated on and near the Mediterranean Sea coast. The capital city of Tripoli in the northwest and the city of Benghazi in the northeast are the largest cities. Both are located along the Mediterranean coast, and between them they contain about a third of Libya's people. Libya is a major oil-exporting country, with oil providing nearly all of its export earnings.

The boundary between Libya and Egypt is geometric. The northern portion of the boundary includes numerous short straight-line segments. The southern three-quarters of the boundary follows the 25th meridian of east longitude. The 25th meridian continues as the boundary between Libya and

Sudan southward to the 20th parallel of latitude, following this parallel westward to the 24th meridian. It then follows the 24th meridian southward to the tripoint between Libya, Sudan, and Chad.

The boundaries between Libya and Chad and Libya and Niger cross uninhabited territory and are also geometric. Most of the boundary between Chad and Libya extends northwestward from the tripoint at latitude 19° 30′ north, longitude 24° east to the point at which the Tropic of Cancer meets longitude 16° east. The boundary then follows another diagonal line southwestward to latitude 23° north, longitude 15° east, passing the tripoint between Libya, Chad, and Niger. The boundary between Libya and Niger also consists of straight-line segments, in this case connecting prominent physical features on the landscape. No paved roads cross either the Libya-Chad or the Libya-Niger boundaries. To the west, the boundaries between Libya and Algeria and between Libya and Tunisia are more complex but also consist of straight-line segments. The northern portion of the boundary between Libya and Tunisia near the Mediterranean Sea is Libya's only border that crosses a populated area.

HISTORICAL CONTEXT

Between 1551 and World War I, Libya was controlled nominally by the Ottoman Empire. However, for most of this time the Ottomans had little real control over present-day Libya, which for practical purposes was governed as an independent country. In 1911, the Ottoman Empire went to war with Italy. After Italy's victory in the war, Italy took control of Libya in 1912. The territory was known as Italian North Africa until 1927, when Italy divided it into two administrative units—Italian Cyrenaica to the east and Italian Tripolitania to the west. The two units were reunited under the name of Libya in 1934. Present-day southwestern Libya, known as Fezzan, was also under the nominal control of Italy. Given the inhospitable climate and lack of water, settlement in Fezzan is limited to oases.

In 1943, the Allies expelled the Italians from North Africa. Britain assumed control of Cyrenaica and Tripolitania while Fezzan, which borders the former French colonies of Algeria, Niger, and Chad, was occupied by French troops. All three regions were united as the independent Kingdom of Libya in 1951. King Idris remained on the throne until he was deposed in a military coup led by Colonel Moammar Gaddafi in 1969.

All of Libya's boundaries were delineated in the late 19th and early 20th centuries by the Italians and neighboring colonial powers. These boundaries have remained stable except for the boundary between Libya and Chad. The two countries disputed sovereignty over a territory known as the Aouzou Strip. The Aouzou Strip is a territory extending between the current Libya-Chad border and a line connecting the Libya-Chad-Niger tripoint and the Libya-Sudan boundary. The strip is about 500 miles long and 60 miles wide. Libya claimed the strip on the grounds that its inhabitants prior to the colonial era were subjects of Libya's precolonial rulers. Sporadic violent skirmishes broke out within the region beginning in 1978 and continuing through the 1980s. Eventually, the dispute was referred to the International Court of Justice, which rejected Libya's claim and awarded the Aouzou Strip to Chad.

CONTEMPORARY ISSUES

With the exception of the Aouzou Strip dispute, Libya's boundaries have remained stable since the early 20th century. That the boundaries have remained uncontested may be related to the fact that they cross uninhabited territory. In 2011, the 42-year dictatorship of Gaddafi was challenged by protestors as part of Arab Spring, when protestors were instrumental in removing the dictatorial regimes of neighboring Egypt and Tunisia. Rebels quickly assumed control of Benghazi, which is the historic capital of Cyrenaica. However, their efforts to advance toward Tripoli and topple Gaddafi from power were unsuccessful. During the summer of 2011, Benghazi remained under rebel control while Tripoli, Tripolitania, and Fezzan remained under the control of Gaddafi's government. Thus, the historic division between Cyrenaica and Tripolitania has been reinforced by ongoing conflict between the rebels in the east and government forces to the west. In August 2011, however, rebel forces took control of Tripoli, and Gaddafi's regime was deposed.

See also   Algeria, Chad, Egypt, Niger, Sudan, Tunisia

Further Reading

Frank Jacobs. "The world's largest sandbox." *New York Times*, November 7, 2011, http://opinionator.blogs.nytimes.com/2011/11/07/the-worlds-largest-sandbox/.

Ronald Bruce St. John. *Libya: From colony to revolution.* London: Oneworld Press, 2012.

Yaroslav Trofimov, Jay Solomon, and Nour Malas. "Arab Spring gives way to an uncertain winter." *Middle East News*, August 23, 2011, http://online.wsj.com/article/SB100014240531119034613045765247016111118090.html.

MOROCCO

OVERVIEW

The Kingdom of Morocco is the westernmost country of North Africa and is located at the northwestern corner of the African continent. Morocco has a land area of 172,487 square miles, slightly larger than California. It has a population of about 33 million, of whom about 80 percent are Arabs.

Morocco is the only country on the African continent that is not a member of the African Union, although it is a member of the Arab League. The economy of Morocco remains closely tied to that of Europe. Northern Morocco has a Mediterranean climate with plentiful winter rains that facilitate agriculture. About 40 percent of the workforce is involved in farming, producing citrus fruits, olives, dates, and other agricultural products typical of Mediterranean climates. Morocco is a popular tourist destination, especially for European tourists visiting the country's beaches, cities, and historic sites.

Morocco borders Algeria to the east and southeast. The former Spanish colony of Western Sahara, over which Morocco claims sovereignty, is located immediately south of Morocco. Morocco has a long

MOROCCO

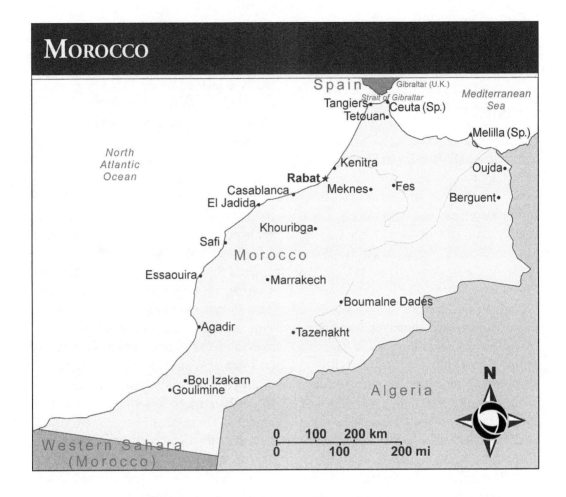

Spain
Gibraltar (U.K.)
Strait of Gibraltar
Tangiers•
Tetouan•
•Ceuta (Sp.)
Mediterranean
Sea

Melilla (Sp.)

North
Atlantic
Ocean

•Kenitra
Rabat★
Casablanca•
El Jadida•
Meknes•
•Fes
Oujda•
Berguent•

•Khouribga

Safi•

Morocco

Essaouira•

•Marrakech

•Boumalne Dadès

•Agadir
•Tazenakht

•Bou Izakarn
•Goulimine
Algeria

N

0   100   200 km
0   100   200 mi

Western Sahara
(Morocco)

coastline on the Atlantic Ocean to the west and another coastline on the Mediterranean Sea to the north. The Strait of Gibraltar separates the Atlantic and the Mediterranean. At its narrowest point, the strait between Morocco to the south and the coast of Spain to the north is less than 10 miles wide. The Spanish exclaves of Ceuta and Melilla are located on the Mediterranean coast of North Africa and are surrounded by Moroccan territory. Ceuta has a land area of seven square miles and a population of 76,000; Melilla has a land area of about five square miles and a population of 73,000.

The boundary between Morocco and Algeria passes through very thinly populated territory to the south and densely populated territory to the north. From the tripoint between Morocco, Algeria, and Western Sahara, the boundary extends northward along the 8° 40′ meridian to 27° 40′ north latitude. It then trends northeastward and remains south of the Atlas Mountains, which separate densely populated northern Morocco from sparsely populated southern Morocco. Much of this boundary follows the Draa River. Near the Algerian town of Beni Ounif, the boundary turns northward, crosses the mountains, and extends through thickly populated territory to the Mediterranean Sea west of the Moroccan city of Oujda.

HISTORICAL CONTEXT

Given its location along the Strait of Gibraltar, coastal Morocco has been an important trading center for more than 2,000 years. The Phoenicians established several ports in present-day Morocco, which later became part of the Roman Empire. Morocco became part of the Umayyad Caliphate in the seventh century AD, and the Moors used Morocco as their base for invading present-day Spain and Portugal. The Alaouite royal family began ruling present-day Morocco in 1664 and has ruled Morocco ever since.

Morocco retained its independence under Alaouite rule during the 18th and 19th centuries while European powers established colonies throughout the remainder of North Africa. France, which controlled neighboring Algeria, and Morocco agreed to their present boundary in 1845. By the end of the 19th century, the French, British, and Ottomans had designs on Morocco. In 1912, Morocco became a French protectorate.

Moroccan opposition to French rule simmered between World War I and World War II and intensified after World War II ended. In 1956, Sultan Mohammed V negotiated a gradual transition to full independence from France, with Morocco becoming a constitutional monarchy. Mohammed V assumed the title of king in the following year. After neighboring Algeria assumed independence in 1962, Morocco laid claim to some Algerian territory that had been ruled by the Alaouites prior to French rule. Border skirmishes between the two countries broke out. The issue was resolved in 1963, when Morocco dropped its claims to this Algerian territory and the two countries agreed to reaffirm their 1845 boundary.

Relationships between Morocco and Algeria deteriorated beginning in 1975 following a dispute over control of Western Sahara, which is located on the Atlantic coast south of Morocco. Spain had ruled this territory as a colony under the name of Spanish Sahara until 1975, when it relinquished its claim to this area. The territory came to be known as Western Sahara. An agreement between Spain, Morocco, and Mauritania, which is located to the south of Western Sahara, specified that Morocco would administer the northern part of Western Sahara with Mauritania in charge of the southern portion. However, Moroccan forces invaded the southern portion of Western Sahara, assumed control of the entire territory, and claimed sovereignty over all of Western Sahara.

CONTEMPORARY ISSUES

The status of Western Sahara, Ceuta, and Melilla are the major boundary-related issues faced by Morocco today. Morocco maintains effective control over most of Western Sahara. However, an insurgent movement known as the Polisario has pushed for full independence for Western Sahara. The Polisario is associated with the Sahrawi Arab Democratic Republic, which claims independent status as a successor state to Spanish Sahara but remains a government in exile. The Polisario has been backed by Algeria, which continues to oppose the expansion of Morocco.

The dispute over the status of Western Sahara continued into the 21st century. In the late 1990s, all parties to the dispute asked former U.S. secretary of state James Baker to serve as a mediator. In 2003, Baker proposed that the Western Sahara continued to be administered by Morocco for four years. After this four-year period ended, a referendum would be held and voters would be given the opportunity to choose among continued autonomy within Morocco, full integration with Morocco, and full independence. However, Morocco rejected Baker's proposal, and it continues to administer much of the area. Thousands of Sahrawi refugees, some claiming human rights violations, have moved to Algeria.

The status of Ceuta and Melilla also remains uncertain. Both of these cities, along with several nearby islands in the Mediterranean Sea, have been under Spanish control for several centuries. A Roman Catholic diocese was established in Ceuta in 1417, and Spain assumed formal sovereignty over the city-state in 1675. Melilla has been controlled by Spain since 1497. Morocco has claimed both cities on the grounds that Spanish control over them represents a carryover from European colonial control over Africa. However, a majority of people in both cities are Roman Catholics of Spanish ancestry. Public opinion surveys confirm that a majority of residents of the two cities prefer that they remain part of Spain as opposed to integration with Morocco.

See also   Algeria

Further Reading

BBC News. "Western Sahara profile." December 9, 2011, http://www.bbc.co.uk/news/world-africa-14115273.

Erik Jensen. *Western Sahara: Anatomy of a stalemate.* Boulder, CO: Lynne Rienner, 2005.

James N. Sater. *Morocco: Challenges to tradition and modernity.* London: Routledge, 2010.

Toby Shelley. *Endgame in the Western Sahara: What future for Africa's last colony?* London: Zed Books, 2004.

OMAN

OVERVIEW

The Sultanate of Oman is located in the southeastern part of Asia's Arabian Peninsula. Oman has a land area of approximately 120,000 square miles, or about the size of New Mexico, with a population of about 3.1 million.

Oman's neighbors are Yemen to the southwest, Saudi Arabia to the west, and the United Arab Emirates to the northwest. Eastern and southern Yemen has coastlines along the Gulf of Oman and the Arabian Sea. Oman also includes two exclaves surrounded by United Arab Emirates (UAE) territory. The larger exclave includes the Musandam Peninsula, which extends northward into the Persian Gulf. Its control of the Musandam Peninsula gives Oman, along with Iran, control over the strategic Strait of Hormuz that connects the Persian Gulf with the Gulf of Oman and the Arabian Sea. At its narrowest point, the Strait of Hormuz between the Musandam Peninsula and the Iranian mainland is 34 miles wide.

OMAN

Strait of Hormuz

Al Khasab•

Qatar

Persian Gulf

Iran

Gulf of Oman

•Al Buraymi

United Arab Emirates

Muscat

Ibri•

Nazwa• •Izki

•Sur

Saudi Arabia

•Ghabah

Oman

Masirah

•Duqm

Dawkah•

•Thamarit

Arabian Sea

Yemen

Salalah•

N

| 0 | 50 | 100 km |
| 0 | 50 | 100 mi |

The Musandam Peninsula is separated from the rest of Oman by United Arab Emirates territory. The Omani-ruled peninsula, known as the Musandam Governate, has an area of about 700 square miles and a population of approximately

29,000. The governate is separated from the rest of Oman by about 40 miles of United Arab Emirates territory. The governate became part of Oman in the 1960s in keeping with the preferences of the local population. The United Arab Emirates claimed the peninsula for a few years after it became independent but abandoned these efforts after about 1980. The smaller exclave, known as Madha, is located about halfway between the Musandam Peninsula and the main territory of Oman. This exclave is about 30 square miles in land area. Within Madha is a small UAE exclave containing the small village of Nahwa.

Oman's boundaries with Yemen and Saudi Arabia are geometric. The boundary between Oman and Yemen is a single straight-line segment extending for nearly 200 miles northwest from the Arabian Sea to the tripoint with Saudi Arabia. The boundary between Oman and Saudi Arabia includes three straight-line segments. The two southernmost and longest segments run from southwest to northeast, with a shorter segment extending northwestward to the tripoint with the United Arab Emirates. This boundary crosses the Rub al Khali, or "Empty Quarter," an uninhabited and almost rainless desert.

The boundary between Oman and the United Arab Emirates is more complex, but it consists of numerous short straight-line segments between the Gulf of Oman and the tripoint between Oman, the United Arab Emirates, and Saudi Arabia. These segments trend generally in a northerly direction from this tripoint to a point near the village of Ar Rawdah. This section of the boundary crosses desert territory that is virtually uninhabited. Near Ar Rawdah,

the boundary trends eastward toward the Gulf of Oman.

HISTORICAL CONTEXT

Present-day Oman includes two distinct territories: the area near the seaport of Muscat along the coast, including Oman's capital city of Masqat, and the interior region known in the 19th century as the Imamate of Oman.

In the early 19th century, the two regions were united as the Sultanate of Muscat and Oman. The sultanate also ruled Zanzibar, which is currently part of Tanzania. Following the death of Sultan Said bin Sultan in 1856, a dispute over succession was mediated by the British. As a result, Zanzibar became independent, and separate rulers were installed in Muscat and Oman. However, the sultan of Muscat was the preeminent ruler. The territory experienced ongoing tension between Muscat, which was more cosmopolitan and secular given its long history as a port and trading center, and Oman, which was much more conservative in religious matters. Tension intensified after oil was discovered in the inland Omani region in the 1930s.

Although Muscat and Oman was never a formal British colony, Britain maintained a strong interest in and effective control of the area because of its importance as a port and as a center for oil production. The British administered the present-day United Arab Emirates, which were then known as the Trucial States, and they delimited the boundary between the Emirates and Oman. The two countries finalized an agreement on the boundary in 2008.

Oman's boundaries with Saudi Arabia and Yemen remained indeterminate until the late 20th century. Oman and Saudi Arabia agreed to their boundary in 1990. Although the territory crossed by the boundary is uninhabited, the formal delimitation of the boundary clarified the division of the region's vast oil reserves between the two countries. Oman and Yemen signed an agreement delimiting their boundary in 1992.

CONTEMPORARY ISSUES

Most of Oman's boundaries cross uninhabited or lightly populated areas, and as a result contemporary Oman faces few boundary conflicts with its neighbors. During the 1960s and 1970s, a guerilla movement fought for the independence of the province of Dhofar, which is located along the boundary between Oman and Yemen. With support from the Soviet Union and from the pro-communist government of what was then the People's Republic of Yemen, rebels fought for Dhofar's independence against the Omani government. Oman was backed by Britain and by the shah of Iran, and a peace agreement was signed in 1976. Today, Oman's location close to Iran has given it a pivotal position in ongoing conflict between Iran and the countries of the Arabian Peninsula. Oman's policy has been to remain neutral in this conflict and to promote diplomatic contacts between the two sides.

See also   Saudi Arabia, United Arab Emirates, Yemen

Further Reading
   Majid Al-Khalili. *Oman's foreign policy: Foundation and practice.* Westport, CT: Praeger, 2009.

   Marc Valeri. *Oman: Politics and society in the Qaboos state.* New York: Columbia University Press, 2009.

PALESTINE OCCUPIED TERRITORIES

OVERVIEW

The Palestine Occupied Territories are located in southwestern Asia. These territories include two distinct regions, the West Bank and the Gaza Strip. The West Bank has a land area of 2,263 square miles and a population of about 3.1 million. More than 80 percent of the West Bank's residents are Palestinian Arabs although about 500,000 Jewish settlers from Israel also live in the West Bank. The Gaza Strip has a land area of 141 square miles and a population of about 1.7 million. A large majority of residents of the Gaza Strip are Palestinians.

The West Bank has boundaries with Israel and Jordan, and the Gaza Strip has boundaries with Israel and Egypt. The Jordan River forms the boundary between the West Bank and Jordan. This boundary extends northward and upstream along the Jordan from the Dead Sea to a point near the village of Tirat Tavi in Israel. From Tirat Tavi, the boundary extends westward to a point near the town of Katsir-Harish. The boundary then turns to the south. West of the city of Jerusalem, it turns eastward and includes the eastern part of the city. The town of Bethlehem, the birthplace of Jesus, is located south of Jerusalem in the West Bank. From Jerusalem the boundary extends southwestward and then turns eastward south and west of the city of Hebron. It then extends eastward to the Dead Sea.

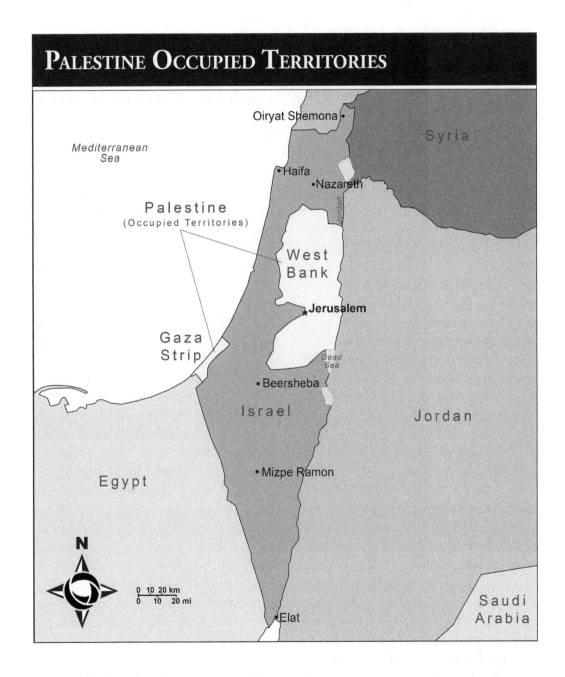

PALESTINE OCCUPIED TERRITORIES

The Gaza Strip is located on the southeastern coast of the Mediterranean Sea north of the boundary between Egypt and Israel. The boundary between the Gaza Strip and Egypt consists of two diagonal segments that extend in a south-southeasterly direction inland from the Mediterranean and pass just to the southwest of the city of Rafah. Together these segments are about seven miles in length. The boundary between the Gaza Strip and Israel extends to the northeast, paralleling the Mediterranean coast between 5 and 10 miles inland. Near the town of Bayt Hanun, the boundary turns northwestward to the Mediterranean. At their closest points, the West

Bank and the Gaza Strip are separated by about 40 miles of Israeli territory.

HISTORICAL CONTEXT

The West Bank and the Gaza Strip were part of the larger area of Palestine, which was ruled by the Ottoman Empire between 1516 and the end of World War I. After World War I ended, the United Nations granted Britain a mandate over Palestine and Transjordan, which became the present-day country of Jordan. During the late 19th century, European Jews began to promote Zionism, or the movement of European Jews to Palestine with the eventual idea of creating a Jewish state there. Hundreds of thousands of Jews moved to Palestine between World War I and World War II, and many thousands more moved there after the end of the Holocaust in Europe. By the late 1940s, over a million Jews, most of whom were of European ancestry, were living in Palestine.

In 1947, the United Nations called for the division of the British Mandate into a Jewish state, an Arab state, and a free city of Jerusalem. The Jewish state became the state of Israel, which declared its independence in 1948. Shortly thereafter, Israel was attacked by forces from Egypt, Syria, Iraq, and Jordan. Jordan captured and annexed the West Bank. By this time, hundreds of thousands of Palestinian Arabs had been displaced by Jewish settlers. Many moved across Israel's borders to the West Bank with others moving to Lebanon, Jordan, and other countries. The Palestine Liberation Organization (PLO), which is recognized currently as the legitimate representative of the Palestinian people in the region by many in the international community, was founded in 1964.

The West Bank remained under Jordanian control until 1967, when it was captured by Israeli forces during the Six-Day War. Israel occupied but did not annex the West Bank. However, the Israeli government encouraged Israeli farmers and settlers to move into the West Bank. The founding and maintenance of these Israeli settlements intensified tensions between the PLO and the Israeli government. Meanwhile, Jordan continued to claim the West Bank until 1988, when Jordan relinquished its claim and offered support to the PLO's claim over the region. The PLO and its legislative organization, the Palestinian National Council, declared Palestine (including the West Bank and the Gaza Strip) to be an independent state in 1988.

In 1993, the PLO and the Israeli government negotiated the Oslo Accords, which were intended to provide a framework for the eventual settlement of the ongoing dispute over control of the West Bank. Under the Oslo Accords, responsibility for the administration of the West Bank was divided between Israel and the Palestinian Authority, which was established as the administrative arm of the PLO in 1994. However, Israel did not recognize Palestine as an independent state and has yet to do so.

The Gaza Strip was also part of Britain's League of Nations mandate. In 1949, Israel and Egypt agreed to the boundary between the Gaza Strip and Israel. The boundary between Egypt and present-day Israel, south of the Gaza Strip, had been agreed upon previously by Egypt and the Ottoman Empire in 1906. The Arab population of the Gaza Strip was augmented by the arrival of thousands of Palestinian refugees from Israel.

The Gaza Strip had nominal autonomy until 1959, when it was occupied by Egypt. Israel took over control of the Gaza Strip during the Six-Day War in 1967. The peace treaty between Israel and Egypt, signed by both countries in 1979, specified that Egypt would give up its claim to the Gaza Strip whereas the Sinai Peninsula, which had been occupied by Egypt since the Six-Day War, would be returned to Egypt. Israel continued to occupy the Gaza Strip until 1994. At that time, administration of most of the Gaza Strip was turned over to the Palestinian Authority. In 2005, the Israeli armed forces withdrew from the Gaza Strip, and Israeli civilians were instructed to leave the area. However, Israel remains in control of the Gaza Strip's airspace and its territorial waters on the Mediterranean Sea. In the early 21st century, Palestinian organizations were accused of launching missiles and rockets into Israel. Israel responded by attacking the Gaza Strip in 2009.

CONTEMPORARY ISSUES

The major issue facing Palestine is its possible status as an independent state. This debate is ongoing. About 140 countries have recognized Palestine as an independent state, although the United States has yet to do so. Palestinian leaders continue to criticize the maintenance of Israeli settlements in the West Bank and have pointed out that an independent Palestine would comprise only a small percentage of the territory that had been occupied by Palestine prior to the Zionist movement. Armed hostilities between Israel and some Palestinian organizations continue, especially in and near the Gaza Strip. Palestine currently holds observer status at the United Nations but has petitioned for full membership in the UN.

See also   Egypt, Israel, Jordan

Further Reading

Robert M. Danin. "A third way to Palestine." *Foreign Affairs*, January/February 2011.

Jeremy R. Hammond. "The future is Palestine." *Foreign Policy Journal*, July 20, 2011, http://www.foreignpolicyjournal.com/2011/07/20/the-future-is-palestine.

Gregory Harms and Todd M. Ferry. *The Palestine-Israel conflict: A basic introduction.* 2nd ed. London: Pluto Press, 2008.

Nathan Shachar. *The Gaza Strip: Its history and politics—from the pharaohs to the Israeli invasion of 2009.* Eastbourne, UK: Sussex Academic Press, 2010.

Mark Tessler. *A history of the Israeli-Palestinian conflict.* Bloomington: Indiana University Press, 2009.

QATAR

OVERVIEW

The State of Qatar is located on a peninsula extending from the mainland of the Arabian Peninsula into the Persian Gulf. Qatar's land area is 4,416 square miles, slightly smaller than Massachusetts. Its population is 1.7 million.

Qatar's only land neighbor is Saudi Arabia to the south and southwest. The border

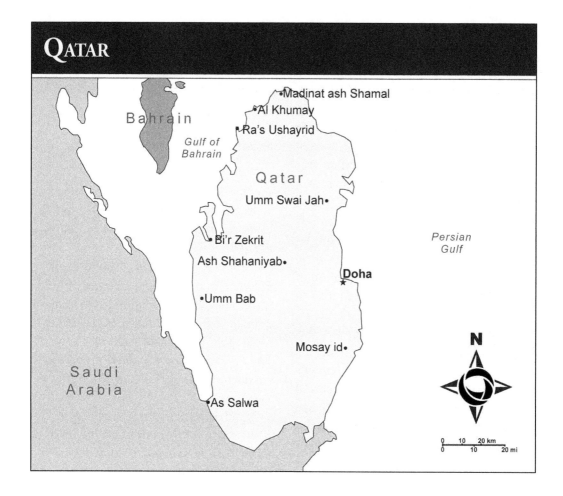

QATAR

Madinat ash Shamal

Al Khumay

Ra's Ushayrid

Bahrain

Gulf of
Bahrain

Qatar

Umm Swai Jah•

Bi'r Zekrit

Ash Shahaniyab•

Doha

•Umm Bab

Persian
Gulf

Mosay id•

Saudi
Arabia

•As Salwa

N

0   10   20 km
0   10   20 mi

between Qatar and Saudi Arabia consists of five straight-line segments. The boundary extends from the tidal inlet of Khor-al-Udeid to the southeast to the bay of Dawhat Salwa, an inlet of the Bay of Bahrain, to the northwest. This boundary crosses uninhabited desert. The Persian Gulf surrounds Qatar to the east, north, and northwest.

Qatar and nearby Bahrain are separated by water. The Qatari coast is approximately 20 miles from the main island of Bahrain. Bahrain's Hawar Islands, south of the main island of Bahrain, are only a mile from Qatar's western coast.

HISTORICAL CONTEXT

Present-day Qatar is located strategically within the Persian Gulf. Qatar's rulers have played an important role in commerce through Persian Gulf and the Indian Ocean for hundreds of years. During the 19th century, the Qatar peninsula was controlled by the royal family of Bahrain until 1872, when it became part of the Ottoman Empire. In 1915, the Ottomans and the British recognized Sheik Abdullah bin Jassim bin Muhammed Al Thani as the ruler of Qatar. Since then, the Qatari throne has been occupied by Sheik Abdullah's descendants. Qatar remains an absolute monarchy although steps are being taken to increase the Qatari people's voice in government.

In 1916, Sheik Abdullah signed an agreement with the British government providing for British protection of Qatar. In exchange, Britain was granted control over Qatar's foreign policy. Large petroleum reserves were discovered in the 1930s. The first oil well was drilled in 1938. Production was halted during World War II but resumed after the war ended. In order to separate Qatari and Saudi oil fields, the boundary between Qatar and Saudi Arabia was agreed upon in 1965.

When signing the 1916 protection agreement, the British negotiated similar agreements with Bahrain and with the seven emirates in southeastern Arabia that would become the United Arab Emirates. During the 1960s, efforts were made to unite the Emirates with Bahrain and Qatar. These efforts were unsuccessful, and in 1971 Qatar declared its independence.

Qatar's substantial wealth derives almost entirely from petroleum exports. On a per capita basis, Qatar produces more oil than any other country in the world. Qatar's oil wealth has attracted a large expatriate population, primarily from India and Pakistan. More than two-thirds of Qatar's population today consists of expatriates.

CONTEMPORARY ISSUES

Qatar and Bahrain have experienced ongoing conflict over control of the Hawar Islands. These islands in the Bay of Bahrain are located only a mile from the Qatari coast at their closest point. The largest island, Hawar, makes up more than 80 percent of the disputed territory. Hawar is about 25 square miles in area with a permanent population of about 4,000. The islands were settled by people from Bahrain in the 19th century. In 2001, the International Court of Justice resolved the dispute in favor of Bahrain.

Currently, efforts are under way to construct a causeway to be known as the Qatar-Bahrain Friendship Bridge to connect Qatar and Bahrain's main island. In 2011, a Bahraini newspaper reported that construction would begin in 2011, with completion and opening scheduled for 2015.

See also   Saudi Arabia

Further Reading

Blake Hounshell. "The Qatar bubble." *Foreign Policy*, May/June 2012, http://www.foreignpolicy.com/articles/2012/04/23/the_qatar_bubble?page=0,1.

Krista E. Wiegand. "Bahrain, Qatar, and the Hawar Islands: Resolution of a Gulf territorial dispute." *Middle East Journal*, 66 (2012), pp. 79–96.

SAUDI ARABIA

OVERVIEW

The Kingdom of Saudi Arabia encompasses about 80 percent of the Arabian Peninsula. It is the home of the city of Mecca, the home of the Prophet Muhammad and the holiest city of Islam. Saudi Arabia has a land area of 830,000 square miles, making it about 25 percent larger than the state of Alaska. Its population is about 28 million.

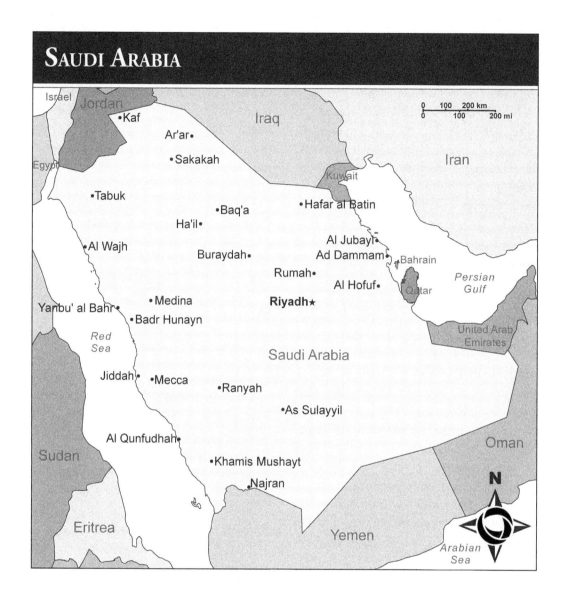

SAUDI ARABIA

Saudi Arabia's neighbors are Jordan to the north, Iraq and Kuwait to the northeast, Qatar to the east, the United Arab Emirates and Oman to the southeast, and Yemen to the south. Western Saudi Arabia fronts the Red Sea while eastern Saudi Arabia has a coastline along the Persian Gulf. Saudi Arabia's western coastline includes a coast along the Gulf of Aqaba, a long and narrow inlet of the Red Sea. Egypt's Sinai Peninsula is located on the opposite shore of the Gulf of Aqaba. Many of Saudi Arabia's boundaries cross uninhabited or very sparsely populated territory. Most of them are straight-line geometric boundaries that in some cases, because of the absence of settlements, have not been delineated or marked with precision.

Saudi Arabia's boundary with Jordan is geometric. From the Gulf of Aqaba, this boundary extends inland along a single segment about 40 miles in length and running from west-northwest to east-southeast. It then turns northeastward, following several segments, before it turns northwestward abruptly. The northernmost part of the boundary consists primarily of a long segment that extends from west-southwest to east-northeast north of the Saudi town of Turaif. Northeast of Turaif, the boundary follows a short segment northeastward to the tripoint between Saudi Arabia, Jordan, and Iraq. From this tripoint the boundary between Saudi Arabia and Iraq consists of several longer straight lines, all of which extend from northwest to southeast. The boundary between Saudi Arabia and Kuwait includes two long, east-west segments at the western and eastern ends, with a more complex series of straight lines running from north-northwest to south-southeast in between.

The border between Saudi Arabia and Qatar crosses an uninhabited desert. It consists of five straight-line segments that extend from the tidal inlet of Khor-al-Udeid to the southeast to the bay of Dawhat Salwa, an inlet of the Bay of Bahrain, to the northwest. Saudi Arabia's boundaries with the United Arab Emirates and Oman cross the uninhabited and virtually rainless desert known as the Rub al Khali, or "Empty Quarter." Most of the boundary between Saudi Arabia and the United Arab Emirates consists of two straight-line segments, with much shorter ones connecting these segments with the Persian Gulf at one end and with the Saudi Arabia–United Arab Emirates–Oman tripoint. The boundary between Oman and Saudi Arabia includes three straight-line segments. The two southernmost and longest segments run from southwest to northeast, with a shorter segment extending northwestward to this tripoint.

The boundary between Saudi Arabia and Yemen is the most complex of Saudi Arabia's boundaries, and it is the only one that follows physical features and cultural considerations. Yemen has claimed the territory that had been considered part of that country prior to the arrival of the Ottomans and later the British. This territory was generally associated with those streams that drain into the Red Sea and the Arabian Gulf. The western portion of the contemporary boundary between Saudi Arabia and Yemen is based on this principle, separating streams that drain into these bodies of water from areas further inland on the Saudi side of the boundary. To the east, the boundary between the two countries crosses the southern portion of the Rub Al-Khali Desert and is a straight-line segment from southwest to northeast.

HISTORICAL CONTEXT

Prior to the 20th century, Saudi Arabia was sparsely populated and located on the geographic and economic periphery of the Arab world. Most of the Arabian Peninsula was controlled by the Ottoman Empire between 1816 and 1918. After the dismemberment of the Ottoman Empire, the area consisted of the kingdoms of Nejd and Hejaz. The kingdoms were united under the rule of the current Saudi royal family in 1932. At that time, a large majority of the people of Saudi Arabia lived in rural areas, and many were nomads.

Saudi Arabia began its transformation from a rural backwater to a wealthy country after the discovery of oil in the 1930s. Saudi Arabia is the world's largest petroleum exporter, and petroleum represents more than 90 percent of the country's export income. In 1933, the Arabian American Oil Company (Aramco) was established through an agreement between the Saudi government and the Standard Oil Company of California. The first commercially successful oil field began production in 1938. Beginning in 1950, Aramco agreed to share its profits with the Saudi government, which bought full control of the company in 1980 and changed its name to Saudi Aramco in 1988. Today, Saudi Arabia produces more than 3 billion barrels of crude oil per year. The need to divide oil fields between Saudi Arabia and its neighbors was an important factor in efforts to delineate many of their boundaries.

Saudi Arabia's population has grown rapidly in the past century. Rapid population growth has been associated with high birth rates as well as a large influx of foreign workers. About a quarter of Saudi Arabia's labor force today consists of foreigners. The population of Saudi Arabia in 1950 was approximately 4 million. At that time, many Saudis lived in rural areas, and some were nomads. Today, more than 88 percent of Saudi Arabia's 28 million people live in urban areas.

Saudi Arabia includes the city of Mecca, which was the home of the Prophet Muhammad and is the holiest city of Islam. Muslims who can afford to do so are expected to make a pilgrimage to Mecca at some point during their lifetimes. Mecca has been an important trading center since ancient times. It became incorporated into Saudi Arabia in 1924. Today, services to Muslim pilgrims provide an important source of income to Mecca's 1.7 million residents. About 3 million pilgrims, the majority of whom come from foreign countries, visit Mecca on pilgrimages each year.

Saudi Arabia's borders were established in the 20th century after Saudi Arabia became a unified kingdom. The most controversial of these borders was the boundary between Saudi Arabia and Jordan. Although most of the frontier region between these countries consists of uninhabited or sparsely populated desert, the major point of contention was access to the Gulf of Aqaba such that Jordan would have a seaport. Prior to World War II, what is now Jordan was controlled by the British, who attempted to negotiate the boundary between Jordan and Saudi Arabia. The boundary issue remained unsettled after Jordan became independent in 1946. In 1965, however, Jordan and Saudi Arabia agreed to their present boundary. The agreement specified that Jordan would have a coastline of about 12 miles on the Gulf of Aqaba, centered on the city of Aqaba. In exchange, Jordan ceded territory inland to Saudi Arabia.

Much of the boundary between Saudi Arabia and Iraq was agreed upon by Saudi Arabia and Britain, which at that time held a League of Nations mandate over Iraq, through the Treaty of Al Uqayr in 1922. The two countries could not agree on the eastern segment of the border just west of its tripoint with Kuwait. Thus a territory of about 2,500 square miles became a neutral zone. The neutral zone was divided between the two countries in 1975, with Saudi Arabia becoming sovereign over the southern half and Iraq becoming sovereign over the northern half.

The Treaty of Al Uqayr also established a border between Saudi Arabia and Kuwait. A second, slightly smaller neutral zone was established south of Kuwait. In 1966, the countries agreed to divide administration of this neutral zone, which then became known as the Divided Zone. Each country is responsible for governing a portion of the Divided Zone, but the two countries share oil wealth from the Divided Zone equally. Oman and Saudi Arabia agreed to their boundary in 1990. Although the territory crossed by the boundary is uninhabited, the formal delimitation of the boundary clarified the division of the region's vast oil reserves between the two countries. In 2000, Saudi Arabia and Yemen agreed to the Treaty of Jeddah, settling their long-standing boundary dispute.

CONTEMPORARY ISSUES

Most of Saudi Arabia's boundaries, which were agreed upon during the 20th century, are stable. Many cross uninhabited territory and are demarcated only approximately. Since the mid-20th century, most boundary conflicts involving Saudi Arabia are related to control of oil reserves. Thus control of the lucrative and profitable oil deposits along the present-day boundary between Saudi Arabia and Oman became an issue in the delineation of the boundary between these two states until this boundary was agreed upon in 1990.

Saudi Arabia's relations with some of its neighbors remain tense. In 1991, Saudi Arabia backed the U.S.-led invasion of Iraq during the Persian Gulf War. Iraq broke off diplomatic relations with Saudi Arabia, and diplomatic relations resumed

only in 2009. However, Saudi government officials remain concerned about the possibility of Iraqi expansion into its territory.

See also   Iraq, Jordan, Kuwait, Oman, Qatar, United Arab Emirates, Yemen

Further Reading

Anthony H. Cordesman. "Saudi Arabia and Gulf security." Center for Strategic and International Studies, May 17, 2010, http://csis.org/publication/saudi-arabia-and-gulf-security.

Bernard Haykel. "Saudi Arabia's Yemen dilemma." *Foreign Affairs*, June 14, 2011.

Thomas W. Lippman. *Saudi Arabia on the edge: The uncertain future of an American ally.* Dulles, VA: Potomac Books, 2012.

SYRIA

OVERVIEW

The Syrian Arab Republic is located along the eastern shore of the Mediterranean Sea. It has a land area of 71,479 square miles, the size of Washington State. Syria's population is about 22.5 million.

About 90 percent of Syria's people are Syrian Arabs, with Kurds making up about 9 percent of the population. About three-quarters are Sunni Muslims, with 12 percent Shi'ites and 10 percent Christians. Islam is the state religion. Much of Syria is a desert, and many of the people live along the Mediterranean coastline or in the valley of the Euphrates River, which is part of the Fertile Crescent in the eastern part of the country. Syria's economy is based

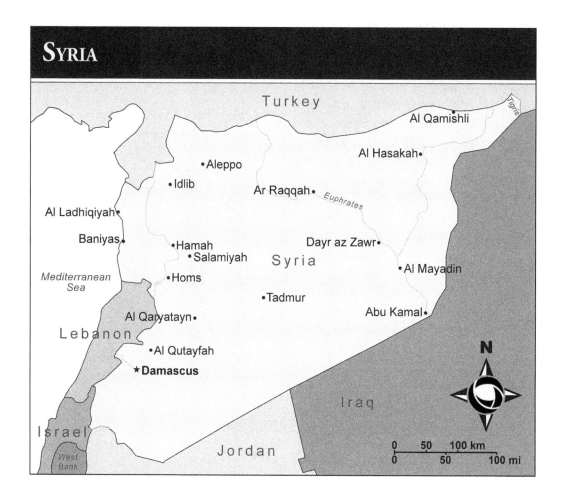

SYRIA

Turkey

Al Qamishli

Al Hasakah

•Aleppo

•Idlib

Ar Raqqah•   Euphrates

Al Ladhiqiyah

Baniyas

•Hamah

•Salamiyah

Dayr az Zawr•

Syria

•Al Mayadin

Mediterranean
Sea

•Homs

•Tadmur

Abu Kamal•

Al Qaryatayn•

Lebanon

•Al Qutayfah

★Damascus

Iraq

Israel

West
Bank

Jordan

Tigris

0   50   100 km
0   50   100 mi

N

on agriculture in the Euphrates valley and in various oases, along with petroleum and natural gas production, manufacturing, and tourism. Syria's capital city of Damascus is one of the oldest continuously inhabited cities in the world.

Syria's neighbors are Turkey to the north, Iraq to the east, Jordan to the south, and Israel and Lebanon to the southwest. Western Syria has a coastline on the Mediterranean. The boundary between Turkey and Syria is primarily geometric, consisting of many short segments that extend in a west-to-east direction from the Mediterranean to the tripoint between Syria, Turkey, and Iraq. This tripoint is located on the Tigris River, which forms the short northern section of the border between Syria and Iraq. The boundary between Syria and Iraq then trends to the southwest and consists of several straight-line segments that extend southwestward to the Euphrates River. From the Euphrates, the boundary is a single segment that runs from northeast to southwest to the tripoint with Jordan. This boundary crosses uninhabited desert. The line marking the boundary between Syria and Iraq continues southwestward to become the boundary between Syria and Jordan for about half that boundary's length. To the west, the boundary becomes more complex. Much of it follows straight-line segments northwestward to the Yarmouk River. The Yarmouk, which is a tributary of the Jordan River, forms the western end of the boundary as it flows from east to west.

The boundary between Syria and Israel is contested. The original boundary extended from the tripoint between Israel, Syria, and Jordan on the Yarmouk River northward to the Sea of Galilee. From the Sea of Galilee, it continued northward along the Jordan River to a tripoint between Syria, Israel, and Lebanon. In 1967, however, Israel occupied the Golan Heights region east and northeast of the Jordan River. This area has been occupied by Israel since 1967. North of the Golan Heights, the boundary between Syria and Lebanon extends in a generally northeastward direction as far as the Lebanese village of Karha. This boundary follows the Jabal Al-Sharqi Mountains, which separate the two countries. From Karha, the boundary turns westward to the Mediterranean. This boundary follows the Nahr el-Kebir River, which is often called the Kebir, before it empties into the sea.

HISTORICAL CONTEXT

Present-day Syria's history dates back more than 5,000 years. It was part of the Roman Empire and later the Eastern Roman Empire until 628, when it was conquered by the Umayyad Caliphate. During the Middle Ages, it was contested among various empires until it was taken over by the Ottoman Empire in 1516.

After the dissolution of the Ottoman Empire, the League of Nations divided administration of the former Ottoman territories east of the Mediterranean between France and Britain. France was awarded a mandate over present-day Syria and Lebanon, with a mandate over Transjordan and Palestine (today's Jordan, Israel, and Palestine) awarded to Britain. This division established the boundaries between Syria and Jordan and Syria and Israel. France divided its mandate into six administrative regions, or "states." The State of Greater Lebanon became the independent country of Lebanon, while the other five became Syria.

France and newly independent Turkey agreed in principle on their boundary in 1923, and the actual boundary was delineated in 1926. Syria became independent in 1946. In 1958, Syria and Egypt merged as the United Arab Republic, but this union dissolved in 1961, and Syria resumed its independent status.

Conflict with Israel dominated Syria's foreign policy from 1948, when the State of Israel achieved independence. After the Arab-Israeli War of 1948, Syria and Israel signed an armistice in 1949. Syria and its allies attempted to retake the Golan Heights in 1973, but the two countries agreed to a cease-fire in 1974. This agreement left Israel in control of the Golan Heights, although Syria continued to claim the area. In 2012, rebels encouraged by the success of antigovernment efforts elsewhere in the Arab world have made efforts to topple the autocratic government of Syria.

CONTEMPORARY ISSUES

Many of Syria's boundaries are contested. In many cases, these issues stem from decisions made during the period of French mandate between World War I and World War II. However, the more recent issue of control over the Golan Heights has been the dominant issue involving Syria's boundaries since its independence.

Much of this conflict between Syria and Israel has involved control of the Golan Heights. The Golan Heights is a region of about 450 square miles located east and northeast of the Jordan River, which represented the original boundary between Israel and Syria. As its name implies, most of the Golan Heights region consists of highlands and mountains, and the region is of considerable military and strategic importance.

The Golan Heights were part of the French mandate over Syria and Lebanon after World War I and remained part of Syria after Syria became independent in 1946. In 1967, Israel occupied the Golan Heights during the Six-Day War. Syria attempted to regain control of the region in 1973, but its efforts were unsuccessful, and in 1974 the two countries signed a cease-fire agreement ending armed hostilities. Israel continues to administer the Golan Heights, although it has not made any formal attempts to annex the territory. Negotiations have continued on an ongoing basis since that time, with both sides claiming the region. One issue of dispute is access to the Sea of Galilee, which is a major source of fresh water in this desert area. Syria claims access to the eastern shore of the Sea of Galilee, whereas Israel claims that the entire lake was part of the British mandate of Transjordan and Palestine and should be regarded as Israeli territory.

Syria has also experienced boundary conflicts with Turkey and Lebanon. The conflict originated over control over Hatay Province, which is located near what is now the northwestern corner of Syria. The League of Nations included Hatay as part of the French mandate of Syria and Lebanon. However, Turkey claimed the territory on the grounds that a majority of its residents were Turkish. In 1939, a referendum over its status was held in Hatay. After a majority of voters supported union with Turkey, Turkey annexed the province. However, Syria claimed that the transfer of Hatay from the French mandate to Turkey was illegal. Even today, Syria's official maps show Hatay as Syrian territory.

Tensions between the two countries intensified during the Cold War. During the late 1950s and early 1960s, Syria came to be allied with the Soviet Union, which provided substantial military assistance to Syria. Tensions between pro-Soviet Syria and pro-Western Turkey escalated, and each side accused the other of massing troops near the border. Tensions have eased since 2000, although Turkey continues to demand that Syria recognize Hatay as part of Turkey.

Syria has also experienced ongoing boundary tensions with Lebanon. In 1976, Syria entered Lebanon's civil war. Syrian troops remained in Lebanon after the war ended in 1990. Lebanon saw Syria's ongoing presence as an illegal occupation and accused Syria of meddling in Lebanon's internal politics. Large numbers of Syrians moved to Lebanon after the war ended in search of employment. However, Lebanon expressed concern that the influx of Syrians depressed wages in Lebanon and amounted to Syrian colonization of Lebanon. These concerns were intensified after Lebanon, under pressure from Syria, granted Lebanese citizenship to about 200,000 Syrian natives living in Lebanon in 1994. Not only did Syria claim sovereignty over the entire French mandate, but it also justified its occupation of southern Lebanon on the grounds that control of the area was needed to defend both countries against Israel. Tensions eased after 2000, and Syria withdrew its troops from Lebanon in 2005. Diplomatic relations between Syria and Lebanon resumed in 2008.

Within Syria, some members of the Alawite community have pushed for political independence from Syria. The Alawites live along the Mediterranean Sea coast directly north of the boundary between Syria and Lebanon. Most Alawites practice an offshoot of Islam that is more closely related to the Shi'ite branch of Islam, whereas about three-quarters of Syria's people are Sunni Muslims. Sunnis consider the Alawites to be heretics, and the Alawites claim ongoing discrimination on the part of the Syrian government. The independence claim of the Alawites is also justified on the grounds that this region was administered separately from the rest of Syria during the period between World War I and World War II.

See also   Iraq, Israel, Jordan, Lebanon, Turkey

Further Reading

Fouad Ajami. *The Syrian rebellion.* Palo Alto, CA: Hoover Institution Press, 2012.

Financial Times. "Syria: Turkey's biggest foreign policy dilemma." June 30, 2012, http://gulfnews.com/news/region/syria/syria-turkey-s-biggest-foreign-policy-dilemma-1.1041137.

Suzan Fraser. "Turkey, Iraq, and Syria tussle over water rights in light of drought." *Huffington Post*, September 3, 2009, http://www.huffingtonpost.com/2009/09/03/turkey-iraq-and-syria-tus_n_276406.html.

TUNISIA

OVERVIEW

The Tunisian Republic is located on the southern shore of the Mediterranean Sea, midway between the Strait of Gibraltar and the Suez Canal. Tunisia has a land area of 63,170 square miles, slightly smaller than Wisconsin. Its population is about 11.2 million.

Tunisia's neighbors are Algeria to the west and Libya to the south. Northern and eastern Tunisia adjoin the Mediterranean Sea. The boundary between Tunisia and Algeria is geometric and consists of short straight-line segments. The border region near and immediately south of the Mediterranean Sea is densely populated. The southern half of the boundary crosses the northern Sahara Desert, and much of this area is uninhabited.

The tripoint between Tunisia, Algeria, and Libya is located two miles north of the Libyan town of Ghadamis. From this tripoint, the boundary between Tunisia and Libya trends to the northeast. It also includes numerous short straight-line segments. Only that portion of the boundary adjacent to the Mediterranean, just west of Libya's capital of Tripoli, crosses inhabited territory.

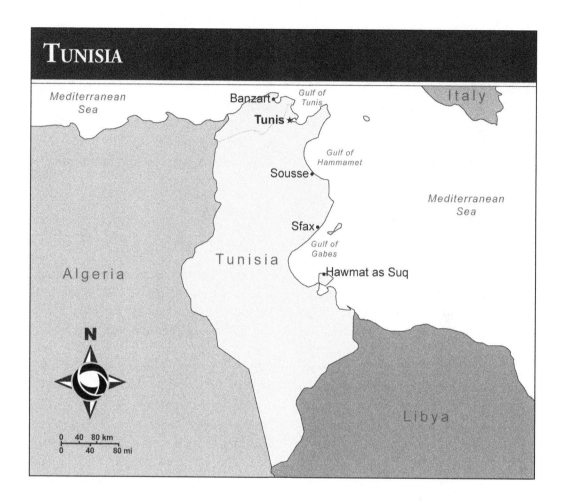

HISTORICAL CONTEXT

Present-day Tunisia is the site of the ancient city of Carthage. During the third and fourth centuries BC, Carthage and Rome vied for political and economic supremacy in the western Mediterranean region. Carthage was incorporated into the Roman Empire in 149 BC and remained under Roman control until the fifth century AD. In the eighth century, the area was conquered and annexed by the Umayyad Caliphate.

Tunisia became an autonomous region under the nominal control of the Ottoman Empire beginning in 1705. During the early 19th century, the coast of present-day Tunisia was the home of the "Barbary Pirates," who were confronted by the United States in America's first foreign military engagement after its independence. In 1883, Tunisia became a French protectorate. The boundaries between Tunisia and its neighbors were agreed upon by French and Italian colonial rulers of Tunisia, Algeria, and Libya during the early 20th century.

Before World War II, Italy controlled Libya, whose capital city of Tripoli is located only 60 miles east of the Tunisia-Libya boundary. The Italians used Tripoli as a base of operations to control North Africa during World War II. Tunisia was the scene of fierce fighting between the Axis powers and the Allies before the Allies secured North Africa in 1943. The Allies later used North Africa as a base from which to launch an offensive into Italy, effectively knocking Italy out of the war.

Tunisia became independent in 1956. The royal family that had reigned over the area since the early 18th century was deposed the following year, and Habib Bourguiba became the country's first civilian president. Bourguiba implemented numerous reforms intended to modernize Tunisia and integrate its economy with Europe and the West. He was named president for life in 1975 but was forced out of office in 1987 because of his advanced age and poor health. Bourguiba was succeeded by Zine al Abidine Ben Ali, who came to be regarded as a dictator and whose regime was marked by corruption. The Arab Spring rebellion that spread throughout Southwest Asia and North Africa in 2011 began in Tunisia in late 2010. Ben Ali and his family fled Tunisia on January 14, 2011. The ouster of the Ben Ali regime represented the first successful overthrow of a dictatorship within Southwest Asia and North Africa.

CONTEMPORARY ISSUES

Tunisia's boundaries have been stable since independence. A minor boundary dispute with Algeria was settled in 1993. Since that time, the two countries have cooperated on international development projects. A joint oil-production venture known as Numhyd was established in 2003. Relationships between Tunisia and Libya have occasionally been strained, although the two countries have made efforts to cooperate with each other. The status of many Tunisian workers who have moved to oil-rich Libya in search of employment opportunities has been an issue of dispute between the two countries.

See also Algeria, Libya

Further Reading

Christopher Alexander. *Tunisia: Stability and reform in the modern Maghreb.* London: Routledge, 2010.

Mohamed El Dahshan. "Tunisia stakes a claim." *Foreign Policy*, May 21, 2012, http://transitions.foreignpolicy.com/posts/2012/05/21/tunisia_stakes_a_claim.

Azzedine Layachi. "Meanwhile in the Maghreb." *Foreign Affairs*, March 31, 2011.

TURKEY

OVERVIEW

The Republic of Turkey is located between the Mediterranean Sea and the Black Sea in western Asia and southeastern Europe. It is one of three countries, along with Russia and Egypt, whose land territory straddles two continents. Turkey's largest city, Istanbul, is located partly in Europe and partly in Asia.

Turkey's overall land area is 302,535 square miles, slightly smaller than Texas and Louisiana combined. The Asiatic portion of Turkey, encompassing the Anatolian Plateau, contains about 97 percent of Turkey's land area. Asiatic and European Turkey are separated by the Bosporus, the Sea of Marmara, and the Dardanelles. The Bosporus and the Dardanelles are straits

TURKEY

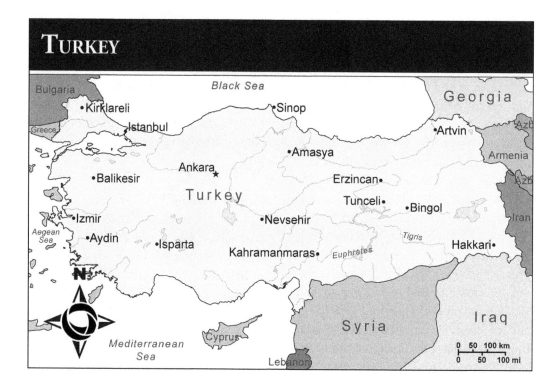

that connect the Sea of Marmara with the Black Sea and the Aegean Sea, which is part of the Mediterranean Sea, respectively. European Turkey, which contains the remaining 3 percent of Turkish territory, is located in the southeastern portion of the Balkan Peninsula. Turkey is also sovereign over more than 100 islands in the Aegean, Mediterranean, and Black seas and the Sea of Marmara. Turkey's population is about 75 million.

The European portion of Turkey has boundaries with Greece and Bulgaria, while Asiatic Turkey borders Georgia, Armenia, Iran, Iraq, and Syria. Turkey also has a short boundary with the Azerbaijani exclave of Nakhchivan. The boundary between Turkey and Bulgaria extends westward and inland along the Rezovska River upstream from its mouth in the Black Sea.

The boundary reaches the confluence between the Rezovska and the Dvina Rivers, and then follows the Dvina upstream until it turns in a northwesterly direction and follows short, straight-line segments to the tripoint between Turkey, Bulgaria, and Greece on the Maritsa River. Most of the boundary between Turkey and Greece follows the Maritsa River southward to the Mediterranean, with a small section of Turkish territory located west of the Maritsa, which is also known in Greece as the Evrus or Hebros River.

Turkey's boundary with Georgia extends eastward from the Black Sea. Beginning on the Black Sea coast between the Turkish town of Sarp and the Georgian town of Sarpi, it follows short, straight-line segments inland and eastward, then turns southeastward to the tripoint between

Turkey, Georgia, and Armenia just east of Turkey's Lake Cildir. The boundary between Turkey and Armenia continues along straight-line segments in a southeasterly direction until it reaches the Arpa River. From there it follows the Arpa downstream and southward to its confluence with the Aras River, which is also known as the Araxes River. The Aras, which flows eastward to the Caspian Sea, is the boundary between Turkey and Armenia eastward to the tripoint between Turkey, Armenia, and Nakhchivan. About 15 miles downstream from this tripoint is the tripoint between Turkey, Nakhchivan, and Iran.

The boundary between Turkey and Iran extends northwestward along the Qareh Su River, which is a tributary of the Aras. It then follows straight-line segments in a westerly direction, passing near Mount Ararat, which is the highest mountain in Turkey. The boundary then turns southward near the Iranian village of Siru Ma'qui. It continues southward along short straight-line segments to the tripoint between Turkey, Iran, and Iraq. The region on both sides of the boundary is rugged and mountainous, with low population densities. From this tripoint, the boundary between Turkey and Iraq extends in a westerly direction into the broad floodplain of the Tigris and Euphrates rivers. It follows straight-line segments through this region until reaching the Nahr al Khabur River, which it then follows to its confluence with the Tigris River near the tripoint between Turkey, Iraq, and Syria. The boundary between Syria and Turkey continues westward, following the Tigris briefly and then following numerous short straight-line segments before reaching the Mediterranean Sea south of the Turkish town of Samandag.

HISTORICAL CONTEXT

Turkey's location between the Mediterranean and Black seas and at the crossroads between Europe and Asia has made it an area of great strategic importance since ancient times. The ancient city of Troy was located on the Aegean Sea coast south of the Dardanelles. Troy was the site of the Trojan Wars, which were described in Homer's *The Iliad* and *The Odyssey* and are believed to have taken place approximately 1250 BC. Most of present-day Turkey was conquered by the Persian Empire during the sixth and fifth centuries BC and by Alexander the Great in about 334 BC. By the first century BC, all of present-day Turkey had been incorporated into the Roman Empire.

Around AD 330, the Roman emperor Constantine established an imperial residence at Byzantium (present-day Istanbul). The city was renamed Constantinople after Constantine's death. In AD 476, the Roman Empire was divided between the Western and Eastern Roman Empires, and Constantinople became the capital of the Eastern Roman Empire, or Byzantine Empire. The Byzantine Empire continued to rule the area until the 11th and 12th centuries AD, after which conflicts associated with the Crusades as well as internal divisions caused it to fragment. The Anatolian Plateau was fragmented politically until the 15th century. In 1453, Constantinople was conquered by the Ottomans, who had arisen in the Balkan Peninsula in the early 14th century. By the early 16th century, the Ottoman Empire controlled all of present-day Turkey. At its height, the Ottoman Empire also included much of southeastern Europe along with much of the territory along the coasts of the eastern Mediterranean and the Black Sea, including what is today Egypt, Israel, Lebanon, and most of Iraq.

The Ottoman Empire was dismembered after World War I, and the sultanate of the Ottoman Empire was abolished formally in 1922. After World War I, a strong Turkish nationalist movement had emerged and worked to end the Allied occupation of the Anatolian Peninsula. In 1923, the Treaty of Lausanne was signed by Turkish nationalist leaders and by the British Empire, France, Italy, Japan, Greece, Romania, and the Serb-Croatian-Slovene State (which would later become Yugoslavia). Under terms of the Treaty of Lausanne, the Turkish Republic was recognized as the successor state to the Ottoman Empire.

With minor adjustments, the treaty established the boundaries of Turkey as they exist today. These boundaries were delineated before and during the process of treaty negotiation. Turkey's boundaries with Greece and Bulgaria were specified as part of the treaty. The boundaries between Turkey and Georgia, Armenia, and Azerbaijan were agreed upon between representatives of the remnants of the Ottoman Empire and the Soviet Union, which controlled all three of these now-independent countries, in 1921. The boundary between Turkey and Iran, which had been established under terms of the treaty, was modified by a series of adjustments agreed upon by both countries between 1932 and 1937.

In exchange for international recognition of its sovereignty over the territories contained within its boundaries, the Turkish Republic gave up any claims to former Ottoman territory outside of these boundaries. The Turkish nationalist leader, Mustafa Kemal, became the head of the new Turkish state and took the name Ataturk, or "Father of the Turks." Turkey has been a multiparty democracy since 1945, except for brief periods of military rule following coups d'état in 1960, 1971, 1980, and 1997. In 1947, the United States established the Truman Doctrine, which guaranteed American support for resistance to the potential communist takeover of Turkey. Turkey joined the North Atlantic Treaty Organization in 1952 and has applied to join the European Union.

CONTEMPORARY ISSUES

With minor exceptions, Turkey's boundaries have remained stable since the Republic of Turkey came to be recognized as the successor state to the Ottoman Empire in 1923. However, Turkey has been involved in a variety of yet-unresolved conflicts with its neighbors.

Turkey and Syria have contested control over Hatay Province, which is located on the northeastern coast of the Mediterranean along the frontier between southern Turkey and northwestern Syria. Hatay contains the ancient city of Antioch, which is believed to be the first place in which followers of Jesus Christ used the term *Christian* to describe themselves. Antioch was also a major battleground during the Crusades. Today, Hatay has a land area of 2,086 square miles (slightly smaller than Delaware) and a population of about 1.5 million.

After World War I, the League of Nations gave control of Hatay to the French mandate over Syria and Lebanon.

However, after independence the Republic of Turkey claimed Hatay on the basis of a claim that the majority of Hatay's residents were Turks. In a referendum conducted in 1939, a majority of voters expressed support for uniting Hatay with Turkey, and Turkey claimed the province. However, Syria claimed that the League of Nations mandate overrode the referendum and that Hatay was Syrian territory. Turkey continues to occupy Hatay today and regards Hatay as Turkish territory. Syria continues to contest this claim, and Syrian maps produced today identify Hatay as Syrian rather than Turkish territory.

Turkey and Greece have been involved in an ongoing dispute about rights in the Aegean Sea between the two countries. The Aegean contains hundreds of islands. Most of the islands, including Crete, Rhodes, Lesbos, and Santorini, are part of Greece although a few are under Turkish sovereignty. Some of the Greek islands, including Rhodes and Lesbos, are located less than 10 miles from the Turkish mainland. Although sovereignty over the individual islands is generally uncontested except for control of a few small, uninhabited islands off the Turkish coast, conflicts remain over the division of the Aegean between Turkish and Greek territorial waters. The conflict extends also to control of airspace over the Aegean.

The status of Turkey's Kurdish population is a matter of considerable international importance. The Kurdish are a distinctive nation whose people live in southeastern Turkey, northwestern Iran, northern Iraq, and northwestern Syria. Most Kurds are Muslims, and the Kurdish language is related most closely to other Indo-European languages spoken in Iran, Pakistan, and India in contrast to Turkish, which is not an Indo-European language.

The total population of Kurds worldwide, including those who have left their ancestral region and have moved to Europe and North America, is estimated at 30 to 35 million. However, the Kurds are a minority in each state in which they live. The Kurds are one of the largest nations of the world by population that are not associated with a sovereign state. The United Nations estimates that Kurds comprise about 20 percent of Turkey's population, including a large majority of people residing in southeastern Turkey near its boundaries with Iran, Iraq, and Syria. After World War I, calls on the part of Kurdish leaders for an independent, sovereign Kurdish state were rejected, and the Kurdish population was divided among Turkey, Iran, Iraq, and Syria on the basis of the 1923 boundaries that are still in use.

On several occasions since the 1920s, the Turkish government has moved to quell rebellions and calls for an independent Kurdish state. In 1937 and 1938, an estimated 50,000 Kurds were killed and thousands more were relocated forcibly to other areas in an effort to disperse the Kurdish population. Kurdish leaders accused the Turkish government of actual and cultural genocide. Protests have continued to the present day, with some Kurdish activists calling for outright independence and others demanding more Kurdish autonomy within Turkey. In part because of its ongoing opposition to Kurdish autonomy and independence, the government of Turkey has actively opposed secessionist movements in other countries such as Spain and Italy.

Turkey, Iraq, and Syria are also disputing water rights. Most of Iraq's people live in the Mesopotamian valley formed by the Tigris and Euphrates rivers, upon which they have depended for irrigation for thousands of years. However, both of these major rivers rise in Turkey. Beginning in the 1970s, Turkey's government planned and promoted the Southeastern Anatolia Project, whose purpose was to promote economic development in this historically impoverished region. Several dams were constructed along the Tigris and the Euphrates with the idea of diverting water in these rivers to irrigate crops in the arid regions of southeastern Turkey. The dams also allowed for the provision of hydroelectric power and for flood control. Once these dams were constructed and went into operation, however, the amount of water flowing in the Tigris and Euphrates into downstream Syria and Iraq has declined. Occasionally, the rivers have dried up during unusually dry periods. Iraq and Syria have accused Turkey of diverting the upstream waters of the Tigris and Euphrates illegally, therefore reducing the stream flow on which these countries have long depended.

See also   Armenia, Bulgaria, Georgia, Greece, Iran, Iraq, Syria

Further Reading

Mustafa Aydin and Kostas Ifantis (eds.). *Turkish-Greek relations: Escaping from the security dilemma in the Aegean.* London: Routledge, 2004.

Suzan Fraser. "Turkey, Iraq, and Syria tussle over water rights in light of drought." *Huffington Post,* September 3, 2009, http://www.huffingtonpost.com/2009 /09/03/turkey-iraq-and-syria-tus_n_276 406.html.

Stephen Kinzer. *Crescent and Star: Turkey between two worlds.* New York: Farrar, Straus and Giroux, 2008.

Denise Natali. *The Kurds and the state: Evolving national identity in Iraq, Turkey, and Iran.* Syracuse, NY: Syracuse University Press, 2005.

UNITED ARAB EMIRATES

OVERVIEW

The United Arab Emirates (UAE) is located in the southeastern portion of the Arabian Peninsula. The UAE is a federation of seven emirates, or small kingdoms, each of which is ruled by a hereditary monarch who has absolute authority within his emirate. The seven emirates that make up the UAE include Abu Dhabi, Ajman, Dubai, Fujairah, Ras al-Khaimah, Sharjah, and Umm al-Quwain. The total area of the UAE is 32,278 square miles, about the size of South Carolina.

The population of the UAE is approximately 9 million. About half live in Abu Dhabi or in Dubai, which have dominated the federation politically and economically since its inception. Given the very dry desert environment of the region, a large majority of residents of the UAE live along the country's coast on the Persian Gulf. With the sixth-largest amount of proven oil reserves in the world, the United Arab Emirates has one of the world's highest per capita incomes. The UAE's oil wealth has attracted large numbers of workers from overseas. As a result, about 60 percent of the UAE's people are expatriates. The largest populations of expatriates living in

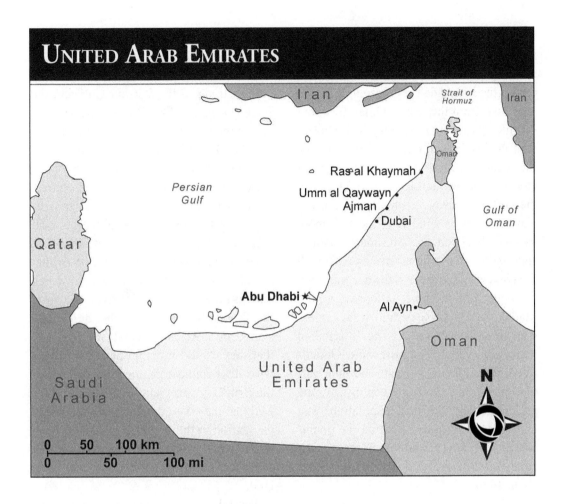

UNITED ARAB EMIRATES

Iran

Strait of
Hormuz

Iran

Persian
Gulf

Oman

Ras al Khaymah

Umm al Qaywayn

Ajman

Dubai

Gulf of
Oman

Qatar

Abu Dhabi

Al Ayn

Oman

United Arab
Emirates

N

Saudi
Arabia

| 0 | 50 | 100 km |
| 0 | 50 | 100 mi |

the UAE come from India, Bangladesh, and Pakistan.

The United Arab Emirates's land neighbors are Saudi Arabia to the south and west and Oman to the east. To the north, the UAE has a long coastline on the Persian Gulf, with a shorter coastline on the Gulf of Oman to the northeast. The UAE is separated from Qatar by the Persian Gulf and from Iran by the Persian Gulf and the Strait of Hormuz. The boundary between the United Arab Emirates and Saudi Arabia consists primarily of two straight-line segments, both extending in a southeasterly direction. A much shorter straight line

extending from south-southwest to north-northeast connects the western of these two segments with the Persian Gulf, and another connects the easterly segment to the tripoint between the United Arab Emirates, Saudi Arabia, and Oman.

The boundary between the United Arab Emirates and Oman extends northward from this tripoint following shorter straight-line segments. This section of the boundary crosses desert territory that is virtually uninhabited. Near the Omani village of Ar Rawdah, the boundary begins to extend in a generally easterly direction until it reaches the Gulf of Oman. The UAE also borders two Omani exclaves located to the north of Oman's main territory. The larger and more northerly of these exclaves includes the Musandam Peninsula, which is separated from the rest of Oman by about 40 miles across UAE territory. The Musandam Peninsula is of considerable strategic importance because it adjoins the Strait of Hormuz connecting the Persian Gulf with the Gulf of Oman. A smaller Omani exclave known as Madha is located about halfway between the Musandam Peninsula and Oman's main territory. A small UAE exclave known as Nahwa, containing a village by that name, is located within Madha. The land area of this exclave is less than three square miles. The Musandam Peninsula, which comprises the Omani-ruled Musandam Governate, became part of Oman in the 1960s in keeping with the preferences of the local population. The United Arab Emirates claimed the peninsula for a few years after it became independent but abandoned these efforts after about 1980.

HISTORICAL CONTEXT

The United Arab Emirates is located along trade routes that have been used for thousands of years, both on land and by sea. The site of Dubai has been a trading center for more than 2,000 years. Fishing and pearl diving have also been major contributors to the economy of the area since ancient times. Pearls extracted from oysters caught off the Dubai coast were traded throughout Southwest Asia and the Mediterranean countries. During the Middle Ages, ships from Dubai went as far away as China.

Following Vasco da Gama's circumnavigation of Africa in the late 15th century, European mariners began efforts to control trade in the Persian Gulf and the Indian Ocean. At first, Portugal became the dominant European power in the region, but the British achieved dominance during the 19th century. British naval ships patrolled the coastlines in order to combat pirates who were attempting to seize British ships. In 1853, sheiks ruling the local emirates along what had become known as the Pirate Coast signed a treaty with Britain and agreed to a maritime truce, after which what is now the UAE came to be known as the Trucial States. In a further agreement signed in 1892, the Trucial States agreed that they would not sign any agreements with other countries without the consent of the British government. The British promised that they would guarantee freedom of navigation in the Persian Gulf and protect the Trucial States in the event of attacks from foreign powers, either by sea or by land.

Pearl diving remained a mainstay of the economy of the Trucial States throughout the 19th century. In the early 20th century, however, the invention of artificial pearls caused the pearl-diving industry to collapse. In response, the Trucial States looked for other sources of revenue. In 1929, Sheik Rashid bin Saeed al-Maktoum of Dubai decided to reinvigorate international trade by making Dubai a duty-free center. He also enlarged the city's port facilities and had coastal areas near Dubai dredged in order to make the city a deepwater port. In the 1960s, valuable oil deposits were discovered in Abu Dhabi. Revenues from oil exports made the Trucial States wealthy.

The United Arab Emirates achieved full independence in 1971. The two largest and wealthiest emirates, Abu Dhabi and Dubai, federated initially after Abu Dhabi agreed to allow Dubai to retain its status as a duty-free port. Once Abu Dhabi and Dubai federated, they invited the other five emirates to join the federation. Wealth from oil exports and trading resulted in very rapid population growth. Dubai's population was estimated at 20,000 in 1950. The first official census, taken in 1968, counted 58,971 people. The UAE government estimated that about 1.4 million people lived in Dubai in 2006, and the population is believed to have passed the 2 million mark. Dubai has worked actively to promote international tourism in addition to its trading activities.

CONTEMPORARY ISSUES

Once the United Arab Emirates gave up its claim to Oman's Musandam Peninsula in 1980, the UAE's land boundaries have remained uncontested. However, the United Arab Emirates and Iran dispute control over the islands of Abu Musa, Greater Tunb, and Lesser Tunb. These islands are located in the Persian Gulf near the entrance to the Strait of Hormuz. The largest of the three islands, Abu Musa, is about 4.6 miles in land area with a permanent population of about 2,000. Abu Musa is equidistant between the UAE and Iran, and the main shipping lanes on the Persian Gulf into the Strait of Hormuz are located just north of the island on the Iranian side. Thus, the UAE has been very reluctant to give up control of both sides of these important shipping lanes to Iran.

Abu Musa and the Tunb Islands were long controlled by Persia. However, Britain claimed the islands formally in 1908 and assigned sovereignty over them to the Emirate of Sharjah. After Sharjah became part of the UAE in 1971, the UAE reasserted its claim to them. Once the British relinquished control of the islands and British forces withdrew from them, Iran occupied and took control of them, justifying its occupation on the grounds that the islands had been under Persian jurisdiction historically. The UAE, meanwhile, claimed the islands on the grounds that it was the successor state to the British, who had controlled and administered them between 1908 and 1971. The UAE took its case to the United Nations Security Council in 1980, but the Security Council ruled in favor of Iran. The dispute was later referred to the International Court of Justice and remains pending. In April 2012, Iran reasserted its claim to Abu Musa and the Tunb Islands, threatening to use force against the UAE if necessary. The Gulf Cooperation Council, which includes the UAE as well as Bahrain, Kuwait, Oman, Qatar, and Saudi Arabia, condemned Iran's actions, and tensions continue.

See also   Oman, Saudi Arabia

Further Reading

Kourosh Ahmadi. *Islands and international politics in the Persian Gulf: The Abu Musa and Tunbs in strategic context.* London: Routledge, 2008.

Christopher M. Davidson. *Dubai: The vulnerability of success.* New York: Columbia University Press, 2008.

Jim Krane. *City of gold: Dubai and the dream of capitalism.* New York: St. Martin's Press, 2009.

YEMEN

OVERVIEW

The Republic of Yemen occupies the southern and southwestern portion of the Arabian Peninsula. In addition to the mainland, Yemen's land area includes about 200 islands in the Red Sea and the Gulf of Aden. The largest of these islands are Kamaran in the Red Sea and Socotra in the Gulf of Aden southeast of mainland Yemen. Socotra is especially notable because it has been isolated from continental landmasses for millions of years, making it home to a very large number of endemic plant and animal species. Including its islands, Yemen has a total land area of 203,796 square miles, making it slightly smaller than Texas. Its population is about 25 million, of whom more than 99 percent live on the mainland.

Yemen's land neighbors are Saudi Arabia to the north and Oman to the east. Yemen has coastlines on the Gulf of Aden to the south and the Red Sea to the west. Yemen is separated from the African country of Djibouti by the Bab el Mandab, or Mandab Strait, which connects the Gulf of Aden and the Red Sea. At its narrowest point, the Bab el Mandab separating Yemen from the African country of Djibouti to the southwest is about 25 miles wide.

The western portion of the boundary between Yemen and Saudi Arabia follows physical features. Much of this boundary is located along the drainage divide between streams that empty into the Red Sea on the Saudi side of the border and those that drain into the Gulf of Aden on the Yemeni side of the border. However, given the very dry climate in both countries, many of these streams are intermittent and dry up in times of sparse rainfall. Beginning at the coast of the Red Sea, the boundary extends in a generally northeastward direction through the Tihama Mountains. East of these mountains, the boundary extends along the drainage divide eastward. The eastern portion of the boundary between Yemen and Saudi Arabia crosses uninhabited territory and is delineated only approximately. The boundary between Yemen and Oman is a single straight-line segment extending about 200 miles in a south-southeasterly direction from the tripoint between Yemen, Oman, and Saudi Arabia to the northwest to the Gulf of Aden to the southeast. This boundary also crosses uninhabited desert.

HISTORICAL CONTEXT

Yemen's location along the Red Sea and the Gulf of Aden has given the area considerable strategic importance for several thousand years, and its location has made Yemen an important trading center. Moreover, Yemen is the only country on the Arabian Peninsula that contains land that has sufficient rainfall to support agriculture. In combination, these factors have meant that Yemen has been contested among various kingdoms since ancient times.

European interest in present-day Yemen began in the 16th century. In 1838, the sultan of the local Lahej state ceded an area of about 75 square miles along the Gulf of Aden, about 100 miles east of the Bab el

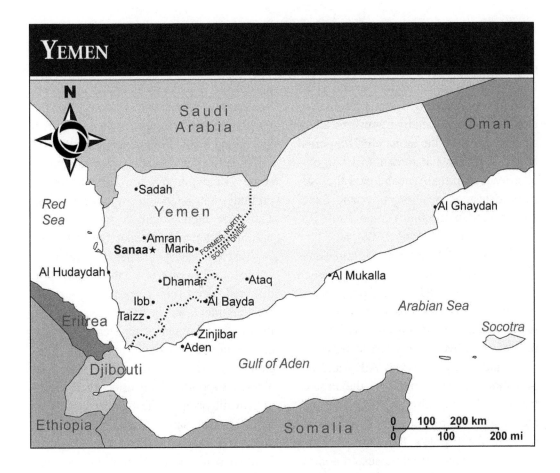

YEMEN

N

Saudi
Arabia

Oman

•Sadah

Red
Sea

Yemen

•Al Ghaydah

FORMER NORTH
SOUTH DIVIDE

•Amran
Sanaa★ Marib•

Al Hudaydah•

•Dhamar

•Ataq

•Al Mukalla

Arabian Sea

Ibb•

Taizz•

••Al Bayda

Socotra

Eritrea

•Zinjibar
•Aden

Gulf of Aden

Djibouti

Ethiopia

Somalia

0   100   200 km
0   100   200 mi

Mandab, to the British. Britain established the port of Aden, which became an important trading and naval center. From Aden, Britain worked to control the coastal regions of present-day Yemen in order to protect trade through the Gulf of Aden, the Bab el Mandab, and the Red Sea. British efforts to secure control over these trade routes intensified after the Suez Canal opened in 1869. In 1872, Britain and the Ottoman Empire came to an informal agreement over control of what is now Yemeni territory, with the Ottomans controlling the northern portion of the territory and the British controlling Aden and the southern coast. This informal agreement was formalized by the signing of a treaty between Britain and the Ottoman Empire in 1904.

For most of the 20th century, Yemen was two separate states known informally as North Yemen and South Yemen. Essentially, North Yemen was that part of Yemen that had been under Ottoman rule, and South Yemen was the territory that had been under British rule and included the port of Aden. North Yemen contained about a third of the land area of present-day Yemen, but about three-quarters of present-day Yemen lived in North Yemen.

In 1918, the portion of Yemen that had been ruled by the Ottoman Empire declared its independence after the Ottoman Empire collapsed. This area became the Mutawakelite Kingdom of Yemen. In 1962, the royal family was deposed in a coup d'état, and the country was renamed the Yemen Arab Republic. Several years of civil war ensued between Arab nationalist forces, supported by Egypt, and advocates of restoring the monarchy, supported by Saudi Arabia and Jordan. In 1970, royalist leaders formally abandoned their efforts to restore the monarchy, and Saudi Arabia recognized the Yemen Arab Republic.

Meanwhile, Aden was administered as part of British India until 1937, when the British detached Aden from the rest of India and established Aden as a separate crown colony. Britain also maintained protectorates over nearby territories to the north and east of the city. Aden and the protectorates were united as the Protectorate of South Arabia in 1963. In 1967, the country became independent under the name of the People's Republic of South Yemen. A Marxist regime seized control of the government in 1970 and changed the name of the country to the People's Democratic Republic of South Yemen. North Yemen and South Yemen merged formally as the Republic of Yemen in 1990, becoming a multiparty state. In 1994, a brief civil war between some Southern secessionists who wished to redivide the country and the government broke out, but the secessionists were defeated quickly, and Yemen remained united.

The boundaries between the two Yemens and Saudi Arabia were contested throughout most of the 20th century. During the early 1930s, Prince Feisal, a Saudi military leader and a future king of Saudi Arabia, led an expeditionary force into what is now northern Yemen and secured control of Yemeni territory. The imam of the Mutawakelite Kingdom asked the reigning king of Saudi Arabia to resolve the dispute. The rulers of Yemen and Saudi Arabia agreed to what is essentially the current boundary between the two countries by signing the Taif Agreement in 1934.

After the Taif Agreement was signed, some Yemenis argued on historical grounds that some territory north of the Taif Agreement boundary was rightfully part of Yemen as opposed to Saudi Arabia. Because the Taif Agreement expired after 20 years, the issue of control over these disputed territories reopened. Boundary tensions increased in the 1960s, after the imam's government was overthrown and after Saudi Arabia supported efforts to restore the Yemeni monarchy. Reunified Yemen supported Iraq after its invasion of Kuwait prior to the Persian Gulf War in 1991, and Saudi Arabia retaliated by deporting several hundred thousand Yemeni workers whose remittances were an important source of revenue for Yemen. The boundary dispute was resolved finally in 2000, when Yemen and Saudi Arabia signed the Treaty of Jeddah. The Treaty of Jeddah reaffirmed the boundary between the two countries as had been delineated in the Taif Agreement. The treaty also established maritime boundaries in the Red Sea.

CONTEMPORARY ISSUES

Yemen's boundaries with its neighbors are stable, although relationships between Yemen and Saudi Arabia have occasionally been strained. Some of the tension has involved control of offshore oil deposits in the Red Sea. The rights and status of

Yemenis working in oil-rich Saudi Arabia have been a matter of concern. Because Yemen and Saudi Arabia have about the same populations, some Saudis have been concerned that their country will be flooded with immigrants from much poorer Yemen. Yemen has also been involved in a dispute with Eritrea over control of the Hamish Islands in the Red Sea. This dispute was resolved through an agreement between the two countries signed in 1998. Tensions between the northern and southern portions of Yemen are ongoing, with some in southern Yemen wanting to secede from Yemen and redivide Yemen into two separate countries.

See also Oman, Saudi Arabia

Further Reading

Bernard Haykel. "Saudi Arabia's Yemen dilemma." *Foreign Affairs*, June 14, 2011.

Michael Horton. "Why Southern Yemen is pushing for secession." *Christian Science Monitor*, December 15, 2009, http://www.csmonitor.com/World/Middle-East/2009/1215/Why-southern-Yemen-is-pushing-for-secession.

James Traub. "Nation-building in the Yemen." *Foreign Policy*, May 18, 2012, http://www.foreignpolicy.com/articles/2012/05/18/nation_building_in_the_yemen.

EAST AND CENTRAL ASIA

CHAPTER 5

EAST AND CENTRAL ASIA

Asia is the largest and most populous continent in the world, and more than half of the world's people live in Asia. Asia is divided into several distinct regions on the basis of its physical geography, including the high mountains that dominate the center of the continent. For the purposes of this book, Asia is divided into three groups of countries. Southwest Asia, including the Arabian Peninsula, is covered in chapter 4. South and Southeast Asia, from Pakistan eastward to Indonesia and the Philippines off the mainland coast of Asia, is covered in chapter 6. This chapter includes discussion of the countries of East Asia and Central Asia. These countries are located in, north of, and east of the Himalaya Mountains and nearby mountain ranges, which are the highest mountains in the world.

East Asia includes China, Japan, North Korea, South Korea, and Taiwan. Historically, East Asia has been isolated from other major population centers by the Pacific Ocean to the east, Siberia to the north, the Himalayas and other high mountains to the west, and rugged uplands to the south. This isolation has contributed to the distinctive civilization of East Asia. It has been reinforced by the fact that very few people live in any of the regions bordering East Asia.

East Asia is one of the most heavily populated areas of the world. More than 1.5 billion people, or about 22 percent of the world's population, live in East Asia. In many parts of East Asia, a majority of people live in cities. Japan, South Korea, and Taiwan are heavily urbanized. However, a majority of China's people continue to live in rural areas. Throughout East Asia, rural populations are concentrated on flatter, fertile lowlands suitable for cropping. For example, more than 100 million people live in China's Sichuan Province, which is only slightly larger in land area than California. Rural areas that are too dry, cold, or steep for agriculture are sparsely populated.

Relative to most other parts of the world, the countries of East Asia have experienced considerable political unity. Most of China has been unified politically for more than 2,000 years. Likewise, Japan and Korea have each been unified throughout most of their histories. Linguistic and religious similarities within each culture have contributed to its cultural uniformity. Cultural and political unity also helped East Asia resist European colonization.

Central Asia includes countries located between Russia to the north, Southwest Asia to the west, South Asia to the south, and East Asia to the east. Countries located within this region include the eight former Soviet republics of Georgia, Armenia, Azerbaijan, Kazakhstan, Uzbekistan, Turkmenistan, Tajikistan, and the Kyrgyz Republic. The region also includes Afghanistan and Mongolia. Georgia, Armenia, and Azerbaijan are located between the Black Sea and the Caspian Sea, and the others are located east of the Caspian Sea. Thus, the region is largely landlocked, and it is distant from the world's oceans. With the exception of Georgia and Armenia, the large majority of people living in Central Asia are Muslims. Most speak Indo-European languages, many of which are related to the languages of Turkey or Iran.

Much of Central Asia is mountainous, although there are also extensive areas of flat land. The Himalayas, the Pamirs, and other very high mountain ranges are located in the southern part of the region. The high mountains block warm, moist winds from the Indian Ocean. As a result, most of Central Asia has a continental climate with warm to hot summers and cold winters. Most of the region is classified as steppe or desert, with less than 20 inches of precipitation per year. Desertification, or expansion of the desert, has been a major issue in Central Asia.

Environmental conditions in Central Asia affect population distributions. Much of the area is sparsely populated. Few people live in very arid or highly mountainous areas. As in Southwest Asia and North Africa, most people live near reliable supplies of water such as rivers, oases, and lakes or in cities. Pastoral nomadism remains prevalent in some rural areas of Central Asia, as is the case in Southwest Asia and North Africa. Birth rates in many parts of Central Asia are high, and in many places populations are increasing rapidly.

Historically, Central Asia has been a crossroads of cultures. Since the days of the Roman Empire, overland trade between Europe and East Asia has been undertaken on roads and caravan routes that cross Central Asia. The term "Silk Road" has been applied to these trade routes because silk produced in China was in high demand in Europe. However, many other goods were traded in both directions between East Asia and Europe along the Silk Road. The Silk Road was also an important conduit for the movement of ideas and innovations. Chinese inventions such as gunpowder, fireworks, and paper reached Europe along the Silk Road, although trade levels declined with the development of sea routes between Europe and Asia beginning in the 15th century. Cities along the Silk Road were important centers of commerce, scholarship, and learning during the Silk Road's heyday in the Middle Ages. In contrast to East Asia, Central Asia has generally lacked a history of political unity. Rather, Central Asia has been contested among various cultures for thousands of years. Today, many of the states of Central Asia contain multiple nations, whereas many of the largest nations of Central Asia, including the Uzbeks, Armenians, and Pashtuns, have been split among various states. Ethnic conflict has characterized Central Asia throughout its history, and especially since boundaries separating the sovereignty of different states were delineated.

AFGHANISTAN

OVERVIEW

The Islamic Republic of Afghanistan is located in south-central Asia. Its land area is 251,772 square miles, approximately the size of Texas. Afghanistan's population is about 30 million. Its population is divided among multiple nations. The largest national group in Afghanistan is the Pashtun, who make up about 42 percent of the population. About 27 percent are Tajiks, and nearly 10 percent each are Uzbeks and Hazaras. Most Tajik and Uzbek Afghans live near the borders between Tajikistan and Uzbekistan, respectively. The term *Afghan* comes from an alternative name for the Pashtun people, but today it is used to describe any citizen of Afghanistan.

Landlocked Afghanistan has boundaries with Iran to the west, Turkmenistan to the northwest, Uzbekistan and Tajikistan to the north, and Pakistan to the east. Afghanistan also includes the Wakhan Corridor, a long and narrow strip of territory about 150 miles long and 10 to 30 miles wide extending east-northeastward from the main portion of the country. The Wakhan Corridor is sparsely populated, with only about 12,000 people living in an area of more than 20,000 square miles. Afghanistan and China have a short boundary at the eastern end of the Wakhan Corridor.

From the tripoint between Afghanistan, Iran, and Pakistan, the boundary between

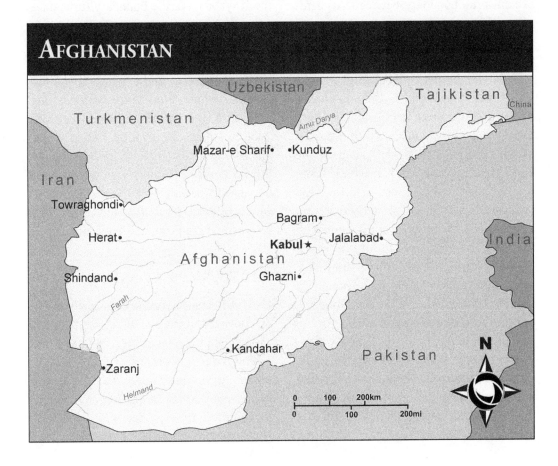

Afghanistan and Iran follows a diagonal segment about 70 miles in length northeastward. The boundary then forms a rough semicircle north and west around Iran's Hamoun Protected Area, then extends along straight-line segments to the Harirud River. It follows this stream northward and downstream to the tripoint between Afghanistan, Iran, and Turkmenistan.

The boundary between Afghanistan and Turkmenistan extends northeastward, following numerous short straight-line segments through arid, rugged, and sparsely inhabited terrain to the Amu Darya River. The boundary then turns eastward, following the Amu Darya upstream and eastward to the tripoint between Afghanistan, Turkmenistan, and Uzbekistan. The river then becomes the boundary between Afghanistan and Uzbekistan. The Amu Darya and its tributaries form most of the boundary between Afghanistan and Tajikistan.

From the tripoint between Afghanistan, Uzbekistan, and Tajikistan, the boundary between Afghanistan and Tajikistan continues eastward and upstream to the Amu Darya's origin at the confluence of the Panj River and the Vakhsh River. From this confluence, the boundary follows the Panj upstream in a northeasterly direction and then southward to its confluence with the Pamir River near the western end of the Wakhan Corridor. It then follows the Pamir upstream and eastward. Here the boundary separates the Wakhan Corridor from Tajikistan. At the extreme eastern end of the Wakhan Corridor, in the high peaks of the Pamir Mountain range, is Afghanistan's short and not clearly demarcated boundary with China. Most of this boundary is more than 16,000 feet above sea level, and it is located along the drainage divide between streams flowing westward into Afghanistan and Central Asia and those flowing eastward into China.

Afghanistan's longest boundary is with Pakistan. This boundary extends southwestward from the southern side of the Wakhan Corridor toward the tripoint between Afghanistan, Pakistan, and Iran. From the Wakhan Corridor, it follows numerous short straight-line segments in a southwesterly direction, then turns more to the south. At this point the boundary moves from very high mountains to less rugged terrain. The Khyber Pass, which has been used since ancient times to connect Central Asia and the Indian subcontinent, is located near the boundary west of the Pakistani city of Peshawar. From the Khyber Pass, the boundary turns once again to the southwest. Except for the section near Peshawar and the Khyber Pass, this boundary passes through inaccessible, mountainous, and dry terrain and has few inhabitants. West of the Pakistani city of Quetta, the boundary turns westward once again to the tripoint between Afghanistan, Pakistan, and Iran. Although the most of the boundary region is sparsely populated, the process of boundary delineation split the ethnic Pashtun community between Afghanistan and Pakistan.

HISTORICAL CONTEXT

Afghanistan has been a crossroads of civilizations and the scene of clashes between various empires, based both internally and externally, for thousands of years. Central Asian, European, Middle Eastern, South Asian, and East Asian cultures have fought for control of the region now known as Afghanistan throughout its history. During the first millennium BC, modern-day Afghanistan was part of the Persian Achaemenid Empire before it was conquered by Alexander the Great in around 340 BC. In the seventh century AD, Muslim invaders from Persia brought Islam to Afghanistan.

In the 10th century AD, most of present-day Afghanistan was unified under the rule of the Ghaznavid dynasty. The Ghorid dynasty took over the area in the 12th century, and in turn the Ghorids were displaced by the Mongols in the 13th century. Between the 16th and 18th centuries, modern Afghanistan was divided between an Uzbek sphere of influence in the north, a Persian sphere of influence in the west, and an Indian sphere of influence in the southeast.

Europeans began to move into modern Afghanistan in the early 19th century. Afghanistan became a buffer between Russian expansion from the north and British expansion from the south. Recognizing Afghanistan as a buffer between the two empires, Britain and Russia established Afghanistan's boundaries in the 19th century. These boundaries approximate the current boundaries between Afghanistan and its neighbors. The boundaries cut across territories occupied traditionally by various nations in the area, contributing to many conflicts after independence.

British troops invaded Afghanistan in 1839 but were repulsed by Afghan armies. In 1878, a second war broke out between the British, moving northward from India, and Afghanistan. At the end of this war, Britain took control of Afghanistan's foreign relations and defense, but Afghanistan was permitted to retain its internal sovereignty. The Durand Line, which separated Afghanistan from British India but cut across territory inhabited by the Pashtun population, was agreed upon as the boundary in 1893. In 1919, Afghanistan's King Amanullah Khan declared Afghanistan to be a fully independent country. Given its location between the Soviet Union to the north and the pro-American government of the shah of Iran to the south, Afghanistan was affected strongly by the Cold War.

In 1979, the Soviet Union invaded Afghanistan from the north. The Soviet invasion was resisted strongly by most Afghans. The Afghans were aided with weapons and funds from the United States, Saudi Arabia, and Pakistan. War between the Soviets and Afghanistan continued for the next 10 years, resulting in the deaths of more than a million Afghan soldiers and civilians. Millions of other Afghans fled the country and moved to Pakistan, Iran, Europe, or the United States as refugees.

Soviet forces were withdrawn in 1989 in light of the impending collapse of the Soviet regime. After the Soviets left, the country was reconstituted as the Islamic State of Afghanistan. Civil war broke out among factions struggling to control the government. In the early 1990s, the Taliban became an important faction fighting for power in Afghanistan. The Taliban originated among Afghan refugees in Pakistan and was made up primarily of Pashtuns from the southern part of Afghanistan. The Taliban seized control of the country in 1996, although the Taliban government was recognized only by Pakistan, Saudi Arabia, and the United Arab Emirates.

The Taliban regime was known for its radical interpretation of Islam, its strict adherence to Sharia law, and its suppression of women. The Taliban also gave support to the radical Islamist terrorist group Al Qaeda, allowing Al Qaeda to use Afghanistan as its base of operations. After Al Qaeda's attacks on the United States killed 3,000 people on September 11, 2001, the United States and several allies initiated military attacks on the Taliban regime in Operation Enduring Freedom. Saudi Arabia and the United Arab Emirates withdrew their recognition of the Taliban, leaving Pakistan as its only ally. After two months of fighting, the Taliban government was toppled, and Hamid Karzai, an opponent of the Taliban, was installed as Afghanistan's president. Karzai was elected in his own right in 2004 and reelected in 2009, although the Karzai government has been accused of widespread corruption. Thousands of American soldiers were stationed in Afghanistan to protect against further attacks by the Taliban and to train Afghan soldiers to protect the country. However, by 2010 the Taliban had regained control of several portions of Afghanistan, especially in Pashtun-dominated areas in eastern and southern Afghanistan. Pakistan has been accused of abetting the Taliban and allowing them to use Pakistan as their base of operations. By 2012, more than 2,000 American soldiers had lost their lives in Afghanistan.

CONTEMPORARY ISSUES

Afghanistan's fragile regime faces many challenges. Foremost among these is the status of the Taliban, who continue to fight to regain control of Afghanistan's government. The United States has announced its intention to withdraw its forces from Afghanistan. Whether the Afghanistan government can resist further attacks

by the Taliban without significant external support remains uncertain.

A related issue involves relationships between Afghanistan and Pakistan. Except for the region near Peshawar and the Khyber Pass, most of the boundary between Afghanistan and Pakistan is located in extremely rugged and isolated territory. The inaccessibility of the boundary region has allowed Taliban fighters and Al Qaeda's leaders to operate with little interference, threatening continued attacks on the Afghan government by the Taliban and other radical Islamist organizations.

After several decades of war, contemporary Afghanistan is lacking in infrastructure and is one of the poorest countries in the world. Complicating its poverty is its economic dependence on the production of opium poppies, which are exported and used to make opium, heroin, and other illegal drugs. Although opium addiction is a significant problem within Afghanistan, most of Afghanistan's opium poppies are exported. These exports are estimated to bring $4 to $5 billion into Afghanistan. Much of this trade is illegal, with opium being smuggled across Afghanistan's poorly demarcated borders into Central Asia and also into Pakistan. Afghan officials and foreign experts have had little success in persuading Afghan farmers to give up opium poppy production in favor of other crops, whose production and sale is far less lucrative.

See also   China, Iran, Pakistan, Tajikistan, Turkmenistan, Uzbekistan

Further Reading

Stephen Biddle, Fotini Christia, and J. Alexander Their. "Defining success in Afghanistan: What can the United States accept?" *Foreign Affairs*, July/August 2010, http://www.foreignaffairs.com/articles/66450/stephen-biddle-fotini-christia-and-j-alexander-thier/defining-success-in-afghanistan.

Stephen Tanner. *Afghanistan: A military history from Alexander the Great to the war against the Taliban*. Cambridge, MA: De Capo Press, 2009.

Peter Tomsen. *The wars of Afghanistan: Messianic terrorism, tribal conflicts, and the failures of great powers*. Philadelphia, PA: Perseus Books, 2011.

Declan Walsh. "UN horrified by surge in opium trade in Helmand." *Guardian*, August 27, 2007, http://www.guardian.co.uk/world/2007/aug/28/afghanistan.drugstrade1.

ARMENIA

OVERVIEW

The Republic of Armenia is a former Soviet republic that is located in the Caucasus Mountains of southwestern Asia. Armenia has a land area of 11,484 square miles, about the size of Maryland. Its population is about 3.4 million.

Armenia is located between the Black Sea and the Caspian Sea but is landlocked. Most of its landscape is mountainous and rugged. Armenia has boundaries with Turkey to the west, Georgia to the north, Azerbaijan to the east, and Iran to the south. In addition, southwestern Armenia borders the Azeri exclave of Nakhchivan. In general, Armenia's boundaries were drawn in order to separate people belonging to the Armenian nation from other national groups, and more than 98 percent of Armenia's citizens today are of Armenian heritage. The Arme-

nian language is Indo-European, and most Armenians are Christians.

The boundary between Armenia and Turkey follows the Aras River northwestern and upstream from the tripoint between Armenia, Turkey, and Nakhchivan. It continues along the Aras to its confluence with its tributary, the Arpa River, which is known also as the Akhurian River. It then follows the Arpa further upstream to a point near its source in Lake Arpi near the northwestern corner of Armenia. The tripoint between Armenia, Turkey, and Georgia is located at the northwest corner of Lake Arpi National Park, which contains the lake.

The boundary between Armenia and Georgia extends in an easterly direction into mountainous and heavily wooded terrain. Most of this boundary follows drainage divides or mountain peaks, although the Debed River forms a short portion of the boundary. The Debed segment of the boundary is located less than 50 miles west of the tripoint between Armenia, Georgia, and Azerbaijan near the crest of the Lesser Caucasus Mountains. The boundary between Armenia and Azerbaijan extends along the peaks of the Lesser Caucasus in a southeasterly direction, continuing to the tripoint between Armenia, Azerbaijan, and Iran on the Aras River. From this tripoint, the Aras forms the boundary between Armenia and Iran and between Armenia and Nakhchivan, continuing upstream and northwestward to the tripoint between Armenia, Nakhchivan, and Turkey.

HISTORICAL CONTEXT

Archaeologists have discovered evidence of permanent settlement in present-day Armenia at least 6,000 years ago.

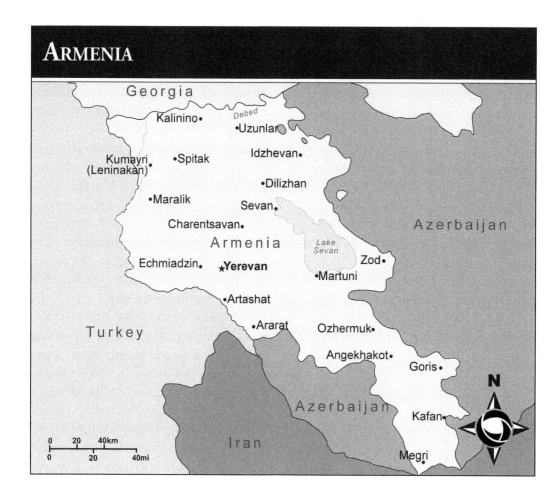

Armenia's capital city of Yerevan is believed to have been founded in 782 BC. The Kingdom of Armenia was established in about 600 BC and remained in control of much of the present-day country until 66 BC, when the Roman general Pompey established a Roman protectorate. The Romans maintained a presence in Armenia for the next 500 years, although the local Arsacid dynasty continued to rule the Kingdom of Armenia under Roman supervision between AD 54 and AD 428. In AD 301, Armenia became the first country in the world to declare Christianity its state religion.

During the Middle Ages, control of Armenia was contested among Byzantines, Turks, and Arab kingdoms and empires. Persia and the Ottoman Empire fought for control of Armenia in the 16th, 17th, and 18th centuries. Russia entered the struggle for influence in Armenia in the early 19th century. After a war between Russia and Persia in the 1820s, Russia took control of the area around Yerevan. After having taken control of Yerevan, Russia pushed to expand its territorial control westward toward the Black Sea. A brief war between Russia and the Ottoman Empire broke out, after which present-day Armenia was divided between the Russians and the Ottomans.

Before and during World War I, the Ottomans massacred Armenians in an ethnic-cleansing effort that became known as the Armenian Genocide or the Armenian Massacre. An estimated 1 to 1.5 million Armenians were killed. Thousands more were forced to march from Armenia through Turkey to modern-day Syria, sometimes without food or water, and many perished en route. During this period, hundreds of thousands of Armenians were deported or fled the country, moving as refugees to other parts of the Middle East, Europe, and the United States.

Armenia declared independence as the Democratic Republic of Armenia in 1918. However, the Democratic Republic was invaded and overthrown by Soviet troops. Armenia was annexed to the Soviet Union and became part of the Transcaucasian Soviet Federated Socialist Republic (TSFSR) in 1922 along with Azerbaijan and Georgia. The TSFSR was dissolved in 1936, and Armenia became the Armenian Soviet Socialist Republic. Nationalist sentiment in Armenia intensified, especially after the 1970s. Armenian nationalists also pushed for reunification between Armenians inside and outside of the Armenian Soviet Socialist Republic. Armenia declared its independence in 1990, and its independence was recognized fully by the international community after the Soviet Union broke up in 1991.

Soon after independence, war broke out between Armenia and Azerbaijan. Conflict centered on the district of Nagorno-Karabakh, a majority of whose residents are of Armenian ancestry but which is surrounded and controlled by Azerbaijan.

Many Armenians in Nagorno-Karabakh demanded unification of the district with Armenia. The Nagorno-Karabakh War began in 1991 and lasted for three years. At least 30,000 Armenians and Azeris were killed and many more left the region as refugees. By 1994, Armenian troops had seized control of about 14 percent of Azerbaijan's land area, including Nagorno-Karabakh. After a cease-fire agreement was negotiated and implemented in 1994, Armenia retained control of this territory and was accused by Azerbaijan and some international observers of ethnic cleansing. The United Nations called upon Armenia to withdraw from Azeri territory in 2008. Meanwhile, Nagorno-Karabakh had declared itself independent, but this declaration of independence is unrecognized by the international community.

CONTEMPORARY ISSUES

Armenia's relationships with both Azerbaijan and Turkey are strained. In addition to the question of Nagorno-Karabakh's status, the situation in Nakhchivan remains uncertain. Nakhchivan is separated from the rest of Azerbaijan by a strip of Armenian territory 30 to 40 miles wide, but a majority of its residents are ethnic Azeris. During the Nagorno-Karabakh War, Armenian troops invaded and then blockaded Nakhchivan, contributing to economic problems there.

Armenia and Turkey have had a long history of antagonism dating back to the Armenian Genocide of the early 20th century. Although persecution of Armenians ended after the Republic of Turkey emerged as the successor state to the Ottoman Empire, Turkey has never acknowledged or apologized for the Armenian Genocide. Although Turkey was quick to recognize Armenian independence from the Soviet Union, tensions between the two countries continued, and Turkey closed its border with Armenia in 1993. Efforts have been made to improve these relationships, and in 2009 the two countries signed an agreement to open negotiations with the intent of reestablishing diplomatic relations and lifting the border blockade.

See also   Azerbaijan, Georgia, Iran, Turkey

Further Reading

Thomas de Waal. *Black garden: Armenia and Azerbaijan through peace and war.* New York: NYU Press, 2003.

Thomas de Waal. "Stuck in 1915: How Turkey and Armenia blew their big chance at peace." *Foreign Policy*, April 25, 2010, http://www.foreignpolicy.com/articles/2010/04/15/stuck_in_1915.

Galib Mammadov. "Nagorno-Karabakh conflict: Armenia's victory or nightmare?" *Foreign Policy Journal*, October 13, 2011, http://www.foreignpolicyjournal.com/2011/10/13/nagorno-karabakh-conflict-armenias-victory-or-nightmare-2/.

Simon Payaslian. *The history of Armenia.* New York: Palgrave, 2003.

AZERBAIJAN

OVERVIEW

The Republic of Azerbaijan is one of three former Soviet republics located in the Caucasus Mountains of southwestern Asia. Azerbaijan's land area is 33,436 square miles, slightly larger than South Carolina.

Its population is about 9.3 million. About 90 percent of Azerbaijan's people are ethnic Azeris, most of whom are Shi'ite Muslims and whose language is related closely to Turkish. In addition to its main territory, Azerbaijan's territory also includes the exclave of Nagorno-Karabakh, which is administered as the Nakhchivan Autonomous Republic. This exclave is separated from the main territory of Azerbaijan by a strip of Armenian territory averaging 20 to 30 miles in width.

Azerbaijan has boundaries with Russia to the north, Georgia to the northwest, Armenia to the west, and Iran to the south. The Nakhchivan Autonomous Republic has a very short boundary with Turkey. To the east, Azerbaijan has a coastline along the Caspian Sea. Its capital city of Baku is the largest city and busiest port on the Caspian Sea. The boundary between Azerbaijan and Russia extends southwestward from the Caspian Sea into the Caucasus Mountains. Some of this boundary follows the Samur River. Near Mount Bazarduzu, the highest peak in Azerbaijan, the boundary turns northwestward and follows the contour of the Caucasus Mountains to the tripoint between Azerbaijan, Russia, and Georgia. This tripoint is located at the northern end of Zagatala State Reserve, a nature preserve in Azerbaijan.

The boundary between Azerbaijan and Georgia is highly irregular and follows a combination of mountain ranges, drainage divides, and short straight-line segments. It extends in a generally southward direction toward a point north of Azerbaijan's Mingacevir Reservoir on the Kura River. From this point, the boundary trends northwestward close to the course of the Kura. It turns back southwestward to the tripoint

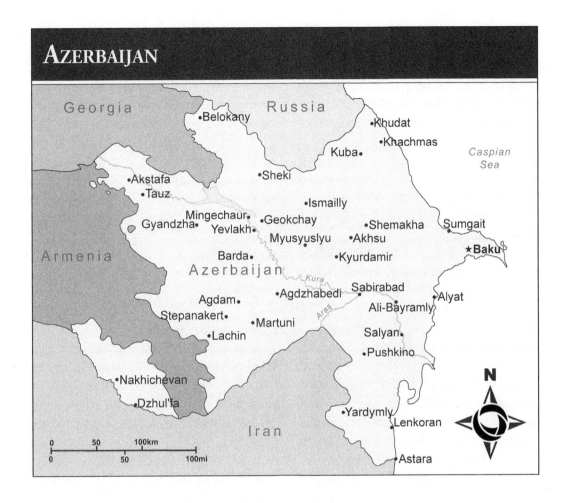

AZERBAIJAN

between Azerbaijan, Georgia, and Armenia. From this tripoint, the boundary between Azerbaijan and Armenia extends in a southeasterly direction along the Lesser Caucasus Mountains to the tripoint between Azerbaijan, Armenia, and Iran on the Aras River. The boundary between Azerbaijan and Iran follows the Aras downstream and northeastward toward the Caspian Sea. Near the Iranian town of Parsabad, the boundary turns southeastward and then eastward, reaching the Caspian Sea at the town of Astara.

The exclave of Nakhchivan has a land area of 2,071 square miles and a population of about 420,000. Nakhchivan borders Armenia to the northeast and Iran to the southeast. The Aras forms the boundary between Nakhchivan and Iran and the very short boundary between Nakhchivan and Turkey at the northwestern corner of the exclave.

HISTORICAL CONTEXT

Present-day Azerbaijan's recorded history dates back 3,000 years. During the sixth century BC, the region became part of the Achaemenid Empire based in Persia. It was conquered by Alexander the Great in the fourth century BC and was ruled by various successor kingdoms for the next 2,000 years. Many Azeris became Christians in the early Christian era, but most became Muslims several hundred years later. The Safavid dynasty controlled Iran as well as all of modern-day Azerbaijan beginning in the early 16th century. The Safavids converted the Azeri population from Sunni to Shi'ite Islam. Various kingdoms and khanates ruled present-day Azerbaijan after the Safavid dynasty collapsed in the mid-1700s.

In the early 19th century, Russia began to move southward into present-day Azerbaijan. The Russian Empire annexed most of Azerbaijan in 1813. The territory remained part of the Russian Empire until the empire collapsed during the Russian Revolution in 1917. Azerbaijan federated briefly with Georgia and Armenia as the Transcaucasian Federative Republic and then became the Azerbaijan Democratic Republic in 1918. Motivated in part by a desire to control the important oil port of Baku on the Caspian Sea, however, the Soviet Union invaded and took over the republic in 1920.The Soviets incorporated Azerbaijan into the Soviet Union as the Azerbaijan Soviet Socialist Republic. During this period, the Soviets drew the boundaries among Azerbaijan, Armenia, and Georgia. However, the borders cross mountainous and often unoccupied territories and have not been delineated precisely. Smuggling of illegal drugs, weapons, and other goods across all of these boundaries has been reported often.

Protests against the Soviet regime and calls for Azeri independence intensified in the late 1980s as the Soviet Union began to disintegrate. Some protestors called for unity between Azeris in the Azerbaijan Soviet Socialist Republic and ethnic Azeris living across the boundary in northern Iran. In 1990, armed skirmishes broke out between proindependence Azeris and the Soviet government. Soviet troops fired on protestors in Azerbaijan's capital city of Baku, killing more than 100 Azeri civilians in what would come to be known as Black January. Black January galvanized Azeri support for independence, and Azerbaijan declared its independence from the collapsing Soviet Union in December 1991.

CONTEMPORARY ISSUES

Since independence, Azerbaijan has been dealing with internal and external ethnic violence. Much of this conflict has involved neighboring Armenia, which is predominantly Christian and whose language is unrelated to the Turkic Azeri language.

Conflict was especially intense in the Nagorno-Karabakh region of west-central Azerbaijan. Nagorno-Karabakh has a land area of approximately 1,700 square miles, slightly larger than Rhode Island, and an estimated population of 150,000. About two-thirds of Nagorno-Karabakh's people are ethnic Armenians. As anti-Soviet sentiment intensified during the late 1980s, Armenians in Nagorno-Karabakh began to demonstrate in support of unification with Armenia. Although the Soviets had granted Nagorno-Karabakh limited autonomy within the Azerbaijan Soviet Socialist Republic, upon independence Azerbaijan established firm control over the territory.

In December of 1991, residents of Nagorno-Karabakh voted in a referendum to make Nagorno-Karabakh an independent state. However, the referendum was boycotted by ethnic Azeris. Nevertheless, Nagorno-Karabakh declared its independence although its independence has not been recognized by the international community. Shortly thereafter, the Nagorno-Karabakh War broke out between Azerbaijan and Armenia. Soldiers and mercenaries from other countries participated in the war, including Muslim fighters from Afghanistan and Russia's breakaway republic of Chechnya who fought on the side of Azerbaijan. By early 1994, Armenia had captured and occupied Nagorno-Karabakh and other portions of western Azerbaijan, including about 14 percent of Azerbaijan's territory. More than 30,000 people were killed and thousands more were displaced as refugees.

A cease-fire was negotiated with the help of the Russian government in 1994, although each side has accused the other of violating the cease-fire agreement. Armenia was accused by Azerbaijan of ethnic cleansing and genocide, and in 2008 the United Nations General Assembly passed a resolution calling on Armenia to withdraw its forces from all of Azerbaijan's territory.

The status of the exclave of Nakhchivan has also been contested. Although Nakhchivan is nearly surrounded by Armenian territory, the majority of its people are Azeris. During the Nagorno-Karabakh War, Armenian forces invaded Nakhchivan, and Armenia continues to blockade the region. Nevertheless, the international community recognizes Nakhchivan as an integral part of Azerbaijan. The blockade has contributed to economic distress in the region, and many people from Nakhchivan have moved to Turkey in search of employment and economic opportunity.

Azerbaijan and Georgia dispute a small area along their boundary that is occupied by the David Gareja Monastery, which is located on the border southeast of the Georgian capital city of Tbilisi. The monastery was founded by a Georgian Christian monk, St. David Garejeli, after whom the monastery was named. It remains an area used by the Georgian Christian community and is visited frequently by Georgian pilgrims. Part of the monastery complex is located on the Azeri side of the boundary, although Georgia claims the entire complex on the grounds of its historical and cultural significance to Georgians. Azerbaijan has rejected a Georgian offer to exchange other territory along the border for the entire Gareja Monastery area.

Azerbaijan is also involved in disputes with Iran, Russia, Kazakhstan, and Turkmenistan over access to the Caspian Sea. The main issue of dispute has been the delineation of maritime boundaries within the Caspian Sea. This is a significant concern because of the large deposits of oil and natural gas under and near the Caspian Sea. As a major oil-producing country, Azerbaijan remains anxious to protect its considerable oil wealth. The issue of transporting oil out of Azerbaijan to Europe has also been controversial. Given that the Caspian Sea has no direct outlets to the open sea, much of the oil produced in Azerbaijan is transported via pipelines. Given political instability in the Caucasus region, questions about where to locate and how to operate pipelines remain significant to Azerbaijan and its neighbors.

See also   Armenia, Georgia, Iran, Russia

Further Reading

Svante E. Cornell. *Azerbaijan since independence.* Armonk, NY: M. E. Sharpe, 2010.

Thomas de Waal. *Black garden: Armenia and Azerbaijan through peace and war.* New York: NYU Press, 2003.

Charles King. *The ghost of freedom: A history of the Caucasus.* New York: Oxford University Press, 2009.

Anar Valiyev. "Azerbaijan and Turkmenistan's dispute over the Caspian Sea: Will it impede the Nabucco project?" George Washington University, Program on New Approaches to Research and Security, Eurasia Policy Memo No. 87, 2009, http://www.gwu.edu/~ieresgwu/assets/docs/pepm_087.pdf.

CHINA

OVERVIEW

The People's Republic of China is the dominant country of East Asia. With a land area of 3,704,427 square miles, China is approximately the size of the United States and is the fourth-largest country by land area in the world behind Russia, Canada, and the United States. It has a population of about 1.3 billion, making it the most populous country in the world. About 18 percent of the entire population of the world lives in China.

China has boundaries with North Korea to the northeast, Russia and Mongolia to the north, Kazakhstan and Kyrgyzstan to the northwest, Tajikistan and Afghanistan to the west, Pakistan to the southwest, and Nepal, Bhutan, India, Myanmar, Laos, and Vietnam to the south. Thus only Russia has boundaries with more countries than does China. To the southeast and east, China has coastlines on the South China Sea and the East China Sea. Many of China's boundaries follow natural features. Most are located in sparsely populated territory, and thus densely populated eastern China is separated by its boundaries from other major population centers. The concentration of people in eastern China relative to areas in other countries across its boundaries has contributed historically to China's long-standing historical sense of cultural distinctiveness. Historically, the isolation of China has been reinforced by the Great Wall of China, which was built to separate the "civilized" Chinese from the "barbarians" to the north.

The boundary between China and North Korea extends in a northeasterly direction from the Korean Bay, which is part of the East China Sea. It follows the Yalu River upstream to a point near its source at Changbai Mountain, which is called Baekdu Mountain in North Korea. More than 200 inhabited islands are located in the Yalu River. These islands have been divided between China and North Korea on the basis of ethnicity. Northeast of Changbai Mountain, the boundary follows the Tumen River downstream and northeastward to the tripoint between China, North Korea, and Russia.

China has two boundaries with Russia, with the boundary between China and Mongolia separating these boundaries. The eastern boundary between China and Russia extends northeastward from the tripoint between China, Russia, and North Korea, separating the Chinese region of Manchuria from Russia territory to the southeast. The boundary continues northeastward to Khanka Lake, which is shared between

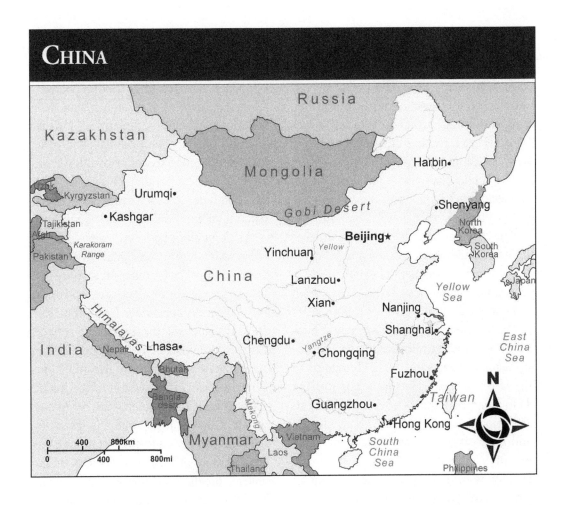

CHINA

the two countries. It follows the Songacha River from the lake to its confluence with the Ussuri River, then continues northeastward along the Ussuri downstream to its confluence with the Amur River near the Russian city of Khabarovsk.

From the confluence between the Ussuri and Amur rivers, the boundary follows the Amur upstream in a northwesterly direction. It then continues in a southwesterly direction along the Amur to the point at which the Amur is formed by the Argun River and the Shilka River. The boundary then follows the Argun, which is the more southerly of the two tributaries, further

southwestward and upstream. At a point near China's Hulun Lake, the Amur's upstream course takes a sharp bend eastward. The boundary between China and Russia, however, turns westward for a short distance to the eastern tripoint between China, Russia, and Mongolia.

The boundary between China and Mongolia connects China's two tripoints with Russia and Mongolia. This boundary extends southward, then turns eastward to a point east of Mongolia's Numrug National Park. It then turns back southwestward, entering and crossing the Gobi Desert. The Gobi is the second-largest desert in the world, after the Sahara Desert of Africa. The harsh terrain of the central Gobi Desert is virtually uninhabited. The boundary between China and Mongolia extends westward across the heart of the desert. It then turns northwestward into the Altai Mountains, where it reaches the western tripoint between China, Mongolia, and Russia. A short boundary between China and Russia connects this tripoint with the tripoint between China, Russia, and Kazakhstan.

The boundaries between China and Kazakhstan and between China and Kyrgyzstan extend in a generally southwesterly direction. These boundaries cross high mountains, and the regions on both sides of the boundaries contain very few people. The boundary between China and Kazakhstan connects the Altai Mountains to the northeast with the main range of the Tian Shan Mountains to the southwest. The tripoint between China, Kazakhstan, and Kyrgyzstan is located near the summit of Victory Peak, which is the highest mountain in the Tian Shan range at an altitude of 24,406 feet above sea level. From this tripoint, the boundary between China and Kyrgyzstan extends in a west-southwesterly direction through the Tian Shan, then turns southward into the Pamir Mountains. Most of this boundary is located at elevations more than 10,000 feet above sea level. The boundary between China, Kyrgyzstan, and Tajikistan is located near the shore of Karakul Lake, which has an elevation of more than 13,000 feet above sea level.

The boundary between China and Tajikistan extends southward from this tripoint. Much of this boundary is located along a drainage divide separating streams flowing eastward into China from those

that become tributaries of the Amu Darya River, which flows westward and empties eventually into the Caspian Sea. The boundary reaches the tripoint between China, Tajikistan, and Afghanistan. Continuing in a southerly direction, China has a short boundary with Afghanistan that is located along the eastern end of Afghanistan's Wakhan Corridor. This short boundary continues to the boundary between China, Afghanistan, and Pakistan.

The boundary between China and Pakistan extends through high mountains. Many parts of the boundary region are contested among China, Pakistan, and India. From the tripoint between China, Pakistan, and Afghanistan, the boundary between China and Pakistan extends southeastward and separates Tibet in southwestern China from Pakistan. This section of the boundary crosses K2, or Mount Godwin Austen, which at an elevation of 28,251 feet above sea level is the second-highest mountain in the world. Southeast of K2, the boundary reaches the disputed region of Jammu and Kashmir in India. Although Jammu and Kashmir is claimed by both Pakistan and India, the northern portion of the territory along the boundary is occupied and administered by Pakistan.

China has three boundaries with India, separated by boundaries between China and Nepal and between China and Bhutan. The two western boundaries are located high in the Himalaya Mountains. The boundary extends past the Pakistan-occupied portion of Jammu and Kashmir to the Indian-occupied northeastern portion of this region. It continues in a southeasterly direction to the western tripoint between China, India, and Nepal. From here it continues southeastward, separating China and Nepal. The world's highest mountain, Mount Everest, is located along the boundary between the Chinese province of Tibet and Nepal. China's border then turns eastward, forming the central boundary between China and India and, further to the east, the boundary between China and Bhutan. The boundary between China and India's state of Arunachal Pradesh is also located in the Himalayas. This boundary extends in an east-northeasterly direction from the eastern tripoint between China, India, and Bhutan to the tripoint between China, India, and Myanmar.

The boundaries between China and its southern neighbors in Southeast Asia also cross mountain ranges that, although not nearly as high as the Himalayas, Pamirs, and Tian Shan Mountains, are very rugged, steep, heavily forested, and, prior to the development of modern transportation, very difficult to cross. The boundaries between China and Myanmar and between China and Laos extend across the Yunnan Mountains separating East Asia from Southeast Asia. Most of the boundary between China and Myanmar follows the drainage divide between tributaries of the rivers of southern and southwestern China to the north and east and the Irrawaddy River basin on the south side of the boundary in Myanmar. Likewise, the boundary between China and Laos separates Chinese rivers from the Mekong River and its tributaries in Southeast Asia. To the east, the boundary between China and Vietnam extends northward to the Red River, which forms a brief section of the boundary. From the Red River itself, the boundary follows a rough semicircle separating the Red River drainage basin in Vietnam to tributaries of the Xi River and other rivers in China.

The eastern section of this boundary follows the Beilun eastward to its mouth in the Gulf of Tonkin, which is part of the South China Sea. Near the Gulf of Tonkin coast, the Chinese city of Dongxing is located across the Beilun from the Vietnamese city of Mong Cai.

HISTORICAL CONTEXT

Historically, China has regarded itself as the center of civilization and the dominant culture of East Asia. China's sense of cultural superiority has been enhanced by its isolation from other major centers of civilization around the world. All of China's land border regions have very few inhabitants, from Siberia and the Gobi Desert to the north to the high mountains of Central Asia to the west to the rugged Yunnan Mountains to the south. The East China Sea and the South China Sea are part of the Pacific Ocean, which is the largest of the world's oceans.

More than anywhere else in the world, most of the heavily populated portions of contemporary China have been unified politically for hundreds of years. Remains of modern humans and their artifacts dating back at least 25,000 years have been found in China by archaeologists. The Shang dynasty, which ruled some of the Hwang Ho River valley, is the first Chinese dynasty whose history is confirmed by written records. The Shang ruled this area during the second millennium BC. The first dynasty to unify most of modern-day eastern China was the Han dynasty, which ruled China between 206 BC and AD 220. The Han also controlled much of present-day Korea, Vietnam, and Mongolia, and they began establishing trade linkages with Europe and the Middle East that would become the Silk Road. Ethnic Chinese are known as Han Chinese people, recognizing this history.

Between the 7th and 19th centuries AD, China was ruled by a succession of dynasties, each of which controlled most of the heavily populated areas of contemporary China. These included the Tang, Song, Yuan, Ming, and Qing dynasties. The Tang ruled from AD 618 to 907 and were succeeded by the Song, which governed from AD 960 until 1279. The Song were deposed by the Yuan dynasty, which was led by descendants of Genghis Khan who invaded China from Mongolia. The Yuan were expelled by the Ming dynasty in 1368. During the late 14th and the 15th centuries, the Ming promoted international commerce. Chinese ships established trading links throughout East Asia, to Southeast Asia, and into the Indian Ocean as far west as the Arabian Peninsula and East Africa. However, the Chinese government withdrew its support for maritime activities in the early 16th century.

The Ming dynasty was overthrown by the Qing dynasty, which originated in Manchuria in northeastern China, in 1644. The Qing ruled China until 1912. By the early 19th century, Europeans had established a significant presence in China. Britain took over Hong Kong and Portugal took over Macau, both of which are located on the southeastern coast of China. European powers, the United States, and Japan carved out spheres of influence along the Chinese coast. In 1894, China was defeated by Japan in the First Sino-Japanese War, and China was forced to cede its influence over Korea to Japan.

Ongoing revolt against Western and Japanese influence culminated in the Boxer Rebellion, which attempted to expel Westerners in northern China by force. Troops from Japan, the United States, and six European countries united to defeat the Boxers, reinforcing the weakness of the Qing regime. As the 20th century dawned, young Chinese reformers began to act to overthrow the dynasty. Many leaders of this reformist movement had been educated in Europe or in the United States. In 1912, the Republic of China was proclaimed in the city of Nanjing, and the last Qing emperor was forced to abdicate.

The nationalist government of the Republic of China remained in power although its control was challenged by both internal and external force. Imperial Japan continued to encroach on China, taking over the Korean peninsula in 1910 and Manchuria in 1937. Conflict between China and Japan continued through World War II. Meanwhile, the nationalist government was threatened by a communist revolutionary movement beginning in the 1930s. Although the nationalists and the communists united against Japan as a common enemy during World War II, civil war between the two sides resumed until the communists proved victorious and seized control of the government. In 1949, the nationalists fled to Taiwan, where they continue to claim their status as the only legitimate government of China. The communists established the People's Republic of China and established firm control of all of the Chinese mainland.

The victorious communists under the leadership of Mao Zedong worked to establish the People's Republic as a largely self-sufficient communist state. Mao's government was aided heavily at first by the Soviet Union, but China broke with the Soviet Union in what would come to be known as the Sino-Soviet Split in the 1960s. As many as 50 million people are believed to have been killed by communist rulers during the 1950s and 1960s.

After more than two decades of isolation from the government, the United States and China established contact with each other in the early 1970s. In 1972, U.S. president Richard Nixon visited Beijing, and diplomatic relations between the People's Republic and the United States were established. After Mao died in 1976, his successor, Deng Xiaoping, led a transition of the Chinese economy away from the centralized planning characteristic of the Mao regime toward a mixed economy in which private enterprise was encouraged. Since the early 1990s, China's economy has grown rapidly, and some observers predict that it will surpass the United States as the leading economy in the world by the middle of the 21st century. However, China's current government has been criticized for human rights violations and contributing to large-scale environmental destruction.

CONTEMPORARY ISSUES

China faces ongoing tensions with many of its neighbors, as well as internally. Three of China's major conflicts involve its relationships with the Uighurs in northwestern China, the Tibetans in southwestern China, and the nationalist government of Taiwan.

Conflicts in northwestern and southwestern China stem from ethnic and national differences between the Han Chinese and other nationalities. About 92 percent of China's people are Han Chinese, with the rest belonging to other ethnic groups. Many of the non-Han Chinese people live in outlying and or relatively inaccessible parts of the country.

One ongoing conflict is taking place between the government of China and the Uighurs (also spelled Uyghurs). About 11.5 million Uighurs live in Central Asia. Most Uighurs live in Xinjiang Province in northwest China, although some Uighurs live in neighboring Russia, Kazakhstan, and Kyrgyzstan. Most Uighurs are Muslims, and they speak a Turkic language that is closely related to the languages of Central Asia rather than being related to Chinese. Religious and linguistic differences have put the Uighurs at odds with the Chinese government, which is officially atheistic. According to Chinese law, men working for the Chinese government are not allowed to grow beards, and women in China are not allowed to wear headscarves in public. Children under 18 are not permitted to attended mosques.

Uighur activists have also accused the Chinese of attempting to dilute their culture by encouraging the migration of Han Chinese into Uighur-majority areas of Xinjiang. In 1949, the population of Xinjiang was 95 percent Uighur; today, it is less than 50 percent Uighur. Indeed, some Uighurs regard the province's name, which means "New Frontier" in Chinese, as offensive. Some Uighurs would prefer that Uighur-dominated territories of northwest China and Central Asia become an independent country named "East Turkestan" or "Uighurstan."

The Chinese government regards Xinjiang as an integral and essential part of China, in part because of its strategic location relative to Russia and Central Asia and also because of the oil-rich province's extensive mineral resources. China has invested large amounts of capital in development projects in Xinjiang, including railroads, highways, factories, dams, and oil pipelines. The Chinese government has encouraged Han Chinese to move to Xinjiang. Today about 75 percent of the residents of Xinjiang's capital city of Urumqi are Han Chinese, and only 13 percent are Uighurs. Uighur activists accuse China of promoting migration of Han Chinese to Xinjiang in order to suppress Uighur culture and encourage the integration of the Uighurs into Chinese culture.

A similar situation prevails in Tibet, which is located high in the Himalayas in southwestern China near its boundaries with Nepal, India, and Pakistan. Tibetans, like Uighurs, are historically and culturally distinct from the Han Chinese. Tibet is often called the "Roof of the World" because of its very high elevation, averaging more than 16,000 feet above sea level. The highest mountain in the world, Mount Everest, is on the border between Tibet and Nepal.

Tibet's population is estimated at between 5 and 6 million. Several hundred thousand Tibetans live in exile outside Tibet in India and other countries, including about 10,000 in the United States. China assumed control of Tibet in 1950. Advocates of Tibetan independence accuse China of genocide against Tibetans, including pushing Tibetans out of Tibet and encouraging non-Tibetans to move into the region. Tibet's spiritual leader, the Dalai Lama, was forced into exile in India. Several thousand Buddhist monasteries have been torn down or damaged, and hundreds of thousands of Tibetans left Tibet as refugees.

The Chinese government opened the Qinghai-Tibet Railroad in 2006. The government argued that it would help the Tibetan economy; some have expressed concern that it will cause environmental damage and dilute Tibetan culture by encouraging more in-migration of Han Chinese, who will see most of the benefits.

Elsewhere, China continues to claim sovereignty over Taiwan while Taiwan also claims sovereignty over the entire country. The controversy dates back to 1949, when the nationalist government of the Republic of China left mainland China after being routed by the communists. At that time, the nationalists claimed that theirs remained the legitimate government of the entire country. The United Nations, the United States, and other Western democracies continued to recognize the nationalist government until the 1970s. In 1971, Taiwan lost its permanent seat on the United Nations Security Council, which awarded this seat to the People's Republic. As more and more countries, including the United States, began to recognize the People's Republic, the People's Republic reasserted that it had territorial sovereignty over Taiwan.

Another ongoing issue is the status of the former European enclaves of Hong Kong and Macau. Hong Kong consists of Hong Kong Island, 260 other islands, and the Kowloon Peninsula on the Chinese mainland near the major city of Guangzhou (formerly known as Canton). Hong Kong has a population of about 7 million. It was occupied by the British in 1841 and officially became a British territory in 1842. Hong Kong became Britain's major East Asian port in the 19th and 20th centuries.

In 1898, Britain and China negotiated a 99-year lease, during which time Britain would control Hong Kong. In the 1980s, China made clear that it expected Hong Kong to be returned to China when the lease expired in 1997. At that time, sovereignty over Hong Kong was transferred to China. Under terms of the transfer agreement, Hong Kong was allowed to retain its capitalistic economy for at least 50 years. However, some Hong Kong residents were uneasy about the transfer, and many left Hong Kong prior to 1997. Those who left tended to be wealthy and/or well-educated business executives, physicians, engineers, and lawyers.

Macau, which is also located along the coast about 50 miles southwest of Hong Kong, is a former Portuguese colony that was established in 1557. Its population is about 550,000. Portugal used Macau as a basis for trade throughout East and Southeast Asia. In 1999, sovereignty over Macau was transferred to the People's Republic. As was the case with Hong Kong, the transfer agreement between China and Portugal stipulated that Macau could retain its economic system and internal autonomy for no less than 50 years.

In 2012, a dispute between China and Japan arose over control of the small, uninhabited Daioyu Islands in the South China Sea. The Daioyu Islands are located north of Japan's Ryukyu Islands and are roughly equidistant from China, Japan, and China. These islands are known as the Senkaku Islands in Japan. Both sides maintain a strong interest in controlling the islands because they are believed to be located near valuable oil and natural gas deposits.

See also Afghanistan, Bhutan, India, Japan, Kazakhstan, Kyrgyzstan, Laos, Mongolia, Myanmar, Nepal, North Korea, Pakistan, Russia, Taiwan, Tajikistan, Vietnam

Further Reading

Gardner Bovingdon. *The Uyghurs: Strangers in their own land.* New York: Columbia University Press, 2010.

Doug Guthrie. *China and globalization: The social, economic, and political transformation of Chinese society.* London: Routledge, 2012.

G. John Ikenberry. "The rise of China and the future of the West: Can the liberal system survive?" *Foreign Affairs*, January/February 2008.

Martin Jacques. *When China rules the world: The end of the Western world and the birth of a new global order.* New York: Penguin, 2009.

Sam van Schaik. *Tibet: A history.* New Haven, CT: Yale University Press, 2011.

Alan Wachman. *Why Taiwan? Geostrategic rationales for China's territorial integrity.* Palo Alto, CA: Stanford University Press, 2007.

GEORGIA

OVERVIEW

Georgia is a state located in the Caucasus Mountains of southwestern Asia. It was one of the constituent republics of the Soviet Union until the collapse of the Soviet Union in 1991. Georgia's land area is 26,911 square miles, the size of West Virginia. It has a population of 4.5 million.

Georgia has boundaries with Russia to the north and east, Azerbaijan to the southeast, and Armenia and Turkey to the south. Western Georgia has a coastline on

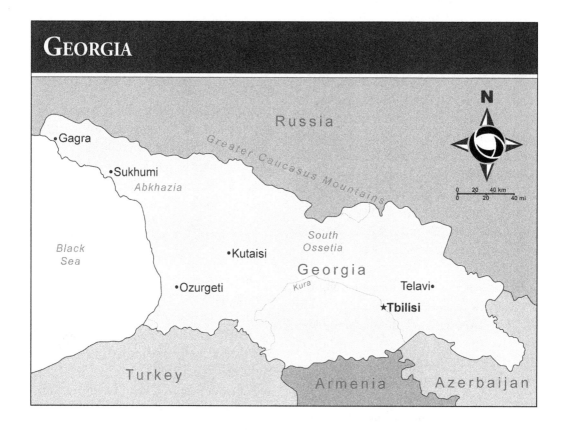

GEORGIA

Russia

Gagra

Sukhumi

Abkhazia

Greater Caucasus Mountains

Black Sea

Kutaisi

South Ossetia

G e o r g i a

Ozurgeti

Kura

Telavi

★Tbilisi

N

0 20 40 km
0   20   40 mi

T u r k e y

A r m e n i a

A z e r b a i j a n

the Black Sea. Two territories in northern Georgia, South Ossetia and Abkhazia, are disputed between Georgia and Russia. Except for Turkey, all of Georgia's neighbors were also part of the former Soviet Union.

Georgia's boundaries with its neighbors are generally cultural boundaries intended to separate ethnic Georgians within Georgia from non-Georgians in neighboring countries. Most of these boundaries cross or extend along high mountain ranges with relatively low population densities. Today almost three-quarters of Georgia's residents are of Georgian ancestry and ethnicity. The existing boundary between Georgia and Russia extends in a southeasterly direction from a point on the Black Sea just south of the Russian resort city of Sochi to the tripoint between Georgia,

Russia, and Azerbaijan. This boundary crosses mountainous, sparsely populated territory. Three national parks—Racha-Lechkhum-Kverno National Park, Tusheti National Park, and Zagatala Nature Reserve—are located adjacent to the Georgian side of the boundary.

From the tripoint between Georgia, Azerbaijan, and Russia, the boundary between Georgia and Azerbaijan also follows mountain range crests, drainage divides, and short straight-line segments. The boundary trends in a generally southerly direction from the tripoint to a point just north of the Mingacevir Reservoir in Azerbaijan. From this point, it trends northwestward and briefly southward to the tripoint between Georgia, Azerbaijan, and Armenia. The boundaries between Georgia and

Armenia and between Georgia and Turkey extend westward and northwestward. The boundary between Georgia and Turkey meets the Black Sea between the Georgian town of Sarpi and the Turkish town of Sarp.

HISTORICAL CONTEXT

Present-day Georgia has been inhabited for at least 3,500 years. It became part of the Roman Empire in 66 BC, and most Georgians converted to Christianity during the fourth century AD. Georgia became united under the Georgian Empire in the 12th and early 13th centuries before the empire was toppled by Mongol invaders. Present-day Georgia was divided among several kingdoms and principalities until the 16th century, when western Georgia became part of the Ottoman Empire and eastern Georgia became part of the Persian Empire.

In the late 18th century, the expanding Russian Empire began to take an interest in Georgia. Russia's Tsar Paul I and Georgia's King George XII signed an agreement in 1800. According to the agreement, Georgia became part of the Russian Empire. The annexation took effect in the following year. In 1805, a Russian military victory over Persian military forces confirmed the incorporation of Georgia into the Russian Empire. Additional wars between Russia and the Ottoman Empire resulted in the capture of additional territory that was transferred from the Ottoman Empire to present-day Georgia.

After the Russian Revolution, Georgia declared independence in 1918. Red Army troops invaded Georgia in 1921, and Georgia came under Soviet rule. During the 1920s and early 1930s, Georgia became a part of the Transcaucasian Soviet Federated Socialist Republic (TSFSR) along with Azerbaijan and Armenia. The TSFSR was dissolved in 1936, and Georgia became the Georgian Soviet Socialist Republic.

As the Soviet Union began to collapse in 1990, Georgia became the first Soviet party to hold a free election in 1990. An anti-communist party known as the Round Table–Free Georgia Party won a majority of seats in Parliament, with the Communist Party finishing a distant second. Georgia declared independence from the Soviet Union on April 9, 1991.

Georgia's declaration of independence left open the question of the status of two majority-Russian areas within the former Georgian Soviet Socialist Republic. South Ossetia, with a land area of 1,506 square miles and a population of 72,000, is located in north-central Georgia just south of the boundary. Abkhazia is located in the northwestern corner of Georgia, with the Black Sea to the west and Russia to the north. Abkhazia has a land area of 3,386 square miles and a population of about 240,000.

With the support of Russia, both South Ossetia and Abkhazia have declared independence. However, their independence has not been recognized by Georgia, and only a few other countries recognize their independence. A war between Abkhazia and the new post-Soviet government of Georgia took place between 1992 and 1993. The conflict was associated with ethnic divisions. Russia supported Abkhazian separatists, while many ethnic Georgians living in the area opposed separation. Some fought with Georgian forces in support of the government. As many as 20,000 people were killed in the war, and more than 200,000 people, primarily ethnic Georgians, were displaced during the conflict.

Another shooting war broke out in 1991 and 1992 between Georgia and Russia over the status of South Ossetia. After Georgia declared itself independent of the Soviet Union in 1990, South Ossetia declared itself to be an independent republic. The 1991 war began when Georgian forces invaded South Ossetia, whose independence was not recognized by the new Georgian government. In 2008, a second shooting war over the status of South Ossetia broke out between Georgia and Russia. Each side accused the other of initiating armed hostilities. Russia gained control of South Ossetia and sent troops across the border between South Ossetia and the rest of Georgia into Georgian territory. The European Union negotiated and implemented a cease-fire, after which Russia withdrew its troops from the rest of Georgia into South Ossetia. Russia remains in de facto control of South Ossetia, while Georgia regards South Ossetia as Russian-occupied territory that has been occupied illegally and remains under Georgian sovereignty.

CONTEMPORARY ISSUES

Many of Georgia's boundaries with its neighbors remain contested, and disputes continue, and these disputes generally involve the ethnicity of local residents in that Georgia wants to incorporate those areas with a majority of Georgians into Georgia. Conflicts over the status over Abkhazia and South Ossetia are ongoing. Georgia continues to claim both of these provinces as integral portions of Georgian territory

while Russia recognizes them as independent sovereign states. In both territories, ethnic Georgians prefer continued integration into Georgia whereas non-Georgians support independence. Elsewhere, portions of the long and complex boundary between Georgia and Russia remain poorly demarcated.

Georgia and Azerbaijan have disputed a section along their boundary. The dispute involves territory occupied by the David Gareja Monastery. The monastery complex is located on the Georgia-Azerbaijan boundary about 40 miles southeast of Georgia's capital city of Tbilisi. It was established in the sixth century AD by St. David Garejeli, an Assyrian monk, and has been occupied and used by Georgian Orthodox monks and religious leaders ever since. The complex was closed by the officially atheist government of the Soviet Union in 1921 but was reopened in 1991 after Georgia became independent. It remains a center of Georgian Orthodox religious activity and is a frequent destination for Georgian pilgrims.

Some of the monastery complex is located across the boundary in Azerbaijan. However, Georgia claims the entire territory on the grounds of its cultural significance to Georgia, a predominantly Christian country, in contrast to Azerbaijan, which is predominantly Muslim. Georgia has proposed to exchange other Georgian territory in exchange for sovereignty over the entire monastery complex, but Azerbaijan has rejected this proposal. Discussions between the two countries over the status of the David Gareja Monastery are ongoing.

See also   Armenia, Azerbaijan, Russia, Turkey

Further Reading

Civil Georgia. "Abkhazia, S. Osse-tia formally declared occupied territory." August 28, 2008, http://www.civil.ge/eng/article.php?id=19330.

Thomas de Waal. *The Caucasus: An introduction*. New York: Oxford University Press, 2010.

Charles King. *The ghost of freedom: A history of the Caucasus*. New York: Oxford University Press, 2009.

JAPAN

OVERVIEW

Japan is an island country located off the coast of mainland East Asia. The Japanese archipelago includes more than 6,800 islands. The four main islands of Japan, from northeast to southwest, are Hokkaido, Honshu, Shikoku, and Kyushu. Together, these four islands comprise more than 97 percent of Japan's overall land area of 145,925 square miles, approximately the size of Montana. Japan's population is approximately 128 million. Honshu is the largest of the four main islands, with about 60 percent of the country's land area. It contains more than 80 percent of Japan's population, including the Tokyo metropolitan area, which is the largest in the world with more than 35 million people.

Japan is situated between the Sea of Japan to the north and west and the Pacific Ocean to the south and east. To the northeast, Hokkaido has a coastline on the Sea of Okhotsk, and southwestern Kyushu has a coastline on the East China Sea that separates Japan from China. As an island country, it has no land neighbors. Japan's closest neighbor by water is Russia. The northern tip of Hokkaido is about 30 miles from Russia's Sakhalin Island across the Soya Strait, which connects the Sea of Japan with the Sea of Okhotsk. Northeastern Hokkaido is even closer. It is separated from the Russian island of Kunashir, which is the southwesternmost of the Kurile Islands. Japan claims Kunashir and three other islands in the Kurile chain to its northeast. The southwest corner of Honshu is about 100 miles southeast of South Korea on the coast of mainland Asia. The west coast of Kyushu is about 400 miles east of mainland China across the East China Sea.

HISTORICAL CONTEXT

Archaeologists have discovered evidence of human habitation on the Japanese islands around 30,000 years ago. The indigenous inhabitants of Japan are believed to have been ancestors of the Ainu, some of whom inhabit northern Japan today. During the first millennium BC, East Asians from present-day China and Korea moved to the islands. They introduced rice cultivation, metalworking, and other components of mainland East Asian culture to Japan and helped to create a distinctive Japanese nationality. Gradually, the Japanese pushed the Ainu and other indigenous peoples to marginal areas. The Ainu were pushed northward, and today most Ainu live in northern Hokkaido.

The Emperor Jimmu has been regarded as the first emperor of Japan. He is believed to have established the first Japanese empire in 660 BC, although his existence and the dates of his reign have not been verified with certainty by historians. The first emperor whose reign has been dated by historians with certainty was the Emperor

JAPAN

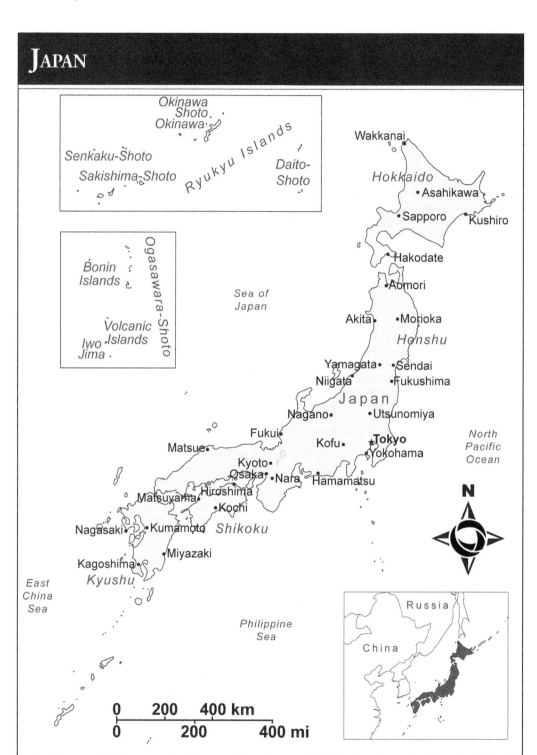

Okinawa
Shoto
Okinawa

Senkaku-Shoto

Sakishima-Shoto

Ryukyu Islands

Daito-
Shoto

Bonin
Islands

Ogasawara-Shoto

Volcanic
Islands
Iwo
Jima

Sea of
Japan

Wakkanai

Hokkaido

•Asahikawa

•Sapporo   •Kushiro

•Hakodate

•Aomori

Akita•   •Morioka

Honshu

Yamagata•   •Sendai
Niigata   •Fukushima

Japan

Nagano•   •Utsunomiya

Fukui•

Matsue•

Kyoto•

Osaka• •Nara

Kofu•   ★Tokyo
         •Yokohama

North
Pacific
Ocean

Hamamatsu

Hiroshima
Matsuyama•
  •Kochi

Nagasaki• •Kumamoto   Shikoku

•Miyazaki

Kagoshima•

Kyushu

East
China
Sea

Philippine
Sea

N

Russia

China

0   200   400 km

0   200   400 mi

Kimmei, who died in AD 571. Control of Japan alternated between the absolute rule of the emperor and domination of the government by powerful families. Beginning in 1185, powerful families known as daimyo, with the support of military warlords known as shoguns, ruled the islands. The emperor became a figurehead whose rule was primarily ceremonial and who had no real power.

European traders and Christian missionaries visited Japan during the 16th and early 17th centuries. In order to halt the spread of Christianity and to control trade with Europe and mainland Asia, the ruling Tokugawa shoguns pursued a policy of strict isolation. Beginning in 1635, trade with Europe was limited to a small artificial island off the coast of the city of Nagasaki in Kyushu. Only the Dutch East India Company was permitted to trade with Japan through this port, and the number of Dutch ships allowed to visit the island was limited strictly. Japanese nationals were forbidden to leave the country, and non-Japanese people could not enter Japan.

Japan's isolation from the rest of the world ended abruptly in 1853, when Commodore Matthew Perry of the United States Navy sailed into the harbor at Yokohama and forced Japan to open itself to trade with the United States and the European powers. In 1868, the last Tokugawa shogun relinquished power. The emperor was given real political power in what came to be known as the Meiji Restoration, establishing the Japanese Empire.

Following the Meiji Restoration, Japan industrialized rapidly. The Japanese Empire also expanded to encompass large portion of mainland East and Southeast Asia. Between 1894 and 1905, Japanese forces were victorious in the First Sino-Japanese War and the Russo-Japanese War, and Japan secured control of Korea, Taiwan, and the southern half of Sakhalin Island north of Hokkaido. Japan invaded and seized control of the Chinese province of Manchuria, north of Korea, in 1931. In 1937, Japan and China went to war a second time as the Japanese Empire made efforts to secure other portions of China. Japan allied itself with Germany and Italy, and it invaded French Indochina, including present-day Vietnam, Cambodia, and Laos, in 1940. The Japanese air attack on Pearl Harbor on the U.S. island of Oahu in Hawaii triggered World War II.

After Allied forces defeated Japan in the war, the empire was stripped of its territories outside the Japanese archipelago. Japan became a republic that was occupied by U.S. forces until 1952. Between the 1950s and the early 1990s, Japan experienced great economic growth, although the Japanese economy has been in recession since the mid-1990s. Japan remains a highly developed country whose standard of living is equivalent to that of the United States, Canada, and most of the European Union.

CONTEMPORARY ISSUES

Although present-day Japan has sovereignty over the Japanese archipelago only, the status of islands to the north and south of Japan's four main islands has been contested. To the north, the Kurile Islands stretch northeastward from off the coast of Hokkaido to the southern tip of Russia's Kamchatka Peninsula. The archipelago, which consists of 56 islands, separates the Sea of Okhotsk from the Pacific Ocean.

In 1875, Japan and the Russian Empire signed the Treaty of St. Petersburg. Under terms of this treaty, Japan was given sovereignty of the 18 southernmost islands in the Kurile archipelago. After World War II, all of the Kurile Islands were returned to the Soviet Union as the successor state to the Russian Empire. However, Japan continues to claim sovereignty over those Kurile Islands located closest to Hokkaido, including Kunashir, Iturup, Shikotan, and the Habamai islets. About 17,000 people live on these four islands whose control remains in dispute.

To the south, the Ryukyu Islands stretch southward and westward from Kyushu toward Taiwan. This archipelago has a total population of about 1.6 million. The United States occupied the largest of these islands, Okinawa, after World War II. In 1972, sovereignty over Okinawa was returned to Japan, but the United States retained military bases on the island. Protests against the American military presence in Okinawa are ongoing. The U.S. Marine Corps and the Japanese government have been working on plans to move the Marine base on Okinawa elsewhere. A secessionist movement to create an independent state in the Ryukyu Islands has been active also. Control of the nearby Senkaku Islands, which are north of the Ryukyu chain, has been contested recently between Japan and China. These islands, which are known in China as the Daioyu Islands, are uninhabited but are believed to be located near valuable undersea oil and natural gas deposits.

The status of the Ainu and other ethnic groups is also an issue of concern. For centuries, ethnic Japanese pushed the Ainu northward into Hokkaido, where most Ainu live today. This process accelerated after the Meiji Restoration, when the Japanese government formally assumed control of Hokkaido and encouraged Japanese people to move there. The indigenous Ainu were encouraged to adopt Japanese names and customs, and they were expected to give up their traditional lifestyles and begin farming. The use of the Ainu language was outlawed. However, discrimination against the Ainu has been reduced in recent years. The Japanese government recognized the Ainu formally as an indigenous group in 2008. The Ainu population in Japan and on Sakhalin Island, which is now part of Russia, has been estimated at 150,000.

On March 11, 2011, an earthquake with a magnitude of 9.0 on the Richter scale struck in the Pacific Ocean off the coast of northeastern Honshu. This earthquake was one of the largest and strongest in recorded history. The earthquake and its associated tsunami resulted in about 16,000 fatalities. An additional 30,000 people were injured and hundreds of thousands of people were made homeless. The earthquake also caused significant damage to the Fukushima nuclear power plant along the coast, creating the world's worst nuclear disaster since the Chernobyl disaster in present-day Ukraine in 1956. Millions of tons of debris washed into the Pacific Ocean, where prevailing currents have moved some of it eastward toward Hawaii and the mainland coasts of Canada and the United States.

Further Reading

BBC News. "Kuril Islands dispute between Russia and Japan." November 1, 2010, http://www.bbc.co.uk/news/world-asia-pacific-11664434.

Kenneth B. Pyle. *Japan rising: The resurgence of Japanese power and purpose.* New York: PublicAffairs, 2008

Brian Salsburg, Clay Chandler, and Heang Chhor. *Reimagining Japan: The quest for a future that works.* San Francisco: VIZ Publishing, 2011.

KAZAKHSTAN

OVERVIEW

The Republic of Kazakhstan is the largest of the five former Soviet republics in Central Asia by land area, although it has fewer people than neighboring Uzbekistan. Kazakhstan's land area is 1,052,085 square miles, nearly twice as large as Alaska. Thus

Kazakhstan is the ninth-largest country in the world by land area. Its population is about 17 million.

Landlocked Kazakhstan is bordered by Russia to the west and north, China to the southeast, and by Kyrgyzstan, Uzbekistan, and Turkmenistan to the southwest. To the west, Kazakhstan has a long coast on the Caspian Sea. To the east, the tripoint between Kazakhstan, Russia, and China is located only 25 miles west of the westernmost point in Mongolia. The boundary between Kazakhstan and Russia is the longest continuous land boundary in the world, longer than the 49th parallel boundary between the western United States and western Canada. It is long and complex, consisting primarily of short straight-line segments.

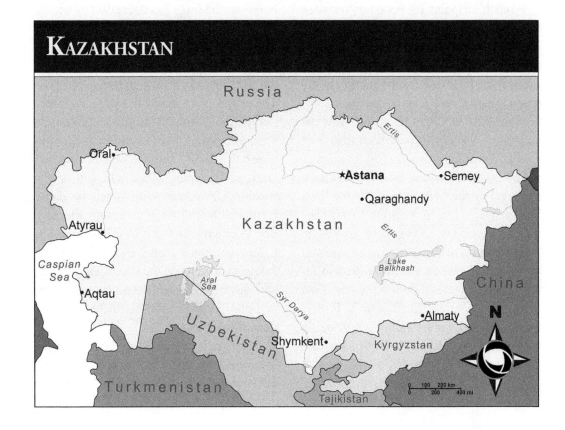

From the Caspian Sea, this boundary extends northwestward through the Ryn-Peski Desert. Most of this boundary follows straight-line segments. Southwest of the town of Saykhin, the boundary turns to the northeast and then to the east. Near Lake Aike on the border, the boundary turns northward again, following a long and complex series of straight-line segments to a point just south of the Russian town of Troitsk. From there, the boundary turns eastward once again. Most of the boundary crosses relatively low, flat steppe land. However, near the tripoint between Kazakhstan, Russia, and China, it ascends into the Altai Mountains. The highest peak in the Altai range, Mount Belukha at 14,784 feet above sea level, is located near the tripoint between Kazakhstan, Russia, and China.

From this tripoint, the boundary between Kazakhstan and China follows straight-line segments southwestward from the Altai range toward the Tian Shan range. The territory along this border is mountainous and sparsely populated. The boundary continues into the Tian Shan to a point near the summit of Victory Peak, which is known also as Jengish Chokusu. This mountain, which at an elevation of 24,406 feet above sea level is the highest peak in the Tian Shan range, is located near the tripoint between Kazakhstan, China, and Kyrgyzstan.

The boundary between Kazakhstan and Kyrgyzstan extends westward from Victory Peak, generally following the Tian Shan. It separates Kazakhstan's former capital city of Almaty from Kyrgyzstan's capital city of Bishkek. Both of these cities are within 25 miles of the boundary. Northwest of Bishkek, the boundary follows the Chu River upstream, then crosses westward to the Talas River. Both of these rivers flow into and dry up in Kazakhstan. It continues briefly along the Talas northwestward and upstream, then trends westward again to the Aksu Zhabagly Nature Reserve, near which is the tripoint between Kazakhstan, Kyrgyzstan, and Uzbekistan.

The boundary between Kazakhstan and Uzbekistan extends in a southwesterly direction from this tripoint to a point south of the Shardara Reservoir. About 500 square miles of Kazakhstan's territory is located south of the reservoir and north of the boundary. From the Shardara Reservoir, the boundary extends northwestward along straight-line segments to the Aral Sea, which is divided between the two countries. The Aral Sea was once the fourth-largest inland saltwater lake in the world, but its surface area has decreased by nearly 90 percent since the 1950s. The shrinkage of the Aral Sea began in the 1950, when the Soviets dammed the Amu Darya and the Syr Darya that flow into the Aral Sea. The dams were constructed in conjunction with the Soviet Union's Virgin Lands Program, which was intended to provide water to irrigate previously uncultivated lands in southern Kazakhstan and northwestern Uzbekistan. However, the dams restricted the inflow of water into the Aral Sea so much that much of it has dried up. Efforts are being made, especially in Kazakhstan, to reverse the depletion process, and water levels are increasing, especially in the northern part of the Aral Sea offshore from Kazakhstan.

From the Aral Sea, the boundary between Kazakhstan and Uzbekistan follows a straight-line segment extending diagonally in a southwesterly direction, then turns directly southward to the tri-point between Kazakhstan, Uzbekistan, and Turkmenistan. The boundary between Kazakhstan and Turkmenistan extends in a generally westward direction to the Caspian Sea. The boundary meets the Caspian Sea north of the town of Bekdash on the Turkmenistan side of the border.

HISTORICAL CONTEXT

Present-day Kazakhstan has been inhabited by people of Turkish origin for at least 1,500 years. Given the generally dry climate, many residents of the region were pastoral nomads. The Turkic Khanate of Gokturk became the first dynasty to establish control of a significant portion of modern Kazakhstan in the sixth and seventh centuries AD. Other locally based kingdoms controlled various portions of the region until it was conquered by the Mongols under Genghis Khan in the early 13th century.

After Genghis Khan's death, the Mongol Empire was divided, and present-day northern and western Kazakhstan came to be ruled by the Mongolian Golden Horde, an empire that controlled present-day south-central Russia as far west as the Black Sea also. Control of what is now southern Kazakhstan was assumed to the locally based Kazakh Khanate in the 15th century.

During the 17th century, Russian soldiers, merchants, and traders began to settle the northern shores of the Caspian Sea, including the northern portion of present-day Kazakhstan. Meanwhile, the Kazakh Khanate expanded northward, squeezing the Golden Horde in between. The Golden Horde requested protection from

the Russian Empire in the 1820s. In the late 19th century, the Russian Empire worked to conquer present-day Kazakhstan and the rest of Central Asia. The conquest was completed during the 1870s. Over the next half century, the Russian Empire encouraged Russian settlers to move into Kazakhstan. Hundreds of thousands of Russian farmers moved to Kazakhstan between 1880 and 1915.

After the Russian Revolution in which the Russian Empire was overthrown in 1917, Kazakhstan declared independence. However, the Soviets reasserted control over Kazakhstan by 1920. The region was named the Kyrgyz Autonomous Soviet Socialist Republic. In 1925, the Soviet government recognized the Kazakhs and the Kyrgyz as distinct national groups, and the name of the republic was changed to the Kazakh Autonomous Soviet Socialist Republic. Kazakhstan was given full-fledged republic status in 1936 as the Kazakh Soviet Socialist Republic (KSSR).

The decades of Soviet rule had profound effects on the KSSR. During the 1930s, widespread famine was followed by a brutal crackdown on dissent by Stalin's regime. Hundreds of thousands of Kazakhs lost their lives. Before and during World War II, Stalin moved many industrial operations to the KSSR, in part to isolate these industries from possible takeover by the Nazis. After the war, the Soviets encouraged people of Russian and other non-Kazakh ethnic backgrounds to move into Kazakhstan. This policy, which encouraged the creation of a common Soviet identity associated with the Russian language, was known as Russification. Many Russian nationals moved to Kazakhstan in order to work in the newly relocated industries. Other Russian emigrants were recruited to farm in Kazakhstan during the Virgin Lands program. By the 1980s, almost half of Kazakhstan's population consisted of ethnic Russians.

As the Soviet Union began to fall apart in the late 1980s, many Kazakhs demanded independence. However, many of the KSSR's residents of Russian ancestry were ambivalent about restructuring Kazakhstan's relationship with Russia. Nevertheless, Kazakhstan became independent in 1991. After Kazakhstan's independence, many ethnic Russians left, and the population of the country is about two-thirds Kazakh today. Nevertheless, a substantial Russian minority remains in Kazakhstan. Substantial mineral deposits have been discovered in Kazakhstan, which has the most oil reserves in Central Asia and is also the second-largest producer of uranium in the world.

The Kazakh government moved the capital from Almaty, just north of the boundary between Kazakhstan and Uzbekistan, to the northern city of Astana in 1997. This was a controversial issue. The official reasons given were that Almaty was located in a seismic zone, with little room to expand because of nearby high mountains, and that Almaty was located near foreign borders. Despite the government's decision to move the capital to Astana, Almaty remains the largest city and the financial center of Kazakhstan.

Astana is located in an area with a large Russian population. Some saw this move as an attempt to integrate the Russian population into Kazakhstan and to increase ethnic Kazakh influence in the northern part of the country, where many people of Russian ancestry live. Given its large Russian population and its very cold climate, many government workers of Kazakh ancestry were unwilling to move to Astana. Other critics of the move to Astana argued that the construction of new government buildings in Astana was an unnecessary expenditure of public funds. The current population of Astana is about 600,000, of whom about 60 percent are of Kazakh ancestry. In 1989, in contrast, only about 17 percent of Astana's residents were ethnic Kazakhs. The increased number of Kazakhs in Astana reflects high levels of government employment there.

CONTEMPORARY ISSUES

In addition to addressing ongoing relationships between ethnic Kazakhs and Russians, Kazakhstan has been involved in conflict with its neighbors concerning access to the Caspian Sea. Kazakhstan, Russia, Azerbaijan, Iran, and Turkmenistan have coastlines on the Caspian Sea. For many years, these countries have disputed the delineation of maritime boundaries within the Caspian Sea, which is actually a lake in that it has no outlets to the open ocean. The Caspian Sea basin is rich in natural resources, and thus the delineation of maritime boundaries between the countries bordering the Caspian Sea is an issue of considerable economic importance.

See also   China, Kyrgyzstan, Russia, Turkmenistan, Uzbekistan

Further Reading
    Jonathan Aitken. *Kazakhstan: Surprises and stereotypes after 20 years of independence*. London: Continuum Press, 2012.

Dilip Hiro. *Inside Central Asia: A political and cultural history of Uzbekistan, Turkmenistan, Kazakhstan, Kyrgyzstan, Tajikistan, Russia, and Iran.* New York: Overlook TP, 2011.

Steve LeVine. *The oil and the glory: The pursuit of empire and fortune on the Caspian Sea.* New York: Random House, 2007.

Daniel Wagner and Luca Costa. "Kazakhstan's balancing act." *Foreign Policy Journal*, June 15, 2011, http://www.foreignpolicyjournal.com/2011/06/15/kazakhstans-balancing-act/.

Pat Walters. "Aral Sea recovery?" *National Geographic News*, April 2, 2010, http://news.nationalgeographic.com/news/2010/04/100402-aral-sea-story/.

KYRGYZSTAN

OVERVIEW

The Kyrgyz Republic is one of the five former Soviet republics located in Central Asia. It has a land area of 77,161 square miles, the size of South Dakota. Its population is about 5.8 million.

Kyrgyzstan is landlocked, with a highly irregular shape and complex borders. Kyrgyzstan has boundaries with Kazakhstan to the north, China to the southeast, Tajikistan to the south, and Uzbekistan to the west. As with the other former Soviet republics in Central Asia, the boundaries of Kyrgyzstan were drawn primarily to separate people belonging to the Kyrgyz nation from other nations. The Kyrgyz, like other nations in the former Soviet Central Asia, are Muslims who speak a Turkic language.

The tripoint between Kyrgyzstan, Kazakhstan, and Uzbekistan is located in the Tian Shan Mountains near the Aksu Zhabagly Nature Reserve in southern Kazakhstan. The boundary between Kyrgyzstan and Kazakhstan extends from this tripoint northeastward and eastward to the Talas River, which forms a small portion of the boundary itself. It extends eastward and extends parallel to the course of the Talas, then turns northward and northeastward again to a point northwest of the Kyrgyz capital of Bishkek. At this point, the boundary turns southeastward and follows the Chu River upstream. It then leaves the Chu and continues in an easterly direction north of Lake Issyk-Kul, which is located entirely in Kyrgyzstan and is the 10th-largest lake in the world by volume of water. It continues back into the main range of the Tian Shan to the tripoint between Kyrgyzstan, Kazakhstan, and China. This tripoint is located near Victory Peak (also known as Jengish Chokusu), which at an elevation of 24,406 feet above sea level is the highest peak in the Tian Shan range.

From the tripoint between Kyrgyzstan, China, and Kazakhstan, the boundary between Kyrgyzstan and China extends in a west-southwesterly direction along the Tian Shan. This boundary then turns southward between the Tian Shan and the Pamir range. The tripoint between Kyrgyzstan, China, and Tajikistan is located high in the Pamir range near Karakul Lake, which at an altitude of over 13,000 feet above sea level is among the highest natural lakes in elevation in the world. From this tripoint, the highly complex boundary between Kyrgyzstan and Tajikistan extends westward, turns northward, and then turns eastward again to the tripoint between

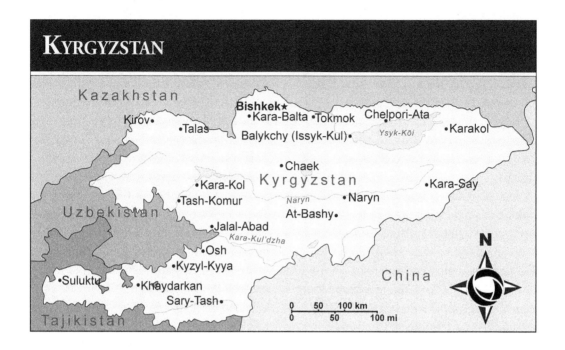

Kyrgyzstan, Tajikistan, and Turkmenistan a few miles north of the town of Batken. The boundary between Kyrgyzstan and Uzbekistan is also highly irregular. It divides the densely populated and fertile Fergana Valley between the two countries. Four Uzbek exclaves south of the boundary are surrounded by Kyrgyz territory, including the Uzbek exclave of Sokh with about 50,000 inhabitants.

HISTORICAL CONTEXT

Kyrgyzstan, like many of its neighbors in Central Asia, is located along major trade routes connecting East Asia, Europe, and Southwest Asia along what came to be known as the Silk Road. It has been an important center for trade for more than 1,000 years, and Lake Issyk-Kul became an important stopping point for caravans laden with trade goods on their way to and from East Asia. In the early ninth century

AD, a Kyrgyz kingdom became dominant in what is now Kyrgyzstan and areas to the north. This kingdom was overthrown by Mongols in the early 13th century, and many people of Kyrgyz nationality moved southward into present-day Kyrgyzstan. After the Mongol Empire's power waned, modern Kyrgyzstan was invaded successively by other Mongol tribes, by the Qing dynasty of China, and by an Uzbek khanate. Throughout this period, many Kyrgyz people were nomads whose day-to-day lives were unaffected by these foreign rulers.

The Uzbek khanate, known as the Khanate of Kokand, was in control of present-day Kyrgyzstan when the Russian Empire expanded into Kyrgyzstan in the second half of the 19th century. Kyrgyzstan was incorporated formally into the Russian Empire in 1876. After the Russian Revolution, Kyrgyzstan became part of the Soviet Union. At first, Kyrgyzstan was an autonomous oblast within the Soviet Union, but it was elevated to full republic status in 1936 as the Kirghiz Soviet Socialist Republic. The borders between Kyrgyzstan and its neighbors, which had been delineated only loosely before the Soviets seized power, were delineated precisely during this period.

The Soviets pursued a policy of Russification, encouraging people of Russian nationality to move into Kyrgyzstan. By 1989, only a minority of the residents of the Kyrgyz capital of Bishkek (then known as Frunze) were of Kyrgyz ethnicity. The Kyrgyzstan Democratic Movement coordinated anti-Soviet activities although many Kyrgyz people preferred continued association with the Soviet Union. A referendum on independence was held in March 1991, and nearly 90 percent of the voters indicated a preference for continued association. However, after the collapse of the Soviet Union in October 1991, proindependence sentiment increased. Kyrgyzstan declared its independence as the Republic of Kyrgyzstan. In 1993, the country's name was changed to the Kyrgyz Republic.

Since independence, Kyrgyzstan has not been fully successful in implementing a stable democracy. The government of Kyrgyzstan's first president, Askar Akayev, was overthrown in 2005 following elections that were regarded widely as corrupt and fraudulent. This overthrow came to be known as the Tulip Revolution. In 2010, riots broke out throughout the country in protest of governmental corruption. Ethnic violence between the majority Kyrgyz and minority Uzbeks also flared up. Although ethnic Kyrgyz people make up about 70 percent of the population of Kyrgyzstan, ethnic Uzbeks are the majority in southern Kyrgyzstan near the Uzbekistan border.

As many as 100,000 Uzbeks left the country after violence broke out, most moving across the border into Uzbekistan.

CONTEMPORARY ISSUES

Ethnic conflicts continue to plague Kyrgyzstan. Although the boundaries between Kyrgyzstan and its neighbors were delineated by the Soviets, with the intention of dividing the populations of the Central Asian Soviet republics along ethnic and national lines, some of the boundaries have not been delineated and marked on the ground. The boundary between Kyrgyzstan and Uzbekistan is contested most strongly, in part because of Kyrgyzstan's recent history of violence between ethnic Kyrgyz and Uzbeks. Conflict also continues over the status of the Sokh enclave and other small Uzbek enclaves that are surrounded by Kyrgyz territory.

See also   China, Kazakhstan, Tajikistan, Uzbekistan

Further Reading

Dilip Hiro. *Inside Central Asia: A political and cultural history of Uzbekistan, Turkmenistan, Kazakhstan, Kyrgyzstan, Tajikistan, Russia, and Iran.* New York: Overlook TP, 2011.

Jim Nichol. "Kyrgyzstan: Recent developments and U.S. interests." Congressional Research Service, January 19, 2012, http://www.fas.org/sgp/crs/row/97-690.pdf.

Willis Sparks and Ana Jelenkovic. "Foreign policy: Why Kyrgyzstan matters." *NPR*, June 16, 2010, http://www.npr.org/templates/story/story.php?storyId=127876051.

MONGOLIA

OVERVIEW

Mongolia is a landlocked country located in east-central Asia. It has a land area of 603,909 square miles, slightly larger than Alaska. Its population is about 2.8 million, making Mongolia one of the most sparsely populated countries in the world.

Mongolia has two neighbors, Russia to the north and China to the south. The western tripoint between Mongolia, Russia, and China is located about 25 miles west of the easternmost point in Kazakhstan. This tripoint is located in the Altai Mountains. From the tripoint, the boundary between Mongolia and Russia extends eastward to Uvs Lake. Uvs Lake is the largest natural lake in Mongolia, but its northern end extends across the boundary into Russia. East of Lake Uvs, the boundary roughly follows the drainage divide between the Yenisey River in Russia and rivers flowing southward into Mongolia. Near the source of the Delgermörön River, the boundary turns northward. The Delgermörön is a tributary of the Yenisey, and north-central Mongolia is located within the Yenisey drainage basin. The boundary turns eastward again northwest of Lake Khovsgol and then extends in an easterly direction to the eastern tripoint. This section of the boundary follows straight-line segments, and the boundary region is very sparsely populated.

From the eastern tripoint, the boundary between Mongolia and China extends in a generally southwestwardly direction into the Gobi Desert. However, the easternmost

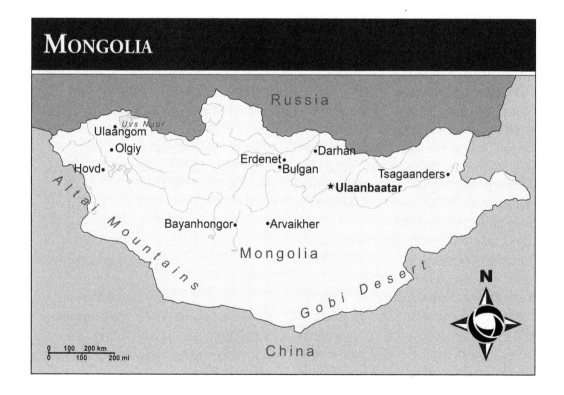

section of the boundary begins in a southerly direction, then turns abruptly eastward to a point near Mongolia's Numrug National Park. From there it turns southwestward, then turns in a more westerly direction into the desert itself. Here it crosses almost rainless and nearly uninhabited territory. West of Great Gobi Park in Mongolia, the boundary turns northwestward into the Altai range. At its westward end, the boundary follows the crests of the high peaks of the Altai.

HISTORICAL CONTEXT

Discoveries of cave paintings and various artifacts confirm that present-day Mongolia has been inhabited by humans for at least 40,000 years. For the last several thousand years, Mongolia has been inhabited by pastoral nomads who traveled great distances on horseback. In the second and third centuries BC, China's rulers began the construction of the Great Wall of China to protect China against Mongol incursions. The Great Wall was expanded, maintained, and protected by soldiers for 2,000 years. The portion of the Great Wall closest to present-day Mongolia is located south of the eastern section of the present boundary between Mongolia and China.

In the late 12th century, a Mongol chieftain by the name of Temujin united most of the nomadic Mongol tribes. Taking the name Genghis Khan, Temujin established the Mongol Empire, which at its height controlled Eurasia from present-day western Russia to Siberia and China. Mongols ruled China as the Yuan dynasty for more than 100 years, until armies of the Ming dynasty pushed the Mongols northward into Mongolia's present-day territory. In the 17th century, China's Qing dynasty took control of present-day Mongolia and incorporated it into China's empire. What is now Mongolia was known at that time as Outer Mongolia, in contrast to Inner Mongolia south and east of Outer Mongolia.

The Qing dynasty collapsed in 1911, and Outer Mongolia declared its independence. During and after World War I, however, Mongolia was invaded by both Chinese and Russian armies. Bolshevik troops seized control of the country and established a communist government, which remained in power until the Soviet Union collapsed in 1991. At that time the country came to be known as the People's Republic of Mongolia. Although Mongolia has more ethnic and cultural affinities with East Asia than with European Russia, Mongolia remained aligned closely with the Soviet Union and supported the Soviets against China during and after the Sino-Soviet Split in the 1950s.

Soviet domination of Mongolia ended with the Peaceful Democratic Revolution in 1990, and the words "People's Republic" were dropped from the country's name. A multiparty democracy was implemented, and Mongolia began a transition toward a market economy. Mongolia's boundaries with Russia and China, which pass through very sparsely populated territory, are stable and uncontested.

See also China, Russia

Further Reading

Daniel Allen. "China breathes new life into Mongolia." *Asia Times Online*, September 1, 2007, http://www.atimes.com/atimes/China_Business/II01Cb02.html.

Uradyn Bulag. *The Mongols at China's edge: History and the politics of national unity*. Lanham, MD: Rowman and Little-field, 2002.

Morris Rossabi. *Modern Mongolia: From Khans to commissars to capitalists.* Berkeley: University of California Press, 2005.

NORTH KOREA

OVERVIEW

The Democratic People's Republic of Korea, which is known generally as North Korea, occupies the northern half of the Korean peninsula in East Asia. North Korea has a land area of 46,528 square miles, about the size of Pennsylvania. Its population is about 25 million.

North Korea has a boundary with the People's Republic of China to the northwest, a very brief boundary with Russia to the northeast, and a boundary with South Korea to the south. North Korea has coastlines on the Korean Bay to the west and the Sea of Japan to the east. Most of the boundary between North Korea and China follows rivers. The boundary extends in a northeasterly direction upstream along the Yalu River to a point near its source on Baekdu Mountain, which is known in China as Changbai Mountain. The Yalu contains more than 200 islands, which have been divided between North Korea and China on the basis of the ethnic backgrounds of their residents. The Tumen River forms the boundary between North Korea and China northeast of Baekdu Mountain as far as the tripoint between North Korea, China, and Russia. The Tumen is also the boundary between North Korea and Russia until it empties into the Sea of Japan. This boundary is less than 10 miles long.

The boundary between North Korea and South Korea crosses the Korean peninsula and is located roughly along the 38th parallel of north latitude. This boundary is located at the center of the Korea Demilitarized Zone, which is about 2.5 miles in width. It is one of the most heavily militarized and fortified borders in the world.

HISTORICAL CONTEXT

The Korean peninsula has been occupied by humans for thousands of years. About 2,000 years ago, the peninsula, along with parts of neighboring Manchuria, was controlled by the Three Kingdoms of Goguryeo to the north, Baekje to the southwest, and Silla to the southeast. The Silla dynasty conquered the other two empires in the seventh century AD and established control over the entire peninsula. The Silla Empire maintained close ties with the Tang dynasty of Korea but retained its status as an independent nation. The Silla regime was toppled by the Goryeo regime in the 10th century, which remained in power until the late 14th century. The country's modern name of Korea was derived from the Goryeo's name.

The Goryeo were overthrown by the Joseon dynasty in 1392, and the Joseon ruled Korea for the next 500 years. In 1897, King Gojong of the Joseon dynasty proclaimed the Empire of Korea. However, the empire was caught in tensions between the Russian Empire and Japan. Korea became a Japanese protectorate in 1907 and was annexed formally into the Japanese Empire in 1910.

Korea remained under Japanese rule until the end of World War II in 1945.

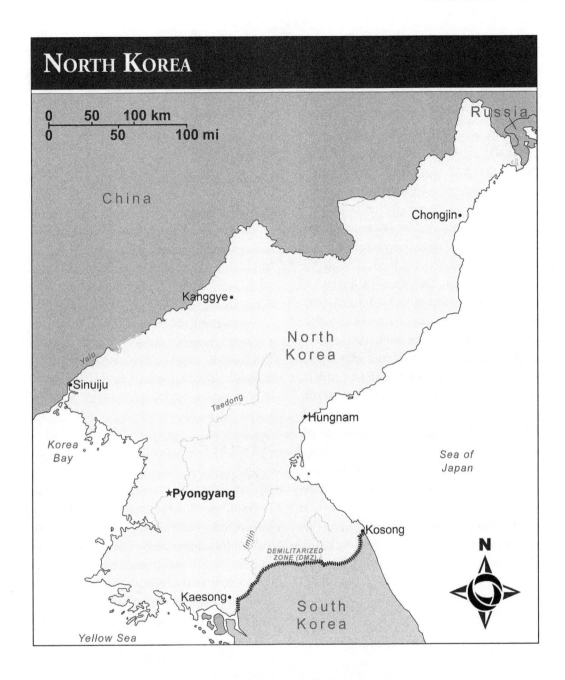

After the war ended, the peninsula was divided into two occupation zones, with a Soviet occupation zone in the north and an American occupation zone in the south. At that time, the United Nations intended that the two sectors would be reunited eventually. However, Soviet forces dominated the northern sector and proclaimed the area north of the 38th parallel as the Democratic People's Republic of Korea while South Korea became independent with American military support. North

Korea soon became a communist dictatorship with aspirations of reunifying the entire country under communist rule.

In 1950, North Korean troops crossed the 38th parallel and invaded South Korea with support from the People's Republic of China and the Soviet Union. The invasion triggered the Korean War. The United States and the United Nations intervened on the side of South Korea. The war lasted three years, and nearly 36,000 American troops and more than 400,000 Korean soldiers were killed in the conflict. In 1953, a cease-fire was agreed upon. The cease-fire agreement established the Korean Demilitarized Zone, located near the points at which the armies of the two countries were stationed.

After the end of the Korean War, North Korea became one of the most isolated countries in the world, with one of the world's most repressive regimes. North Korea's ruler, Kim Il-sung, ruled North Korea as a dictator, with a strong personality cult, until he died in 1994. He was succeeded by his son Kim Jong-Il, who remained in power until his own death in 2011. Kim Jong-Il was succeeded by his son, Kim Jong-un. The economy of North Korea declined steadily, and its decline intensified after the collapse of the Soviet Union in 1991.

CONTEMPORARY ISSUES

North Korea remains one of the most isolated and most repressive regimes in the world, and it continues to push for reunification with South Korea under its communist regime. International observers have pointed out that North Korea's regime has one of the worst records of protecting human rights in the world, with thousands of people incarcerated in concentration camps. Despite its relatively small population, North Korea's army is the fourth largest in the world. In recent years, North Korea pushed the development of nuclear weapons over concerted international opposition.

See also   China, Russia, South Korea

Further Reading

Victor Cha. *The impossible state: North Korea, present and future.* New York: HarperCollins, 2012.

Aiden Foster-Carter. "South Korea–North Korea relations: A turning point?" *Comparative Connections*, 2012, http://csis.org/files/publication/1102qnk_sk.pdf.

Young W. Kihl and Hong Nack Kim. *North Korea: The politics of regime survival.* Armonk, NY: M. E. Sharpe, 2006.

SOUTH KOREA

OVERVIEW

The Republic of Korea, which is known generally as South Korea, is located in East Asia at the southern end of the Korean peninsula. South Korea's land area is 38,691 square miles, slightly smaller than Kentucky. Its population is about 50 million, making it about twice as large by population as neighboring North Korea.

North Korea is South Korea's only land neighbor and is located, as its name implies, to the north of South Korea. It extends across the Korean peninsula in a roughly east-west direction near the 38th parallel of north latitude. The boundary is located at the center of the Korea Demilitarized Zone, which was established at the end of the Korean War and is about 2.5

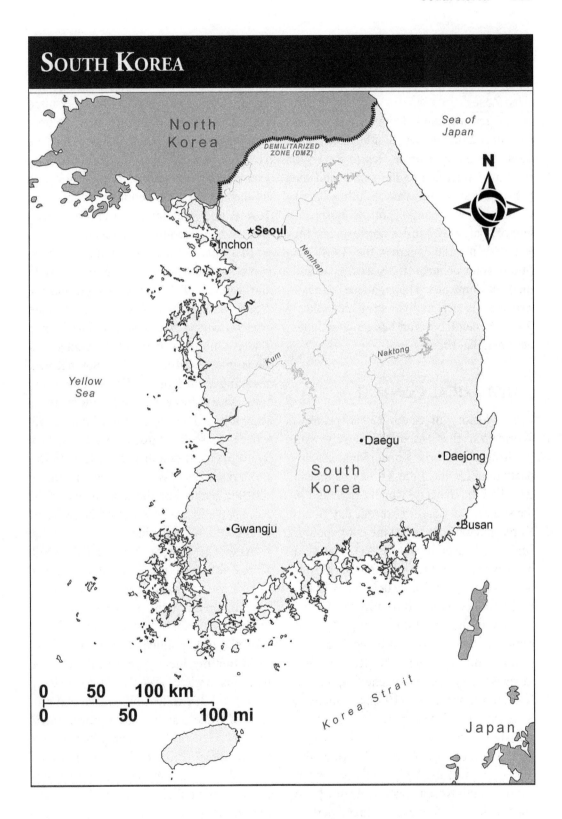

miles wide. Both South Korea and North Korea station large numbers of troops along the edges of the Korean Demilitarized Zone.

The rest of South Korea's territory is surrounded by water. South Korea has coastlines on the Korean Bay to the west, the East China Sea to the south, and the Sea of Japan to the east. South Korea's second-largest city, the port of Busan, is approximately 120 miles northwest of the Japanese mainland across the Tsushima Strait, which connects the Sea of Japan and the East China Sea. The Japanese island of Tsushima is located in the strait about halfway between the South Korean and Japanese mainland coasts.

HISTORICAL CONTEXT

The history of South Korea prior to World War II is associated closely with the history of North Korea. The first dynasty to unify all of the Korean peninsula was the Silla dynasty, which originated in the southeastern part of present-day South Korea and took control of the entire peninsula in the seventh century AD. The Silla dynasty was overthrown by the Goryeo dynasty, from which Korea derives its name, in the 10th century and later by the Joseon dynasty in the late 14th century. The Joseons retained power until the late 19th century, during which the Russian and Japanese empires encroached upon the Korean peninsula. In 1910, Japan annexed Korea as part of the Japanese Empire.

After Japan was stripped of its empire at the end of World War II, under the auspices of the United Nations, what is now South Korea was occupied by the United States while the northern part of the peninsula was occupied by the Soviet Union. The 38th parallel became the boundary between the two occupation zones. During the late 1940s, the United Nations intended that the two occupation zones would eventually be reunified. However, a Soviet-based communist government seized control of North Korea as the Democratic People's Republic of Korea, and it claimed the entire Korean peninsula as a communist dictatorship.

In 1950, North Korea attempted to assert control over the entire peninsula. With the backing of the Soviet Union and the People's Republic of China, North Korean forces invaded South Korea. The United States, with the support of the United Nations, intervened on the side of South Korea, resulting in the Korean War. Over the next three years, more than 400,000 Koreans were killed. The war continued until 1953, when a cease-fire agreement was reached. The agreement established the Korean Demilitarized Zone, which is located north of the 38th parallel on the eastern side of the Korean peninsula but south of the 38th parallel on the western side.

After the Korean War ended, South Korea followed the lead of Japan and other East Asian countries and developed its economy rapidly. However, the government was run by autocratic rulers who tolerated little political dissent. South Korea's first president, Synghan Rhee, ruled until his regime was forced to give up power in 1960 following widespread protests of Rhee's authoritarian government. In 1961, General Park Chung-hee became South Korea's military dictator, and he remained in power until he was assassinated in 1979. Nevertheless, standards of living rose quickly under the Park regime and continue to rise today. The per capita income of South Korea has risen to a level comparable to those of many developed European countries, in sharp contrast to very poor and isolated North Korea. Since Park's assassination, democracy began to take hold in South Korea, and multiparty elections are held on a regular and consistent basis.

CONTEMPORARY ISSUES

South Korea's major foreign policy concern remains its relationship with North Korea. South Korea maintains a large military force against the ongoing threat of another North Korean invasion. Especially since 2000, talks concerning possible reunification of the two Koreas have been held sporadically. Yet ideological differences between the two countries are vast, and neither regime is willing to yield to the other's claims over its territory. Conflict has been intensified in response to North Korea's development and testing of nuclear weapons. The boundary along the Korean Demilitarized Zone remains one of the most heavily militarized boundaries in the entire world, with thousands of troops stationed on both sides.

South Korea and Japan have also disputed the name of the body of water separating the two countries between the east coast of South Korea and the west coast of Japan. This body of water is known generally as the Sea of Japan. However, South Korea has asked that the international community change its name to the East Sea. In 2012, the International Hydrographic Organization considered and declined South Korea's request.

See also   North Korea

Further Reading

Bruce Cummins. *Korea's place in the sun: A modern history.* New York: W. W. Norton, 2005.

Myung Oak Kim and Sam Jaffe. *The new Korea: Inside Korea's economic rise.* New York: AMACOM, 2010.

Esther Pan. "South Korea's ties with China, Japan, and the U.S.: Defining a new role in a dangerous neighborhood." Council on Foreign Relations, February 8, 2006, http://www.cfr.org/east-asia/south-koreas-ties-china-japan-us-defining-new-role-dangerous-neighborhood/p9808.

TAIWAN

OVERVIEW

The Republic of China includes the island of Taiwan off the coast of mainland China along with a few smaller islands nearby. Although the Republic of China's government claims to be the legitimate government of all of China, the republic is generally known by the name of its main island. Taiwan's land area is 13,974 square miles, slightly larger than Maryland and Delaware combined. Its population is about 24 million. About 84 percent of the people are ethnic Taiwanese, and most of the others are of Han Chinese ancestry. At its closest point, the island of Taiwan is less than 100 miles southeast off the coast of mainland China across the Taiwan Strait. Taiwan is about 150 miles east of the southwesternmost of the Ryukyu Islands of Japan, and the southern tip of the island is about 250 miles north of the main island of Luzon in the Philippines.

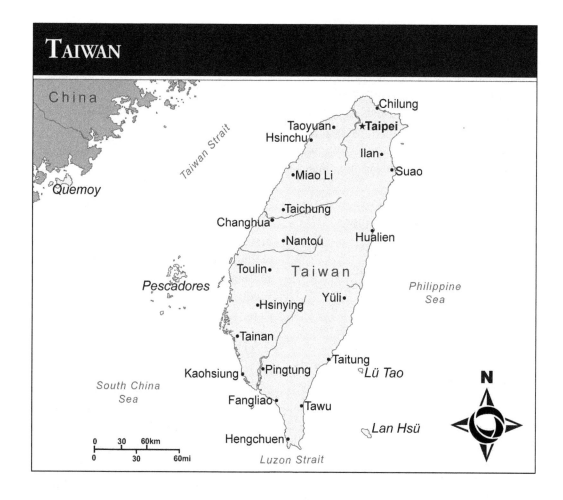

HISTORICAL CONTEXT

Archaeologists have discovered human remains and artifacts on the island of Taiwan that date back to at least 25,000 years ago. Farmers from the Asian mainland are believed to have moved to Taiwan about 5,000 to 6,000 years ago, developing what came to be known as the Dapenkeng culture. Many of the people of the Philippines, Southeast Asia, and the Pacific Islands are believed to be descended from these early inhabitants of Taiwan.

The first Europeans to visit Taiwan were Portuguese settlers who named the island Formosa in 1544. Trading centers on the Taiwanese coast were established by the Dutch and by the Spanish in the 17th century. The Netherlands attempted to establish a Dutch colony on Taiwan, but the Dutch were expelled by Chinese forces in the mid-17th century. The remnants of the Ming dynasty tried to establish Taiwan as a base from which to retake the government of mainland China, but the ruling Qing dynasty took over Taiwan in the early 18th century.

In 1895, Japanese forces defeated China in the First Sino-Japanese War. Under terms of the Treaty of Shimonoseki, which ended the war, Taiwan was ceded to Japan. Taiwan became a base of Japanese military operations against the Republic of China in the 1930s and against Allied forces during World War II.

After World War II, sovereignty over Taiwan was returned to the Republic of China. At that time, China was embroiled in civil war between the nationalist government and communist rebels led by Mao Zedong. The war ended in 1949 with a communist victory, and the communists established the People's Republic of China. However, more than a million nationalist government officials, military leaders, and business owners moved across the Taiwan Strait into Taiwan. The nationalist government's leader, Chiang Kai-Shek, moved the government to Taiwan while retaining its claim over all of China. The nationalist government remains in control of Taiwan today. The People's Republic of China does not recognize Taiwan's government and regards Taiwan as part of the People's Republic.

During the 1950s and 1960s, the People's Republic was isolated from the international community, and the United States, many other Western countries, and the United Nations continued to recognize the nationalists as China's legitimate government. However, the United Nations withdrew its recognition of the nationalists and recognized the People's Republic in 1971. The United States followed suit in 1979. Chiang Kai-Shek maintained authoritarian rule over Taiwan until he died in 1975. After Chiang's death, Taiwan's economy grew rapidly, and the country began a transition toward democracy. The first fully democratic election was held in 1996.

CONTEMPORARY ISSUES

The major foreign relations issue involving Taiwan remains its relationship with the People's Republic of China, which does not recognize Taiwan's government and continues to press its claim of sovereignty over the island. The nationalist government maintains a large military force in response to concerns about a possible mainland Chinese invasion of Taiwan. Taiwan remains concerned also about a possible naval blockade by China. In 1996, the United States and Japan signed a treaty stipulating that the two countries would respond to attacks on the "areas surrounding Japan," but it is unclear whether the two countries regard Taiwan as among these areas. Given the People's Republic's size and economic power, many observers doubt if the United States or Japan would offer military support to Taiwan in response to a possible invasion.

A related issue involves the extent to which Taiwan's residents consider themselves to be Taiwanese. Both the government of Taiwan and the government of the People's Republic regard themselves as the only legitimate government of both Taiwan and the mainland. However, many Taiwanese residents regard themselves as Taiwanese only, rather than as Chinese. Those seeing themselves as Taiwanese also see Taiwan and the People's Republic as separate countries. Public opinion surveys have shown that younger people, who have no memory of China and Taiwan as the same country, are more likely to regard themselves as Taiwanese exclusively.

Further Reading

Shyu-tu Lee, Douglas Paal, and Charles Glaser. "Disengaging from Taiwan: Should Washington continue its alliance with Taipei?" *Foreign Affairs*, July/August 2011.

Shelley Rigger. *Why Taiwan matters: Small island, global perspective.* Lanham, MD: Rowman and Littlefield, 2011.

Alan Wachman. *Why Taiwan? Geostrategic rationales for China's territorial integrity.* Palo Alto, CA: Stanford University Press, 2007.

TAJIKISTAN

OVERVIEW

The Republic of Tajikistan is a former Soviet republic located in Central Asia. Tajikistan has a land area of 55,251 square miles, the size of Illinois. It has a population of about 8 million. Tajikistan is the poorest of the former Soviet republics that became independent after the collapse of the Soviet Union in the early 1990s.

Landlocked Tajikistan is bordered by Uzbekistan to the north and west, Kyrgyzstan to the north, China to the east, and Afghanistan to the south. It is separated from the disputed Indian and Pakistani territory of Jammu and Kashmir by the long and narrow Wakhan Corridor in northeastern Afghanistan. About 80 percent of Tajikistan's population is made up of people of the Tajik nation. The Tajiks are related closely to Iranians. Most are Muslims, and they speak a language that is similar to the Persian language of Iran. Most of Tajikistan is mountainous, with the Pamir Mountains occupying the eastern half of the country, including those parts of Tajikistan that border China and Afghanistan. Much of this region is more than 10,000 feet above sea level, and it contains eight peaks that have elevations of more than

20,000 feet. Eastern Tajikistan is very sparsely populated. The large majority of Tajiks live in the more fertile lower elevations of the western part of the country.

Tajikistan's boundaries are highly complex. Its boundaries with Uzbekistan, Kyrgyzstan, and China were delineated in large part in order to separate Tajik nationals in Tajikistan from other nations living in neighboring countries. The tripoint between Tajikistan, Uzbekistan, and Afghanistan is located on the Amu Darya River northeast of the Afghan city of Mazar-i-Sharif. The boundary between Tajikistan and Uzbekistan follows short straight-line segments in a generally northerly direction to a point near the Tajik town of Panjakent. It then turns to the east, then northward again but in a highly irregular pattern. The northern part of Tajikistan is separated from the rest of the country by a strip of land only 20 miles wide at its narrowest point, and the region between northern Tajikistan and the other main center of population in the southwest is mountainous, with some peaks over 18,000 feet in elevation. This portion of Tajikistan contains part of the fertile Fergana Valley, which is watered by the Syr Darya River. The Syr Darya itself forms a brief segment of the boundary between Tajikistan and Uzbekistan.

The Tajik portion of the Fergana Valley surrounds the Karakum Reservoir. East of the reservoir, a small strip of territory about 25 miles long and three to five miles wide extends eastward from the town of Isfara to the tripoint between Tajikistan, Uzbekistan, and Kyrgyzstan. From this tripoint, the boundary between Tajikistan and Kyrgyzstan extends westward south of the reservoir, then southward, and then back eastward, past Pamirsky National

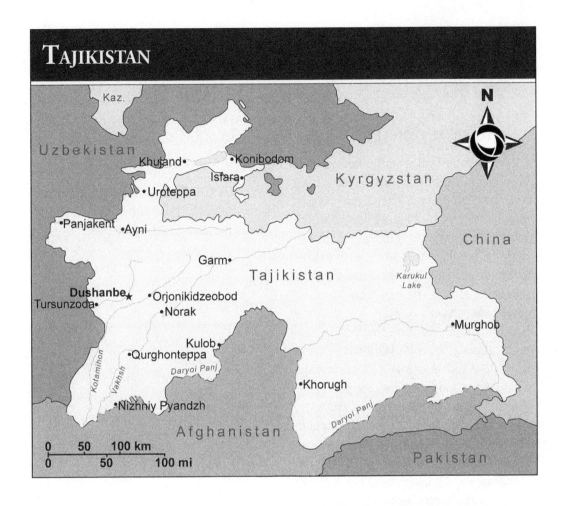

TAJIKISTAN

Park and into the high mountains of the Pamirs to the tripoint between Tajikistan, Kyrgyzstan, and China. This tripoint is located north of Karakul Lake, a natural lake located high in the Pamirs at an elevation of nearly 13,000 feet above sea level.

The boundary between Tajikistan and China follows straight-line segments through the Pamirs, reaching the tripoint between Tajikistan, China, and Afghanistan at the extreme eastern end of the Wakhan Corridor. Some of this boundary is located at the drainage divide between the Amu Darya and streams flowing eastward into China. Most of the boundary

between Tajikistan and Afghanistan follows the Amu Darya and its tributaries. The Pamir River forms much of the border between Tajikistan and the Wakhan Corridor. The Pamir empties into the Panj River, which makes up most of the boundary west of the Wakhan Corridor. The Panj flows northward and then back eastward, descending from the higher elevations of the Hindu Kush as it does so. The Amu Darya is formed by the confluence of the Panj and Vakhsh rivers near the southwestern corner of Tajikistan, and the boundary between Tajikistan and Afghanistan follows the Amu Darya westward and downstream to the tripoint between Tajiki-stan, Afghanistan, and Uzbekistan. Many ethnic Tajiks live on the Afghanistan side of this boundary.

HISTORICAL CONTEXT

The Fergana Valley and other parts of present-day Tajikistan have been settled for at least 6,000 years. The region was part of the Persian Achaemenid Empire, which was overthrown by Alexander the Great in the fourth century BC. Various dynasties controlled modern Tajikistan for the next thousand years. Islam was brought to the area in the seventh century AD, and the Samanid Empire became the first locally based dynasty to rule Tajikistan during the 9th and 10th centuries AD. During the Middle Ages, Tajikistan became part of the Mongol realm. The Emirate of Bukhara, which was centered in the city of Bukhara in present-day Uzbekistan, seized power in 1785 and ruled present-day Tajikistan.

During the 19th century, the Russian Empire began to encroach on Central Asia. Russia took control over the land between the Caspian Sea and the northern bound-ary of Afghanistan between 1864 and 1885. This area, which was called Russian Turkestan by the Russian government, in-cluded all of modern Tajikistan. After the fall of the Russian Empire in 1917, local leaders in Tajikistan and neighboring por-tions of Russian Turkestan agitated for independence. However, the Bolsheviks suppressed these efforts. Tajikistan was in-corporated into the Soviet Union in 1924 as part of Uzbekistan, but it was separated from Uzbekistan in 1929 and became the Tajik Soviet Socialist Republic. As the So-viet Union collapsed, Tajikistan declared independence in 1991. Civil war broke out in 1992 and lasted until 1997.

CONTEMPORARY ISSUES

Many of Tajikistan's boundaries have been defined imprecisely, and efforts are being made to delineate them precisely. The boundary between Tajikistan and China in the Pamirs has been contested since the late 19th century, when Tajiki-stan was controlled by the Russian Empire. China has claimed about 15,000 square miles of territory along the border between Tajikistan and China. The dispute was in-herited by the Soviet Union and later by Tajikistan as successor states to the Rus-sian Empire. In 1996, Tajikistan and China began negotiations to resolve their bound-ary dispute. A 2002 agreement awarded most of the disputed territory to Tajikistan, although Tajikistan ceded several hundred square miles of territory to China. Nego-tiations between Tajikistan and Uzbekistan and between Tajikistan and Kyrgyzstan to define these boundaries more precisely are ongoing.

See also   Afghanistan, China, Kyrgyz-stan, Uzbekistan

Further Reading

George Gavrilis. "The Tajik solution." *Foreign Affairs*, November 22, 2009.

Dilip Hiro. *Inside Central Asia: A po-litical and cultural history of Uzbekistan, Turkmenistan, Kazakhstan, Kyrgyzstan, Tajikistan, Russia, and Iran.* New York: Overlook TP, 2011.

International Boundaries Research Unit. "Tajikistan ratifies demarcation agreement with China in settlement of long-running dispute." January 13, 2011, http://www.dur.ac.uk/ibru/news/bound-ary_news/?itemno=11360&grehref=%2F ibru%2Fnews%2F&resubj=Boundary+n ews%20Headlines.

TURKMENISTAN

OVERVIEW

Turkmenistan is a former Soviet republic in Central Asia. Its land area is 188,456 square miles, slightly smaller than Nevada and Utah combined. Thus, Turkmenistan is the second-largest former Soviet republic in Central Asia by land area. Its population is about 5.3 million. Much of Turkmenistan is arid and covered by deserts.

Turkmenistan, like the other former Soviet republics in Central Asia, is landlocked. Its neighbors are Kazakhstan to the north, Uzbekistan to the northeast, Afghanistan to the southeast, and Iran to the south. Western Turkmenistan has a lengthy coastline on the Caspian Sea. The boundary between Turkmenistan and Kazakhstan extends in an easterly direction from the Caspian. It begins north of the city of Garabogaz, which is known also as Bekdas. The boundary extends eastward just to the north of the Garabogazköl Lagoon, a shallow lake separated by a narrow ridge of land that extends south from the city. East of the lagoon, the boundary extends southeastward and then eastward to the tripoint between Turkmenistan, Kazakhstan, and Uzbekistan west of a national park known as the Kaplankyr Reserve.

The boundary between Turkmenistan and Uzbekistan goes eastward from this tripoint to the reserve along two straight lines that extend in an east-southeasterly direction. From the reserve, the boundary becomes irregular. It extends northward and northeastward to Sarygamysh Lake, which is located on the boundary. It then extends northeastward and then southeastward to the Amu Darya River. The boundary follows the Amu Darya briefly and continues southeastward west of the main channel of the river. Further southeastward, it follows the drainage divide between the Amu Darya on the Uzbekistan side of the boundary and southward-flowing streams in Turkmenistan southeastward to the tripoint between Turkmenistan, Uzbekistan, and Afghanistan.

Most of the boundary between Turkmenistan and Afghanistan extends along numerous short straight-line segments extending in a southwesterly direction. This region is mountainous and dry, with very few residents. The tripoint between Turkmenistan, Afghanistan, and Iran is located on the Harirud River. The boundary between Turkmenistan and Iran follows the Harirud downstream and northward to a point north of the Iranian town of Sarakhs. The boundary turns westward along four straight-line segments, then turns northwestward into the Kopet Dag Mountains west of the city of Ashgabat (which was known as Ashkhabad during Soviet times). The westernmost segment of the boundary follows the Atrek River from its confluence with the Sumbar River westward and downstream to the Atrek's mouth in the Caspian Sea.

HISTORICAL CONTEXT

About 85 percent of Turkmenistan's people are ethnic Turkmens, who are Muslims and speak a Turkic language. Present-day Turkmenistan has a long history of

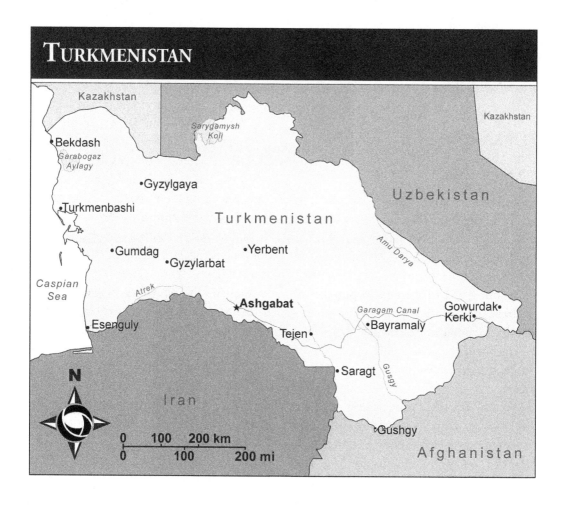

control by empires based outside of the modern country. The region was part of the Persian-based Achaemenid Basin in the first millennium BC. It was conquered by Alexander the Great, then became part of Persia's Parthian Kingdom. In the 10th and 11th centuries, most of modern Turkmenistan was ruled by the locally based Seljuk Empire. The Seljuks were deposed by the Mongols under Genghis Khan in the 13th century. After the Mongols were deposed in the 15th century, Turkmen territory was contested among various empires based in neighboring countries, including modern Iran and Uzbekistan. Several wars among these empires were fought in what is now Turkmenistan.

In the 19th century, the Russian Empire established ports on the Caspian Sea and encroached southward into what is now Turkmenistan. Russia conquered Turkmenistan in the late 19th century, establishing full control of the region by the 1890s. The Russian Empire encouraged ethnic Russians to move to present-day Turkmenistan, where many developed irrigation systems in order to farm this arid region. After the Russian Revolution, Turkmenistan was incorporated into the Soviet Union. Turkmenistan became the Turkmen Soviet Socialist

Republic in 1924. At that time, Soviet officials delineated its boundaries relative to other Soviet republics.

Turkmenistan became independent in 1991 as the Soviet Union collapsed. A former Communist Party leader, Saparmurad Niyazov, became Turkmenistan's first president. Niyazov's rule was autocratic and included a strong personality cult. In 1999, the constitution of Turkmenistan was amended in order to allow Niyazov to serve as the country's president for life. Niyazov remained president until he died in 2006, and his successor has begun transitioning Turkmenistan toward multiparty democracy with free elections.

CONTEMPORARY ISSUES

Turkmenistan is one of five countries (along with Iran, Azerbaijan, Russia, and Kazakhstan) with coasts on the Caspian Sea. For many years, these countries have disputed maritime boundaries within the Caspian Sea. The question of maritime boundaries is important for several reasons. The Caspian Sea basin is rich in oil and natural gas and includes some lucrative fishing grounds. Thus maritime boundaries between the countries bordering the Caspian Sea can have considerable economic impact on these countries.

Transportation is another key issue. The Caspian Sea has no natural outlets to the ocean. However, the Caspian is connected to the Black Sea, and hence to the Mediterranean Sea and the Atlantic Ocean, by canals. The idea of constructing a canal connecting streams flowing into the Caspian Sea to those flowing into the Black Sea was first proposed by the Ottomans in the 16th century and was later pursued

by the Russian czar Peter the Great in the early 18th century. The Volga-Don Canal, connecting these major Russian rivers that empty into the Caspian and Black seas, was finally constructed by the Soviets and opened to shipping in 1952. The canal is now located within Russia. Turkmenistan and the other landlocked countries must rely on the canal for any maritime access to the open ocean. In 1940, the Soviet Union and Iran signed a treaty declaring that the Caspian Sea, with no outflow into the ocean, is a lake and that it was to be divided between Russian and Iranian territories. After the Soviet Union was dissolved, however, the newly independent and landlocked states of Turkmenistan, Kazakhstan, and Azerbaijan proposed that the Caspian be divided in accordance with the length of each country's coastline. The specific maritime boundaries, as well as the question of access to the open sea via the Volga-Don Canal and other artificial waterways, remain unresolved.

See also Afghanistan, Iran, Kazakhstan, Uzbekistan

Further Reading

Dilip Hiro. *Inside Central Asia: A political and cultural history of Uzbekistan, Turkmenistan, Kazakhstan, Kyrgyzstan, Tajikistan, Russia, and Iran.* New York: Overlook TP, 2011.

Adeeb Khalid. *Islam after communism: Religion and politics in Central Asia.* Berkeley: University of California Press, 2007.

Steve LeVine. *The oil and the glory: The pursuit of empire and fortune on the Caspian Sea.* New York: Random House, 2007.

UZBEKISTAN

OVERVIEW

The Republic of Uzbekistan is the second largest of the five former Soviet republics in Central Asia and is the most populous of these five countries. Uzbekistan has a land area of about 173,000 square miles, slightly larger than California. The population of Uzbekistan is approximately 28 million. Most of the people are ethnic Uzbeks, and nearly 90 percent are Muslims. The Uzbek language is Turkic and related to Turkish and other languages of western Asia. Uzbekistan's economy relies heavily on the export of agricultural products and minerals. It is the world's second-leading exporter of cotton, and it also produces gold, copper, uranium, and natural gas.

Uzbekistan borders all four of the other former Soviet republics in Central Asia. Its neighbors are Kazakhstan to the west, north, and northeast, Kyrgyzstan and Tajikistan to the east, and Afghanistan and Turkmenistan to the south. Uzbekistan and tiny Liechtenstein in Central Europe are the only countries in the world that are doubly landlocked—that is, they are landlocked countries themselves whose neighbors are all landlocked also.

In general, Uzbekistan's boundaries were drawn in order to separate ethnic Uzbeks from people belonging to other nations. The boundary between Uzbekistan and Kazakhstan is Uzbekistan's longest boundary. This boundary is geometric. A single straight-line segment extends north-northwest from the tripoint between these two countries and Turkmenistan. Another long segment extends northeastward at a 60-degree angle from the western

boundary. The boundary then extends southeastward as a series of shorter geometric lines.

The boundary between Uzbekistan and Kazakhstan crosses the Aral Sea near the northernmost point along the boundary. At one time, the Aral Sea was the fourth-largest inland body of salt water in the world, with an area about the size of West Virginia. Since the 1960s, the Aral Sea has been shrinking steadily. The shrinking of the Aral Sea began in the 1950s, after the government of the Soviet Union completed efforts to dam the two major tributaries of the Aral Sea, the Amu Darya and the Syr Darya, in order to irrigate crops. By 2007, the Aral Sea had shrunk to only about 10 percent of its size in 1900. The sea had shrunk so much that it had become three separate lakes. Efforts have been made to reverse the long history of environmental damage and water depletion in the Aral Sea, but these efforts have been more successful in wealthier Kazakhstan than in Uzbekistan.

Uzbekistan's northeastern and eastern boundaries are far more complex, with a history of contestation. The boundary with Kazakhstan, after extending in a southeasterly direction for several hundred miles, then turns northeastward. It passes within 10 miles of Uzbekistan's capital city of Tashkent, then continues northeastward through high and sparsely populated mountains to the tripoint between Uzbekistan, Kazakhstan, and Kyrgyzstan.

The boundary between Uzbekistan and Kyrgyzstan crosses the fertile and densely populated Fergana Valley, which owes its fertility to irrigation from the Syr Darya and its tributaries. Four small exclaves belonging to Uzbekistan are located south of

the main boundary and are surrounded by Kyrgyzstan's territory. The largest of these exclaves is Sokh, with a land area of approximately 100 square miles and a population of about 50,000.

West of these exclaves, the highly irregular boundary between Uzbekistan and Tajikistan extends in a generally southward direction, increasing in elevation from north to south. Near Uzbekistan's Zaamin National Park, the boundary turns westward to a point about 25 miles east of the ancient city of Samarkand, which is located along the Silk Road. The boundary then extends in a generally southward direction to the tripoint between Uzbekistan, Tajikistan, and Afghanistan northeast of the Afghani city of Mazar-i-Sharif.

A short boundary between Uzbekistan and Afghanistan on the Amu Darya extends westward to the tripoint between Uzbekistan, Afghanistan, and Turkmenistan. From this tripoint, the boundary between Uzbekistan and Turkmenistan extends in a northwesterly direction. Generally speaking, it follows the drainage divide between the Amu Darya on the Uzbekistan side of the border and southward-flowing streams that flow southward on the Turkmenistan side of the border. Southwest of the city of Urgench, the boundary turns to the north and enters the Amu Darya drainage basin. The Amu Darya itself forms a brief section of the boundary. The river continues northwestward on its course to the Aral Sea near the town of Takhiatash. From that point the boundary becomes highly irregular, extending northwestward and then southwestward to Sarygamysh Lake, which is shared between the two countries. From the lake it extends southwestward and then southward into Turkmenistan's Kaplankyr Nature Reserve, then follows two straight lines extending in a west-northwesterly direction to the tripoint between Uzbekistan, Turkmenistan, and Kazakhstan.

HISTORICAL CONTEXT

Migrants from present-day Iran are believed to have moved into modern Uzbekistan and its neighbors about 3,000 years ago. The major cities of Samarkand, Tashkent, and Bukhara were founded before the fifth century BC. The region was conquered by Alexander the Great, then was ruled by Persian dynasties for the next thousand years.

During the Middle Ages, overland trade between China and Europe developed and expanded. The trade route became known as the Silk Road, some of whose routes went through Samarkand, Tashkent, and Bukhara. Merchants in these and other Uzbek cities profited from their location along the Silk Road and became very wealthy. In the early 13th century, present-day Uzbekistan, including territory along the Silk Road, was conquered by the Mongols, who ruled the region for the next 200 years. Uzbek tribes, from whom the current state derives its name, seized control of the country in the early 16th century and deposed the remaining Mongol rulers. At this time, trade along the Silk Road declined as Europeans developed sea trade to East Asia via the Atlantic and Indian oceans.

During the 19th century, the Russian Empire began to expand into Central Asia, including Uzbekistan. Most of present-day Uzbekistan had been absorbed into the Russian Empire by the 1880s. After the Russian Revolution, control of Uzbekistan passed to the Soviet Union. Uzbekistan became the Uzbek Soviet Socialist Republic in 1924. At that time, boundaries of the republic were drawn by Soviet officials with the intent of separating ethnic and national groups. The original boundaries were adjusted later on several occasions. The Uzbek Soviet Socialist Republic included present-day Tajikistan until 1930, when Tajikistan was elevated to Soviet Socialist Republic status and was separated from the Uzbek Soviet Socialist Republic. The Soviets pursued their policy of Russification and encouraged many ethnic Russians to move to Uzbekistan in order to dilute the dominance of Uzbek culture.

The Uzbek Soviet Socialist Republic was dissolved in 1991, when it became an independent country under its present name of the Republic of Uzbekistan. After independence, the new Uzbek government promoted Uzbek nationalism, and many ethnic Russians left the country. Uzbek's president, Islam Karimov, began ruling as an autocrat, and international observers regarded elections in Uzbekistan as fraudulent. Tensions between moderate and radical Islamic groups have characterized Uzbekistan in recent years.

CONTEMPORARY ISSUES

Uzbekistan and Kyrgyzstan continue to contest their boundary. This disagreement is associated with ethnic conflict. Much of this disagreement is associated with the status of the Uzbek exclaves in Kyrgyzstan. Between 1999 and 2010, Uzbekistan stationed troops, armored vehicles, and military equipment in Sokh in order to reinforce its control over the territory. A major road connecting northern Kyrgyzstan with the rest of the country but extending across Sokh was blocked. In 2010, Uzbekistan agreed to withdraw its armed forces from Sokh, but the status of this Uzbek exclave remains unresolved. Moreover, ethnic Uzbeks in Kyrgyzstan have engaged in armed skirmishes with the Kyrgyz majority. In response to this conflict, an estimated 100,000 people of Uzbek nationality have moved into Uzbekistan as refugees in recent years.

See also Afghanistan, Kazakhstan, Kyrgyzstan, Tajikistan, Turkmenistan

Further Reading

Dilip Hiro. *Inside Central Asia: A political and cultural history of Uzbekistan, Turkmenistan, Kazakhstan, Kyrgyzstan, Tajikistan, Russia, and Iran.* New York: Overlook TP, 2011.

Adeeb Khalid. *Islam after communism: Religion and politics in Central Asia.* Berkeley: University of California Press, 2007.

Colin Mackerras and Michael Clarke (eds.). *China, Xinjiang, and Central Asia: History, transition, and crossborder interaction into the 21st century.* Oxford: Taylor and Francis, 2011.

Pat Walters. "Aral Sea recovery?" *National Geographic News*, April 2, 2010, http://news.nationalgeographic.com/news/2010/04/100402-aral-sea-story/.

SOUTH AND SOUTHEAST ASIA

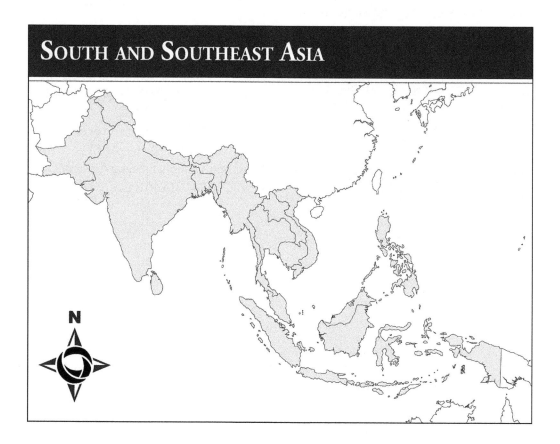

CHAPTER 6

SOUTH AND SOUTHEAST ASIA

South and Southeast Asia includes the countries south of the high mountains of Asia and extends from Pakistan eastward to the Pacific Ocean. It also includes several island countries south and east of the Asian mainland. In South Asia, the region includes the countries of India, Pakistan, Bangladesh, Sri Lanka, Nepal, and Bhutan. The Maldives in the Indian Ocean are also discussed with South Asia. To the east, Southeast Asia includes the mainland countries of Myanmar, Thailand, Laos, Cambodia, and Vietnam as well as the island countries of Indonesia, Singapore, East Timor, and the Philippines. The country of Malaysia is located partially on the mainland and partially on the island of Borneo.

South and Southeast Asia contain a large number of distinctive cultures, religions, and languages. Cultural, religious, and linguistic differences within the region have had major impacts on South and Southeast Asia's political geography for centuries. Hinduism is the major religion of India. More than 80 percent of India's people are Hindus, and the boundary between India and Pakistan was drawn in order to place as many Hindus as possible on the Indian side of the boundary. India's constitution specifies that the country is a secular state. However, some orthodox Hindus have argued

that Hindu principles should govern civil law within India. For example, orthodox Hindus believe that cattle are sacred. Some have argued that Indian law should ban the slaughter of cattle entirely.

In contrast, a majority of people in both Pakistan and Bangladesh are Muslims. Islam spread into India from southwest Asia hundreds of years ago. Some South Asian Muslims are descended from Muslims who moved into South Asia from Southwest Asia. Others are descended from people who converted to Islam from Hinduism. Indonesia and Malaysia are also predominantly Muslim. Buddhism originated in present-day India, but only a small number of people in India today are Buddhists. However, a majority of Sri Lanka's residents are Buddhists. Buddhism is also the dominant religion of most of mainland Southeast Asia, while a majority of Malaysians and Indonesians are Muslims. The Philippines and East Timor are Christian-majority countries. Most of the countries of South and Southeast Asia have experienced considerable conflicts between adherents of their various religions.

Cultural, linguistic, and religious differences between the residents of highland and lowland areas also characterize South and Southeast Asia. Although South and Southeast Asia is one of the most densely populated areas of the world, population densities vary considerably within the region. The valleys of the major rivers, from the Indus in Pakistan eastward to the Mekong in Southeast Asia, support very dense populations. For example, the large majority of people in Myanmar live in the valley of the Irrawaddy River, and the large majority of people in Thailand live in the valley of the Chao Phraya River.

The densely populated valleys of South and Southeast Asia are separated by often rugged mountains. These mountains are found in parts of northern and central Southeast Asia and in parts of northeastern and northern India. These mountainous areas are lightly populated relative to the valleys. Many of these mountainous regions are inhabited by people who are distinct culturally from the majority populations of the lowlands. In some cases these residents are indigenous peoples whose ancestors were driven into the mountains by larger and more powerful lowland cultures.

Geographers and historians have coined the term *Zomia* to describe these mountainous areas, which extend from northwestern Vietnam and neighboring southwestern China westward into India. The term *Zomia* comes from a Cambodian word meaning a mountain dweller or highlander. Tensions between Zomians and people in the lowlands have been ongoing and in several countries have generated ongoing separatist movements.

As with Latin America, most of the region has experienced a history of European colonization. Britain, France, and the Netherlands had extensive territorial claims over parts of the region. Thailand is the only country in South and Southeast Asia that remained independent throughout the colonial era. The boundaries between the countries of South and Southeast Asia, for the most part, were drawn by Europeans. In some cases, as with India and Pakistan, the boundaries were drawn with the specific intention of separating nations and cultural groups. However, South and Southeast Asia's great diversity of nations, cultures, religions, and languages has made the task of matching nations and states impossible. Most South and Southeast Asian countries currently experience internal or external conflicts, many of which are related to these long-standing cultural differences.

BANGLADESH

OVERVIEW

The People's Republic of Bangladesh occupies part of the northeastern portion of the Indian Peninsula in South Asia. Bangladesh has a land area of 56,977 square miles, the size of Iowa. Bangladesh is one of the most densely populated countries in the world. With a population of more than 160 million, Bangladesh is the world's eighth-largest country by population. Much of Bangladesh is located within the combined delta of the Ganges and Brahmaputra rivers. Bangladesh has two land neighbors, India and Myanmar. Bangladesh has a long land border with India to the west, north, and east and a short boundary with Myanmar to the southeast. The Bay of Bengal adjoins Bangladesh to the south.

The boundary between present-day Bangladesh and India was delineated initially in 1947 by the British. In delineating the boundary, the intent of the British was to separate predominantly Muslim

BANGLADESH

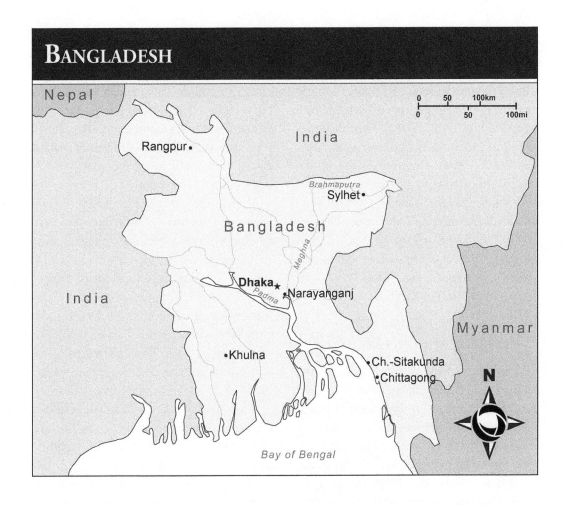

Bangladesh, then East Pakistan, from predominantly Hindu India. Thus, the boundary between Bangladesh and India is a cultural boundary. Today almost 90 percent of Bangladesh's people are Muslims, and about 98 percent are ethnic Bengalis.

From the Bay of Bengal at the southwestern corner of Bangladesh, the boundary between Bangladesh and India extends in a generally northerly direction. It follows distributaries of the Ganges northward to the main channel of the Ganges itself near the village of Ganga. From there, it follows the Ganges upstream and northwestward to a point near the town of Chapai

Nawabganj. It then follows many short straight-line segments. These are oriented northeastward, and then northwestward, and then northward again to a point near the Indian city of Siliguri. From there the boundary turns eastward, following a very complex series of short segments in a generally east-southeastward direction to the Brahmaputra River. Most of the nearly 200 exclaves on either side of the border are located along this section of the boundary.

The boundary crosses the Brahmaputra and turns southward, paralleling the river for about 40 miles. It then turns abruptly eastward along the southern end of the

Khasi Hills in the Indian state of Meghalaya. Near the village of Kalakata, the border turns southward again. It nearly encircles the Indian state of Tripura, coming within 30 miles of the Bay of Bengal coast near the city of Kalidaha. The boundary then turns inland and northeastward. Near the Dampe Tiger Reserve on the Indian side of the boundary, it extends southward and southeastward to the tripoint between Bangladesh, India, and Myanmar. This tripoint is located along the Naaf River. The boundary between Bangladesh and Myanmar follows the course of the Naaf to its mouth in the Bay of Bengal.

HISTORICAL CONTEXT

The flat, fertile combined delta of the Ganges and Brahmaputra rivers has been settled and farmed for thousands of years. The area was ruled for centuries by various dynasties, many of which controlled large portions of the Ganges and Brahmaputra valleys in present-day India and Bangladesh. Islam was introduced into the area in the 13th century. Beginning in the 15th century, present-day Bangladesh was controlled by Islamic dynasties, and by that time the large majority of the population had converted to Islam.

European interest in present-day Bangladesh began in the 15th and 16th centuries after Vasco de Gama first circumnavigated Africa in order to reach India and Southeast Asia. Traders from Portugal, the Netherlands, France, and Britain all attempted to establish influence over the area, which was known as Bengal and was inhabited by people speaking the Bengali language. The eastern portion was predominantly Muslim; the area further to the west was

primarily Hindu. In 1757, the British East India Company established control of the entire region, including the city of Calcutta (present-day Kolkata in India). Britain transferred control of Bengal from the British East India Company to the British Empire in 1858. The territory became part of British India, which also included present-day India and Pakistan.

During the early 20th century, Britain began the process of transitioning British India toward eventual independence. In 1947, Britain decided to divide British India on religious lines, and the two states of India and Pakistan were created. Pakistan included those parts of British India with Muslim majorities. Pakistan included what was then called West Pakistan (present-day Pakistan) and what was then called East Pakistan (present-day Bangladesh).

Although both West Pakistan and East Pakistan were predominantly Muslim, the two portions of Pakistan were divided by 1,000 miles by land and were very different in culture, language, and environment. A majority of Pakistan's residents were Bengalis from East Pakistan, although West Pakistan held the seat of administration and dominated the government. Shortly after independence, Pakistan's founder, Mohammad Ali Jinnah, insisted that Urdu, the language of West Pakistan, be designated as the official language of the entire country. After protests and riots, the government backed down, and Urdu and Bengali were given equal status as official languages in Pakistan.

Throughout the 1950s and 1960s, efforts to promote greater independence or autonomy for East Pakistan continued. In 1970, a cyclone or hurricane devastated East Pakistan. The cyclone resulted in an estimated 250,000 to 300,000 fatalities and made millions of people homeless. East Pakistan's leaders accused the government in West Pakistan of indifference and slow response to the plight of East Pakistan. In parliamentary elections held later that year, the proindependence Awami League won all but two of East Pakistan's seats, giving the league a parliamentary majority. Pakistan's prime minister did not allow the new parliament to convene and sent troops into East Pakistan in order to repress opposition 1971. Thousands of Bengalis were killed by these troops, and an estimated 8 to 10 million refugees crossed the boundary from East Pakistan into India. India intervened into the crisis in support of East Pakistan. In December 1971, Indian forces invaded East Pakistan. West Pakistan's forces surrendered and left East Pakistan. East Pakistan then became fully independent under its present name of Bangladesh.

CONTEMPORARY ISSUES

The boundaries of Bangladesh are generally stable, but tensions between Bangladesh and its neighbors remain. Of particular importance are tensions along the boundary between Bangladesh and India. This boundary separates densely populated areas on both sides and reflects concern about illegal immigration. Millions of Bengalis have moved illegally across the boundary into India.

During the 1980s, India began construction of a fence known as the Indo-Bangladeshi Barrier along the boundary between the two countries. Today the barrier extends along about two-thirds of the boundary, which is about 2,500 miles in length. India maintains a Border Security Force consisting of more than 200,000 personnel to patrol its borders. It has been estimated that nearly 1,000 Bangladeshis have been killed by the Border Security Force since 2000. India has defended its actions on the grounds that many of the victims were potential terrorists, drug traffickers, or smugglers. Bangladesh has protested that the Border Security Force has been ordered to shoot persons crossing the boundary on sight and that many of the victims have been unarmed, innocent civilians.

The status of Bangladesh's numerous exclaves within Indian territory and that of Indian exclaves within Bangladeshi territory also remains uncertain. An estimated 50,000 to 100,000 people live in the nearly 200 exclaves, known as chitmahals, located along the boundary. In 2011, the two countries agreed to implement a swap of territory in order to eliminate the exclaves and regularize the boundary. Individual residents of the chitmahals would be given the option to move and the choice of whether to become citizens of India or Bangladesh. In a separate agreement, Bangladesh and India agreed to swap several hundred acres of territory along the boundary between Bangladesh and the Indian state of Meghalaya in an effort to resolve long-standing tension along that boundary.

Meanwhile, Bangladesh and Myanmar have disputed their maritime boundaries in the Bay of Bengal. Valuable oil and natural gas deposits have been discovered in the area, adding to the tension between the two countries. The dispute was referred to the United Nations International Tribunal for the Law of the Sea. In 2012, the tribunal handed down a binding decision establishing the boundary. With the boundary now resolved, both countries have initiated efforts to begin exploration for oil and natural gas under the Bay of Bengal.

See also   India, Myanmar

Further Reading

Scott Carney, Jason Miklian, and Kristian Hoelscher. "Fortress India." *Foreign Policy*, July/August 2011, http://www.foreignpolicy.com/articles/2011/06/20/fortress_india.

Reece Jones. "Sovereignty and statelessness in the border enclaves of India and Bangladesh." *Political Geography*, 28 (2009), pp. 373–381.

Samudra Gupta Kashyap. "Smuggling thrives as fencing of Indo-Bangla border delayed." *Indian Express*, December 5, 2011, http://www.indianexpress.com/news/smuggling-thrives-as-fencing-of-indobangla-border-delayed/884123/.

David Lewis. *Bangladesh: Politics, economy, and civil society.* New York: Cambridge University Press.

Willem van Schendel. *A history of Bangladesh.* New York: Cambridge University Press.

BHUTAN

OVERVIEW

The Kingdom of Bhutan is located in the eastern portion of the Himalaya Mountains in South Asia. Bhutan has a land area of 14,824 square miles, as large as Maryland and Delaware combined. Its population is approximately 750,000.

Bhutan is landlocked. Its neighbors are India to the southwest, south, and east and the Chinese province of Tibet to the west and north. There are two tripoints between Bhutan, India, and China. The western tripoint is located near the Torsa Strict Nature Preserve in western Bhutan. From that tripoint, the boundary between Bhutan and India extends southward briefly and then turns eastward through the Himalayan foothills. Many areas on both sides of this boundary have been designated as national parks or nature reserves, including the Khaling Wildlife Sanctuary in the southeastern corner of the country.

East of the Khaling Wildlife Sanctuary, the boundary turns northward until it reaches the Kulong Chu Wildlife Sanctuary. The eastern tripoint between Bhutan, India, and China is located at the eastern edge of the Kulong Chu Wildlife Sanctuary. From here the frontier between Bhutan and China extends eastward through higher parts of the Himalayas. Near Bhutan's Jigme Dorji National Park, the frontier turns southwestward to the western tripoint. The boundary between Bhutan and China has not been delineated fully, and Bhutan does not maintain diplomatic relations with China.

HISTORICAL CONTEXT

Although present-day Bhutan has been inhabited for thousands of years, little is known about Bhutan's history until Buddhism was introduced into the area during the eighth and ninth centuries AD. Bhutan has remained independent ever since. During the 19th century, Bhutan's monarchy cooperated closely with the British rulers of British India, but Bhutan maintained its independence. In 1910, Bhutan and Britain

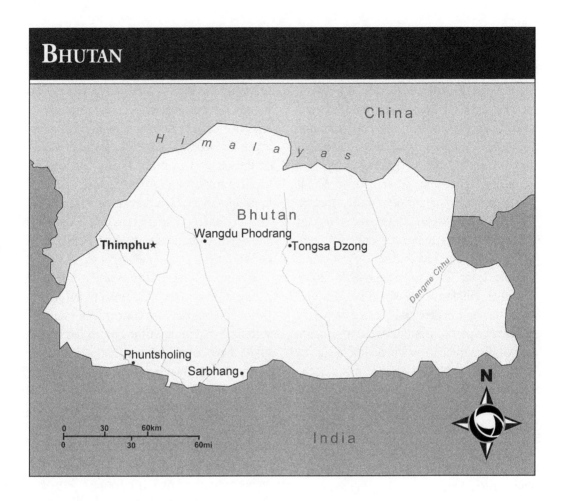

signed the Treaty of Punakha. The treaty affirmed Bhutan's independence and internal autonomy but gave Britain responsibility for Bhutan's foreign affairs.

The Treaty of Punakha remained in effect until India became an independent country in 1947. Bhutan was invited to join India but declined the invitation and retained its independence. Subsequently, Bhutan and India signed a treaty similar to the Treaty of Punakha, and this agreement guarantees India's recognition of Bhutan's sovereignty. Prior to the 1950s, Bhutan was an absolute monarchy. Since then, Bhutan has transitioned from an absolute monarchy to

a constitutional monarchy, with the first democratic elections held in 2008. During the 1990s, the Bhutanese government received international criticism for expelling thousands of Hindu residents of Nepalese ancestry. In the first decade of the 21st century, about 60,000 Bhutanese refugees of Nepali ancestry were resettled in the United States under the auspices of the United Nations.

CONTEMPORARY ISSUES

Since the 1940s, Bhutan has had close relationships with India but strained relationships with China. Historically, Bhutan has had close ties with neighboring Tibet, which like Bhutan is a predominantly Buddhist state. Relations between Bhutan and China deteriorated after China took control of Tibet in 1959. Bhutan and China both claim several small territories along their boundary. In 1998, the two countries signed the Agreement to Maintain Peace and Tranquility on the Bhutan-China Border Areas. Under the terms of this agreement, China reaffirmed its commitment to the recognition of Bhutan's independence and sovereignty. In 2006, however, Bhutan accused China of building roads and bridges within territory recognized as part of Bhutan. In 2010, Bhutan and China agreed to establish a field survey that would be charged with delineating the boundary precisely and with resolving the long-standing territorial dispute between the two countries.

See also   China, India

Further Reading

Mohan Balaji. "In Bhutan, China and India collide." *Asia Times Online*, January 12, 2008, http://www.atimes.com/atimes/China/JA12Ad02.html.

Medha Bisht. "Bhutan's foreign policy determinants: An assessment." *Strategic Analysis*, 36 (2012), pp. 57–72.

BRUNEI

OVERVIEW

The Nation of Brunei, the Abode of Peace, is located on the northern coast of the island of Borneo in Southeast Asia on the South China Sea. Brunei has a land area of 2,226 square miles, making it slightly larger than Delaware. Its population is about 410,000. It includes two land areas that are separated by a narrow strip of Malaysian territory. About 80 percent of Brunei's land area is located in the western portion of the country, which contains about 98 percent of the population. Much of the eastern portion of Brunei, known as the Temburong District, consists of national parks and forest reserves. Borneo is the only island in the world that is divided among three countries (Brunei, Malaysia, and Indonesia).

Brunei is one of the world's last absolute monarchies. The present sultan of Brunei claims descent from a 15th-century sultanate that at one time controlled much of northern Borneo, including present-day Sarawak and Sabah in Malaysia, as well as the Sulu Islands in what is now the Philippines. Brunei is an important oil-producing state, and oil revenues have helped make Brunei one of the wealthiest countries in Southeast Asia. Oil wealth has created employment for foreign workers from India, Bangladesh, the Philippines, and elsewhere.

Brunei's only land neighbor is Malaysia, whose territory is located to the west, south, and east of Brunei. The boundary between the two countries follows drainage divides between rivers, although not all of this boundary has been demarcated clearly. The boundary between western Brunei and Malaysia follows the drainage divide between the Baram River in Malaysia and the Belait River in Brunei. Western Brunei also includes the drainage basin of the Limbang River. East of the Limbang, western Brunei is separated from the Temburong District by a strip of Malaysian territory known as the Limbang District,

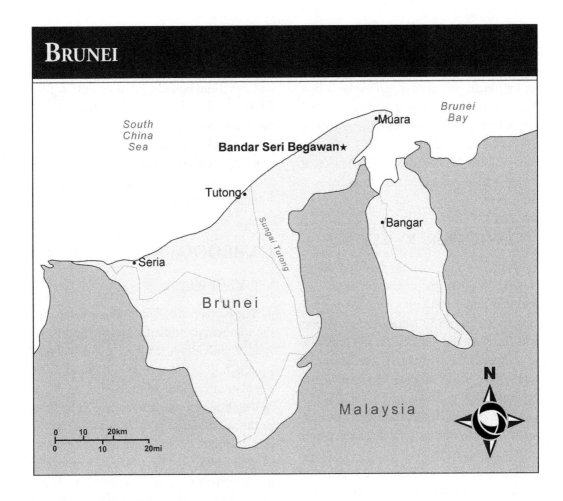

BRUNEI

which extends southward from Brunei Bay on the South China Sea. This territory is about 5 miles wide along the coast and widens to about 20 miles in width further south. The Limbang District and Brunei's Temburong District are separated by the Pandaruan River.

HISTORICAL CONTEXT

Brunei traces its history to a sultanate that arose during the seventh century AD. By the 13th century, the Brunei sultanate controlled present-day Brunei along with most of what are now the Malaysian

provinces of Sarawak and Sabah on the northern coast of the island. The sultanate also controlled the Sulu Islands and parts of Mindanao in the present-day Philippines. The sultanate converted to Islam during the 16th century, and Islam remains the state religion of Brunei today.

Spain invaded and captured the sultanate's capital city of Kota Batu in 1578. The sultanate retained nominal power but lost control of its territories in the Philippines. In 1839, Britain took control of the region. The British separated present-day Brunei from neighboring Sarawak in present-day Malaysia. Brunei became a protectorate of

Britain in 1888, and British resident advisors held real political power. The British resident advisors withdrew in 1959, and political power reverted to the sultan. The British protectorate ended in 1984, when Brunei achieved full independence. Oil was discovered in the late 1920s, and today oil wealth has provided Brunei with one of the highest per capita incomes in the world.

CONTEMPORARY ISSUES

Brunei's relationships with Malaysia involve ongoing disputes over both land and maritime boundaries between the two countries. The 1839 separation of Brunei and Sarawak did not delimit the boundaries between the two clearly, and some of them have still not been defined unambiguously. The Limbang District, which has been claimed by Brunei, has been contested between the two countries since both became independent.

Brunei and Malaysia have also disputed control of offshore areas under the surface of the South China Sea. Brunei claims an exclusive economic zone along the continental shelf within 200 nautical miles of its coastline. This claim would give Brunei exclusive access to resources within much of the southern South China Sea. Malaysia did not recognize Brunei's claim until 2009, when the two countries signed an agreement known as the Letters of Exchange. Under the Letters of Exchange, Malaysia recognized Brunei's access to some oil-rich areas within its claimed exclusive economic zone in exchange for Brunei's giving up its claim to the Limbang District.

See also Malaysia

Further Reading
International Boundary Research Unit. "Brunei and Malaysia move toward land and maritime boundary settlement." March 17, 2009, http://www.dur.ac.uk/ibru/news/boundary_news/?itemno=7724&rehref=%2Fibru%2Fnews%2F&resubj=Boundary+news%20Headlines.

Graham Saunders. *A history of Brunei.* London: Routledge, 2002.

CAMBODIA

OVERVIEW

The Kingdom of Cambodia is located in the southern portion of mainland Southeast Asia. Cambodia has a land area of 69,898 square miles, the size of Oklahoma. Its population is about 15 million.

Cambodia's neighbors are Thailand to the west and north, Laos to the north, and Vietnam to the east and southeast. To the south and southwest, Cambodia has a coastline along the Gulf of Thailand. Many of Cambodia's boundaries with its neighbors follow mountain ranges or drainage divides. This reflects the fact that population densities throughout Southeast Asia are much higher along rivers and in lowland areas than is the case in the mountains.

About two-thirds of Cambodia's boundary with Thailand follows drainage and watershed divides. From the Gulf of Thailand, the boundary stretches northward from the Gulf of Thailand along the crest of the Cardamom Mountains range, which parallels the coast of the Gulf. Thus, a narrow strip of land along the coast, more than 20 miles long and in most places less than a mile wide, is part

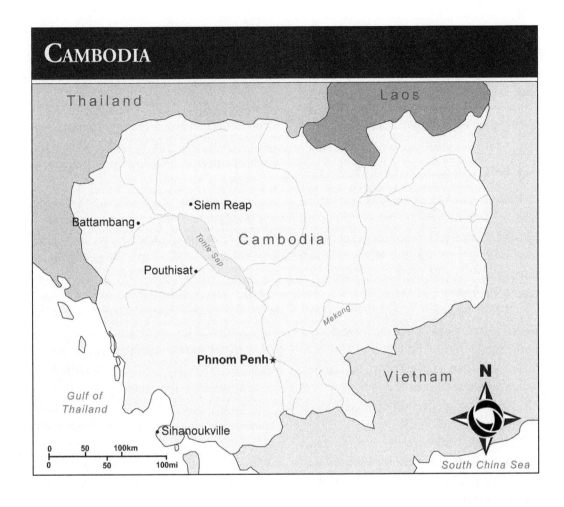

CAMBODIA

Thailand

Laos

•Siem Reap

Battambang•

Cambodia

Tonle Sap

Pouthisat•

Mekong

Phnom Penh★

Vietnam

N

Gulf of
Thailand

•Sihanoukville

| 0 | 50 | 100km |
| 0 | 50 | 100mi |

South China Sea

of Thailand. The boundary then extends inland in a generally northward direction, and then it turns eastward to the tripoint between Cambodia, Thailand, and Laos on the Mekong River. Most of this boundary follows several small rivers and watershed divides. To the east, the boundary between Cambodia and Laos also follows physical features. Much of this boundary is located along drainage divides that are located in sparsely settled areas separating more densely populated valleys. However, some of the boundary follows the Se Kong River, which is a tributary of the Mekong River.

Many portions of the boundary between Cambodia and Vietnam, in contrast, follow geometric lines that separate people on the basis of culture and ethnicity. This is true especially along the southern portion of this boundary, which crosses flat land along the lower reaches of the Mekong. From the Gulf of Thailand, the boundary trends generally eastward to the "Parrot's Beak," where Cambodian territory approaches the densely populated region around Ho Chi Minh City (formerly Saigon) in Vietnam. The Parrot's Beak region was used by North Vietnamese forces as a staging area for military actions in what was then

South Vietnam near the end of the Vietnam War in the early 1970s. From the Parrot's Beak, the boundary follows a combination of short geometric segments and physical features northward to the tripoint between Cambodia, Vietnam, and Laos.

HISTORICAL BACKGROUND

Present-day Cambodia was part of the Khmer Empire, which became the most powerful empire in Southeast Asia during the ninth century AD. The Khmer Empire remained powerful until it collapsed, for unknown reasons, in the early 15th century. The Khmer capital of Angkor is believed to have been one of the largest cities in the world during the 12th and 13th centuries. After the empire collapsed, Angkor was abandoned. Since the late 19th century, Angkor has been excavated and restored by archaeologists.

Cambodia became a French protectorate in 1863. It was administered as part of French Indochina along with Vietnam and Laos from 1863 to 1953, except during World War II, when it was occupied by the Japanese. It became an independent constitutional monarchy in 1953. In 1975, a guerilla organization known as the Khmer Rouge took power. The Khmer Rouge attempted to restructure Cambodian society by forcing people into rural areas and destroying Western-influenced buildings and infrastructure. The Khmer Rouge regime was one of the most brutal and repressive governments in the 20th-century world. Between 1 and 3 million Cambodians are believed to have died from disease, starvation, or political violence under the Khmer Rouge regime during the 1970s and 1980s. A democratic

government was restored in 1993. Cambodia has slowly recovered from the atrocities of the Khmer Rouge regime, but it remains one of the poorest countries in Southeast Asia. With a democratic government in place, foreign investment is increasing. Agriculture, textiles, other light manufacturing, and tourism are major economic activities.

The question of a boundary between Cambodia and Thailand first arose after France established Cambodia as a protectorate in 1863. In 1867, Thailand (then known as Siam) formally recognized French sovereignty over Cambodia. A boundary commission demarcated the border. The commission completed its work in the early 20th century. Since then, the boundary has been modified on several occasions by later agreements between France and Thailand. Cambodia's boundaries with Laos and Vietnam were delineated during the period of French colonial rule in the late 19th and early 20th centuries.

CONTEMPORARY ISSUES

Cambodia's boundaries have not been contested extensively, yet a few issues remain unresolved. The delineation of the boundary between Cambodia and Thailand left open the question of which country had sovereignty over the site of the Preah Vihear Temple. Located along Cambodia's northern boundary, the Preah Vihear Temple was a Hindu temple constructed in the Khmer Empire during the 11th century. One map drawn by the boundary commission placed Preah Vihear on the Thailand side of the boundary, another placed it on the Cambodian side of the boundary.

In 1962, the International Court of Justice ruled that the land on which the temple was located, along with artifacts that had been recovered from the temple, belonged to Cambodia. Thailand protested the court's decision, but Cambodia took possession of the area formally in 1963.

The dispute between the two countries over Preah Vihear continued after the court's ruling, and it intensified in the 1970s after thousands of Cambodian refugees fled to Thailand to escape the atrocities of the Khmer Rouge regime. In 2007, Cambodia announced its intention to request that Preah Vihear be declared a World Heritage Site. Thailand protested that the decision to have the site designated as a World Heritage Site should have been made jointly by the two countries in light of ongoing dispute over its ownership. Armed skirmishes occurred in the area in 2008 and again in 2011.

Cambodia and Vietnam have also been involved in a dispute over control of the island of Phu Quoc. Phu Quoc is located in the Gulf of Thailand, about 8 miles off the Cambodian coast and nearly 30 miles from the nearest point on the Vietnamese mainland. It has a land area of 222 square miles and a population of about 85,000. Despite its proximity to the Cambodian mainland, the French assigned its administration to the province of Cochin China, now part of Vietnam, in 1939. In 1975, Khmer Rouge soldiers captured the island, which was soon recaptured by Vietnamese forces. The dispute over control of Phu Quoc was a cause of the Cambodian-Vietnamese War in 1979. The conflict eased after Vietnam removed its troops from Phu Quoc in the late 1980s. Phu Quoc remains under Vietnamese sovereignty and is the site of an increasingly lucrative international tourism business.

See also   Laos, Thailand, Vietnam

Further Reading

BBC News. "Gunfight on Thai-Cambodia border." October 15, 2008, http://news.bbc.co.uk/2/hi/asia-pacific/7668657.stm.

Joel Brinkley. *Cambodia's curse: The modern history of a troubled land.* New York: PublicAffairs, 2011.

EAST TIMOR

OVERVIEW

The Democratic Republic of Timor-Leste, also known as East Timor, occupies the eastern half of the island of Timor in the Indonesian archipelago. The Savu Sea and the Selat Wetar are located to the north, with the Timor Sea to the south. The country also includes two smaller islands, Atauro and Jaco, and a small exclave on the northwest coast of the main island. The total land area of the country is 5,743 square miles, about the size of Connecticut. Its population is estimated at about 1.1 million. East Timor and the Philippines are the only Catholic-majority countries in Asia.

The island of Timor is the largest of the Lesser Sunda Islands, the rest of which are part of Indonesia. As its name implies, East Timor is located on the eastern portion of the island. East Timor's only land boundary is with the Indonesian province of Nusa Tenggara Timur. This boundary between the main portion of East Timor and Indonesia follows rivers and short

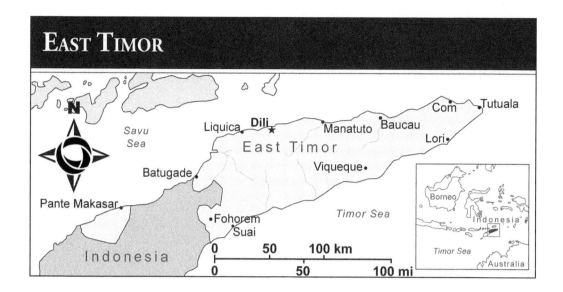

EAST TIMOR

straight-line segments across the island in a roughly north-south direction. The exclave of Oecusse is located about 40 miles southwest of the main portion of East Timor. It has a land area of about 500 square miles and a population of about 60,000.

HISTORICAL CONTEXT

Present-day East Timor is believed by anthropologists to have been occupied by humans for at least 40,000 years. By the 14th century, Timor was involved in trading sandalwood and other products with China and India. Portugal established trading posts on the island in the 16th century. The first of these Portuguese settlements was established at Oecusse in 1556. The port of Dili, which is East Timor's capital city today, was founded in 1769. Portugal claimed the area, including Oecusse, as Portuguese East Timor. The Portuguese and the Dutch, which controlled present-day Indonesia, agreed upon the current boundary between the two colonies in

1916. This agreement confirmed Portuguese sovereignty over Oecusse. Japan occupied East Timor during World War II, but the colony reverted to Portuguese control after the war ended.

Portugal dissolved its colonial empire and granted independence to East Timor in 1975. Nine days later, Indonesian troops invaded East Timor, and Indonesia claimed sovereignty over the newly independent country. Indonesia claimed East Timor as an Indonesian province, and Indonesian troops continued to occupy East Timor until 2000. The period of Indonesian control of the area was marked by violence and brutality. An estimated 100,000 East Timorians were killed or died as a result of famine and starvation between 1976 and 2000. Resistance movements battled the Indonesian occupiers, and the rebels were supported by human rights organizations in Portugal, Australia, the United States, and other countries. In 1999, the United Nations sponsored a referendum in East Timor. A large majority of voters supported East Timor independence, which was recognized by the international community in 2002.

CONTEMPORARY ISSUES

East Timor's sovereignty is now recognized by the international community, but a few issues remain unsettled. Although the boundaries between East Timor and Indonesia were agreed upon in the early 20th century, the boundary has not been demarcated fully. A joint boundary commission known as the East Timor–Indonesia Boundary Committee continues to work to delimit the land boundaries between the two countries. The status of thousands of refugees who fled East Timor prior to independence remains in doubt. Many of these refugees live in Indonesia, and some have refused or resisted repatriation.

East Timor and Australia have disputed their maritime boundary. East Timor is located about 400 miles north of the Australian city of Darwin. The dispute involves control of valuable mineral resources, including billions of dollars' worth of oil and gas reserves in the Timor Sea. Both sides claim revenues from the eventual development of these resources. Resolution of this dispute has been complicated by Australia's involvement in East Timor before and after East Timor became independent. Australian troops have been stationed in East Timor since the United Nations first proposed the referendum on East Timorian independence in 1999. Australia is also a major trading partner and source of aid for East Timor.

See also Indonesia

Further Reading

Irina Cristalis. *East Timor: A nation's bitter dawn.* London: Zed Books, 2009.

Victor Prescott. "The question of East Timor's maritime boundaries." *IBRU Boundary and Security Bulletin*, Winter 1999/2000, pp. 72–82, https://www.dur.ac.uk/resources/ibru/publications/full/bsb7-4_prescott.pdf.

John G. Taylor. *East Timor: The price of freedom.* Sydney: Pluto Press, 1999.

INDIA

OVERVIEW

The Republic of India, located in South Asia, occupies most of the Indian subcontinent. It has a land area of 1,269,219 square miles. Thus India is twice the size of Alaska and is the seventh-largest country in the world by land area. India's population is about 1.2 billion, and it is the second-largest country in the world by population behind only China.

India has land boundaries with Pakistan to the west and northwest, China, Nepal, and Bhutan to the north, and Myanmar and Bangladesh to the east. India adjoins the Bay of Bengal to the southeast and the Arabian Gulf to the southwest. The southeastern coast of India is separated from the island country of Sri Lanka by the Palk Strait, which is about 33 miles wide at its narrowest point.

The boundary between India and Pakistan is a cultural boundary that was drawn by the British in order to separate the Hindu-majority population of India from the Muslim-majority population of Pakistan. From the Arabian Gulf, the boundary

INDIA

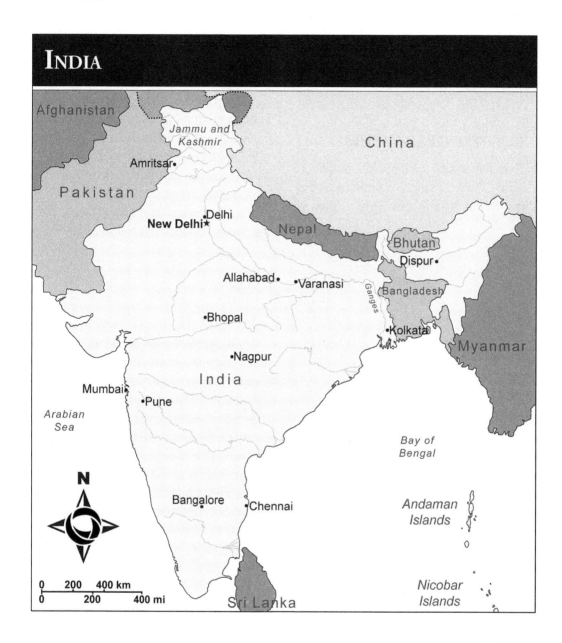

crosses the resource-rich salt marsh of the Rann of Kutch. Northeast of the Rann of Kutch, the boundary follows many straight-line segments northeastward to the Satluj River near the Indian town of Abohar. It follows the Satluj upstream and then extends further northward along straight-line segments to the Ravi River. It extends northeastward and upstream along the Ravi. It then continues northward from the Ravi to the disputed territory of Jammu and Kashmir, which is claimed by both countries, to the frontier between Jammu and Kashmir and China.

India's three boundaries with China are separated by its boundaries with Nepal and with Bhutan. All of the boundaries between India and China are located in the high peaks of the Himalaya Mountains. Although the boundaries cross rugged, sparsely populated, and inaccessible territory, portions of the boundary between India and China have been contested since India became independent in 1947. Both countries claim disputed territory along their border. India's boundary with Bhutan also extends across the high country of the Himalayas. In contrast, much of India's border with Nepal is located in the densely populated Terai Plains, which are part of the valley of the Ganges River. Most of this boundary consists of straight-line segments. The boundary extends from the Terai Plains northward into the Himalayas at both ends of the border. The Kali River, which is a tributary of the Ganges, forms the boundary between India and western Nepal.

The boundary between India and Bangladesh was drawn also to separate people on the basis of religion, with Hindus in India and Muslims in what was then known as East Pakistan. To the west, the boundary extends northward from the Bay of Bengal along distributaries of the Ganges. It follows the Ganges itself briefly and then follows a large number of short straight-line segments further northward until it reaches a point just south of the city of Siliguri. Siliguri is located along the "Chicken's Neck," which separates Bangladesh from Nepal and is only 15 miles wide at its narrowest point. The Chicken's Neck connects the seven states of Northeast India with the rest of the country. This relatively isolated region contains about 8 percent of India's land area but only about 3 percent of its population. Culturally and linguistically, Northeast India is more closely related to Southeast Asia and to neighboring Tibet than it is to the rest of India. Except for the state of Assam in the valley of the Brahmaputra River, much of northeast India is part of the highland region of Zomia.

From near Siliguri, the boundary turns eastward. It follows many short straight-line segments that are oriented in a generally eastward-to-southeastward direction. It crosses the Brahmaputra River and turns to the south. From there it parallels the course of the Brahmaputra for about 40 miles before it turns eastward again. Here it follows the foothills of the mountains of the state of Meghalaya, separating Meghalaya from the Bangladeshi lowlands to the south. The boundary then turns southward again, encircles the Indian state of Tripura, and continues eastward again to the tripoint between India, Bangladesh, and Myanmar. Nearly 200 Indian and Bangladeshi exclaves are located near the boundary, especially in that section of the border separating India from the northwestern portion of Bangladesh.

The boundary between India and Myanmar trends in a generally northeasterly direction from this tripoint to the tripoint between India, Myanmar, and China. More than half of this boundary follows drainage divides, including the drainage divide between streams that empty into the Ganges delta or directly into the Bay of Bengal on the Indian side of the border and streams that empty into the Irrawaddy River on the Myanmar side of the border.

HISTORICAL CONTEXT

Anthropologists have discovered evidence of the occupation of present-day

India dating back about 75,000 years. About 3000 BC, the Indus Valley Civilization became established along the valley of the Indus River in what is now northwestern India and eastern Pakistan. Other dynasties followed the Indus River Civilization. In the fourth century BC, the Maurya Empire took control of most of the Indian subcontinent. After the Maurya Empire fell apart, many different dynasties controlled various portions of present-day India over the next 1,600 years. Most of India was reunited beginning in 1526 by the Mughal Empire, which was established originally by invaders from Central Asia. The Mughal emperors, who claimed direct descent from Genghis Khan, were Muslims although a majority of their subjects continued to practice Hinduism.

The Mughals ruled the Indian subcontinent for the next 200 years, but Mughal control of India weakened in the 18th century. A variety of smaller kingdoms began to seize power in outlying portions of the Mughal Empire, especially in what is today northwestern India. Meanwhile, the British East India Company began to control port cities along India's coast, thereby dominating trade between India and Europe. The weakened state of the Mughal Empire allowed the company to expand its sphere of influence over the Indian subcontinent.

In 1857, a rebellion against company rule known as the Sepoy Mutiny broke out among Indian soldiers serving in the British Army. After the Sepoy Mutiny was put down by British forces, Britain placed the Indian subcontinent under direct control of the British government in 1858. British India included today's India, Pakistan, Bangladesh, and Myanmar. The consolidation of direct British rule over British

India initiated what came to be known as the British Raj. In 1937, what is now Myanmar was detached from British India and became a separate colony. The British signed a boundary treaty with Tibet in 1914, establishing the crest of the Himalayas as the boundary between the British Empire and Tibet.

The British Raj retained control of British India into the 20th century, when agitation for independence became widespread. The Indian leader Mohandas Gandhi, known as the Mahatma, led nonviolent protests against continuing British rule. After World War II, Britain decided to grant independence to British India. Although Gandhi favored a single united India, the British decided to partition British India along religious lines. Areas with Hindu majorities were included within India. Areas with Muslim majorities in northwestern and northeastern India were included within what would become the independent state of Pakistan, which split into Pakistan and Bangladesh in 1971. The partition process resulted in one of the largest mass migrations in world history as Hindus moved into what is now India and Muslims moved into what is now Pakistan. An estimated 15 to 20 million people crossed what would become the boundary. As many as 500,000 people lost their lives, and many more lost their homes, farms, and properties.

India became independent in 1947, and Gandhi, who became the first president of India, was assassinated in 1948. The constitution of India went into effect in 1950. It specified that India would be a secular and democratic state. However, some orthodox Hindus objected to India's status as a secular state, arguing that Indian civil law should reflect Hindu religious principles. Protests against the secular orientation of India began, and these protests continue to the present day.

Newly independent India faced territorial disputes with its largest neighbors, Pakistan and China. Tension with Pakistan centered on control of the province of Jammu and Kashmir, which is claimed by both countries. Jammu and Kashmir extends northward from the main portion of India. The area has a land area of approximately 85,000 square miles and is about the size of Utah, with a population of 13 million.

At the time of partition in 1947, about 75 percent of the people living in Jammu and Kashmir were Muslims. However, the local prince who governed Jammu and Kashmir was a Hindu who preferred making Jammu and Kashmir part of India. Both India and Pakistan claimed Jammu and Kashmir after independence, and wars over control of the territory broke out in 1947, 1965, 1971, and 2001. Jammu and Kashmir became an Indian state, although Pakistan is in de facto control of its northern and western portions. Today Jammu and Kashmir is the only Indian state with a Muslim majority. About 97 percent of people in the Kashmir Valley, which is adjacent to the border with Pakistan, are Muslims. Jammu and Kashmir has an autonomous relationship with India; except for defense and national security, any Indian law must also be ratified by the state's legislature before it applies to Jammu and Kashmir. Indians from other parts of the country are not allowed to purchase land in Jammu and Kashmir.

India and China have also had a contentious relationship over control of territory along their boundary in the Himalayas. After China seized control of Tibet, it claimed the area administered in India by the North East Frontier Agency. War between India and China broke out in 1962. Although territorial control was an important cause of the war, China also objected to India's granting asylum to Tibet's spiritual ruler, the Dalai Lama, as well as thousands of other Tibetan refugees. In December 1962, a cease-fire agreement was negotiated. The agreement established the Line of Actual Control, which separated Indian-occupied territory to the south from Chinese-occupied territory to the north. The Line of Actual Control remains the effective boundary between the two countries. The area that had been administered by the North East Frontier Agency became the Indian state of Arunachal Pradesh, which became a state of India officially in 1987. Arunachal Pradesh has a land area of about 35,000 square miles, the size of Maine, and a population of about 1.5 million. China continues to claim the area.

CONTEMPORARY ISSUES

India's boundaries with Pakistan and China remain contested, and India has also been involved in boundary-related conflicts with Bangladesh and Nepal.

The major point of contention with respect to the boundary between India and Pakistan remains the question of Jammu and Kashmir. Jammu and Kashmir contains numerous shrines and religious sites, both Muslim and Hindu. The presence of these sites along with the cool summer climate of the region has resulted in a substantial increase in tourism. Tourism declined after the 2001 war between India and Pakistan over control of Jammu and Kashmir. Tourism increased toward its pre-2001 levels over the next several years. However, in 2008 violence broke out over access to a cave known as Amarnath, which contains a stalagmite believed by Hindus to contain a representation of the god Shiva. About 400,000 pilgrims visit Amarnath each year. The Jammu and Kashmir government appropriated land to build shelters and way stations for the pilgrims visiting Amarnath. However, the appropriation process displaced many Muslim farmers and their families, angering the Muslim community. Protests escalated into violence that resulted in 15 fatalities, and the Indian Army sent 10,000 troops into the province to try and head off further violence.

Although India continues to claim all of Jammu and Kashmir, insurgent movements continue. Some insurgents want all or part of the state to be annexed to Pakistan, while others want Jammu and Kashmir to become an independent country. However, both India and Pakistan are opposed to independence for Jammu and Kashmir. Pakistan and India have also disputed control of portions of the Rann of Kutch region, which is located at the southwestern end of their boundary along the Arabian Gulf. The Rann of Kutch is rich in natural gas, making the boundary region highly attractive to both countries. The dispute over the Rann of Kutch includes disagreement over maritime boundaries in the Arabian Gulf as well as the boundary on land. Tensions flared in 1999, when the Indian Air Force shot down a Pakistani plane and killed 16 passengers. India justified its actions by claiming that the plane was violating Indian airspace, but Pakistan denied this claim.

Meanwhile, India and China continue to contest control of Arunachal Pradesh. Although the Line of Actual Control remains the de facto boundary, China has not relinquished its claim to Arunachal Pradesh, which it refers to as South Tibet. India, China, and Pakistan also dispute control of a small, uninhabited territory known as Aksai Chin adjacent to the northeastern corner of Jammu and Kashmir.

Although the boundary itself between India and Bangladesh is not contested, there are numerous tensions along the border. Many of these tensions involve illegal migration from Bangladesh into India. The Indian government began constructing a border fence known as the Indo-Bangladeshi Barrier in the 1980s. Today, the barrier encloses about two-thirds of the border. The barrier and other border areas are patrolled by India's Border Security Force, which contains nearly 200,000 troops.

The status of India's exclaves and those of Bangladesh is uncertain, although the two countries have made efforts to resolve the dispute. The population of the nearly 200 exclaves, which are known locally as chitmahals, has been estimated at between 50,000 and 100,000. In 2011, the two countries agreed to swap territories and regularize the boundary in order to eliminate the exclaves. As part of the swapping process, individual residents of the chitmahals would be given the right to choose between Indian and Bangladeshi citizenship and would also be given the right to move across the boundary into their country of choice if necessary.

India and Nepal dispute control over a small territory known as Kalapani, which is located near the western tripoint between Nepal, India, and China. Kalapani has a land area of about 30 square miles. The dispute stems from disagreement about the location of the Kali River, which is also known as the Sarda River in India and the Mahakali River in Nepal. The two countries disagree as to which of two tributaries of the Kali is its source and therefore should form the northernmost segment of the boundary. Nepal regards the Limpiyadhura River as the true source of the Kali, while India claims that the Lipu Lekh River, which is east of the Limpiyadhura, is the true source.

See also Bangladesh, Bhutan, China, Myanmar, Nepal, Pakistan

Further Reading

Scott Carney, Jason Miklian, and Kristian Hoelscher. "Fortress India." *Foreign Policy*, July/August 2011, http://www.foreignpolicy.com/articles/2011/06/20/fortress_india.

GlobalSecurity.org. "India-China border dispute." 2009, http://www.globalsecurity.org/military/world/war/india-china_conflicts.htm.

International Boundary Consultants. "India's boundary disputes with China, Nepal, and Pakistan." May 15, 1998, http://www.boundaries.com/India.htm.

Reece Jones. "Sovereignty and statelessness in the border enclaves of India and Bangladesh." *Political Geography*, 28 (2009), pp. 373–381.

Yasmin Khan. *The great partition: The making of India and Pakistan.* New Haven, CT: Yale University Press, 2007.

C. Raja Mohan. "India and the balance of power." *Foreign Affairs*, July/August 2006.

Surya P. Sebedi. *Dynamics of foreign policy and law: A study of Indo-Nepal relations.* New York: Oxford University Press, 2006.

INDONESIA

OVERVIEW

The Republic of Indonesia is located off the coast of mainland Southeast Asia. The country includes the world's largest archipelago, with more than 17,500 islands of which about 6,000 are inhabited. The overall land area of Indonesia is 735,355 square miles. With a population of about 240 million, Indonesia is the fourth-most populous country in the world after China, India, and the United States.

Indonesia's islands can be divided into three main groups. Most of western Indonesia comprises the Greater Sunda Islands, including the islands of Sumatra, Java, Borneo, and Sulawesi. More than half of Indonesia's residents live on the densely populated island of Java, which is much smaller by land area than either Sumatra or Borneo. East of the Greater Sunda Islands, the smaller Lesser Sunda Islands extend in an easterly direction toward New Guinea, which is the second-largest island in the world. Indonesia also includes the western half of New Guinea, a territory known as Irian Jaya.

Indonesia's three land neighbors are Malaysia, Papua New Guinea, and East Timor. At its closest points, Indonesia is 12 miles from Singapore, about 150 miles south of the Philippines, and 200 miles north of the mainland of Australia. Indonesia and Malaysia share the island of Borneo with Brunei, making Borneo

the only island in the world that is shared among more than two sovereign states. The Indonesian portion of Borneo, known as Kalimantan, occupies the southern portion of the island. It contains about three-quarters of the land area of Borneo and about 70 percent of its population. Most of the boundary between Kalimantan and the Malaysian portion of Borneo follows ridges that form drainage divides between rivers flowing northward into the South China Sea through Malaysia from those flowing southward through Kalimantan into the Java and Celebes seas.

Indonesia and Papua New Guinea share the island of New Guinea, with the Indonesian province of Irian Jaya occupying the western half of the island. The boundary between the two countries extends southward from the Pacific Ocean to the north to the Arafura Sea, north of Australia, to the south. From the Pacific coast, it follows the 141st meridian of east longitude southward to the Fly River. It then follows the Fly River as it bends first southwestward and then southeastward. It continues along the Fly until reaching the 141° 10′ meridian, which it follows southward to the Arafura Sea. Indonesia and East Timor have a common boundary extending across the island of Timor, which is shared between the two countries. The boundary follows river and straight-line segments in a generally north-south direction from the Savu Sea to the north to the Timor Sea to the south.

HISTORICAL CONTEXT

Modern humans are believed to have reached the islands of present-day Indonesia about 50,000 years ago. By the first millennium BC, Indonesian kingdoms had established trade linkages with China, South Asia, and across the Indian Ocean. The earliest settlers of Madagascar off the coast of Africa are believed to have come from Indonesia originally about 2,000 years ago. Many Indonesians, especially on the islands of Java and Sumatra, converted to Islam beginning in the 13th century. Today about 87 percent of Indonesia's people are Muslims.

European traders began to visit the coast of present-day Indonesia in the 16th century. In 1602, the Netherlands authorized the formation of the Dutch East India Company, which soon dominated trade in the area. The Dutch East India Company maintained control of Indonesia's coastal trading centers until it became bankrupt in 1800. The Netherlands then took over administration of the area, naming the colony the Dutch East Indies. The Dutch retained control of Indonesia until World War II, when it was occupied by the Japanese. Shortly after Japan surrendered to the Allies in August 1945, the Indonesian nationalist leader Sukarno declared Indonesia to be an independent country. The Dutch refused to recognize Sukarno's claim and continued to contest control of Indonesia until 1949, when they recognized Indonesia's independence. However, the Netherlands retained control of the western half of New Guinea. The Dutch intended Dutch New Guinea to become a separate independent country. However, Indonesian troops invaded Dutch New Guinea in 1961. The United Nations took over administration of Dutch New Guinea in 1962, and sovereignty over this area, now known as Irian Jaya, was transferred to Indonesia the following year. Indonesia annexed Irian Jaya formally in 1969.

The boundary between Indonesia and Malaysia on Borneo was first agreed upon in principle by the Netherlands and Britain, as the colonial powers controlling these present-day countries respectively, in 1846. In 1891, the Netherlands and Britain signed a second agreement to determine the land border more precisely. The boundary was maintained by Indonesia and Malaysia as the successor states of the two colonial powers. In 1975, Indonesia and Malaysia undertook a joint boundary survey that was completed in 2000. Indonesia's boundaries with Papua New Guinea and with East Timor were also determined by the Dutch in agreement with Australia and Portugal, respectively.

CONTEMPORARY ISSUES

Indonesia's land boundaries are generally uncontested. However, in recent years several issues involving Indonesia and its neighbors have arisen.

One of these issues was the status of East Timor, which was a Portuguese colony in contrast to the rest of Indonesia, which was under Dutch administration. Indonesia claimed sovereignty over the entire island of Timor, and Indonesian forces occupied East Timor shortly after Portugal granted East Timor independence in 1975. Indonesia occupied East Timor from 1976 to 2000 and claimed it as an Indonesian province. In 1999, the United Nations sponsored a referendum in East Timor concerning its future. A large majority of voters supported East Timor independence, which was granted formally in 2002.

The status of a long-standing separatist movement in the province of Aceh appears to have been resolved also. Aceh is located in northwestern Sumatra at the extreme western end of the country. Historians believe that Islam first reached Indonesia through Aceh during the 13th century. Between 1500 and 1800, a powerful sultanate based in Aceh controlled much of the trade going through Sumatra as well as along the nearby Malay Peninsula on the mainland. After the Dutch took formal control of the Dutch West Indies, they met with fierce resistance in Aceh, which refused to accept Dutch authority. The Netherlands declared war on Aceh in 1873, and over the next 30 years, an estimated 50,000 to 100,000 people are believed to have lost their lives.

The war between the Netherlands and Aceh ended formally in 1904, but Aceh separatists continued to resist Dutch rule. After independence, the Free Aceh movement arose and led efforts to resist integrating Aceh into the rest of Indonesia. Guerilla warfare erupted in 1975 and continued for the next three decades.

Aceh was hit very hard by the Indian Ocean tsunami of December 2004. Given its location close to the epicenter of the earthquake that caused the tsunami, most of the fatalities and property damage suffered in Indonesia as a result of the earthquake took place in Aceh. The large majority of the 170,000 residents of Indonesia who lost their lives in the earthquake and tsunami were residents of Aceh, and an estimated 500,000 residents of the province were left homeless.

The suffering in Aceh brought international attention to the province, including the state of the Free Aceh movement. Peace talks resumed in early 2005, and a peace agreement was signed by Indonesia's government and leaders of the Free Aceh movement ending armed hostilities. The agreement granted Aceh considerable autonomy relative to the rest of Indonesia.

To the east, separatists have demanded independence for the Indonesian portion of New Guinea for many years. Indonesia is sovereign over the western half of the island, while the eastern half is part of the independent country of Papua New Guinea. Western Indonesia was a Dutch colony known as Netherlands New Guinea until it became part of Indonesia in 1962. The area was known as Irian Jaya until its name was changed to Papua in 2001.

The population of Papua, which includes the Indonesian provinces of Papua and West Papua, is about 3 million, or slightly more than 1 percent of Indonesia's population. In contrast to the large majority of Indonesians, who practice Islam, the majority of people in Papua are Christians. Separatist activists have argued that Papua was added to Indonesia in 1962 without regard to the will of the Papuan population. They are also concerned that Indonesia's government has encouraged large numbers of non-Papuans to move to New Guinea, diluting the local culture. They also argue that profits from the extraction of Papua's substantial natural resources are flowing to other parts of Indonesia and that Papuans are suffering from the consequences of large-scale environmental damage. However, the Indonesia government has refused to give serious consideration to granting Papua its independence.

See also   East Timor, Malaysia, Papua New Guinea

Further Reading

Dewi Fortuna Anwar. "A journey of change: Indonesia's foreign policy." *Global Asia*, September 2009, https://globalasia.org/V4N3_Fall_2009/Dewi_Fortuna_Anwar.html?PHPSESSID=8ac93a07dc4d30ecb7907a8d6395a30f.

Luke Hunt. "Love thy neighbor." *Diplomat*, October 6, 2010, http://thediplomat.com/2010/10/06/love-thy-neighbour/.

Michelle Ann Miller. *Rebellion and reform in Indonesia. Jakarta's security and autonomy policies in Aceh.* London: Routledge, 2009.

Bilveer Singh. "Indonesia and the challenge of Papuan separatism." Institute for Defence Studies and Analysis, August 25, 2010, http://www.idsa.in/idsacomments/IndonesiaandthechallengeofPapuanseparatism_bsingh_250810.

LAOS

OVERVIEW

The Lao Democratic People's Republic is located in Southeast Asia. Laos has a land area of approximately 91,430 square miles, about the size of Kansas. It has a population of 6.8 million.

Laos is landlocked. Its neighbors are Myanmar to the northwest, China to the north, Vietnam to the northeast and east, Cambodia to the south, and Thailand to the west. Most of Laos's boundaries follow rivers or drainage divides associated with Southeast Asia's major river, the Mekong. Many cross rugged, heavily forested, and lightly populated terrain and recognize historic separation of various local cultural groups in the region.

The Mekong River forms the boundary between Myanmar and Laos. This stretch of the Mekong flows through rugged and sparsely populated country, and there are no bridges across the river between Myanmar and Laos. At the tripoint with China, the upper reaches of the Mekong become the boundary between Myanmar and China. The Laos-China boundary trends northeastward and is located along drainage divides between tributaries of the Mekong.

The long boundary between Laos and Vietnam also passes through mountainous and lightly populated terrain. In general, this boundary follows the drainage divide between the Mekong on the Laotian side and streams emptying directly into the South China Sea on the Vietnamese side. Much of the boundary between Laos and Cambodia follows drainage divides, although the Se Kong River, which is a major tributary of the Mekong, forms some of the boundary.

The entire boundary between Laos and Thailand follows rivers or drainage divides, and the Mekong forms more than half of the boundary. South of the tripoint between Laos, Thailand, and Myanmar, the boundary runs westward along a mountain range that defines the drainage basin of the Nam Kak River, a tributary of the Mekong. The boundary returns to the Mekong for much of the boundary's length except at its southern end, where it again follows drainage divides.

HISTORICAL CONTEXT

France absorbed Laos into its colony of French Indochina, which also included Vietnam and Cambodia, in 1893. Laos's boundaries were established by treaties and agreements between France and its neighbors shortly after Laos was absorbed into French Indochina. France signed boundary agreements with Thailand in 1894, China in 1895, and Britain (which controlled Myanmar) in 1896. France regarded Laos as one of several provinces of French Indonesia, and it determined boundaries between Laos and other provinces that would become the independent states of Vietnam and Cambodia.

Laos and the rest of French Indochina were occupied by Japan during World War

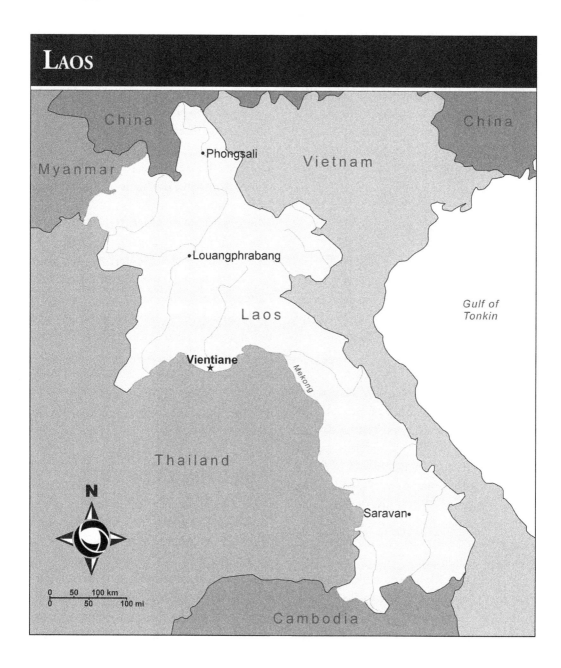

LAOS

China

•Phongsali

Vietnam

China

Myanmar

•Louangphrabang

Laos

Gulf of
Tonkin

Vientiane
★

Mekong

Thailand

N

Saravan•

0   50   100 km
0   50   100 mi

Cambodia

II. After the war ended, the area reverted to French control. Following several years of conflict, Laos along with Vietnam and Cambodia became independent in 1954. With minor adjustments, the boundaries between Laos and its neighbors as established by the French remain intact.

CONTEMPORARY ISSUES

The major issue facing Laos has involved its boundary with Thailand. A dispute involving sovereignty over four villages near the border broke into a shooting war in 1987 and 1988. The Thai-Laotian Border

War lasted for three months and resulted in about 1,000 casualties before a ceasefire was declared. A joint boundary commission was established in 1996 and was charged with resolving the question of sovereignty over the disputed villages, and the process of border demarcation continues. Laos is also an active member of the Mekong River Commission, which is charged with the management of the Mekong River. Laos has proposed to construct a dam on the upper reaches of the Mekong, but the downstream countries of Cambodia and Vietnam have expressed concern about the possible effects of the dam on water supplies and the natural environment downstream from the site of the proposed dam.

See also Cambodia, China, Myanmar, Thailand, Vietnam

Further Reading

Ruth Banomyong. *Laos: From buffer state to crossroads?* Chiang Mai, Thailand: Silkworm Books, 2007.

Francois Molle, Tira Foran, and Mira Kakonen (eds.). *Contested waterscapes in the Mekong region: Hydropower, livelihoods, and governance.* London: Routledge, 2009.

MALAYSIA

OVERVIEW

Malaysia is located in Southeast Asia. The overall land area of Malaysia is 127,355 square miles, slightly larger than New Mexico. Its population is about 30 million.

Malaysia is divided geographically between the Malay Peninsula on the Southeast Asian mainland and the provinces of Sarawak and Sabah on the island of Borneo. The Malayan peninsula contains about 40 percent of Malaysia's land area but about three-quarters of its population. Sarawak and Sabah are known collectively as East Malaysia. Sarawak is

slightly smaller than Peninsular Malaysia by land area, but it has a population of 2.6 million. Sabah, northeast of Sarawak, is somewhat smaller by land area than Sarawak but has a larger population, with about 3.4 million people.

Malaysia's land neighbors are Thailand, north of the Malay Peninsula, and Indonesia and Brunei on Borneo. Malaysia is separated from the island state of Singapore by the Straits of Johor, which are less than a mile wide at their narrowest points. Malaysia and Singapore are connected by the Johor-Singapore Causeway and by the Malaysia-Singapore Second Link Bridge, both of which are used heavily. Sabah, which is located along the northeastern coast of Borneo, is separated from the nearest islands of the Philippines by about 50 miles across the Sulu Sea.

The boundary between the Malay Peninsula and Thailand extends from the Straits of Malacca to the west to the Gulf of Thailand, which is part of the South China Sea, to the east. This boundary crosses drainage divides on the west and in the central portion of the boundary, with streams flowing westward into the Straits of Malacca on the Malaysian side of the boundary and those flowing northward and eastward into the Gulf of Thailand on the Thai side of the border. To the east, the Golok River forms the boundary until it empties into the Gulf of Thailand. This boundary was established by Britain and Thailand, then known as Siam, in 1909.

Malaysia's international boundaries on Borneo separate the Malaysian provinces of Sarawak and Sabah from Indonesia and Brunei. The boundary between Malaysia and Indonesia crosses the drainage divide between rivers flowing northward into

the South China Sea from those flowing southward across the Indonesian region of Kalimantan into the Java Sea and the Celebes Sea. Brunei is located on the northern coast of Borneo between Sarawak to the west and Sabah to the northeast. The boundary between Malaysia and Brunei follows drainage divides. Brunei includes two distinct land areas separated by a narrow strip of Malaysian territory known as the Limbang District.

HISTORICAL CONTEXT

The Malay Peninsula has been settled by humans for more than 40,000 years. By the first century BC, trade relationships had been established between Malay kingdoms and both India and China. The culture of the Malay Peninsula was influenced by India, and Hinduism and Buddhism came to be well established. The Buddhist Srivijaya Empire ruled the peninsula between the 7th and 13th centuries AD. Later, the peninsula was contested by kingdoms based in present-day Thailand, Cambodia, and Indonesia. Islam was introduced into the area during the 13th and 14th century, and Islam remains the primary religion of Malaysia. In 1402, the Islamic Sultanate of Malacca was established and soon began to control the peninsula.

In 1511, a Portuguese navy attacked and captured the city of Malacca on the southwestern coast of the peninsula. The Netherlands took over Malacca in 1641. In the late 18th century, the British East India Company began to establish a presence in the Malay Peninsula by leasing the city of Penang, northwest of Malacca. The Dutch ceded Malacca to Britain in 1824. By 1900, most of the mainland portion of present-day

Malaysia was governed by the British as the Federated Malay States. Meanwhile, the sultanate of Brunei granted Sarawak to an Englishman, James Brooke, in 1842. Brooke and his descendants served as rajahs of the independent Kingdom of Sarawak until 1946, when the right to rule Sarawak was ceded to the British crown. Britain obtained Sabah, which was then known as British North Borneo, from the sultanate of Sulu in the present-day Philippines in 1878.

The Malay Peninsula, Sarawak, and Sabah were occupied by Japanese forces during World War II, with nationalist sentiment increasing after the expulsion of the Japanese at the end of the war. In 1948, Britain established the Federation of Malaya. The federation became an independent state within the British Commonwealth in 1957. In 1963, Singapore, Sarawak, and Sabah joined the federation, which was renamed Malaysia.

Singapore left the federation and became an independent country in 1965. A major issue associated with Singapore's departure was ethnicity because people of Malay ancestry were a minority in Singapore, which had a majority-Chinese population, but a majority in the Malay Peninsula. Today about 50 percent of Malaysia's people are ethnic Malays, 26 percent are of Chinese ancestry, and 8 percent are of Indian ancestry. Most of the others are descended from the indigenous peoples of Sarawak and Sabah. The majority of Malaysians of Chinese and Indian ancestry live in cities; people of Malay ancestry are more likely to live in rural areas.

People of Malay ancestry are known as Bumiputras. The word *Bumiputra* comes from a Malay word meaning "son of the soil." According to Malaysia's constitution, a Bumiputra is a person who "professes the religion of Islam, habitually speaks the Malay language, conforms to Malay customs and is the child of at least one parent who was born within the Federation of Malaya before independence of Malaya on the 31st of August 1957." After Sarawak and Sabah became part of the independent country of Malaysia in 1963, the definition of a Bumiputra was expanded to include descendants of the indigenous peoples of these provinces, although these persons are not ethnic Malays. Malaysian law privileges Bumiputras in various government programs such as government contracting and admission to schools and universities.

CONTEMPORARY ISSUES

Malaysia's land boundaries are generally uncontested. However, Malaysia and its neighbors have attempted to resolve disagreements concerning their maritime boundaries. A maritime boundary was delineated between the Malayan sultanate of Johor, at the southern end of the Malay Peninsula, and Singapore in 1824. The boundary has been in effect ever since, but it was considered an internal, subnational boundary until Singapore left the Federation of Malaysia in 1963. In 1979, Malaysia and Singapore began to dispute the specific location of their maritime boundary. Both states claimed the island of Pedra Branca, which was awarded to Singapore by the International Court of Justice in 2008. Malaysia and Thailand have agreed to their continental shelf boundary in 1971 and their territorial sea claims in 1979. However, Indonesia also claims territory on the potentially mineral-rich continental shelf of the Gulf of Thailand. Indonesia's claims overlap those of Malaysia and Thailand. The three countries began efforts to resolve the dispute by creating a joint development area, within which profits associated with the extraction and sale of mineral resources would be shared.

Relations between Malaysia and the Philippines have occasionally been strained. Much of this tension involves religion, especially in Muslim-majority areas within the Catholic-majority Philippines. Some Muslim-dominated communities in the Philippines have advocated the possibility of unification with Malaysia. Meanwhile, the Philippines has claimed Sabah as a former part of the sultanate of Sulu, although this claim is dormant and has not been pursued.

See also   Brunei, Indonesia, Thailand

Further Reading

Amitav Acharya. *Constructing a security community in Southeast Asia: ASEAN and the problem of regional order.* London: Routledge, 2009.

Luke Hunt. "Love thy neighbour." *Diplomat*, October 6, 2010, http://the diplomat.com/2010/10/06/love-thy-neighbour/.

Johan Saravanamuttu. *Malaysia's foreign policy: Alignment, neutrality, and Islamism.* Singapore: Institute for Southeast Asian Studies, 2010.

MALDIVES

OVERVIEW

The Republic of Maldives is an island country in the Indian Ocean. The country includes an archipelago of more than 1,100 islands, of which about 250 are inhabited. Most of the islands are small; the total land area is only 115 square miles, or less than twice the size of the District of Columbia. The population is about 330,000. The northernmost islands are located about 300 miles southwest of the southern tip of India. The capital city, Male, is about 450 miles southwest of Sri Lanka.

HISTORICAL CONTEXT

The Maldives are believed to have been settled originally by Dravidians from present-day Kerala and Sri Lanka about 2,000 years ago. Most residents of the Maldives were Buddhists until the 12th century AD, when the last Buddhist king of the Maldives converted to Islam, which remains the dominant religion of the country today. Portugal established a settlement on the Maldives in 1558. After local forces drove the Portuguese out, the Netherlands assumed control of the Maldives in the 17th century. Britain assumed control of the Maldives, as well as Sri Lanka, in 1796. The Maldives became independent in 1965.

The Maldives are very low-lying islands. The highest point in the entire country is only about eight feet above sea level. The threat of sea-level rise associated with global warming is thus a major threat to the country, especially given predictions that melting ice caps in the Antarctic, Greenland, and elsewhere could cause global sea levels to rise. Measurements of average sea level demonstrated that the average sea level in the Maldives has risen about eight inches since 1900. A global sea-level rise of 10 feet would mean that the entire country would be underwater. Most of the Maldives's islands were flooded in the 2004

MALDIVES

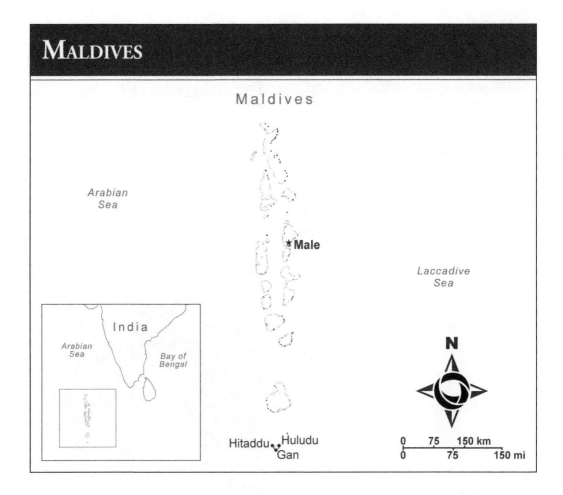

Indian Ocean tsunami, which killed 108 people in the country and caused extensive damage. Leaders in the Maldives are looking seriously into the possibility of moving the entire population elsewhere should sea-level rise continue. In 2008, the Maldives's president announced that he was considering the purchase of land in India, Australia, or Sri Lanka in the event that the islands become inundated and their people would be forced to relocate.

Further Reading

Justin Hoffmann. "The Maldives and rising sea levels." *ICE Case Studies*,

2007, http://www1.american.edu/ted/ice/maldives.htm.

Rasheep Ramesh. "Paradise almost lost: Maldives seek to buy a new homeland." *Guardian*, November 9, 2008, http://www.guardian.co.uk/environment/2008/nov/10/maldives-climate-change.

MYANMAR

OVERVIEW

Myanmar, which is also known as Burma, is the largest country by land area on the Southeast Asian mainland. Myanmar

MYANMAR

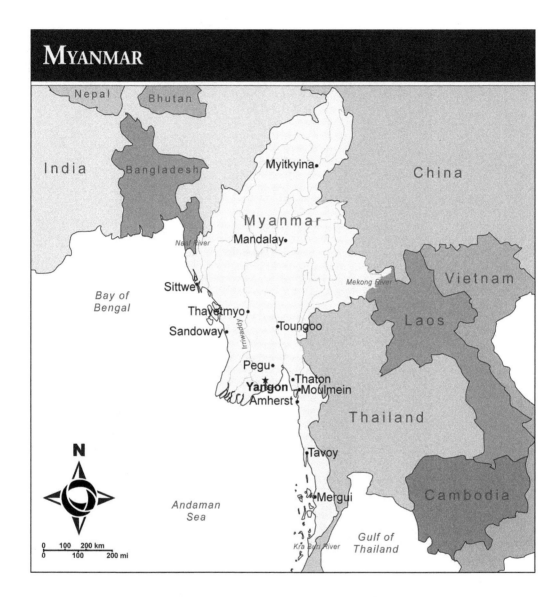

is slightly larger in land area than the state of Texas, with a population of about 58 million.

Myanmar's neighbors are Bangladesh and India to the west, China to the north and east, Laos to the east, and Thailand to the east and south. Western Myanmar has a long coastline on the Bay of Bengal. For hundreds of years, Burmese culture and economic activity have centered on the

Irrawaddy River, which flows through the center of the country and enters the Andaman Sea south of Myanmar's capital and largest city, Yangon. Many of Myanmar's boundaries follow physical features, and many of its boundaries separate the Irrawaddy drainage basin from neighboring countries and cultures. The large majority of Myanmar's people live in the valley of Irrawaddy.

The Naaf River, an estuary of the Bay of Bengal, forms the short boundary between Myanmar and Bangladesh. Most of the much longer boundary between Myanmar and India follows drainage divides or natural watercourses, while the remainder consists of straight-line segments. Much of this boundary is located in mountainous areas including the Dawna and Bilauktaung ranges, and at several points it is located along the drainage divide between the valley of the Irrawaddy on the Burmese side of the border to the east and rivers flowing directly into the Bay of Bengal on the Indian side of the border to the west. The general trend of this boundary is from northeast to southwest.

Myanmar's irregular boundary with China trends from west to east before trending southeastward. The western section of the boundary coincides generally with the area drained by the Irrawaddy River, with areas north and east of the Irrawaddy drainage basin on the Chinese side of the border. To the east and south, the boundary follows several rivers and in some places follows drainage divides. The Mekong River forms much of the short boundary between Myanmar and Laos. The much longer border between Myanmar and Thailand also follows natural features including mountain ranges and rivers. The Kra Buri River, which is also known as the Pakchan River, forms the southern portion of the Myanmar-Thailand boundary that extends through the Isthmus of Kra.

HISTORICAL CONTEXT

Most of modern-day Myanmar was part of the Kingdom of Myanmar, which had ruled over the area since the ninth century. In 1752, the Konbaung dynasty was established. Konbaung rulers controlled much of Myanmar along with parts of British-ruled northeastern India. Conflicts between Myanmar and British India led to three wars, which took place between 1824 and 1885. After the Third Anglo-Burmese War, the Burmese kingdom was disestablished, and Myanmar became part of British India. It remained part of British India until 1935, when Britain began to administer Myanmar as a separate colony. However, the boundary between Myanmar and British India was not defined clearly after the two colonies were separated. The Government of India Act of 1935 stated merely that Myanmar would consist of territories east of Bengal (present-day Bangladesh) and what are now the Indian states of Assam and Manipur. The intent of this act was to separate people of Burmese culture from those of Indian culture as much as possible; hence, much of the boundary is located on drainage divides or along mountain ranges.

Myanmar remained a British colony from the late 19th century until it became independent in 1948. After independence, Myanmar formalized its boundaries with its neighbors. Myanmar and China agreed upon its boundary in 1960, and the boundary between Myanmar and India was formally demarcated by international agreement in 1967.

CONTEMPORARY ISSUES

Although one rationale for drawing Myanmar's boundaries was to separate the Burmese population and culture from those of its neighbors, there are many minority populations in Myanmar. About two-thirds of the population is ethnic Burmese. The rest belong to 135 ethnic groups recognized officially by the governments. The two largest ethnic groups are the Shan (9 percent of the population) and the Karen (7 percent). Both the Shan and the Karen live in eastern Myanmar along the border with Thailand. Both groups claim that they are victims of discrimination and persecution by the Burmese-dominated government, and both have pushed for independence or greater autonomy.

The fact that much of the boundary between Myanmar and Thailand is located in rugged, heavily forested terrain has helped the Shan and Karen efforts to oppose the government. Guerillas opposed to the Myanmar government can escape easily across the poorly maintained border into Thailand when threatened by government troops and security forces. Myanmar has accused Thailand of harboring these Shan and Karen activists. An estimated 2 million residents of Myanmar, many of whom are of Shan or Karen ancestry, now live as refugees in Thailand. In 2009, thousands of refugees moved into China following skirmishes between local ethnic minority populations and the Burmese army.

Ongoing tension between Myanmar and Thailand is exacerbated by several other boundary-related issues. Heavily deforested Thailand has been accused of illegal logging on the Burmese side of the border. At the same time, Thailand has accused the Burmese government of working actively with local populations to smuggle illegal drugs across the boundary into Thailand. Smuggling of gemstones is also a significant issue. Myanmar produces 90 percent of the world's rubies, and many international observers have accused Myanmar's repressive government of using profits from mining and selling these rubies to finance activities that suppress human rights and otherwise repress minority populations. In 2008, the United States banned the import of these "blood rubies" from Myanmar. However, many rubies continue to be smuggled across the boundary into Thailand, from which they are sold illegally on international markets.

The boundaries between Myanmar and its western neighbors, Bangladesh and India, are much more stable and less controversial. However, the three countries have become involved in an acrimonious dispute over maritime boundaries, which have yet to be demarcated unambiguously, in the Bay of Bengal. The disagreement has intensified following the discovery of potentially lucrative oil deposits in the disputed area. In 2012, the United Nations International Tribunal for the Law of the Sea issued a ruling establishing the boundary and resolving the dispute between Myanmar and Bangladesh. Resolution will allow both countries to begin oil and gas exploration.

See also   Bangladesh, China, India, Laos, Thailand

Further Reading

Jared Bissinger. "The maritime boundary dispute between Bangladesh and Myanmar: Motivations, possible solutions, and implications." *Asia Policy*, 10 (2010), pp. 103–142.

Jessica Harriden. "Making a name for themselves: Karen identity and the politicization of ethnicity in Burma." *Journal of Burma Studies*, 7 (2002), pp. 84–144.

Dan McDougall. "The curse of the blood rubies: Inside Burma's brutal gem trade." *Daily Mail*, September 18, 2010, http://www.dailymail.co.uk/home/moslive/article-1312382/The-curse-blood-rubies-Inside-Burmas-brutal-gem-trade.html.

NEPAL

OVERVIEW

The Federal Democratic Republic of Nepal is located in the Himalaya Mountains of South Asia between India and China. The highest mountain in the world, Mt. Everest, is located on the boundary between Nepal and China. Nepal has a land area of 56,827 square miles, about the size of Iowa. Its population is about 30 million,

with the majority living in the lowland areas in the southern and central parts of the country.Nepal contains three distinct physiographic regions. The southern part of Nepal, known as the Terai Plains, is part of the Indo-Gangetic Plain, which extends across northern India. This area is heavily agricultural and has Nepal's densest rural population. The Hill Region of Nepal, located north of the Indo-Gangetic Plain, has altitudes of between 3,000 and 8,000 feet above sea level. This area contains Nepal's capital city of Kathmandu. The rapidly growing Kathmandu metropolitan area has a population of nearly 7 million.

Nepal is a long, narrow country whose land area extends from northwest to southeast. Its neighbors are India to the west, south, and east and China to the north. The southern boundary between Nepal

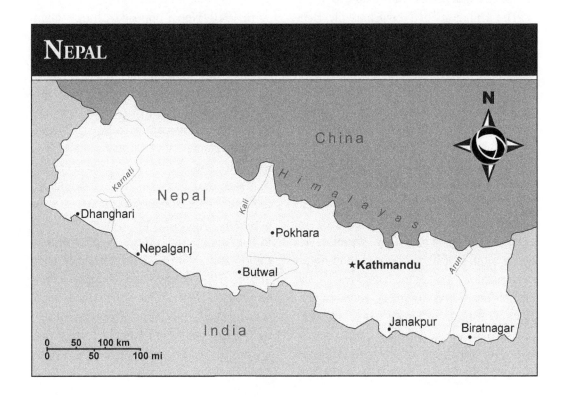

NEPAL

China

Nepal

Dhanghari

Karnati

Kali

Himalayas

Pokhara

Nepalganj

★Kathmandu

Arun

Butwal

Janakpur

Biratnagar

India

0   50   100 km
0   50   100 mi

and India is composed primarily of long straight-line segments through the Terai Plains. On both ends, the boundaries extend northward from the Terai Plains into the Himalayas. The western boundary follows the Kali River, a tributary of the Ganges, for the entire length of the boundary. The boundary between Nepal and China follows the crest of the Himalayas with tripoints between Nepal, India, and China at each end.

HISTORICAL CONTEXT

Present-day Nepal was ruled by a series of dynasties for more than 2,000 years before the Kingdom of Nepal was unified under King Prithvi Narayan Shah in 1768. Prithvi Narayan Shah's descendants continued to rule Nepal under the country's monarchy was abolished in 2008.

The Kingdom of Nepal and the British East India Company, which controlled neighboring portions of India, disputed control of the region during the late 18th and early 19th centuries as Britain expanded its sphere of influence in the northern portion of the Indian subcontinent. In 1814, British forces attacked the Kingdom of Nepal in the Anglo-Nepalese War, also known as the Gurkha War. After the war ended, Britain and the Kingdom of Nepal signed the Sugauli Treaty in 1816. Under terms of the Sugauli Treaty, Nepal ceded about a third of its territory, including all of its territory west of the Kali River, to the British East India Company. In exchange, Britain recognized Nepalese independence and recognized the Shah dynasty as sovereign over Nepal. The territories ceded from Nepal to the British East India Company

under terms of the Sugauli Treaty are now part of India.

During the 1850s, power in Nepal was seized by the Rana family, which reduced the Shah family's role to a ceremonial one. Nepal was isolated largely from the outside world until the mid-20th century. Nepal and the People's Republic of China agreed to the crest of the Himalayas as their common boundary in 1960.

CONTEMPORARY ISSUES

Nepal's location has made it a buffer state between China and India. Nepal's status as a buffer state has influenced Nepal's foreign policy and boundary issues throughout the 20th and early 21st centuries. Nepal has been careful to maintain a balance between its relationships with the two major powers while preserving its own autonomy and independence.

In 1910, Nepal opposed China's claim of sovereignty over Tibet and supported Tibetan independence. In 1950 and 1951, the People's Republic of China invaded Tibet and incorporated Tibet forcibly into the People's Republic. Nepal opposed this invasion, in part because the Nepalese government saw China as a threat to its own borders. Nepal signed a Treaty of Peace and Friendship in 1950, but by the late 1950s, Nepalese officials became concerned about undue Indian influence in Nepal's internal affairs. Nepal resumed diplomatic relations with China in 1955 and in 1956 recognized Chinese sovereignty over Tibet. India and China went to war in 1962, and Nepal maintained neutrality. In recent years, Nepal's foreign policy has come to be oriented more to China. China began constructing a railroad from

Tibet's capital of Lhasa into Nepal, thus connecting Nepal by rail with China's railroad network.

Nepal and India continue to dispute a small area near the western tripoint between Nepal, India, and China. The dispute arose over conflicting interpretations of the Sugauli Treaty associated with which tributary of the Kali River is the northernmost segment of the boundary. The area in dispute is about 30 square miles in size and contains three villages. It has value to both countries as a source of hydroelectric power. Negotiations between the two countries to resolve the dispute are ongoing.

See also   China, India

Further Reading

Sudha Ramachandran. "Nepal to get China rail link." *Asia Times*, May 15, 2008, http://www.atimes.com/atimes/South_Asia/JE15Df01.html.

Sanjay Upadhya. *Nepal and the geostrategic rivalry between China and India.* New York: Routledge, 2012.

PAKISTAN

OVERVIEW

The Islamic Republic of Pakistan occupies the western portion of the Indian subcontinent in South Asia. It has a land area of 307,374 square miles, about the size of Texas and Louisiana combined. With a population of about 180 million, Pakistan is the sixth-most populous country in the world.

Pakistan's neighbors are Iran to the west, Afghanistan to the northwest and west, China to the northeast, and India to the east. Southern Pakistan has a coastline along the Arabian Gulf and, in the southwest, the Gulf of Oman. The boundary between Pakistan and Iran follows a series of short-line segments, drainage divides, and short segments along rivers northward from the Gulf of Oman to the tripoint between Pakistan, Iran, and Afghanistan. Most of the boundary between Pakistan and Afghanistan crosses the high peaks of the Pamir and Hindu Kush mountain ranges. The boundary region is very rugged and inaccessible.

From the tripoint between Pakistan, Afghanistan, and China, the boundary between Pakistan and China extends southeastward, again crossing very high, rugged mountains in the Himalayas. This boundary is in dispute because the territory of Jammu and Kashmir is located along the border and is claimed by both Pakistan and India. Pakistan has de facto control of the northern and western portion of Jammu and Kashmir, and much of this part of the territory adjoins Chinese territory.

South of Jammu and Kashmir, the boundary between Pakistan and India is a cultural boundary that separates predominantly Muslim Pakistan from predominantly Hindu India. South of Jammu and Kashmir, the boundary extends along the Ravi River, which is a tributary of the Indus River, southwestward. The Ravi enters Pakistan east of the city of Lahore, and from there the boundary follows short segments southward to the Satluj River, which is another tributary of the Indus. A few miles south of the Pakistani town of Haveli, the Satluj flows into Pakistan. From the Satluj, the boundary follows straight-line segments that extend in a

PAKISTAN

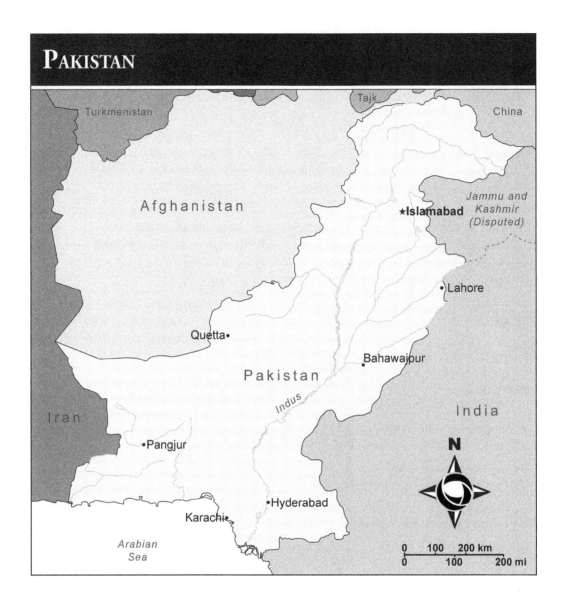

generally southwesterly direction. Along the Arabian Gulf, the boundary crosses the Rann of Kutch, which is one of the largest salt marshes in the world.

HISTORICAL CONTEXT

The valley of the Indus River, which is the major river of Pakistan, was the site of one of the oldest civilizations in the world. The Indus Valley Civilization arose around 6,000 years ago, and its two major cities, Harappa and Mohenjo-Daro, were established nearly 3,000 years BC. Much of present-day Pakistan was occupied subsequently by a succession of empires. The first Indo-Aryan civilization, known as the Vedic civilization, was established by Indo-Aryan migrants from present-day Iran. The Indo-Aryans, whose descendants now occupy much of Pakistan along with northern India and Bangladesh, are believed to have developed Hinduism. The Vedic civilization was supplanted by the Achaemenid Empire of Persia, the Greek Empire of Alexander the Great, and the Mauryan Empire based in eastern India. Beginning in the seventh century AD, a majority of people living in present-day Pakistan converted from Hinduism or Buddhism to Islam. The Mughal Empire ruled what is now Pakistan beginning in 1526.

In the 19th century, the British East India Company established increasing control over present-day Pakistan. The British cemented control of the area via a series of wars during the 19th century, and the area became part of British India. During the early 20th century, Britain initiated efforts to transition British India toward independence. A major concern was whether to divide British India into different sovereign countries on the basis of religion. Support for dividing British India was especially strong in the Indus Valley and other Muslim-majority areas because a substantial majority of British India's residents were Hindus. In 1933, supporters of an independent Muslim-majority country in the northwestern part of British India coined the word *Pakistan*. The name is an acronym derived from the names of the five Muslim-majority provinces in and near the Indus Valley: Punjab, the Afghan Province (which is known now as the North-west Frontier Province), Kashmir, Sind, and Baluchistan.

British India was partitioned in 1947, and Pakistan and India became independent. Independent Pakistan included present-day Pakistan, then known as West Pakistan, and present-day Bangladesh, then known as East Pakistan. Although the two components of Pakistan were both predominantly Muslim, they were separated by 1,000 miles by land, and their environments, cultures, and economies were very different. Efforts to separate the country into two separate countries occurred in East Pakistan during the 1960s and 1970s. In 1971, the government of Pakistan sent troops into East Pakistan. Armed conflict broke out, and thousands of East Pakistanis were killed and millions moved into India as refugees. India supported East Pakistan's independence, and Indian troops with the support of local independence activists invaded East Pakistan in order to expel West Pakistan's troops. West Pakistan's forces surrendered in December 1971, after which Pakistan was divided. West Pakistan retained the name of Pakistan, and East Pakistan became the independent country of Bangladesh.

Many of Pakistan's other boundaries were determined during the period of British colonial rule. The boundary between Pakistan and Iran was agreed upon by Britain and the Persian Empire in 1893. In the same year, the boundary between British India and Afghanistan was agreed upon in principle. Pakistan and China agreed to their boundary in a series of agreements between 1961 and 1965.

CONTEMPORARY ISSUES

Pakistan and India have had a tense relationship since both became independent in 1947. The major issue of contention between the two countries has been the status of Jammu and Kashmir. Jammu and

Kashmir is an area of about 85,000 square miles, approximately the size of Utah, with a population of about 13 million. The northern portion of Jammu and Kashmir borders China and Afghanistan and is located in the Himalayas.

A majority of the population in Jammu and Kashmir are Muslims. However, during the days of the British Empire, Jammu and Kashmir was ruled by a Hindu prince who decided to make it part of India at the time of independence. At the time of independence, about 75 percent of the people were Muslims. After independence, India claimed Jammu and Kashmir. Jammu and Kashmir is an Indian state, although Pakistan remains in control of the northern and western portions of the territory. Wars over the territory have broken out between India and Pakistan in 1947, 1965, 1971, and 2001. Pakistan does not recognize Indian sovereignty over Jammu and Kashmir, and it regards the territory as "occupied by India." China also claims portions of northeastern Jammu and Kashmir.

Pakistan and India have also disputed control of portions of the Rann of Kutch region along the Arabian Gulf. The boundary dispute has focused on Kori Creek, which flows into the Arabian Gulf about 10 miles southeast of the current boundary. The two countries fought a brief war over the region in 1965. In 1999, the Indian Air Force shot down a Pakistani military plane over the Kori Creek region, claiming that the Pakistani plane was violating Indian airspace. The Rann of Kutch is rich in natural gas, making the boundary region highly attractive to both countries. The dispute over the Rann of Kutch includes disagreement over maritime boundaries in the Arabian Gulf as well as the boundary on land.

See also   Afghanistan, China, India, Iran

Further Reading
Robert Johnson. *A region in turmoil.* London: Reaktion, 2005.

Robert D. Kaplan. "What's wrong with Pakistan?" *Foreign Affairs*, July/August 2012, http://www.foreignpolicy.com/articles/2012/06/18/whats_wrong_with_pakistan?page=0%2C0.

Aparna Pande. *Explaining Pakistan's foreign policy: Escaping India.* London: Routledge, 2011.

Declan Walsh. "Afghanistan war logs: Secret war along the Pakistan border." *Guardian*, July 25, 2010, http://www.guardian.co.uk/world/2010/jul/25/afghanistan-war-pakistan-border-taliban.

PHILIPPINES

OVERVIEW

The Republic of the Philippines is an island country off the coast of Southeast Asia. The archipelago comprising the Philippines contains 7,107 islands, of which about 2,000 are inhabited. The overall land area is 115,831 square miles, the size of Arizona. The population of the Philippines is about 98 million, making the Philippines the 12th-largest country in the world by population.

Geographically, the islands of the Philippines are divided into three major groups. These are Luzon and its neighbors to the north, the Visayas in the central portion, and Mindanao and its neighbors to the south. Luzon is the largest island in the Philippines. It contains more than a third of the Philippines's land area, and it is the fourth-largest island in the world by

PHILIPPINES

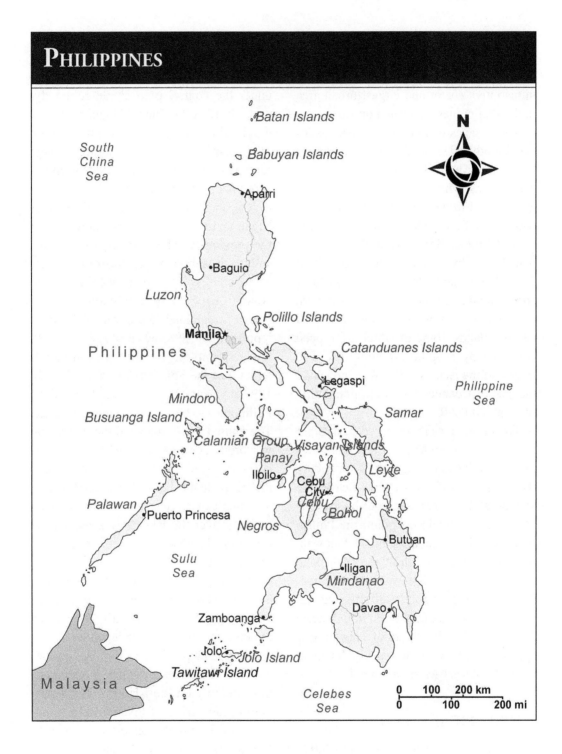

population, with nearly 50 million people, or about half of the country's total population. The Manila metropolitan area, the administrative center and largest urban area in the Philippines, is located on Luzon.

The Visayas include several islands located south and west of Luzon and north of Mindanao. About 20 million people live in the Visayas. Mindanao, the southernmost main island in the Philippines, is the second-largest Philippine island by both land area and population. It is slightly smaller than Luzon by land area, but with about 23 million inhabitants has only half of Luzon's population density. The southern portion of the Philippines contains several nearby islands, some of which have been contested by neighboring countries. The largest of the islands is Palawan, an island the size of Connecticut with a population of about 800,000.

The Philippines is separated from other East Asian and Southeast Asian countries by the South China Sea to the west and by the Sulu Sea and the Celebes Sea to the southwest. Its closest neighbor by water is Malaysia. At its closest point, the Philippines island of Balabac, south of Palawan, is about 50 miles north of the Malaysian territory of Sabah on the island of Borneo. The Philippines is about 250 miles northwest of the island of Sulawesi in Indonesia and about 250 miles south of Taiwan. It is approximately 500 miles east of Vietnam on the Southeast Asian mainland.

HISTORICAL CONTEXT

Artifacts dating back more than 50,000 years have been discovered and excavated on several Philippine islands by archaeologists. By about 1000 BC, kingdoms and chiefdoms had arisen throughout the islands. However, at no time prior to European colonization were the islands united under the control of a single ruling dynasty. In 1521, Ferdinand Magellan visited the Philippines in his circumnavigation of the earth and claimed the archipelago for Spain. Magellan was killed by indigenous people in the island of Cebu. Permanent Spanish settlement of the Philippines began in 1565, and the Spanish took over the previously inhabited town of Manila and made Manila the administrative center of the colony. The islands were named in honor of King Philip II of Spain.

Spain remained in control of the Philippines until 1898, when sovereignty was transferred to the United States in the aftermath of the Spanish-American War. In 1899, an insurgent movement declared the Philippines to be an independent republic. The United States disputed the claim, and war broke out between the Filipino insurgents and American forces. The war ended in 1901, when Filipino forces surrendered to American troops and American sovereignty over the islands was recognized formally. Japan invaded and seized the Philippines in 1942 and remained in control of the colony until the end of World War II. The United States continued to govern the Philippines as a colony until 1946, when the Philippines became independent.

Since independence, the Philippines has dealt with secessionist movements, most notably on the island of Mindanao. During the period of Spanish rule, a majority of Filipinos converted to Roman Catholicism. However, some areas of the Philippines have Muslim majorities. About a third of Mindanao's people are Muslims, and most Muslims on Mindanao live in the southern part of the island closest to heavily Muslim Malaysia and Indonesia. Islamic separatists have sought independence or more local autonomy for Muslim-dominated areas of Mindanao and nearby islands for many years. Muslims living in the Philippines are known as Moros, and a group known as the Moro Islamic Liberation Front has pushed for greater autonomy for the Moro population of the Philippines.

In 1989, the Philippine government approved the creation of the Autonomous Region in Muslim Mindanao. The provinces included in the Autonomous Region are located in southwestern Mindanao and have a combined land area of about 10,500 square miles, the size of Maryland, and a combined population of 4.5 million. Sharia law is practiced in this region, but it applies only to Muslims and cannot be practiced in conflict with the Constitution of the Philippines.

Religious conflict has also occurred on the island of Palawan, which is located west of Mindanao and extends southwestward toward Borneo. In 2001, Palawan voted against joining the Autonomous Region in Muslim Mindanao. However, some Muslim activists in southern Palawan want more autonomy or to join with Muslim-majority Malaysia to the south.

CONTEMPORARY ISSUES

The Philippines along with other countries that adjoin the South China Sea remain involved in ongoing dispute over the Spratly Islands, which are located above valuable oil and gas deposits. The status of the Autonomous Region in Muslim Mindanao remains uncertain. Another

movement for more local autonomy is found in the Cordillera region in the interior portion of northern Luzon. Most residents of this region are of indigenous rather than Filipino ancestry, and they have claimed to be ignored and/or discriminated against by the central government based in Manila. The Philippines have also claimed sovereignty over the Malaysian province of Sabah in northeastern Borneo, but in recent years the Philippine government have not pressed this claim.

See also   Indonesia, Malaysia

Further Reading

IRIN News. "Mindanao separatist hardliners against peace talks with government." February 8, 2011, http://www.irinnews.org/Report/91864/PHILIP-PINES-Mindanao-separatist-hardliners-against-peace-talks-with-government.

Julminir I. Jannaral. "Government urged to reassert Sabah claim." *Manila Times*, June 11, 2012, http://www.manilatimes.net/index.php/news/regions/24640-govt-urged-to-reassert-sabah-claim.

Greg Rushford. "Asia's next tiger." *Foreign Policy*, June 19, 2012, http://www.foreignpolicy.com/articles/2012/06/19/asias_next_tiger.

SINGAPORE

OVERVIEW

Singapore is an island country located off the coast of the Malay Peninsula between Malaysia to the north and Indonesia to the south. It includes the main island of Singapore along with 62 small nearby islands. The total land area of Singapore is

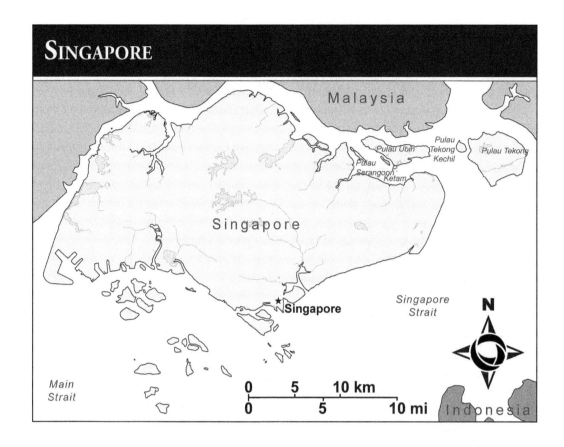

SINGAPORE

274 square miles, or about four times as large as the District of Columbia. Its population is about 5 million.

As an island country, Singapore has no land boundaries. However, it is located very close to both Indonesia and Malaysia. The Straits of Johor separate Singapore from Malaysia. The straits are less than a mile wide at their narrowest point and are crossed by the Johor-Singapore Causeway and by the Malaysia-Singapore Second Link Bridge. Both carry thousands of people across the straits every day. Singapore is separated from Indonesia's Riau Islands by the Strait of Singapore, which at its narrowest point is about 12 miles wide. Maritime boundaries have been delimited through both the Straits of Johor and the Strait of Singapore. Both are located midway between the shorelines of the respective countries.

HISTORICAL CONTEXT

Singapore was known to the Romans. Given its location along the major trade route between India and China, Singapore has been an important trading and commercial center for at least 2,000 years.

The modern state of Singapore was founded by Great Britain in the early 19th century. At that time, the Netherlands controlled what is today Indonesia. In doing so, they controlled trade between East Asia and Europe and charged high tariffs and tolls to merchant ships from other countries. The British determined to challenge the Netherlands for economic supremacy in the region. In 1819, the British East India Company signed a treaty with Sultan Hussein, the shah of Johor. Johor, which is located on the southernmost part of the Malayan Peninsula and is today part of Malaysia, was then in control of Singapore. This treaty gave the company the right to establish a trading post on the island. The Port of Singapore was established on the site of a small Malay village on the southern side of the island facing the Strait of Singapore. A second treaty between the company and the shah of Johor, signed in 1824, gave the company ownership of the entire island of Singapore. Singapore became a British colony in 1826.

Singapore became independent in 1963 as part of the Federation of Malaysia, which also included Malaya on the Asian mainland and Sarawak and Sabah on the island of Borneo. In 1965, Singapore was expelled from the federation and became an independent country. A major issue associated with Singapore's departure was ethnic conflict. A majority of people throughout Malaysia were of Malay ancestry, whereas more than two-thirds of Singapore's residents were of Chinese ancestry. Many in Singapore believed that Malaysia's affirmative action programs privileged Malays and discriminated against people of Chinese descent.

Singapore moved quickly to solidify its position as an independent country. At the time, some believed that a small island, with no natural resources and high unemployment, could not be a viable state. In order to strengthen its position, Singapore emphasized a policy of export-led industrialization, producing goods for export and using profits to expand its industry. Singapore also continued to emphasize international trade. The Port of Singapore is currently the busiest port in the world. Electronics and biotechnology are also emphasized in Singapore's economy. These efforts have contributed to the fact that Singapore today is the wealthiest country in Southeast Asia.

The maritime boundary between Singapore and Malaysia was first created in 1824 as part of the treaty between the British East India Company and the shah of Johor. In 1979, a dispute between Singapore and Malaysia over the maritime boundary's location arose. Both countries claimed the small island of Pedra Branca. In 2008, the International Court of Justice resolved the dispute by awarding Pedra Branca to Singapore. The maritime boundary between Singapore and Indonesia was first delineated by the Anglo-Dutch Agreement between Britain and the Netherlands in 1824. This agreement established Malaya and Singapore as a British sphere of influence and established a Dutch sphere of influence over the Dutch East Indies, or present-day Indonesia. The boundary was reaffirmed by an agreement between Singapore and Indonesia in 1973.

See also Indonesia, Malaysia

Further Reading

Andi Arsana and Farid Yuniar. "Geospatial aspects of maritime boundary delimitation in the Singapore Strait involving Indonesia, Malaysia and Singapore." *FIC Congress 2010: Facing the Challenges—Building the Capacity*, 2010, http://www.fig.net/pub/fig2010/papers/ts01i%5Cts01i_arsana_yuniar_3939.pdf.

Kate Hodal. "Singapore's maids to get a day off." *Guardian*, March 6, 2012, http://www.guardian.co.uk/world/2012/mar/06/singapore-maids-one-day-off-a-week.

Saw Swee-hock. *The population of Singapore.* 3rd ed. Singapore: Institute for Southeast Asian Studies, 2012.

SRI LANKA

OVERVIEW

The Democratic Socialist Republic of Sri Lanka occupies the island of Sri Lanka, which is located off the southeastern coast of India. Sri Lanka has a land area of 25,332 square miles, the size of West Virginia. Its population is about 22 million. Sri Lanka is separated from the mainland of India by the Palk Strait, which is 33 miles wide at its narrowest point.

Sri Lanka contains two major population groups, the Sinhalese and the Tamils. Almost 75 percent of Sri Lankans are Sinhalese. About 12 percent are Tamils whose ancestors moved to Sri Lanka from Tamil Nadu in southeastern India. Most Tamils in Sri Lanka live in the northern and eastern portions of the country. Most

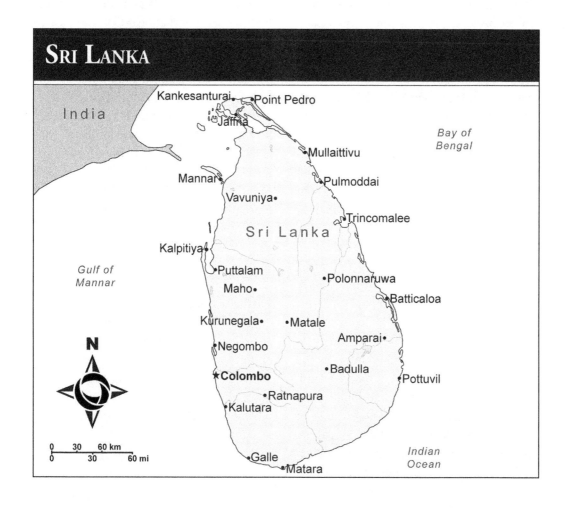

Sinhalese are Buddhists, and most Tamils are Hindus.

HISTORICAL CONTEXT

Sri Lanka has been settled for at least 125,000 years. The first Sri Lankan kingdom in recorded history was the Kingdom of Tambapanni, which according to ancient records was established in 543 BC. Various dynasties ruled Sri Lanka continuously from that time until 1815, when the last monarch was deposed by the British.

The Portuguese established the city of Colombo, which is the capital city of Sri Lanka today, along the southwest coast of the island in 1517. Portugal named the island Ceilao, which was translated into English as Ceylon. While Portugal controlled Colombo and other coastal areas, the Sri Lankan monarchy remained in control of interior areas of the island and rebuffed Portuguese efforts to depose it. In 1638, the Sri Lankan king signed an agreement with the Dutch East India Company, enlisting the company's assistance in trying to expel the Portuguese. In 1656, Dutch forces took control of Colombo. However, contrary to the terms of the treaty, the Dutch refused to leave Colombo. Britain took possession of Sri Lanka in 1796 and increased its control over the entire island. In 1815, the last native monarch, Sri Vikrama Rajasinha, was deposed by British forces and was exiled to India. The British remained in control of Ceylon until independence was granted in 1948. The country changed its name from Ceylon to its original name of Sri Lanka in 1972.

After independence, ethnic tensions between the majority Sinhalese and the minority Tamils arose. Many Tamils regarded themselves as victims of discrimination and as underrepresented in the country's government, and many demanded more autonomy or independence for Tamil-majority areas in northern and eastern Sri Lanka. In the early 1980s, a guerilla movement known as the Liberation Tigers of Tamil Eelam, or Tamil Tigers, became active in promoting Tamil independence. An ongoing war between the Tamil Tigers and the Sri Lankan government caused more than 80,000 fatalities between the mid-1980s and 2009.

By early 2009, the Sri Lankan army had reduced Tamil Tiger–held territory to a small strip of land on the east coast. In May 2009, the Tamil Tigers acknowledged having lost their effort to promote Tamil independence, and the Sri Lankan government declared victory.

Further Reading

J. Jeganaathan. "Sri Lanka's post-war foreign policy strategy: Europeans out and Chinese in?" Institute for Peace and Conflict Studies, April 21, 2011, http://www.ipcs.org/article/china/sri-lankas-post-war-foreign-policy-strategy-europeans-out-and-3359.html.

Lasanda Karakulassunya. "Post-conflict Sri Lanka: External factors, perceptions, and misperceptions." *Sunday Times*, June 24, 2012, http://www.sundaytimes.lk/120624/columns/post-conflict-sri-lanka-external-factors-perceptions-and-misperceptions-4134.html.

Matthew Weaver and Gethin Chamberlain. "Sri Lanka declares end to war with Tamil Tigers." *Guardian*, May 19, 2009, http://www.guardian.co.uk/world/2009/may/18/tamil-tigers-killed-sri-lanka.

THAILAND

OVERVIEW

The Kingdom of Thailand is a constitutional monarchy that occupies the central part of mainland Southeast Asia. It has a land area of 198,115 square miles, slightly smaller than Colorado and Wyoming combined. Thailand's population is about 68 million. The large majority of Thailand's people live in and near the valley of the Chao Phraya River, an area including the capital city of Bangkok. Most of the outlying areas of Thailand, including the regions near most of its boundaries, are hilly and less densely populated. Nearly all of Thailand's boundaries follow physical features and extend through terrain that is sparsely populated relative to the rest of Southeast Asia, with its dense population. Thailand is the only country in Southeast Asia that never became a colony of a European colonial power.

Thailand's neighbors are Myanmar to the west, Laos to the north and northeast, and Cambodia to the east. Thailand has coasts on the Andaman Sea to the southwest and on the Gulf of Thailand to the south and southeast. The Thai mainland also extends southward to encompass part of the Isthmus of Kra, which separates the Andaman Sea and the Gulf of Thailand. South of the Isthmus of Kra, Thailand and Malaysia share a boundary at the northern end of the Malay Peninsula.

Thailand's longest boundary is its western boundary with Myanmar. This boundary follows mountain ranges, drainage divides, and rivers. To the south, the boundary follows the Kra Buri River, which is also known as the Pakchan River.

The Kra Buri empties into the Andaman Sea west of the Isthmus of Kra, and the boundary follows the river northward and upstream. North of the Isthmus of Kra, the boundary runs northward through more rugged, mountainous terrain. In general, this boundary separates streams that flow into the drainage basis of the Chao Phraya in Thailand from those that flow into the Irrawaddy in Myanmar. The boundary between Thailand and Laos extends southeastward from the tripoint between Thailand, Laos, and Myanmar. All of this boundary follows rivers or drainage divides, with Southeast Asia's largest river, the Mekong, forming more than half of this boundary.

The boundary between Thailand and Cambodia also follows rivers and drainage divides. The boundary extends westward from the tripoint between Thailand, Cambodia, and Laos on the Mekong. Near the Roneam Doum Sam Wildlife Sanctuary in Cambodia, it turns southward again and eventually follows the crest of the Cardamom Mountains, which parallel the coast of the Gulf of Thailand. This boundary separates a strip of Thai territory about 20 miles long and less than a mile wide along the coast from Cambodian territory inland.

The boundary between Thailand and Malaysia is located at the southern end of the Isthmus of Kra. The boundary extends from the Straits of Malacca, at the south end of the Andaman Sea, to the west to the Gulf of Thailand to the east. From the west, it crosses drainage divides between streams emptying into the Gulf of Thailand on the Thai side of the border to the north and east from those emptying into the Andaman Sea and the Straits of Malacca on the Malaysian side of the border.

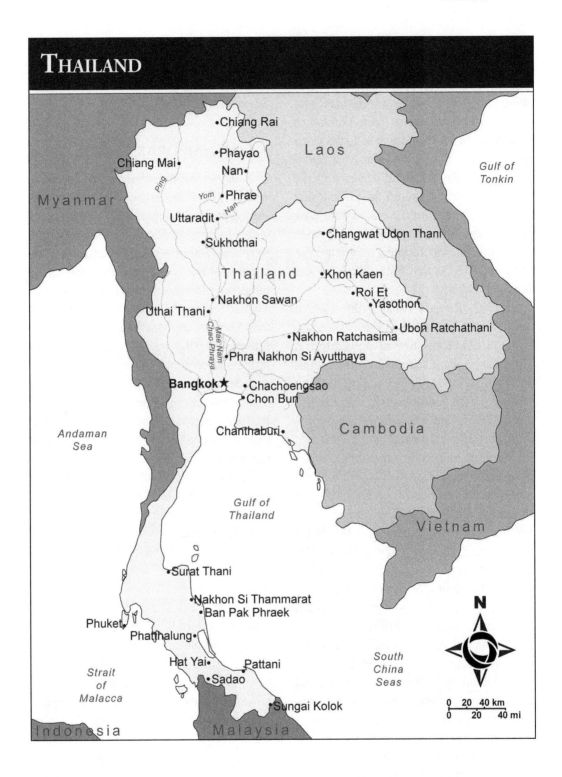

HISTORICAL CONTEXT

The ancestors of today's Thai people are believed to have migrated into the Chao Phraya valley from Yunnan in southwestern China more than 1,000 years ago. Between the 9th and the 14th centuries, present-day Thailand was part of the Khmer Empire, centered in present-day Cambodia. The Ayutthaya Kingdom took power in the 14th century and remained in power until it was toppled by a Burmese army in 1767. At that time, Thailand was known as Siam.

In 1782, Rama I became the king of Siam. Rama I established the Chakri dynasty, which continues in power today. The Chakris were successful in maintaining Siamese independence during the 19th and early 20th centuries, whereas the rest of Southeast Asia was divided among the European colonial powers. Siam remained an absolute monarchy until 1932, when it began to transition to a constitutional monarchy. The name of the kingdom was changed from Siam to Thailand in 1939. The name reverted to Siam in 1945, but it was renamed Thailand once again in 1949. Siam's ability to maintain its independent status throughout its history may also have resulted from tensions between Britain and France. Britain controlled Myanmar, which was part of British India until 1937, whereas France controlled French Indochina, including Vietnam, Cambodia, and Laos. Neither colonial power wanted the other to take control of Siam. The Siamese Kingdom negotiated boundary agreements with Britain and France during the late 19th centuries. During World War II, Thailand was allied with Japan. However, it adopted a pro-Western position during the Cold War, generally supporting the United States against the interests of the Soviet Union and China.

CONTEMPORARY ISSUES

Today, Thailand experiences problems with several of its neighbors as well as with separatist movements and organizations within its own boundaries. Within Thailand, separatist activities have emerged on the Isthmus of Kra. Conflict is associated with religious differences. Nearly 95 percent of Thailand's people are Buddhists, and less than 5 percent are Muslims. However, Muslims make up the majority of the population in the southern part of the Isthmus of Kra near the boundary with Malaysia, which has a Muslim-majority population. The Thailand government has stationed about 60,000 troops in and near this border region. Since the beginning of 2008, more than 600 persons, both soldiers and civilians, have lost their lives in the conflict.

The Thai government has given serious consideration to a proposal to construct a canal across the Isthmus of Kra, which is only about 30 miles wide at its narrowest point. Proponents of constructing the canal argue that it would reduce shipping times between India and East Asia and would allow Thailand to capture some of the lucrative trade currently controlled by Singapore. The canal has yet to be constructed, however, because the terrain is rugged and mountainous and because financing may be difficult. Early in the 21st century, China considered constructing and underwriting the costs associated with building the canal.

To the northwest, Thailand and Myanmar have experienced ongoing conflict over territory along their boundary. The boundary region is rugged and heavily forested. It can be considered part of Zomia and is inhabited by people who are neither ethnic Thai nor ethnic Burmese. The two largest ethnic groups in the area are the Shan and Karen. Shan and Karen guerillas have initiated actions against the Burmese government but can escape easily across the boundary when sought by Burmese police or armed forces. Myanmar has accused Thailand of harboring these Shan and Karen activists. An estimated 2 million Shan and Karen people are believed to live currently as refugees in Thailand.

Thailand and Myanmar have also contested other cross-border activities. Thailand has been deforested, whereas much more of Myanmar's landscape along the border remains in forest cover. Myanmar has accused Thailand of illegal logging on the Burmese side of the boundary. Meanwhile, the Thai government has accused Myanmar of smuggling illegal drugs and gemstones across the boundary. Myanmar produces almost 90 percent of the world's rubies. The repressive government of Myanmar has been accused of using the profits associated from the mining, processing, and sale of these rubies to finance police and military activities that repress the rights of minorities within Myanmar. Although the United States has banned the import of these "blood rubies" from Myanmar, international observers have contended that many are still smuggled across the boundary from Myanmar into Thailand and then sold illegally.

Thailand has also experienced territorial disputes with both Laos and Cambodia. A territorial dispute over control of four villages along the boundary between Thailand and Laos resulted in a shooting war in 1987 and 1988 and has not been resolved fully. Thailand and Cambodia contest control of the Preah Vihear Temple, which was constructed in the 11th century by the Khmer Empire. The dispute arose when separate boundary commissions drew different maps. One map placed Preah Vihear on the Thai side of the border, with the other assigning Preah Vihear to Cambodia. The International Court of Justice ruled in favor of Cambodia in 1962.

However, the dispute continued and intensified after Cambodia announced its intention to have Preah Vihear declared a World Heritage Site. Thailand protested that it was given no input into this decision. Armed skirmishes occurred in the area around Preah Vihear in 2008 and again in 2011.

See also   Cambodia, Laos, Myanmar

Further Reading

Chris Baker and Pasuk Phongpaichit. *A history of Thailand.* New York: Cambridge University Press, 2010.

Bertil Lintner. "The battle for Thailand: Can democracy survive?" *Foreign Affairs*, July/August 2009.

Tanvi Pate. "Myanmar-Thailand border dispute: Prospects for demarcation." Institute for Peace and Conflict Studies, July 8, 2010, http://www.ipcs.org/article/southeast-asia/myanmar-thailand-border-dispute-prospects-for-demarcation-3186.html.

VIETNAM

OVERVIEW

The Socialist Republic of Vietnam occupies the mainland portion of eastern Southeast Asia. The long and narrow country has a land area of 128,565 square miles, slightly larger than New Mexico. Its population is about 93 million, and it is the 13th-largest country in the world by population.

Vietnam has boundaries with China to the north and with Laos and Cambodia to the west. The South China Sea adjoins Vietnam to the east, and southern Vietnam has a short coastline on the Gulf of Thailand. Vietnam's two major population centers are located on opposite sides of the country, including the valley of the Red River near the Chinese boundary to the north and the delta of the Mekong River to the south. Central Vietnam is populated much more sparsely.

The boundary between Vietnam and China extends westward from the Gulf of Tonkin, which is a part of the South China Sea. It follows the Beilun River inland from its mouth on the Gulf of Tonkin. It then extends westward and northward following numerous short straight-line segments and drainage divides separating tributaries of the Red River from streams flowing northward into China. Near the town of Dong Van, it turns southwestward and continues to follow short straight-line segments to the Red River. It follows the Red River briefly upstream in a northwesterly direction and then turns westward again through steep and rugged mountains until it reaches the tripoint between Vietnam, China, and Laos.

From this tripoint, the boundary between Vietnam and Laos also extends across the Hoang Lien Son mountain range. As elsewhere in Southeast Asia, these mountainous areas are lightly populated and considered part of Zomia as compared to the more densely populated lowlands along river valleys. Most of this boundary follows the drainage divide between streams flowing directly into the South China Sea on the Vietnamese side of the boundary and streams that flow into the Mekong on the Laotian side of the boundary. The boundary approaches the South China Sea coast in several places, and Vietnam is less than 40 miles wide at its narrowest point. To the south, population densities increase. The boundary between Vietnam and Cambodia extends southward and southwestward from the tripoint between Vietnam, Cambodia, and Laos. As it descends from the mountains into the flat and fertile delta of the Mekong, it includes straight-line segments intended to separate people of Vietnamese origin from those of Cambodian origin. Vietnamese territory also includes the island of Phu Quoc in the Gulf of Thailand. Phu Quoc is 30 miles west of the southwestern corner of mainland Vietnam but only 8 miles south of the Cambodian mainland. Control of Phu Quoc was contested between Vietnam and Cambodia for many years.

HISTORICAL CONTEXT

The Han Chinese dynasty began to control the Red River valley in present-day northern Vietnam about the second century BC. Vietnam continued under Chinese domination until AD 938, when a

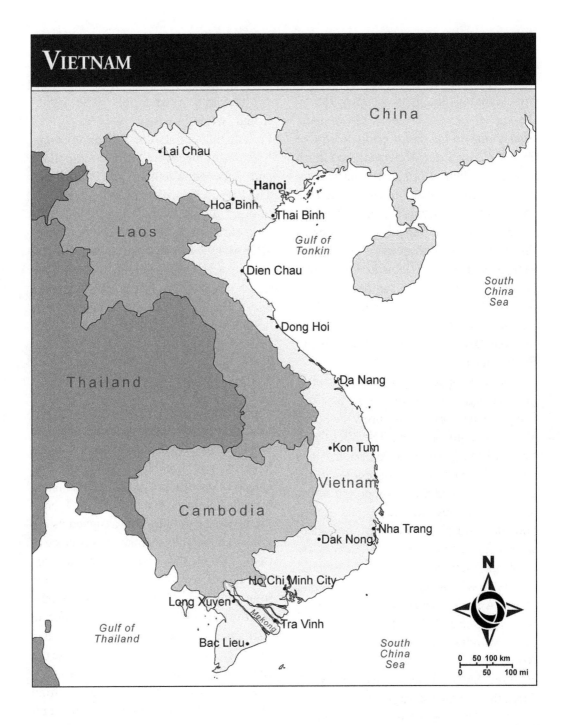

Vietnamese army expelled Chinese rulers and established an independent kingdom. Vietnamese dynasties controlled the country for most of the next 900 years. Both the Mongols and the Ming dynasty tried unsuccessfully to regain control of Vietnam.

France initiated efforts to establish control of Vietnam during the 19th century. In 1885, Vietnam became part of French

Indochina along with Laos and Cambodia. Japan occupied French Indochina during World War II. After the war ended, pro-communist guerillas occupied Hanoi, the capital city of present-day Vietnam. France sent troops in an effort to restore French colonial rule. However, the French abandoned their efforts and granted independence to Vietnam in 1954. Vietnam was partitioned between North Vietnam, ruled by pro-Soviet and pro-Chinese forces that had led guerilla activity against the French, and South Vietnam, which was governed by rulers who had been loyal to the French prior to independence. The 17th parallel of north latitude was recognized as the boundary between North Vietnam and South Vietnam.

With the support of North Vietnam, a guerilla organization known as the Viet Cong began efforts to overthrow the South Vietnamese government. The Viet Cong regarded the government of South Vietnam as the continuation of a colonial regime. The United States supported South Vietnam, and by the late 1960s almost 500,000 American military personnel were stationed in Vietnam. U.S. involvement in Vietnam became highly controversial within the United States, and 58,000 Americans were killed in Vietnam between 1965 and 1975. The United States began withdrawing its troops in 1973. In April 1975, North Vietnamese forces captured Saigon (today's Ho Chi Minh City), the capital and largest city of South Vietnam. The South Vietnamese government collapsed. Several hundred thousand refugees, many of whom had served in the South Vietnamese armed forces or the South Vietnamese government, left the country, and many moved to the United States. North Vietnam and South Vietnam were reunited as the Socialist Republic of Vietnam in 1976.

Vietnam's boundaries were established while Vietnam was a part of French Indochina. The French drew the boundaries between Vietnam and Laos and between Vietnam and Cambodia. The French regarded these boundaries as internal divisions, but they became the boundaries among the three countries after they were granted independence. France and China agreed originally to the border between French Indochina and China in 1885. The boundary was delineated fully in 2009.

CONTEMPORARY ISSUES

Vietnam's relationship with Cambodia has been uneasy. In particular, control of Phu Quoc has long been contested between Vietnam and Cambodia. Although Phu Quoc is closer to the Cambodian mainland than the Vietnamese mainland, the French rulers of French Indochina assigned its administration to the Vietnamese province of Cochin China. Cambodian forces captured Phu Quoc in 1975, although they were soon expelled. Vietnam and Cambodia went to war in 1979. The war resulted in Vietnamese occupation of the Cambodian capital of Phnom Penh. As Vietnamese occupation of Cambodia ended and tensions eased, Vietnamese troops withdrew from Phu Quoc, which is an important tourist resort today. Vietnam is one of several countries that have continued to contest control of the Spratly Islands in the South China Sea.

See also: Cambodia, China, Laos

Further Reading

Ramses Amer and Nguyen Hong Thao. "The management of Vietnam's border disputes: What impacts on its sovereignty and regional integration?" *Contemporary Southeast Asia*, 27 (2005), pp. 429–452.

Francois Molle, Tira Foran, and Mira Kakonen (eds.). *Contested waterscapes in the Mekong region: Hydropower, livelihoods, and governance.* London: Routledge, 2009.

Dustin Roasa. "The terrible tiger." *Foreign Policy*, April 17, 2012, http://www.foreignpolicy.com/articles/2012/04/17/the_terrible_tiger.

N

CHAPTER 7

AUSTRALIA AND OCEANIA

Australia and Oceania includes countries located in or on the coast of the Pacific Ocean east of the Asian mainland and north and east of the large and populous countries of Indonesia, Malaysia, Singapore, the Philippines, and Taiwan off the mainland coast. Except for Australia, which occupies the entire continent of that name, all of these countries occupy islands. With the exceptions of Australia, New Zealand, and Papua New Guinea, these countries have small populations. Many are isolated from one another as well as from the mainlands of Asia, Australia, and the Americas.

Anthropologists believe that the territories occupied by these countries were settled originally by migrants from eastern Asia and particularly from the present-day Philippines, Taiwan, and Indonesia. The continent of Australia is believed to have been settled originally about 40,000 years ago by people moving eastward and southward from New Guinea and other islands of present-day eastern Indonesia. Later, other settlers moved westward from the islands near the mainland and settled the many small islands that dot the western half of the Pacific Ocean. Over time, settlement proceeded from west to east. The last major group of islands to be settled was the islands of New Zealand, which were populated by Maori settlers who moved to New Zealand from the north less than a thousand years ago.

The islands of the Pacific Ocean form three distinct groups: Micronesia, Melanesia, and Polynesia. Micronesia consists of the portion of the western Pacific Ocean near and north of the equator, north of New Guinea, and east of the Philippines. As the name implies, most of the islands and countries of Micronesia are small in both land area and population. The independent countries of Micronesia include the Federated States of Micronesia, Kiribati, Marshall Islands, Nauru, and Palau. The U.S. possessions of Guam, the Northern Mariana Islands, and Wake Island are also located in Micronesia. Together, the independent countries and U.S. colonies of Micronesia have a combined land area of less than 1,300 square miles, smaller than Rhode Island, and a combined population of less than 600,000.

Melanesia is located to the south of Micronesia. Most of it lies south of the equator. This region contains many larger islands and a much larger population. The largest country in Melanesia is Papua New Guinea, which occupies the western half of the island of New Guinea, which it shares with Indonesia. Melanesia also includes islands east of New Guinea, south of Micronesia, and northeast of Australia.

In addition to Papua New Guinea, the independent countries of Melanesia are Fiji, Solomon Islands, and Vanuatu. Melanesia also includes several islands that remain colonies of foreign powers. The largest of these is New Caledonia, which is a French colony.

Polynesia is located in the central Pacific to the east of Micronesia and Melanesia. It extends from New Zealand to the south northward and eastward to include the U.S. state of Hawaii. Polynesia includes the independent countries of Samoa, Tonga, and Tuvalu. In addition, the original Maori settlers of New Zealand were Polynesians although a large majority of New Zealanders today are of European ancestry. Many islands in Polynesia are also colonies, including American Samoa and the French colonies of Tahiti and Bora Bora.

Australia, New Zealand, and Oceania were all settled by Europeans during the 17th, 18th, and 19th centuries. Europeans quickly displaced and overthrew indigenous kingdoms and seized political power. As Europeans seized power, many indigenous residents of Australia and Oceania died from exposure to European diseases. Many others were enslaved or forced to move away from their homelands. In some cases, notably Australia and New Zealand, the arrival of large numbers of migrants of European origin overwhelmed the indigenous populations, who soon resorted to minority status and were often victims of discrimination. In other places, such as Papua New Guinea, relatively few Europeans established settlements locally. However, Europeans retained firm control over their colonies' politics and economies.

Prior to the arrival of Europeans, most residents of Australia and Oceania supported themselves through a combination of subsistence agriculture, fishing, and hunting and gathering. Today, Australia and New Zealand have well-developed postindustrial economies and are integrated firmly into the global economy. Their per capita incomes are comparable to those of the United States, Western Europe, and Japan. The colonial process disrupted the traditional economies of the islands of Oceania. Fishing and agriculture continue to be important components of the economies of many of these island countries, although in many cases subsistence farming and fishing have been replaced by commercial farming and fishing. In addition, the economies of many of Oceania's countries are also reliant on tourism and mining.

AUSTRALIA

OVERVIEW

The Commonwealth of Australia includes the entire continent of Australia, along with the island of Tasmania and several smaller islands. The continent of Australia is located in the Southern Hemisphere and separates the Indian and Pacific Oceans. The total land area of the Commonwealth of Australia, including its offshore islands, is 2,941,299 square miles. Thus, Australia, which is the sixth-largest country in the world by land area, is slightly smaller in land area than the United States exclusive of Alaska and Hawaii. Australia's population is about 24 million. The large majority of Australians live on or

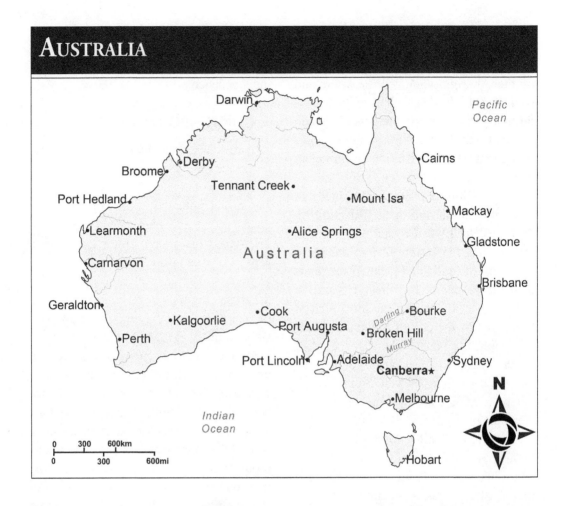

AUSTRALIA

near the coast, whereas much of the interior is desert territory that is sparsely populated or uninhabited.

Australia's nearest neighbor by water is Papua New Guinea. The two countries are separated by the Torres Strait, which is about 93 miles wide at its narrowest point and separates Australia's Cape York Peninsula from the island of New Guinea. Australia is also sovereign over the Torres Strait Islands within the strait. Australia is separated from Indonesia's portion of New Guinea by about 150 miles. At its closest point, the Australian mainland is

separated from the island of Timor, which is divided between Indonesia and East Timor, by about 350 miles. New Zealand is located approximately 900 miles east of the southeastern coast of Australia.

HISTORICAL CONTEXT

Australia was first settled between 40,000 and 60,000 years ago. Ancestors of Australia's original inhabitants, sometimes known as Aborigines, are believed to have migrated from the islands of what is today Indonesia. At that time, the earth was experiencing the most recent Ice Age, and sea levels were significantly lower than they are today. Hence the ancestors of the Aborigines moved eastward and southward by land as well as by boat. Anthropologists have estimated that between 500,000 and 1,000,000 Aborigines were living in Australia at the time of European contact.

Several European mariners visited the coast of Australia during the 17th and 18th centuries. In 1770, Captain James Cook sailed along the eastern and southeastern coasts of Australia and claimed the lands along these coasts for Great Britain. In 1788, a fleet of 11 English ships arrived at the site of the city of Sydney in order to establish a penal colony for English convicts. The area around this settlement became the colony of New South Wales. About 160,000 convicts were resettled in Australia over the next 80 years.

The English sailor Matthew Flinders circumnavigated Australia between 1801 and 1803 and in doing so demonstrated that Australia was a separate continent. During the 19th century, additional English settlements were established in what are today the Australian states of Victoria, Queensland, South Australia, and Western Australia. Tasmania, which was administered jointly with New South Wales beginning in 1788, became a separate British colony in 1825.

The six British colonies in Australia federated officially in 1901 to form the Commonwealth of Australia. The commonwealth became a dominion within the British Empire in 1907. In 1931, the British government enacted the Statute of Westminster, which gave each dominion of the British Empire the option of legislative equality with the United Kingdom itself. Australia ratified the Statute of Westminster in 1942, thereby achieving full independence.

CONTEMPORARY ISSUES

Australia and nearby countries have experienced ongoing disputes over maritime boundaries and maritime mineral rights. Large and potentially very lucrative deposits of oil and natural gas have been discovered under the Timor Sea, which separates Australia from Indonesia and from East Timor. Relationships among the three countries have been affected by the fact that Australia recognized Indonesia's claim over East Timor in 1975—a claim that led to 27 years of discord and unrest before East Timor's independence was recognized in 2002. After East Timor became independent, Australia and East Timor initiated negotiations over the division of revenues from oil and natural gas production in the Timor Sea. In 2007, the two countries agreed to a 50-year revenue-sharing plan, but the specific maritime boundary between the two countries was not determined. Australia is also one of seven countries that have made territorial claims in Antarctica, although these territorial claims are not recognized by the international community in accordance with the Antarctic Treaty.

Further Reading

Stewart Firth. *Australia in international affairs: An introduction to Australian foreign policy.* Sydney: Allen and Unwin, 2011.

Frank Welsh. *Australia: A new history of the Great Southern Land.* New York: Overlook TP, 2008.

FEDERATED STATES OF MICRONESIA

OVERVIEW

The Federated States of Micronesia is an island country located in the western Pacific Ocean near the equator. The country is an archipelago of 607 islands that are divided into four major groups: Yap, Chuuk, Pohnpei, and Kosrae. These islands are spread across nearly 1 million square miles of the Pacific. The overall land area of the Federated States of Micronesia is 271 square miles, or about four times the size of the District of Columbia. The population is about 115,000. The federated states are about 500 miles west of the Marshall Islands, about 900 miles east of Palau, and about 900 miles northeast of Papua New Guinea.

HISTORICAL CONTEXT

The islands comprising the present-day Federated States of Micronesia, which are known as the Caroline Islands, were settled about 3,000 to 4,000 years ago by Micronesian settlers whose ancestors are believed to have originated in the Philippines. Europeans first sighted the Caroline Islands in the 16th century, and by the early 19th century, they had come under Spanish influence. Spain incorporated the islands into the Spanish East Indies, which was based in the Philippines and administered from the Philippine capital of Manila. In 1899, Spain transferred sovereignty over the Caroline Islands to Germany. Japan took over the islands in 1914 and remained in control of the archipelago until World War II, when they were pushed out by American forces in 1944. In 1947, the United Nations awarded a mandate over the present-day federated states, along with present-day Palau and the Marshall Islands, to the United States. This mandate was known as the Trust Territory of the Pacific Islands.

In 1979, the four states of Yap, Chuuk, Pohnpei, and Kosrae agreed to federate and became the independent federation. Palau

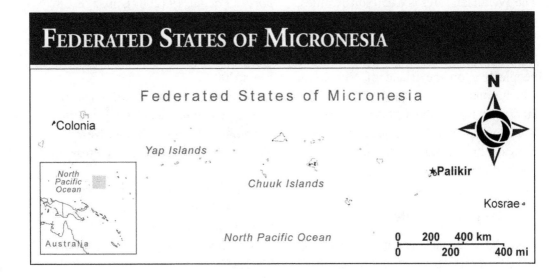

FEDERATED STATES OF MICRONESIA

and the Marshall Islands were invited to become part of the federation, but both declined, and both later became independent states. The Northern Mariana Islands also declined to participate in the federation. This territory remains under U.S. administration. The federation signed a Compact of Free Association with the United States in 1986. The compact guaranteed full independence to the federation, but the United States remained responsible for the country's defense.

See also   Palau

Further Reading
John Haglelgam. "Federated states of Micronesia." *Contemporary Pacific*, 24 (2012), pp. 136–142.

FIJI

OVERVIEW

The Republic of Fiji is an island state located in the western Pacific Ocean. Fiji is an archipelago consisting of more than 800 islands, of which 110 are inhabited. The overall land area is 7,056 square miles, or the size of Connecticut and Rhode Island combined. Fiji's population is about 850,000. About three-quarters of Fiji's people live on the island of Viti Levu, which contains more than half of Fiji's land area. Fiji is about 500 miles east of Vanuatu and about 400 miles northwest of Tonga. Fiji is about 1,300 miles directly north of the North Island of New Zealand.

HISTORICAL CONTEXT

Fiji has been inhabited by Austronesian and Melanesian peoples whose ancestors arrived from the west between 3,500 and 5,000 years ago. Fiji was sighted by the Dutch explorer Abel Tasman in 1643, and Europeans began to establish permanent settlements on the islands in the early 19th century. In 1874, Fiji became a British colony. Contract laborers were brought from British India to work on sugar plantations on the islands. Today about 54 percent of Fiji's people are of Melanesian ancestry, and about 37 percent of Fiji's people are Indo-Fijians of South Asian ancestry.

Fiji became independent in 1970. Since that time, Fiji's politics have been dominated by tensions between the Melanesian Fijian and Indo-Fijian communities. Fiji has been under military rule on several occasions following coups d'état in 1987, twice in 2000, and in 2006. Fiji and Tonga have disputed control of the Minerva Reefs, which are two partially submerged and uninhabited atolls located in the Pacific between the two countries.

Further Reading
Alumita L. Durutalo. "Fiji." *Contemporary Pacific*, 19 (2007), pp. 578–582.
Stewart Firth (ed.). *Globalisation and governance in the Pacific Islands.* Canberra: Australian National University Press, 2006.
Stephanie Lawson. *Tradition versus democracy in the South Pacific: Fiji, Tonga, and Western Samoa.* New York: Cambridge University Press, 1996.
One News. "Showdown between Tonga and Fiji looms." June 11, 2001, http://tvnz.co.nz/world-news/show-down-between-tonga-and-fiji-looms-4221560.

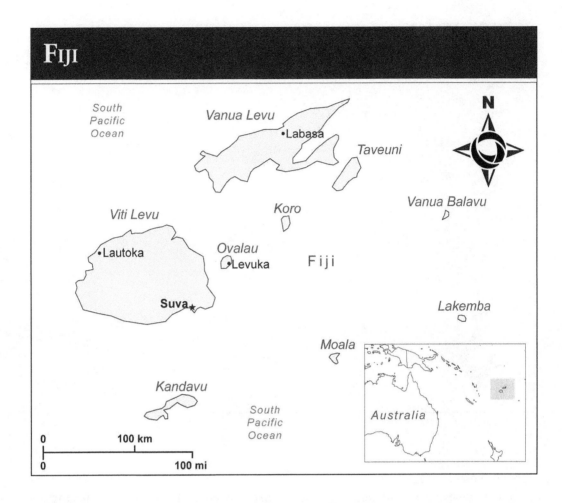

KIRIBATI

OVERVIEW

The Republic of Kiribati is an island country in the Pacific Ocean. The country is located just north of the equator and just west of the International Date Line. It includes 33 islands, with a total land area of 313 square miles. The islands are scattered over nearly a million square miles of ocean, but the land area is only about one-quarter the size of Rhode Island. The population of Kiribati is about 105,000. The closest independent country to Kiribati is Samoa, which is located approximately 750 miles southwest of Kiribati's capital city of Tarawa.

HISTORICAL CONTEXT

The islands comprising present-day Kiribati are believed to have been settled by Micronesians who arrived from the west between 1,000 and 4,000 years ago. Subsequently, the population was augmented by Polynesian invaders from Samoa and Melanesian invaders from Fiji. Intermarriage and cultural mixing have resulted in a homogeneous indigenous population. Today

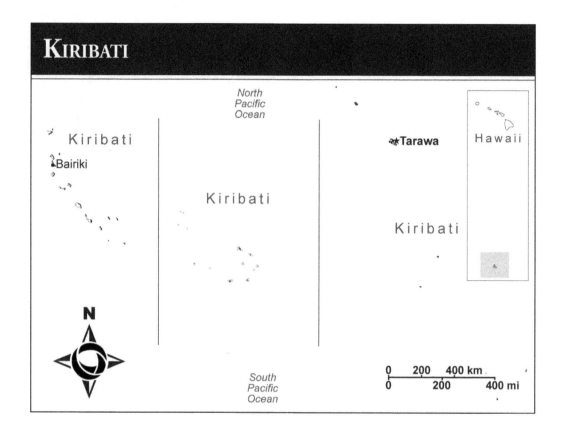

about 99 percent of Kiribati's people are of mixed Micronesian, Polynesian, and Melanesian ancestry.

Europeans first spotted the islands in the 16th century. The islands comprising Kiribati were named for a British seafarer, Thomas Gilbert, in 1820. The country's present name is a pronunciation of "Gilbert" in the indigenous Gilbertese language. In 1892, Britain established the protectorate of the Gilbert and Ellice Islands, which are located 1,000 miles southwest of Kiribati and are now the country of Tuvalu. The Gilbert and Ellice Islands became a crown colony in 1916. They were captured and occupied by Japan during World War II. The waters off the coast of the Gilbert Islands were used extensively for nuclear testing by the United States and Britain during the 1950s and 1960s. The Gilbert and Ellice Islands were separated administratively in 1975, and the Gilbert Islands became fully independent under the name Kiribati in 1979.

CONTEMPORARY ISSUES

Following independence, Kiribati claimed the Phoenix and Line Islands, which were British possessions along the equator east of the Gilbert Islands. In 1983, Britain agreed to relinquish its claim to the Phoenix and Line Islands. In 1994, Kiribati moved the International Date Line eastward so that all of its territory would be to its west.

The possible impacts of rising sea levels on Kiribati have become an issue of major concern. Most of the islands are atolls that rise only a few feet above sea level. The highest point in Kiribati is at 266 feet above sea level on the island of Banaba, but this island has only 300 residents. Most climatologists predict that continued global warming will cause sea levels to rise as much as 20 feet or more over their present levels. If this occurs, nearly all of Kiribati would be submerged. Two small atolls have already been submerged.

Kiribati's leaders have taken steps to address the problem of sea-level rise. With support from the World Bank and the United Nations Development Program, Kiribati has initiated a plan intended to mitigate the impacts of rising sea levels. The plan includes coastal zone management initiatives and laws intended to reduce coastal erosion. Recognizing the possibility that these initiatives may not be successful in combating the impacts of long-term sea-level rise, government officials in Kiribati have explored the possibility of moving the population to other places. In March 2012, Kiribati's president announced support for a plan to purchase 6,000 acres on the island of Viti Levu in Fiji with the idea of moving some or all of Kiribati's people to this territory should the islands become inundated by ocean waters in light of rising sea levels.

Further Reading

Paul Chapman. "Entire nation of Kiribati to be relocated after rising sea level threat." *Telegraph*, March 7, 2012, http://www.telegraph.co.uk/news/world-news/australiaandthepacific/kiribati/9127576/Entire-nation-of-Kiribati-to-be-relocated-over-rising-sea-level-threat.html.

MARSHALL ISLANDS

OVERVIEW

The Republic of the Marshall Islands is an island country located in Micronesia in the west-central Pacific Ocean. The country includes 34 islands, of which 24 are inhabited. Most of the islands are atolls, which are islands formed from coral reefs that are generally only a few feet above sea level. Because most of the land in the Marshall Islands is only slightly above sea level, the Marshall Islands are highly vulnerable to the possibility of rising sea levels. The total land area of the Marshall Islands is about 70 square miles. The country's population is about 75,000. The Marshall Islands are about 700 miles north of Nauru and 800 miles east of the Federated States of Micronesia.

HISTORICAL CONTEXT

Micronesian peoples first settled the Marshall Islands between 3,000 and 4,000 years ago. A Spanish navigator, Alonso de Salazar, became the first European mariner to sight the islands. Spain claimed sovereignty over the islands in the early 19th century. In 1884, Spain transferred sovereignty over the islands to Germany.

After World War I, Germany was stripped of its overseas colonies, and the League of Nations gave a mandate over the

MARSHALL ISLANDS

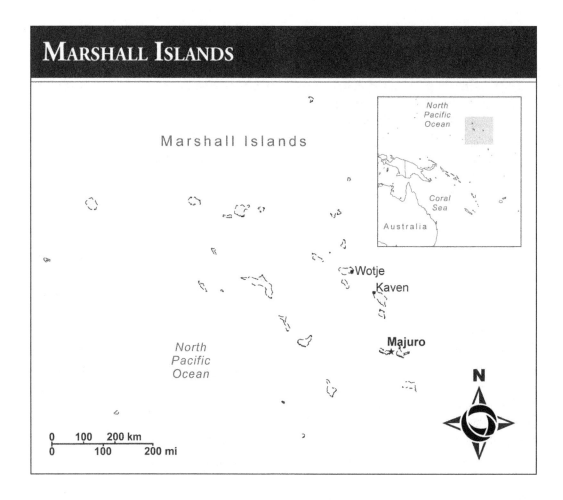

islands to Japan. United States forces invaded the Marshall Islands during World War II and expelled the Japanese in 1944. After World War II ended, the islands became part of the U.S.-administered Trust Territory of the Pacific Islands along with Palau and the Federated States of Micronesia. The United States used the area as a testing ground for nuclear weapons, and since 1956 the U.S. government has paid nearly $1 billion in compensation to Marshall Islanders who were exposed to radiation from these nuclear tests. The Marshall Islands became independent in 1986. The contemporary relationship between the Marshall Islands and the United States is governed by the Compact of Free Association, which specifies that the United States remains responsible for the country's defense. Marshall Islanders have the unrestricted right to live and work in the United States. The Marshall Islands claims the U.S. territory of Wake Island, a small coral atoll located about 900 miles to the northwest of the Marshall Islands.

Further Reading

H. M. Barker. *Bravo for the Marshallese: Regaining control in a post-nuclear, post-colonial world.* Belmont, CA: Thomson/Wadsworth, 2004.

NAURU

OVERVIEW

The Republic of Nauru is located in Micronesia in the Pacific Ocean. With a land area of 8.1 square miles, it is one of the world's smallest countries. Nauru's population is about 9,500, making it the smallest sovereign country in the world following Vatican City. Nauru is about 180 miles west of Kiribati, its closest maritime neighbor.

HISTORICAL CONTEXT

According to anthropologists, Nauru has been occupied by Micronesian peoples for at least 3,000 years. By the early 19th century, 12 indigenous tribes controlled various parts of the island. European contact with Nauru began in 1830, when Western whaling and trading ships began to land on the island and established trade relationships with the indigenous inhabitants. Western traders brought firearms and alcoholic beverages, whose impact disrupted the island's long-standing relationships among the 12 tribes and resulted in significant population declines. Many other

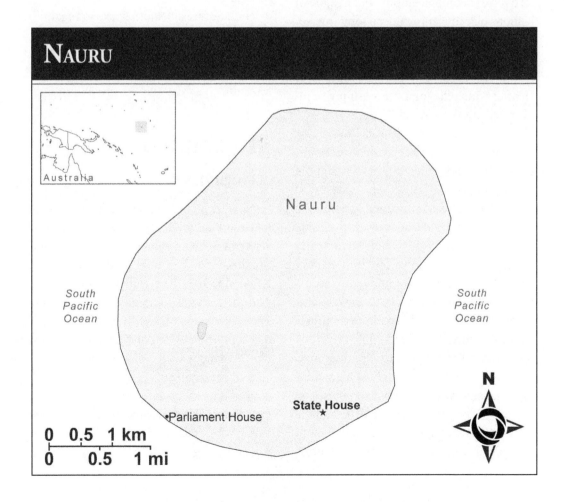

NAURU

Australia

Nauru

South
Pacific
Ocean

South
Pacific
Ocean

State House
★

•Parliament House

N

0   0.5 1 km
0   0.5   1 mi

indigenous residents of Nauru died from tuberculosis, influenza, and other Western diseases to which they had no immunity.

In 1886, an agreement between Germany and Britain gave Germany the right to control Nauru. Germany annexed Nauru formally in 1888. In 1900, large quantities of phosphates, which originated from the droppings of millions of seabirds, were discovered on Nauru. Subsequent mining and export of these phosphate deposits made Nauru one of the richest colonies in the world over the next several decades.

Nauru was occupied by Australian troops during World War I. After the Treaty of Versailles stripped Germany of its overseas colonial empire, the League of Nations placed Nauru under a joint trusteeship that included Australia, New Zealand, and the United Kingdom. Japan occupied Nauru for three years during World War II, after which the joint trusteeship was reaffirmed by the United Nations in 1947. Nauru became independent in 1968.

Nauru continued to prosper economically from phosphate exports throughout the 20th century. However, widespread and extensive environmental destruction took place during decades of strip-mining of phosphate deposits, which were nearly exhausted by the end of the 20th century and whose depletion removed Nauru's only major export. In 1989, the government of Nauru sued Australia in the International Court of Justice to hold Australia responsible for damage to Nauru's environment resulting from phosphate mining. The suit was settled out of court, and Australia along with New Zealand and the United Kingdom agreed to pay damages to Nauru's government. However, Nauru's economy all but collapsed in the 1990s as phosphate mining was phased out. More than half of Nauru's workers are unemployed. Many others have left the island to seek employment in Australia, New Zealand, or other Pacific islands. Recent discoveries of additional phosphate deposits have encouraged some Nauru leaders to develop this resource while seeking a long-term solution to Nauru's economic difficulties.

Further Reading

Carl N. McDaniel and John M. Gowdy. *Paradise for sale: A parable of nature.* Berkeley: University of California Press, 2000.

Nick Squires. "Nauru seeks to regain lost fortunes." *BBC News*, March 15, 2008, http://news.bbc.co.uk/2/hi/programmes/ from_our_own_correspondent/7296 832.stm.

NEW ZEALAND

OVERVIEW

New Zealand is located in the southwestern Pacific Ocean. New Zealand consists of two main islands, North Island and South Island. The total land area of New Zealand is 103,483 square miles, about the size of Colorado. The population of New Zealand is about 4.5 million. About three-quarters of New Zealand's people live on North Island, which contains about 40 percent of the country's land area. New Zealand is one of the most isolated countries in the world. It is located about 900 miles east of Australia and 600 miles south of Fiji and Tonga.

NEW ZEALAND

Three Kings Islands.

South
Pacific
Ocean

Australia

New Zealand

Auckland

North Island

•Hamilton

•Gisborne

Tasman
Sea

•Palmerston North

★Wellington

New Zealand

South Island

Christchurch

Chatham Islands

Dunedin

Invercargill

Stewart Island

Bounty Islands

The Snares.

Antipodes Islands

N

Auckland Islands

South
Pacific
Ocean

0   100   200 km
0   100   200 mi

Campbell Island

HISTORICAL CONTEXT

Anthropologists believe that New Zealand was first settled by humans in the 13th century AD. The first settlers of New Zealand were the Maoris, who are Polynesians believed to have migrated southwestward from islands in the central Pacific Ocean. The Dutch explorer Abel Tasman visited New Zealand in 1642, but Europeans did not visit the area again until James Cook circumnavigated and mapped the islands in 1769. Cook's voyage initiated a period of sustained European and American contact with New Zealand. Many Maoris died, primarily from exposure to European diseases. However, the Maori survived, and Maoris comprise about 15 percent of New Zealand's current population.

In 1840, representatives of the British government and several hundred Maori chiefs signed the Treaty of Waitangi. The treaty established British sovereignty over New Zealand, while the Maoris were given the same rights as British subjects. However, the treaty remains controversial. Although its language guarantees Maori rights, in practice the Maoris were victims of ethnic discrimination. The treaty was also interpreted by British authorities as allowing the taking of ancestral Maori lands. Pressure on Maori lands intensified in the late 19th century as more and more migrants from the British Isles and other European countries arrived.

New Zealand was made a crown colony of the British Empire in 1841. After New Zealand declined to become a part of Australia in 1901, it became a dominion of the British Empire in 1907. As a dominion, New Zealand had autonomy over its internal affairs, but Britain remained in charge of its foreign policy and military activities. In 1926, the British government announced the Balfour Declaration (a document separate from the Balfour Declaration of 1917 concerning the status of what is now Israel, Palestine, and Jordan). The Balfour Declaration of 1926 specified that all dominions of the British Empire would have equal status and that Britain would relinquish its control over their foreign policies, subject to approval by each individual dominion. This policy was given legal effect by the Statute of Westminster, which was enacted in 1931. However, New Zealand did not agree to relinquish British control over its foreign affairs until 1947, when the New Zealand Parliament passed the Statute of Westminster Adoption Act.

CONTEMPORARY ISSUES

Given its isolation from other countries, New Zealand has no significant controversies concerning its territorial sovereignty. However, in 1923 New Zealand claimed the territory south of the 60th parallel of south latitude and between the 160th meridian of east longitude and the 150th meridian of west longitude southward to the South Pole. This area of mainland Antarctica and nearby parts of the Southern Ocean are known as the Ross Dependency. The terms of the Antarctic Treaty, which was signed in 1959 and went into effect in 1961, specify that territorial claims south of the 60th parallel are no longer recognized by the international community and were suspended.

Further Reading

Tom Brooking. *The History of New Zealand.* Westport, CT: Praeger, 2004.

Ralph Lattimore and Shamubeel Faqub. *The New Zealand economy: An introduction.* Auckland: Auckland University Press, 2012.

PALAU

OVERVIEW

The Republic of Palau is located in the Pacific Ocean east of the Philippines and south of Japan. Palau includes 8 major islands and over 200 smaller islands. The overall land area of Palau is 177 square miles, about two and a half times the size of the District of Columbia. The population is about 22,000, of whom about two-thirds live on the main island of Koror. Palau is about 500 miles east of the Philippine island of Mindanao and about 500 miles north-northeast of the Indonesian island of Halmahera and its province of Irian Jaya on New Guinea. It is about 2,000 miles south of Tokyo.

HISTORICAL CONTEXT

The original settlers of present-day Palau were Micronesians whose ancestors are believed to have come from the Philippines

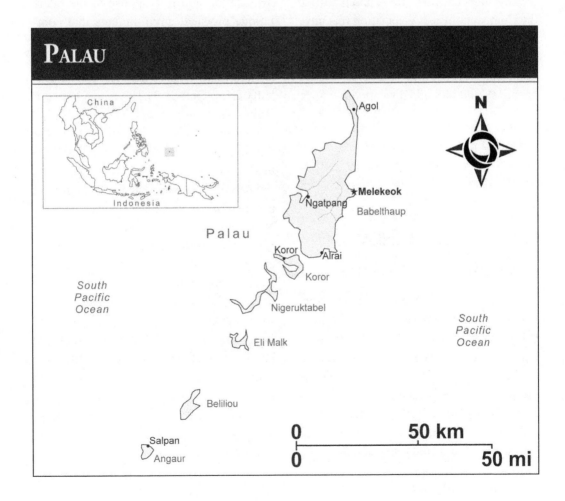

between 3,000 and 4,000 years ago. Spain claimed Palau in the 19th century. After Spain was defeated in the Spanish-American War, the islands were sold to Germany in 1899. Germany transferred the islands to Japan in 1914. During World War II, the islands were invaded by U.S. troops who seized control of them in 1944. After the war ended, the United Nations assigned a mandate over Palau, along with the Federated States of Micronesia and the Marshall Islands, to the United States as the Trust Territory of the Pacific Islands. In 1979, Palau declined to join the Federated States of Micronesia, most of which are more than 900 miles east of Palau. Palau became independent in 1994, and it ratified the Compact of Free Association that gave the United States continued responsibility for the defense of Palau. Palau's constitution forbids the use and storage of nuclear, chemical, and biological weapons.

Further Reading

Donald R. Shuster. "Republic of Palau." *Contemporary Pacific*, 19 (2007), pp. 194–205.

PAPUA NEW GUINEA

OVERVIEW

The Independent State of Papua New Guinea is an island state in the western Pacific Ocean that straddles the equator. Papua New Guinea includes the eastern half of the island of New Guinea, which is the second-largest island in the world following Greenland. It also includes many offshore islands. The largest and most populated of these islands are Bougainville,

New Britain, and New Ireland. The overall land area of Papua New Guinea is 178,703 square miles, making it slightly larger than California. The population is about 6.3 million.

Papua New Guinea has the most cultural diversity of any state in the world today. Its 6.3 million people speak more than 800 distinct, mutually unintelligible languages. The cultural diversity of Papua New Guinea is paralleled by its unmatched biodiversity. Some anthropologists see the high levels of biodiversity in Papua New Guinea as related to its high level of cultural diversity in that many of Papua New Guinea's cultures evolved in isolation and in response to the many unique physical environments that comprise the country.

Papua New Guinea's only land neighbor is Indonesia, which occupies the western half of New Guinea. The boundary between Papua New Guinea and Indonesia bisects the island. From north to south, it begins at the 141st meridian of east longitude and extends southward to the Fly River in the central part of the island. The Fly is the largest and second-longest river on the island of New Guinea. The boundary follows the Fly south-southwestward and downstream, extending west of the 141st meridian. The river bends south-southeastward, and the boundary continues along the river until the river course reaches the 141° 10` meridian. From this point, the boundary follows that boundary southward to the Arafura Sea. Papua New Guinea is separated from the Australian mainland by 93 miles across the Torres Strait, which connects the Arafura with the Coral Sea, which is part of the southwest Pacific Ocean.

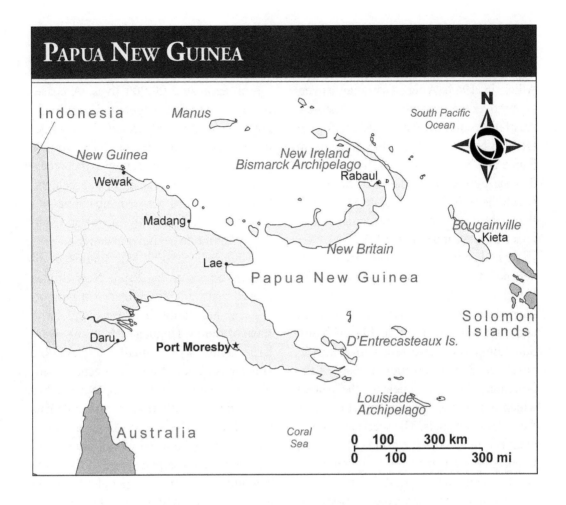

PAPUA NEW GUINEA

HISTORICAL CONTEXT

Anthropologists believe that the island of New Guinea was first settled between 50,000 and 70,000 years ago by people who migrated eastward from Southeast Asia. The large offshore islands are believed to have been settled by people from mainland New Guinea between 20,000 and 35,000 years ago.

New Guinea was sighted by European explorers in the 16th century. Germany claimed the northeastern quarter of mainland New Guinea in 1884, naming this colony German New Guinea. The southeastern quarter, known as Papua, became a British protectorate in 1884. The British authorized Australia to administer Papua in 1906. In 1920, German New Guinea was assigned to Australia as a League of Nations mandate.

In 1941, Japan invaded and occupied much of the island of New Guinea as well as the offshore islands of New Britain, New Ireland, and Bougainville. Both the mainland and the islands were the scene of fierce fighting between the Japanese and the Allies, including troops from the

United States and Australia. Australian sovereignty over eastern New Guinea was reaffirmed after Japan's surrender to the Allies in 1945. After Australian sovereignty over the two colonies was restored, Australia combined Papua and the former German New Guinea into the Territory of Papua and New Guinea. Australia and Indonesia agreed upon the boundaries between the territory and Indonesia in 1973. Papua New Guinea became independent under its present name in 1975.

After Papua New Guinea became independent, secessionists on the island of Bougainville declared Bougainville's independence from Papua New Guinea under the name of the Republic of North Solomons. The name refers to Bougainville's geographic position as part of the Solomon Islands archipelago, the rest of which is now the independent country of the Solomon Islands. The secession movement was fueled by ethnic and cultural differences between residents of Bougainville and the mainland. As well, valuable copper deposits were discovered on Bougainville, giving the island a significant source of wealth. Bougainville claimed that it was receiving less than 1 percent of the total profits from mining operations but that it was suffering from substantial environmental damage and degradation.

In 1976, secessionists on Bougainville agreed to accept Papua New Guinea sovereignty in exchange for Papua New Guinea promises of substantial autonomy and eventual independence for Bougainville. However, Papua New Guinea did not follow through on its promise of independence, and a second secessionist movement developed in the late 1980s. In 1990, the Papua New Guinea government sent troops into Bougainville to reinforce its authority. Civil war broke out and continued through the 1990s, claiming an estimated 20,000 lives. A ceasefire agreement was negotiated in 1998. In 2001, New Zealand brokered an agreement between the Papua New Guinea government and the Bougainville secessionists. Under terms of the agreement, Bougainville was granted substantial autonomy, with the possibility of an eventual referendum on independence.

Extensive cultural and linguistic diversity in present-day Papua New Guinea caused considerable problems in promoting communication between people who speak different languages. Not only were large numbers of mutually unintelligible languages spoken by the indigenous peoples of the country, but people needed to communicate with traders and colonists from Europe, Southeast Asia, and elsewhere. Throughout the world, pidgin languages have developed in order to promote communication among people living in areas with substantial linguistic diversity. Pidgin languages are characterized by simple sentence and grammatical structure and vocabularies that are derived from many linguistic traditions.

The pidgin language that developed in and near present-day Papua New Guinea has evolved into an official national language. This language is known as Tok Pisin (literally "Talk Pidgin"). Tok Pisin is derived from the indigenous languages of New Guinea and nearby islands, English, and German. About 80 percent of the vocabulary is from the Indo-European languages, 14 percent from the languages of New Guinea and nearby Melanesia, and the rest from other origins.

After Papua New Guinea became independent, Tok Pisin was taught in schools. Debates in the Papua New Guinean parliament are conducted in Tok Pisin. Newspapers, magazines, and books are published in Tok Pisin. Today, Tok Pisin is one of three official languages of Papua New Guinea, along with English and Hiri Motu, which is one of the most widely spoken indigenous languages. The ability to speak, read, and write Tok Pisin is recognized as a mark of national identity among citizens of Papua New Guinea.

CONTEMPORARY ISSUES

Papua New Guinea remains aligned closely with Australia, which provides substantial aid to Papua New Guinea. The boundary between Papua New Guinea, while settled, is porous and patrolled poorly. Australia continues to assist Papua New Guinea's efforts to protect its border with Indonesia in order to restrict smuggling of weapons and contraband and prevent illegal drug trafficking. Ongoing conflict in Indonesia's Irian Jaya, which occupies the western half of the island of New Guinea, has resulted in a substantial flow of refugees into Papua New Guinea.

See also Australia, Indonesia

Further Reading

Diana Glazebrook. "More than a matter of distance: Refugees in Papua New Guinea." *Cultural Survival*, May 5, 2010, http://www.culturalsurvival.org/publications/cultural-survival-quarterly/papua-new-guinea/more-matter-distance-refugees-papua-new-gu.

Anthony Matthew. "Bougainville and Papua New Guinea: Complexities of secession in a multi-ethnic developing state." *Political Studies*, 48 (2000), pp. 724–744.

Geoff Smith. *Growing up with Tok Pisin: Contact, creolization, and change in Papua New Guinea's national language.* London: Battlebridge, 2002.

SAMOA

OVERVIEW

The Independent State of Samoa is located in the Pacific Ocean. It contains part of the Samoan Islands, the remainder of which comprise the American colony of American Samoa. The country includes two main islands, Upolu and Savai'i, along with eight small islands. The overall land area of Samoa is 1,133 square miles, about the size of Rhode Island. Upolu and Savai'i contain about 99 percent of this territory. The overall population of Samoa is about 185,000, of whom about three-quarters live on Upolu. Aside from American Samoa, Samoa's nearest neighbors by water are Tonga, 500 miles to the south-southwest, and Tuvalu, 500 miles to the northwest. Samoa is about 1,500 miles north-northeast of New Zealand and about 1,500 miles northeast of the Australian mainland.

HISTORICAL CONTEXT

Samoa has been inhabited by Pacific Islanders for about 3,000 to 4,000 years. The islands were sighted by the Dutch navigator Jacob Roggeveen in 1722 and by the French explorer Louis-Antoine de Bougainville in 1768. Bougainville named the islands the Navigator Islands. During the late 19th century, control of Samoa was

SAMOA

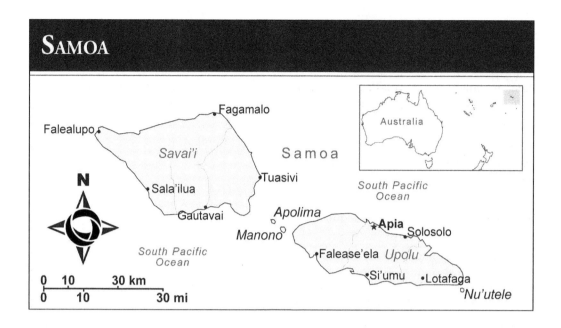

disputed between Germany, the United Kingdom, and the United States. In 1899, the three powers agreed to the Tripartite Convention, which divided the islands between Germany and the United States. Germany obtained sovereignty over the islands that make up the Independent State of Samoa today.

After World War I, former German colonies throughout the world were assigned to various countries via League of Nations mandates. Administration of German Samoa was assigned to New Zealand. New Zealand's mandate over the islands was reaffirmed by the United Nations after World War II. New Zealand continued to administer the islands until they were granted independence in 1962 under the name of Western Samoa.

Western Samoa changed its name to the Independent State of Samoa in 1997. In 2011, Samoa moved from the east to the west of the International Date Line, thereby advancing its time ahead by 24 hours. This change reflected Samoa's increasing economic ties with Australia and New Zealand, both of which are also west of the International Date Line.

Further Reading

Stephanie Lawson. *Tradition versus democracy in the South Pacific: Fiji, Tonga, and Western Samoa.* New York: Cambridge University Press, 1996.

Cluny Macpherson and La'avasa Macpherson. *The warm winds of change: Globalisation in contemporary Samoa.* Auckland: Auckland University Press, 2010.

USA Today. "Samoa, Tokelau cross International Date Line." December 30, 2011, http://www.usatoday.com/news/world/story/2011-12-30/samoa-tokelau-dateline/52283026/1.

SOLOMON ISLANDS

OVERVIEW

The Solomon Islands are an island state located in the southwestern Pacific Ocean. The country consists of 922 islands, of which 347 are inhabited. The overall land area of the country is 10,965 square miles, the size of Maryland. The population is about 550,000.

The Solomon Islands' closest neighbor by water is Papua New Guinea. The island of Bougainville, which is part of Papua New Guinea politically but part of the Solomon Islands archipelago geologically, is less than 5 miles northwest of the small island of Ovau in the Solomon Islands and is 40 miles west of the larger, populated Choiseul Island. The Solomon Islands are about 400 miles northwest of Vanuatu and about 1,000 miles northeast of the coast of Australia.

HISTORICAL CONTEXT

The Solomon Islands, including Bougainville, have been inhabited for more than 30,000 years by people of Melanesian ancestry. Even today, nearly 95 percent of Solomon Islands people are Melanesian. In 1568, the Spanish explorer Alvaro de Mendana de Neira became the first European navigator to visit the islands. During the 19th century, many indigenous residents of the islands were kidnapped and transported to Australia and Fiji to work on sugar plantations in a practice known as "blackbirding."

In the late 19th century, European powers became more interested in formal control of the islands. Germany established a protectorate over Bougainville and the northern portion of the Solomon Islands in 1885, while the United Kingdom established a protectorate over the southern portion of the archipelago in 1893. Germany

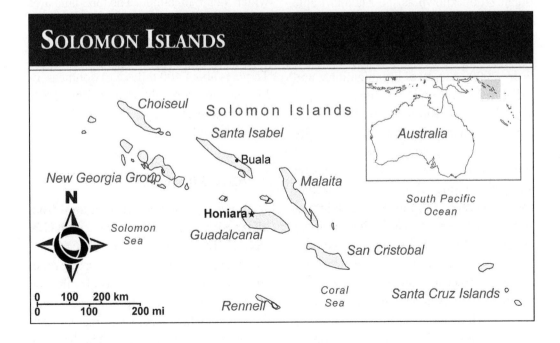

SOLOMON ISLANDS

transferred sovereignty over its protectorate, except for Bougainville, in 1900. Japan occupied the islands in January 1942. Later that year, a U.S. Marine Corps division landed on the island of Guadalcanal in the Solomon Islands. The islands were the scene of fierce fighting between American and Japanese forces until the Japanese withdrew from Guadalcanal at the end of 1942, although fighting continued on Bougainville until 1945.

After World War II ended, the British regained control over its protectorate. Self-government was introduced gradually. In 1978, the Solomon Islands were granted full independence. Shortly after independence, civil war broke out. The Isatabu Freedom Movement, centered on Guadalcanal, worked to separate Guadalcanal from the rest of the country. The movement proposed to change the island's name to Isatabu and to restrict migration rights from other islands. Another guerilla organization known as the Malaita Eagle Force supported the rights of people from the island of Malaita who had migrated to Guadalcanal.

In 2000, the two organizations and the government of the Solomon Islands signed the Townsville Peace Agreement, which was named for the Australian city where it was negotiated, ending the hostility. However, continuing ethnic tension along with rising crime rates and ineffective local security induced the Solomon Islands parliament to ask for international assistance. In 2003, a security force consisting of troops from Australia and New Zealand arrived to promote the restoration of order. This Regional Assistance Mission, which includes representatives from 15 countries, remains in the Solomon Islands and continues to be charged with maintaining order.

Further Reading

John Braithwaite, Sinclair Dinnen, Matthew Allen, Valerie Braithwaite, and Hilary Charlesworth. *Statebuilding as peacebuilding in Solomon Islands.* Canberra: Australian National University Press, 2010.

H. C. Brookfield. *Colonialism, development, and independence: The case of the Melanesian Islands in the South Pacific.* New York: Cambridge University Press, 2010.

TONGA

OVERVIEW

The Kingdom of Tonga is an island country located in the South Pacific Ocean. Tonga is an archipelago of 176 islands, of which 52 are inhabited. The total land area of Tonga is 289 square miles, or about four times the size of the District of Columbia. Tonga's population is about 105,000. Tonga is about 400 miles east-southeast of Fiji, its closest neighbor, and about 1,300 miles northeast of the city of Auckland in New Zealand.

HISTORICAL CONTEXT

Tonga was settled by migrants from Melanesian islands in the western Pacific Ocean between 3,000 and 3,500 years ago. Dutch explorers became the first Europeans to visit the islands in 1616. By the end of the 18th century, European traders and missionaries had established regular contact with the islands. In 1845, the chief

TONGA

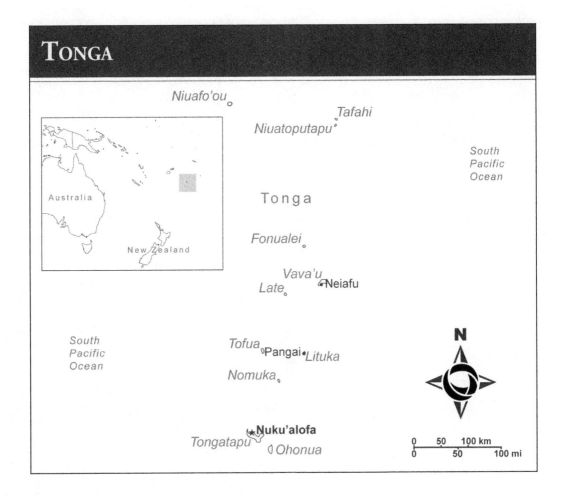

Taufa'ahau Tupou completed military conquest of islands throughout the archipelago and was proclaimed king of Tonga. The Tongan monarchy has remained in power since that time, and Tonga never became a formal European colony.

In 1900, Tonga became a protectorate of the British Empire. It was administered as part of the British Western Pacific Territories, which was headquartered in Fiji, from 1901 to 1952. Tonga became an independent member of the British Commonwealth of Nations in 1970 and joined the United Nations in 1999. Tonga has retained cordial relationships with nearby countries. However, Tonga and Fiji contested control of the Minerva Reefs, which are uninhabited and partially submerged at high tide and are located between the two countries.

Further Reading

Stephanie Lawson. *Tradition versus democracy in the South Pacific: Fiji, Tonga, and Western Samoa.* New York: Cambridge University Press, 1996.

One News. "Showdown between Tonga and Fiji looms." June 11, 2001, http://tvnz.co.nz/world-news/showdown-between-tonga-and-fiji-looms-4221560.

TUVALU

Nanumea
Lolua

Kulia Niutao
Tonga Nanumanga

South Pacific
Ocean

Australia

New Zealand

Tanrake Nui

Vaitupu
Asau

Nukufetau
Savave

Tuvalu

Funafuti
Funafuti

Nukulaelae
Fangaua

N

South Pacific
Ocean

0   50   100 km
0   50   100 mi

Niulakita

TUVALU

OVERVIEW

Tuvalu is an island country located in the central Pacific Ocean. It includes nine small islands and many tiny islets with a combined land area of about 10 square miles. Thus only Vatican City, Monaco, and Nauru among the world's sovereign states have smaller land areas. Tuvalu's population of about 10,500 makes it the third-smallest country in the world by population, with only Vatican City and Nauru having fewer people. Tuvalu is about 500 miles north of Fiji, 800 miles northeast of Vanuatu, and 1,000 miles east of the Solomon Islands.

HISTORICAL CONTEXT

The first settlers of present-day Tuvalu were Polynesians, who are believed by many anthropologists to have arrived from Samoa around 2,000 years ago. A Spanish explorer, Álvaro de Mendaña y Neyra, was the first European to visit Tuvalu in 1568. However, the islands were not known to have been visited by Europeans again until 1781. The archipelago was given the name of the Ellice Islands in 1819.

In 1892, the Ellice Islands became a British protectorate. They were administered as part of the British Western Pacific Territories between 1892 and 1916. In 1916, they became part of the Colony of the Gilbert and Ellice Islands, along with present-day Kiribati. In a 1974 plebiscite, residents of the Ellice Islands voted to separate from the Gilbert Islands as a separate dependency. The Ellice Islands became a fully independent member of the British Commonwealth in 1978, when the country's present name of Tuvalu was adopted. Tuvalu became a member of the United Nations in 2000.

Further Reading

Gerard A. Finan. "Small is viable: The ebbs and flows of a Pacific atoll nation." East-West Center Working Paper #15, 2002, http://scholarspace.manoa.hawaii. edu/bitstream/handle/10125/3614/PID-Pwp015.pdf?sequence=1.

VANUATU

OVERVIEW

The Republic of Vanuatu is an island country located in the South Pacific Ocean. Vanuatu is an archipelago consisting of 82 islands, of which 65 are inhabited. The archipelago stretches in a north-south direction, and the northernmost and southernmost islands are separated by about 800 miles. The total land area of Vanuatu is 4,710 square miles, making it slightly smaller than Connecticut. Most of the islands are volcanic in origin, and much of the land surface is steep, rocky, and unsuitable for agriculture. The total population of Vanuatu is about 230,000. Vanuatu's closest neighbor by water is the French territory of New Caledonia, about 300 miles to the south. The closest sovereign state is the Solomon Islands, 500 miles to the northwest. Vanuatu is about 1,000 miles northeast of the coast of Australia.

HISTORICAL CONTEXT

Anthropologists believe that present-day Vanuatu was settled originally by

Melanesian people who may have arrived from New Guinea or the Solomon Islands 5,000 to 6,000 years ago. The first European explorer to visit the archipelago was the Portuguese mariner Pedro Fernández de Quirós, who spotted the island of Espiritu Santu in 1606. In 1774, Captain James Cook visited the islands and gave them the name of the New Hebrides. During the 19th century, settlers from both Britain and France claimed land in the New Hebrides and used this land to grow cotton, coffee, bananas, and other tropical crops for export. Polynesians, some of whom were kidnapped from islands in the central Pacific, were brought to the New Hebrides to work on these plantations.

France and Britain disputed sovereignty over the New Hebrides during the 19th century. In 1878, the two countries agreed that the islands should be regarded as neutral territory. France and Britain agreed to administer the New Hebrides jointly in 1906. In the 1960s, the British proposed transition toward independence. France was opposed to independence for Vanuatu. French opposition to independence stemmed in part from France's concern that independence sentiment would spread to New Caledonia, which has substantial

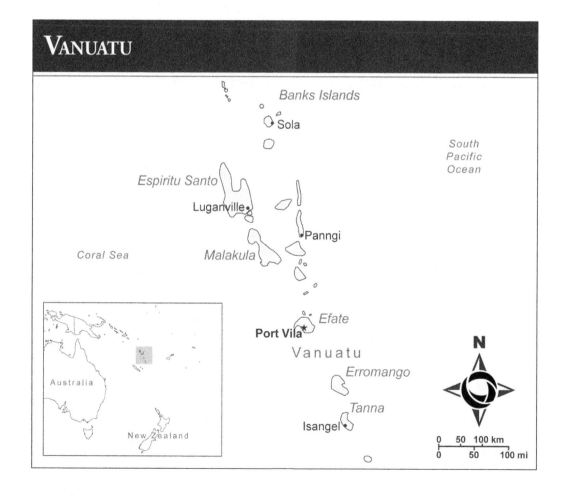

mineral wealth and is one of the leading nickel-producing areas of the world. Despite French opposition, Vanuatu became fully independent in 1980.

CONTEMPORARY ISSUES

Currently, Vanuatu and France are involved in a dispute about sovereignty over the Matthew and Hunter Islands, which are located southeast of the Vanuatu archipelago and east of the main island of New Caledonia. The two islands are uninhabited, are separated by about 45 miles of ocean, and have a combined land area of about half a square mile. Despite the small size of the Matthew and Hunter Islands, both countries remain interested in sovereignty over them because of the possibility of control of undersea minerals and resources in accordance with the Law of the Sea Treaty's definition of an exclusive economic zone surrounding land.

Further Reading

Howard van Trease. *The politics of land in Vanuatu: From colony to independence.* Honolulu: University of Hawaii Press, 1990.

SELECTED BIBLIOGRAPHY

Darin Acemoglu and James Robinson. *Why nations fail: The origins of power, prosperity, and poverty.* New York: Crown Business, 2012.

John Agnew. *Geopolitics: Re-visioning world politics.* London: Routledge, 2003.

John Agnew. *Globalization and sovereignty.* Boulder, CO: Rowman and Littlefield, 2009.

Lydia L. Bean and Fred M. Shelley. "Borders and vulnerability." In *World minds: Geographical perspectives on 100 problems*, edited by Donald G. Janelle, Barney Warf, and Kathy Hansen. Dordrecht: Kluwer, 2004, pp. 461–466.

Zbigniew Brzezinski. *Strategic vision: America and the crisis of global power.* New York: Basic Books, 2012.

Allen Buchanan and Margaret Moore (eds.). *States, nations and borders: The ethics of making boundaries.* New York: Cambridge University Press, 2003.

Saul Bernard Cohen. *Geopolitics: The geography of international relations.* 2nd ed. Boulder, CO: Rowman and Littlefield, 2008.

Simon Dalby (ed.). *The geopolitics reader.* London: Routledge, 2006.

Klaus Dodds (ed.). *Geopolitics.* 2 vols. Thousand Oaks, CA: Sage 2009.

Niall Ferguson. "Sinking globalization." *Foreign Affairs*, May/June 2005, pp. 64–77.

Colin Flint. *Introduction to geopolitics.* London: Routledge, 2006.

Ernest Gellner and John Breuilly. *Nations and nationalism.* 2nd ed. Ithaca, NY: Cornell University Press, 2010.

E. J. Hobsbawm. *Nations and nationalism since 1780: Programme, myth, reality.* New York: Columbia University Press, 2012.

Samuel P. Huntington. *The clash of civilizations and the remaking of world order.* New York: Simon and Schuster, 1996.

Reece Jones. "Categories, borders, and boundaries." *Progress in Human Geography*, no. 33 (2009): pp. 174–189.

Rhys Jones, Michael Woods, and Martin Jones. *An introduction to political geography: Space, place, and politics.* London: Routledge, 2012.

Robert D. Kaplan. *The revenge against geography: What the map tells us about coming conflicts and the battle against fate.* New York: Random House, 2012.

Norrie MacQueen. *Colonialism.* London: Longman, 2007.

John O'Loughlin, Lynn Staeheli, and Edward Greenberg (eds.). *Globalization and its outcomes.* New York: Guilford, 2004.

Joe Painter and Alex Jeffrey. *Political geography.* Thousand Oaks, CA: Sage, 2009.

J.R.V. Prescott. *Political frontiers and boundaries.* London: Routledge, 1990.

Victor Prescott and Clive Schofield. *The maritime boundaries of the world.* Leiden, Netherlands: Brill, 2005.

Dani Rodrik. *The globalization paradox: Democracy and the future of the world economy.* New York: W. W. Norton, 2012.

Clive Schofield. *The razor's edge: International boundaries and political geography.* New York: Springer, 2002.

Fred M. Shelley and Colin Flint. "Geography, place, and world-systems analysis." In *A world-systems reader*, edited by Thomas D. Hall, pp. 69–82. Lanham, MD: Rowman and Littlefield, 2000.

Neil Smith and David Harvey. *Uneven development: Nature, capital, and the production of space.* 3rd ed. Athens: University of Georgia Press, 2008.

Lynn A. Staeheli. "Political geography: Where's citizenship?" *Progress in Human Geography*, no. 35 (2011): pp. 393–400.

Gearoid O Tuathail and Fred M. Shelley. "Political geography and the new world order." In *Geography in America at the dawn of the 21st century*, edited by Gary Gaile and Cort Willmott, pp. 164–184. New York: Oxford University Press, 2003.

Immanuel Wallerstein. *The uncertainties of knowledge: Politics, history, and social change.* Philadelphia, PA: Temple University Press, 2004.

INDEX

ABOUT THE AUTHOR

Fred M. Shelley is professor of geography and environmental sustainability at the University of Oklahoma. He earned his PhD at the University of Iowa in 1981 and has taught also at the University of Southern California, Florida State University, and Texas State University–San Marcos. His research interests include political geography, economic geography, geography of the global economy, and the historical and cultural geography of the United States within the world economy and the global polity. He is the author or editor of 14 books and over 100 journal articles and book chapters on these and related subjects. He is a former member of the Council of the Association of American Geographers (AAG) and a former president of the Political Geography Specialty Group of the AAG.